D1592317

**FOR REFERENCE**

Do Not Take From This Room

# Ethnic Groups of Europe

**Forthcoming *Ethnic Groups of the World* titles**

*Ethnic Groups of Africa and the Middle East*
*Ethnic Groups of North, East, and Central Asia*
*Ethnic Groups of South Asia and the Pacific*
*Ethnic Groups of the Americas*

# Ethnic Groups of Europe

## AN ENCYCLOPEDIA

Jeffrey E. Cole, Editor

Ethnic Groups of the World

ABC-CLIO

Santa Barbara, California • Denver, Colorado • Oxford, England

**Library of Congress Cataloging-in-Publication Data**

Ethnic groups of Europe : an encyclopedia / Jeffrey E. Cole, editor.
    p. cm. — (Ethnic groups of the world)
   Summary: "This comprehensive survey of ethnic groups of Europe reveals the dynamic process of ethnic identity and the relationship of ethnic groups to modern states"— Provided by publisher.
   Includes bibliographical references and index.
   ISBN 978-1-59884-302-6 (hardback) — ISBN 978-1-59884-303-3 (ebook)
1. Ethnology—Europe—Encyclopedias.   2. Ethnicity—Europe—Encyclopedias.   3. Europe—Ethnic relations—Encyclopedias.
I. Cole, Jeffrey, 1958–
   D1056.E838   2011
   305.80094'03—dc22     2011000412

ISBN: 978-1-59884-302-6
EISBN: 978-1-59884-303-3

15  14  13  12  11    1  2  3  4  5

This book is also available on the World Wide Web as an eBook.
Visit www.abc-clio.com for details.

ABC-CLIO, LLC
130 Cremona Drive, P.O. Box 1911
Santa Barbara, California 93116-1911

This book is printed on acid-free paper ∞

Manufactured in the United States of America

# Contents

# Introduction

## How to Use This Book

This volume contains more than 100 descriptions of ethnic and national groups in Europe, as well as a number of sidebars highlighting related issues. Each entry provides a capsule summary of a group followed by an account of origins and early history, cultural life, and recent developments. Collectively, the entries highlight the dynamic process of ethnicity: ethnic groups may persist for centuries, but they change and often branch into new groups or merge into other populations. Driving this dynamism are a number of factors, among them migration, war, religion, and, especially since the 19th century and continuing to the present day, nation-building. While most individual entries chronicle the changing fortunes of single groups, the process of ethnicity is perhaps best seen in regional context. Readers are encouraged to peruse entries covering neighboring groups, such as the Bulgarians, Macedonians, and Greeks, for example, or the Danes, Norwegians, and Swedes, to gain an appreciation for the ways ethnic and national identities are constructed and contested. This introduction discusses the concept and practice of ethnicity (and nationalism), and then addresses historic and contemporary trends in Europe. The short essay on methodology that follows this essay explains the criteria for inclusion in the volume.

## Ethnic Groups, Nations, and States

It is tempting to regard ethnic groups as fixed and enduring. But ethnicity is better described as a process that combines two mutually reinforcing forms of identification. First, an ethnic group refers to a population that regards itself as a people bound by common origins, shared experience and culture, and quite possibly a distinct language and religious practice. Second, this act of self-identification is always made with reference to other groups with whom the ethnic population interacts or shares an area or both. The setting for interethnic interaction is usually a society, an orbit of patterned social relations typically framed by the political boundaries of a kingdom, nation-state, or empire.

Of course, to understand any ethnic group it is important to grasp the distinct cultural content of its identity. This content can and often does change over time. New expressions and forms enrich and alter languages, people take up new livelihoods as old industries fade, and the content and context of faith may change with the development of heresies and establishment of new orthodoxies. A passing acquaintance with English history, for example, demonstrates such changes. The English language gained thousands of new expressions and words with the 11th-century invasion of French-speaking Normans (themselves Frenchified Vikings), the English population adopted Protestantism when Henry the VIII broke with Rome, and a nation of farmers became factory workers with industrialization. Along each point in this historical arc, people in the country saw themselves as properly English—though of course more exclusive local identities or, later, the more inclusive British identity featured prominently in people's lives too. Most of the entries in this volume demonstrate similar processes of change and continuity in ethnicity identity and experience.

Anthropologists, who study ethnicity in contemporary cross-cultural contexts, have confirmed both the fluid nature of the cultural content of group identity and the tendency of people to regard identity as fixed and inviolate. Anthropology's most powerful insight, however, has been the revelation of the signal importance of interaction, or boundary maintenance, in ethnicity. It is no exaggeration to say that ethnic categories persist precisely because of interaction; far from dissolving ethnic identity, interaction enacts it by publicly contrasting group membership. Distinctions between groups are frequently preserved through mutually exclusive definitions of group belonging, reinforced through prohibitions on intermarriage, for example, or restrictions on social interaction. Yet, even in the rare cases in which people routinely move from one group to another, distinct ethnic categories persist because new members adopt the appropriate code of behavior and self-identification.

It is worth stressing that a concern for one's ethnicity is unevenly distributed. If a group is geographically concentrated in a homeland, members residing along ethnic borders are far more conscious of the requirements for publicly demonstrating adherence to their group. Likewise, individuals who frequently interact with other groups, such as traders or migrants or political leaders, are typically quite attentive to the needs of ethnic boundary maintenance. Finally, relations between groups strongly influence the tenor of interethnic relations, including the relative porosity of borders, group autonomy, and the extent and forms of interaction. A group may interact easily with others and live in mixed neighborhoods or regions, or they may interact rarely with others and only then hedged with restrictions. Economically, a group may enjoy more or less parity with others, or possess much less or more in the way of access to valued resources and livelihoods. Politically, a group may enjoy autonomy in terms of decision making and dispute resolution, or it may participate on equal footing with other similar groups within the same society, or it may be plainly dominant or subordinate. The entries in this volume describe virtually every possible combination of social, economic, and political relations among ethnic groups in Europe.

This volume adopts an inclusive definition of the term *ethnic group*. The entries to follow describe indigenous populations such as the Saami of Scandinavia, dispersed minorities such as Jews and Roma, distinct and regionally based populations such as the Avars and Dargins in Dagestan in the southern reaches of the Russian Federation, and nationalities such as Bulgarians and Norwegians. While populations such as the Saami, Roma, and Avars accord with the common usage of the term *ethnic group* as minority in a larger social system, the inclusion of nationalities under this general rubric requires explanation. As many commentators have noted, the principal difference between ethnic groups and nationalities is that the latter are defined by a political boundary, possess the institutional forms of a nation-state (or subsections thereof), and do not necessarily claim shared ancestry. The French, to take an oft-cited example, typically regard themselves as such by virtue of membership and participation in a republic defined by political boundaries and shared political process and democratic ideals. The French state does not recognize ethnicity (or the related category of race), and individual immigrants are expected to become French by adopting the laws and customs of the land. And yet some very influential French politicians do hold essentially an ethnic (some would say racial) view of the nation. Thus, ethnic nationalists such as Jean Marie Le Pen claim that certain kinds of immigrants (Muslim or dark-skinned or both) cannot become "real" French, even if they hold French citizenship. A number of other entries, for example those on successor states to the Soviet Union or the states emerging from the former Yugoslavia, also reveal the contemporary power of ethnic definitions of the nation. Indeed, the journal *Nationalities Papers: The Journal of Nationalism and Ethnicity* is devoted to just such questions with a geographical focus on Central Europe, the Balkans, the former Soviet Union, and Caucasus as well as the Turkic world and Central Asia. Nor is the relevance of ethnicity to nationality solely contemporary. The treatment of group history—a part of every entry—reveals the ethnic core of many of today's nationalities, including those like the French that tend to stress their civic as opposed to ethnic nature. This is not to say that all nationalities stem from ethnic cores, nor to dismiss the very real distinctions between ethnicity and nationality, or between ethnic and civic forms of national identity. It is to argue, however, that treating these diverse forms of social organization between the covers of a single volume is merited, given similarities in the process of identity formation and in observable patterns of interaction.

There are also educational and practical motives for this inclusive approach to ethnicity in Europe. This encyclopedia is one of several projected volumes designed to cover ethnic groups around the world; all volumes share the same four-part entry template, the contents of which include nationalities as well as ethnic populations; and all are geared to a general readership in terms of language and presentation. Because the primary purpose of the project is educational, rather than advancing a theoretical argument for a specialist readership, nationalities are included along with more conventionally defined ethnicities. Moreover, the exclusion of nationalities would have entailed unbalanced geographical coverage, with a focus on the former Soviet Union, where there are countless recognized ethnicities, for reasons discussed at some length below. With this volume's more inclusive approach, readers can appreciate the differences and similarities between nations and ethnic groups, as well as the contours and consequences of interactions between such populations.

## Patterns and Prospects

The model and reality of the nation-state is the single most important context for understanding ethnic groups. In Europe, the model came to prominence in the 19th century, inspiring many peoples to demand independence; it was sanctified in the principle of the right to self-determination espoused by U.S. President Woodrow Wilson and utilized in the Treaty of Versailles at the conclusion of World War I; and it is given tacit support by the criteria of admission (statehood) for highly influential supranational organizations such as the United Nations and the European Union. True, several notable multinational (or multiethnic) states exist, such as Spain and the United Kingdom, as do self-consciously civic nations with recognized linguistic diversity, such as Switzerland. And it could be persuasively argued that the pure nation-state is in fact a rarity. However, the notion that statehood is the ultimate legitimate form of political organization for a given people has inspired and continues to inspire ethnic groups seeking independence (sometimes referred to as ethno-national movements). Conversely, the conviction that states should represent the interests of a people united by common culture, not to mention the evident political dividends of cultivating common cause in an era of popular democracy, has been used to justify, at least until recent decades, the promotion of national cultures as well as the suppression of regional and ethnic diversity and autonomy. And of course dispersed populations without a state, such as Jews and Roma, are at a distinct disadvantage in such a world.

These twin processes are clearly manifest in the realm of language use and policy. Because of its close association with group identity, language often acts as a key indicator of group membership. Where a dominant language exists, national elites have typically established academies to safeguard the purity of their tongue and celebrate its beauty, as in the case of the academies of Sweden and France. Where ambiguity resides, aspiring nationalists have turned to identifying the dialect(s) that can serve as the basis of a distinctive national language. In the 19th century, Norway was under nominal Swedish control and much of its elite culture and written language (*riksmål* or *bokmål*) was essentially Danish, thanks to nearly 300 years of earlier Danish control. Such was the popular and political support for a distinctive Norwegian tongue that *nynorsk*, the creation of language reformer Ivar Aasen based on rural western dialects, became the second official language in 1885. To take a contemporary example, Montenegro, which had remained part of Serbia after the break-up of the former Yugoslavia in the early 1990s, declared independence from Serbia in 2006. While a slim majority of Montenegrins see themselves as distinct from Serbs, many regard themselves as Serbs and all acknowledge a shared history and culture, including language. Significantly, the 2007 constitution declared as the official language the Ijekavian variant of the Shtokavian dialect of Serbo-Croatian—just as the Croatian Constitution identifies Croatian as its official language and Serbia's as Serbian. (The principle difference is that Croats use the Latin alphabet, Serbs the Cyrillic.) In most cases past and present, the official language is promoted above regional dialects or minority languages and is taught in schools, ensuring its dominance.

Borders also play a signal role in relations between ethnic groups and states. If we are a nation within our own state, then the treatment of our cousins abroad can become a foreign policy issue. Such concern can take many forms. A state may officially recognize conationals abroad, as does Slovenia, and perhaps extend to conationals streamlined access to residency and eventual citizenship, as in the case of ethnic Germans (*Aussiedler*) welcomed home to Germany from Eastern Europe. Or a state may lay claim to ethnic minorities abroad in a bid for symbolic gains. For example, Bulgaria, Turkey, and Greece all claim kinship with the Slavic-speaking Muslim Pomaks, who reside in these respective countries as well as in Romania, Macedonia, and Albania. Bulgarians also say that Macedonians are really their own kinsmen, while Greeks insist that only they may accurately use the term *Macedonian* because they claim that the ancient Macedonians—most notably Alexander the Great—were Greek. Needless to say, Macedonians reject such claims and assert their own autonomy as *the* Macedonian people.

War provides a dramatic and traumatic context for ethnic conflict. At the end of the Greco-Turkish War (1919–1922), for example, some 2 million people were relocated in what was one of Europe's largest population exchanges. Out of the ashes of the multiethnic Ottoman Empire, Turkey and Greece sought to establish themselves as nation-states, and consequently all Greek Orthodox believers in Turkish territory were sent to Greece and all Muslims in Greek territory were removed to Turkey.

At the risk of engaging in sweeping generalization, it might be stated that within Europe far greater numbers of ethnic groups and perhaps a greater incidence of ethno-national claims are found in the Balkans and Central and Eastern Europe. In part, this is the result of timing, namely the earlier formation of nation-states in Western Europe. In the days before widely acknowledged minority rights and identity politics, modernizing states to the west consciously eroded the material and symbolic supports of ethnic and regional populations. Language policies outlawing or restricting the use of local language exemplify this process. Breton was long forbidden in French schools in Brittany, for example, and students in 19th-century Ireland once wore around their necks tally sticks that recorded the punishable infractions of speaking Gaelic in school. Also important to the relative paucity of ethno-nationalism in the contemporary West is the widespread recognition of ethnic minority rights as well as, in a number of cases, forms of political autonomy. (These are described in more detail below.)

To the east, ethnic groups and forms of nationalism seem to prevail, not least because of the longevity of multinational empires and, later, the policies of the former Soviet Union. The Russian Federation and other successor states to the Soviet Union represent enormous ethnic diversity—indeed, nearly a third of this volume's 100-plus entries are devoted to ethnic and national groups in just the European sphere of the country. Considering the magnitude of such diversity, the Russian situation merits close attention. Current ethnic diversity there stems in large measure from the demographic legacy of the sprawling Russian Empire, most of the territories of which were reacquired by the Bolsheviks in the years immediately following the Russian Civil War. The Soviet Union's self-consciously novel nationalities program, however, did much to promote—and sometimes destroy—ethnic and national identity. Lenin and Stalin, the architects of the plan, adopted the Wilsonian principle of the right to self-determination as a necessary step in the advance of international socialism. They had paid close attention to the disintegration of the Austro-Hungarian Empire, noting the power of nationalism to inspire people as well as the economic development that appeared to accompany this powerful cross-class mobilization. By cultivating nationalism among the constituent peoples of the USSR, they hoped to harness this seemingly inevitable modernizing force. At the same time they were keenly aware of the historical animosity toward Russians harbored by many of the peoples formerly subjugated by the empire. By supporting the right to self-determination of non-Russians, Lenin and Stalin hoped to gain their allegiance to the socialist cause.

The resulting program, often labeled "indigenization" (*korenizatsiya*), was initiated in the 1920s. Groups were granted what amounted to the forms and institutions of the nation-state, namely a homeland, national culture, and official language. Peoples were typically granted a territory in which they comprised the majority and could influence affairs. The size and type of territory varied, from Soviet Socialist Republics (SSRs) for the most populous peoples like Ukrainians, to Autonomous Soviet Socialist Republics (ASSRs) for regionally significant populations like the Kalmyks and Udmurts, to smaller units such as Autonomous Oblasts for peoples such as the Adygey and Chechens, to still smaller Autonomous Okrugs for populations such as the Komi. Whenever possible, the collectivization of agriculture and establishment of industry secured the economic base for socialist development. Indigenous elites were promoted to positions of leadership; by cultivating local power holders of proletarian origins, the Soviets aimed to avoid the plague of "bourgeois" nationalism by which capitalists endeavor to direct the currents of nationalism for their own ends. National cultures were documented and celebrated in folklore studies and enshrined in museums. National languages were also established. In cases of literate peoples such as Belarusians, the national tongue was standardized and indigenous literature supported. In the case of nonliterate peoples, of whom there were many in the southern, northern, and eastern reaches of the USSR, teams of linguists and ethnographers established written languages, typically using the Latin script rather than the Cyrillic, which would have recalled perhaps the heavy-handed Russification policies of the empire. In this fashion dozens of written languages were established by the mid-1930s and, together with the construction of a school system, secured significant gains in literacy rates among non-Russians.

Local elites welcomed at least some of these developments and willingly accepted greater power within their territories. Overall, the indigenization campaign clearly demonstrates the power of the central state to set conditions for the maintenance and even creation (and destruction) of ethnic groups. For example, the Balkars and Karachay, two Turkic-speaking and Muslim populations in the central North Caucasus, were long considered a single people. The dialects upon which their written languages were based in the 1920s are virtually identical, and both groups have long histories as pastoralists. For census purposes, however, the groups were considered distinct. In the case of the Balkars, they were named after one of their five loosely affiliated tribes (the Malquar), and their official language was based on the dialect of two others (the Bakhsan and Chegem). In a similar fashion the closely related Adyghs and Kabards were deemed distinct, as were the Dargins and Avars in Dagestan.

As Terry Martin describes in *The Affirmative Action Empire*, Soviet policy toward non-Russians ran on two tracks, sometimes reinforcing, sometimes contradictory. Soft-line institutions like the nationalities office entertained amicable relations with non-Russians and concerned themselves with folklore and language and museums, while hard-line institutions such as the secret police and Communist Party exercised vigilance over minorities and utilized violence, intimidation, and other measures in the name of socialism. The principle message was that non-Russian nationalism was not an end in itself, but rather a stage on the road to international socialism. By the late 1930s the program, never popular with the Russian-dominated Communist Party, was curtailed and a new era of Russification was begun, this time under the rubric "Friendship of Peoples." Latin script was dropped in favor of Cyrillic to facilitate communication in Russian; non-Russian identity became suspect, especially for cross-border populations; and the hegemony of ethnic Russians in the organs of state and economy was all but assured. Following World War II, Stalin chose to punish peoples who had supposedly collaborated with Nazis. Whole populations, such as the Balkars, Chechens, Ingush, Kalmyks, and Karachays, were stripped of their property and banished to Central Asia. Only after Stalin's death were these groups rehabilitated and allowed to return to their homelands. However, they often returned to find others, competing ethnic groups or Russians or both, in their houses and farms—a point of interethnic tension that remains raw even today.

Subsequent to the breakup of the USSR, ethnicity has featured predictably and prominently in political conflict, both domestic and international. Within Russia itself, the nationalist agenda of Vladimir Putin's administration has rolled back whatever gains for ethnic recognition emerged in the brief period of ethnic revival in the 1990s. In the key area of education, for example, Russian continues to dominate as the language of instruction while offerings in indigenous languages shrink. Thus few young Mari and Mordvin are proficient in the tongue of their grandparents, with deleterious effects on ethnic identity. Some groups, typically far from Moscow and keenly aware of past and present Russian attempts at dominance, have taken up arms in a quest for autonomy. The bloodiest such uprising has taken place in Chechnya, where some ethnic Chechens have been fighting Russian forces or their Chechen allies since 1994.

Ethnicity has also figured in headline-grabbing clashes with former Soviet republics (SSRs). Take the case of the Ossetians, a population whose territory spans the Georgia-Russia border. Objecting to the invasion of the Georgian army (1990–1992) after South Ossetia's declaration of independence, Russia recognized South Ossetian autonomy in a move receiving virtually no support from the international community of states. For its part, Georgia decried Russia's activities as a thinly veiled attempt to stoke an Ossetian independence movement within its borders and regarded Ossetians with suspicion. In 2008 the Russian army invaded Georgian territory and together with South Ossetian separatists established control over the disputed territory, which again declared its independence from Georgia. For the foreseeable future Ossetian ethnicity will be inextricably linked to the struggle between Georgia and Russia.

In a number of former SSRs, elites have pursued an aggressive nationalist agenda and attempted to de-Russify their countries. In 1991, Estonia denied citizenship to nearly one-third of its population, on the grounds that they or their parents had entered during the USSR's illegal annexation of the country (1940–1989). In response to the concerns of Western development organizations and especially the European Union, to which Estonia successfully sought admittance, Estonia was required to demonstrate attention to minority rights and a pathway to citizenship. Estonians, still smarting from half a century of Soviet domination, have made proficiency in Estonian the principal requirement for citizenship, a challenge that relatively few ethnic Russians have been able to accomplish. Given the presence of ethnic Russians in a number of former Soviet republics, ethnicity will continue to figure in domestic and international politics for some time.

Current EU protections of ethnic minorities build on legislation initiated in the immediate post–World War II period. Revolted by the atrocities committed by the Nazis in their quest to establish a new racial order in Europe, a number of European countries repudiated racism and established prohibitions on expressions of racial ideology. The following decades would see additional prohibitions on other forms of discrimination, including those based on nationality and ethnicity. Notwithstanding these laws, ethnic discrimination and even violence has not disappeared, a sorry fact most clearly manifested in the mistreatment of the Roma, Europe's largest and most dispersed ethnic minority. Also important to ethnic relations has been a trend in some countries toward decentralization. Rejecting the centralization of power and suppression of ethnic minorities characteristic of the Franco period, in the late 1970s Spaniards granted a significant measure of political autonomy to 17 autonomous regions. In Catalonia, the Basque area, and Galicia—the homelands of recognized historical nationalities—the Catalan, Basque, and

## European Union Policy on Minorities

Countries seeking admittance to the European Union (EU) must demonstrate respect for and protection of minority rights at legislative, institutional, and practical levels. The process of creating/amending national legislation to meet the antidiscrimination requirements, the so-called Copenhagen (1993) criteria adopted into EU primary law under the Amsterdam Treaty (1997), emphasizes the reduction of disadvantages and the assurance of equal opportunity for all citizens. Members of national minorities should be free to express, preserve, and develop their distinctive culture and practices, including their language, as long as democratic procedures, the rule of law, and the rights of others are respected. In practice, this policy concerns groups who self-identify on the basis of ethnic, linguistic, or religious criteria; such groups include peoples long resident as well as recent arrivals. European minority policy also draws support from the Council of Europe (an organization distinct from the EU), which issued the Framework Convention for the Protection of National Minorities (1995). The absence of common systematic monitoring of government policies and practices toward minorities, and the nonapplicability of Copenhagen criteria to EU member states, however, undermines postenlargement minority protection.

*Sergiu Gherghina*

Galician languages share co-official status with Castilian (Spanish). Out of this new political environment has emerged a sense of compatible, dual identities combining the national and the regional. Similar patterns of dual identification appear to be developing in the United Kingdom as well, another state that has adopted the devolution of political power. It is an open question whether some form of European identity will emerge out of the manifold cross-border interconnections supported by the European Union, and join regional and national forms of identification. If it does, it would surely be of such a civic quality that the term *ethnic* would scarcely apply—unless European Union politics takes an unlikely ethnic turn.

No review of ethnicity in contemporary Europe would be complete without consideration of postwar immigration. In broad strokes, former colonial powers such as France, the United Kingdom, and the Netherlands drew on their (former) overseas territories to meet the labor demands of the economic boom of the 1960s and early 1970s. Countries without such an option, such as Germany and Switzerland, drew on countries along the Mediterranean. Policy makers envisioned such flows as temporary, but by the 1970s the many immigrants decided to settle, creating in effect new ethnic communities, often of non-European origins. Starting in the late 1980s, former labor exporters such as Italy and Spain became destinations for immigrants hailing from around the globe. Ethnic diversity has increased still more with the recent eastward expansion of the EU and the consequent increase in intra-European population flows. While hard times and a less than enthusiastic reception from the majority population have greeted many immigrant groups, as a rule it has been those of non-European origins who have endured the greatest hardship. Despite the fact that many are often born and raised in Europe, these groups face the highest unemployment, experience pronounced discrimination, and live in the most undesirable areas with the worst schools and other services.

In the vocal opinion of the European ethnic nationalists who have gained increasing popular support across the continent, these immigrant-origins populations will remain forever foreign by virtue of their background and religion and therefore cannot and will not fit into European society. In some countries these ethnic nationalist forces have succeeded in passing restrictive citizenship laws that make very difficult the naturalization of legal immigrants and their children, a course of action that impedes the successful integration of newcomers. Some commentators prefer to describe the situation of non-European origins populations in terms of racism, a term that both acknowledges the colonial past of many even as it stresses the severity of their disadvantage and the essentialist claims of their detractors. Regrettably, this volume can offer only limited coverage of ethnicity as it relates to immigration. This limitation stems in large measure from the nature of the entry template described above, which privileges ethnic and national populations indigenous to Europe (recall that the title refers to ethnic groups *of,* not in, Europe). Within this constraining framework, immigration is addressed in two ways. Short sidebars give key facts concerning such settled immigrant populations, for example regarding people of Turkish origins in Germany and Algerian origins in France. And, where appropriate, entries include information on immigration trends and the relation of immigrant identity to national identity. Recent scholarship on immigration issues has contributed especially to our understanding of citizenship and cognate issues of belonging and identity. Readers interested in learning more about these issues of signal importance to Europeans will find several relevant titles listed below.

In sum, in Central and particularly Eastern Europe, ethnicity today tends to involve interaction among indigenous groups, interactions that range from harmonious coexistence to vigorous ethno-nationalist claims and even violence. Given the recognition of minority rights and the significant degree of political autonomy afforded many recognized indigenous ethnicities to the west, the term ethnicity there most commonly calls to mind populations, whether recent immigrant or settled, of non-European origins. In view of their origins, claims of an ethno-national stamp are simply not conceivable; rather their principle concern is the recognition of their civic and human rights (including, in some cases, the right to be different) and better prospects for advancement within their adopted societies and cultures.

## Further Reading

Brubaker, Rogers. *Nationalism Reframed: Nationhood and the National Question in the New Europe.* New York: Cambridge University Press, 1996.

Cordell, Karl, ed. *Ethnicity and Democratization in the New Europe.* London and New York: Routledge, 1999.

Eriksen, Thomas Hylland. *Ethnicity and Nationalism: Anthropological Perspectives.* 2nd ed. London: Pluto, 2002.

Fowkes, Ben. *Ethnicity and Ethnic Conflict in the Post-Communist World.* New York: Palgrave, 2002.

Gammer, Moshe, ed. *Ethno-nationalism, Islam, and the State of Disorder in the Caucasus: Post-Soviet Disorder.* London: Routledge, 2008.

Gellner, Ernest. *Nations and Nationalism.* Ithaca, NY: Cornell University Press, 1983.

Karner, Christian. *Ethnicity and Everyday Life.* London and New York: Routledge, 2007.

Joppke, Christian. *Citizenship and Migration.* Cambridge: Polity, 2010.

Koopmans, Ruud, Paul Statham, Marco Giugni, and Florence Passy. *Contested Citizenship: Immigration and Cultural Diversity in Europe.* Minneapolis: University of Minnesota Press, 2005.

Mandel, Ruth. *Cosmopolitan Anxieties: Turkish Challenges to Citizenship and Belonging.* Durham, NC: Duke University Press, 2008.

Martin, Terry. *The Affirmative Action Empire: Nations and Nationalism in the Soviet Union, 1923–1939.* Ithaca, NY: Cornell University Press, 2001.

Panayi, Panikos. *An Ethnic History of Europe since 1945: Nations, States, and Minorities.* Harlow, England: Longman, 2000.

Richmond, Walter. *The New Caucasus: Past, Present, Future.* London: Routledge, 2008.

Smith, Anthony. *Ethno-symbolism and Nationalism: A Cultural Approach.* London and New York: Routledge, 2009.

# Methodology

As explained in detail in the introduction, this volume adopts an inclusive approach to the treatment of ethnic groups, including indigenous peoples without states such as the Saami, dispersed religious and ethnic minorities such as Jews and Roma, distinctive regional populations such as Catalans and Bretons, and nationalities such as Russians and Serbs. Despite differences in scale and organization, in all cases there exists a group consciousness or identity grounded in shared experience and history as well as acknowledgment of group identity on the part of others, particularly the state. However, excluded from the list of entries are those populations that are not generally acknowledged to be ethnically distinct. For this reason the residents of Gibraltar, that polyglot and cosmopolitan British overseas territory, are not included, nor are the people of San Marino, a microstate that is essentially Italian in all but passport and tax code, nor are residents of the decidedly multiethnic microstate of Vatican City. As a rule, regional populations, who may in fact share important experiences and a dialect, have not been included unless acknowledged as distinct in some way, most commonly by the government of the country in which they live. Thus the Frisians and Friulians, whose languages are granted co-official status along with the national tongues in their respective regions, receive entries, whereas the Sicilians and Bavarians, whose dialects do not receive such status, have no separate entry.

Starting with this inclusive approach, groups were selected on the basis of size and geography. As for size, the minimum population for inclusion was set at 20,000, a figure that ensured the volume would cover approximately 100 groups, in accordance with the publisher's projections for the volume. Thus Monegasques, the 5,000 or so passport holders of tiny Monaco, do not receive an entry. Whenever possible, small groups receive mention in treatments of larger, related groups, as in the case of the Ramaniotes (Greek-speaking Jews) who were incorporated into Sephardic Jewish communities, or that of the Kaitags and Kubachins who are considered subgroups of the Dargins. Additionally, some sidebars highlight populations mentioned in larger entries, such as Irish Tinkers and Ulster Protestants, or provide concise descriptions of distinctive border areas, such as Alsace and Tyrol.

The final criterion for inclusion in the volume is that a group must have a historic homeland as well as a continued presence in Europe, as conventionally defined. Thus there is no treatment of the Ubykh, a Muslim people long resident in the northwest Caucasus who fled the advancing Russian Empire forces in 1864, settled mostly in western Turkey, took up farming in preference to their former nomadic existence, and adopted as their language Turkish or Circassian. Groups whose members are found both inside and beyond the borders of Europe are not described in this volume if the majority of their numbers currently reside outside of Europe. For this reason the Meskhetian Turks, a Georgian population exiled to Central Asia by Josef Stalin in the 1940s and still concentrated in Kazakhstan and Azerbaijan, will be treated in the volume on ethnic peoples of Asia.

# A

## Abazin

The Abazin live in the Northern Caucasus region, particularly in the Adygheya and Karachaevo-Cherkessia republics of the Russian Federation. They call themselves Abaza, Ashywua, or Ashkarywua, the latter two names referring to their two major tribes. Historically, the Abazin have practiced herding and some farming. They live on the northern parts of the Great Caucasus range, in the valleys of the Kuma and Great and Little Zelenchuk rivers. They also live on the northeastern shores of the Black Sea basin in a tier starting from Sochi down to the borders of contemporary Abkhazia. The most recent data show their numbers in the Russian Federation near 40,000; smaller numbers also live in Turkey, Syria, and Jordan. The Abazin language belongs to the West Caucasian subgroup of the North Caucasian language family, a subgroup consisting of Abazin (i.e., Abaza), Abkhaz, Adygh, Kabardinian, and Ubykh languages. The Abazin are Sunni Muslims. They are often confused with the Abkhaz (Apsywua), a related people now resident in Abkhazia. Some Circassians use the term Abazin for Abkhaz living outside of Abkhazia, but the two populations should be distinguished on the basis of the strong self-consciousness of the Abazin people about their identity.

One theory says that in the distant past the Ashywua and Ashkarywua split from the Abkhaz in search of meadows for their herds in the northern plains of the Caucasus Mountains. Some accounts say that they are a Black Sea people with strong ties to Asia Minor as well. Yet others consider the Abazin a separate ethnic group and explain the similarity of the Abazin and Abkhaz languages as the result of historical relations. Abazin dialects are understandable for Abkhaz speakers.

On the eve of the Russian Empire's campaign in the Caucasus, the numbers of Abazin were estimated at around 45,000; about 10,000 remained in Russian territory at the end of the 19th century. The Ashywua subgroup consists of six families: Loo, Bibard, Darykua, Kylych, Jantemir, and K'achua. The Ashkarywua subgroup consists of seven families: Bashylby, Barakey, Mysylbiy, Kyzylby, Shegerey, T'am, and Bagh. In the face of Russian forces most of the Ashkarywua fled to the Ottoman Empire in the second half of the 19th century. They are now found in different parts of Turkey, Syria, and Jordan.

Abazin literature is predominantly oral, identified with the epic tradition of the Caucasus nations. The first written forms of Abazin literature were published by the famous Abazin literary figure Tobil Talustan in 1920s in the Soviet Union. The Abazin national movement tried to establish a homeland within the Karachaevo-Cherkessia Republic in 1991 but failed. Following a referendum in 2005, an Abazin national district was formed in 2006. After a transitional period and reorganization of the administrative districts in northern Karachaevo-Cherkessia, in December 2007 elections were held to elect a 15-member parliament and a president of the Abazin national district. The population of the Abazin national district is estimated at 15,000. Its capital is the village of Psyzh.

*Hasan Ali Karasar*

**Further Reading**

Danilova, E. N. *Abaziny: Istoriko-etnograficheskoe Issledovanie Khozyastva i Obshinnoy Organizatsii XIX vek (Abazins: Historical-Ethnographic Study of Agriculture and Communitarian Organization in the 19th Century).* Moskva: Izdatel'stvo Moskovskogo Universiteta, 1984.

Pershits, A. I. *Abaziny: Istoriko-Etnograficheskii Ocherk (Abazins: Historical-Ethnographic Essays).* Cherkessk: Karachaevo-Cherkesskoe Otdelenie Stavropol'ckogo Knizhnogo Izdatel'stva, 1989.

# Abkhaz

The Abkhaz (or Abkhazians) are indigenous to the Caucasus region and the autochthonous people of Abkhazia, a Black Sea republic whose self-declared independence is recognized by Russia and Nicaragua but disputed by the remainder of the international community, which accepts Georgia's right to the territory. Less than 100,000 now live in Abkhazia, and the number of native Abkhaz speakers has dwindled during the last century through Russification. While Christianity, Islam, and paganism have coexisted among the Abkhaz for centuries, seven decades of Soviet rule has created a largely nonreligious people. In the 14th and 15th centuries, some Abkhazians moved to the North Caucasus, and their descendants became known as Abazinians. There is also a large diaspora in Turkey, mostly descendants of those expelled by the Russian empire in the late 19th century.

At the end of the 8th century, following a dilution of Byzantine power, an Abkhazian kingdom emerged, which encompassed the whole of western Georgia with its capital in Kutaisi. The kingdom consolidated Abkhazian tribes and thrived for two centuries before being superseded in 978 by a new state, known as the Kingdom of Abkhazians and Kartvelians. Ruled by the Bagrationi family, the capital remained in Kutaisi until 1122, when the expulsion of the Arab emirate of Tbilist facilitated a move to that city. The kingdom succumbed to Mongol invasions in the 13th century, never to reappear, and was replaced by numerous smaller principalities, including Abkhazia, now ruled by the Chachba (Sharvashidze) family. The Abkhaz were in regular battle with the neighboring principality of Mingrelia, an ethnic Georgian region ruled by the Dadiani family.

Extensive interaction with the Genoese in the 14th and 15th centuries was eclipsed by the rise of Ottoman power in the region. The Turks brought Islam, which gradually replaced Christianity as the dominant religion in Abkhazia, though traditional paganism remained influential. The Ottomans were dislodged in turn by an expanding Russian empire and in 1810 Abkhazia became an unruly

Svetlana and Anatoly Vosba paint a newspaper kiosk that is decorated with the Abkhaz flag in Sukhumi, the capital of the Georgian breakaway region of Abkhazia. Once the Soviet Union's most prestigious piece of real estate, Abkhazia is now, after its 1992–1993 war for independence from Georgia, sadly reduced. (Corbis)

Russian protectorate. Sporadic attacks on Russian power through the decades culminated in large-scale rebellions in the 1860s and 1870s. These were ruthlessly suppressed and led to the forced resettlement of up to 200,000 Abkhaz to Turkey, an event known in Abkhaz folklore as *amha'dzhyrra* (exile). Leaderless and bereft of its indigenous people, Abkhazia came under direct Russian rule and was repopulated with Mingrelians and a host of other nationalities including Armenians, Russians, and Greeks.

Famed for their food, wine, and dancing, the Abkhaz are influenced by their Black Sea location, which has exposed them to traders and invaders over many centuries.

Their proximity to the mountain peoples of the north Caucasus, neighboring Kartvelians, and the eclectic mix of peoples that have inhabited the republic have also left their mark. A fundamental part of Abkhaz national culture is *'apswara*, which is roughly translated as "Abkhaz-ness" or "Abkhaz world view." A high premium is placed on personal and familial honor, and chastity is prized and expected of Abkhaz women. The culture is conservative, patriarchal, and clannish, with family, locality, and personal contacts as key features. People bearing the same surname are considered relatives.

Abkhaz is a northwest Caucasian language, which, though ancient, was bereft of an alphabet until 1862 when an adaptation of Cyrillic was introduced. During the 1930s, a Georgian script for Abkhaz was imposed before Cyrillic was reintroduced following Soviet leader Joseph Stalin's death in 1953. The Cyrillic alphabet continues to be used.

The collapse of the Russian Empire in 1917 facilitated the emergence of the Democratic Republic of Georgia, incorporating a recalcitrant Abkhaz population that, in 1919, was granted autonomy within the new state. A completely new dispensation followed the consolidation of Bolshevik power in Russia. The Red Army invasion obliterated Georgian independence and, in February 1921, both Georgia and Abkhazia were made Soviet Socialist Republics within the Soviet Union. Amendments later that year and in 1925 diluted Abkhazia's status until, in 1931, it was reduced to an autonomous republic within Georgia. A "Georgianization" policy was rigorously pursued during the 1930s and 1940s, accompanied by substantial Georgian migration to the region. The worst of the repression ended with the departure of Stalin and Lavrentiy Beria (both ethnic Georgians) in 1953 and, though conditions largely improved for the Abkhaz during the remainder of Soviet rule, there were popular demands for secession from Georgia in 1957, 1964, 1967, 1978, and 1989. As Soviet power declined and Georgian nationalists sought independence, the Abkhaz tried first to remain within the Soviet Union before opting for independence. The bitter Georgian-Abkhaz war of 1992–1993 claimed about 10,000 lives, with Russian military support for the Abkhaz proving decisive. Approximately 250,000

ethnic Georgians (many of them Mingrelians) were expelled from Abkhazia. A ceasefire, which gave Russia a central role in the region, remained largely intact until 2008.

Demography continues to challenge the Abkhaz; their dwindling numbers put them at risk of assimilation or being overwhelmed by other nationalities. Though renowned for their longevity, the last Soviet census in 1989 indicated that the Abkhaz constituted only 17.8 percent (93,267) of Abkhazia's 525,061 residents. The Abkhaz government census of 2003 estimated there were 215,972 living in Abkhazia of whom 94,606 (43.8%) were ethnic Abkhaz. These figures are almost certainly inaccurate, not least because of a desire to inflate Abkhaz numbers at the expense of other nationalities.

Abkhazia has adopted a presidential form of government. The first incumbent (1994–2005), war-hero Vladislav Ardzinba, enjoyed early popularity, though the later years of his presidency were marked first by increasing authoritarianism and then by very poor health. The task of ruling Abkhazia fell largely to Raul Khadjimba, a former KGB agent, popular with the Kremlin. A standoff developed during the 2004 presidential election, when Khadjimba refused to accept defeat at the hands of Sergei Bagapsh. The solution brokered, which saw the pair run on a unity ticket, with Khadjimba running as Bagapsh's vice-presidential candidate, was overwhelmingly endorsed by the Abkhaz electorate. Though seats for the 35-member Peoples Assembly are hotly contested, the legislature plays a minor role in the republic's political life.

On August 26, 2009, following a brief war that primarily involved Russian and Georgian forces, the Kremlin issued a decree recognizing Abkhazia as an independent state. Only Nicaragua followed suit. The absence of recognition will do little to stop extensive Russian investment and influence in Abkhazia. While this Russian presence will bring economic dividends for those living in Abkhazia, it will also increase the risk of more intensive Russification. The position of Georgians expelled from Abkhazia as a result of the 1992–1993 and 2008 wars remains unresolved.

*Donnacha Ó Beacháin*

### Further Reading

Coppieters, Bruno, Ghia Nodia, and Yuri Anchabadze, eds. *Georgians and Abkhazians: The Search for a Peace Settlement.* Köln: Bundesinstitut für Ostwissenschaftliche und Internationale Studien, 1998.

Hewitt, George B. *The Abkhazians: A Handbook.* London: Curzon, 1998.

Suny, Ronald Grigor. *The Making of the Georgian Nation.* 2nd ed. Bloomington: Indiana University Press, 1994.

# Adyghs

Adyghs, known also as Circassians in English and Cherkesy in Russian, live in northwestern Caucasus. As of 2002, there are 108,100 Adyghs residing in the Republic of Adygheya, located between the Kuban and Laba rivers, with another 49,500 in the northern Karachaevo-Cherkessia Republic, both parts of the Russian Federation. Some 15,800 Adyghs live in the neighboring Krasnodar region. They speak Adygh, a Caucasian language, and most practice Islam. The exonym Cherkesy (Circassian) also includes the closely related Abkhazians, Kabards, and Ubykhs. In the pre-Soviet period the Adyghs and Kabards were actually considered one people. With Russian conquest of the Adygh territories starting in 1864, many of the mountain people left and became refugees in the Ottoman Empire. Surviving Adyghs settled all over the Ottoman Empire and can therefore be found today in small diaspora settlements spread over a vast area, from the Balkans in the west to Anatolia in the east. A few hundred live in the Republic of Macedonia and in Bulgaria, while most of those living in Kosovo left in 1998, when they were repatriated to the Republic of Adygheya. There are still several Çerkez (Adygh) villages in the western and central Anatolian part of Turkey with a total population of about 700,000, but settlements can also be found numbering about 15,000 in Israel, 40,000 in Lebanon and Syria, about 20,000 in and around Amman in Jordan, and fewer numbers in Egypt and even Libya. Immigrant communities from Syria exist in New Jersey and other parts of the United States. Some have also arrived as guest workers from Turkey and live nowadays in Germany and the Netherlands. According to some estimates, the world population of Adyghs is between 800,000 and 1 million.

The Adyghs are recognized in the sources since the 13th century, when they were dispersed over a much larger area around the Don River and the Caucasus Mountains. At that time and in the following centuries, they were dispersed by Mongols, several Turkic peoples, and Russians, and had to retreat to their contemporary mountainous homeland. The Adyghs lived and still live as pastoralists and farmers in the mountains.

The Russian Empire's war of conquest against the Caucasian peoples lasted for more than a century. The mountaineers put up fierce resistance, and the difficult conditions also contributed to the slow pace of the conquest. When their leader Shamil capitulated in 1859 and the Chechen-Dagestani resistance was broken, the Russians completed the conquest of the Adygh and other Circassian territories in 1864. The Circassians who survived the war and did not accept Russian rule left their mountains and sought refuge in the Ottoman Empire. Nearly half a million are said to have been deported or fled, and many died during the journey. One closely related Circassian group was the Ubykhs, who died in large numbers when escaping Russian troops. Only a few survived and they have now all disappeared; the last speaker of the Ubykh language died in 1992.

After the revolutions in 1917–1918, the Adygh territory was established as an autonomous region (oblast) in 1922. It went through several administrative changes during the 1920s and 1930s. In 1937 Adygheya was incorporated into the Krasnodar region. Adygheya changed its status to that of a republic within the Russian Federation in 1991.

In 2002, the Adyghs constituted only 24 percent of the population in Adygheya; Russians made up 64 percent, Armenians 3 percent, and Ukrainians 2 percent. Adygheya is now highly industrialized, especially in food production. The Adyghs remain a rather rural people, although many live in cities.

Most Adyghs are Sunni Muslims belonging to the Hanafi School of jurisprudence. Popular religion includes many pre-Islamic elements. The Adygh language belongs, together with Ubykh and Kabardian, to the northwestern or Abkhazo-Adyghean group of Caucasian languages. It is divided into several dialects: Abadzekh, Bzchedugh, Chemgwi, and Shapsug. A written Adygh language was developed in the 1920s, based on the Chemgwi dialect. It was written with Arabic script, which was replaced by the Latin alphabet in the late 1920s. However, at the end of the 1930s, Soviet authorities ordered the Adygh language to be written in the Cyrillic alphabet. Most Adyghs use their native language as their first language, although a majority of them are bilingual, also speaking Russian. There is an increasing interest in using the language in various domains, such as newspapers and for radio broadcasts. However, since Russian is the dominant language in Adygheya, the future of the local languages is under threat.

*Ingvar Svanberg*

**Further Reading**

Akiner, Shirin. *Islamic Peoples of the Soviet Union.* London: KPI, 1986.

Cornell, Svante, and Ingvar Svanberg. "Russia and Transcaucasia." In *Islam Outside the Arab World*, eds. David Westerlund and Ingvar Svanberg. Richmond: Curzon, 1999.

Jaimoukha, Amjad. *The Circassians: A Handbook.* London: Routledge, 2001.

Olson, James S. *An Ethnohistorical Dictionary of the Russian Soviet Empires.* Westport, CT: Greenwood Press, 1994.

# Ajarians

The Ajarians (Ajars, Adjars, Adzhars) belong to the large family of ethnic Georgians, together with Mingrelians, Abkhazians, Svans, Lezgins, and about 20 other groups. More than 300,000 Ajarians live in an autonomous province in southwestern Georgia; others reside elsewhere in Georgia and in nearby Turkey. Largely known as "Georgian Muslims," they call themselves *Ach'areli* (pl. *Ach'arlebi*). In 1926 Ajar, a derivative of this name (*Acar* in Turkish) was adopted formally. The local dialect of Georgian contains both Laz and Turkish influence, and the Ajars' written language is Georgian. In "Marxism and the National Question" (1913), Josef Stalin, himself a Georgian by background and the leading Bolshevik expert in ethnicity, observed that they were a people "who speak the Georgian language but whose culture is Turkish and who profess the religion of Islam."

During antiquity, Ajaria was part of Colchis and Caucasian Iberia. Colonized by ancient Greeks in the 5th century BCE, the region fell under Roman control three centuries later. Local tribes, believed to be of Hun origin, adopted Christianity in the 4th century, to be replaced by Islam during Ottoman rule in the 17th through 19th centuries. As a part of the region of Egrisi, in the 9th century CE it was incorporated into the unified Georgian Kingdom. The Ottomans administrated the area from 1614, when conversion to Islam occurred, until being forced to cede area by the expanding Russian Empire in 1878.

Vestiges of earlier Christian practice do remain, for example, in the crosses laid traditionally on bread and cakes, and in the recurrent decorative crosses encircled with a vine leaf, found even in mosques. Remains of churches and monasteries are maintained with their Byzantine-style icons, and Christian graves are protected and cared for. Though a significant percentage of Ajarians remain Sunni Muslims, with the collapse of the Soviet Union and reestablishment of Georgia as an independent state, voluntary reconversion to Christianity has accelerated, especially among the young. Curiously enough, in the regional capital city of Batumi, there are now 14 Christian churches and only one mosque.

In accordance with the terms of the Russo-Turkish Treaty of March 16, 1921, the city of Batumi on the Black Sea, after a brief British occupation, was ceded to Georgia along with lands to its north. A few months later, on July 16, 1921, the Soviet regime established the Ajarian Autonomous Republic, with a capital in Batumi and comprising 1,120 square miles in southwestern Georgia. Ajarians were spared the fate of the other neighboring Muslim peoples of the northern Caucasus—the Meskhians (also known as "Meskhetian Turks"), Hemshins (Islamicized Armenians), and others—who were deported by Stalin to Central Asia.

According to the last reliable census (1989), 324,806 Ajarians reside in the Ajarian Autonomous Republic of Georgia, where they constitute 82.8 percent of its population. Ajarian settlements are also found in nearby Georgian provinces and parts of neighboring Turkey. During the turmoil that followed Georgia's 1991 independence, their regional leader, Aslan

Abashidze, turned Ajaria into a personal fiefdom, an undeclared but de facto independent state for more than a decade. By 2004, when Abashidze was compelled to flee, the region had been incorporated into the Republic of Georgia as an autonomous republic.

*Stephan E. Nikolov*

**Further Reading**

Greene, T. *The Forsaken People: Internal Displacement in the North Caucasus, Azerbaijan, Armenia and Georgia.* Washington, DC: The Brookings Institute, 1996.

# Albanians

Albanians inhabit parts of the Balkan Peninsula and are mostly concentrated in Albania, a country in southeastern Europe, where they make up about 95 percent of approximately 3.5 million inhabitants (Greeks, Vlachs, Roma, Macedonians, Serbs, and Bulgarians make up the remaining 5%). Unlike most other European countries, Albania is predominantly rural: according to the Albanian Institute for Statistics (INSTAT), about 42 percent of the population lived in urban centers in 2001. The capital city of Tirana boasts the greatest concentration of Albanians, and the next most densely populated cities include Elbasan in central Albania, Shkodër in the north, Korcë in the east, and Durrës and Vlorë on the Adriatic coast. Additional countries in the Balkans with significant numbers of Albanians include Kosovo (about 1.8 million or 90% of the population), the Republic of Macedonia (about 500,000 or 25% of the population), and Montenegro (about 55,000 or 8% of the population). Albanian diasporic communities are found elsewhere in Europe (mainly Greece, Italy, Germany, and Switzerland) and also in Turkey, Egypt, and the United States.

Albanians converse in the Albanian language. A distinctive branch of the Indo-European language family, Albanian is written in Latin script and spoken in two main and mutually intelligible dialects: Gheg (northern) and Tosk (southern). The geographical boundary between the two dialects is roughly marked by the Shkumbin River, which cuts across Albania. Tosk was pronounced the base for the standardized literary language in 1952, but nonetheless the use of Gheg remains widespread in Kosovo and Macedonia. With reference to religious identity, the Albanian constitution ensures freedom of religious belief and expression, but demographic figures regarding religious affiliation are currently unavailable because the most recent census, which took place in 2001, did not include any such questions. At present, there is a widespread tendency among Albanians in Albania to identify as Roman Catholic whereas Albanians in Kosovo and Macedonia are predominantly Muslim.

Since the end of World War II, archaeological evidence has been deployed to support the hypothesis of the origin of Albanians from the Illyrians, who once inhabited parts of present-day Albanian territory. It is generally accepted that peoples who spoke a different language from Greek or Latin, and to whom the Greeks and Romans referred as Illyrians, inhabited

Ethnic Albanians near the town of Domorovce in Kosovo Province wave Albanian national flags to protest Serbian roadblocks in August 2000. (Department of Defense)

the Balkan Peninsula by the seventh century BCE. Nonetheless, the hypothesis of the descent of Albanians from Illyrians remains somewhat controversial, especially with regard to the peoples who inhabit the wider coastal region of Epirus, stretching across northwestern Greece and southern Albania. Ptolemy of Alexandria, the notable astronomer, in the second century CE makes the first historical references to a free Illyrian tribe of the "Albanoi" and their town "Albanopolis," which is located within present-day Albania. The term "Albanoi" derives from the Latin *albus*, which means "white," and, according to some theories, translates into "people dressed in white." Alternative theories assume that the term refers to the whiteness of the nearby mountains.

The area where present-day Albania lies was colonized by Greece in the 7th century BCE, was subjugated by the Roman Empire in the 2nd century BCE, and became part of the Byzantine Empire in the 4th century CE. Its rich history includes invasions and conquests by Huns, Visigoths, Ostrogoths, Slavs, Normans, and Venetians. Between 1334 and 1347, the area became part of the Great Serbian Empire under Stefan Dušan. Toward the end of the 14th century, the Venetians established themselves in what are now northern Albania and the Montenegrin coast (Albania Veneta in Italian, or "Venetian Albania"). In 1478, according to the provisions of a peace agreement that ended a multiyear war between the Venetians and the Ottoman Turks, and after more than two decades of successful armed resistance by Albania's notable military leader and national hero Gjergj Kastioti (otherwise known as Skanderbeg; 1405–1468), the territory of present-day Albania became a Turkish province. Under Ottoman rule, Albanians were classified as Muslim and received education in the Turkish, not Albanian, language for an interesting reason: education in the Ottoman Empire had a religious character and schooling was provided in Turkish (for Muslims), Greek (for Orthodox Christians), and Italian (for Catholics). The years of Ottoman rule, especially the weakening of Ottoman power in the late 19th/early 20th centuries, were critical to the awakening of Albanian national consciousness and the development of modern Albanian identity.

When the Roman Empire was divided in 395, Albania came under Constantinople's administrative rule and Rome's ecclesiastical jurisdiction. After the Great Schism of 1054, whereby the Eastern Orthodox Church was divided from the authority of the Roman Catholic Church, north Albania became Roman Catholic, the south Greek Orthodox. It is not certain whether the Catholic cause was furthered under Venetian rule, but it is certain that the Greek Orthodox religion was practiced by Albanians until the Ottoman conquest. Following the Ottoman invasion at the end of the 15th century, Islam gradually spread in Albania. From the mid-16th century onward, the Bektashi, a Shiite dervish order preaching tolerance toward all non-Muslim creeds, gained influence and popularity in Albania. Bektashi places of worship (*tekkes*) spread in the country, and the shrine of legendary warrior-saint Sari Saltik in Krujë became a center of worship. At the beginning of the 19th century additional *tekkes* were established in the towns of Gjirokaster, Tepelena, and Janina.

Under Ottoman rule, Roman Catholicism in Albania suffered a severe blow. The Ottoman administration, however, recognized the patriarch of Constantinople as the spiritual leader of Orthodox Christians, and the Albanian Orthodox Church, founded by Bishop Fan Noli in Boston, Massachusetts, in 1908, was recognized as autocephalous by the patriarchate of Constantinople in 1937. Up to the end of World War II, 70 percent of Albanians in Albania were registered as Muslim (largely belonging to the Sunni branch of Islam and some to the Shiite order of Bektashi), 20 percent Eastern Orthodox (mostly in the south), and 10 percent Roman Catholic (mostly in the north). Starting in 1944, many religious leaders were imprisoned or

executed and all religious groups were subject to persecution. During communist rule (1944–1989), the practice of religion was declared illegal (in 1967) and Albania was proclaimed an atheist state—the first in the world. Albanian folk culture was also suppressed under communist rule. Folk mythology and beliefs that have survived to this day are replete with references to taboos, vampires, witchcraft, dragons, and monsters such as the *kulshedra*.

The Ghegs, who live in the northern mountainous regions, were traditionally herders and were organized around the exogamous, patrilineal clan (*fis*) whereby people claim descent from a common, sometimes fictitious, male ancestor. Until the 1950s, when the communist regime tried to eliminate clan rule, it was common for extended families, consisting of the nuclear families of many brothers, to live together in an extended household (*shtëpi*, which means "house"). Land was owned communally by the clan. Additionally, before Albania came under communist rule, everyday life among the Ghegs was regulated by the *kanun*, a code of customary laws that has been passed on orally from generation to generation in the form of proverbs and common sayings. There are numerous versions of the *kanun* that are named either after areas or after reputable agnatic clan rulers and ancestors, who allegedly created the *kanun*. The *kanun* of Lekë Dukagjin, an affluent Albanian clan chieftain (*bajraktar*) and contemporary of Skanderbeg, is the best-known and most widely practiced customary law; its adherents include Albanians in the North Albanian Alps, Shkodër, Dukagjin, western Kosovo, and Albanian populations in parts of Serbia, Montenegro, and Macedonia. Consisting of 1,262 articles that are presented in 12 books, the *kanun* covers all aspects of everyday life such as work, marriage, gender roles, personal honor, family and economic organization, and land and livestock, and continues to regulate social status, especially with reference to blood feuds and conflict reconciliation.

While the autonomous Gheg herders in the rugged mountains of northern Albania have traditionally regulated daily life using the laws of the *kanun* and shown strong-willed resistance to both Ottoman and Communist rule, the Tosks have led a different lifestyle because of the geographical specificities of the regions they inhabit. Living in the easily accessible southern lowland plains, the Tosks came under firm Ottoman control and were better integrated into the larger system of Ottoman governance. Traditionally, they were tenant farmers organized in a semifeudal system whereby the Muslim landowning nobility (*beys*), and not clan chiefs as was the case in the northern mountains, had political and economic control over the latifundia (*çiftliks*). Similarly to the clan chiefs, the beys in effect became autonomous rulers. This system of land tenure lasted well into the 20th century, albeit with some modifications. After 1946, however, the communist government expropriated farmland and distributed it among the farmers who were dependent on the landowners. Later, all land was nationalized, private ownership was abolished, and people were organized in cooperatives.

A process of land privatization has begun since the collapse of socialism, accompanied with various challenges including the establishment of institutions for land and property management. Albania remains one of the poorest countries in Europe: according to the 2005 Living Standard Measurement Survey conducted by the INSTAT, 18 percent of Albanians live on less than U.S. $2 a day. In general, rural areas and the mountainous areas in the north continue to be poorer and less developed than urban areas and the lowlands in the south.

Albanian epic songs and ballads, mostly preserved in northern Albania and Kosovo, are part of a rich Albanian oral tradition. The songs are commonly woven around such themes as warfare, sacrifice, and honor (*besa*). Albania also has an old tradition of embroidery, silver and gold filigree making, pottery making, and wood carving. Notable Albanian figures include nun and philanthropist Mother Teresa, painter Ibrahim Kodra, and writer Ismail Kadare. Also well known is the Franciscan missionary Shtjefën Gjeçov, who assembled the Albanian proverbs and sayings making up the *kanun* and codified them in paragraphs and articles in the 1920.

With the weakening of the Ottoman Empire in the late 19th century, Albanian intellectuals feared that Albanian-populated territories would be partitioned between Greece and Serbia. Therefore, they formed the League of Prizren in 1878 as a way of promoting the use of a unified Albanian language, hence strengthening Albanian national consciousness and preparing the ground for an independent Albanian state. Even though the Turks crushed the efforts of the League of Prizren three years later, attempts to achieve Albanian cultural recognition within the Ottoman Empire continued. In 1908, when the Young Turks rose to power in Istanbul, Albanians were temporarily granted linguistic rights, and additional democratic reforms for Albania were discussed. The new Turkish government failed to carry out these reforms, however, and Albanians engaged in a new armed struggle between 1910 and 1912. Albania remained part of the Ottoman Empire until 1912 when the First Balkan War broke out. On November 28 of that year, Ismail Kemal, who is widely recognized as the father of Albanian independence, organized a national assembly at the city of Vlorë and became the president of a provisional government. The Great Powers recognized Albanian independence after the London Conference of July 1913.

During World War I Albania was occupied by the Allies, and in 1924 became a monarchy under the tutelage of Italy. As a socialist republic led by Enver Hoxha, Albania was kept isolated from the rest of the world from 1946 until Hoxha's death in 1985. Since the collapse of the communist regime in 1989, Albania has gradually developed into a democracy. The Democratic Party of Albania (PDS) won a decisive victory in the 1992 parliamentary elections, and its leader, Sali Berisha, became Albania's first noncommunist president. In early 1997, however, the PDS bore the brunt of a severe financial crisis after several popular financial pyramid schemes collapsed. Many Albanians who had invested their life savings in the schemes took to the streets in protest and toppled the government. The country descended into anarchy after hundreds of thousands of weapons were looted from government armories and some 2,000 people were killed in uncontained rioting.

President Berisha declared a state of emergency, and in March 1997 the United Nations Security Council endorsed a proposal by the Organization for Security and Cooperation in Europe (OSCE) to deploy a multinational protection force in Albania in order to help restore order and provide humanitarian aid. The presence of the multinational force provided the security needed for the organization of parliamentary elections that were held in June of that year and resulted in a clear victory of the Socialist Party of Albania (PSS), the reformed Communist Party. Thereafter the rule of law was gradually reestablished.

Albania is a member of a number of international organizations, including the United Nations, the OSCE, and the World Trade Organization. The country became a member of the North Atlantic Treaty Organization in 2008, and applied to join the European Union in April 2009.

Before and after World War II, Greece asserted ownership of the southern part of Albania, arguing that its inhabitants are ethnically Greek. In 1987 Greece renounced any territorial claims against Albania, and a year later the two countries signed a cross-border trade agreement. Nonetheless, tense relations between Greece and Albania continued and gave rise to mutual recriminations through the mid-1990s. Also, before Kosovo declared its independence from Serbia in 2008, attempts by the Serbian (and earlier, Yugoslav) authorities to keep the Albanian population in Kosovo under firm control significantly strained regional relations with Albania. The district of Mitrovica in northern Kosovo remains the apple of discord between Serbs and Albanians. Relations between

Albania and neighboring Macedonia have also often been strained, mainly by Albania's support of the requests for greater cultural and political rights made by the Albanian community in Macedonia (which amounts to about 25% of the Macedonian population).

During the communist era and until 1991, when a strict pronatalist law in effect prohibited contraception and restricted abortion, the size of the population nearly tripled, rising from about 1.2 million in 1945 to about 2.9 million in 1985. Albania's annual rate of population increase between World War II and the collapse of the communist regime in 1989 averaged about 2.5—the highest in Europe. The results of the most recent census in 2001 show that the population has declined since 1989, probably diminished by mass migration to Western Europe during the 1990s. Albania has the youngest population in Europe: in the mid-1990s the average age was 26 and more than a third of the total population was under 15 years of age. The U.S. Census Bureau figures in 2008 placed life expectancy at 78 years.

*Vasiliki Neofotistos*

## Further Reading

Durham, Edith. *High Albania.* Boston: Beacon Press, 1905.

Jacques, Edwin E. *The Albanians: An Ethnic History from Prehistoric Times to the Present.* Jefferson, NC: McFarland, 1995.

Pettifer, James, and Miranda Vickers. *The Albanian Question: Reshaping the Balkans.* London: I. B. Tauris, 2007.

Schwandner-Sievers, Stephanie, and Bernd Jürgen Fischer, eds. *Albanian Identities: Myth and History.* Indiana: Indiana University Press, 2002.

Shytock, Andrew J. "Autonomy, Entanglement, and the Feud: Prestige Structures and Gender Value in Highland Albania." *Anthropological Quarterly* 61 (1988): 113–118.

Skendi, Stavro. *The Albanian National Awakening: 1878–1912.* Princeton, NJ: Princeton University Press, 1967.

Vickers, Miranda. *The Albanians: A Modern History.* London: I. B. Tauris, 1995.

## Andorrans

Andorrans, who call themselves *Andorrencs* in Catalan, *Andorranos* in Castilian, and Andorrans in English and French, reside in the Principality of Andorra. Within this small, mountainous homestead, Andorrans have negotiated cultural autonomy, economic autarky, and political distinction between France and Spanish Catalonia for more than a millennium. At the same time, they share pervasive Roman Catholicism; Catalan, the enclave's official language; and many other cultural traits of food, family, and everyday life with these close neighbors. Yet, among contemporary residents, the actual citizens of Andorra constitute only 35.7 percent of the 76,874 residents, fewer than the resident Spanish population (37.4%). Beyond its history of cross-border exchanges, banking, shopping, and tourism have made contemporary Andorra a European crossroads in which cosmopolitan development challenges centuries of isolation.

Andorra emerged as a separate polity within the Marca Hispanica, or Spanish March, that Charlemagne established in 795 along the Pyrenees as a border with

Two Andorran women wearing contrasting clothing styles lean on stone wall. (B. Anthony Stewart/National Geographic Society/Corbis)

Iberian Muslims; the national anthem still refers to "Charlemagne, my father." (The name Andorra may also reflect earlier Basque roots.) In 819, sovereignty was granted to the Count of Urgell in Catalonia, from whom it passed to the Bishop of Seu d'Urgell. Since the 13th century, this cleric has been titular coprince of Andorra with the Count of Foix, whose rights eventually accrued to the president of the French state. A new constitution establishing clear local control was promulgated in 1993.

Andorra's traditional economy depended for centuries on agriculture, herding, mining and ironwork, and textiles, supplemented by smuggling of goods and peoples across borders; by 1950, its population only numbered 10,000, with the power of patriarchal stem families remaining strong. Traditional architecture remains visible in the slate-roof homes and churches of the countryside, some of which go back to Romanesque times. *Festes majors* (primary feasts), with traditional banquets and dances such as the *marratxa, contrapàs,* and *sardana* mark the lives of these settlements as well as the nation, in a calendar that shares major Catalan feasts like Sant Jordi (April 23) and Santa Llucia, before Christmas.

In the last 50 years, increased connections by roads and communications technologies have led to intense growth and modernization. Andorra's "offshore banking" has enriched the state, while 11 million tourists now seek its mountain resorts and shopping opportunities each year. Labor immigration and retirement have also diversified cities like Andorra la Vella and Escaldes-Engordany, which include Portuguese and Hindu communities. Nonetheless, while Andorrans now rank among the healthiest and longest-living people in the world, modernization and immigration have also stimulated new demands for what Joan Becat calls an "Andorrization of Andorra."

*Gary Wray McDonogh*

### Further Reading

Becat, Joan. "Les portugais seront-ils les meilleurs Andorrans?" (Are the Portuguese the Best Andorrans?) *Revue Européenne des migrations internationals* 13 (1997): 135–156.

d'Argemir, Comas, and J.J. Pujadas. *Andorra: Un Pais de Frontera (Andorra: A Frontier Country).* Barcelona: Alta Fulla, 1997.

Degage, Alain, and Antoni Duro. *L'Andorre (Andorra)*. Paris: P.U.F., 1998.

McDonogh, Gary. *Iberian Worlds*. New York: Routledge, 2008.

# Arbëreshë

The Arbëreshë or Arbareschi (also known as the Albanians of Italy) live in southern Italy. They descend from Albanian migrants, follow the Greek Orthodox faith, and speak Arbërisht, a dialect that has developed in the course of over 500 years of residence in Italy. Arbëreshë was the term self-designation of Albanians before the Ottoman invasion of the 15th century; similar terms are used for Albanian origins populations living in Greece ("Arvanitika," the Greek rendering of Arbëreshë) and Turkey ("Arnaut," Turkish for the Greek term Arvanitika). The Arbëreshë process of settlement in Italy started in the 15th century and it continued through different migratory waves until the 18th century. Today, Arbëresh villages and communities can be found in several southern Italian regions (Abruzzo, Basilicata, Campania, Molise, Puglia, and Sicily), especially in Calabria. The estimated number of members of the Arbëresh community in Italy is about 100,000.

The earliest known Albanian/Arbëresh presence in Calabria dates back to the 14th century, when, in order to repress a rebellion of the nobility, King Alfonso V of Aragon employed Albanian troops, who were then rewarded with land in the area around Catanzaro. Over the years, other Albanian troops were deployed in Sicily and Apulia and similarly rewarded. Finally, the invasion of Greece by the Ottoman Empire in the 15th century caused a massive flow of the Albanian communities residing there toward Sicily, especially Piana. In the 20th century, following a common pattern in southern Italy, some Arbëreshë left their villages and emigrated either to northern Italy or abroad (especially the United States).

Today the Arbëreshë show a high level of insertion in Italian society, despite the fact that they often live in enclaves or areas that are ethnically homogenous. Traditional customs survive, especially during marriages and religious celebrations such as the epiphany, but their vitality varies between settlements. While several groups have promoted independent radio broadcasts and newspapers, and several university centers are devoted to the study and defense of the culture, recent research shows that linguistic competency in Arbërisht is shrinking among the youngest members of the community and that a growing number of insiders reject traditional culture. However, the Greek Orthodox religion is still observed by Arbëreshë.

Arbëreshë have long contributed to Albanian culture, and many Arbëreshë intellectuals, who maintained throughout the centuries a profound attachment to their native country, played an important role in the emergence of Albanian nationalism. Although Arbëreshe literature developed of its own accord, it may be considered an integral part of Albanian culture. Well-known intellectuals include Jeronim De Rada, Nicolò Brancato, Nicola Figlia di Munxifsi, Jul Variboba, and Nicola Chetta.

Under Italian law, Arbëreshë are a protected linguistic minority (under Law 482 of 1999). Their territories are considered bilingual by the state, and the Italian regions hosting Arbëreshë settlements and other minority groups, in agreement with the interested groups, must implement initiatives aimed at supporting the survival of the culture and the language.

*Pietro Saitta*

**Further Reading**

Altimari, F., and L. M. Savoia. *I dialetti italo-albanesi (Italian-Albanian Dialects)*. Roma: Bulzoni, 1994.

Cassiano, D. *La cultura minoritaria arbëreshe in Calabria (The Minority Culture of the Arbëreshe in Calabria)*. Cosenza: Edizioni Brenner, 1981.

Derhemi, E. "Features of Dysfunctional Attrition in the Arbresh of Piana degli Albanesi." *International Journal of the Sociology of Language* 178 (2006): 31–52.

Elsie, Robert. 2006. "The Hybrid Soil of the Balkans: A Topography of Albanian Literature." In *History of the Literary Cultures of East-Central Europe*, eds. M. Cornis-Pope and M. Neubauer, 283–301. Amsterdam: J. John Benjamins, 2006.

# Aromanians

Aromanians (Romanian: *Aromâni*; Greek: *Αρμάνο*□) inhabit the southern Balkans and are found in Greece, Albania, the Republic of Macedonia, Romania, and Bulgaria. They call themselves Aromanian (i.e., *Romans, Armãnj, Rrãmenji, Rrãmãnji*). Since they were usually concentrated in small isolated areas, in the past neighboring majority populations often called them by place names: for example, *frasheroti* in Albania; *muzakiri* in the region of Muzakiya; *Moglen,* or *Meglen Vlachs* in Macedonia; and *Gramusteni* and *Pindeni* in Greece. Balkan neighbors also referred to them as "Vlachs," a pejorative term for any outsider, especially a shepherd. (In a neutral and widespread sense, Vlach refers to southeastern European populations descending from Latinized pastoralists, the largest modern groups of which are Romanians and Aromanians.) Enumerating the Aromanian population is difficult because national censuses do not record them as a separate ethnic group and because the processes of assimilation into other groups and misidentification are ongoing. According to calculations of Aromanian NGOs, out of a total of 100,000–200,000, up to 100,000 Aromanians reside in Greece, 40,000–45,000 in Serbia, 26,000–30,000 in Romania, and around 10,000 each in Bulgaria and Macedonia—roughly one-tenth the number at the beginning of the 20th century. Virtually all Aromanians are Eastern Orthodox Christians. They speak a Romance language related to the Romanian spoken in Romania. Aromanians use the Latin alphabet in Romania; the Cyrillic in Serbia, Bulgaria, and Macedonia; and Greek letters in Greece. Among the most polyglot of Balkan peoples, Aromanians are typically fluent in the official languages of the countries in which they reside as well as in Aromanian.

In the absence of written records and other forms of evidence, the origins of the Aromanian language remain unknown. From CE 165–275 the Aromanian homeland was incorporated into the Roman Empire as Dacia Traiana. During this period roads and trade routes penetrated the inland hills more than ever, bringing herders from the hills into contact with Roman culture. It is not a coincidence that surviving Vlach communities are present in areas near the ancient Via Egnatia, the infamous Roman military and trade route connecting the Adriatic with the Aegean. A number of scholars suggest that Vlachs in fact descend from Roman colonists. However, these colonizers rarely came from Rome itself and did not speak Latin as a first language. Further, it is hard to believe that urbanized colonists would in such numbers turn to a nomadic way of life; it is much more likely that native peoples adopted a simplified form of Latin and other aspects of Roman culture. Other investigators posit a link with the non-Hellenic Balkan tribes such as Thracians and Illyrians, especially the Macedons, implying that in the 6th century CE Aromanians went down to the Pindus while Slavs massively settled into Illyria. It is believed that by about the 10th century the Aromanian language had differentiated itself from the northern Vlach language that would become modern Romanian. Romanian and especially Greek historians' claims that their peoples are the lineal descendants of the Vlachs correspond with geopolitical claims. For instance, if Vlachs are in fact the hitherto unrecognized offspring of ancient Greeks, then Greece can justify further demands on historically disputed Balkan lands.

From the 6th century CE on, written references to the Vlachs can be deduced from Latin place names. Bulgarian scriptures from the 10th century make reference to Vlachs and to areas designated as Great and Little Wallachia, which roughly correspond to the location of present Vlach populations. About that time close connection among numerous Aromanian groups was probably broken, and they were exposed to various outside influences. By the mid-14th century Serbs occupied most of the Aromanian parishes. This was soon followed by five centuries of Ottoman rule, from when accounts of Vlachs are few and meager. Modernization, the introduction of multiple state borders, and animosity between Balkan states during most of the 20th century, together with the denial of a distinctive Aromanian culture and vigorous assimilation practices by dominant populations, shattered Aromanian specificity.

According to fading Aromanian tradition, each step in human existence is the work of providence. Though they strictly observe Orthodox holidays, and practically submit their own seasonal activities to the prescribed calendar, they seldom attend church and do not require clergy to mark weddings, baptisms, funerals, or important life events. Their principal dedication is the pagan devotion to the fecundity of nature. Belief in life after death was deeply rooted, and elaborate funeral rites were observed; though prohibited by law, custom called for the reburial of the deceased 40 days after death, a possible vestige of Orphic culture. (Orphic funerary customs are thought to involve the actual or imitated dismemberment of the corpse believed to represent the Greek god Dionysus, who was then reborn. Orphic eschatology laid great emphasis on reward and punishment after death, when the soul was believed to be free to achieve its true life.) Communication with ancestors was practiced in many circumstances and in various ways. Aromanians have created an abundant narrative popular culture, including ballads, epic and lyric songs, fairy tales, proverbs, and brainteasers, though such forms lack the imaginary creatures and occurrences common in so many traditions. Aromanians commonly heal with herbs and other mixtures. Traditional body tattoos distinguish some Vlach groups. Unique among all European peoples for the extent to which their culture amalgamates both Roman and Hellenic heritages, their customs have come under special protection of UNESCO and the Council of Europe.

Traditionally, Aromanians were herders living in isolated areas. Their home bases were ample villages, with homes built of stone, located high in the mountains. Theirs was a mobile life. Within the Ottoman Empire, Aromanian muleteers and merchants enjoyed a virtual monopoly on redistributive and mercantile functions along the inland routes of the Balkans; some ventured as far north as Vienna, Odessa, Leipzig, and Warsaw. Until the beginning of 20th century, Aromanian shepherds would spend time from the Orthodox feasts of St. George's Day (April 23, old style) to St. Cross Day (September 14) moving through main mountainous pastures before heading south for wintering close to the Aegean Sea. These seasonal migrations were made by communities of 50–100 people, comprising rich and poor families as well as servants. They kept horses and large flocks of sheep and fashioned cheeses such as the yellow cheese, kashkaval. Before the coming of the railway they furnished central markets with such primary products as meat, wool, and dairy products.

Aromanians have long been the targets of discrimination. Some authors, aiming apparently to minimize any contribution of the Aromanian to local culture, point to the absence of written laws and literature. In addition to their notable economic contribution, Aromanians seem to have respected, not ignored, Classical and Byzantine civilization, just as they did that of neighboring peoples. They played a not-insignificant role in the historical process in southeastern Europe. Culturally, the Aromanians remain the most Hellenophile among the Slav, Latin, Albanian, Turkic, Roma, and other minorities still living on Greek territory. Those Aromanians who had the opportunity to educate themselves distinguished themselves during the Ottoman epoch; in fact, Aromanians owned some of the first printing presses. Animosity from dominant populations was a constant preoccupation for Aromanians, however. For example, Turks and Arnaut (Albanian) hordes sacked the predominantly Aromanian center of Moskopolje in 1769 and again in the next century. Since the early 20th century, Romania has established schools catering to Aromanians inside Romanian as well as in neighboring countries.

Aromanians were crucial in the establishment of the Philike Hetairea rebellion and in the eviction of Turks from Greece, as well as later in the Ilinden uprising in Macedonia. In 1923, the few who converted to Islam during Ottoman rule joined the retreating Turks and were further assimilated into Turkish society. Owing to anti-Vlach prejudice, many educated Aromainans have melded with the surrounding majority populations. With their remarkable ability for hard work and adaptation, Aromanians have made important contributions to the public life of the countries in which they reside. According to local Aromanian association sources, many prominent figures in the history of Balkan peoples have Aromanian backgrounds, although official histories do not accept this because it conflicts with national myths. Aromanians have never received any political representation, let alone statehood, with a rare exception in 1941 when Fascist Italy, invading Greece, tried to create the puppet Aromanian Pindic Principality. During the communist period their unique identity was officially denied. Even after recent democratic reforms, local nationalistic parties in Serbia, Macedonia, Bulgaria, Albania, and Greece, fearing a "menace to the national unity" and groups "serving alien interests," have resisted the extension of any cultural rights or forms of self-government for Aromanians. Notwithstanding the efforts of Aromanian associations to sustain their language and traditions, permanent settlement in towns has eroded the pastoral life and with it their culture.

*Stephan E. Nikolov*

**Further Reading**

Gossiaux, Jean-François. *Pouvoirs ethniques dans les Balkans* (*Ethnic powers in the Balkans*). Paris: Presses Universitaires de France, 2002.

Stephenson, Paul. *Byzantium's Balkan frontier: A Political Study of the Northern Balkans, 900–1204*. Cambridge, NY: Cambridge University Press, 2000.

Winnifrith, Tom J. *The Vlachs—The History of a Balkan People*. New York: St. Martin's Press, 1987.

## Ashkenazic Jews

The term Ashkenazic typically refers to East European Jewry. Ashkenaz appears as the name of a person, the son of Gomer, grandson of Japheth, and great-grandson of Noah, in Genesis (10:3) and 1 Chronicles (1:6). Jeremiah (51:27–28) refers to Ashkenaz as a kingdom. These sources associate Ashkenaz with a region of ancient Assyria or Armenia, but by the 12th century, rabbinic writings, including those of Rabbi Shelomoh ben Yitshak Troyes (known as Rashi, 1040–1105 CE), used the term to refer specifically to "Germany" or "Germans." Ashkenaz most usually refers to a geographic location but has also been used to refer to a culture and a people. The term now commonly refers to the area along the banks of the Rhine (especially near the towns of Mainz, Worms, and Speyer) where a distinct Jewish culture developed that was carried throughout the world, especially to Eastern Europe, by Jews who trace their roots to this region. Historians have yet to adequately explain how the term came to be preferred over other regional names such as Rhineland or Lotharingia/Lorraine. While some scholars limit the term to describe the area of northwestern Europe and the German cultural areas of Central Europe where Jews resided, Ashkenaz is in wide use as a reference to the lands and culture of East European Jewry, whether that culture was developed in Europe or in lands to which European Jews migrated, especially the United States and Israel. The term denotes an origin group within the larger Jewish community and is used in contrast to Sepharad, a common Hebrew term for the Iberian Peninsula used to designate Jews (known as Sephardic Jews or Sephardim, with origins in Spain and Portugal before the expulsion of 1492). Jews from different origin groups display noticeable variations, especially in liturgical rites and the pronunciation of Hebrew. The diverse customs of Ashkenaz (*minhag Ashkenaz*) reflect the decentralized communal organization in France and Germany yet unite Ashkenazic Jews conceptually. While the total number of Ashkenazic Jews living in the small communities of Western Europe in the early Middle Ages has been difficult for historians to determine, it is known that approximately 200,000 Jews lived in France and the Holy Roman Empire in 1300 CE. Hebrew and Aramaic were the languages of the religious texts of the Jews of Ashkenaz, while Jewish dialects spoken during the period of early Ashkenaz in northwestern Europe developed into Yiddish, the distinct Jewish language spoken by approximately 11 million Ashkenazic Jews before World War II. Over time, however, Ashkenazic Jews throughout Europe also adopted the many non-Jewish vernaculars spoken by their Christian neighbors, sometimes to the detriment of their knowledge of Yiddish and Hebrew. Ashkenaz is often used in a broad sense to refer to the geographic areas where Yiddish-speaking Jews dominated Jewish popular culture in the 19th and early 20th centuries.

A group of *Ashkenazim* in Jerusalem, about 1876. (Library of Congress)

Many historians describe early Ashkenaz as a Jewish society that adhered strictly to Jewish law as interpreted in rabbinic writings. The Talmudic commentator Rashi is a central figure of Ashkenaz; his writings remain standard texts of study for all students of Jewish religious learning. Also of importance are the works of the tosaphists, rabbis centered in France and Germany from the 12th to 14th centuries whose commentaries are still studied. Especially noteworthy are those of Rabbi Ya'akov ben Me'ir of Ramerupt, a grandson of Rashi (known as Rabenu Tam, ca. 1100–1171). The intellectual achievements of these rabbis distinguished the Jewish culture of northern Christian Europe from previous Jewish cultures developed in other regions and set new law and practices to be followed by future generations. An ideology of martyrdom rooted in the experiences of the violence of 1096 is often seen as characteristic of Ashkenaz.

The violence of Christian Crusaders in that year led some Jews to kill themselves and their families in order to avoid baptism. These acts of religious heroism, by perhaps as many as a thousand Jews, both men and women, led to the development of an ideology of martyrdom that had a profound impact on Jewish collective memory. This martyr culture included new rituals for memorializing the dead that are still in practice today. These rituals, including the *yortsayt*, the practice of recalling the death of a loved one on the yearly anniversary of the death, are examples of how Ashkenazic Jews modeled their practices on Christian behavior. The Hasidei Ashkenaz, or Pietists of Ashkenaz, resisted innovation and instead focused on ascetic practices as the basis of moral teachings. The *Sefer Hasidim* (*Book of the Pietists*), to which Rabbi Yehudah ben Shemu'el the Pietist (ca. 1150–1217) contributed, is a collection of writings detailing these practices. Many historians have also noted the positive view of women held by Ashkenazic Jews, as part of an emphasis on the pure nature of the Jewish family. The understanding of Ashkenaz as a place where Jews lived strictly in accordance with Jewish law has been challenged by historians who also see variations in practice among the Ashkenazic Jews of the medieval and early modern periods. In spite of periodic anti-Jewish violence and differences in religious belief, Jews interacted closely with Christians in Ashkenaz, often drawing on Christian practices to develop new religious customs. Jews and Christians in the early Middle Ages have often been described as living in a symbiotic relationship, separate from each other in many ways but living

in small communities where they gained firsthand knowledge of the other group's religious, social, and cultural behaviors.

From the 12th through the 14th centuries, Ashkenazic Jews migrated east, primarily to the lands that would make up the early modern Polish-Lithuanian Commonwealth. Jewish life in the Polish-Lithuanian Commonwealth was conditioned by numerous pacts and privileges throughout the early modern period. Jews were, however, able to develop *kehillot*, or institutions of self-government that regulated Jewish religious practice and community life. Living primarily in small towns and working mostly in local and international trade and as merchants and craftsmen, Jews developed a culture based on the teachings of early Ashkenaz, but with local modifications. For example, Ashkenazic liturgical rites in Bohemia differed from those in Lithuania. Cracow's Rabbi Moses Isserles (known as Rema', 1520–1572) offered legalistic interpretations of Jewish law in accordance with Ashkenazic custom and in opposition to the rulings of Yosef Karo (1488–1575), who followed Sephardic tradition. Generations of legalists have looked to Isserles as a practical authority in Jewish law.

The Khmel'nyts'kyi massacres of 1648–1649 (known in Ashkenazic tradition as *gzeyres takh vetat*), coinciding with Cossack and Ukrainian peasant uprisings against the Polish nobility in the Polish-Lithuanian Commonwealth, led some Ashkenazic Jews to migrate to Western Europe and some to the Americas. This was the start of Ashkenazic communities in the Americas, which would in time numerically overtake Sephardic settlements. Approximately

40,000 Jews, or one-third of those in the 17th-century Polish-Lithuanian Commonwealth, lived in lands affected by the violence. Estimates of casualties vary widely, but at least thousands were killed. Less than 50 years later, though, many Jewish refugees returned to Ukrainian lands, stabilizing communities that would grow significantly in later years.

After the late 18th-century partitions of Poland, most of the Jews of Ashkenaz came under the rule of three absolutist states in Eastern Europe, the Russian, Prussian, and Austrian empires. As a result of Enlightenment ideas and the spread of nationalism throughout Europe in the late 19th century, East European Jews would find themselves, sometimes simultaneously, committed to traditional Jewish religious ideals, dedicated to evolving ideas of Jewish nationalism, attracted to non-Jewish cultures, and engaged in various nationalist and/or radical movements. Zionism, the movement to found a home for the Jewish nation, attracted many Jews acculturated to but alienated from non-Jewish cultures and their corresponding nationalist movements. Born in Budapest, the journalist and writer Theodor Herzl (1860–1904) spurred concrete political action that would ultimately result in the mobilization of the Jewish community toward the goal of a territorial nation-state. With the growth of Zionism as a national movement came the rebirth of Hebrew as a spoken language in the late 19th and early 20th centuries, alongside Yiddish and the non-Jewish vernaculars increasingly spoken by Jews educated in modern, secular institutions. Many Ashkenazic Jews fled Eastern Europe at the turn of the 20th century in search of better economic opportunities and greater political, religious, and social freedoms and in response to periodic outbursts of anti-Jewish violence. Like earlier migrants, these Jews took with them the culture of Ashkenaz, including its religious values, Yiddish linguistic heritage, and newly formed political ideas.

The largest Jewish origin group, Ashkenazic Jews made up 90 percent of the world's total of 16,500,000 Jews before the outbreak of World War II in 1939. The events of World War II and the Holocaust (1939–1945) devastated the Jewish communities of Europe, reducing the total Jewish population by more than one-third. The populous Jewish communities of Central and Eastern Europe became numerically insignificant after the war, while larger populations of Jews remained in the Soviet Union and, to some extent, in Western Europe. The center of Ashkenazic life thus shifted from Europe to the United States and Israel, in whose formation in 1948 Ashkenazic Jews played a key role, realizing the dream of many Zionists to create a territorial nation-state on geographical territory that Jews regarded as their homeland. Ashkenazic Jews maintained many aspects of the culture of early Ashkenaz in those places to which they had migrated, from Australia to the Americas. Hebrew, championed by Zionists of varying ideological inclinations, became the language of daily life in Israel, while Yiddish waned, victim of the wartime deaths of a majority of its speakers and negative perceptions of diaspora Jewry. By 1970, over 80 percent of the world's Jews lived in the United States, the Soviet Union, and Israel. International recognition of the Yiddish culture of Eastern Europe came with the awarding of the 1978 Nobel Prize in Literature to Isaac Bashevis Singer (1935–1991), a Yiddish writer from Poland whose stories and novels reflect deep knowledge of prewar Jewish life and the postwar reality of life as a Jew in the Ashkenazic diaspora. After the collapse of the Soviet Union, many former Soviet Jews migrated to the West, resulting in small but significant increases in the Jewish population of Western Europe, including Germany. Today Ashkenazic Jews make up less than 75 percent of the world's total Jewish population, reflecting the losses of World War II. While the dispersion of Ashkenazic Jews has made reference to Ashkenaz as a physical location increasingly problematic, distinct cultural differences among Ashkenazic Jews, Sephardic Jews, and other Jewish origin groups remain.

*Sean Martin*

**Further Reading**

Biale, David. *Cultures of the Jews: A New History.* New York: Schocken Books, 2002.

Fishman, Joshua A. *Never Say Die! A Thousand Years of Yiddish in Jewish Life and Letters.* The Hague: Mouton Publishers, 1981.

Friesel, Evyatar. *Atlas of Modern Jewish History.* New York: Oxford University Press, 1990.

Glinert, Lewis, ed. *Hebrew in Ashkenaz: A Language in Exile.* New York: Oxford University Press, 1993.

Hirschler, Gertrude, ed. *Ashkenaz: The German Jewish Heritage.* New York: Yeshiva University Museum, 1988.

Malkiel, David. *Reconstructing Ashkenaz: The Human Face of Franco-German Jewry, 1000–1250.* Stanford, CA: Stanford University Press, 2009.

Marcus, Jacob R. *The Jew in the Medieval World: A Source Book, 315–1791.* New York: Atheneum, 1973.

## Austrians

Austrians live in Austria, a parliamentary democracy in central Europe with a population of just over 8 million. Most Austrians are German-speakers whose main religious affiliation is Catholicism. Austrians are better described as a national group than an ethnic one. Prior to 1918, the term "Austria" encompassed broadly the lands and peoples of the House of Habsburg, of which the German-speakers represented a minority. Between 1867 and 1918, Austria represented one constitutional half of the Austro-Hungarian Empire, or Dual Monarchy. Both under the Habsburg and post-1918 eras, German-speaking Austrians did not refer to themselves as Austrians, but as Germans. The difficulty of encapsulating what "Austrian" and "German" meant to the inhabitants of Austria over the course of centuries also carried through to the post-1918 era and it has only been during the years of the Second Austrian Republic (1955 to the present) that the term "Austrian" has gained popular resonance.

The land around the Danubian Basin that makes up modern-day Austria was first mentioned in historical records as a military outpost, or march, of Charlemagne's Holy Roman Empire. In CE 996, more than 100 years after the collapse of the Carolingian Empire, historical records referred to an eastern march of the Bavarian Duchy, in Latin, *terra orientalis*, or

A couple in traditional costumes, Altaussee, Austria. (Corel)

in the vernacular *Ostarrichi*, from which the later German word for Austria (*Österreich*) derived. This land was given by Charlemagne's successor, Otto I, to the Babenberg dynasty, relatives of the Hohenstaufens in nearby Bavaria. The Babenburgs ruled over Austria for the next 250 years, during which time they established their residence in Vienna and extended the territory further south to include the duchy of Styria. In 1278, sometime after the last Babenburg died without an heir in 1246, the newly crowned king of the Germans, Rudolf of Habsburg, defeated Bohemian King Otakar II to succeed the Babenbergs as the ruling dynasty over Austria. The House of Habsburg would rule over Austria for the six and half centuries until the end of World War I.

The Habsburgs expanded their territories early on in their reign, acquiring the duchies of Carinthia, Carniola, Tyrol, Istria, and Gorizia within a century of the coming to power of Rudolf, the first Habsburg duke of Austria. But it was during the era of the Habsburgs as Holy Roman Emperors from 1452 until 1804 that the House of Austria became a world power. Less than a century after Frederick III was crowned emperor in 1452, he and his successors had acquired possessions spanning Europe and South America through a series of marital alliances with other European dynasties. In 1521, the Habsburgs split into Spanish and Austrian branches, with the former being the larger. By 1526 the two branches of the family controlled Burgundy, Spain, and Portugal and their overseas territories, as well as the kingdoms of Poland and Bohemia. Parts of central and eastern Hungary were captured by the Ottoman Turks in the first Ottoman-Habsburg war in 1529 and later regained by the Habsburgs at the end of the 17th century in the second major conflict with the Ottoman Empire. The next aggressor to challenge Habsburg rule was Napoleon, who crowned himself Holy Roman Emperor in 1804. Francis II was forced to abdicate his title and crown himself Francis I of Austria, formally dissolving the Holy Roman Empire two years later in 1806. In 1809 Napoleon entered Vienna and forced Francis to sign a peace agreement relinquishing territory and in excess of 3 million of his Austrian subjects. After Napoleon's defeat in 1815, Austria regained land in Tyrol, Salzburg, and Lombardy and expanded further south into the Mediterranean provinces of Dalmatia, Venetia, and Istria. From 1815 to the empire's collapse in 1918, Austria included more than 12 distinct ethnic groupings, some officially recognized as constituent nationalities, others, like Jews and Muslims, having no legal recognition in the empire.

Austria's cultural influences reflect the historical patterns of dynastic rule and intermingling of ethnic groups that have been the hallmark of Austrian history for more than a millennium. Under the Carolingian and Ottonian empires, a mixture of Roman and Germanic influences shaped the early culture of the Austrian duchy. The vernacular language was Germanic in origin, deriving from the dialects of the Bavarian tribes, who extended east and south in the duchy, and the Alemanni tribes in the west. In addition a local dialect was spoken by the remaining Roman Christian tribes (Romansch) in the western territories. A number of Roman cultural practices in agriculture, viticulture, and road building also survived and were integrated with late medieval German traditions in farming. Later during the Renaissance and Baroque periods, a prominent Italian influence marked the architecture, music, and dress of the Habsburg dynasty and aristocracy. Spanish influences were also evident during the era of the Spanish Habsburgs in theater and equestrian sports. After the Napoleonic Wars, French Empire interior styles came to influence middle-class domestic tastes in furniture and other household objects during the Biedermeier era (ca. 1815–1848).

An important shift in Austrian cultural practices was reflected in the Biedermeier

preference for domesticity. The growing economic and cultural aspirations of the emerging middle classes in the early 19th century contrasted with the imperial grandeur and dynastic privileges of the earlier baroque and reform eras. The baroque period of Catholic ascendancy in the wake of the Turkish defeat, followed by the half-century era of reform and "enlightened despotism" during the successive reigns of Maria Theresa and her son Joseph II (1740–1790), which emphasized the place of the state in economic, political, social, and religious affairs, concentrated entirely on the whims and needs of the ruling aristocracy and the imperial court. But after the specter of Napoleon had retreated, the voices and tastes of the urban middle classes began to emerge onto the empire's political and cultural landscape. The growth of a German-speaking public administration and secular education system during the reform era was one of the factors in this shift from imperial to middle-class political culture during the 19th century. Economists, bankers, civil servants, lawyers, university professors, and their families, required houses close to the central financial, political, and academic districts of the city. At the same time, these influential families of the German middle classes became the new arbiters of artistic and musical taste as they sought to patronize painters and musicians for their domestic salons.

Reading, too, was a hallmark of all things domestic and middle class. A predilection for historical themes characterized the Romantic poetry and literature of the late 18th and early 19th centuries. Romanticism also gave rise to another cultural movement of literary nationalism as the various Slavic, Hungarian, Romanian, and German renaissances in language and literature flourished and eventually led to political movements for independence in the empire. New literary forms of nationalism, coupled with the imperial laws on censorship in the post-Napoleonic era, proved a lethal combination in the liberal and national revolutions in 1848.

The 1848 revolution in the Habsburg dominions was initially a German affair, concentrated on liberal demands for constitutional reform and rivalry between Austria and Prussia for the crown of the German Confederation, which had been created in 1815. Several Austrian liberals were present at the General Assembly in Frankfurt in 1848–1849 to decide on a new constitution, but uprisings across the Habsburg monarchy prompted a General Assembly in Vienna, where just over half of the 303 deputies elected to the parliament were Germans. The leading Czech representative, František Palacky, called for an alliance of the empire's majority Slav population as an autonomous unit within the empire alongside the German and Hungarian parts. However, the Czech pan-Slav vision failed and the Hungarians were to be the sole beneficiaries of the 1848 revolutions, eventually winning the 1867 Compromise (Ausgleich) Agreement that granted full autonomy to the Hungarian state except in dynastic and military affairs. After 1867, "Austria" referred only the Austrian state within the Dual Monarchy of Austria-Hungary.

As a conservative reaction against the nationalist demands of the non-German groups, and in part as an attempt to reassert the imperial legitimacy of the Habsburg throne, Austrian culture witnessed a historicist turn in the imperial capital, Vienna. The long reign of Francis Joseph (1848–1916) was associated with a large-scale renovation project to create a prominent boulevard ring with imperial monuments and buildings built in neo-Gothic and neo-Classical styles. Outside the capital, in the German provinces of the empire, and especially in regional centers where German-speaking middle classes felt aggrieved by the increasing demands of the non-German population, German culture became the antithesis of Slavic and Jewish culture. Local German artwork, wood carvings, dress, songs, dialect, and especially schools were held up as examples of a dominant German influence over an undeveloped Slavic preculture. In contrast to both historicist and folk national movements, Austria also witnessed an international modernist movement whose spiritual and cultural center was cosmopolitan Vienna. The leading group of writers and artists at the forefront of this Austrian art nouveau movement, known as Secessionism, were Jewish. However, their intellectual and artistic contribution to what would later be regarded as quintessentially Austrian culture by the end of the 20th century was derided by the German nationalist purveyors of Austrian culture at the beginning of that century.

The humiliating defeat in World War I, the subsequent dismemberment of the Austro-Hungarian Empire in 1918, and the Allied moratorium on any union between Germany and Austria, left outside commentators to muse that Austria was "the state that no one wanted." In the words of

French Foreign Minister Georges Clemenceau, Austria was "what was left over from the rest." But seen in the context of its centuries-long history, imperial collapse was simply another reconfiguration of the many ethnic groups that had made up the territory of Austria from the Middle Ages. The period of the First Austrian Republic (1918–1938) was marked by political bipolarity between the two major German parties, the Social Democrats and the Christian Socialists, whose power bases were split respectively between Vienna and the provinces, with an assortment of agrarian and German-nationalist parties making up the rest of the political spectrum. The emergence of the Austrian Nazi Party as an electoral contender in the early 1930s prompted the ruling Christian Social Party to end parliamentary rule and establish a dictatorship under Chancellor Engelbert Dollfuss in 1933. Launching a civil war against the Social Democrats in 1934, the new Austrian state banned all opposition parties and aligned its domestic and foreign policy first with Fascist Italy and then with Nazi Germany. Austria's annexation (Anschluss) to Nazi Germany in March 1938 reduced the Austrian state to a German border province of the Third Reich until the end of World War II.

Austria regained its independence in 1955 following a 10-year occupation by British, French, American, and Soviet troops. Socialists and conservatives initially forged a coalition between 1945 and 1966, with both sides committed to shaping a new Austrian republican identity. Following a decade of socialist rule in the 1970s, a coalition between the socialists and the right-wing Freedom Party in 1983 signaled the reentry of right-wing politics into the Austrian government. The decade of the 1980s also coincided with growing international scrutiny of the wartime record of Austria's presidential candidate, Kurt Waldheim, prompting the first public debate about Austria's National Socialist past. In 1991 the socialist chancellor, Franz Vranitzky, was the first Austrian leader to acknowledge publicly Austria's responsibility for Nazi crimes in World War II. However, right-wing politicians and activists continue to deny that Austrians perpetrated the genocide against Jews, while simultaneously campaigning against ethnic minorities and immigrant groups who currently represent around 10 percent of Austria's population.

With the waves of refugees and migrants from former Yugoslavia in the 1990s, and right-wing attempts to abolish minority rights for Slovenian-speakers in Austria's southern provinces, Austrians have had to confront another aspect of their past—their relations with neighboring states that once belonged to the Habsburg domains. Since Austria's accession to the European Union in 1995, Austrians enjoy good relations with other European member states. Despite the EU's political sanctions on Austria after the country elected right-wing leader Jörg Haider to a coalition government in 2000, Austrians remain overwhelmingly positive about the European Union. Public debates surrounding Austria's complex history and identity in Europe continue to be triggered by significant anniversaries. While the births and deaths of popular Austrian composers of the Habsburg era has attracted international festivals and tourism in the small alpine country, other anniversaries commemorating the end of the empire, the Austrian dictatorship, the Anschluss, and the end of Allied occupation, attract polarized debate from Austrians.

*Julie Thorpe*

**Further Reading**

Beller, Steven. *A Concise History of Austria.* Cambridge: University of Cambridge Press, 2006.

Brook-Shepherd, Gordon. *The Austrians: A Thousand Year Odyssey.* London: HarperCollins, 1997.

Kann, Robert A. *A History of the Habsburg Empire, 1526–1918.* Berkeley: University of California Press, 1974.

# Avars

The Avars are an indigenous people who reside in the mountainous central western districts of the Russian Federation's Republic of Dagestan in the northeast Caucasus. The Avar language belongs to the Avar-Ando-Tsez subgroup of the Nakh-Dagestani or Northeast Caucasian group of languages. Avars adhere to Sunni Islam. According to the 2002 Russian census, the number of Avars in all of Russia was 814,473. In Dagestan proper there were 758,438, making Avars, at 29 percent of Dagestan's population, the single largest ethnic group in a land known for its extraordinary ethnic diversity. These population figures include 12 other much smaller ethnic groups—Andis, Archins, Akhvakhs, Bagulals, Bezhtins, Botlikhs, Ginukhs, Godoberins, Gunzibs, Didois, Karatins, Tindals, Khvarshins, and Chamalais. These groups all developed and lived

alongside the Avars for centuries, and, as a rule, members of these groups all speak Avar in addition to their native tongues and routinely identify themselves as Avars depending on context. It should be noted that the Avars of the Caucasus are not related to that of the better-known nomadic Avars who invaded Europe in the 6th century. Indeed, the designation "Avar" for this Caucasian population came into wide use only at the beginning of the 20th century. The Avars traditionally referred to themselves as *ma'arulal.* (Some suggest that this ethnonym derives from *me'er*, the Avar word for "mountain," but others dispute this etymology.) As late as the 1950s the older generations of Avars preferred this term. Neighboring ethnic groups know the Avars by a wide variety of names.

The ancestors of the Avars are believed to have formed part of Caucasian Albania. Archeological evidence points to a substantial Christian influence in Dagestan before the arrival of Islam. During the 7th century, Arab-Muslim forces of the Arab Caliphate invaded the southern parts of what is today Dagestan and captured the city and gateway of Derbent. The Avars joined the Khazars in resisting the newcomers and their faith. Gradually, however, Islam spread northward, and by the 11th century it had established itself among the Avars. Although Christianity retained a presence in the Avar lands until as late as the 16th century, already by the 14th century Islam was dominant. Reflecting their reception of Islam through the Arab Caliphate, the Avars, like the vast majority of indigenous Muslims of the northeast Caucasus, are Sunni Muslims of the Shafi'i School. By contrast, the Turkic peoples of the North

Caucasus and the indigenous Muslims of the northwest Caucasus, who for long were under the influence of the Crimean Tatars, are Sunnis of the Hanafi School.

Through most of history, the Avars remained divided among many different communities whose social structures varied from the egalitarian to the feudal. During the 16th century, however, a group of Avar elites who claimed descent from the Arab governors of Khunzak founded what became known as the Avar Khanate. Although the khanate never united all of the Avar lands, it came to dominate upper Dagestan politically and culturally, and in the 17th century saw the codification of Avar customary law. The Avars supported a high culture of scholarship in Arabic, Islamic law, and the Islamic sciences. Avar experts in these fields acquired reputations throughout the Caucasus and far beyond in the greater Middle East.

The Russian Empire made its first formal claim over the Avars in 1727 when the Avar Khanate agreed to become a protectorate. The relationship between the khanate and the Russian Empire, however, was volatile. The approach of Russian power toward the Caucasus posed the most comprehensive challenge Avar society had yet seen. In the 1820s a vigorous response from the Avars and other North Caucasian mountain peoples to the political, economic, and cultural destabilization wrought by Russia's advance began to build in the form of a religiously inspired movement of cultural and military resistance. The leaders of this movement were all sheikhs of the Naqshbandi Sufi brotherhood, and all were Avars. In 1829 a number of Sufi adepts who called upon the mountaineers to observe their Muslim faith more rigorously and to unite against Russian power in a holy struggle declared the Avar Ghazi Muhammad imam of Dagestan. Following Ghazi Muhammad's death in combat, his followers named Hamza Bek, an Avar notable, as the second imam. In 1834 Hamza Bek slew the Avar ruling house, and that same year he was killed in retaliation.

What became known as the Great Caucasian War, however, only intensified when the rebels subsequently recognized the Avar Sheikh Shamil as the third imam. For fully a quarter of a century until his surrender in 1859, Shamil led the Avars, Chechens, and other mountain peoples of the northeast Caucasus in a protracted and violent struggle against the Russian Empire. In the process, Shamil became the most famous Avar in history, gaining renown not just in the Caucasus but in Europe and throughout the Muslim world, where today he is remembered as a heroic defender of the faith who defied the tsar and his armies.

The Russian Revolution of 1917 and the fall of the Russian empire gave the Avars and other mountaineers a brief and confused period of independence. During this time the Avar livestock baron and scholar of Islam Najmuddin Hotsatli (Gotsinskii) attempted to recreate Shamil's imamate, but in 1920 the Bolsheviks overwhelmed his forces and those of other anticommunist leaders. They then incorporated Dagestan into the Russian Soviet Federative Socialist Republic as an autonomous Soviet socialist republic.

The geography of Dagestan—rugged mountains cut by unnavigable rivers running through steep valleys—severely complicates communications. One consequence has been Dagestan's exceptional linguistic and ethnic diversity. Indeed, among the Avars one finds considerable linguistic variation between villages.

A form of Avar known as *bolmats* provided the basis for the literary and later standard form of Avar. Two slightly variant accounts of the origins of this language exist. One holds that it derives from a form of Avar known as "the guest's language," which arose after centuries of interaction at bazaars and with travelers to provide a common language to Avars. Another contends this language derived from efforts to facilitate intertribal relations, especially on matters of common defense, from the 16th century onwards. The Avars' central location meant the Avar language also sometimes served as a common language among Dagestan's other highlanders.

With the spread of Islam, Avar scholars began writing texts in the Arabic language. The earliest writing of the Avar language in Arabic script dates to sometime between the 12th and 14th centuries. Around the turn of the 17th and 18th centuries the Avar scholar Dibirqadi of Khunzakh developed a formalized system for writing Avar in Arabic. Although it is not known whether Avars wrote in their language prior to Islam, there is evidence to suggest that they were familiar with the Caucasian Albanian and Georgian alphabets.

In 1928 the Bolsheviks banned the Arabic script and introduced a Latin script for Avar. Ten years later Soviet authorities replaced the Latin script with the Cyrillic, which following some modifications remains in use today. Currently, in schools Avars are instructed in their native language up through the third grade. Sixty-five percent of Avars speak Russian as a second language; that percentage exceeds 80 percent among those living in cities.

Although linguistic Russification threatens to overtake the indigenous languages in Dagestan's swelling cities, Avar in the villages is in no immediate danger. Moreover, radio and television broadcasts are made in Avar, and books, magazines, a republic-wide newspaper, and several local newspapers are all published in Avar. Dagestan's capital, Makhachkala, has an Avar musical-dramatic theater.

The traditional economic activities of the Avars were farming and herding livestock. The lands in which the Avars lived can be divided into three zones. In the foothills, rain-fed farming predominated. The Avars in this zone cultivated wheat, barley, and later corn using a two- and three-field system of rotation with some fertilization. They raised large-horned livestock, primarily sheep. In the second zone, the higher foothills, where farmers had pursued terraced farming from the Bronze Age onward, the Avars developed agriculture to a very advanced level. They sowed wheat, barley, oats, beans, lentils, linen, and hemp, and used water-powered wheels to mill their grain. Animal husbandry predominated in the third zone, the higher mountain regions, where arable land was scarce and crops were limited primarily to small quantities of barley and rye.

Famous Avars of the contemporary period include Dagestan's most renowned poet, Rasul Gamzatov (b. 1923), five-time world champion in freestyle wrestling Ali Aliev (1937–1995), Olympic champion in freestyle wrestling Zagalav Abdulbekov

(b. 1945), and test pilot and Hero of the Soviet Union Magomed Tolboev (b. 1951).

Dagestan is the poorest and least developed region of Russia; it has suffered economically and otherwise from the upheaval associated with the breakup of the Soviet Union. In recent decades, the Avar population has been growing rapidly, from 483,000 in 1979 to 601,000 in 1989 and nearly 815,000 in 2002, the most recent year for which data is available. Although such rapid growth contrasts sharply with the general trend inside the Russian Federation where the overall population has begun to decline, it conforms to the dominant pattern in the North Caucasus of surging populations. Reflecting a more general trend of urbanization in Dagestan, today more than 40 percent of Avars live in cities. Deteriorating conditions in the villages contribute to the stream of youth going to the lowlands, which exacerbates the already considerable problem of urban unemployment.

Ethnic identity is a critical factor in contemporary Dagestani politics. Because of their status as Dagestan's largest ethnic group and their traditional prominence among the mountaineers, including their leading role in the Great Caucasian War, Avars regard themselves as the rightful elite of Dagestan. Their chief rivals are the Dargins, who constitute Dagestan's second largest ethnic group but who lack the cultural cohesiveness of the Avars. Ethnic tensions, a decline in the legitimacy of government authorities, the collapse of the economy and of industry in particular, wars in neighboring Chechnya, low-level but chronic violence, and ongoing corruption combine to make Dagestan one of the least stable parts of Russia. Unlike many of Dagestan's smaller ethnic groups, however, the Avars face no short-term prospect of cultural assimilation.

*Michael A. Reynolds*

## Further Reading

Golden, Peter B. "Avars." In *Encyclopaedia of Islam Three*, eds. Gudrun Krämer, Denis Matringe, John Nawas, and Everett Rowson. Leiden: Brill, 2010. *Brill Online.*

Islammagomedov, A. I. "Avartsy." In *Narody Dagestana*, eds. S. A. Arutiunov, A. I. Osmanov, and G. A. Sergeeva, 115–148. Moscow: Nauka, 2002.

Magomedov, Murad, and Istoriia Avartsev. *The History of the Avars.* Makhachkala: Dagestanskii Gosudarstvennyi Universitet, 2005.

# B

## Balkars

The Balkars call themselves *malqar* (pl. *malqarla*). Over 80 percent of the contemporary Balkar population—108,500, according to the 2002 Russian census—lives in the Russian republic of Kabardino-Balkaria, a still largely unsettled mountainous region located in the central part of the northern Caucasus. The Balkars constitute 12 percent of the inhabitants in Kabardino-Balkaria, while ethnic Russians account for 25 percent and Kabards 55 percent. Only a few thousand Balkars live scattered in other areas of the former Soviet Union, for instance in Kazakstan and Kyrgyzstan, where they were forced to settle in 1944. There are also still a few Balkar villages in the province of Tokat in Turkey. Most Turkic-speaking Balkars are Sunni Muslims.

The origin of the Balkars is only fragmentarily known. However, Turkic-speaking groups have inhabited the mountain areas of the northern Caucasus since early medieval times. From 1219 to 1223 the Mongols conquered the mountains, and the inhabitants became part of the Kipchak Khanate. In 1260 the region was divided again, and the Balkars belonged to the Noghai Horde. The area was later part of the Ottoman Empire, Persia, and Russia. It was finally incorporated, although with some autonomy, into the Russian empire in 1827.

Still in the mid-18th century these mountain inhabitants, who called themselves *taulu* (mountaineers), lived as shepherds and cattle pastoralists in the river valleys of the Terek region in Caucasus. These Turkic-speaking mountain inhabitants were divided into five tribes: the Bizingi, Chegem, Kholam, Malqar, and Urusbiy. Among the Russians and European visitors they were known as Mountain Tatars (*Gornii Tatar*). One of these mountain tribes called themselves *malqar*, a name said to derive from a legendary ruler of the Caucasus Mountains, Malkhar Khan, who conquered the area in the 9th century. The Mountain Tatars had their native religion until premodern times; vestiges are still found in Balkar popular religion. However, many of these Turkic-speaking mountaineers converted to Islam during the long Avar revolt led by Imam Shamil in Daghestan in the mid-19th century. With increasing integration to Russia, many Balkars abandoned their pastoral way of life for agriculture. In order to escape the wars in Caucasus, many Balkars moved to Anatolia, where they were allowed to establish their own villages on lands previously used by nomadic Balkars.

The Balkars developed their modern national identity during the early 20th century. They were integrated into the Soviet system after 1920 and the Balkar nation was created in accordance with the Soviet nationalities policy. The nation-building involved the five above-mentioned tribal groups, and the ethnonym Balkar (derived from the tribal name *malqar*) was introduced for census purposes and for the introduction of an alphabet. Together with the Kabards, who speak a Caucasian language related to Adygh, the Balkars were organized into a national territory in 1922, which was elevated into an Autonomous Soviet Socialist Republic in 1936. Persecution of religion and cultural aspirations was a part of the Stalinist policy in the area, and during the Nazi occupation in the autumn of 1942, some Balkars were said to have collaborated with the Germans. During the occupation the Nazi troops dissolved the general unpopular collective farms (*kolkhozes*) and opened up the mosques that the Bolsheviks had closed.

In the spring of 1944, a year after the Soviet reconquest of the region, almost all Balkars—together with Chechens, Karachays, Ingush, and others—were deported from their native land in the northern Caucasus to Central Asia. They became scapegoats for the Soviet shortcomings during the war. Many did not survive the hardship of this forced exile. According to the 1939 census there were 42,700 Balkars. Of them, only 37,400 reached their new settlements in Central Asia. This mortality constituted almost a fifth of the total Balkar population. However, after Stalin's death, the exiled nations of the Caucasus were rehabilitated and in the late 1950s they were allowed to return to the reorganized Kabardino-Balkar autonomous region. Many did not manage to return until the late 1960s and they were not allowed to settle in their former homes in the mountain areas, but in foothills. Many nowadays therefore live in the cities of Nalchik, Chegem, and Baksan.

Balkars are still rather rural, at least compared to their Kabard and Russian neighbors, who are industrial workers within the oil and coal industries. Balkars earn a living as farmers and cattle breeders. Some Balkar farmers are very successful with their Angora goats.

Since the Balkars were never allowed to rebuild their homes in the mountains, a feeling of discrimination informs their postwar identity. There are some tensions between Balkars and the Kabard majority in the territory. In November 1991, there were media reports that a Balkar congress had adopted a declaration about national sovereignty in the southern part of the republic. A few years later a Balkar separatist movement evolved, led by Sufyan Beppaev, a former military leader in the Transcaucaus region. However, the separatist movement was suppressed by the Kabardinian republican leadership, and Beppaev retreated in 1998 from the claims. There are still very few Balkars in decision-making positions in the Kabardino-Balkar Republic.

Most Balkars are Sunni Muslims of the Hanafi juridical school. However, the majority remain rather indifferent to their religion, not only having been affected by the communist atheist campaigns in the past, but also by tradition. No Islamic movements are active in their region, and very few religious activities, other than the more popular rites, are followed.

The Balkar language, which belongs to the western subgroup of the Kipchak or northwestern branch of the Turkic languages, is very closely related to Karachay, and Balkar-Karachay was for a long time actually considered a single written language. It was first written in 1924 with a Latin script, but it was replaced with Cyrillic in 1939. Nowadays Balkar is considered to be a separate language. An attempt to reintroduce the Latin script in the 1990s has failed. The Balkar Turkic is divided into three dialects: Bakhsan-Chegem, Kholam-Bezinga, and Malqar dialect. The Bakhsan-Chegem dialect is the basis for written Balkar and is almost identical with the Karachay Turkic. The Balkars have a large oral literature, but their interrupted history in the 20th century means that very few modern books have been produced.

*Ingvar Svanberg*

**Further Reading**

Akiner, Shirin. *Islamic Peoples of the Soviet Union: A Historical and Statistical Handbook.* London: KPI, 1986.

Conquest, Robert. *The Nation Killers: The Soviet Deportation of Nationalities.* London: MacMillan, 1970.

Pröhle, Wilhelm. "Balkarische Studien" ("Balkar Studies"). *Keleti Szemle*, vol. 15 (1914–1915), pp. 164–276, and vol. 16 (1915–1916), 104–243.

# Bashkirs

The Bashkirs (self-designation *bašqort*; pl. *bašqortlar*), estimated at 1.8 million, live south of the Ural and on the adjacent plains. The greater part of the Bashkir people live in their own territory that nowadays forms a constituent republic known as the Republic of Bashkortostan, a part of the Russian Federation that borders both Asia and Europe. There is also a significant diaspora living in other parts of the Russian Federation, with 166,300 in the district of Chelyabinsk, 53,300 in Orenburg, 52,300 in Perm, 37,300 in Sverdlovsk, 17,500 in Kurgan, 7,800 in Samara, 2,300 in Sakha, and 41,100 in Tyumen, as well as 20,000 in the neighboring Republic of Tatarstan. About 1,300 are found in Belarus, 24,000 in Kazakhstan, 3,300 in Kyrgyzstan, 700 in Latvia, 700 in Lithuania, 600 in Moldova, 5,000 in Tajikistan, 2,600 in Turkmenistan, 4,300 in Ukraine, and 41,000 in Uzbekistan. Only a few Bashkirs have settled outside the former Soviet Union, where they are mostly recent emigrants. Most Turkic-speaking Bashkirs are Sunni Muslims.

Bashkirs are mentioned in medieval sources, for instance by the Franciscan friar William of Rubruk who travelled through their territory in 1253. When the Mongol Golden Horde was divided in the 14th century, the Bashkirs were included in the Kazan and Siberian Khanates. After the Russian Tsar Ivan IV conquered Kazan in 1552, the Bashkirs became subjects of the Muscovites. However, many Bashkirs continued to resist the tsarist armies and they were not fully conquered until the suppression of the Pugachev Rebellion in 1773–1775. The Orenburg muftiate was created during the reign of Catherine II in 1788. It was later moved to Ufa (capital of Bashkiria) and the city became the main spiritual center for the Muslims in Russia until the 1990s.

The Russian colonial rule included the immigration of Russians and Tatars to the area, recruitment of soldiers for the armies, as well as high taxation burdens that forced Bashkir pastoralists to adopt a more settled life. However, at the turn of the 20th century, most were still living in the countryside as

Bashkir woman in traditional dress, Ural Mountains, Russian Federation. (Sergey Prokudin-Gorsky/Galerie Bilderwelt/Getty Images)

peasants and herdsmen. Wild beekeeping has for centuries been important among the Bashkirs, and apiculture remains a kind of key symbol for their ethnic culture. Honey is nowadays exported overseas, and many Bashkirs continue to keep beehives as a pastime. Bashkir horses have also been famous within and outside Russia.

During the civil war after the Russian Revolution in 1917, Bashkiria enjoyed a brief period of autonomy, but eventually became part of the Soviet Union. Many Bashkirs died during a famine in 1921. Within Russia it formed an autonomous republic, although Moscow ruled without any real participation from the Bashkirs

until the Soviet Union fell apart in 1991. As herdsmen and peasants, the Bashkirs were forced to participate in the collectivization system. The Bashkir population, around 715,000 in 1926, remained mainly a rural population throughout the century.

Oil was discovered in 1932 and this caused rapid industrialization in Bashkiria. Other mineral resources further contributed to the development, making the area's economy relatively prosperous. Workers moved in from other parts of the Soviet Union to work in the oil fields and the heavy industries that developed within Bashkiria. However, the Bashkirs themselves suffered from the Stalinist purges and World War II. Many Bashkirs died during another famine in the early 1930s, and large losses were experienced during the war.

The Bashkir state proclaimed sovereignty on October 11, 1990. In the fall of 1994 an agreement on division of powers between the central government in Moscow and the authorities was signed in Ufa, the capital of the republic. Bashkortostan, with a population of 4.1 million (29.8 percent Bashkirs, 36.3 percent Russians, 24.1 percent Tatars, and some 70 other nationalities in 2002) is now highly industrialized. Fuel, energy, and chemical products make up the main part of its exports. It is an ethnically divided country and tension between Bashkir and Tatar activists have been reported; corruption is widespread and protests have occurred, but in general it is a rather stable society. Bashkirs within their own territory are clustered in rather rural areas, while the diaspora consists mainly of industrial workers who usually go to Russian schools and follow Russian cultural practices. They are thus also more assimilated into the majority populations.

The Bashkirs converted to Islam in medieval times. They are Sunni Muslims and belong to the Hanafi School. Since the early 1990s, there has been a kind of religious revival in the Republic of Bashkortostan. There are now around 800 mosques within the territory, Muslim festivals are celebrated, and popular religion thrives with, for instance, pilgrimages to graves of holy men. There is also increasing activity by Islamist and Sufi movements originating in Turkey. However, the Bashkirs are rather secularized, and religion plays a minor role in politics and daily life. The religion remains an important part of the Bashkir national identity, though. A small group of Orthodox Christian Bashkirs, the so-called Nagaibäks (9,600 in the 2002 census), still live in the Chelyabinsk region.

The Bashkir language, which belongs to the northern subgroup of the Kipchak or the northwestern branch of the Turkic languages, is divided into three major dialect groups: the mountain or eastern dialects; the northwestern dialects; and the steppe or southwestern dialects. The last dialects are strongly influenced by the Kazan Tatar language, while the others are closer to Kazak. Standard Bashkir, which is based on the eastern dialects, was developed as a written language after 1917. During the first years of its existence it was written in Arabic, but the Latin alphabet replaced it in 1927. Since 1940, Bashkir language has been written with the Cyrillic script. Tatar written language has been widely used among the Bashkirs. Many Bashkirs, especially the educated groups and those living in diaspora, use Russian rather than their native tongue. Most Bashkirs are bi- and trilingual. Others have increased their identification with the Bashkir language since the establishment of the republic.

Since the early 1990s, there has emerged an increasing national consciousness and cultural revival among the Bashkirs. This has renewed interest in their native language and culture.

*Ingvar Svanberg*

**Further Reading**

Akiner, Shirin. *Islamic Peoples of the Soviet Union*. London: KPI, 1986.
Cornell, Svante, and Ingvar Svanberg. "Russia and Transcaucasia." In *Islam Outside*

the *Arab World*, eds. David Westerlund and Ingvar Svanberg. Richmond: Curzon, 1999, 402–419.

Gorenburg, Dmityr. "Identity Change in Bashkortostan: Tatars into Bashkir and Back." *Ethnic and Racial Studies* 22 (1999): 554–580.

Poppe, Nicolai. *Bashkir Manual.* Bloomington, IN: Mouton, 1964.

# Basques

The Basques live on both sides of the western Pyrenees in Spain and France. Out of the total population of 3 million the majority live in the Spanish autonomous regions of the Basque Country and Navarre, respectively 70 and 20 percent. The Northern Basque Country, which is part of the French department of the Atlantic Pyrenees, comprises 10 percent of the Basques. Today's Basques are predominantly city dwellers. The agglomeration of Bilbao is by far the most important urban area with almost 1 million inhabitants, followed by the metropolitan areas of Donostia/San Sebastian and Pamplona (each totaling some 320,000 inhabitants), Vitoria-Gasteiz (240,000 inhabitants), and the Bayonne-Anglet-Biarritz area on the French-Basque coast with some 112,000 inhabitants. Most Basques are Roman Catholics, though secularization is increasing. In Euskara, the Basque language, Basques are named *euskaldunak* (Basque speakers). Euskara is the only non-Indo-European language of Europe and does not have any linguistic relations with other languages. The languages spoken in Euskal Herria, as many Basques call the greater Basque country, are

respectively Spanish, French, and Basque. Originally language distinguished the Basques from neighboring groups. At present many Basques use French or Spanish in the private and public spheres. During the last three decades Euskara has revived as a consequence of regional policies in Spain. The distinction between Basques, Frenchmen, or Spaniards is blurred because of intermarriage and the long duration of cultural homogenization politics in the two states. Basques do not agree among themselves about who is Basque and who not. According to survey research most Basques in the areas where Euskara is spoken would see language as the most important denominator. For the majority who live in Spanish or French-speaking areas, however, to be born and living on Basque soil makes somebody Basque. As a result of cultural mixing many Basques identify themselves as hybrids in the sense that they combine Basque and Spanish, or Basque and French, identities.

The historical origins of the Basques are all but clear. In classical antiquity there is written evidence that they were living in and near the western Pyrenees. When the Romans colonized the Iberian Peninsula, the Basques (whom they called Vasconians) lived in a more sizable area than the present-day territory extending from the Pyrenees in the north to the plains along the River Ebro in the south. During the Roman era Latin spread to the economically most integrated parts of the empire, in particular the southern lowlands. The isolated and poor mountainous Basque heartland held little attraction for Roman exploitation. Like Latin, the Romans spread Christianity relatively more in the south than in the mountainous north. Scarce historical

Traditional Basque dancers hold torches in Bilbao's San Mames soccer stadium during a celebration of the official Basque language, Euskera, Saturday December 26, 1998. (AP/ Wide World Photos)

sources indicate that full Christianization occurred somewhere between the 8th and 10th centuries.

During the Middle Ages the Basques lived in the Kingdom of Navarre, reigned from Pamplona. Navarre reached its maximum dimensions under King Sancho the Great (1004–1035) extending far beyond the limits of today's Euskal Herria. The kingdom shrank and was divided between Spain and France in the 16th century. With the Treaty of the Pyrenees (1659) the Basque realm was definitively divided between France and Spain. Basque nationalism still glorifies the ancient kingdom as the old Basque heartland. Paradoxically most inhabitants of the present-day Charter Community of Navarre see themselves more as Navarrese than Basque.

Initially both states respected local privileges or *fueros* (Basque: *foruak*; French: *fors*). From the Middle Ages onward local privileges evolved to provincial charters. The charter for Biscay (Bizkaia) became a symbol of Basque autonomy. The Castilian kings had the obligation to go to the town of Gernika (Guernica). Under an ancient oak tree the king gathered with local representatives to swear loyalty to Biscay's *fueros*. Today Gernika and the tree continue as symbols of Basque self-government, democracy, and equality.

The *fueros* first eroded in the north because of centralizing efforts of the French kings. The French revolution gave a definitive push to the incorporation of the north, which in 1790 became part of the Atlantic Pyrenees, a department twice as big as the northern Basque area. In Spain the *fueros* lasted longer. During the 19th century they were increasingly under state pressure and were finally abolished in 1876.

The end of the *fueros* caused resentment among many Basques who were deprived from self-rule. The resulting frustration was at the origins of early nationalism. Sabino de Arana y Goiri, a son of a Carlist middle-class family, was the inventor and organizer of Basque nationalism. In a rapidly industrializing Bilbao flooded by migrants from Spain's interior, he promoted nationalism. Arana portrayed the Basques as a superior race, far more devout than their Spanish neighbors. In 1895 he founded the Basque nationalist Party (EAJ-PNV; Euzko Alderdi Jeltzalea-Partido Nacionalista Vasco). Nowadays the PNV is the oldest substate nationalist party of the world, claiming more autonomy and promoting Basque culture, but stripped of its initial racism and religious orthodoxy.

Up to the modern era Basques were devout Catholics compared to their neighbors. Basques were overrepresented in monasteries in France and Spain. The traditional right of inheritance contributed to the high proportion of Basques who obeyed the call. The oldest son was the only child entitled to inherit the family farm or *baserri.* Younger brothers had to find a livelihood elsewhere. Many did so as priests or migrants. The number of occupations has decreased dramatically over the last 50 years. Secularization is reflected in the number of civil weddings, which equals consecrated ones in the Autonomous Community of the Basque Country, the most urbanized of the Basque regions.

After the dictatorship of General Franco (1939–1975) Spanish democracy was restored. Euskara, repressed during the dictatorship, experienced a remarkable revival, particularly in the Basque Autonomous Community, now free to pursue its own language policies. The Charter Community of Navarre started to favor Basque from the 1980s, but only in Basque-speaking and mixed Basque-Castilian zones of the north. In both communities many children who do not speak Euskara at home are now receiving Basque-medium or bilingual education. They are taught in a new language (*Euskara batua* or Unified Basque, standardized in 1968) that is dissimilar to the Basque dialects of Biscayan (west), Zuberoan (northeast), and Roncalese (east). As a result of language policies, there are nowadays considerably more new Basque speakers (*euskaldunberriak*) who are proficient in Basque, but do not speak the language in the private sphere. In the Basque-speaking areas usage in the private sphere is diminishing because of migration to the urban areas of France and Spain and an extremely low birthrate compared to other European regions.

From 2000 onward, after 130 years of French assimilation policies, France has reversed its policy towards Euskara. Schools are now massively adopting bilingual education, which has become very popular. Paradoxically, in the Basque-speaking rural interior of Zuberoa (Soule) bilingual schools are less popular because of the dialect gap with standardized Basque and a strong tendency to migrate to French cities caused by agricultural decline. Despite the promotion of Basque under different state and regional administrations, there are still doubts about its capacity to survive.

The lifestyles of the Basques are deeply influenced by their exposure to Spanish and French cultures. In France the Basques have a French timetable, in Spain a Spanish one. French Basques have early lunches and dinners and short lunch breaks, unlike their southern peers. Typical for the south, until recently, were the so-called *cuadrillas*, informal groups of friends of the same age who spend part of their free time in the evening visiting bars (*el poteo*), where they have drinks and eat small snacks (*pintxos*). Cuadrillas have lost much importance in the urban areas as youth find more attractive other activities such as sports, advanced study, and recreational activities (e.g., discotheques). Even in small towns and villages, young people prefer to join sport clubs instead of cuadrillas.

The following Basque habits and institutions have survived the exposure to French or Spanish culture.

- *Pelota* is played with a hard ball that rebounds from a walled court. Several varieties of pelota exist.
- *Txokos*, gastronomic societies, are particularly prominent in Gipuzkoa and Spanish Navarre.
- *Bertsolaritza*, a tradition invented in about 1800, consists of improvised poetry sung at popular festivals.
- Stone lifting, rowing, and other sports requiring much physical strength continue in popularity.
- *Mendigoitzaleak*, mountaineers' clubs, originally an urban invention (Bilboa 1903), have spread throughout the southern Basque realm.

- *Ikastolak*, self-financed Basque-medium schools, a reaction to education in Spanish (1920s), have not at all disappeared. They mushroomed under late Francoist dictatorship (1970–1977). Nowadays regional authorities support ikastolak.
- Among modern more universal sports, bike racing is popular in Euskal Herria. The taste for other modern sports is often in line with popularity within the respective states, as for instance rugby in the north or soccer in the south.

Like the Carlist wars of the 19th century, the Spanish Civil war (1936–1939) was fought between Basques themselves. Navarre and the province of Alava (Araba) fought with Franco's army, while two coastal provinces joined the Republicans. During the dictatorship Alava and Navarre enjoyed a preferential regional status (*régimen especial*) within the Spanish administration. Repression, antileft and anti-Basque, was harsh in the two coastal provinces. Unionism strongly rooted in the Bilbao area, with its heavy industries, Basque culture, and language in the small towns and countryside of Gipuzkoa and Bizkaia, became important targets of repression. The legacy of repression is a lack of loyalty to the Spanish state in the north compared to Alava and Navarre.

As a reaction to persecution of the left and of Basque nationalism, a group of students of the Catholic university of Deusto in Bilbao began to mobilize people during the late 1950s. Ten years later this group, named ETA (*Euskadi ta Askatasuna*/ Basque Homeland and Freedom), started to use violence. They claimed an independent and socialist Euskal Herria. Up to the early 1980s violence spiraled, resulting in a death toll of 800 (1969–2009). Initially ETA gained much support. However, its support base has been gradually eroding from the end of the 1980s. Political parties connected with ETA are now banned by the Spanish authorities. The 2009 elections for the Basque autonomous parliament were the first ones without any representation with an ETA connection. The banning of ETA-linked parties represents several political dilemmas. First, Basque nationalism has now lost its majority in the Basque parliament because of the absence of radical nationalism. Second, radical nationalists, numbering approximately 100,000 voters, feel unrepresented. Third, liberal democracy would be in peril with parties that threaten statewide parties and their representatives by condoning violence. Today ETA violence continues at low intensity. After two ceasefires (1998–1999; 2006) the widely spread hope for a negotiated end of violence has evaporated. ETA's sectarianism and the hard line of the center-right Partido Popular are held responsible for the failure of peace processes.

The devolution of powers in Spain has led to nation-building and rebasquization policies in the Basque Autonomous Community and a modest support for Euskara in Navarre governed by center-right antinationalists. On the French side nationalist mobilization is weak. The nationalists' claim is modest and state-abiding compared to their Spanish counterpart—a Basque *département* within France. In contrast, the nationalists of the south have state-challenging claims. The moderate parties (the PNV and its split-off Eusko Alkartasuna) demand cosovereignty of the Autonomous Community with Spain, while the former radical ones and the neoradical party Aralar want an independent Euskal Herria.

A challenge faced by many Basques is how to cope with cultural extinction, particularly in the regions where sufficient political support is missing, like in Navarre and France. Rural decline and concomitant depopulation menace the last rural strongholds of Basque culture. In the cities Basques are continuously exposed to Spanish or French culture. The economic problems vary considerably from place to place. The Basque Autonomous Community is one of Spain's core regions, coping with problems of transforming an old industrialized area into a postmodern service economy. There, congestion and environmental issues are high on the political agenda. Pamplona and Vitoria-Gasteiz have experienced a boom during the last decades up to the 2009 credit crisis. In France there is huge discrepancy between the urbanized coastal fringe and the depopulating rural interior. The major complaint is the shortage of housing for young natives caused by the pressure on the housing market by outsiders who buy second homes. Mass tourism has led to a folklorization of Basque culture. Given the fragmented administrative, political, and cultural landscape of Euskal Herria it is almost impossible to find pan-Basque solutions to these challenges.

*Jan Mansvelt Beck*

**Further Reading**

Bray, Z. *Living Boundaries, Frontiers and Identity in the Basque Country.* Brussels: PIE Peter Lang, 2004.

Collins, R. *The Basques.* London: Basil Blackwell, 1986.

Corcuera Atienza, J. *The Origins, Ideology and Organization of Basque Nationalism, 1876–1903.* Reno: University of Nevada, 2008.

Heiberg, M. *The Making of the Basque Nation.* Cambridge: Cambridge University Press, 1989.

Lecours, A. *Basque Nationalism and the Spanish State.* Reno: University of Nevada Press, 2007.

Mansvelt Beck, J. *Territory and Terror, Conflicting Nationalisms in the Basque Country.* London/New York: Routledge, 2005.

Muro, D. *Ethnicity and Violence: The Case of Radical Basque Nationalism.* London: Routledge, 2008.

# Belarusians

Belarusians or Belorussians (Belarusian: Беларусы, *Bielarusy*; earlier spelled Belarussians, Byelorussians, and Belorusians)—are an Eastern Slavic ethnic group and the dominant population of the Republic of Belarus (before 1991 the Byelorusian Soviet Socialist Republic). Belarusians also form minorities in neighboring Poland (especially in the former Bialystok province), Russia, Lithuania, Ukraine, and Kazakhstan. There are currently about 11.5–12 million people who associate themselves with the Belarusian ethnicity, of which 10 million reside within Belarus. The name "Belaya Rus" first appears in the 13th century. The term derives from the word "Bela"—"white" in the meaning of "free, independent"—and refers also to the color of the national costumes and to the historical impact of Balts ("Balta" in Lithuanian means "white"). However, the use of the name "White Russians" is misleading, and some Belarusians regard it as insulting because of its association with the White Russian troops that fought the Bolsheviks during the Russian Civil War (1918–1922). Belarusians speak Belarusian, a Slavic language, and are predominantly Eastern Orthodox, with small Catholic and Uniat (Eastern Rite) denominations in the northwestern areas.

Most Belarusians today consider themselves descendants of the Dragoviches, Kriviches, and Radimiches, Eastern Slav tribes who moved into the region between the 6th and 8th centuries CE, settling in the western and northwestern parts of what is presently Belarus. They merged freely with the indigenous Balt tribes, especially in the northwest. Belarusian people trace the roots of their culture and nationhood to the Old Rus state—known as the Kievan Rus (9th–11th century), in particular, the vassal Principality of Polatsk—and to Samogitiya (part of Lithuania). During the Middle Ages Belarusians were identified as Rusyns or Ruthenians as well as "Litviny" (Litvins, or Lithuanians). This later term refers to the state of the Grand Duchy of Lithuania (Litva, Great Litva), part of which was White Ruthenian lands after the 13th to 14th centuries. The Ruthenian language, which later evolved into modern Belarusian, was the official language there. For this reason many historians argue that the medieval Grand Duchy of Lithuania was the first Belarusian nation state. In 1569, following the signing of the Union of Lublin, the Belarusians acceded to the Polish "commonwealth" (*Rzeczpospolita*) and fell under Poland's control. During the three partitions of Poland

Belarusian women near the village of Timirazyev cut wheat as part of a harvest celebration. (AFP/Getty Images)

(1772–1795) Belarusians were incorporated into the Russian Empire under Catherine the Great. According to the doctrine called Pan-Slavism that was prevalent in the Russian Empire during 19th century, the Belarusians and "Malorusi" (literally "Petite Russians," i.e., the Ukrainians) were merged into Russians, collectively known as "Velikorusi" (Great Russians).

Next to the Russian and Ukrainian, Belarusian belongs to the Eastern branch of the Slavic division of the Indo-European language family. Together with Russians and Ukrainians, Belarusians share Orthodox Christianity, Old Orthodox Church Slavonic, and the Cyrillic alphabet complemented with certain symbols to accommodate the special spelling. Belarusian literature dates from the 11th century.

The development of the Belarusian people owes much to Baltic tribes, with a particularly strong Lithuanian impact in western Belarus; in fact, in the areas bordering Lithuania residents continue to practice Lithuanian-Belarusian bilingualism. The Belarusians became distinct from their neighbors in language, customs, and material culture about the end of the 12th century. In the 14th century, while being incorporated to Lithuania, Belarusians never lost their national identity. Moreover, with the translation of the Bible in 1517, Belarusian emerged as the dominant language and the vehicle for legislation.

In 1696, the Polish Sejm (Diet) banned the use of Belarusian in the official interaction and record keeping. During this period, Catholic and Polish influences were resisted by the Orthodox Church and brotherhoods (*bratchyny*). Modeled on Western European confraternities and trade guilds, brotherhoods initially concerned themselves with religious and charitable activities; later they took up the defense of the Orthodox Church as well as Belarusian and Ukrainian autonomy. Certain Belarusian cultural peculiarities, especially in the rural dwellings and woodlands, are preserved to this day, including the clothing, embroidery, a diet based mainly on potatoes, the wedding cake, and elements of architectural design. Distinctive rituals include Maslenitsa (the sending off of winter, celebrated before Lent) and Kupala (originally a pagan rite of summer, celebrated in the third week of June).

Despite having a population the size of an average European country and residing in an area as large as Britain, of all the major nations in the USSR the Belarusians were in the greatest danger of losing their distinctive identity during Soviet rule. Belarusians were portrayed by Communist authorities as a backward population, writing in a damaged form of Russian, dressing with embroidered shirts and straw hats, dancing the Lyavoniha national dance, continuously celebrating Stalin as the "Father of the Peoples." Of the 540–570 authors published in Belarus in the 1920–1930s, at least 440–460 (80%) were repressed; together with those Belarusians who fled the country, Belarusians make up one-quarter of the total number of the writers and artists repressed in the USSR. The language issue has been crucial for Belarusian national consciousness. In the last decades of the 20th century, about one-third of Belarusians—predominantly the more educated—considered Russian as their native language, the highest percentage in any Soviet Republic outside of Russia. Russian rapidly replaced the native language in schools, particularly in secondary and university education. It was claimed that Belarusian could be heard only in the countryside among peasants and at the Republican Writers' Union, where authors were directed by Communist authorities to write in Belarusian. (The only path to a career in the creative arts lay in the union.) Despite systematic repression, Belarus contributed considerably to Soviet literature, drama, and poetry. One of the most prominent artists of the 20th century, Marc Chagal, was born and began his career in Belarus, and the best pop group in the USSR, Pesnyary, was from the republic.

After World War I the Belarusians briefly attained statehood, as the ephemeral Belarusian National Republic under German occupation. On January 1, 1919, in the city of Smolensk, the Soviet Socialist Republic of Belarus (SSRB) was founded, and in 1922 the Byelorussian Soviet Socialist Republic, together with other territorial units, became a constituent member of the Soviet Union (USSR). Under the Treaty of Riga (1921) Western Belarus was ceded to Poland only to be retrieved in 1939 under the Soviet agreement with Nazi Germany. During the Stalinist repression (1930s), at least 300,000 intellectuals, members of the cultural and artistic elite, and wealthy peasants were shot, and close to 1 million were exiled to Siberia and Central Asia. During the German occupation of World War II, which lasted more than three years, the republic lost about a third of its population (almost 3 million) and perhaps half of its infrastructure and productive capacity. More than 200 cities, towns, and district centers, and more than 9,000 villages were completely or partially destroyed. Moscow ceded Belarusian territory to Poland and Lithuania; moreover, retaliatory operations against the anti-Soviet resistance continued long after the end of the war. As a consequence, the population of Belarus reached its prewar level (10 million) only in the late 1980s. Under the Soviet system, Belarus did not benefit from the fact that it was formally a United Nations founding member, and an ethnic Belarusian, Andrey Gromyko, was from 1957 until 1985 the Soviet Minister of Foreign Affairs, a full member of the highest ruling body in the USSR, Politbureau, and a ceremonial head of state during the last years of his life.

Belarus suffered considerable environmental damage under the Soviet regime. After the Chernobyl nuclear disaster (1986), the radioactively contaminated areas coincided with those characterized by extreme industrial and chemical pollution. More than 200,000 hectares tainted with radioactive caesium-137 remain unfit for agricultural purposes, and 1.685 million hectares of Belarus's vast forests remain contaminated with radioactive elements. This catastrophe affected the destinies of millions of Belarusians, who have suffered rising levels of thyroid cancer, leukemia, mental disorders, and disabilities in adolescents.

Belarus achieved full independence with the dissolution of the Soviet Union in December 1991—an event that formally occurred on its soil, at the Belovezha summit of the presidents of Russia, Ukraine, and Belarus. Under its first president,

Alyaksander Lukashenka (elected in July 1994), Belarus sought closer integration with Russia, on which it is heavily dependent economically. Lukashenka describes himself as having an "authoritarian ruling style," and he is often described as a dictator. The country's constitution was changed in 1994 to allow Lukashenka to remain in office for a third term, with the specter of an unlimited regime. The Belarusian government has been criticized for human rights violations. Belarus is the only European state that retains the death penalty.

*Stephan E. Nikolov*

**Further Reading**

Korosteleva, Elena A., Colin W. Lawson, and Rosalind J. Marsh, eds. *Contemporary Belarus: Between Democracy and Dictatorship.* London and New York: Routledge Curzon, 2003.

Marples, David R. *Belarus: A Denationalized Nation.* New York: Harwood Academic, 1999.

Silitski, Vitali, and Jan Zaprudnik. *Historical Dictionary of Belarus.* 2nd ed. Lanham, MD: Scarecrow Press, 2007.

Vakar, Nicholas P. *Belorussia: The Making of a Nation. A Case Study.* Russian Research Center Studies, no. 21. Cambridge, MA: Harvard University Press, 1956.

Zaprudnik, Jan. *Belarus: At a Crossroads in History.* Boulder, CO: Westview Press, 1993.

# Bosniaks

Bosniaks (Bosnian: *Bošnjaci*, sg. *Bošnjak*; in English also spelled Bosniacs; before 1993 known as Muslimani, i.e., Bosnian,

Yugoslav, or Serbo-Croat-speaking Muslims) are a Muslim Slav nation in the former Yugoslavia. They live mostly in Bosnia-Herzegovina, which they look to as their homeland (*matična država*), and in the adjoining Sandžak region of southern Serbia and northern Montenegro, but also in the other Yugoslav successor states. From 1878, many emigrated to remaining Ottoman lands. Later flows of political exiles since 1945, economic migrants since the 1960s, and refugees in the 1990s have brought a Bosniak diaspora of perhaps half a million to German-speaking countries, Scandinavia, North America, and Australia. In the most recent census in Bosnia-Herzegovina (1991), Bosniaks were not a category, but there were 1,902,956 Muslimani (43.5% of the republic's population); many of the 242,682 who declared themselves Yugoslavs would also be likely to identify as Bosniaks today. One current estimate is about 2.2 million Bosniaks in Bosnia-Herzegovina, some 48 percent of a total population of 4.6 million. Some 300,000–350,000 live in other former Yugoslav countries; they make up the majority (52.6%) in the Sandžak, according to the 2002–2003 censuses. Their religion and identification with Ottoman cultural tradition distinguishes them from the Croats and Serbs, with whom they until recently shared a language. Bosniaks now refer to their language as Bosnian. Like Croatian, the written language is based on the *Ijekavian* dialect (spoken in much of Croatia, Bosnia-Herzegovina, and Montenegro, but not in Serbia) and written in Latin script, and is distinguished mainly by a greater frequency of Oriental loan words and an additional -h–(/x/) in some

words (e.g. kahva, coffee). The language distinguishes Bosniaks from other Muslim communities in the former Yugoslavia, which speak Albanian, Turkish, Romani, or Macedonian. The status of the Bosnian Muslims as a separate nation has been contested, and the recent (1993) adoption of *Bosniak* (a word used in Ottoman times) as their ethnonym was in part intended to put a stop to claims that they were ethnic Croats or Serbs of Muslim faith. The Muslim Slav communities in Montenegro and southern Kosovo are divided over whether to identify as Bosniaks, or as Muslimani or Goranis, respectively.

Bosniaks, like Croats and Serbs, derive from the South Slavs that arrived in the area in the fifth century. They identify with the medieval Bosnian state under Ban Kulin (r. 1180–1204) and King Tvrtko (r. 1353–1391). The conquest of Bosnia by Mehmet II (1463) made it an administrative province (at various times *sancak*, *eyelet*, or *vilayet*) of the Ottoman Empire. Ancestors to the Bosniaks adopted Islam under Ottoman rule from the 15th century onward; by the 17th century, there was a Muslim majority. In the past, Islamization was explained variously as the result of forced conversion, conversion by a feudal class seeking to retain its privileges, and the mass conversion of a heretic Bosnian church. The evidence, however, points to a gradual, noncoercive process of conversion from folk Christianity to folk Islam, affecting different social strata and religious confessions; driven by the relative legal, economic, and psychological advantages of belonging to the dominant religion; and meeting scant resistance from Christian clergy, who were few and weakly organized.

Bosnian Muslims (known as Bosniaks) pray during the Eid al-Adha festival in the city of Banja Luka in January 2006. Located in the Bosnian Serb political entity, the Republika Srpska, Banja Luka witnessed horrific ethnic cleansing operations during Bosnia-Herzegovina's civil war. Across the nation, churches and mosques were leveled by warring factions of Bosniaks, Serbs, and Croats. Since the war ended in 1995, there has been a major religious revival among the country's three major faiths: Islam, Orthodox Christianity, and Roman Catholicism. (AFP/Getty Images)

Though the Muslims were regarded as Turks on account of their religion and participation in Ottoman culture, Bosnia was not significantly settled by ethnic Turks, and the Muslim population remained Slavic-speaking. An Ottoman urban civilization developed in Sarajevo, Travnik, Mostar, and other towns, fostered by the endowments of notables like Sarajevo's Ghazi Husrev-Bey, with learning and arts in Turkish, Persian, and Arabic as well as a vernacular literature in Arabic script (*alhamiado*). The Muslims also participated in the oral culture of epic song in the Slav vernacular. Bosnia lay on the border between the Ottoman and Habsburg empires, and

the many wars and growing tax pressures were a heavy burden. The 19th century saw a number of local rebellions, both by local Muslim notables (against Ottoman modernizing and centralizing reforms, between 1821 and 1850), and by Christian peasants, the latter leading eventually to the involvement of European powers and the Ottoman loss of Bosnia to Austria-Hungary.

Bosniaks are traditionally Sunni Muslims of the Hanafi School. The main Sufi orders today are the Naqshbandiyya and Qadiriyya; many others, including those with more heterodox tendencies, have been present in history. Local religious practices of note include the *mevlud* celebrations with recitations of pious poetry on the Prophet's birthday as well as on other festive occasions; the *tevhid* commemoration of the dead and the women's *tevhid* in private homes, with Qur'an recitation and prayers; visiting the roofed tombs (*turbeta*) of Muslim saints and martyrs; and pilgrimages with open-air devotions at particular prayer sites (*dovišta*), some of which have become annual mass events. Contemporary religiosity ranges from the nonpracticing secularist, through an easy-going faith stressing ethical principles and local traditions, to more rigid forms of piety that have recently asserted themselves, including salafi influences associated with the Middle East.

Reformers and traditionalists in the first half of the 20th century debated how to adapt to life in a non-Muslim state. Muslim family and personal status law remained under sharia court jurisdiction until 1946. Under socialist rule, these and other Islamic institutions were suppressed. The recognition of Muslims as a nation led to a cautious religious revival in the 1970s, with the founding of an Islamic newspaper and a theological faculty. Since the fall of socialism, through the 1992–1995 war and postwar years, religion has had a high public profile, and has spurred considerable growth in Islamic institutions (schools and higher education, publishing, etc.). Nearly all religious life is organized by the Islamic Community, headed by a *reisu-l-ulema* (Grand Mufti), which is recognized under the 2004 law on freedom of religion and religious communities.

The Bosnian Muslim population has historically been associated primarily with the urban life of traders and craftsmen. In the Bosnian borderland, unlike other Ottoman lands, the estates of military leaders often became hereditary, and there developed an indigenous Muslim nobility whose land was farmed by Christian customary tenants (*kmets*). There were also Muslim peasants farming their own land. Agrarian reforms in the 20th century did away with the Muslim landlord class, but many common family names incorporate titles like *beg* or *aga*. In the socialist period Bosnia-Herzegovina underwent rapid urbanization and the development of some heavy industry. Male seasonal labor migration to countries like Germany and Switzerland has been significant in the later 20th century. There is a pronounced social divide between city and countryside, and urbanites worry that their modern and cosmopolitan lifestyle is undermined by an influx of peasants displaced by the war.

Bosniaks have lived closely mixed with Croats and Serbs, often in adjacent or shared villages and neighborhoods, and have participated with these and other groups in Bosnia's social, economic, and cultural life through shared institutions. In the early 20th century, some Muslim intellectuals promoted Croat or Serb nationality, but most Muslims opted instead to identify themselves as nationally "undetermined" (*neopredeljeni*), until they were offered the option to be Muslims in an ethnic or national sense. Important traditional forms of artistic expression include the sevdalinka love songs and oral folk epics and ballads, and lively literary production and award-winning cinema have developed.

In recent times, Bosnia-Herzegovina has been a part of Austria-Hungary (occupied 1878, annexed 1908), the first Yugoslavia (1918–1941), the fascist NDH state, and Socialist Yugoslavia (1945–1992) before

## Bosnia-Herzegovina: War and Refugees

In the final years of the Socialist Federal Republic of Yugoslavia (1943–1992), a fierce struggle erupted among the constituent republics and autonomous regions. Croatia's vote for seceding from the federal structure was followed by the Yugoslav National Army's seizure of one-third of Croatian territory, while Bosnia-Herzegovina's declaration of independence resulted in the siege of its capital, Sarajevo, in April 1992. Some 250,000 Bosnians, most of whom were Bosnian Muslims, lost their lives in the ensuing four years of war. The breakup of the former Yugoslavia was one of the major refugee-producing events in the last decade of the 20th century: more than 1 million Bosnians were displaced internally and another 1 million fled the country in search of safety. About 130,000 refugees have been resettled in the United States. Other destinations for refugees from Bosnia-Herzegovina include Germany, Austria, Great Britain, Australia, and Canada, where Bosnians build new livelihoods while seeking to heal the wounds of wartime.

*Fethi Keles*

becoming independent. Austro-Hungarian rule left a lasting administrative, legal, educational, and architectural legacy. Many Muslims emigrated to Ottoman lands; others remained and slowly integrated into the new institutions. Political mobilization of Muslims under the new system began with a successful movement for Muslim autonomy in matters of education and administration of the religious endowments (1899–1909). Muslim parties, the MNO party (established 1906), and its successor the JMO (established 1919) joined shifting coalitions in ultimately unsuccessful attempts to prevent agrarian reform and keep Bosnia intact. In socialist Yugoslavia under Tito, from 1968 onward, the Communist Party recognized Muslims as a sixth nation (*narod*) in the country's nationalities system, though the Muslims, unlike the other nations, did not have a republic to themselves, or national institutions to promote their identity.

Economic crisis, the collapse of socialism, and the first free elections (1990) brought an uneasy coalition of nationalist parties to power. The SDA party of Alija Izetbegović (1925–2003), a broad national movement with a pan-Islamist current, gained the Bosniak vote and has been a dominant force in Bosniak politics since. Bosnia's subsequent declaration of independence from a dissolving Yugoslavia triggered the 1992–1995 war, in which Bosnian Serb and Croat forces supported by Belgrade and Zagreb respectively fought the Bosnian government to partition the country along ethnic lines. The brutal ethnic cleansing of the civilian population, the genocide in Srebrenica (1995), and the siege of Sarajevo left at least 64,000 Bosniaks killed or missing, more than half of

## Srebrenica

Srebrenica (Srebrenitza), a town located in contemporary eastern Bosnia-Herzegovina, was the site of a mass murder planned and executed by the Serbian Army and paramilitaries against the local Bosnian Muslim (Bosniak) population in the 1991–1995 war in the Balkans. The town was declared a safe haven as per a United Nations Security Council Resolution in 1993; however, approximately 8,000 Bosniaks were killed in a series of attacks in July 1995 by forces led by Ratko Mladić, who faced no resistance from the Dutch peacekeepers on duty. In an award made in 2007, the International Court of Justice decided that the killings amounted to genocide. The Dayton Agreement of 1995, which ended the war, divided the country into two political entities, the Federation of Bosnia and Herzegovina, and the Serb Republic (Republika Srpska), and left Srebrenica to the control of the latter entity. Approximately 2,000 of the Bosniaks who fled Srebrenica and surrounding areas at various stages of the war, including the time of the massacre, have entered the United States as UN-recognized refugees and they currently live in Syracuse, New York.

Bosnian Muslim women pray in front of a marble stone with the inscription "Srebrenica, July 1995," which was unveiled in the village of Potocari near Srebrenica, Bosnia, on July 11, 2001. The monument marks the reburial site for victims of Europe's worst massacre in 50 years. (AP/Wide World Photos)

*Fethi Keles*

them civilians. The war experience has greatly affected all facets of Bosniak life, and it has left the challenge of rebuilding a devastated society and economy in a weak, decentralized, ethnically divided state.

*Christian Moe*

## Further Reading

Babuna, Aydın. "National Identity, Islam and Politics in Post-Communist Bosnia-Herzegovina." *East European Quarterly* 24, no. 4 (2006): 405–438.

Bringa, Tone. *Being Muslim the Bosnian Way: Identity and Community in a Central Bosnian Village.* Princeton, NJ: Princeton University Press, 1995.

Friedman, Francine. *The Bosnian Muslims: Denial of a Nation.* Boulder, CO: Westview Press, 1996.

Malcolm, Noel. *Bosnia: A Short History.* Rev. ed. London: Macmillan, 1996.

## Bretons

Bretons live mainly in the Brittany region of western France. The population of the four administrative departments of Brittany plus the Loire-Atlantique department was about 4.365 million in 2007. The three largest cities in Brittany are Nantes, Rennes, and Brest. There are also significant Breton diasporas in Paris, other French cities, and in several foreign countries. Bretons are of Celtic cultural origin, the primary language linked to the ethnic group is Breton (although all Breton speakers also speak French), and their religion is predominantly Roman Catholic. Gallo, a Romance language that is now nearly extinct, was traditionally spoken throughout the eastern part of Brittany. The Breton language has undergone a rapid decline in the number of speakers over the past century. In 1900 there were probably about 1.3 million Breton speakers. By the 1980s the number of Breton speakers had decreased to about 600,000, and by 2007, language use surveys suggest that there were fewer than 200,000 speakers. Perhaps 35,000 of these speak it on a daily basis, and 70 percent of Breton speakers today are past 60 years old. Breton ethnic identity is self-ascribed, situational or contextual, and frequently performative in a folkloric setting. Major bases of ethnic identity for Bretons include territory, race and ancestral origins, expressive culture (music, dance, costume), and language. Surveys also suggest that only a small but significant minority of the region's total population claims a strong Breton ethnic identity or affiliation. The historical processes of the stigmatization,

devalorization, and marginalization of Breton language and culture within the larger French nation-state and society partially explain the ambiguous status of ethnic identity in the region.

The Celtic Bretons originally settled in western France through multiple waves of migration from the British Isles that began in the 3rd century CE as Bretons fled invading Angles and Saxons. Bretons developed an independent and well-organized state structure that lasted from the 9th to the early 16th centuries. In 1488, the Breton army was defeated by the French, and in 1532 a treaty unified Brittany and France. Brittany retained significant fiscal and

A woman wears a traditional Breton headdress during a *tromenie*, or hilltop pilgrimage, in Locronan, France. (Christophe Boisvieux/Corbis)

administrative autonomy, however, until 1789. Subsistence agriculture and fishing were the major traditional sources of livelihood for the Breton people until the mid-20th century. Throughout the 19th and the first half of the 20th centuries, the French state gradually extended its control over the region. Processes of modernization, including the construction of railroads and highways, compulsory public education in the French language, military conscription, rural-urban migration, and industrialization, led to the greater linguistic, cultural, and economic assimilation of Bretons into the French nation-state. Today Bretons live in an economically developed and technologically advanced contemporary nation-state structure. The principal foundations of Brittany's economy today include agriculture (especially pork, dairy, and vegetable crop production), food processing, fishing, industrial production (most notably automobiles and electronics), tourism and second home construction, a significant service sector, and a large public-sector labor force (including universities and military installations).

Brittany was traditionally a rural agrarian society until the second half of the 20th century (although there were also urbanized elites from an early period and a growing professional middle class after the mid-20th century). The prevailing image of Brittany centers around rural and rustic small villages, and the Breton people are also known for their deep religiosity and their commitment to the Catholic faith. Catholic rituals of baptism, marriage, and funerals are still important today. Brittany's complex religious landscape includes a large number of saints, religious festivals known as pardons, and collective pilgrimages to chapels and sacred saint locations. Bretons also have some culturally distinctive beliefs about death, souls, and the afterlife. Family, marriage, and kinship were other important pillars of Breton society. Ethnic group relations within Brittany have three important aspects. First, Bretons have long interacted with tourists and non-Bretons who have second homes in the region. Some of these outsiders are French people (often from the Paris area) and others are from foreign countries (Germany and Britain, among others). Relationships between Bretons and these outsiders are generally harmonious, but may also be tinged with resentment and mild conflict. Second, Bretons have long had cultural, intellectual, and political ties with peoples from the other Celtic nations (Scots, Irish, Welsh, Cornish, and Manx) and with some other ethnic minorities within France and Europe (Basque, Occitan, and Catalans, among others). Finally, new postcolonial and racially diverse immigrants have also started to live in Brittany.

Brittany has a long history of ethnoregionalist and nationalist social movements beginning at the end of the 19th century. Throughout the first half of the 20th century, these political parties were mainly on the right ideologically, and during World War II some Breton nationalists actively collaborated with the German occupiers. After the war, some of the Breton nationalists were executed, imprisoned, or punished with civil penalties for this collaboration by the French state. When the Breton movement reemerged in the 1960s, it was reconstituted primarily as a set of small leftist and autonomist political groups with a largely middle-class, intellectual, and urban-dwelling membership. Three of the principal parties operating today are the Union Democratique Breton (Democratic Breton Union), the Parti Breton (Breton Party), and Emgann (a Breton neologism suggesting struggle or combat). The Union Democratique Breton was founded in 1964 as a socialist autonomist party. This party has approximately one thousand active members and includes several local elected officials. The Parti Breton was founded in 2002 as a social democratic and nationalist political party. This party claims about 400 active members, participates in electoral politics, and also has a small number of local elected officials. Emgann was founded in 1982 as an anticapitalist and antiracist leftist nationalist party. This group is even smaller, does not participate in electoral politics, and has ambiguous links with the Breton Revolutionary Army (a banned terrorist group under French law).

Breton ethnonationalist parties today share several broad goals: greater political and economic autonomy for Brittany (or actual independence from France in some cases), the administrative reunification of the department of Loire-Atlantique with Brittany, and official French state recognition and preservation of the Breton language. Breton ethnoregional activists have employed protests, rallies, marches, and electoral politics as their main strategies to pursue their goals. Violence has never played a major role in Breton nationalism; however, between 1966 and 1978, the Front de Libération de la Bretagne (Breton Liberation Front) carried out approximately 200 bombings of symbolic and infrastructural manifestations of French state power in Brittany (but without killing anyone). Although the political Breton movement is relatively small and marginal, cultural movements in the region—those groups devoted to the preservation and folkloric performance of traditional or neotraditional Breton costume, dance, music, and sports—are far larger and more actively influential in contemporary Brittany. Organizations supporting the teaching of the Breton language, such as the Diwan schools, are also an important part of this cultural movement.

The future of Breton ethnicity in the early 21st century is problematic and difficult to predict. The Breton language represents an all-too-familiar case of language disappearance and death. Given the current age distribution of Breton speakers, the small number of children and young adults enrolled in Breton language instruction, the absence of official French state recognition for the language, and the limited availability of mass media in Breton, it appears likely that Breton will be moving toward functional extinction within the next few decades. Bretons have in many ways been assimilated into broader French society and culture, as well as into European and global cultural identities. Although some facets of Breton ethnicity have displayed great resilience, major questions to ask include, what does it now mean to be Breton? And how will Breton ethnic identity be shaped, articulated, and expressed in the future?

*David Maynard*

## Further Reading

Badone, Ellen. *The Appointed Hour: Death, Worldview and Social Change in Brittany.* Berkeley: University of California Press, 1989.

Broudic, Fanch. *Parler Breton au XXI siecle: Le nouveau sondage de TMO regions* (*Speaking Breton in the 21st Century: The New Survey of the TMO Regions*). Brest: Emgleo Breiz, 2009.

Helias, Pierre-Jakez. *The Horse of Pride: Life in a Breton Village*. New Haven, CT: Yale University Press, 1978.

McDonald, Maryon. *"We Are Not French!"*: *Language, Culture and Identity in Brittany*. London: Routledge, 1989.

Monnier, Jean-Jacques, et. al. *Toute l'Histoire de la Bretagne* (*The Complete History of Brittany*). Morlaix: Editions Skol Vreizh, 1996.

Skol Vreizh. *Histoire de la Bretagne et des pays celtiques* (*History of Brittany and the Celtic Countries*). 5 vols. Morlaix: Editions Skol Vreizh, 1989.

# Bulgarians

Bulgarians (Bulgarian: *bulgartsi*) are a Slavic people chiefly concentrated on the Balkan Peninsula. The Republic of Bulgaria is home to nearly 7 million of the 9 million Bulgarians worldwide, with minorities in neighboring Romania, Turkey, Greece, and Serbia. Communities in Ukraine (over 200,000) and Russia (over 330,000) were founded by émigrés in the 19th century, while hundreds of thousands of Bulgarians emigrated to Western Europe (500,000), North America (200,000), and South America (100,000) in the post-1989 period. Primarily Orthodox Christians who speak Bulgarian, a South Slavic language, Bulgarians have historically defined themselves in opposition to aspects of Greek, Turkish, and Romanian culture, while sharing broad parallels with (Slavic) Serbians. The latter led to minor disputes regarding the identity of the population of border territories. Bulgarian scholars often emphasize shared history, linguistic links, and customs to claim Macedonians as part of the Bulgarian people, disputing the claim to an independent Macedonian ethnicity.

Accepted scholarly opinion holds Bulgarians to be the fusion between Slavic tribes and Bulgar nomads (referred to as "proto-Bulgarians" in Bulgaria) who settled in the Balkans in the 7th century; however, popular discourse in contemporary Bulgaria often emphasizes an earlier Thracian heritage. In CE 640, the Khanate of the Onogur Bulgars to the north of the Black Sea fragmented into several tribes following their conquest by the Khazars. One group, led by Khan Asparukh, migrated southwest and founded a new state in the Danubian plain (today divided between Romania and Bulgaria), annexing local Slavic tribes in the process. The new state pressed the boundaries of the Byzantine Empire, leading to endemic warfare but allowing Byzantine influence to permeate the new state. Khan Boris embarked on a policy of forced Christianization in the 860s. Byzantine influence accelerated under Simeon I, who founded the First Bulgarian Empire in 914 and in 927 gained recognition for the Bulgarian Patriachate, the first Orthodox Church independent of Constantinople. In the 9th and 10th centuries the towns of Pliska, Ohrid, and Preslav emerged as key centers of Slavonic Orthodoxy, developing the Slavonic rite and translating and disseminating Latin and Greek texts. Continued rivalry saw the end of the Bulgarian Empire in 1018 at the hands of Byzantine Emperor Basil Boulgaroktnos, "Basil the Bulgar-slayer."

Bulgarians perform in traditional costume during Trifon Zarezan (Vine Grower's Day) in the village of Ilindenci. This festival celebrates wine and includes rituals for an abundant grape harvest. (EPA Photo/Mladen Antonov)

A second Bulgarian Empire was founded in 1185, which fragmented by the late 13th century, and the smaller successor states were first vassalized, then annexed outright by the Ottoman Empire during the period of 1376–1396.

The nearly five centuries of Ottoman rule are popularly characterized in Bulgaria as the *Tursko igo* ("Turkish Yoke"). The initial postconquest period saw religious toleration, relative administrative autonomy for Christians, and a lighter tax burden since the expansionist Ottoman Empire was fueled by conquest rather than by the taxation imposed by the Bulgarian Empire and Church. Bulgarian Christians did face higher taxes than Muslims and were subject to the *devşirme*, a "child tax" in which children were enslaved, converted to Islam,

and raised to serve in the Janissary corps or other state duties. Additional laws restricted Christians from church construction and limited church height, forbade certain kinds and colors of clothing, and restricted the ownership of weapons. Such material restrictions may have inspired the historic conversion of some Bulgarian communities to Islam (see POMAK). Although the Ottoman market created some economic opportunities and a prosperous class of Bulgarians emerged (the *chorbadzhiia*, Bulgarian for "providers of soup" to the needy), the administrative breakdown of the empire in the 18th century led to the victimization of both Christian and Muslim peasants by local administrators, bandits, and mutinous army units. Bulgarian popular memory accords little good to the

Ottoman period, depicted as a period of cultural and ethnic slumber for the Bulgarian nation.

Bulgarian cultural life incorporates both unique features, shared heritage with other Balkan peoples, and Turkish elements. Cultural and economic ways of life were profoundly altered in the late 19th century by modernization, which saw traditional folk customs eclipsed by Westernization. Bulgarians are overwhelmingly Orthodox Christians, with small and relatively recent Protestant, Catholic, and Muslim communities. Bulgarian Orthodoxy encompasses some pagan traditions outside of Christian dogma. These include *Baba Marta* ("Grandmother March") on March 1, gifting friends and family with red-and-white tassels or bracelets for good health and spirit; entombing symbolic offerings in the foundations of new buildings; and *kukeri*, a rural celebration of masked, animal-hide, and bell-bedecked dancers who celebrate spring and drive away evil influences. Secularism, particularly in the socialist era, has undermined the expression of religious belief, but Bulgarian Orthodoxy is still popularly seen as integral to Bulgarian identity.

Ottoman conquest transformed agriculture in Bulgaria, with indigenous noble landowners either assimilated or dispossessed of the best land in the plains and valleys. Towns became increasingly Turkish centers of administration and commerce. Most Bulgarians historically lived in self-sufficient peasant households, with alpine communities raising goats and sheep and trading in wool. Bulgarian independence was marked by relatively egalitarian landholding (although Turkish estates were confiscated). Occupations no longer strictly follow ethnic lines today, although the Turkish ethnic minority dominates regional industries (mining in the southeast, tobacco growing in the south) and the Roma minority is generally segregated into lower-class roles. Although agriculture remains an important sector of the country's economy, Bulgaria today is predominantly urban with nearly three-quarters of the population living in towns and cities, including one-fifth of the population dwelling in the capital of Sofia alone.

During Ottoman rule Muslims predominated in administrative and military positions, while Greeks (and Hellenized Bulgarians) took the leading role in the hierarchy of the Orthodox Church. The autonomous Archbishopric of Ohrid, the last vestige of the medieval autocephalous Bulgarian church, was abolished in the 18th century. These divisions shaped ethnic rivalries during the revival (*vuzrazhdane*) period, with Bulgarians seeking greater control over ecclesiastical and secular administration: the *Istoriia Slavianobulgarskiia* of St. Paisii Hilendarski, written in 1762, is typical in exhorting Bulgarians to feel pride and avoid Hellenization. State rivalries with neighboring Serbia, Greece, and Romania emerged in the late 19th century, fueling ethnic tensions in disputed borderland areas. Ethnic violence, however, remained relatively rare. The Bulgarian independence struggle saw attacks against Muslim and Christian communities, and the Balkan Wars of 1912–1913 saw targeted attacks against rival ethnicities by each combatant. Ethnic tensions within 20th-century Bulgaria occasionally flared up against the Muslim Turkish and

Pomak communities, who were subjected in the 1870s, 1910s, 1930s, 1950s, and 1970s–1980s to assimilation campaigns and who responded by emigrating in the hundreds of thousands. The historic Greek population located in the southwest and along the Black Sea Coast was exchanged for the Bulgarian population of western Thrace in the 1923 Greco-Bulgarian population exchange. The contemporary ethnic climate is relatively peaceful, although far-right political elements occasionally indulge in antiminority rhetoric.

Medieval Bulgarians employed distinctive artistic and architectural elements, including interlacing patterns of plant life, the use of ceramic tile to create mosaics, and a distinctive church-building pattern featuring four raised towers. Byzantine influence displaced this, introducing painted frescoes (examples are preserved at Boyana Church, near Sofia). Icon painting, as with other Orthodox peoples, is common and celebrated, although the distinctive Bulgarian art of stone icon carving is now rare. Bulgarian songs and dances are similar to those of other Balkan peoples, but Bulgarian folk costume is notable and diverse. Women traditionally wore aprons and dresses, while men wore trousers, shirts, wide belts, and vests; outerwear was colorful (often red) and heavily embroidered, the patterns falling along regional lines. Traditional entertainments and costume have been supplanted by modern European styles since the early 20th century, but continue to be celebrated and performed by heritage troupes.

Modern Bulgarian history is marked by the drive for independence, expansion, and modernization of the Bulgarian state. The last century of Ottoman rule in Bulgaria witnessed the twin drives of state failure and reform. The former, most notably the *kurdzhaliistvo* ("brigandage") of the 1790s through 1820, saw the breakdown of central authority and the emergence of local warlords and bandits who victimized local peasantry (both Christian and Muslim). The latter, particularly the Tanzimat period of 1839–1876, saw attempts at centralization and modernization of the Ottoman state and military, fueling economic prosperity as Bulgarian-inhabited regions became key suppliers of cloth and iron for the new military units. The influx of wealth helped drive the second phase of the Bulgarian Revival, which saw both the dissemination of nationalism as a philosophical and political ideal and the patronage of local schools and churches with the intent to foster Bulgarian identity against the pressures of a Turkish Ottoman state and a Greek Orthodox hierarchy. Demands for increased independence were met first by the creation of the autocephalous Bulgarian Exarchate Church in 1870, and the creation of an autonomous principality (under a German prince) following the Bulgarian Uprising of 1876 and Ottoman defeat in the Russo-Turkish War of 1877–1878.

The Kingdom of Bulgaria had initially been envisioned as encompassing a vast expanse that would have incorporated nearly all ethnic Bulgarian communities in the Balkans, but Russia was forced to accede to rival great power demands and the resulting state of 1878 comprised less than half of modern Bulgaria. The new state focused on the incorporation of Bulgarian communities in the region into a single state, leading to conflicts over borderlands with

Greece (in Macedonia and Thrace), Romania (in Dobrudzha), and Serbia (in Macedonia and around the Timok River basin). The most critical conflict concerned geographic Macedonia, with Bulgarian scholars and politicians claiming its Christian Slavic inhabitants as conationals. The goal of unification with Macedonia drove Bulgaria's participation in the Balkan Wars of 1912–1913, World War I, and World War II. Bulgaria was defeated in the last three of these wars, losing territory and leaving substantial minority populations outside of state borders. The failure to reclaim Macedonia (chiefly split between Greece and Yugoslavia) was compounded by socialist Yugoslavia's recognition after 1944 of a Macedonian nation. The relationship between Macedonian and Bulgarian identity remains a controversial one in Bulgaria today, and although the government recognizes the Republic of Macedonia as a state, many Bulgarians consider the Macedonian ethnicity to be a subset of Bulgarians.

The attention to foreign policy and expansion by the Bulgarian government meant the neglect of domestic development, particularly with regard to the peasantry. Although a peasant-centered regime came to power in 1919, it was overthrown by a rightist coup d'état in 1923. Only after the socialist assumption of power in 1944 (Bulgaria formally becoming a republic in 1946) did domestic development touch the majority of the state's inhabitants. Urbanization and industrialization were matched by state efforts to bring electricity, transportation links, education, and medical treatment to rural areas. The booming centrally planned economy of the 1940s and 1950s faced increasing stagnation by the late 1970s. The state responded with limited reforms and by appeals to nationalism, but both policies were superseded by reforms in the Soviet Union, the Soviet refusal to use force to maintain socialist rule in Eastern Europe (the Gorbachev Doctrine), and the revolution of 1989.

The period since 1989 has been marked by the transition to political pluralism and a more open economic market. The loss of former Soviet bloc markets has meant a sustained decline in the standard of living; this, along with widespread corruption in government and the growth of organized crime, has resulted in widespread frustration. One sign of this frustration has been the frequent change between ruling government parties, which have included the socialists, the center-right, and a personal party led by the former king, Simeon II. Although populist (and xenophobic) extremist parties have received substantial protest votes and a great deal of attention in the Western media, the political and ethnic climate remains stable. Demographically, however, continued economic problems have led roughly 1 million citizens to emigrate (out of the 8 million citizens inhabiting the country in 1989). This raises popular concerns both that Bulgarians may be assimilated within Europe as a whole and lose their identity, and that the faster-growing Muslim minorities might assume more control within the country. Accession to the European Union in 2007 was popularly seen as a route to economic development, but also reinforced concerns that Bulgarian culture might be diluted. This provides context for the Bulgarian government's symbolic challenges to the EU on cultural issues, notably to gain recognition for *evro* as an alternate spelling (in Cyrillic) and pronunciation for the Euro, both reflecting Bulgarian usage.

*James Frusetta*

## Further Reading

Crampton, Richard J. *Bulgaria*. Oxford: Oxford University Press, 2007.

Fine, John V. A., Jr. *The Early Medieval Balkans*. Ann Arbor: University of Michigan Press, 1991.

Fine, John V. A., Jr. *The Late Medieval Balkans*. Ann Arbor: University of Michigan Press, 1994.

MacDermott, Mercia. *Bulgarian Folk Customs*. London: Jessica Kingsley, 1998.

Shay, Anthony. *Balkan Dance*. Jefferson: McFarland, 2008.

Todorova, Maria. "The Course and Discourses of Bulgarian Nationalism." In *Eastern European Nationalism in the Twentieth Century*, ed. Peter Sugar. Washington, DC: American University Press, 1995, 55–102.

# C

## Carpatho-Rusyns

Carpatho-Rusyns are a small East Slavic people. The identity of this population has been much disputed, with several nationalities laying claim to the group. For example, in Poland they were seen as a lost tribe, in Hungary as Slavophone Hungarians; in Slovakia they were considered Eastern Rite Slovaks, while in Ukraine they were considered a subethnos of Ukrainians, and in Russia members of the greater East Slavic Rus nation. Various parts of the Carpatho-Rusyn population have been referred to as Rusyn, Rusnak, Rusyn-Ukrainian, some variant of Ruthenian, Lemko, Boiko, and even Russian. In the main, Carpatho-Rusyns are Greek-Slavonic Rite—that is, Eastern Rite—Christians, a feature they share with other East Slavic peoples. They live in the most western extension of East Slavdom, and their traditional homeland spans the south side and part of the north side of the northeast arc of the Carpathian Mountains in Central Europe. This territory includes the northeast part of the Presov region of eastern Slovakia, Subcarpathian Ukraine (Zakarpatska Oblast), part of the Maramures district of north-central Romania, and the Lemko Region of southeast Poland. There are also compact Carpatho-Rusyn settlements in Serbia, Croatia, and Hungary, a sizable diaspora in North America, and small numbers in South America and Australia. The total number of Carpatho-Rusyns living in Europe is a matter of some contention since there is no Carpatho-Rusyn political entity of any sort and various countries use different ways to count their inhabitants. Carpatho-Rusyns are recognized as a distinct group in all countries where they exist with the exception of Ukraine, which prefers to identity Carpatho-Rusyns as a subsection of the Ukrainian nation.

The Carpatho-Rusyn homeland was arguably populated by Slavs since at least the sixth century CE. Slavs existed beyond the northern horizon of Greek, Roman, and Byzantine historians. Present-day scholars generally locate the Slavic homeland somewhere north of the Carpathians and perhaps even touching those mountains. Slavs broke onto the historical stage in the sixth century when they appeared on the Danube river frontier of the Eastern Roman Empire, eventually flooding south into the Balkans where they are known today as "South Slavs." Other Slavs went East and north into Ukraine and Russia while others went west and northwest to the Czech lands and Poland. The Carpatho-Rusyns either migrated into the Carpathian valleys at that time or were already there unnoticed by Roman and Greek writers. The "Mission to the Slavs" of saints Cyril and Methodius in the ninth century brought Christianity to the region and the rooting of that faith may have occurred then or a bit later, from disciples of Cyril and Methodius who were based in Bulgaria. Eventually Kievan influence became dominant in religious activities. The form of Eastern Rite (Greek or Byzantine Ritual) Christianity accepted by the Carpatho-Rusyns includes married priests and was originally conducted in the Carpathian version of Church Slavonic.

Today the everyday Rusyn language exists in four mutually intelligible forms and is written in the Cyrillic or accented Roman alphabets. Outside observers in the 19th and early 20th centuries especially noted that Carpatho-Rusyns were profoundly conservative, shunning innovation, with archaic elements in religious life and even pagan carry-overs in village activities. They were further distinguished by the celebration of holidays, their social relations, their customs, and their traditions. Carpatho-Rusyns, on the whole, were never city dwellers but rather farmers and herders of cattle and especially sheep. These herders practiced seasonal migration for pasture, summering in high altitudes and wintering in valleys. Their villages, usually established along watercourses, were self-sufficient but cash poor. Male Rusyns traveled down to the plains on both sides of the mountains in the spring and summer to work as manual laborers on the estates of Hungarian, Polish, and German landowners, returning in the fall to their mountain homes. Rusyn tinkers also traveled great distances offering their repair services, while others gathered up the heavy oil that seeped from the ground in the Lemko Region to sell as medicine or lubricant.

Beginning in the 1880s, nearly half of all Carpatho-Rusyns moved to the Americas for work, particularly the United States. Many returned to their homeland and made the trip several times until World War I effectively cut off immigration. Since Carpatho-Rusyns came from the Hungarian Kingdom and the Austrian Empire (that is, Austria-Hungary) they were listed as Hungarians or Austrians when they crossed borders. An estimation of 250,000 immigrants who came to the United States alone is not unreasonable. Both in the homeland and the diaspora Carpatho-Rusyn solidarity has been rooted in their Eastern Rite Christianity, mutually celebrated holidays, social relations, customs, and traditions. The most important factor is the feeling of *nash* ("ours") or the sense of being different.

The entire Carpatho-Rusyn homeland was contained within the Austro-Hungarian state before World War I. After the war the Subcarpathian portion enjoyed semiautonomy as part of Czechoslovakia. This part was seized by the Soviet Union in 1944 and attached to Soviet Ukraine. The Lemko Region, despite attempts by Lemkos to attach it to Subcarpathia in 1918–1920, was awarded to Poland during the peace settlement of World War I. The area was depopulated during and after World War II (1944–1947) by the Polish Communist regime; Lemkos were deported to Ukraine or northern or western Poland. Only a small percentage of Lemkos returned to their homeland after the 1956 political changes. The Presov and Subcarpathian Rusyns/Rusnaks have mainly remained in place. In both world wars the Lemko and Presov regions suffered mightily when the Russian and later Soviet forces attempted to cross the Carpathian mountain passes in order to invade Hungary. From 1944 to 1989 all Carpatho-Rusyns were administratively identified as Ukrainians by Communist authorities.

Since 1990, there has been a large-scale Carpatho-Rusyn renaissance, and in the 21st century Carpatho-Rusyns have been accepted by most scholars as a Fourth East Slavic nation alongside the Russians, Belarusians, and Ukrainians. With the collapse of communism many Carpatho-Rusyns have supported Rusyn societies in Poland, Slovakia, Subcarpathia, Romania, Serbia, Croatia, Czech Republic, and Germany as well as the United States and Canada. Codified versions of Rusyn language are taught in schools wherever Carpatho-Rusyns exist. Within Ukraine's Subcarpathian Province (Zakarpatska Oblast), Carpatho-Rusyns have been recognized as distinct, while the government in Kiev continues with the subethnos concept, refusing to recognize a distinct Carptho-Rusyn ethnic group.

*Paul J. Best*

**Further Reading**

Best, Paul, and Stanislaw Stepien, eds. *Is There a Fourth Rus? Concerning Cultural Identity in the Carpathian Region.* Higganum, CT: South-Eastern Research Institute and the Carpathian Institute, 2010.

Horbal, Bogdan. *Lemko Studies: A Handbook.* New York: East European Monographs, 2010.

Magocsi, Paul Robert, and Ivan Pop, eds. *Encyclopedia of Rusyn History and Culture.* Rev. and expanded ed. Toronto: Toronto University Press, 2005.

Plishkova, Anna. *Language and National Identity: Rusyns South of Carpathians.* Trans. Patricia Krafcik. New York: East European Monographs, 2009.

# Catalans

Catalans—referred to in English as Catalonians, in French as *Catalans*, and in Castilian as *Catalanes*—are citizens of an autonomous community of the Spanish state whose capital is Barcelona. According to the Catalan Statistical Institute, 7.2 million people now live in this Mediterranean coastal community, 70 percent clustered around Barcelona. Historically, contiguous territories across the Pyrenees in France also constitute the millennial heartland of Catalonia (Catalunya, Cataluña, Catalogne), while its imperial influence spread further around the Mediterranean. Catalan is an official language of Catalonia as well as the independent Pyrenean Principality of Andorra (77,000 residents) and claims some 200,000 speakers in the south of France and roughly 20,000 in the Sardinian city of Alghero (l'Alguer), a legacy of the early modern Catalan-Aragonese Mediterranean empire. Related Catalan histories, cultures, and tongues form central elements in the contemporary ethnic identities of other Spanish contiguous communities including inland Aragon, coastal Valencia, and the Balearic Islands. These communities manifest different ecosystems, stronger impact from Arab occupation, and divergent strategies of agricultural, commercial, and political development; in the present, their languages and other markers of identity also embody different relations to Spain and the Castilian language. Descendants of Catalans, meanwhile, played important roles in Spain's late colonial foundations, especially in the Caribbean and the Philippines; other Catalans sought refuge from the Franco regime (1936–1975) across the Americas. The reconstruction of a Catalan polity within a post-Franco Spanish state has revitalized language, culture, and the international standing of the nation and has repositioned Barcelona as a European capital and global destination for diverse immigrants. Yet, Catalans do not forget the struggles of the past while their cosmopolitan future raises questions about a vital and changing culture.

Catalonia's coasts constitute a zone of prehistoric Mediterranean activity overlaid by centuries of contact with Phoenicians, Greeks, Carthaginians, Romans, and Arabs; Tarragona was a Roman capital. A distinctive Catalan identity can be traced to the Frankish reconquest of former Visigothic realms from the Arabs; Franks created a *Marca Hispanica* (Spanish March) along the Pyrenees in the eighth century. Rousillon (Roselló) was captured in 760; Girona, in 785 and Barcelona in 801. Count Guifré I, called *el Pelós* ("the Hairy") made Barcelona and surrounding territories hereditary domains in 897; his grandson, Borrell II, effectively claimed independence from the Carolingians in 987—celebrated subsequently as the birth of Catalonia.

Children wander around a booth at a street market selling flags during the celebrations of the Catalonian National Day (Diada) in Barcelona on September 11, 2005. Many Catalans demonstrate annually to demand recognition of their national rights and liberties, as well as for a greater degree of self-governance. (AFP/Getty Images)

Frankish leaders repopulated war-weary regions with farmsteads (*masies*) built around strong stem family inheritance and independent production of grains, wine, and meat as they revitalized cities like Barcelona and Tarragona. In 1150, the dynastic marriage of Ramon Berenguer IV of Catalonia and Peronella (Petronilla) of Aragon united those territories as the Kingdom of Aragon and Principality of Catalonia. In the 13th century, King Jaume I conquered Mallorca and Valencia. Later kings added Menorca, Sicily, Sardinia, and Naples to an empire that ranged from North Africa to Greece, despite profound internal divisions, wars with Castile, and a crisis of succession.

Catalan society, while deeply Roman Catholic, encompassed polyglot populations of Muslims, Jews, and Mediterranean traders; Catalan maritime law became a standard for the Mediterranean. From 1238 onwards, Catalan parliaments and rulers also adopted distinctive constitutions ensuring laws and rights. Catalan traditions of literature, music, art, religious thought, and architecture emerged in the Middle Ages and Renaissance, alongside popular cultural features such as its Mediterranean cuisine. The philosopher/novelist Ramon Llull (1232–1316), the great historical chronicles, the novelist Joanot Martorell (1413–1468) who was author of *Tirant Lo Blanch*, and poets such as Ausiàs March (1397–1459) all contributed to Catalonia's position in European culture.

In 1469, another dynastic marriage of Ferran (Ferdinand) of Catalonia-Aragon and Isabel of Castile-Leon underpinned a new peninsular unity evident in the defeat of the last Muslim rulers of Granada in 1492, the expulsion of peninsular Jews, and increasing constraints on Muslim, converts, and Gypsies across the peninsula. Meanwhile, the expansion of Castile's claims in the New World and wars in Europe furthered the interests of the Habsburgs, who had inherited the Spanish throne through marriage to Ferdinand and Isabel's daughter, Juana. This imperial vision undermined Catalonia's prosperity and Mediterranean interests. In 1640, Catalans revolted against encroachment on their rights in the Reaper's War (*Guerra dels Segadors*), which led to the proclamation of a Catalan republic under the French. Defeat in 1659 led to division of the polity as Catalonia north of the Pyrenees became incorporated into France, which eliminated most Catalan institutions and public use of Catalan. In the War of Spanish Succession (1705–1714), Iberian Catalans supported a contender to the throne whom they thought likely to ensure their political interests. Military defeat here led to division of Catalonia and Aragon and suppression of Catalan constitutions, institutions of governance, and learning as well as repression of the Catalan language.

In the 18th and 19th centuries, Iberian Catalans revitalized their economy through strong agricultural and viticultural trade and successful engagement with the Industrial Revolution, facilitated by new access to Spain's New World colonies and the Philippines. Banking, industry, and commerce, in turn, underpinned growing mid-century claims to political rights and a cultural renaissance (the *Renaixença*). By the turn of the century, an expanding Barcelona was again a cradle for European arts, including architects Antoni Gaudí and

Lluís Domènech I Muntaner, artists Santiago Russinyol, Ramon Casas, Isidre Nonell, and a young Pablo Picasso; and writers Narcís Oller, Jacint Verdaguer, and Dolors Monserdà. Popular expressions like the working-class choirs founded by Anselm Clavé, revitalized traditions (the now iconic circle dance of the *sardana*), folklore studies, and appreciation of the countryside meant that variegated ideas of Catalan identity imbued a complex society. Two Barcelona World's Fairs, in 1888 and 1929, claimed an international spotlight as well. Tensions existed, nonetheless, between urban and rural populations, especially in 19th-century civil conflicts over the role of tradition, church, and government. These were eclipsed by the end of the century by violent struggles between the Catalan bourgeoisie and workers, whose origins and interests sometimes spread beyond the Catalan polity. In Barcelona, socialists and anarchists clashed with conservative Catalan elites, notably in the destructive urban riots of the 1909 Tragic Week.

By 1914, Catalan politicians including Enric Prat de la Riba and Josep Puig I Cadafalch negotiated limited self-government through the Mancomunitat de Catalunya, which promoted local infrastructure and vital cultural and scientific institutions. After another period of violent class conflict, this state recognition ended in 1925 under the Spanish dictatorship of Miguel Primo de Rivera (1923–1930). Shortly thereafter, many Catalans joined other Spaniards in welcoming the second Spanish Republic, although Francesc Macià proclaimed a short-lived Catalan Republic in 1931 before agreeing to an autonomous government, the Generalitat de Catalunya, within Spain. This Generalitat promoted a more secular, leftist Catalanism, emphasizing language, rights, and history, against opposition from Catalan and Spanish conservatives. Another proclamation of independence in 1935 received a harsher response, revealing the intensity of divisions that erupted across Spain with the Civil War (1936–1939).

In this war, Catalonia became a battleground not only between conservatives and leftists, but among Catalan leftists who fought among themselves before Barcelona fell to Franco and his Axis allies in 1939. Later, the centralized fascist regime of Francisco Franco identified Catalans as enemies, suppressing political agents and institutions and attacking Catalan culture. Many public uses of the Catalan language (especially in schools and mass media) were prohibited, streets renamed, and monuments replaced. Catalonia was flooded with immigrants from other parts of Spain and, after the 1960s, sun-seeking tourists from northern Europe. Industry and banking established new alliances that polluted cities and countryside. For decades, Catalan identity became oppositional and privatized around domestic spheres and memories, sustained by Catalans in exile in France and the New World, including Josep Tarradellas, head of the Generalitat in exile, and cellist Pau Casals. Despite the close identification of the Catholic Church with the Franco regime, Vatican recognition of Catalan as a vernacular liturgical language and communities based in Catholic schools and institutions, including the Catalan patronal abbey of Montserrat, became important features in the renewal of nationalist issues and debates.

After Franco's 1975 death, Catalan demands spilled into the streets. On the 1977 *Diada*—the Catalan national holiday commemorating the fall of Barcelona to the Bourbon claimants and their allies in 1714—more than 1 million people took to the streets waving the *senyera*, the red-and-yellow-striped Catalan flag, and singing Catalan anthems. As Spain evolved into a constitutional monarchy with democratic institutions, Catalans of many political and social backgrounds became active spokesmen in defining a more decentralized state and asserting Catalonia's distinctive place within it. In 1977, Josep Tarradellas returned from exile to assume duties as the president of the Generalitat as an autonomous community in Spain defined by the four core provinces of Catalonia around Barcelona (the Balearics, Valencia, and Aragon soon established similar regimes). Over the next decade, the generally conservative leaders of the Generalitat and those of myriad local governments, including the Socialists in Barcelona (PSOE/PSC), fostered political, economic, and cultural campaigns to rebuild and publicize Catalan traditions. Reclaiming spaces for the Catalan language in classrooms, media, and streetscapes was a primary goal, as was preservation and appreciation of Catalonia's history, natural resources, and monumental past. Meanwhile, social issues of immigration from Andalusia and Catalan citizenship grew with the collapse of many older industrial firms, causing crises across Catalonia. Spain's 1986 entry into the European Union and the 1992 Barcelona Olympics helped spur Barcelona's redevelopment and the city's claims as a global attraction. While the Generalitat and Barcelona municipality competed with each other over responsibilities and recognition surrounding the 1992 Olympics, local strengths have supported a stronger international role for Catalonia within a changing Europe.

In subsequent decades, Catalans have continued their active stewardship of their territory, language, and culture, especially in opposition to claims of the Spanish state. Conflicts range from rights of language, to control of finances, education, and police, to the location of historical archives. Within a complex, changing Spain, Catalan politicians have leveraged their positions in shifting Spanish governments to ensure increasing autonomy in governance, planning, and control. At the same time, Catalans have stressed their cosmopolitan history through connections with Europe and strategies of leadership for the wider Mediterranean. Catalan Gypsies, for example, have reasserted themselves within transnational culture and debates while Barcelona has become a seat for Mediterranean conferences and events. As a relatively wealthy, peaceful, and generally successful ethnic-national unit, Catalans have often sought to be a model for conflictive zones in Europe and around the world and innovators in design, ecological planning, and other areas. Political figures such as Pasqual Maragall, mayor of Barcelona and then president of the Generalitat, and cultural figures such as writers Salvador Espriu, Mercè Rodoreda, and Manuel de Pedrolo, opera star Montserrat Caballé, artists Salvador Dalí, Joan Miró, and Antoni Tàpies, chef Ferran Adrià, architects, scientists, and reformers all have reaffirmed the vitality of contemporary Catalan culture and society.

At the same time, as a global tourist center, Catalans have faced questions about the commodification of local culture and history into mass-market paellas, placeless pubs, fast-food outlets, and Gaudí knick-knacks. Immigration from Africa, Latin America, China, and the Indian subcontinent have raised issues about culture and polyphony, including the language choice of immigrants (for example, Latin Americans who speak Castilian as their native language), immigrants' religious presence in an increasingly secular population, and local confrontations with neighbors who do not look "like us." Declining rates of reproduction among Catalan and Spanish populations as well as economic crises have also challenged the relationship of an evolving Catalonia and new global populations. Yet history, institutions, and past survivals also underscore the continuing strength and repeated reinvention of Catalans as an ethnic group and a nation in the new European century.

*Gary Wray McDonogh*

**Further Reading**

Amelang, James. *Honored Citizens of Barcelona*. Princeton, NJ: Princeton University Press, 1986.

Elliott, J. H. *The Revolt of the Catalans*. Cambridge: At the University Press, 1963.

Hughes, Robert. *Barcelona*. New York: Knopf, 1992.

McDonogh, Gary Wray. *Good Families of Barcelona*. Princeton, NJ: Princeton University Press, 1986.

McRoberts, Kenneth. *Catalonia: Nation Building without the State*. Ontario: Oxford University Press, 2001.

Robinson, William, Jordi Fargà, and Carmen Belen Lord. *Barcelona and Modernity.*

Cleveland, OH: Cleveland Museum of Art, 2006.

Sobrequés i Callicó, Jaume. *Història de Catalunya (History of Catalonia)*. Bristol: Editorial Base, 2007.

Solis, Fernando. *Negotiating Spain and Catalonia*. Barcelona: Intellect Books, 2003.

Woolard, Kathryn A. *Double Talk: Bilingualism and the Politics of Ethnicity in Barcelona*. Stanford University Press, 1989.

# Chechens

The Chechens are the largest Muslim group living in Russia's north Caucasus and, according to a 1989 Soviet census, numbered 956,879 at that time. They currently live in the Russian Federation, although segments of the population have been fighting Moscow for independence since 1994. The Chechens who call themselves *Nokchi* or *Vainakh* have been restless subjects of the Russian and Soviet states ever since they and their related neighbors, the Ingush, were conquered by Imperial Russia in 1861. Chechens observe Islam and speak an ancient local language that belongs to the northeastern branch of the Caucasian language family and is unrelated to Indo-European languages such as Russian, French, English, or German.

The Chechens are among the oldest peoples in Europe and are indigenous to the Caucasus Mountains. The traditionally pagan and animist Chechens converted to Sunni Islam between the 17th and 18th centuries under the influence of missionaries from the neighboring mountainous region of Dagestan. Like many peoples in the northern Caucasus, the Chechens adopted

A Chechen grandma with her granddaughter. (Joan Piven/Dreamstime)

a tolerant mystic form of Islam known as Sufism that blended many of their ancient pagan beliefs with mainstream Sunni Islamic beliefs. Their frontier form of Islam displayed none of the puritanical traditions found in Saudi Wahhabi Islam.

Historically the Chechens were formed into clans known as *teips* and these united during time of trouble or invasion to form greater alliances known as *tukhums*. The various tukhums then united under their respective elders to defend their home villages and *ka'am* (nation) from external attacks. When the Christian Russian invaders first entered their republic, Islam also provided a rallying call for the Chechens to unite with other Muslim groups to wage a unified jihad (holy war).

The Chechens first began to clash with the Russians and their Cossack frontier forces when the latter began to expand into the North Caucasus flank during the 18th and 19th centuries. Such dynamic leaders as the legendary mountain guerrilla leader Imam Shamil from Dagestan unified the Chechens with fellow Caucasian Muslim nations to wage a jihad against the transcontinental Russian Empire. The Russians responded to this stubborn defense with brutal scorched-earth tactics that saw scores of Chechen villages burnt and their populations massacred. Russian policies such as cutting down the forests where the Chechen guerillas hid, the collective punishment of villagers for ambushes on Russian troops, and the construction of fortresses in Chechen lands, such as the fortress city of Grozny, enabled the Russians to subdue the outnumbered Chechens.

While the Chechens were nominally subdued by the Russians after the 1861 defeat of Imam Shamil, this highland people never really accepted Russian rule and revolted several times during the tsarist period. The traditionally Muslim, clan-based society of the Chechens was subjected to sometimes violent attempts to assimilate and minimize minority identity during the early Soviet period. In the first decades of Soviet rule the Chechens suffered from the execution of their community leaders, forced collectivization of their property, and violence. During the early Soviet period Chechnya remained one of the least developed of the Russian provinces.

One cannot understand the Chechens of today without exploring the ways in which the memory of these traumas shaped their collective identity and the views toward their powerful Russian neighbors. Special mention should be made of the total deportation of the Chechens by Soviet leader Josef Stalin on February 23, 1944. Using false charges of mass treason against the Chechens and other distrusted minorities in the region (such as the Crimean Tatars, Ingush, Kalmyks, Karachay, Balkars, and Volga Germans), Stalin had this entire people transported from their mountain homeland to the depths of Central Asia during World War II. KGB documents that were declassified in the early 1990s brought to life the horrors of deportation that saw as many as one in three Chechens die. In the process villages were burnt, Chechens were executed en masse, and many survivors died from diseases, exposure, and hunger.

The vast majority of Chechen deportees were shipped on trains to the frozen wastes of the Central Asian republic of Kazakhstan, where they gradually began to rebuild their lives. In their absence tens of thousands of Russians were settled in the Chechens' former homeland. At this time ancient cemeteries were ploughed over, mosques destroyed, books in Chechen burnt, and the land "de-Chechenized" and given Russian names.

After more than a decade of living in so-called special settlement camps, the Chechens were released from their exile in 1957 by the new Soviet leader, Nikita Khrushchev. Thousands of Chechen exiles began to stream back to their former homeland where they clashed with Russians who had settled in their homes and villages during their absence.

After several years of struggle the vast majority of Chechens resettled in their homeland, where they continued to face discrimination. While the Chechens made up the majority of the Chechen-Ingush Autonomous Soviet Socialist Republic, the republic administration was dominated by ethnic Russians. Although the Chechen capital of Grozny grew to be the largest city in the north Caucasus, Chechens were often denied residency permits there. They also suffered from workplace and educational discrimination and from anti-Islam campaigns.

With the collapse of the Soviet Union in 1991 an indigenous Chechen leadership rose up to declare independence for the Chechen republic. Under the leadership of a Chechen Air Force general named Djohar Dudayev (a rare Chechen who rose in the Soviet system), the Chechens moved to create an independent state known as Ich-keria. Russia's president at the time, Boris Yeltsin, saw this act of secession as intolerable. The Russians feared a domino effect and were convinced that if Chechnya were allowed to secede, then other ethnic Muslim republics in the region would soon follow suit.

Finally, in the fall of 1994, the Russians decided to launch an invasion of the breakaway Chechen republic and forcefully bring it back into the Russian fold. Moscow's hopes for a swift victory were dashed when Chechen street fighters and guerillas destroyed Russian invading divisions and launched a full-scale partisan war. After losing approximately 7,500 soldiers and killing roughly 35,000 Chechen civilians, the Russians decided to withdraw their troops from the unpopular Chechen conflict in 1996. The humiliated Russians were forced to sign a treaty that gave Chechnya de facto independence.

But stability did not come to the long-suffering Chechens. From 1996 to 1999 a lawless situation prevailed in Chechnya as the new Chechen president, a secular moderate named Aslan Mashkadov, vied for control with more radical commanders such as war hero Shamil Basayev. As the anarchy in Chechnya spread to neighboring Russian republics, the Russian government used two events as a pretext for reinvading. The first was an August 1999 incursion into the neighboring Russian Muslim republic of Dagestan by more than a thousand Chechen and Arab raiders, led by the radical commander Shamil Basayev. The second was a series of unexplained bombings in Moscow and other Russian cities that were blamed on the Chechens by the hawkish new Russian president, Vladimir Putin. In October 1999 Russia reinvaded Chechnya and launched the second Russo-Chechen War.

The Russian invasion stalled in the winter of 1999–2000 as the Chechens turned the urban maze of Grozny into a guerilla ambush zone. But in February the Russians finally broke into the city. Chechen rebels nonetheless managed to escape from the Russian encirclement and make their way into the forested mountains of the south. There they waged a hit-and-run campaign that began to lose its momentum when a powerful Chechen religious leader named Ahmed Kadyrov went over to the Russians. Since the 2004 killing of Ahmed Kadryov, his son Ramzan Kadyrov has ruled as the pro-Russian president of Chechnya. Ramzan Kadyrov and his Russian allies have been effective at hunting down and killing such Chechen rebel leaders as Shamil Basayev and former president Aslan Mashkadov. The Russian government has also been quite successful in conflating its war against secessionist Chechen rebels with the U.S. war on Al Qaeda. But so far the closest link between the Chechen insurgents and Al Qaeda has been the existence of an Arab volunteer unit that fought alongside the Chechens.

The war was declared over by the Russians in 2008, although low-level insurgency and terrorism continues in Chechnya and surrounding republics such as Dagestan and Ingushetia. Such peace has, however, come at a price and Ramzan Kadyrov and his followers have been accused of numerous crimes against humanity. Among them have been the targeted assassination of journalists, critics, and opponents.

Today Chechnya exists in a sort of limbo—officially it is part of the Russian Federation, but in fact it is an autonomous state ruled by Ramzan Kadyrov and his militiamen.

*Brian Glyn Williams*

## Further Reading

Baiev, Khassan. *The Oath: A Surgeon Under Fire*. New York: Walker Books. 2004.

Smith, Sebastian. *Allah's Mountains: The Battle for Chechnya*. London: Tauris. 2006.

Williams, Brian Glyn. "Allah's Foot Soldiers An Assessment of the Role of Foreign Fighters and Al-Qa'ida in the Chechen Insurgency." In *Ethno-Nationalism, Islam and the State in the Caucasus: Post-Soviet Disorder*, ed. Moshe Gammer. London: Routledge, 2007.

Williams, Brian Glyn. "The Russo-Chechen War: A Threat to Stability in the Middle East and Eurasia?" *Middle East Policy* 8, no. 1 (March 2001): 128–148.

# Chuvash

The Chuvash call themselves *Chavash*. Their central Russian geographical location is considered the borderline between the Turkic speaking and Finno-Ugric speaking people in Russia. The total population of Chuvash people is estimated at 2 million; most reside in the Chuvash Autonomous Republic while others live in the neighboring autonomous republics of Tatarstan and Bashkiria as well as other parts of the Russian Federation. Along with the Gagauz of Moldova, the Chuvash are the only (Russian) Orthodox Christian Turkic-speaking people.

Most historians agree that they are the direct descendants of the Volga Bulgar (Bolgar in some sources) Khanate, a Turkic state that flourished from the middle of the 7th through the middle of the 13th centuries in the Volga-Kama basin. The region was once home to the Schytian and Hunnic civilizations, and the Volga Bulgars are thought to descend themselves from the Huns in this region. Volga Bulgars used the ancient Turkic runic alphabet; after the end of 10th century, with their conversion to Islam, they adopted the Arabic script. Contrary to official Turkish historiography, which considers the Central Asian Karahanids as the first Turkic state to adopt Islam as an official religion in CE 932, the Volga Bulgars adopted Islam as their state religion in 922, a decade before the Karahanids, making them the first Turkic speakers to convert to Islam en masse. Remnants of their great mosques and architecture can still be seen in the Bulgar city on the shores of Volga River. During the Middle Ages, the Bulgars gained fame for their commercial activities and highly cultured society. They accumulated great wealth thanks to their close relations with the Turkic Khazar Empire in the south, which interestingly had adopted Judaism as a state religion. One of the ruling tribes of the Volga Bulgar state was the Suvar, a name that current Chuvash nationalists prefer to use as their ethnonym as well.

With the arrival of the Mongols of Batu Khan in 1236, the Bulgar state was destroyed and its residents became subjects of the Golden Horde for the next 300 years, contributing to the Turkification of the population. Soviet/Russian historiography argues that during this period the Chuvash were forced into the forests to the northwest and west where Finno-Ugric peoples,

A Chuvash folk group meets a tourist ship on the embankment of the Volga river in Cheboksary city, the capital of Chuvashia. (Mikhail Epishin/Dreamstime)

especially the Mari, live. This line of reasoning holds that Chuvash ethnicity was born of the mixture of Turkic Bulgars and Finno-Ugric Mari. However, there is no evidence, especially linguistic, for this claim. The Chuvash in fact lived under the Golden Horde, and following its disintegration in 1437 they became subjects of the Kazan Khanate. It is known that the Chuvash aristocrats (called Tarkhans) were at the service of the armies of the Kazan Khanate. Again, Soviet/Russian historiography claims that the Chuvash people voluntarily joined the Russian state under Ivan Grozny (the Terrible) in 1551, just a year before the fall of Kazan to the Russians. This kind of "voluntary reunion with

Russia" rhetoric has been and still is a part of a Russian historiography attempting to explain the expansion of the Russian state in its early phases. Actually, the Chuvash became Russian subjects only after the fall of Kazan in 1552. From that time until the beginning of 19th century, Chuvash peasants were subject to their own *yasak* (law) in which they rendered labor to Chuvash lords in exchange for food, particularly milled grain or bread. However, most Chuvash derived a livelihood from hunting, fishing, and intervillage commerce.

The Chuvash were active participants in the peasant-Cossack rebellions of Razin (1670–1671) and Pugachev (1773–1775). With reforms to the institution of serfdom in the 19th century, Russian landless peasants as well as some lords staked claims to land within Chuvash territory. In 1920, a Chuvash Autonomous Oblast (Region) was created within the Russian Soviet Federative Socialist Republic (RSFSR). The Chuvash region fed Moscow during the 1921–1923 famine. As a result, in 1925 the area became the Chuvash Autonomous Soviet Socialist Republic (ChASSR) within the RSFSR. After the dissolution of the Soviet Union in 1991, the Chuvash Autonomous Republic remained within the Russian Federation. The Chuvash people constitute the majority in the Chuvash Republic, one of the few regions in the Russian Federation where ethnic Russians are a clear minority. The republic is one of the important industrial centers of the Volga basin, hosting factories for farming equipment, beverages, and furniture.

Culturally they are divided into three parts: Upper (Hill), Central (Meadow), and Lower (Southern) Chuvash. They speak the ancient Ogur Turkic dialect, making them the only Turkic people having this characteristic. That is why their dialect is one of the most difficult to understand among all the surviving Turkic dialects. The Chuvash are (Russian) Orthodox Christians. However, they were not considered true believers by their Russian neighbors. Their religious practice in fact contains elements from paganism, Islam, and Tengrism. It is known that their mass conversion to Russian Orthodoxy took place in the second half of the 19th century under the Russian Empire. Before this, they practiced a mix of faiths, especially Tengrism, a pre-Islamic Turkic religion positing a number of minor deities as well as a dominant sky god. The Chuvash still have traditional healers in the villages and in the cities, practicing using herbs and ancient rituals. One can also see holy sites all over the country where the Chuvash make sacrifices. Chuvash literature stands out in central Russia. Chuvash author/poets such as Pyotr Khuzangai and Mishshi Yukhma have been translated into several languages all over the world. Chuvash poetry is distinguished from other minority literature in the Russian Federation with its strong emphasis on the inner world of the individual rather than the classical pastoral themes.

*Hasan Ali Karasar*

**Further Reading**

Denisov, Petr Vladimirovich. *Religioznye verovaniya Chuvash: Istoriko-etnograficheskie Ocherki* (*Religious Beliefs of Chuvash: Historical-Ethnographic Essays*). Cheboksary: Chuvashskoe gos. izd-vo, 1959.

Flippov, Leonid Klavdievich. *Etnonim Chuvash i Predystoriya Chuvashskogo Etnosa: Istoriko-Lingvisticheskoe Issledovanie* (*The Chuvash Ethnonym and Prehistory of the Chuvash Ethnos: Historical-Linguistic Studies*). Saratov: Saratovskiy gos. Universitet, 2008.

Iukhma, Mishshi. *Drevnie Chuvashi: Istoricheskie Rasskazy* (*Ancient Chuvashes: Historical Stories*). Cheboksary: Chuvash kn. iz-vo, 1996.

Rona-Tas, Andras. *Chuvash Studies*. Budapest: Akademiai Kiado, 1982.

# Cornish

The Cornish are a Celtic people whose name derives from the county of Cornwall, situated in the far southwestern corner of the United Kingdom. Cornwall has an area of 1,376 square miles (3,563 square kilometers) and a population of 534,300. The county's administrative hub (and Cornwall's only city) is Truro, on the south coast. Some 37,500 identified themselves as Cornish in the United Kingdom (UK) Census (2001), all but 3,700 of whom lived in Cornwall. Many Cornishmen, known as "Jacks," emigrated as miners to the United States (specifically California), Canada, South Africa, and elsewhere. Cornish are predominantly Christians.

Cornwall has been settled at least since Paleolithic times. The Cornish descend from the ancient Britons and define themselves as ethnically distinct from the (Anglo-Saxon) English. Wales and Cornwall were the last bastions of British culture until the 10th century when the region became a constituent part of the Kingdom of England. It is probable that the last king of Cornwall, Dungarth, died in 876. Cornish culture continued to weaken throughout medieval and early modern times with the centralization of British government.

The Cornish have practiced Christianity since the arrival of Irish missionaries in the early medieval period. They stood against liturgical changes generated by the Reformation and suffered for it. The Methodist revival had an impact in the 19th and 20th centuries but church attendance has dropped rapidly in Cornwall in recent decades, as it has in the rest of the United Kingdom.

"Cornish" as an ethnic category has undergone something of a resurgence in contemporary British identity politics. It is recognized by a number of official bodies as one of the Celtic nations (along with Wales, Brittany, and others). Mebyon Kernow presents itself as the Cornish nationalist party, standing for greater Cornish autonomy. This rediscovery of Cornish nationhood has been stimulated by the slow but steady revival of the Cornish language since the publication in 1904 of Henry Jenner's *Handbook of the Cornish Language*. While everyday life is conducted almost entirely in English, Cornish is currently spoken by 3,000–4,000 enthusiasts and taught in over 50 primary schools. The Cornish language has been recognized by the UK government as an official minority language since 2002. A standard written form of the language was established in 2008, and bilingual street and shop signs are becoming increasingly common. As in the case of Welsh, the language suffered from aggressive Anglicization until it died out as a living language in the 18th century.

Given its extensive coastline, with the Atlantic to the northeast and English Channel to the south, fishing has long been a major industry. One of the world's largest natural harbors, Falmouth remains an important port. Tin mining became an important industry in the medieval period and expanded throughout the Industrial Revolution. However, the decline of tin mining is now complete. Apart from agriculture, the only major industry in Cornwall since the mid-20th century is tourism. The country is blessed with a relatively warm climate and a rugged coastline with many sandy beaches.

The Cornish flag—named after Saint Piran, the patron saint—comprises a white cross on a black background. The county motto is *onen hag oll* (one and all).

Famous Cornish people include inventors Humphrey Davy (1778–1829) and Richard Trevithic (1771–1833), writer and English scholar Arthur Quiller-Couch, Nobel Prize–winning novelist William Goldman, astronomer John Couch Adams (discoverer of the planet Neptune), and Captain William Bligh, who famously suffered mutiny on his ship the *Bounty*. The Cornish developed their own form of wrestling and have a passion for rugby union. For three decades from the early 1880s a group of 50 or so artists settled in the small fishing town of Newlyn, influenced by the Impressionists and led by Frank Bramley and Stanhope Forbes, forming what came to be called the Newlyn School. A few decades later, a number of highly regarded modernist painters and sculptors began working in and around St. Ives, including Barbara Hepworth, Ben Nicholson, and Patrick Heron, some of whose work can be seen at the Tate St. Ives Gallery.

*Peter Collins*

## Further Reading

Halliday, Frank Ernest. *A History of Cornwall*. Thirsk: House of Stratus, 2001.

Payton, Philip. *Cornwall: A History*. Fowey: Cornwall Editions, 2004.

## Corsicans

Corsicans, known in French as *le peuple Corse* and in Corsican as *u Populu Corsu*, are French citizens who trace their origins to the indigenous people of the Mediterranean island of Corsica. An estimated 294,000 people reside on the island (2009), though approximately 10 percent are of foreign origin, the majority from North Africa. Two port cities are the population hubs on the island—Ajaccio, with approximately 64,000 residents; and Bastia, with approximately 44,000. Despite this significant urban population, 276 of the island's 360 communes are rural villages, most nestled in the mountainous interior. Villages remain the symbolic core of Corsican identity, and Corsicans typically maintain two residences, working in the cities during the week and commuting home to their family's village on weekends. Widespread migration to the French mainland and colonies from the island during the 20th century increased the Corsican diaspora to nearly double the island population. The principal religion of Corsicans is Christianity (Roman Catholicism). For more than 200 years, Corsica's official language has been French, and it is spoken in all administrative and political domains. However, the indigenous Corsican language (*Corse* in French, *u corsu* or *Lingua Corsa* in Corsican), which developed from Latin and was heavily influenced by Tuscan Italian between the 11th and 18th centuries, has been preserved in the interior villages. Corsicans have been actively fighting for cultural and political recognition (in some cases sovereignty) for the last 40 years in a movement for cultural reacquisition, the Riacquistu, and the closely linked Nationalist movement.

Corsica's history is one of constant invasion and occupation in which the indigenous population has been continually oppressed and exploited. The island was conquered by the Greeks in 565 BCE, Carthaginians 300 years later, and then

A man dines with the beach in background in Corsica, France. Corsica is an island in the Mediterranean that was ruled in succession by the Pope, Pisa, and Genoa. Corsicans gained independence from Genoa in the 18th century, but the island was then annexed by France. (Corel)

taken over by the Roman Empire for 500 years, during which time Latin and Christianity infused the local culture. After the fall of Rome, Corsica was invaded by Vandals, the Byzantine Empire, Ostrogoths, Lombards, and Saracens (Moors). Pisa and Genoa launched a joint attack in the early 11th century, and Pisa then ruled and colonized the island from the late 11th century to the end of the 13th century, replacing Latin with Italian as the primary language. In 1284, the Genoese expelled the Pisans and became harsh rulers of the Corsican people for the next 600 years.

Finally, in the 18th century, under the leadership of the Corsican Pascal Paoli, the population rose in revolt. Soliciting help from France in 1756, Paoli's army succeeded in defeating the Genoese and liberating the island. Paoli declared Corsica an independent nation, established a democratic government and universal suffrage, wrote a constitution (with the aid of Jean-Jacques Rousseau), opened a university, challenged the dominant system of family and clan-based politics, and created a Corsican currency. Independence lasted just 14 years. In the treaty of Versailles (1768), the French bought the island from the Genoese. After a short-lived and violent resistance, aided briefly by the English, Corsica was defeated at the battle of Ponto Novu in 1769 and has remained French since. For Corsicans today, Paoli is considered the babbu di a patria (father of the homeland), and his reign is a symbol of their struggle for cultural and political sovereignty.

Until the 20th century, Corsican life was primarily agro-pastoral. Year-round crops of chestnuts, olives, honey, wine, wheat, and village garden plots were complemented by seasonal hunting and fishing, as well as the cheese, milk, and wool produced by the transhumant goat and sheep herders (*bergers*), whose nomadic existence is today revered as a symbol of Corsican tradition. The basic socioeconomic unit was the extended family, followed by the village and neighboring villages, and land was often communally owned. Economic activity was based primarily on inner exchange of natural products between regions. Until the 20th century, the bureaucratic influence of Italy and then France remained weak in the inner villages, and Corsica's local political life was dominated by deeply entrenched family and village affiliations known as the clan (*partitu* in Corsican), which until the 1930s preserved a culture dominated by family honor and vendetta.

Though Christianity was strongly implanted during Roman rule and each village has a church and a patron saint, traces of pre-Christian beliefs remain, including the *mazzeri* ("dream-hunters"), gifted shaman-like members of the society who are able to predict and sometimes prevent the death of community members, and signatore, capable of detecting and driving away the evil eye.

A rich musical tradition also developed over the centuries, including the *voceri*, laments for the dead; *baddate*, bandits' laments; *nanne*, lullabies; *tribbiere*, threshing songs; *chamji et respondi*, improvised poetic debate; and *paghjella*, polyphonic songs. These were orally transmitted musical forms that varied by region and were sung spontaneously, more like speech than the performed lyrical music of the Western tradition.

At the turn of the 20th century, agricultural crisis ravaged the island, and the two world wars decimated the island's population (an estimated 20,000 Corsicans died), leading to the demise of the traditional Corsican way of life. The Corsican economy was left in ruins, and France made only minimal efforts to industrialize Corsica, establishing a few unsuccessful asbestos and lead mines in the 1920s. Nearly half a million Corsicans emigrated from Corsica during the first half of the 20th century, searching for employment. A vast proportion went to the French colonies, where they found work as administrators. By 1950, Corsicans, then only 1 percent of France's population, composed 20 percent of colony administrators. Young people were encouraged to learn French and to leave the island for a better life. In this context traditional life became synonymous with rural poverty.

In the late 1960s, influenced by the anti-Vietnam War movement and postcolonial sentiment inspired by Algerian liberation, Corsican students in French universities awakened to their own unique cultural identity. Young cultural militants flooded back to the island, attempting to regain their heritage from the brink of extinction. Between 1960 and 1980, the Corsican population rose from 170,000 to 240,000. Cultural militants involved in the Riacquistu rejected the dominant anti-Corsican stereotypes and turned their attention toward traditional language, music, pre-Christian belief systems, cuisine, village life, and customs, as well as traditional artisanal craftsmanship and modes of agricultural production.

The passion for cultural revitalization was, in the 1960s and 1970s, inseparable from the bourgeoning and violent Nationalist movement, embodied primarily in the activities of two groups—the FLNC (Front de Liberation Nationale de la Corse), a clandestine group that used explosives to demand full independence and national sovereignty; and ARC (Action Regionaliste Corse/Action pour la Renaissance de la Corse), a nonviolent group looking for increased autonomy from France. These groups focused on exposing French political oppression and economic neglect of Corsica. In 1962, the French state allocated the majority of funds from France's first program for Corsican economic development, SOMIVAC (Societé pour la Mise en Valeur d'Agricole de la Corse) to the 18,000 *pied noirs* returning from Algeria, rather than the island population. Corsicans were enraged, and Nationalist activity surged.

The efforts of the Riacquistu and the Nationalist movements combined with French president François Mitterrand's novel attention towards "diversity" during the 1980s resulted in remarkable stride toward the recognition of Corsican identity, language, and heritage. While Corsican remains on UNESCO's list of potentially endangered languages, it is increasingly used in books, newspapers, and local media. Corsican language pedagogy is now officially recognized in the educational curriculum on the island, with bilingual schools optional as early as elementary school. The Universita di Corsica Pascal Paoli opened in 1981, and includes a Corsican Studies Department. Ethnographic museums detail Corsican cultural heritage, and hundreds of popular local musical groups, including some of international acclaim (A Filetta, I Muvrini, and Petru Guelfucc), celebrate traditional Corsican repertoire. In 1991 the island was granted a special statute and became the only region in France to have its own regional government—the Collectivité Territoriale—distinguishing it from other French regions and overseas territories. In 2002, the Collectivité was given full responsibility for its own cultural policy, and a significant portion of its budget, which has increased from 87.2 million Euros in 1992 to 636.6 million in 2008, is dedicated to the preservation of Corsican culture.

These efforts have coincided with a focus on traditional products as well as eco and cultural tourism designed to bring people to the island and incite development without corrupting the Corsican landscape or tradition. Despite these efforts, the Corsican economy remains among the poorest in France. Today, commercial services and employment in the public sector by the French state account for 70 percent of the island's economic activity; agriculture and industry represent a mere 7.4 percent. There is a strong sense that the aid provided by the French state, and increasingly by the European Union (EU), is not sustainable. Given the island's feeble production, economic sustenance points toward commercial tourist development, which is at odds with the widespread cultural and environmental preservationist goals.

The Nationalist movement was, from its inception, prone to divisiveness. Local family and village interests often trumped loyalty to the Nationalist cause, resulting in factionalism and violent intergroup conflict in the 1980s and 1990s, locally called *le guerre* (the war). This, combined with suspected illegal activity and mafia connections of the FLNC, island-wide bombings that have discouraged external investment in island development, and the 1998 Nationalist assassination of the French prefect, Claude Érignac, has resulted in public rejection of the Nationalist movement—only 6 percent of the voting population are registered Nationalists.

While most Corsicans feel that the Riacquistu has been vital in the preservation of Corsican identity and heritage, there is a growing sentiment that the standardization that has taken place as the language is put into grammar books and the culture into museums is itself a source of cultural corruption. There is a fear that the source of the Corsican people's heritage and language, its spontaneity and naturalness, may be lost in translation, threatening the very core of what militants have fought so hard to preserve.

*Sarah H. Davis*

## Further Reading

Bithell, Caroline. *Transported by Song: Corsican Voices from Oral Tradition to World Stage.* Maryland: Scarecrow Press, 2007.

Candea, Matei. *Corsican Fragments: Difference, Belonging and the Intimacies of Fieldwork.* Bloomington: Indiana University Press, 2010.

Jaffe, Alexandra. *Ideologies in Action: Language Politics on Corsica.* New York: Mouton de Gruyter, 1999.

Ravis-Giordani, G. *Atlas Ethnohistorique de la Corse* (*Ethnohistorical Atlas of Corsica*). France: Comité des travaux historiques et scientifiques, 2004.

# Cossacks

Cossacks (*Kazaki* in Russian, *Kozaki* in Ukrainian) reside in Russia and Ukraine, especially in the southern Russian federal units of Don, Krasnodar, and Stavropol, together with Volgograd further east. Five main Cossack groups can be discerned today, associated with their respective geographical origins: Ukrainian Cossacks, Don Cossacks, Volga Cossacks, Kuban Cossacks, and Terek Cossacks. Cossacks are predominantly Slavs; they speak Russian or Ukrainian languages and profess Russian Orthodox Christianity. It is difficult to enumerate Cossacks since many were assimilated into Russian and Ukrainian populations during the Soviet era when Cossack identity was subject to persecution. Even today Cossack is not included as an ethnic category in Russian National Surveys. According to Russian authorities, an estimated 3.5–5 million Cossacks resided in Russian territory in the mid-1990s. Cossack ethnicity itself remains a subject of political and scholarly dispute, since the Cossacks are distinguished from their Russian and Ukrainian neighbors primarily by their role as state warriors in tsarist Russia.

As Mongolian rule disintegrated in parts of present-day Ukraine and Russia in the 15th century, there arose mobile communities of Tatar freemen organized democratically and dependent for survival on military prowess. Known as Cossacks, these groups sometimes preyed on peasant populations. In the 15th and 16th centuries, the repressive policies of the Moscow-based state produced flows of refugees; joining the Cossacks, these

Riders wearing ca. 1910s-era Cossack military uniform perform during a festival outside the southern Russian city of Rostov-on-Don in 2005, to mark the 200th birthday of the Don Cossacks' capital Novocherkassk. The flags are Russian national, (right), and of the Don Cossacks, who fought against Soviets in 1918–1920. Cossacks were mounted peasant-soldiers, who by the late 18th century became a privileged military class in Russia. There were 11 Cossack communities, each named for its location. Cossacks' traditions and customs continue to survive, notably in the Don and Kuban regions. (AP/Wide World Photos)

refugees made the Slavic element predominant among Cossacks. From the 16th to 18th centuries an expanding Russian state incorporated Cossacks as border guards and soldiers. The free Cossacks continued, however, to be a nuisance to the early Russian state, as they provided refuge for subjects escaping legal punishment and they sought allegiance where it strategically suited them. Several famous peasant revolts in Russian and Ukrainian history have been instigated by Cossacks, including one headed by the Don Cossack, Stenka Razin, in 1667–1671, and another led by the Ukrainian Cossack, Bohdan Khmelnytsky, in 1648.

One may distinguish between those Cossack communities that spontaneously formed, and those that were established on the initiative of the Russian state. Of the former category, Cossack communities had been formed by the end of the 16th century along the River Dnepr (the Zaporozhian Cossacks), River Don (the Don Cossacks), and Volga River (the Volga Cossacks). The Russian government later established the following hosts: the Kuban Cossacks, Orenburg Cossacks, Amur Cossacks, Siberian Cossacks, and Astrakhan Cossacks, among others. Cossacks never constituted a single community, organization, or territorial entity; each of the Cossack groups had its own distinct traditions. The Don Cossacks developed into sedentary farming communities, where members resided with their families. Zaporozhian Cossacks established an exclusively male community, where men resided in a military camp and political center (*Sich*); women and children lived outside the camp. The Russian army dispersed the Zaporozhian Cossacks in 1775; its members were resettled in territory conquered along the Kuban River in northwestern Caucasus and later incorporated in the Kuban Cossack Host.

The Cossacks represented a military resource for competing states, and their services were sought out by Poland-Lithuania, the Ottoman Empire, and Russia. Over time, the Russian state tightened its grip on Cossacks, and succeeded in incorporating the largest number of Cossacks as a permanent part of its army. The Russian Empire formed new hosts by moving Cossacks from other hosts, and by incorporating ordinary soldiers and peasants into these communities. The Kuban Cossack host was established this way, and the Kuban Cossacks played an important role in the Russian conquest, settlement, and colonization of the northwestern Caucasus. In 1914 there were 11 Cossack Hosts spread over a large territory stretching from the River Don in the west to the Rivers Amur and Ussuri far to the east. The symbiosis of Cossacks and empire grew, and Cossacks became known as defenders of the tsar, orthodoxy, and fatherland. During the Russian revolution (1917) Cossacks fought on both sides, though the majority fought with tsarist troops. After the defeat some Cossacks fled to Turkey, Europe, and North and South America. Under Soviet rule the remaining Cossacks experienced persecution, exile, and execution. With the exception of World War II, Cossacks were stripped of military position and privileges, and it was dangerous, especially in the prewar years, to wear uniforms or to voice a Cossack identity.

The ethnic identity of Cossacks was linked to their special role in the Russian tsarist state from the 17th century. By 1875 the military service for a Cossack male lasted 20 years and began at age 18. Cossacks served in the cavalry, and besides their excellent horsemanship they were famed for their abilities as scouts, pickets, patrolmen, and for their general hardiness; they were also well known as storm troops used to curb internal rebellions. Military status was hereditary, and Cossack boys were trained from an early age in horsemanship and military skills. Cossacks integrated useful knowledge, clothing, and technology from non-Russian neighbors, and in their appearance, horsemanship, military technique, and warrior ethics they were closer to Caucasian mountaineers and Turkish nomads than to Russian peasants.

Family life was ordered by patriarchy. The father of the house held great authority and represented the household in communal gatherings. Cossack livelihoods combined military service and farming. Men were the main property owners, but the wife could become a proprietor if widowed and without grown-up sons. Each household was allocated house lots and farmland; communal land was allocated to households through need assessments. Officers received more land than ordinary soldiers. As originally male communities, Cossacks long took wives from neighboring ethnic groups, and by marrying a male Cossack the woman automatically lost her previous identity and became a Cossack (*kazachka*). This practice was altered by 19th-century state policies restricting the entry of outsiders, male or female, into existing Cossack communities. In the past, the youngest son was typically heir to his family's house and expected to reside with and care for his parents. It was not uncommon, however, for all grown sons to settle near their parents or, if required by the exigencies of military life, to accompany them in a new location identified by tsarist authorities. The practice of settling near parents remains common in rural areas even today, at least early in marriage.

Cossacks celebrated masculinity. Bodily strength, endurance, bravery, toughness, and camaraderie were considered important virtues, clearly deriving from military activity. However, the Cossack way of life depended on women for the preservation of local livelihoods, childrearing, and defense during the prolonged absences of the men. In the face of a high mortality rate among men, women played, and continue to play, an important role as conveyors of the traditional social order, rituals, and religious practices.

During Soviet persecution, Cossack traditions, songs, and rituals were kept secretly alive within the family alongside photographs of their forefathers. Cossacks have been cherished objects of literature and national myth making. In Russian national mythology they represent the very core of historical Russianness. Today, Cossacks are associated with acrobatic dance, horsemanship, and a singing tradition conveyed by touring Cossack choirs.

Cossacks lived in rural areas, where they were given special rights to natural resources. The Cossack communities had a democratic system of rule where the community leader, the *ataman* (Russian) or *hetman* (Ukrainian), was elected for three or four years in the communal gatherings but could be replaced at any time. In the rural settlements (*stanitsa*) where Cossacks resided and ruled, Russian peasant migrants and migrants of other ethnicities rented land and were not allowed to vote in communal gatherings. Viewing the Cossacks as repressive landowners (*kulaks*), the Soviets abolished their privileges and seized much property from the wealthiest Cossacks. In 1917, a secret decree from Trotsky ordered a pogrom against the Cossacks, to crush them once and for all. The communist policies killed many Cossacks, removed important dimensions of the Cossack culture, and relegated them to the past. As a result it was difficult to carry out historical studies of the Cossacks.

Gorbachev's glasnost policies (1980s) opened up new opportunities for archival study, and small clubs devoted to the study of Cossack history appeared in Moscow, St. Petersburg, and regional centers elsewhere in Russia. These history clubs were rapidly transformed in the turmoil of the 1990s into a politically significant Cossack movement. In the Krasnodar territory, the bedrock of the Kuban Cossacks, the Cossack organization is represented at village (*stanitsa*), municipality, and regional administrational levels. These organizations are open to all Russian Orthodox men, and do not use Cossack descent as a criterion for membership. For this reason, many Cossack descendants refuse to join them, as they firmly believe that descent should play a central role. When the Soviet state crumbled, Cossack paramilitary troops stepped in on their own initiative to maintain law and order. The Cossack organization was granted recognition through the establishment of public financial support, the founding of military academies for Cossack recruits, and separate Cossack military units in the Russian army during Yeltsin's presidency. Support is nevertheless not firm, and many of the decrees granting Cossacks special rights have stalled in the Duma. Cossacks are proponents of Russian nationalism and have been involved in violent episodes directed at other ethnic and religious minorities. The support of the Cossack movement and its political projects has lost some of its clout, as the Russian state has become consolidated. Cossackdom nevertheless remains a potent political symbol in Russia.

*Hege Toje*

**Further Reading**

Longworth, Phillip. *The Cossacks*. London: Constable, 1969.

O'Rourke, Shane. *The Cossacks*. New York: Manchester University Press, 2007.

O'Rourke, Shane. *Warriors and Peasants: The Don Cossacks in Late Imperial Russia*. New York: St. Martin's Press, 2000.

Seaton, Albert. *The Horsemen of the Steppes: The Story of the Cossacks*. London: Bodley Head, 1985.

Skinner, Barbara. "Identity Formation in Russian Cossack Revival." *Europe-Asia Studies* 46, no. 6 (1994): 1017–1037.

Toje, Hege. 2006. "Cossack Identity in the New Russia: Kuban Cossack Revival and Local Politics." *Europe-Asia Studies* 58, no. 7 (2006): 1057–1077.

# Crimean Tatars

Crimean Tatars are the native Turkic people of the Crimean peninsula, located on the northern shores of the Black Sea. According to the 2001 census, the population of Crimea (Ukraine) is 2,031,000, of which the Crimean Tatars constitute around 15 percent (Russians make up 65–70% and Ukrainians 10–15%). Apart from those who returned to Crimea from exile under the Soviets, there are also Crimean Tatars living elsewhere in Ukraine, Uzbekistan, the Russian Federation, Tajikistan, and other ex-Soviet Republics. It is estimated that the total population of Crimean Tatars ranges from 300,000 to 500,000 within the territory of the former Soviet Union (except Ukraine). Large diasporic communities of Crimean Tatars also reside in other countries, such as Turkey (around 5,000,000), Romania (30,000), the United States (30,000), Bulgaria (15,000), and Germany (20,000). Crimean Tatars adhere to Sunni Islam. Their language includes elements of Kipchak and Oghuz, the two principal Turkic groups. In terms of grammar and vocabulary, modern Crimean Tatar language is closely related to the Turkish spoken in Turkey.

The earliest known existence of Turkic peoples in Crimea dates to the time of the Huns who, during their westward drive, invaded parts of the Crimean peninsula in the second half of the 4th century CE. By the end of the 7th century, Crimea had become part of the Turkic Khazar Empire. With the gradual disintegration of the Khazar Empire, a new wave of Turkic peoples, the Pechenegs, invaded the steppes north of the Black Sea, and a large group of them forced their way into Crimea, where they settled down during the early 10th century. Within less than a century, another influx of Turkic horsemen, the Cumans (Kipchaks), followed the Pechenegs. The Cumans dominated Crimea for more than two centuries, with the exception of certain coastal cities ruled by the Byzantines and later by the Venetians and Genoese. The Cumans left a very strong cultural and linguistic legacy in the contemporary culture of Crimean Tatars.

In the 1240s, the armies of the Mongol Genghis Khan occupied Crimea. Soon after, when the Great Chinghiside Empire practically disintegrated, Crimea became part of the western branch of the Mongolian Empire, the Golden Horde. Within less than a century, the Golden Horde became thoroughly Turkified and Islamicized, as ethnic Turkic peoples far outnumbered Mongolians. Several Turkic tribes and groups settled in Crimea then and gradually amalgamated with the conquered population, which also included many Turkic elements. Thus, Turkification and Islamization of the largest part of the peninsula ensued throughout this era. Since the 13th century the Turkic-Muslim (as well as the Turkified and Islamicized) population of Crimea has come to be called "Crimean Tatars."

Upon the disintegration of the Golden Horde, a Chinghiside prince, Hacı Geray, after unsuccessfully attempting to seize the throne of the Golden Horde, settled in Crimea and declared himself the Khan of Crimea around 1428. His domains included Crimea and the Kipchak Steppes situated north of the Crimea. In 1475, Mengli Geray I concluded an agreement with the Ottoman Empire whereby the Crimean Khanate accepted Ottoman overlordship. Henceforth, Crimean Tatar armies joined the military expeditions of the Ottomans upon the request of the Sultan.

The Crimean Khanate remained a mighty power in Eastern European politics for the succeeding three centuries. As its dominions extended from the North Caucasus to the Dnestr River, the khanate essentially played the role of a buffer state between Muscovy and the Ottoman territories. During the 16th and 17th centuries, the Crimean Khanate effectively curbed the southward expansion of Muscovy. The Treaty of Küçük Kaynarca in 1774 terminated the Ottoman suzerainty over the khanate. Following a decade of civil strife actively provoked by Russia, Empress Catherine II formally annexed Crimea to the Russian Empire in 1783.

The characteristic feature of Russian rule was vigorous effort by the tsarist administration to colonize and Slavicize Crimea. Repressive Russian rule and the large-scale expropriations led to massive emigration of Crimean Tatars to Ottoman Turkey. As a result, from the 1860s on, Crimean Tatars effectively lost their status as the majority population in the Crimea.

Still, the national education drive of the Crimean Tatar reformist İsmail Bey Gaspıralı resulted in initiating a wholesale national movement. By the 1910s, a Crimean Tatar intelligentsia and a number of underground groups aiming at the liberation of the Crimean Tatar people came into existence. With the outbreak of the March 1917 Revolution in Russia, these nationalist groups soon took control of Crimean

Tatar affairs in Crimea. In November 1917, direct democratic elections led to the formation of a Crimean Tatar Qurultay (National Parliament). In December, the Qurultay declared an independent Crimean Democratic Republic. After a brief armed struggle, Russian Bolsheviks invaded the peninsula and succeeded in overthrowing the newborn republic. Up to 1920, Crimea changed hands three times between the White and Red Russian armies, neither of which sympathized with the national aspirations of Crimean Tatars.

In November 1920, the Red Army finally invaded and occupied Crimea, and in October 1921, the Crimean Autonomous Soviet Socialist Republic (Crimean ASSR) was declared. Crimean Tatars, like other national groups in the Soviet Union, suffered under the dekulakization, that is, the collectivization of agriculture, the famines, and the Great Terror of the 1920s and 1930s. By 1938, the Crimean Tatar national intelligentsia was virtually liquidated.

Soon after the beginning of the German-Russian war during World War II, the German armies occupied Crimea in the fall of 1941. In April 1944, however, the Red Army recaptured the peninsula from the Germans. On May 18, 1944, the entire Crimean Tatar population, to the last person, was deported from Crimea by the People's Commissariat for Public Affairs (Narodnyy Komissariat Vnutrennikh Del—NKVD) and Red Army troops. The dreadful journey, which took place in sealed cattle cars crammed with people without adequate food, water, or sanitary and medical care, lasted at least three weeks and cost half of the deportees their lives. The cars were destined for the Urals,

Siberia, and Central Asia, where survivors were assigned to special settlements resembling concentration camps without adequate housing, means of subsistence, or social facilities, and without permission to leave their designated settlements for 16 years.

In the meantime, the authorities eradicated virtually every trace of Crimean Tatar culture. Russian toponyms replaced all Tatar ones, while even the term "Crimean Tatar" was removed from the encyclopedias and censuses. A massive settlement of Russians in Crimea commenced. In 1954, Crimea was incorporated into the Ukrainian SSR.

In 1956, the Crimean Tatar National Movement was formed in exile to demand the return to the homeland. It became one of the earliest national-democratic movements in the post-Stalinist Soviet Union. The Soviet response was the imprisonment, arrest, and harassment of the activists of the movement. However, the Crimean Tatar National Movement, with the conspicuous support of the Crimean Tatar population in exile, continued its activities. The flow of petitions with tens of thousands of signatures, numerous deputations to Moscow, and mass demonstrations and meetings persisted. This state of affairs lasted until Gorbachev's policies of perestroika and glasnost.

In July 1987, the Crimean Tatar National Movement organized its first public meeting on Red Square in Moscow. Following this event, the government formed a number of successive state commissions to deal with the Crimean Tatar problem, but none took any concrete or constructive steps to enable Crimean Tatars to reclaim their homeland. Frustrated by such delays, a centralized Organization of the Crimean Tatar National Movement (OCTNM) formed in exile in 1989, defied the Soviet authorities, and urged exiled Crimean Tatars to return to the Crimea illegally.

In January 1991, the leadership of the Crimean regional Communist Party declared the establishment of the Crimean ASSR. Crimean Tatars vigorously opposed this new formation, arguing that this did not constitute the reestablishment of the former Crimean ASSR in which Crimean Tatars had enjoyed their preeminent status as the native people. Upon the initiative of the OCTNM, elections for the Qurultay were conducted among Crimean Tatars in exile and in Crimea. On June 22, 1991, the second Qurultay convened in Akmescit (Simferepol). The Qurultay thereupon delegated its powers between its plenary sessions to the Millî Meclis (National Council), which was elected from among the Qurultay deputies.

Although the Qurultay and Millî Meclis have not been granted an unequivocal recognition on the part of the Ukrainian government since their foundation, they act as de facto representative bodies of the Crimean Tatar people. Throughout the 1990s a number of diplomatic crises occurred between Ukraine and Russia over the status of Crimea. While the Russian population of the peninsula stood for the annexation of Crimea to Russia, the Crimean Tatars staunchly refused such a possibility and defended the Ukrainian territorial integrity.

Currently, the problems of Crimean Tatar returnees are still far from being solved. The issues of the restoration of their rights previous to the deportation, the threateningly high rates of child deaths, low living standards, landlessness, and unemployment as well as the strong desire for national educational and cultural institutions continue to trouble Crimean Tatar society.

*Hakan Kirimli*

## Further Reading

Allworth, Edward, ed. *Tatars of the Crimea: Their Struggle for Survival*. Durham, NC: Duke University Press, 1988.

Kırımal, Edige. *Der nationale Kampf der Krimtürken* (*The National Struggle of the Crimean Tatars*). Emsdetten/Westfallen: Lechte, 1952.

Kırımlı, Hakan. *National Movements and National Identity among the Crimean Tatars (1905–1916)*. Leiden: E. J. Brill, 1996.

Lazzerini, Edward James. "İsmail Bey Gasprinskii and Muslim Modernism in Russia, 1878–1914." PhD diss., University of Washington, 1973.

Sheehy, Ann, and Bohdan Nahaylo. *The Crimean Tatars and Volga Germans: Soviet Treatment of Two National Minorities*. London: Minority Rights Group, 1989.

## Croats

Croats, or Croatians (*Hrvati*, pl.), are the majority population in Croatia, a southeastern European country with 4 million people (2001) having Zagreb as its capital. A worldwide diaspora, estimated at about the same size, includes those living in the neighboring countries of Bosnia-Herzegovina, Serbia, and Slovenia after the dissolution of Yugoslavia; descendants of Croats who moved to present-day Austria,

Hungary, the Czech and Slovak Republics, Italy, and Romania between 16th and 18th centuries; descendants of those who moved mainly in response to economic (1870s–1914) and political causes (after World War II) to North and South America, Australia, and New Zealand; and Croats who emigrated between the 1960s and 1980s to central Europe and Scandinavia as well as the newest wave of emigrants from the early 1990s. Croats speak Croatian, a South Slavic language, and use the Latin alphabet.

Historically, Croatia has been a land of turbulent population movements and significant borders. The area divided the Western from the Eastern (later Byzantine) Roman Empire in the 5th century and Western from Eastern (Orthodox) Christianity since the Great Schism in the mid-11th

century. Religion has figured importantly in Croat identity, as Roman Catholicism has long differentiated them from the Orthodox Serbs and other eastern neighbors as well as the Muslim Bosniaks. Croatian culture has been formed on Roman foundations, with Christian, Reformation, Renaissance, and Baroque influences, which spread from European courts and cities, and on vernacular traits such as Slavic agricultural practice and Christian church rites in the old-Slavic language with the Glagolitic script (*Glagoljica*), which was maintained into the 20th century.

By the ninth century, the Croats established two areas of domination: one between Sava and Drava Rivers in the north (Pannonian Croatia), and the other in the hinterland of the eastern Adriatic coast (Dalmatian Croatia). The dukes of the latter

Folk dancers, Dubrovnik. (Corel)

were installed as kings in the 10th and 11th centuries: some of them managed to unify all Croatian territories in one Kingdom. From the beginning of the 12th to the 16th centuries Croatia was united with Hungary under a common king; in 1526 both Croatian and Hungarian crowns were consigned to the Habsburg dynasty (until 1918). The history of the cities on the eastern Croatian Adriatic coast was marked by political struggles for dominance, mostly between the Venetians and the rulers of the hinterland; Dubrovnik (Ragusa) remained an independent Republic (until 1808). From the end of the 15th to the end of the 17th centuries, the Ottomans conquered great parts of Croatia, provoking Croatian migration westwards (the old disapora) as well an influx of eastern peoples (mostly Orthodox Christians) to Croatia. In the borderland, which was under direct Hapsburg administration, a military organization (*Vojna krajina*) was constituted that lasted far into the 19th century and shaped a specific social and economic system due to military service and privileges of the population.

In the 19th century Croatia was territorially, politically, and culturally disunited, and regionalism ran high. Modernization and a national revival movement inspired by the ideal of South Slavic unity were promoted by the fledgling middle classes. A standard language was created based on one regional dialect, demands for territorial unification were articulated, and many cultural and educational institutions were founded, including the Academy Library, the Academy of Science and Art, the Matrix Croatica, and the Art Gallery. In 1848, serfdom was abolished and a manifesto for civil and democratic reforms as well as for greater autonomy was proclaimed (these were only partially realized until 1918).

In the 20th century, Croats entered into several state unions with other South Slav populations. In the first half of the 20th century they joined the Kingdom of Serbs, Croats, and Slovenes (later the Kingdom of Yugoslavia), with the ruling Serbian crown dynasty. During World War II the independent State of Croatia, collaborating with fascism and Nazi Germany, was established. The Yugoslav Communist Party headed the antifascist movement; in 1945, it took power of the new Socialist Yugoslav state, in which Croatia numbered one of the federal republics.

Ethnologists identify three regional cultures within Croatian traditional culture: Pannonian in the north, Dinaric in the central and southern area, and Adriatic along the coast. While the boundaries of culture areas are not sharply drawn, ways of life in these regions do express the influence of the Austrians and Hungarians (central European), Ottomans (Balkan), and the Venetians and other Italians (Mediterranean), respectively.

Traditional Pannonian agriculture devoted equal attention to grain farming and livestock (cattle, pigs, horses). Viticulture was important in the western part. The relative prosperity of the inhabitants could be seen in people's costume and jewelry, cuisine, furniture and other household appointments, and wedding celebrations. Linen and cotton fabrics prevailed in clothing, home spun on horizontal weaving looms. The costumes were roomy, often richly puckered, mostly white, with woven or embroidered ornamentation. Settlements were clustered or organized into perpendicular streets (the result of the 18th-century planned resettlement), while the houses from the 19th century were made of clay mixed with chaff and brick. Multiple family households or *zadruge* (sg. *zadruga*) were common until the 1930s. In recognition of their economic contribution, women enjoyed a certain independence and respect.

A distinctive feature of traditional Dinaric culture (so named for the Dinaric mountain range) was stock raising of both Alpine and transhumant types. Sheep rearing and milk processing were retained until the mid-20th century, as was the production of woolen fabrics on vertical weaving looms and garments with ornamentation in the weave of the material and its embroidery. Wood carving of furniture, cooking utensils, and musical instruments, a male skill, was highly valued. The houses in spread-out settlements were made of wood (oak logs or trimmed wooden planks). The Dinaric region was characterized by patrilinearity, patriarchy, and multiple-family households. While the latter have disappeared, a powerful echo of patriarchy reverberates in the area.

Traditional Adriatic culture was connected above all with the sea, and many derived a livelihood from seafaring, shipbuilding, trade, and utilization of the products from the sea (fish, corals, sponges). Constantly struggling with the lack of fertile land and water, people managed to grow olives, grapes, figs, and vegetables, and rear sheep and goats. Stone was used to build houses in closely built villages, to build shepherd shelters, and to shape vessels for storing oil and wine (though the latter were also made of animal skin). With the men working at sea and, at the turn of the 20th century, emigrating overseas, women had to take over men's work. This labor gave the women an important role in the nuclear family unit, but the public sphere remained a male prerogative. Much more than elsewhere, the rural way of life in this area was influenced by outside forces such as the ancient, neighboring urban centers and the faraway places visited by seafaring male emigrants.

With the conversion of the Croats to Christianity, pagan beliefs and rituals were incorporated into Christian thought and transformed into what we today call folk customs. Noteworthy traditional holidays included Christmas Eve (characterized by the Christmas tree and, until the 1930s, by the burning of a yule log, or *badnjak*), Holy Week (nocturnal processions organized by confraternities in Dalmatia), Easter (decorated eggs), and midsummer solstice (bonfires). Rural carnivals featured personages (draped in sheep fleece, bells, etc.) and head masks (made of leather and wood), practices and symbols that lost their meaning as ancient fertility cults and are recognized today as risqué spectacles. Urban carnivals, on the other hand, might express social criticism through the destruction of the carnival effigy. Weddings consisted of complex ritual events, including the transportation of the bride's trousseau and symbolic fertility rituals conducted by the bride. Laments for the deceased characterized death rituals, as did feasting ceremonies. There were many beliefs connected with the dead, as well as many beliefs in fairies, vampires, witches, and mythic female beings that determine the fate of children. Folk beliefs have disappeared or are fading away, but persist in myths, legends, tales, and poems.

The music styles differ by region, ranging from narrow intervals style (which is characteristic for varieties of *ojkanje* singing in the Dinaric region, and the genres in so-called "Istrian scale" on the northern coast, that is, Istria and Quarnero Bay) to widespread style called *na bas*, that is, *on bass* (two-part singing with cadences in perfect fifths, which originates from eastern Croatia), to major-minor tonal frameworks (typical for some genres and areas in central Croatia and especially for Dalmatian klapa singing). Among aerophones, *gajde* and *dude* (instruments from the family of bagpipes) are typical for eastern and central Croatia, *mišnice/diple* (double clarinet with or without windbag) for Dinaric region and parts of coastal area, and a pair of *sopile/roženice* for Istria and Quarnero Bay. Soloist chordophones are used to accompany singing (a bowed chordophone gusle in the Dinaric region), dance (a bowed chordophone *lijerica* in southern Dalmatia), or in both functions (a long-necked lute *tambura samica* in eastern Croatia). Among ensembles, the most frequent are *tamburitza* ensembles (consisting of long-necked lutes in various sizes, shapes, tunings, and number of strings), which started to form in the mid-19th century in both urban and rural settings, and have served in different periods as the Croatian national symbol. *Kolo*, or circle-dance, is the most popular dance form, spread in varied forms throughout Croatia. Since the 1930s, festivals of traditional music and dance have strongly influenced their preservation and revival. The most prominent is the International Folklore Festival, held in Zagreb since 1966.

A number of major events strongly influenced the reshaping of traditional culture in the past hundred years or so: most notably, industrialization, urbanization, major ideological changes (communism/socialism 1945–1990 and democratization afterwards), and fluctuations in the political borders. The imposition of the communist worldview repressed religious practice into the private sphere and promoted secular traditions, some of which were linked to the political regime (e.g., Youth Relay Race). Due to recently reawakened national self-awareness and touristic incentives, certain aspects of traditional culture have been revitalized or reinvented. Examples include the production of folk costumes, the traditional carnival, tamburitza-playing, lace-making, reenactments of medieval or Roman tournaments, multipart singing of chording structure known as klapa-singing, and reinterpretations of traditional tunes as part of world music trends.

The late 20th century saw various attempts at greater national autonomy within socialist Yugoslavia. The first, the so-called Croatian Spring in 1971, was followed by Communist purges but paradoxically resulted in greater autonomy being given to republics in the Constitution of 1974. The proclamation of Croatian independence (1991) caused rebellion among the Serbian minority in Croatia and armed conflict between Croatia and Serbia (assisted by the Yugoslav army), which spilled over into neighboring Bosnia and Herzegovina. The war ended with the forceful recapture (1995) and peaceful reintegration (1998) of Croatian territories occupied by the Serbs. The war resulted in hundreds of thousands of refugees and internally displaced persons on all sides, who found refuge in third countries or in their ethnic homelands. The status of the neighboring Bosnian and Herzegovinian Croats, who possess double citizenship and are recognized as a constituent people in both Croatia and Bosnia and Herzegovina, has been controversial. Today, Croatia hosts about half a million members of ethnic minorities, many of whom are Serbs.

The transitional 1990s brought to the fore political democracy, economic restructuring from socialist to capitalist economy, and changes in social structure, most notably the impoverishment of the middle class. Given one of the lowest total fertility rates (1.4) in Europe, Croatia is projected to lose 30 percent of its population by 2050. Croatia is also challenged—politically, economically, and socially—by the process of accession negotiations with European Union. And global culture makes itself felt every day in all spheres of life, from popular culture to cultural tourism.

*Jasna Čapo and*
*Valentina Gulin Zrnić*

**Further Reading**

Bošković-Stulli, Maja. *Kroatische Volksmärchen (Croatian Folk Tales)*. Düsseldorf–Köln: Eugen Diederichs Verlag, 1975.

Čapo Žmegač, Jasna. *Strangers Either Way: The Life of Croatian Refugees in Their New Home*. New York: Berghahn Books, 2007.

Čapo Žmegač, Jasna, et al., eds. *Kroatische Volkskunde/Ethnologie in den Neunzigern (Croatian Folklore/Ethnology in the Nineties)*. Vienna: Institut für Europäische Ethnologie, 2001.

Goldstein, Ivo. *Croatia: A History*. London: Hurst, 1999.

Lozica, Ivan. *Poganska baština (Pagan Heritage)*. Zagreb: Golden Marketing, 2002.

Rihtman-Auguštin, Dunja. *Christmas in Croatia*. Zagreb: Golden Marketing, 1997.

Vitez, Zorica, and Aleksandra Muraj, eds. *Croatian Folk Culture at the Crossroads of Worlds and Eras*. Zagreb: Klovićevi dvori, 2000.

# Cypriots, Greek

Greek Cypriots live on Cyprus, an island that has been divided since 1974. After the 1974 division, almost all Greek Cypriots live in the south side, and the other major ethnic group, the Turkish Cypriot minority, on the north. The population of Greek Cypriots currently living in Cyprus is around 650,000. In addition, it is estimated that up to 500,000 Greek Cypriots live outside Cyprus, the major concentrations being in the United Kingdom (270,000), Australia, South Africa, Greece, and the United States. Greek Cypriots are Greek speakers and follow the Christian Orthodox religion. Most of them would identify themselves as members of the Greek nation, while a sizeable minority would claim to be Cypriots first, in an expression of affinity with Turkish Cypriots.

Greek Cypriots trace their origins to the first arrival in Cyprus of the Mycenaean Greeks around 1400 BCE, claiming racial, cultural, and historical continuity from that period to the present. This view has been disputed by various academic scholars who see the emergence of a Greek identity in Cyprus as a result of the emergence and spread of nationalism, mostly during the 20th century. The island of Cyprus was ruled by many powers, the latest being the Ottomans from 1571 to 1878 and the British from 1878 to 1960, at which point Cyprus became an independent state. The origins of the current Turkish Cypriot population of Cyprus can be traced to the Ottoman Period.

Greek Cypriots follow the Christian Orthodox dogma. Most gained a livelihood from agriculture until the influx of industrialization during the early decades of the 20th century. The southern port city of Limassol became the island's first industrial city, and it is here that the Communist Party of Cyprus (AKEL) traces its roots, leading to a strong tradition of leftist politics, which included the Turkish Cypriots and is still a powerful force today. Later, the main

economic activities of Greek Cypriots became tourism, services, and trade. Until the 1950s, the two major ethnic groups, Greek Cypriots and Turkish Cypriots, coexisted in relative peace while left-wing organizations, especially trade unions, provided the most significant platforms for interethnic cooperation focusing on workers' struggles. Greek Cypriots have considered Greece to be their main political ally. Turkey and at certain periods the Turkish Cypriots have been regarded as their major enemies.

One of the distinguishing cultural characteristics of Greek Cypriots is their local dialect, sometimes called *kypreika* (Cypriot). While standard Greek is taught at school, in daily life and especially in informal situations the dialect is often employed in order to create a sense of intimacy and

Traditional dancers celebrate a national holiday in Cyprus. (EPA Photo/Katia Christodoulou)

equality among speakers. However, depending on the social context, a speaker of the dialect also risks being labeled negatively as a "peasant" (*horkatis*). The Greek Cypriot dialect has influences from ancient Greek, Italian, Turkish, and English, among others. The degree of intelligibility of the dialect by, say, an Athenian Greek varies, from extreme difficulty to more or less full understanding, depending on the dialect employed. While the limited amount of poetry and literature written in the dialect is now considered traditional, often dismissively so in the sense of being considered old-fashioned, the dialect is undergoing a revival through Cyprus-produced television series and Internet blogs. More than any other medium, the blogs currently explore, experiment, and play with the full range of linguistic possibilities commonly available to Greek Cypriots: standard Greek, the dialect, and English.

During the early course of the 20th century, while Cyprus was a British colony, Greek and Turkish nationalisms spread in Cyprus, with Greek-speaking Orthodox Christians identifying themselves as Greek, and Turkish-speaking Sunni Muslims as Turks. The Greek Cypriots (around 80% of the total population, according to 1960 official survey figures) demanded *enosis*, the Union of Cyprus with Greece. During 1955, EOKA (National Organization of Cypriot Fighters) was set up to lead an armed struggle aiming to bring about union with Greece. Turkish Cypriots (18% of the total population) demanded *taksim*, the partition of Cyprus, setting up their own armed organization called TMT (Turkish Resistance Organization) in 1958. Neither aim of the two major ethnic groups

was successful; instead the island became an independent republic in 1960. Yet, the two communities continued to pursue their opposed goals, leading to the eruption of interethnic violence in 1963 and the withdrawal of Turkish Cypriots, who suffered most in terms of casualties and the displacement of around a fifth of their population, into armed enclaves. By 1967 interethnic violence abated, but a different conflict emerged this time among Greek Cypriots. The Greek Cypriot leadership gradually edged away from the goal of union with Greece, especially after 1967 when a military junta grabbed power in Greece. But a small group of Greek Cypriot right-wing extremists, backed by the junta, calling themselves EOKA B, and insisting on union, launched a coup against the president of the Republic of Cyprus, Archbishop Makarios, in July 1974. In reaction to the coup, Turkey launched a military offensive in Cyprus that divided the island along an east-west axis, claiming this was necessary for the protection of the Turkish Cypriot community and within Turkey's rights as guarantor power, which had been granted to Turkey (along with Greece and Britain) by the constitution of Cyprus. This conflict led to further displacements of Greek Cypriots to the south side, and Turkish Cypriots to the north side, with Greek Cypriots bearing the heavier casualties (around 170,000 persons people killed and missing). During 1983, the Turkish Cypriot leadership declared its own state in the north, the Turkish Republic of Northern Cyprus, which has since remained internationally unrecognized, except by Turkey. Throughout this period, Cyprus witnessed another, externally less visible conflict, between forces of the right and of the left within each side, with significant incidents of violence against the left. Leftists were often branded as traitors in their own community, either for cooperating with the other ethnic group, or for being communists, a political designation considered to lie outside the dominant definitions of both Greek and Turkish identities.

The two sides have since 1978 agreed that a solution to what has been known as the Cyprus Problem should take the form of a bizonal, bicommunal federation with political equality of the two ethnic groups. Negotiations are still continuing to reach a political settlement. A major watershed in these negotiations was the jointly negotiated United Nations-finalized plan for a solution (known as the Annan Plan) that was accepted by the majority of Turkish Cypriots but rejected by Greek Cypriots in simultaneous referenda during April 2004. The Greek Cypriot rejection rendered this international effort unsuccessful. The Greek Cypriot-controlled Republic of Cyprus has successfully negotiated its entry into the European Union, formally entering during May 2004. The Turkish Cypriot side, that is, the TRNC, however, remains outside the EU pending the political settlement of the conflict.

*Yiannis Papadakis*

**Further Reading**

Attalides, Michael. *Cyprus: Nationalism and International Politics*. New York: St Martin's Press, 1979.

Calotychos, Vangelis, ed. *Cyprus and Its People: Nation, Identity and Experience in an Unimaginable Community, 1955–1997*. Boulder, CO: Westview Press, 1998.

Hill, George. *History of Cyprus* (4 vols.). Cambridge: Cambridge University Press, 1940–1952.

Panteli, Stavros. *A History of Cyprus: From Foreign Domination to Troubled Independence*. London: East-West, 2000.

Papadakis, Yiannis. *Echoes from the Dead Zone: Across the Cyprus Divide*. London: I. B. Tauris, 2005.

# Cypriots, Turkish

Turkish-Cypriot identity is tightly connected to the dispute over sovereignty in Cyprus, commonly known as the Cyprus Problem. Variability in the designation attests to this, as different designations are linked to political orientation, ranging from a thesis of common belonging to the Turkish race that identifies the group as Turks of Cyprus to a thesis of common belonging to the land of Cyprus alongside other groups (mainly Greek Cypriots) where the group may be defined as Cypriotturks. In a similar fashion, views of Cyprus itself differ, so that the Turkish Republic of Northern Cyprus (TRNC), which governs the northern part of the island, regards this area as the homeland for Turkish Cypriot nationalists, whereas others envision a future state governing the entire island, where power will be shared with Greek Cypriots. The Cyprus problem is considered the main cause of out-migration waves that created large diaspora communities, primarily in English-speaking countries and Turkey. The political dispute also feeds into population estimates, which range from 500,000 in Cyprus to 500,000 around the world. Religion and language are less disputed, with the overwhelming majority of Turkish

Cypriots being secular Sunni Muslims and speaking a dialect of Turkish.

The beginnings of the formation of the community are traced to the Ottoman Empire's ending Venetian rule in Cyprus in 1571. Some conversions have been recorded from Catholicism to Islam, in the early days, while nearly 65,000 people were settled among the existing 200,000 Orthodox Christian locals. By the end of the Ottoman period (1878), the local ruling class consisted of the Orthodox and Muslim religious elite, Ottoman officials (military and bureaucrats), landowners, and merchants, while the rest of the population (excluding urban artisans) lived in rural areas and subsisted on agriculture.

The island was leased to the British in 1878, annexed in 1914, and declared a British crown colony in 1925. The British infused preexisting Ottoman legal and administrative systems with secularist and capitalist ideals, worsening Turkish Cypriots' socioeconomic status and resulting in large emigration movements as the Muslim Ottoman ruling class lost its significance and Muslim nomadic pastoralists lost out to the mainly sedentarized Orthodox farmers during the process of land registration. The Muslim religious institution

Turkish Cypriots hold blue European Union (EU) flags with the map of Cyprus in the center during a demonstration on the Turkish side of Nicosia on January 14, 2003. Tens of thousands of Turkish Cypriots rallied on their side of the world's last divided capital in support of a UN plan to reunify the east Mediterranean island ahead of its entry to the EU, which is opposed by Rauf Denktash, leader of the Turkish Republic of Northern Cyprus. (AFP/Getty Images)

(Evkaf) also lost control of large portions of its landed resources in the same period.

Although most Turkish-Cypriots are Sunni Muslims, many insist they are not religious and ignore Islamic food taboos. Yet, secularism is less fiercely guarded than in Turkey, and head scarves are allowed in public buildings. Syncretic practices also exist, particularly among small rural communities who had lived with Greek-Cypriots prior to the division, while the group known as "linen-cottons" (*linobambaci*), who underwent a number of conversions between Islam and Christianity in the last few centuries before being forced to fix their identity within one of the two communities with the formation of the state, is now legendary.

Artistic traditions common to other Cypriot groups are also celebrated, including the tradition of improvised banter singing (*çatisma* or *atişma*) and regional traditional crafts like wood carving, lace embroidery, and silk cocoon art. Recent literary achievement has been heavily influenced by the political conflict, for example, Mehmet Yashin's poetry and Derviş Zaim's films, while achievements of diaspora artists have been largely unconnected to Cyprus, for example, artist Tracey Emin and designer Husseyin Chalayan.

The militarization of Cypriot society in the 1950s and 1960s turned many males into veterans of battles with Greek Cypriots. With the setup of autonomous state structures, this experience became a factor in deciding employment in the expanding civil service, which currently employs close to 20 percent of the TRNC's working population. Turkish Cypriots often distinguish themselves by their higher living standard from Turks (thought to constitute up to 50% of the TRNC population), who were settled on the island after 1974, as many Turks are laborers, although Turkish nationals are also students, soldiers serving in the Turkish military, and civil servants (notably in the police), or involved in the tourism business. At the fringes of Turkish Cypriot society are Cypriot Muslim Roma, numbering a few thousand individuals, mostly manual laborers traditionally involved in recycling scrap metal, who were itinerant up to the 1974 war, after which they were settled in particular locations in northern Cyprus until the early 2000s, when a significant number moved to the south part of the island.

By the time of independence in 1960, Turkish Cypriots were constituted as a minority community of 18 percent, with a strong Turkish national consciousness, whose continuing existence on the island was thought to be under threat by belligerent Greek Cypriot nationalists. By 1963, efforts to forge a partnership state broke down and Greek Cypriot paramilitaries began to attack Turkish Cypriot civilians. Turkish Cypriot leaders set up self-administered enclaves into which the majority of the community withdrew, leaving the structures of the state to Greek Cypriot control. Negotiations with the Greek Cypriot leadership failed repeatedly until, following a coup in 1974 instigated by the Greek military dictatorship seeking to oust the Greek Cypriot president and impose on the island union with Greece, the Turkish military staged an operation to save Turkish Cypriots from feared massacre. The military took control of the northern part of the island, and approximately 40,000 troops have remained stationed there since, following repeated failures to reach an agreed settlement with the Greek Cypriot leadership. The area under the military's control was unilaterally declared independent in 1983, forming the TRNC, which has since remained unrecognized by the international community.

The TRNC government was led by the nationalist veteran Rauf Denktash until 2003, when he was ousted from the presidency by Mehmet Ali Talat, following a series of massive demonstrations against Denktash's uncompromising stance on the political agreement and expectations that a solution formula could be found before 2004, when the Republic of Cyprus acceded to the European Union (EU), so that the northern part of the island could also become part of the EU. The change in leadership enabled the tabling of a settlement plan by the United Nations, which was in the last instance rejected by the Greek Cypriot public at referendum, despite Turkish-Cypriot acceptance. Since then, the Turkish Cypriot leadership has called on the international community to recognize its efforts towards reaching a peace agreement and implement policies against the territory's global economic and political isolation, which renders it perpetually dependent on Turkey.

*Murat Erdal Ilican*

**Further Reading**

Çevikel, Nuri. *Kıbrıs: Akdeniz'de bit Osmanlı Adası (1570–1878) (Cyprus: An Ottoman Island in the Mediterranean 1570–1878)*. Istanbul: Tarih İnceleme, 2006.

Cobham, Claude Delaval. *Excerpta Cypria: Materials for a History of Cyprus*. Cambridge: Cambridge University Press, 1908.

Kızılyürek, Niyazi. *Milliyetçilik Kıskacında Kıbrıs (Cyprus in the Claws of Nationalism)*. Istanbul: İletişim, 2002.

Navaro-Yashin, Yael. *The Make-Believe Space: Administration, Materiality and the Affects in Northern Cyprus*. Durham: Duke University Press, forthcoming.

Patrick, Richard. *Political Geography and the Cyprus Conflict: 1963–1971*. Ontario: University of Waterloo, 1976.

Volkan, Vamik. *Cyprus—War and Adaptation: A Psychoanalytic History of Two Ethnic Groups in Conflict*. Charlottesville: University Press of Virginia, 1979.

## Czechs

Czechs are a nation of 10 million, who live in the territory of the Czech Republic, the frontiers of which correspond to those of the medieval Kingdom of Bohemia and Margravate of Moravia. Czech-speaking minorities in Austria, Romania, Croatia, and Ukraine have been almost completely assimilated. The Czech language belongs to the West Slavic group. The dominant religion until World War II was Catholic with 15 percent minority of various Protestant churches. Today, more than 50 percent of Czechs declare themselves to be nonconfessional.

West Slavic ancestors of the Czech population came to their present territory in the sixth century, probably from East-Central Europe. They settled the cultivated areas of the country and Czechicized the local population, possibly composed of Celtic and Germanic tribes. Beginning in the ninth century they were incorporated into the early medieval state of Great Moravia and at the same time were Christianized through the Eastern Church (Greek) mission. With the destruction of this state by the Magyar invasion after 900, Bohemia was transformed into a principality (which later also included Moravia) and accepted the dominance of the Western (Latin) Church. One of the first Christian Princes, Wenceslas (Vaclav, died 935), was sanctified and declared the protector of the land of Bohemia. In following centuries princes of Bohemia had to accept their subordinate position in the newly created Holy Roman Empire, but they gradually enlarged their autonomy, until they achieved the status of Kingdom of Bohemia in 1212. Lands of the Crown of Bohemia included Moravia and later also Silesia and Lusatia.

During the 13th and 14th centuries, German-speaking colonists were invited by Czech kings to settle and cultivate the woody and hilly border areas of Bohemia and Moravia; the wealthier immigrants assumed leading positions in newly founded towns. Consequently, a German-speaking minority inhabited the historical territory of the Czech state, which was surrounded on all sides, except the East, by German-speaking populations. The language of administration switched, however, from Latin to Czech during the 15th century, as a result of the successful Hussite revolution, which was a kind of Reformation one century before Luther. Its initiator, Jan Hus, who was executed by the Roman Catholic Church in 1415, was and still is a part of national myths. The Hussites introduced utraquism (communion was offered in the form of bread and wine to laity as well as priests) and the Czech language in church

services, abolished celibacy for priests, nullified the secular dominance of the church, and defended themselves against several crusades. Even though they did not achieve full victory, Bohemia and Moravia (and later all lands of the Crown of Bohemia) became a biconfessional state. The period also saw the development of literature in the Czech language, which emerged as a codified printed language during the 16th century.

The lands of the Crown of Bohemia became a part of the Habsburg Empire in 1526, and afterward autonomy and religious tolerance became gradually limited. The unsuccessful upheaval of Protestant Estates against the Habsburg policies in 1618–1620 figured in the beginning stages of the Thirty Years' War (1618–1648) and totally transformed the political and religious situation; the forceful Counter-Reformation introduced Catholic confession as the only form allowed and introduced the German language step by step, first into higher levels and later into all levels of administration and education. Protestant nobility and intellectuals were expelled and replaced by foreign (above all German, but also Italian, Spanish, and Irish) nobility. Czech intellectual life declined, and the Catholic Church achieved full control over all areas of cultural life. For all these reasons, the defeat of the Bohemian armies in November 1620 at White Mountain is regarded as a national tragedy. During the 17th and 18th centuries, Czech-language literature was devoted almost exclusively to religious topics.

The Czech-speaking ethnic core nation nevertheless survived as a majority of the population in the countryside and among middle and lower classes in most towns, even though its numerical predominance fell to around 65 percent as a result of assimilation into German culture. The enlightenment initiated increasing scholarly interest in the Czech language, literature, and customs, and the history of the kingdom.

This circumstance was important for the success of national agitation, initiated in the early 19th century with the goal of achieving the all-important attributes of a fully formed nation with a highly developed culture, full social structure, and political autonomy. During the first half of the 19th century, this initiative gradually gained support, becoming a mass movement characterized by a liberal democratic program by the middle of the century. The first national institutions were the Patriotic Museum (founded 1818) and the so-called Matice ("mother"), the central institution for self-financing the printing of Czech-language scientific books. The first literary journals were published in the 1820s, and the first novels appeared in the 1840s. The most important authors were poet Karel Hynek Mácha, playwright Josef Kajetán Tyl, and novelist Božena Němcová. The leading personality of this national movement was the historian František Palacký, and the national liberal program was developed by his younger friend Karel Havlíček.

Czech national identity, defined linguistically, was not, however, the only one emerging in the territory of Bohemia and Moravia. Some citizens identified themselves in terms of Austrian or German identity on the basis of language use, while identification in terms of land survived from earlier times as well. Indeed, given that all intellectuals and socially upwardly mobile people had to be bilingual, multiple identifications, both competing and compatible, were common up until 1848.

The revolution of 1848 played a decisive role in the formation of Czech national identity. The originally unified revolutionary movement disintegrated in May, when German-speaking intellectuals and bourgeoisie decided to participate in elections to the parliament in Frankfurt, which aimed to effect the political unification of the German nation. Czechs refused to participate, declaring that they did not regard themselves as members of the German nation. Thus began the rivalries and conflicts between Germans and Czechs in Bohemia, and with some delay in Moravia also. On the whole, Czechs belonged to lower and middle classes and their culture was less developed than the German one.

During the second half of the 19th century, the Czech national movement achieved important successes not only in mobilizing broadly among the masses in the towns and countryside, but also in competing with Germans in the field of culture and education. A rich Czech culture emerged, including novels, poetry, painting, and above all music (national opera), with international renown garnered by Bedřich Smetana and Antonín Dvořák. Most important, works of Western literature were translated into Czech. In 1881 the Czech National Theater was opened, thanks to fund-raising. By the 1880s, a fully formed Czech society had emerged, complete with its own social structure, including entrepreneurs, academics, and professionals. Czech was a language of higher education in an increasing number of high schools, and in 1882 the Charles University in Prague was divided into German and Czech schools. The ambitious Czech bourgeoisie tried, sometimes rather successfully, to compete with the stronger class of German industrialists. Political representation in the period of the 1860s through the 1880s was reduced to two national parties, but by the end of the 19th century only the more radical Young Czech Party survived. At the same time new Czech political parties were formed, corresponding to the internal stratification of the Czech society (for example, the Agrarian Party, Social Democrats, and the People's Party).

Since Bohemia and Moravia continued to be part of the Habsburg Empire, German remained the dominant language in government administration, economy, and public life of the empire, and Czechs had to struggle to preserve their language. The self-conscious Czech leadership demanded the equality of Czech and German in administration and public life. This demand created much tension between Czechs and Germans living in Bohemia and Moravia, who refused to learn the totally different Czech language, regarding it as underdeveloped and unacceptable in the higher social strata in which they traveled. Consequently, social and economic tensions, where counterparts differed in language, were translated into national terms. Relations of power were upended with the birth of an independent Czechoslovakia in 1918. Germans in Bohemia and Moravia were transformed from a dominant nation into a national minority, though with all cultural and political rights of equal citizens in the new state.

While Czech lands to the south, west, and north bordered German-speaking populations, to the east, in the territory of the Kingdom of Hungary, were Slovaks, whose vernaculars the Czechs understood. Czech patriots often regarded Slovaks and their culture as a part of their own nation, and some Slovak intellectuals, especially Protestants such as the poet Ján Kollár and politician Vavro Šrobár, shared this opinion. This was the point of departure for the concept of a single Czechoslovak nation, which became the official state ideology of the Czechoslovak Republic, declared as independent in 1918 after the breakdown of the Austro-Hungarian Empire in World War I. In this state, Czechs, as the more highly educated and economically stronger population, assumed the dominant role. Efforts to integrate Slovaks into one nation with Czechs during the two interwar decades failed. The Slovak ethnic identity was not extinguished; on the contrary, it was transformed into a national one.

The well-organized, prosperous, and democratic Czechoslovak Republic existed only 20 years, but secured a place in national mythology until recent times. Its first president, T.G. Masaryk, originally a professor in sociology, was widely regarded as a moral authority and is still appreciated as one of the most important national figures.

In October 1938, under the terms of the Munich treaty, Germany was granted the authority to occupy German-inhabited areas of Czechoslovakia. In March 1939 the interwar Czechoslovak republic was split and the Czech lands were occupied by Nazi Germany as the Protectorate of Bohemia and Moravia. Germanization and persecution provoked among the Czech population strong hatred of Germans, which escalated toward the decision, approved by the victorious Great Powers after World War II, to expel the German minority from the territory of restored Czechoslovakia during the years 1945–1946. At the same time, Czechoslovakia was (re)constructed as a state of two nations—Czechs and Slovaks, each having full cultural autonomy. Nevertheless, the Slovaks felt politically underprivileged in the binational state. Under the Communist dictatorship established in February 1948, Slovak attempts to achieve a higher degree of autonomy were oppressed. Only in October 1968 did Slovakia achieve the political status of an autonomous republic, and in 1992, after the breakdown of Communist rule, politicians of both nations decided to divide the republic into two independent national states. This was a notable challenge above all for Czechs, since their identity permanently included the Czechoslovak component. A rather strong regional identity survived in Moravia, but all efforts to define this regional identity as a national one after 1990 failed: Moravian Nationalist Parties received less than 1 percent of votes in elections. The Czech Republic is now an almost mono-ethnic nation-state, with some hundreds of thousands of minority Gypsies (Roma), but many among them regard themselves as Czechs or Slovaks. Their number is increasing, while the Czech population is slightly decreasing as the result of a sinking birth rate. During the last two decades the number of inhabitants increased as a result of immigration: today, almost 5 percent of inhabitants are foreigners, most notably Slovaks, Ukrainians, and Vietnamese. The political representatives decided to enter the North Atlantic Treaty Organization in 1999, and the republic joined the European Union with a favorable vote in the 2004 plebiscite.

*Miroslav Hroch*

## Further Reading

Agnew, Hugh LeCain. *The Czechs and the Lands of the Bohemian Crown.* Stanford: Hoover Institution Press, 2004.

Krejčí, Jaroslav. *Czechoslovakia at the Crossroads of European History.* London: I. B. Tauris, 1990.

Mamatey, Victor S., and Radomir Luza, eds. *A History of the Czechoslovak Republic 1918–1948.* Princeton, NJ: Princeton University Press, 1973.

Morison, John, ed. *The Czech and Slovak Experience.* New York: Macmillan, 1992.

Sayer, Derek. *The Coasts of Bohemia: A Czech History.* Princeton, NJ: Princeton University Press, 1998.

Seton-Watson, Robert S. *A History of the Czechs and Slovaks.* Hamden, CT: Archon Books, 1965 (1st ed. 1943).

Teich, Milulas, ed. *Bohemia in History.* Cambridge: Cambridge University Press, 1998.

# D

## Danes

Danes mainly live in Denmark, a nationally and socially homogeneous state situated in southern Scandinavia at the entrance to the Baltic Sea, bordering Germany to the south. The Kingdom of Denmark consists of Denmark, the Faroe Islands, and Greenland. Denmark's capital, Copenhagen, is located on the eastern edge of the country on the island of Zealand (Sjælland) and larger Copenhagen comprises almost a third of the population (5.5 million in 2009). Around half a million are immigrants or descendants of immigrants who arrived within the last 50 years. Danes speak Danish, a language dating back to the Old Norse known from the Icelandic Sagas. More than 80 percent of Danes are members of the Evangelical Lutheran Church; 4–5 percent profess Islam, mostly recent immigrants and their descendants. Danes consider themselves a nationality and reserve the word "ethnic" to describe minority groups of recent immigrants, mostly of Turkish, Arab, Pakistani, Moroccan, Somali, or Bosnian background. The age-old minority of German speakers in southern Jutland is labeled a "national minority" although all speak fluent Danish. The Faroese and the Greenlanders are not considered minorities but "nationalities" in their own right with their own emerging nation-states within the still existing Danish commonwealth (*Rigsfællesskab*).

"Danes" and "Denmark" appear in written sources dating as far back as the 9th century. For more than 400 years the Danish monarchy used its geopolitical position to rule a dominion in Northern Europe that was formalized in the Kalmar Union from 1397 to 1523. Despite heavy territorial losses in the 17th century, in the 18th century the multinational monarchy still ranked as a medium-sized European power at the level of Prussia and Sweden (which then possessed present-day Finland). Thanks to Norway, Denmark possessed the third largest navy in Europe. According to an agreement with Russia, the Danish king gained unchallenged possession of all Holstein in 1773. Thus, the foundations were laid for a great reform process throughout the multinational state from 1784 to 1814, a process initiated primarily by representatives of the German-speaking aristocratic elite within the composite state. Until the loss of the Norwegian part of the realm in 1814, the name Denmark referred to a composite state, typical of European territorial states of the era. The official name of this mid-sized sovereign power was the Danish Monarchy or Oldenbourg Monarchy.

In addition to the four main realms, the composite state included Iceland, the Faroe Islands, and Greenland. Originally affiliated with Norway, these three countries in the course of the 17th and 18th centuries gradually came under direct rule from

103

Danes dressed in folk costume, Denmark. (Corel)

Copenhagen. Finally, the Danish monarchy in this period acquired a number of colonies in the West Indies (today the Virgin Islands), West Africa (Christiansborg in today's Ghana), and India (Frederiksnagore, today Serampore outside Calcutta, and Tranquebar in the south). By virtue of this colonial empire, Denmark played a role, however small, in the Atlantic trade triangle between a European center, the slave-producing West Africa, and the sugar-growing West Indies, complemented by a stake in the East Asian trade. The multinational character of the realm is evidenced by the fact that by the end of the 18th century the biggest cities of the composite state were Copenhagen in Denmark proper, Altona and Kiel in Holstein, Flensburg in Schleswig, and Bergen in Norway, while the seaports of Charlotte Amalie in St. Thomas in the West Indies and Frederiksnagore in India were second and sixth, respectively, measured by trade volume.

The monarchy survived the Napoleonic Wars, albeit in an amputated form after the loss of Norway in 1814. In this situation, the National Liberals (1830–1848) proposed an ethnic and historical definition of the nation. This program clashed with demands for a united Germany from the elites in Holstein and Schleswig. The result was civil war between Danes and Germans from 1848 to 1851, ending with a temporary Danish victory. An abortive attempt to annex Schleswig in 1863 led to complete defeat and the subsequent collapse of the National Liberals. The loss eventually led to the national and eventually social unification of the remaining Danes.

Only in the 19th century, after the dissolution of the multicultural and multilingual state (Helstaten) in 1864, did the core provinces became a nation-state with a political culture based on identity between language, people (folk), nation, state, and religion. Owing to a combination of outside pressures and initiatives from below, primarily from the class of peasant farmers, helped by a deliberate demarcation from Germany and all things German, modern democratic Denmark emerged in the 19th century. In this period Danes acquired their own undisputed national identity, language, and sovereign state. The process can be traced to a large class of relatively well-to-do peasants turned independent farmers (themselves created by the enlightenment reforms of the late 18th century) who succeeded in establishing control over the rump state. This identity-forming process did not occur without opposition, primarily from the elites in Copenhagen in alliance with the old manorial class. Nevertheless, in the second half of the 19th century, peasant farmers gradually took over from the former ruling elites, the civil servants, and the manorial class. The cultural, economic, and political awakening of the newly formed farmers typifies Danish nationalism and national identity. Agrarian Denmark was able to rise to prominence thanks to the relative weakness of the Danish bourgeoisie and the country's late industrialization. (Industrialization did not get under way until the 1890s and was not dominant until the 1950s.)

The middle peasants developed a consciousness as a separate class and saw themselves as the backbone of society, culturally as well as economically. That their ideology supported free trade is not surprising, as they from the 1880s relied heavily on the export of bacon and butter to the rapidly developing British market. More surprising is the fact that, because of their struggle with the existing urban and academic elites, their ideology at times did contain strong libertarian elements that transgressed their narrow economic and social interests. The peasant-farmers' movement achieved a cultural and political hegemony after they succeeded in establishing an independent culture with its own educational institutions as an alternative to the old educational system. The success of their alternative educational system was a result of the unique organization of the agrarian sector and the industries that processed their products, the cooperative. The basic unit of agrarian production remained the independent farms, which were somewhat larger than the European average. However, local cooperatives were responsible for most of the processing of dairy and meat produce into exportable goods. Cooperative associations were run democratically, with members participating equally, regardless of their initial investment.

The intellectual preparation for participating in the cooperatives was laid by the training that the sons and daughters of the peasant farmers received in the so-called folk high schools. These institutions were founded by the peasant farmers themselves. Although not run democratically, through the content and form of their teaching, which was less formal and without a fixed curriculum, they helped establish an independent mind and self-consciousness towards the upper and urban classes in the peasants, which helped them establish a virtual cultural hegemony and a strong relatively democratic nationalism.

The defeat of the German Reich in World War I enabled Denmark to retrieve the Danish-speaking part of North Schleswig. Because of clumsy attempts to Germanize them, the Danish-speaking North Schleswigers had become ardent Danish nationalists, organizing a sort of parallel society. Even though Denmark remained neutral in World War I, the German defeat opened up the possibility for a referendum over national affiliation, and in 1920 half of the old province of Schleswig was united with Denmark.

The peasant farmers had successfully established an ideological hegemony over the rest of the population in the 19th century. Later the working class successfully organized trade unions and the Social Democratic Party. This party and associated organizations soon became the largest political party, which in close collaboration with a centrist party of social liberals (the Radikale Venstre, which literally means the radical left) succeeded in organizing a welfare state encompassing all Danish citizens under the slogan "Denmark for the People" (1934). Despite this success, Social Democracy never won the absolute majority of its sister parties in Sweden and Norway and thus always had to govern in coalition. In response, the workers' movement adopted the core values of liberalism, social harmony, and nationalism promoted by the peasant farmers. These peasant values, together with the particular Lutheran version of Protestantism, constitute an ideological hegemony shared across party

lines to the present. In combination with later historical experiences this explains the particularities of the Danish path to modernity and the efficiency of the so-called Danish model of "flexicurity" in the globalizing world of the 21st century.

With a little over 92 percent of the population on the labor market, Danes today have the second highest percentage of people in formal occupation in the world (surpassed only by Sweden). This statistic is reached because virtually all women work outside the home, a circumstance made possible by the very high number of children in child care and kindergartens.

Today, Danes have a double history. Denmark refers to a typical multinational nation-state with a long-standing role in European politics; at the same time, this very same name refers to an atypically homogeneous small nation-state. This duality is nicely reflected in the existence of two national anthems: "Kong Christian" ("King Christian"), a martial song written in 1779, praises the warrior king who defeats the enemies of the country—and politely forgets how he lost everything in the end. The other song is "Der er et yndigt land" ("There is a lovely land"), which was written in 1819, praising the beauty of the friendly and peaceful country and its inhabitants. This latter is sung at national football games, regardless of the result. Denmark, Danes, and Danish national consensus are caught between competing and at times even antagonistic notions of Danishness.

This contradiction is revealed in attitudes toward religion. Denmark is one of the most secularized countries in the world. Church attendance is below 10 percent, apart from the great occasions in life such as baptism, confirmation, wedding(s), funerals, and Christmas. Yet official life is very much organized according to Lutheranism, from the official holy days to the requirement for the ruling monarchy to belong to the Evangelical Lutheran Church. Despite secularism, there are no indications of an imminent separation of state and church as happened in Sweden (2000).

Denmark and the Danes thus represent a number of paradoxes. These derive from two pasts, one as a relatively large composite state of the general West European pattern, the other a more recent history as a small, homogenous nation-state now faced with the challenges of globalization and immigration. These challenges create tensions that sometimes bring Denmark into the headlines of the world as in the so-called cartoon crisis, when a Danish newspaper printed satirical drawings of the prophet Mohammed and attracted heavy criticism from the Muslim world for blasphemy. The debate quickly escalated into a confrontation over free speech versus religious feelings. But behind it lay a Danish small-state innocence and lack of knowledge of the rest of world, despite Denmark's great success as an exporter.

*Uffe Østergaard*

**Further Reading**

Campbell, J. L., J. A. Hall, and O. K. Pedersen, eds. *National Identity and the Varieties of Capitalism. The Danish Experience.* Montreal: McGill-Queen's University Press, 2006.

Jespersen, K. V. *A History of Denmark.* London: Palgrave Macmillan, 2004.

Nye, David. *Introducing Denmark and the Danes.* Odense: CBS Press and University Press of Southern Denmark, 2006.

Østergaard, Uffe. "The Danish Path to Modernity." *Thesis Eleven* 77 (2004): 25–43.

Østergaard, Uffe. "Peasants and Danes— National Identity and Political Culture in Denmark." *Comparative Studies in Society and History* 34, no. 1 (1992): 3–27.

Sørensen, Ø., and B. Stråth, eds. *The Cultural Construction of Norden.* Oslo: Scandinavian University Press, 1997.

# Dargins

Dargins refer to themselves as *Dargan* (s) and *Darganti* (pl) and collectively as *Dargwa*. They are an indigenous people of the northeast Caucasus residing in the central districts of the Dagestan Republic. The total Dargin population in the Russian Federation stood at 510,156 in 2002. Of this number, 425,526 lived in the Dagestan, making them the second largest ethnic group there after the Avars. Almost all Dargins are Sunni Muslims of the Shafi'i School. The Dargin language belongs to the Nakh-Dagestani branch of the North Caucasian family of languages. Some scholars suggest that the Dargins do not represent a specific ethnicity so much as a combination of multiple ethnic groups. It is worth noting that the Kaitags and Kubachins are considered Dargin subgroups.

The earliest written reference to the Dargins is found in a 10th-century Arabic-language manuscript that mentions the Kaitags and Kubachins. The first written use of the ethnonym Dargin occurred in the 14th century, when Arabic-language

A Dagestani couple poses for a photograph, ca. 1907. The mountainous region of Dagestan has historically been one of Russia's most ethnically diverse regions. (Library of Congress)

manuscripts describe an attack by Timur (Tamerlane) upon the Darga. The Dargin were part of, or under the influence of, Caucasian Albania and later the Khazar Khanate, and are believed to have been formidable opponents of the Arab-Muslim conquerors who arrived in southern Dagestan in the 7th century. The Dargins inhabited the Caspian coast before being pushed up into the subalpine and mid-alpine zones of central Dagestan by the recently arrived Turkic Kumyks in the 12th century. In the 14th century the armies of Timur exacted great damage upon the Dargin. During the 12th and 13th centuries a feudal Kaitag entity under a hereditary ruler known as the

Utsmi emerged. Following the decline of the Golden Horde this principality, known as the Utsmiyat, became a major power in Dagestan. Dargin villages that did not fall under the Utsmiyat organized themselves into free unions and often waged war with it. In addition to infighting among themselves and their neighbors, the Dargins suffered from successive invasions from Iran, the last of which culminated in the defeat of the army of Nadir Shah in 1741.

In 1819 the Imperial Russian Army captured Akusha, the center of Dargin settlement and power, and thereby brought the Dargins under nominal Russian control, but the Russians would not consolidate their hold over the Dargins until 1844. The Dargins by and large did not take part in the Great Caucasian Wars of the 19th century. They were not part of Sheikh Shamil's Imamate and only occasionally participated in Shamil's struggle against the Russians. By contrast, Dargins did play a major role in the 1877 Caucasian uprising against the Russian Empire.

Up until the Soviet period, the Dargins remained an undefined ethnicity. Russian sources of the 18th and 19th centuries commonly refer to the Dargins using the terms Tavliny or Tavlintsy, derived from the Kumyk word for mountaineer, or as Lezgin, a name Russians commonly used to refer to all Dagestani mountain peoples. Dargin neighbors such as the Avars, Laks, and Kumyks tended to label them according to the name of the largest or nearest union of Dargin villages.

Dargins inhabit all geographic zones of Dagestan, from lowland to mountain regions. Agriculture, horticulture, and the raising of livestock (especially sheep, goat, cattle, and horses) all constituted important components of traditional economy. Dargin material culture is the same as that of the other Dagestani peoples, and their dress also belongs to the general regional type. The carrying of arms, and in particular the *kinjal* (a dagger), traditionally was mandatory for Dargin men. Today, Dargins, especially those in cities, dress in the general European style. Culturally specific forms of dress are worn only by the elderly or for ceremonial events.

The village community, or *jamaat* (Arabic for group or congregation) served as the fundamental unit of traditional Dargin society. The chief authority was the village qadi (judge trained in Islamic law) who would oversee village administration together with the village elders. Questions of pressing importance to the *jamaat* as a whole were decided at gatherings where all adult free males participated. Two or more *jamaats* could form a union, and multiple unions formed a super-union. Questions of war and peace and major legal questions would be decided at the level of the union or super-union at a general meeting. A council consisting of 12 to 15 *qadis* and respected elders would decide matters in the periods between general meetings.

A combination of customary law (*adat*) and Islamic law (sharia) regulated the social life of the Dargins. Unions of *jamaats* developed their own combinations of law, and some codified them. The codex of the Kaitag Utsmi Rustem Khan of the 17th century became well known throughout Dagestan. Dargin social and legal norms resembled those of their neighbors, with sharia covering questions of inheritance, marriage, and religious observation, and *adat* regulating criminal matters, especially vendetta. The Dargins, like most Dagestanis, long considered the practice of vendetta an essential part of masculine honor. Dargin families are patrilineal, and organized into clans (*tukhums*) said to share common ancestry.

The Dargin language has 15 recognizable dialects, and some scholars question whether it is possible to assert that there is a single Dargin language. In the 1920s Soviet authorities selected the Akusha dialect to serve as basis for the literary form of Dargin. Although taught in schools, literary Dargin never became a common language of communication. Avar, Kumyk, Azeri, and Russian have all exerted influence on the Dargin language and its dialects. Most Dargins are bilingual; nearly 70 percent are fluent in Russian. Indeed, Dargins most often use Russian as their language of common communication. Local dialects, however, remain in use in villages.

At the beginning of the 20th century, the Dargins were slowly assimilating to their neighbors, the Avars and Kumyks. Soviet authorities, however, disrupted this process by acknowledging Dargin as an official ethnicity and classified the smaller Kaitags and Kubachins as related ethnicities. The period of Soviet rule saw other enormous changes in Dargin life in addition to the bureaucratic codification of Dargin identity and language. Among these changes were the destruction of traditional agriculture and home industries by increased urbanization, and also the achievement of virtually universal literacy.

Urbanization threatens the preservation of distinct ethnic identities in Dagestan, as Dagestan's cities are all multiethnic, and life in the cities undermines village traditions and promotes the use of Russian as a common language of communication. Similarly, the erosion of material culture continues. Among the Dargin, the process of ethnic consolidation has halted and the question of a common Dargin language remains open as the role of Russian as a common language only increases.

*Michael A. Reynolds*

## Further Reading

Quelquejay, Ch. "Darghin." In *Encyclopaedia of Islam*, 2nd ed., ed. P. Bearman et al. Leiden: Brill, 2009, 2:141.

Aliev, A. I., and Z. A. Nikol'skaia. "Dargintsyi." In *Narody Dagestana: Sbronik Statei (The Peoples of Dagestan: A Collection of Articles)*, eds. M. O. Kosven and Kh.-M. O. Khashaev. Moscow: Izdatel'stvo Akademii nauk SSSR, 1955, 68–101.

Osmanov, M. O. "Dargintsy." In *Narody Dagestana (The Peoples of Dagestan)*, eds. S. A. Arutiunov, A. I. Osmanov, and G. A. Sergeeva. Moscow: Nauka, 2002, 289–321.

# Dutch

The Dutch (in Dutch: *Nederlanders*) are a Germanic people living in the Netherlands, a constitutional monarchy in Western Europe with some 16.5 million inhabitants. Their homeland is sometimes referred to as Holland, although Holland is only a region within the Netherlands, albeit the cultural, economic, and political center of the Netherlands and one of the most densely populated areas in Europe. Amsterdam, Rotterdam, The Hague, and Utrecht are major Dutch cities. In the 19th and 20th centuries, many Dutchmen emigrated for economic reasons to countries such as New Zealand, Australia, South Africa, Canada, and, particularly, the United States. It is estimated that some 4 million Americans are of Dutch descent, some of them—including presidents Theodore Roosevelt, Franklin D. Roosevelt, and Martin Van Buren—being descendants of inhabitants of the 17th-century Dutch colony New Netherland in present-day New York and New Jersey. Historically, the two most important religions among the Dutch have been the (Calvinist) Dutch Reformed Church and the Roman Catholic Church, though

Protestant dissenters and Jews were significant minorities. Today, the Dutch are one of the most secular peoples in the world. The word "Dutch" has the same etymological origin as Deutsch (German), meaning "those who speak a popular language (and not Latin)." Despite grammatical similarities, Dutch cannot be considered a variant of German, but is rather a proper Germanic language spoken by some 23 million people in the Netherlands, Belgium (by the Flemish), and the Caribbean (in Suriname and the Netherlands Antilles). In South Africa, some 6 million descendants of Dutch colonists speak Afrikaans, a language similar to Dutch.

The word "Netherlands" means "Low Countries," an expression that refers to a geographical area that was bigger than the present-day Netherlands. The flatness of the country and the struggle against the ever-threatening sea are strong metaphors in the definition of Dutch identity. Exemplary are the 17th-century landscape paintings with a high sky to accentuate the flatness, and the major Dutch hydraulic works to protect the country against the sea by a network of dikes. Popular symbols such as wooden shoes and windmills to drain water also represent a nation where people had to adapt to life on marshy ground. Sailing and ice skating are sports with a long tradition in the country, with its abundance of lakes, rivers, and canals, not to mention a long seashore. Although soccer and cycling are commercially more important, no other sporting event arouses more Dutch enthusiasm than the 125-mile-long Elfstedentocht, an ice-skating tour in the northern province of Friesland.

In the Middle Ages, the Low Countries comprised an area roughly equivalent to the present-day Netherlands, Belgium, Luxembourg, and the extreme northwest of France. Located between the German Empire and the Kingdom of France, the Low Countries often fell victim to the expansionist policies of these major military forces. As was the case with northern Italy, the Low Countries were involved in international trade from the early Middle Ages, giving rise here too to wealthy cities such as Bruges, Ghent, and Ypres. These cities used their influence to acquire special rights—so-called "liberties"—from their sovereigns in return for taxes. To underline their privileged status within the feudal society, important cities would build their own belfry, or city tower; it was in these monuments to civic pride that the documents granting their special status were proudly housed.

In the 15th century, the Low Countries formed a political unity under the rule of the (French) Dukes of Burgundy, which were later succeeded by the Habsburg Dynasty. In the early 16th century, the Habsburg Dynasty reached its height with Charles V ruling over an empire "where the sun never sets," from the German Empire, Southern Italy and the Low Countries to the Kingdom of Spain and the Spanish colonies in the Americas and Asia. In order to tighten control over the Low Countries, Charles V, and later his son Philip II, imposed a policy of increasing centralization. The unpopularity of this policy boosted the Protestant challenge to the monopoly of the Catholic Church. The combination of discontent with Philip's policy and anger over the persecution

Dutch girl in Hague rose garden, Holland. (Corel)

of Protestants led to an anti-Spanish uprising in 1566.

The leader of the uprising, Prince William of Orange, relied heavily on radical Calvinist forces (*geuzen*), but also included moderates and even Catholics in his camp. The printing press played an important role in William's propaganda policy, an example being the song "Wilhelmus," the world's oldest national anthem. Although the uprising originally began in defense of traditional liberties, it radicalized in 1581 with the Act of Abjuration, in which the rebellious provinces unilaterally rejected their (Spanish) sovereign. This historical decision, which completely disregarded the political conventions of the time, served as an example to later events of world importance such as the American Revolution and French Revolution.

In consequence of a 1648 peace agreement, the Low Countries were divided. The southern Low Countries remained part of Spain, whereas the north became an independent republic under the name United Provinces of the Netherlands. The Dutch Republic soon developed into one of the most powerful nations in Europe. With the creation of the East India Company (1602) and the West India Company (1621), it became a major player in Europe's colonial expansion.

Itself the result of a war for traditional liberties, the country adopted a tolerant policy regarding ethnic and religious minority groups. This policy attracted tens of thousands of Protestant refugees from the southern Low Countries, Eastern Europe, England, and France, as well as Sephardic and Ashkenazi Jews. It should be said that this tolerance was rarely defended as a matter of principle; it was rather the result of circumstances, inspired by pragmatic and often opportunistic considerations as well as commercial good sense. Protestant dissenters, Jews, and particularly Catholics did not have the same rights as Calvinists, and critical thinkers such as Spinoza or Descartes were confronted with serious difficulties in the dissemination of their ideas. Yet, there was undoubtedly greater freedom in the Dutch Republic than anywhere else in 17th-century Europe.

The Eighty Years' War against Spain as well as the 17th-century Dutch golden age laid the foundations of Dutch (Calvinist) identity. Painting has traditionally been seen as the quintessential reflection of the cultural construction of the Netherlands. Painters such as Rembrandt van Rijn and Johannes Vermeer depict the Netherlands as a nation of proud, self-confident burghers, who cherish such Calvinist virtues as modesty, a strong work ethic, and abhorrence of exuberance. Another famous Dutch symbol, the tulip, refers to the involvement in international trade and the incorporation of foreign elements. The flower was originally imported from Turkey but adapted itself so well to the Dutch soil that it induced an authentic tulip boom. An often oversimplified vision of the Netherlands as the cradle of tolerance, freedom, and critical thinking continues to exist today. Such glorifications of the golden age neglect the dark sides of the 17th-century Netherlands, most notably its involvement in the slave trade.

A joint attack by English, French, and German forces in the disaster year of 1672 marks the end of the golden age. The Treaty of Westminster concluded the war and ceded New Netherland to the English. In 1795, a French Napoleonic army conquered the Netherlands. During the period of French rule that lasted until 1813, the Dutch colonial possessions were "protected" by Great Britain and some (the Cape Colony, Guyana, and Ceylon) were never returned.

In consequence of the lack of centralization, Dutch society never formed a unity. Catholics in particular had difficulties in identifying themselves with the way the Dutch nation had been defined ever since the 17th century. The segregation of Dutch society according to different religions and ideologies is traditionally referred to as "pillarization." From the late 19th century on, Protestants, Roman Catholics, and Social Democrats constituted the three main pillars. These pillars all had their own institutions: from newspapers and youth clubs to brass bands. As the three pillars were roughly of the same size, and a fourth, neutral, nonpillarized group represented an important counterbalance, none of them ever had a realistic chance to take control over the country. Therefore, Dutch society was characterized by politics of accommodation. The elite of each group played an important role as mediators; by reaching compromises behind the scenes, they were able to avoid direct confrontation.

World War II is generally considered to be the second period of essential importance for the formation of Dutch identity. One could argue that while the Eighty Years' War formed the basis of Dutch (Calvinist) identity, it was World War II that truly united the nation. During the German occupation in World War II, 73 percent of the Jewish population was transported to Nazi death camps, the largest percentage in Western Europe. Despite the fact that solidarity with the Jews was rather limited, Anne Frank later became a symbol of the nation's suffering under German rule. The occupation also led to a change in the structure of Dutch society. The fact that all groups were suddenly confronted by a common enemy induced mutual solidarity. Queen Wilhelmina, who led the resistance from her exile in London, became a symbol of this newly achieved unity. Ever since, the color of the monarchy—orange—is prominently present in any celebration of Dutch unity. As Dutch unity was achieved at a time of war, Germany is traditionally seen as the quintessential enemy of the Dutch people. In consequence of the process of European integration, however, anti-German feelings have considerably waned.

After the recognition of Indonesia's independence in 1949, the Netherlands transformed itself from a colonial empire with a predominantly provincial mentality into a small nation with a predominantly international mentality. Whereas the Netherlands had traditionally been considered a profoundly religious country with rather conservative moral values, the country's capital, Amsterdam, and its playful anarchist Provo movement became a symbol of progressiveness. The Netherlands was far more radical than any other country in applying the progressive philosophy of the 1960s to political practice. Whether in the case of same-sex marriage, abortion, or the legalization of soft drugs, prostitution, and euthanasia, Dutch legislators were European front-runners. Simultaneously,

the Netherlands developed into one of the most secular countries in the world.

The 1960s were also the beginning of another important change in Dutch society: the arrival of immigrants. When the colonial era came to an end, thousands of people from the former colonies came to the Netherlands and were given Dutch citizenship. Ever since, these groups have formed important ethnic minorities. Eurasians from Indonesia form the largest of these minority groups. Other ethnic minorities with links to the Netherlands' colonial past are the Surinamese, Moluccans, and Antilleans. The booming economy in the 1960s also urged the need for guest-workers. The first group came from southern Europe (Italy, Greece, Spain, Portugal); later, large groups from Morocco and Turkey followed. Although originally invited for a limited period of time, many guest-workers preferred not to return to their homeland; they were granted Dutch citizenship and given the right to be reunited with family members from their country of origin.

Whereas it was assumed that integration would occur naturally, Muslim communities especially isolated themselves from Dutch society. Several neighborhoods in the largest cities became predominantly Moroccan or Turkish, where a new generation grew up that had to find its way between the traditionalist values of their parents and those of the predominantly secular and extremely liberal Dutch society. These challenges have led to a heated debate on the future of the Netherlands and what it means to be Dutch in the 21st century. The killings of the populist politician Pim Fortuyn in 2001 and the film director

Theo van Gogh in 2004, both known for their critical views on Islam, stirred up emotions. Whereas the focus tended to be on internationalization and the promotion of diversity, this has now shifted to the importance of finding new strategies to foster bonds between the different ethnic and religious groups.

*Jeroen DeWulf*

## Further Reading

Besamusca, Emmeline, and Jaap Verheul, eds. *Discovering the Dutch. On Culture and Society of the Netherlands.* Amsterdam: Amsterdam University Press, 2009.

Buruma, Ian. *Murder in Amsterdam: The Death of Theo van Gogh and the Limits of Tolerance.* New York: Penguin Press, 2006.

Lechner, Frank J. *The Netherlands: Globalization and National Identity.* New York: Routledge, 2008.

Resch, Marc. *Only in Holland, Only the Dutch: An In-Depth Look into the Culture of Holland and Its People.* Amsterdam: Rozenberg, 2004.

Schama, Simon. *The Embarrassment of Riches: An Interpretation of Dutch Culture in the Golden Age.* New York: Knopf, 1987.

Van Oostrom, Frits, ed. *A Short History of the Netherlands.* Amsterdam: Amsterdam University Press, 2008.

# E

## English

The English are native to England, one of the four home nations of the United Kingdom. The population of England at the time of the 2001 census was 51,092,000, which is 84 percent of the total UK population. With 383 people per square kilometer, it is the most densely populated country in Europe; it is also an urbanized country, with more than 96 percent of the population living in towns and cities. Mainland England constitutes the southern two-thirds of the island of Great Britain, bounded by Scotland to the north, Wales to the west, and the English Channel to the south. The capital of England (and the United Kingdom) is London, the largest urban area in Europe, with a population of over 8 million. While the largest English population is in England, there are substantial populations who claim English descent in the United States, Canada, Australia, and New Zealand, all former colonies of the United Kingdom. The English language is widely spoken in these countries but also in the 53 British ex-colonies, now independent states, that comprise the Commonwealth of Nations. The largest religion in England is Christianity, with the Church of England, the official state church, holding a special constitutional position.

The genesis of English ethnicity is complicated and contentious. It has long been held that the English emerged after the Anglo-Saxon invasions of Britain in the 5th–7th centuries. Up until that point a number of British or Celtic tribes vied with the Roman forces of occupation, which had arrived in Britain under the command of Julius Caesar in CE 43. By 750, the Anglo-Saxons occupied most of present-day England. The Celts, speaking Brythonic languages such as Cornish, Cumbric, and Welsh, held on for several centuries in the Southwest, Northwest and Northeast, West Midlands, and Yorkshire. However, from the first Roman invasion up to this time, peoples of what are currently the British Isles mixed and mingled: the population of England cannot be described as purely Anglo-Saxon. The population was later subjected to recurrent raids from Scandinavia, from the Vikings, Danes, and Jutes. A final major invasion took place following the Battle of Hastings in 1066, with an influx of Normans from what is now France. Throughout this period, people from Ireland, Wales, and Scotland further augmented and complicated the "English stock."

The English nation-state began to form when the Anglo-Saxon kingdoms united against Danish Viking invasions, beginning around 800. Over the following 150 years England was for the most part a politically unified entity, and remained permanently so after 927, when Athelstan of Wessex established the nation of England after the Battle of Brunanburh. The

A brass band plays on Victory in Europe Day in Hyde Park, London, England. (Corel)

Norman conquest of England led by William the Conqueror in 1066 ended Anglo-Saxon and Danish rule of England, as the new Norman elite replaced virtually all of the Anglo-Saxon aristocracy and church leaders. Within a century of the invasion the Normans had adopted the English language. Wales was annexed by England by the Laws in Wales Acts of 1535–1542, which incorporated Wales into the English state. In 1328 England recognized Scotland's independence in the Treaty of Edinburgh-Northampton. Catholicism was replaced as the national religion following the English Reformation, instigated by King Henry VIII. The first of the great European revolutions erupted in England in 1642. The English Civil War between Monarchists and Republicans, led by Oliver Cromwell, resulted in the establish-ment of the Commonwealth (1649–1660). The monarchy was restored in 1660, when Charles II was crowned king. Union between Scotland and England was achieved with the Acts of Union in 1707, and the United Kingdom of Great Britain came into being that same year. In 1776, after a decade of conflict, the United States published the Declaration of Independence and the United Kingdom lost its major colony. The United Kingdom of Great Britain and Ireland came into being in 1801 with another Act of Union.

From the 19th century, the history of England is bound up with the history of the United Kingdom. But the economic transformation that came to be called the Industrial Revolution began in and around Manchester in the county of Lancashire, with the rapid growth of the cotton industry.

The value of cotton exports increased from £23,253 in 1701 to £5,406,501 in 1800, and by 1830 cotton exports accounted for just over half of Britain's total exports. These goods were produced almost entirely in England. This facilitated the rapid growth in the British, and therefore English, economy during the 19th century. The 19th century also saw the Anglo-British overseas dominions multiply. During the Imperial Century (1815–1914) approximately 10 million square miles of territory and about 400 million people were added to the British Empire. This was also a time when many major wars were fought—all on foreign territories, in defense of England's (and Britain's) economic interests. War dominated the history of England in the first half of the 20th century, with the country playing a leading role in two World Wars, against Germany and its allies on both occasions. Decolonization was gradual but gained pace after 1945, with many ex-colonial states coming together to form the British Commonwealth.

Since 1536, the Church of England has been the official church in England. Almost all 50 English cities have an Anglican cathedral, and the smallest administrative unit in the country remains the parish. While the British monarch is supreme governor of the Church of England, its spiritual leader is the archbishop of Canterbury. Other significant Christian faiths include Methodism, Catholicism, and Pentecostalism. Muslims make up the largest number of non-Christians, whose ranks also include Sikhs, Buddhists, and Jews. England has a large and growing atheist and agnostic population, like many West European countries.

The patron saint of the English is Saint George, and his day is celebrated on April 23. The national flag of England is a red cross on a white background (St. George's Cross), which forms part of the British flag (the Union Jack). Other significant national symbols include the Tudor rose, the nation's floral emblem; and the oak tree, representing the nation's strength and endurance. The national coat of arms of England, featuring three lions, dates back to its adoption by Richard the Lionheart in the 13th century. While "God Save the Queen" serves as the national anthem of the United Kingdom, England has generally relied upon the hymn "Jerusalem" and the patriotic song "Land of Hope and Glory" to mark historic events.

The English have an impressive tradition in the arts. English painting probably reached its peak in the 18th and 19th centuries, exemplified by Sir Joshua Reynolds, George Stubbs, and Thomas Gainsborough. Print-making reached new heights in the work of William Hogarth. The late 18th century and the early 19th century was perhaps the most successful period in British art, producing William Blake, John Constable, and J. W. M. Turner (1775–1851), who influenced the later impressionists. Significant modern artists include the sculptors Jacob Epstein and Henry Moore and the painters Lucian Freud, Francis Bacon, and David Hockney. Early English architecture is best represented in the great cathedrals. There have been a number of internationally prominent English architects, especially from 1650 to 1850, most notable among them Sir Christopher Wren. More recently, Sir Norman Robert Foster has won acclaim.

The traditional folk music of England is centuries old and has contributed to such forms as sea shanties, jigs, hornpipes, and dance music. Brass bands have always played an important role, especially for the working classes in the industrial towns and mining areas. Important figures in the classical tradition include Thomas Tallis, William Byrd, and John Dowland in the 16th century; in the 17th century, Henry Purcell; in the 18th century, John Gay and G. F. Handel; and in the 19th, Edward Elgar. Since the 1960s, popular music has grown significantly in range and significance. Many contemporary musical genres have origins or strong associations with England, such as hard rock, glam rock, prog rock, heavy metal, mod, britpop, drum and bass, punk, indie, acid house, and some of the most famous of all rock bands are English, such as The Beatles.

England has produced many writers of the first rank. The period of Old English literature provided the epic poem *Beowulf* and saintly hagiographies. The best-known secular prose is the *Anglo-Saxon Chronicle*. Middle English literature emerged with Geoffrey Chaucer's *The Canterbury Tales*. In the 16th century, William Shakespeare emerged as the greatest of all English writers. He wrote more than 30 plays, all of which are still performed today. Aphra Behn (1640–1689) was a prolific dramatist of the Restoration and was one of the first English professional female writers. Some of the most prominent philosophers of the Enlightenment era were John Locke, Thomas Paine, and Jeremy Bentham. More radical elements were later countered by Edmund Burke, regarded as the founder of conservatism. Daniel Defoe published *Robinson Crusoe*, perhaps the first novel written in English, in 1719. The English played a significant role in the Romantic movement, especially the poets George Byron, John Keats, Percy Shelley, William Blake, and William Wordsworth, and the gothic novelist Mary Shelley, who wrote *Frankenstein*. Standing outside this group was perhaps the greatest English novelist of the era, Jane Austen (1775–1817). In response to the Industrial Revolution, agrarian writers looked to find a way between liberty and tradition; William Cobbett, Gilbert Chesterton, and Hilaire Belloc were main exponents. Empiricism continued through John Stuart Mill and Bertrand Russell. The novel developed rapidly in the 19th century (Charles Dickens, Thomas Hardy, the Brontë sisters), while H. G. Wells developed the genre of science fiction and Arthur Conan Doyle pioneered the detective novel with his character Sherlock Holmes (1882–1941). During the 20th century England continued to produce novelists such as Virginia Woolf, George Orwell, D. H. Lawrence, T. S. Eliot, C. S. Lewis, William Golding, Agatha Christie, and J. R. R. Tolkien, author of *The Lord of the Rings*, as well as the playwrights John Osborne, Alan Ayckbourn, and Harold Pinter. Renowned English writers for children include Enid Blyton, Beatrix Potter, Lewis Carroll, Kenneth Graham, Roald Dahl, and J. K. Rowling, author of the Harry Potter series.

The English are a sporting nation and codified many sports in the 19th century that are now played globally, of which football (soccer) is the most popular. Sheffield FC, founded in 1857, is the world's oldest club still playing. The Football Association is the oldest of its kind, and FA

Cup and The Football League were the first cup and league competitions respectively. The Premier League is currently the world's most lucrative football league and is considered one of the best.

The English have been an imaginative and inventive people. The modern scientific method was developed by Francis Bacon. There have been numerous influential English scientists, but towering above them all is Sir Isaac Newton, who developed the laws of motion and gravity and infinitesimal calculus, and Charles Darwin, who developed evolutionary theory. Notable developments include the modern computer (by Alan Turing); the World Wide Web, along with HTTP and HTML (by Tim Berners-Lee); performance of the first blood transfusion; the electric motor; the microphone; steam engines; the seed drill; the jet engine (by Frank Whittle); and many modern techniques and technologies used in precision engineering. The structure of DNA was discovered by Francis Crick and others.

England has had a significant cultural and legal impact on the wider world as the place of origin of the English language; the world's oldest parliamentary system; the Church of England; and English law, which forms the basis of the common law legal systems of many countries around the world. The English have long been pioneers in public education, and the literacy rate is over 99 percent. English universities tend to have a strong reputation internationally in two disciplines: history and research output. The University of Cambridge has produced 83 Nobel Laureates to date.

The English theater is thriving and has been at least since the early 16th century. Several of the most popular English actors have won Academy Awards (Oscars) including Alec Guinness, Anthony Hopkins, Charles Laughton, Laurence Olivier, and Daniel Day-Lewis (twice); and Best Actress, including Vivien Leigh, Julie Christie, Maggie Smith, Glenda Jackson, Helen Mirren, and Kate Winslet. There are hundreds of drama schools in England, among which the Royal Academy of Dramatic Arts is the most prominent. Comedy has been central to popular culture since the heyday of the music hall of the 19th and early 20th centuries. Popular stand-up comics include the double act Morecombe and Wise. Comedy shows, for example, *The Goon Show* (radio) and *Monty Python's Flying Circus* (television), have been described as quintessentially English. In recent years sit-coms such as *Dad's Army* and sketch shows such as *The Two Ronnies* have been very popular. The mass media plays a continuing, significant role in English culture. The British Broadcasting Corporation provides national and local radio stations, as well as considerable foreign broadcasting. Television has become a major focus of popular culture in England. Soap operas such as *Coronation Street* and *East Enders* continue to capture the public's imagination. The English also like police dramas; some of the most popular have been *Inspector Morse* and *A Touch of Frost.*

England's mixed market economy is among the largest in the world. One of the world's most highly industrialized countries, England is a leader in the chemical and pharmaceutical sectors and in key technical industries, particularly aerospace, the arms industry, and the manufacturing side

---

## British Asians

According to the last census (2001), there are more than 2.3 million British Asians in the United Kingdom, 95 percent of which are in England. In the terminology of the British census, British Asians descend from immigrants from South Asia, a population comprised primarily of Indian, Pakistani, and Bangladeshi origins. While the presence of immigrants from the Indian subcontinent dates to the establishment of the East India Company, the largest numbers arrived after World War II to work in factories and the public sector; and also in the 1960–1970s when many Asian merchants left the former territories of British East Africa (or were expelled, as in the case of Uganda). The term British Asian is debated. Some argue it reflects colonial ideology and cite differences in language, religion, and culture obscured by the term. British Asians constitute the UK's largest nonwhite ethnic group, comprising more than 4 percent of the total population and more than half of nonwhite. Their presence is evident in literature, music, cinema, and food, with Chicken Tikka Masala now considered Britain's national dish.

*Jeffrey E. Cole*

---

of the software industry. London is home to the London Stock Exchange, the main stock exchange in the United Kingdom and Europe's largest.

Recent English history is inextricably tied up with British history. Examples include the conflict between Catholics and Protestants in Northern Ireland as well as Welsh and Scottish devolution. The late 1990s saw a resurgence of English national identity, spurred by devolution in the 1990s of some powers to the Scottish Parliament, the National Assembly for Wales, and the Northern Ireland Assembly. A rise in English self-consciousness has resulted, with increased use of the English flag. Opinion polls show support for a devolved English parliament from about two-thirds of the residents of England as well as support from both Welsh and Scottish nationalists.

The English have long been a hybrid nation, and post–World War II immigration, mostly from Commonwealth nations, has continued the trend. Apart from English, the most significant languages spoken in England include Bengali and Panjabi. One result of accelerated immigration was a wave of urban riots that swept through England in the early 1980s. Ethnically, 91 percent of the population chose to self-identify in 2004 as "white," 4.6 percent as "Asian or British Asian," 2.3 percent as "Black or Black British," and the rest as mixed, Chinese, or "other," according to the population survey conducted by the Office of National Statistics. The distribution of ethnic minority groups is far from even. For example, while 2 percent of the population of England and Wales is Indian, the proportion of Indians in the Midland city of Leicester is 25.7

## Black British

According to the last census (2001), there are over 1.1 million Black British in the United Kingdom, with the overwhelming majority living in the London area. In the terminology of the British census, Black British descend from immigrants from the Caribbean, Africa, and elsewhere. In a more inclusive political usage dating to the 1970s, the term refers to all nonwhite Britons, especially those of South Asian and African/Caribbean origins. While the presence of persons of African descent dates to the slave trade, many Black British descend from immigrants from the British West Indies, especially Jamaica, who arrived in the years following World War II. Since the 1980s, most new Black British have arrived from former colonies in sub-Saharan Africa; Black Africans endure the highest levels of poverty of any nonwhite population in the UK. Black British constitute the UK's second–largest nonwhite ethnic group, comprising 2 percent of the total population and about one quarter of nonwhites. Their presence is evident in literature, music, cinema, intellectual life, and sports.

*Jeffrey E. Cole*

percent. As in the case with ethnicity in general, the English are best described as those who consider themselves to be English; while 58 percent of white people described their nationality as "English," the vast majority of nonwhite people considered themselves "British." There has also been considerable intermarriage; in 2001, 1.31 percent of England's population called themselves "mixed," a figure that is likely to grow.

*Peter Collimns*

### Further Reading

Ackoyd, Peter. *Albion: The Origins of the English Imagination.* London: Chatto & Windus, 2002.

Colls, Robert. *Identity of England.* Oxford: Oxford University Press, 2002.

Kumar, Krishan. The *Making of English National Identity.* Cambridge: Cambridge University Press, 2003.

Paxman, Jeremy. *The English: A Portrait of a People.* Harmondsworth: Penguin, 1999.

Young, Robert J. C. *The Idea of English Ethnicity.* Oxford: Blackwell, 2008.

## Estonians

Estonians are the majority population in the Baltic country of Estonia (930,219 according to the general census of 2000, constituting 68.6% of the country's total population). The biggest Estonian diasporas live in Finland (36,000), Russia (30,000), Sweden (26,000), the United States (25,000), Canada (22,000), and Australia (6,300). Less than a third of Estonians define themselves as religious; of those who do, the majority are Lutheran. Although Estonia is one of the three Baltic countries, Estonians are linguistically unrelated to Latvians and Lithuanians. The Estonian language belongs to the Baltic-Finnic branch of the Finno-Ugric group of languages that are unrelated to the Indo-European languages. A Finno-Ugric people, Estonians are closely related to the Finns.

The name "Eesti" (the Estonian word for "Estonia") is believed to derive from "Aesti" (also "Aestii"). This term was allegedly used by ancient Germanic peoples to describe the people who lived in the area located northeast of the Vistula River. The first known reference to the term dates back to CE 98, when the Roman historian Tacitus mentioned it in his treatise *Germania*. In Scandinavian sagas the area south of the Gulf of Finland was called Eistland and its population the *eistr*. Early Latin variants of the name Estonia were Estia and Hestia.

Old East Slavic chronicles referred to early Estonians as Chudes.

The territory of contemporary Estonia was most probably settled at around 8500 BCE, immediately after the Ice Age. Traces of ancient hunting and fishing communities in northern Estonia (near the town of Kunda) constitute the oldest known evidence of settlement in the region. It is not clear what language(s) the early inhabitants spoke, but it is highly probable that by 3000 BCE at the latest, speakers of early Finno-Ugric languages had migrated to Estonia. These people most likely came from the middle Volga region of Russia. Estonian had evolved into a distinct language by around CE 500. By then also a political system had emerged based on patriarchal clans headed by elders. From the 9th century onwards, Vikings sporadically

Five women in Estonian national costume, Estonia. (Corel)

attacked the territory of contemporary Estonia, but these attacks were unsuccessful and the region remained virtually independent until the 13th century.

In the early 13th century, southern Estonia was invaded by German crusaders while northern Estonia fell under the control of the Danish crown (until 1346). Up until 1918 Estonians were subject to various periods of Danish, Teutonic, Polish, Swedish, and Russian rule. The economic and cultural elite during most of that era was predominantly German. The native population was obliged into serfdom that was abolished only in 1816–1819. Subjected to numerous wars and epidemics throughout these six centuries, the number of ethnic Estonians periodically decreased. The decline was most drastic in 1620–1640 when the population dropped to 70,000–100,000.

Estonian ethnic awareness and sense of nationhood are relatively recent. The ethnonym *eestlane* ("Estonian") came into wider usage only in the early 19th century, gradually replacing the term *maarahvas* ("country people"). Garlieb Merkel (1769–1850), a Baltic German Estophile, was the first to describe Estonians as a distinct nationality. The earliest university-educated intellectuals who considered themselves Estonians emerged as late as in the 1820s. Estonian ethnic awareness and nationalist feelings strengthened considerably during the era of Estonian national awakening (*ärkamisaeg* in Estonian) in the second half of the 19th century. On February 24, 1918, Estonia was declared independent.

During the early years of World War II, Estonia was occupied first by the Soviet Union (1940) and subsequently by the Third Reich (1941). An estimated 90,000 Estonians died during the war, about 60,000 during the Soviet and 30,000 during the Nazi occupation. In 1944, Estonia was reincorporated into the Soviet Union. Its cultural and political institutions were reorganized, and Estonian language and culture were heavily suppressed. The majority of the Estonian national elite fled Estonia before 1944 or were imprisoned, deported, and executed. Tens of thousands of Estonians, mostly women, children, and elderly, were deported to concentration camps in Siberia in 1941 (approximately 10,000 individuals) and in 1949 (21,000). Between 1945 and 1989, the share of ethnic Estonians in the total population of Estonia dropped from 96 to 61 percent, primarily lessened by mass immigration from Russia and other parts of the Soviet Union into urban areas and industrial northeast Estonia.

The Estonian language is fairly homogeneous, although historically three groups of dialects, the northeast, northern, and southern, could be distinguished. A distinct feature of the language structure is the contrast of three degrees of consonant and vowel length. For example, the pronunciation of the vowel "u" is short in the word *tuli* (fire), long in *tuuline* (windy), and overlong in *tuul* (wind). Estonian language also has a characteristic Baltic-Finnic consonant gradation, in which consonants alternate in certain contexts. There are 14 cases in Estonian, and these are generally marked by adding suffixes to the noun's stem, although in many cases the root of the noun may also change. Estonian vocabulary has been greatly influenced by loans from German and Russian, and more recently also from Finnish and English.

Cultural and religious influences from Finland and Scandinavia have played an important role in Estonia for centuries. Myths based on animistic beliefs dominate Estonian mythology. According to the ancient Estonian cosmology, the world turned around a tree or a pillar, to which the skies were attached. The pantheon consisted of various deities associated mainly with natural phenomena. Legends about giants (e.g., Kalevipoeg, Suur Tõll) were common and point to Germanic and Scandinavian cultural influences.

Estonians were Christianized in the early 13th century by the Teutonic knights. During the Reformation, Lutheranism spread to Estonia (in 1523). Evangelical Lutheranism is the dominant religion also nowadays, although less than a quarter of ethnic Estonians define themselves as active believers.

Very few literary works in Estonian were published before the 19th century, owing to the domination of Estonia by foreign rulers. The oldest known records of written Estonian can be found in *Heinrici Chronicon Livoniae* (*Chronicle of Henry of Livonia*, 1224–1227) and in *Liber Census Daniae* (*The Danish Census Book*, 1241). Both contain Estonian place and family names. The first known book in Estonian was published in 1525 but was later destroyed. The oldest book of which a few pages have survived until our times is a translation of the Lutheran catechism by Wanradt and Koell (1535). The New Testament was translated into southern Estonian in 1686 and into northern Estonian in 1715. In his translation of the Bible (1739), Anton Thor Helle united the two dialects. During the so-

called Estophile period (1750–1840), literary works in Estonian (mainly moral tales) written by Baltic Germans proliferated. The Estonian national epic, *Kalevipoeg* (*The Son of Kalev*), published in 1857–1861, is partly a compilation of authentic folk tales and partly a creation of Friedrich Reinhold Kreutzwald. The internationally most acknowledged and most widely translated writers in modern Estonian literature are Jaan Kross and Jaan Kaplinski.

Runic (or runo-) singing (*regilaul*) was common in Estonia until the 18th century and is still performed as part of the folkloric tradition. Characteristic of the runic songs are the trochaic four-foot line as its dominant meter, assonance, alliteration, repetition, and parallelism. Estonians often refer to themselves as a "singing nation" for whom singing has not only cultural but also political meaning. The tradition of song festivals (*laulupidu*) dates back to the era of Estonian national awakening; the first song festival was held in 1869. These nationwide events, organized every four or five years, are said to have united the whole nation in its struggle for national independence before 1918 and also during the period of the Soviet occupation. The Estonian independence movement in the end of the 1980s is often referred to as the "Singing Revolution." In September 1988, nearly three hundred thousand Estonians gathered in the Song Festival Grounds in Tallinn to sing patriotic songs.

Today's Estonians are highly urbanized—approximately 70 percent of the population lives in cities or towns. Yet a majority of Estonians maintain at least some rural ties, often possessing a summer cottage that is considered a characteristic feature of Estonian life.

Contemporary Estonian cuisine is not very distinctive; historically it has been highly seasonal and characterized by simple peasant food. The most typical foods include black bread, pork, potatoes, and dairy products.

Out-migration from Estonia has occurred in three big waves. Before the country's independence in 1918, sizable groups of farmers and workers moved mainly to the Russian empire and the United States. The second big wave occurred during World War II. In September 1944, when the Germans retreated from Estonia and Soviet troops returned, approximately 70,000 Estonians fled to the West (44,000 to Germany, 25,000 to Sweden, and 5,000–6,000 to Finland). Many of the refugees later moved on further to Canada, the United Kingdom, the United States, and Australia. Some of the refugees and their descendants returned to Estonia after the nation regained its independence in 1991. The third wave of out-migration from Estonia, still ongoing, started in the late 1980s and has intensified since 2004 when Estonia joined the European Union. It is estimated that 150,000–200,000 ethnic Estonians currently live abroad.

After regaining independence, the proportion of ethnic Estonians in the country's total population has increased from 61 to nearly 69 percent (2000), mainly owing to large-scale emigration of ethnic Russians. However, since 1991 the population growth in Estonia has been negative. The total fertility rate is low (1.4 children born per woman in 2006), and during the two decades of political and economic transition, life expectancy at birth has dropped considerably, especially for men.

*Toomas Gross*

## Further Reading

Hiden, John, and Patrick Salmon. *The Baltic Nations and Europe: Estonia, Latvia and Lithuania in the Twentieth Century*. New York: Longman, 1994.

Lieven, Anatol. *The Baltic Revolution: Estonia, Latvia, Lithuania and the Path to Independence*. New Haven and London: Yale University Press, 1993.

Loit, Aleksander, ed. *National Movements in the Baltic Countries during the 19th Century*. The Seventh Conference on Baltic Studies in Scandinavia, Stockholm, June 10–13, 1983. Stockholm: Almqvist & Wiksell International, 1985.

Petersoo, Pille. "Reconsidering Otherness: Constructing Estonian Identity." *Nations and Nationalism* 13 (2007): 117–133.

Raun, Toivo U. *Estonia and the Estonians*. 2nd updated ed. Stanford: Hoover Institution Press, 2002.

Raun, Toivo U. "Nineteenth- and Early Twentieth-century Estonian Nationalism Revisited." *Nations and Nationalism* 9 (2003): 129–147.

Taagepera, Rein. 1993. *Estonia: Return to Independence*. Boulder, Co: Westview Press.

# F

## Faroese

The Faroese, also known as the Faroe Islanders, inhabit the basaltic North-Atlantic ocean archipelago of the Faroe Islands, about 404 miles (650 kilometers) from the Norwegian west coast. The total Faroese population counts around 60,000 people, of which a quarter live outside the Faroe Islands. The main diasporic population is based in Denmark. The rest of the Faroese abroad, less than 1,000 persons, reside primarily in Norway and Iceland. The native language of the Faroese is a West-Nordic language, closely linked to Icelandic. Faroese language is rooted in ancient Norse, which belonged to the Germanic language group. The Faroese are Christians in faith, of which more than three-quarters are members of the national Lutheran Protestant church. The Plymouth Brethren, an evangelical Christian community, is the strongest of several free churches in Faroese society.

The Faroese are descendants of Vikings from western Norway who settled the Faroe Islands in the early 9th century. Irish monks searching for solitude had inhabited the remote islands for short periods in earlier centuries, but they escaped before the Vikings colonized the archipelago. The Faroese have through language, place-names, architecture, and traditions very close cultural bonds to the Norwegian peasant and fishing communities of their Viking ancestors. The Faroese lived in small autonomous village communities spread out on 17 of the 18 islands comprising the windswept archipelago until the modern era. The Faroese were mainly sheep farmers until large-scale fishing in the 19th century turned a poor feudal agricultural society into a modern industrial society.

The Faroese never had an independent state, but were, because of the peripheral location and small size of the islands, largely self-ruling during long periods in the Middle Ages. The Faroese were subjugated to

Girl in Faroese national costume using a mobile phone during St. Olaf's Day. (Gaja/Dreamstime.com)

Norwegian rule for eight centuries (1030–1816), before they came under Danish control. The Danish influence on the Faroese culture and society has been very deep the last 200 years. In the 1880s the Faroese patriotic movement, with the landowner and politician Jóannes Patursson as leading figure, started its national "awakening project" that mobilized Faroese people to defend their culture and language against Danish imperialism. In 1909 the movement also got a political dimension, when the Independency party (Sjálvstýrisflokkurin) was established as a counteraction against the new pro-Copenhagen Unionist party (Sambandsflokkurin). In 1948 a home-rule resolution was introduced in the Faroe Islands.

The Faroese have a strong cultural identity with the language in its inner circle. The Faroese are usually considered relatively homogeneous culturally, even if there are important subgroups delineated by affiliation to village/region, family, religion, and lifestyle. The rich cultural heritage from the premodern era is mainly preserved through oral traditions, as the written Faroese language was not systematically developed until the mid-19th century. The oral traditions embrace tales, poems, ballads, and songs that have been transmitted from one generation to the next for many centuries. More than 90 percent of the Faroese population is attached to the Christian faith that has totally dominated as a belief system on the islands since the 11th century. The Faroese often split themselves into binary poles regarding belief: on the one side are the believers who belong to a myriad of evangelical free churches; on the other side are the nonbelievers who are modern passive members of the national church.

Paganism, belief in the old Nordic mythology, has no function in Faroese faith today, even if many people identify with heathen Vikings when describing the roots of their cultural identity.

The Faroe Islands underwent a huge societal shift during the second half of the 20th century, a turbulent process of change that has resulted in a culture and people with one leg planted in traditional society and the other in late modern globalized society. The Faroese are indeed Nordic and European people, but they are from the northern outskirts of the continent, hence also somehow untouched by many facets of cultural modernization; for example, remnants of vanished European culture, such as the Faroese ring-dance, still exist in Faroese cultural life. Another essential characteristic of the Faroese is the strong role and function kinship has on the islands, compared to the more individualized egocentric social structure of continental European neighbors. The kinship-based Faroese consider family as the main social and cultural capital needed to succeed in life on the islands.

The Faroese are famous for their excellent skills in navigation and shipping. Faroese sailors work in all the corners of the earth. In many Faroese villages and towns all men of working age are part of local fishing and international cargo ship crews. It is not unusual for mariners to be away from home for four to six months before getting vacation. Children from such families do not spend much time with their fathers, hence the everyday household issues are under their mothers' strict control. The capital of the Faroe Islands, Torshavn, deviates from traditional farming and fishing villages, because Torshavn as the administrative center of society has a strong academic middle-class population working in the service sectors—schools, financial institutions, public offices, and so forth. There used to be a deep contrast between rural and urban lifestyles, but today's youth generation is building bridges across the gap with the help of new technologies of communication and information (such as the Internet).

The Faroese, a small hidden ethnic group and community in a misty northern corner of Europe, lived a silent life without extensive interaction with continental power centers for centuries, but that is not the case anymore. The economic crisis that hit society in 1989–1992 changed the Faroe Islands radically, linking the local economy closely to global financial structures. The 1990s were marked by a restructuring of the collapsed economy as well a growing cultural globalization following the presentation of new electronic media in the Faroe Islands. Today, three essential questions regard the future of the Faroese: Is fish still the gold of the Faroese, or do they need novel large-scale economic ventures? Are young Faroese people still going to turn home after higher education abroad? Are Faroese going to establish an independent state or are they going to stay within the state of Denmark?

*Firouz Gaini*

**Further Reading**

Petersen, Katrin, ed. *The Faroe Islands*. Kopavogur, Iceland: Printskill, 2006.

Powell, F. York. *Faereyinga Saga: the Tale of Thrond of Gate*. Burnham-on-Sea, Somerset: Llanerch, 1995.

Proctor, James. *The Faroe Islands*. Chalfont St Peter: BRADT Travel Guides, 2004.

Schei, Liv Kjorsvik. *The Faroe Islands*. Edinburgh: Birlinn, 2003.

Taylor, Elizabeth. *The Far Islands and Other Cold Places*. St. Paul, MN: Pogo Press, 1997.

# Finns

Ethnic Finns (*Suomalainen*) live mainly in the territory of the modern nation-state of Finland (Suomi), although during the last two centuries many have migrated and Finns now reside in Sweden, Canada, the United States, Australia, and countries around the world. The political borders and the cultural borders of the Finnish nation are not a perfect match. There are approximately 5.3 million residents of Finland (2009), with 93 percent of the population defining themselves as ethnic Finns and 91 percent speaking Finnish as their mother tongue. There is an east-west cultural boundary that is sometimes referred to as the "hard bread" versus "soft bread" distinction. "Hard bread" is the eastern area, Finnish-speaking, with its distinctive social structure and cultural patterns, and "soft bread" is the western area, where Swedish speakers (5.6% of the population) and general European cultural patterns are found. The cultural boundary also extends east and south of the nation-state, to include groups who speak related Finno-Ugric languages, such as Ingrians and Viena Karelians (in Russia) and Estonians. The Saami inhabit the far northern regions of Finland and neighboring nation-states. There is an ancient religious boundary between

Lutherans (82.5% of the population) and the Eastern Orthodox religion, which is found mostly along the eastern boundary and among related ethnic groups in Russia. The boundary of Finland and Russia has changed many times, most recently in 1944, so that the old mercantile city of Viipuri and portions of the territory of Karelia are now in Russia. Finnish-speaking Tampere is an industrial city surrounded by farmland in the central Häme region, and Helsinki, on the southern coast, was designed as the capital city in the early 19th century. In the west, the medieval city of Åbo (Turku) is a center for Swedish-speakers. During the 20th century, there has been a steady migration from the countryside to urban centers, with the expansion of the greater Helsinki region and other towns and cities. It is quite common, however,

for people to maintain a cottage and sauna near a lake in the countryside where they migrate for the summer months.

Based on linguistic and cultural evidence, it is thought that several thousand years ago small groups of hunter-gatherers migrated into the territory from both the west and the east. The Vikings came from the west while Finno-Ugric speakers came from the Urals and parts of Siberia into Europe through northern and southern routes. Some of these northern groups settled in the general region of Finland and Estonia, while some southern groups eventually settled in what is today Hungary. A common cultivating/hunting economy characterized what is called the Early Proto-Finnic Period (about 3,500 years ago), and common cultural traits related to hunting, such as the bear cult, can be found across the

Market Square, Turku, Finland. (Corel)

northern Finno-Ugric cultural area into Siberia.

Historically, the territory between the Scandinavian Peninsula and Russia was a battleground between empires with shifting boundaries. The Finnish population was Christianized by Swedish crusaders in about 1100. In 1323, Finnish territory came under the rule of the Swedish crown as Sweden expanded its power across the region to Russia. The Treaty of Pähkinäsaari in 1323 recognized the east-west divide between the Catholic Church and the Eastern Orthodox Church, which also became a significant cultural border. Gradually, a territory known as Finland emerged, first including only the southwestern area of the present Finland in a treaty signed in 1595, and then expanding to include eastern Finland, in 1616. During the 600-year period of the Swedish Empire's influence, the Lutheran Church was established as the state church (after the Swedish Reformation of 1527), a system of taxation was established, and men were recruited to serve in the Swedish army. Swedish was the language of the empire—and remained the language of bureaucracy until the late 19th century—and Lutheran ministers and civil servants were the local representatives of the Swedish crown. In particular, it was the job of the Lutheran ministers to record all births, marriages, deaths, and movements of the local population in each parish, with the result that one can find some of the earliest population records in the world in this former empire. In 1809, as the result of the defeat of Sweden, the territory of Finland became a Grand Duchy of the Russian Empire, and it remained part of Russia until December 6, 1917, when Finland was granted independence by V.I. Lenin, two months after he led a successful revolution against the Russian Empire.

Empires are characterized by national diversity and the Swedish and Russian empires were no exception. As a result, citizenship and nationality were separate identities, and the Finns continued to regard themselves as Finnish under both empires. While the politics of empire were somewhat distant from the people, the Lutheran Church had a more direct influence through its bureaucratic practices and especially because of the need to translate the Bible into Finnish. It was the job of the Lutheran minister to test his parishioners to ensure that they could read and understand the Bible. Bishop Michael Agricola was the first to create Finnish-language literary texts, with an ABC book in Finnish in approximately 1543, a translation of the New Testament (1548), and a translation of parts of the Old Testament (1551). The first Finnish grammar was produced in 1649.

In the 18th century, Henrik Gabriel Porthan (1739–1804) was the first scholar to collect field materials for a comparative study of Finno-Ugric languages, thus opening the way for several important 19th-century field expeditions to study Finno-Ugric groups in Russia. In 1863, as part of the establishment of a national educational program, Finnish was recognized as a national language. Alexis Kivi began writing poetry, plays, and novels in Finnish; his popular novel, *Seven Brothers*, was published in 1870. At the end of the 19th century it was the mission of ministers and schoolteachers to prepare the rural population, through literacy, for eventual political independence. As a result of this period of activity in the late 19th century, women's suffrage was guaranteed in the parliamentary reform of 1906.

The territory of Finland consists of two-thirds forestland and one-tenth water. In this northern ecological zone, the population in the east and north subsisted mainly by swidden cultivation, hunting and fishing, and forestry, while an agrarian-peasant economy developed in the south and west of Finland. The distinctive patterns follow land and soil types; swidden cultivation— burn beating in forest lands—was suited to regions where field cultivation was not possible. By contrast, the south and west of Finland were characterized by intensive agriculture and animal husbandry. While there were centuries-old iron foundries and pockets of industry and mercantile capitalism, Finnish society was predominantly agrarian before 1950.

Swidden cultivation was suitable to the hilly terrain of eastern and northern Finland and it was typically found in the regions of Savo and Karelia. Trees were burned and crops were planted in the clearances— during the first year rye and barley, in following years, turnips or flax, and after the late 18th century, oats. The clearances also served as pasture for cattle and provided a supply of small game, birds, and berries. Swidden cultivation was labor-intensive and it did not produce much wealth. The basic tools were an axe and a light plough; all other tools were fashioned of wood and stone as needed. It was common practice for a man to walk through the countryside with his axe on his back and work wherever he was needed. The basic social unit was an extended family, which included adopted members and workers and could number several dozen people—up to 100 in some recorded cases. The family farmed, kept cattle, hunted, fished, and gathered. Until the 17th century, families utilized forest land as they needed it, with seasonal trips to fishing saunas on shores of lakes in the summer and trapping routes with saunas in the forest in the winter. As the government began to collect taxes and regulate land and inheritance in the 17th century, a type of house society developed. The house, surrounded by small storage houses, barns, and outbuildings, was named for the man who built it and was headed by both a male (*isäntä*) and female (*emäntä*) head of household. Usually they were a married couple and their sons would inherit the house when the couple became old or at their death. However, if there were no sons, a daughter's husband or another man would be brought in as *isäntä*, and that man would inherit the house. This practice maintained the gendered division of labor and the continuity of the house. The winter and summer solstice marked the calendar year and there was an annual cycle of markets and feast days that were times for arranging marriages and for important social occasions. By the early 20th century, wage labor and new patterns of village life had replaced swidden cultivation and house society.

It was in the context of the culture of these eastern swidden regions that Elias Lönnrot made a systematic collection of Finnish folk poetry about the hero Väinämöinen. From 1831 to 1833, Lönnrot made five field trips to Karelia to collect versions of this poetry. In 1835, he published the poetry as the *Kalevala*, the national epic of Finland (a second and expanded edition was printed in 1849). The *Kalevala* became a politically significant symbol of national culture as well as establishing a method for collecting folk poetry and related genres that became the basis of Finnish folklore studies.

The publication of the *Kalevala* heightened an interest in folk culture and, with the spread of literacy at the end of the 19th century, village teachers, artists, and folklorists were interested in collecting oral traditions. Local people were also encouraged to record these genres in their village (and in local dialect) and send them to the Finnish Folklore Archives in Helsinki, where this extensive collection of primary data is housed. For about 20 years before and after independence, Finnish artists appropriated Finnish folk culture to build a sense of national identity; for example, Jean Sibelius composed the Finlandia symphony. However, the attempt at national identity was not completely successful because there were major class differences, especially between the landed classes and the tenant farmers and landless workers. This tension became obvious shortly after independence in the short civil war in the winter of 1918, and continued for some years after. The nation finally drew together during the Winter War of 1939–1940, when the Soviet Union attacked Finland and the population—where men walked or skied to join the fighting and young women volunteered to help on the front—organized a defense. That war ended with the Soviet Union moving into eastern regions of Finland, but it remains a deeply symbolic war in Finnish historical memory because a unified national effort saved the Finnish nation. These working-class soldiers were the subject of Väino Linna's popular postwar novel, *The Unknown Soldier* (1954). In 1941, this time allied with Germany, Finland reclaimed the eastern territory and again fought with the Soviet Union. Defeated in June 1944, 420,000 people left their homes to be resettled within the newly drawn borders of Finland. This resettlement was the evacuation of Karelia, a territory that is still symbolically significant as part of the cultural region of the Finns.

Finnish folk culture has been transformed into an urban, high-tech society, with a national government that encourages international cooperation. Finland became a member of the European Union in 1995 and laws and institutions have been changed to meet EU regulations. The number of immigrants has risen steadily since 1990—in part related to EU membership—but immigration remains relatively low and is carefully controlled by national laws. The largest immigrant population is Russian while other groups come mainly as refugees or asylum seekers—such as Somalis, Kurds, and Bosnians. Multiculturalism and the practical problems of a multicultural welfare state are popular topics for research and in the media. President Martti Ahtisaari (1994–2000), who earlier served as the UN Commissioner to supervise independence for Namibia, won the Nobel Peace Prize in 2008 for his work in international arbitration. This changing Finnish community is reflected in art and conversation; it is the subject of Aki Kaurismäki's films, *The Man without a Past* (2002) and *Lights in the Dusk* (2006). However, some practices continue with steady repetition: the winter and summer solstice still mark the calendar year, saunas remain central to work and socializing, the cautionary tales of the Kalevala continue to resonate, and social gatherings work best when organized by male and female cooperation.

*Karen Armstrong*

**Further Reading**

Armstrong, K. V. *Remembering Karelia*. Oxford: Berghahn Books, 2004.

Honko, L., S. Timonen, M. Branch, and K. Bosley. *The Great Bear: A Thematic Anthology of Oral Poetry in the Finno-Ugrian Languages*. Helsinki: Finnish Literature Society, 1993.

Sarmela, M. "Swidden Cultivation in Finland as a Cultural System." *Suomen Antropologi* (*Journal of the Finnish Anthropological Society*) 4 (1987): 241–262.

Sarmela, M. *Suomen Perinneatlas* (*Atlas of Finnish Ethnic Culture*). Helsinki: Finnish Literature Society, 1994.

Talve, I. *Finnish Folk Culture*. Helsinki: Finnish Literature Society, 1997.

Virtanen, L., and T. DuBois. *Finnish Folklore*. Helsinki: Finnish Literature Society, 2000.

# Flemish

The Flemish (Dutch: *Vlamingen*), also called Flemings, are a Germanic people living in Belgium, a constitutional monarchy in Western Europe with some 10 million inhabitants. With 6 million people, the Flemish form the majority of the Belgian population. Flanders, the Flemish homeland, is located in the north of Belgium, whereas the French-speaking south of Belgium, homeland of the Walloons, is called Wallonia. Although the Flemish and the Dutch share the same language (Dutch), the mentality is quite different. Flanders is a traditionally Catholic region, while Calvinism shaped Dutch identity. Although since the 1960s religion no longer plays an important role in the increasingly secular Flemish and Dutch societies, the Flemish continue to experience the Dutch as "different." In its written form, there is little difference between the Dutch spoken in Flanders and that of the Netherlands; however, the Flemish speak Dutch with a different accent. Together with the Dutch and the Surinamese, the Flemish form a Dutch Linguistic Union (Dutch: *Nederlandse Taalunie*) in order to handle all issues related to the Dutch language in close collaboration.

The word "Flanders," originally meaning "land near the sea," refers to a geographical area that used to be quite different. By Flanders we mean today the entire Dutch-speaking part of Belgium, whereas in the Middle Ages Flanders was a county, roughly equivalent to the present-day Belgian provinces of East- and West-Flanders, the northwestern part of France (a region called "French-Flanders"), and the southwestern part of the Netherlands (a region called "Zeeland Flanders"). The largest part of present-day Flanders originally pertained to the Duchy of Brabant and the Prince-Bishopric of Liège.

Although Flanders had to accept the king of France as its sovereign, it retained considerable political autonomy. An important characteristic of medieval Flanders was its involvement in international trade, which brought wealth and prominence to cities such as Bruges, Ghent, and Ypres. Their main source of income was the production

People participate in a unity march in Brussels on May 16, 2010. Around 2,000 people have marched for unity in Belgium less than a month before a general election when nationalist Flemish parties will petition for more power to be transferred from the federal state to the regions. Belgium is divided into Dutch-speaking northern Flanders and French-speaking southern Wallonia with bilingual Brussels in between. Sign reads in Flemish, French, and German "Yes, we want to live together." AP/Wide World Photos

of luxury textiles, hence the importance of the cloth halls. During the Middle Ages, there was a constant struggle between the king of France and Flemish cities for more autonomy. This struggle led to several battles, most notably the Battle of the Golden Spurs in 1302 when—for the first time in European history—an army of (French) knights was defeated by an irregular army. In exchange for payment of taxes, these cities negotiated "liberties," or special rights, from their rulers. In celebration of their distinctive status within the feudal order, Flemish cities constructed a city tower, or belfry, to house these prized documents. They also expressed their wealth by building magnificent Gothic churches,

often equipped with a *carillon* (belfry) in its highest tower. Still today, *carillioneur* is considered one of the most honorable professions in Flanders.

In the 15th century, Flanders, as well as the remaining territories of the Low Countries (an area roughly equivalent to the present-day Netherlands, Belgium, Luxembourg, and the extreme northwest of France), formed a political unity under the rule of the (French) Dukes of Burgundy. The Burgundians dedicated a substantial part of their wealth to culture in order to compete for prestige with the king of France. Painting flourished, most notably in the work of the Flemish Primitives. A splendid example is Jan van Eyck's *The*

*Mystic Lamb.* The Dukes of Burgundy deliberately promoted the more obedient Brabant to the detriment of the recalcitrant Flemish cities, hence the choice for Brabantic cities such as Leuven as the first university of the Low Countries (in 1425), Brussels as the administrative capital, and Antwerp as the main seaport.

The unity of the Low Countries was preserved when they became ruled by the Habsburg Dynasty in the late 15th century. This dynasty reached its height with Charles V ruling over a vast empire incorporating the German Empire, the Low Countries, Southern Italy, and the Kingdom of Spain as well as the Spanish colonies in the Americas and Asia. Charles V and later his son Philip II imposed a policy of centralization in an attempt to secure control over the Low Countries. However, dissatisfaction with this policy lent support to the Protestant churches that challenged the monopoly of the Catholic Church. Discontent with Philips' policy and outrage over the persecution of Protestants fueled an anti-Spanish uprising.

The Low Countries were divided following the 1648 peace agreement. The south remained part of Spain, while the north became an independent republic. The Dutch blockade of the river Scheldt, which cut off Antwerp's access to the sea, had dramatic consequences for the southern economy; tens of thousands of people, often members of the economic and intellectual elite, emigrated to the Dutch Republic. Spain reinforced its authority in the south in the context of the Counter-Reformation. This new spirit of Catholic self-confidence reflected itself in the work of the Baroque master Pieter Paul Rubens.

In 1815, the Low Countries were again reunited in consequence of the restructuring of Europe after Napoleon's defeat in Waterloo. This reunification did not last long, as the deeply Catholic south distrusted the northern Protestant King William I; William's language policy favoring the use of Dutch also contributed to the failure. After the separation of the Low Countries, French had become the dominant language of the political elite in the south. A coalition of Francophone and Catholic forces led, in 1830, to an anti-Dutch uprising and eventually the independence of the southern Low Countries that adopted the name "Belgium."

The elites behind the revolution determined that the (only) official language of Belgium would be French, despite the fact that the majority of the population was Dutch-speaking and did not understand French. Only the wealthy Dutch-speaking families—particularly in Brussels—could afford French education for their children, while the poor majority stayed behind as second-rate citizens. The main reason why the northern part of Belgium remained Dutch-speaking was its poverty. Had all people then had access to (French) education, Belgium nowadays probably would be an entirely French-speaking country.

The birth of a distinctive Flemish identity in Belgium can only be understood in connection to the Romantic Movement. As a typical reflection of Romantic nostalgia, a group of intellectuals glorified the Middle Ages and favored the resurrection of the once-powerful county of Flanders. They opportunistically named the entire Dutch-speaking north of Belgium "Flanders" and wanted to prevent its Frenchification. A famous example of the cultural production of this "Flemish Movement" is Hendrik Conscience's novel *The Lion of Flanders* (1838), in which the Battle of the Golden Spurs is interpreted as a Flemish struggle against French domination. His novel inspired both the Flemish flag and anthem.

By the end of the 19th century, the Flemish Movement developed into a pressure group and was particularly successful among members of the Catholic Workers' Movement. At the same time, an economic shift was taking place. In Wallonia, the importance of the once-lucrative metallurgic industry suffered dramatically from competition from the German Ruhr, whereas in Flanders the expansion of the port of Antwerp attracted ever more investors. In 1866, Antwerp was the first city to adopt Dutch as its official language and remained, ever since, a center of Flemish nationalism.

In 1914–1918 Flanders was at the front of World War I; the many casualties are remembered in the poem "In Flanders Fields" by Canadian soldier John McCrae. Both during World War I and World War II, Germany occupied Belgium and tried to win Flemish support by promising further language reforms, including a Dutch-speaking university. Although the large majority of the Flemish Movement refused cooperation, some of its radical members did eventually collaborate. This led to considerable loss of credibility and to harsh repressions after each war. Nevertheless, the dismantlement of the Belgian state as it had been created in 1830 was inexorable. In 1962, a language border between the two communities was officially established. The consequent political reforms divided Belgium into an exclusively Dutch-speaking Flanders and an exclusively French-speaking Wallonia. The city of Brussels remained as the only officially bilingual part of Belgium.

Belgium has thus developed into a patchwork of two opposing interpretations of nationalism. On the one hand, the Belgian state—represented by the federal parliament and the monarchy—still reflects a common, bilingual Belgian identity. The communities, on the other hand, are established according to monolingual criteria. This unusual construction, so complex that it is sometimes referred to as "the Belgian Labyrinth," has in recent years led to several political crises. Whereas Walloons are reluctant to continue the process of dismantlement of the Belgian state, the Flemish, who see themselves as supporting poorer Wallonia, generally favor greater regional autonomy in most government functions. Radical groups, who represent about a quarter of the Flemish population, even demand independence.

The future of Brussels remains uncertain. As Brussels is a historically Dutch-speaking city, located within Flemish territory, Flanders considers it its capital. Yet, as today the vast majority of its population is French-speaking, Wallonia seeks an alliance with Brussels. In view of its international position as capital of the European Union, however, Brussels is increasingly devolving into neither a Flemish nor a Belgian, but a global city.

*Jeroen DeWulf*

## Further Reading

Barnard, Benno, et al. *How Can One Not Be Interested in Belgian History? War, Language, and Consensus in Belgium Since 1830.* Gent: Academia Press, 2005.

Cook, Bernard A. *Belgium: A History*. New York: Peter Lang, 2002.

Deprez, Kas, and Louis Vos, eds. *Nationalism in Belgium: Shifting Identities, 1780–1995*. New York: St. Martin's Press, 1998.

De Vries, André. *Flanders: A Cultural History*. Oxford/New York: Oxford University Press, 2007.

Nicholas, David. *Medieval Flanders*. London/New York: Longman, 1992.

Prevenier, Walter, and Wim Blockmans. *The Burgundian Netherlands*. Cambridge: Cambridge University Press, 1986.

# French

French people are generally defined as the residents and citizens of France, or in some cases, as descendants of former residents of France. As of 2008, there were approximately 66 million people living in metropolitan France and its overseas territories, which include Martinique, Guadeloupe, French Guiana, French Polynesia, New Caledonia, Mayotte, Saint-Pierre-et-Miquelon, and Wallis and Futuna. It is estimated that there are an additional 40 million people of French descent living around the world, principally in the United States, Canada, Argentina, and Brazil. Although people of French descent may consider themselves French, membership in the French nation is usually defined by citizenship and other cultural factors, thus limiting the ability of noncitizens to claim French identity. Since the late 19th century, debates about what defines French identity have divided people into two camps. One view focuses on the role of descent and history in defining who is French, while the other draws on adherence to French values and allegiance to the French nation as key factors in French identity. French is the dominant language among French people; in fact, the use of French is often considered to be a defining feature of French identity. Catholicism is the largest religion among French people, but a slight majority of French people now identify with other religions or with none at all.

Since the end of the 19th century, successive French governments have worked to construct a unitary narrative describing the development of France and of the French people. This narrative sometimes starts as far back as 15,000 years ago, with the people who left cave paintings in Lascaux and other parts of southern France. However, narratives more often begin with the Celtic tribes of Gaul, who settled in most regions of what would become France around 600 BCE. Most of this area was conquered by the Roman Empire around 58 BCE. One of the key figures from this period was Vercingetorix, a Gaulish chief who was defeated by the Romans at the Battle of Alesia. His ability to unite Gaulish tribes is often invoked as a precursor to the unification of France today. The plucky—but fictional—character of Asterix, chief of a Gaulish village that successfully resists the Romans, has also contributed to the manner in which this period is invoked as a part of French history. Roman rule, which lasted for nearly 500 years, helped established economic ties across the region, began linguistic unification (although French per se did not exist at the time), and began the spread of Christianity.

As the Roman Empire weakened in the 5th century, Gaul was invaded by a series of barbarian tribes including most notably the Franks, from whom the name "France"

French youths run past the Arc de Triomphe during Armistice Day ceremonies in Paris. (AFP/ Getty Images)

eventually came. Perhaps more significantly, the Franks established two dynasties that ruled much of Gaul until the end of the 10th century. The Merovingian and Carolingian dynasties began the work of unifying Gaul and contributed several notable figures to French national mythology. These include Clovis, who made Paris his capital and who reinforced the country's allegiance to the Catholic Church, Charles Martel, who defeated an Arab invasion in Poitiers in 732, and Charlemagne, who established what would become known as the Holy Roman Empire and presided over the development of very close ties between the church and state. These rulers and their dynasties have become important symbols in modern identity narratives in France, but it is important to note that the people who lived in Gaul under their rule did not identify as French, did not speak French,

and from a cultural perspective had significant differences among themselves.

The beginnings of a distinctly French state—as opposed to dynasties more interested in rebuilding the Holy Roman Empire or regional fiefdoms—are usually attributed to the monarchy of Hughes Capet, which began in 987. Over the following seven centuries, Capet and his successors expanded the territory under French control and established the idea of France as a distinct country, differentiated from England or Spain, and strengthened the state. The city of Paris grew significantly as the center of state power. Kings such as Phillip II and St. Louis (Louis IX) expanded and consolidated French control over much of the territory that is part of France today. The French monarchy also launched a number of crusades during this period, violently enforcing the Catholic faith within

France as well as waging war in the Holy Land and further linking the French state with the Catholic Church. In the early part of the 15th century, Joan of Arc, a peasant girl, helped organize an army to defeat the English, encouraged King Charles VII, and was eventually burned at the stake. Her story became one of the founding myths of French identity, drawing together both the monarchy and the commoners and illustrating the tension between French nationalism and allegiance to the Catholic Church. The identity of France as a Catholic country and the close ties between the Catholic Church and the state were reinforced during the Reformation and Counter-Reformation, most notably during the reign of Henri IV, a Protestant who converted to Catholicism upon ascending to the throne. Yet French Catholicism took on a particularly national character, as French kings and their ministers—including those affiliated with the Catholic Church, such as Cardinal Richelieu, prime minister for Louis XIII in the 17th century—asserted the interests of the French state over those of Rome.

By the second half of the 17th century, under the rule of Louis XIV, the French state had become very centralized. This was symbolized by the gathering of the nobility at Versailles and by the development of a large and ramified bureaucracy devoted to maintaining a standing army, imposing taxes, and tracking the population by recording births, marriages, and deaths. The spread of literacy in the 17th and 18th century, combined with the development and popularization of enlightenment thinkers and writers (including Voltaire, Rousseau, Montesquieu, and Diderot, among many others) contributed to the growth of a significant public sphere in which vigorous political, scientific, and philosophical debate contributed to a growing sense of French identity. These debates helped undermine the legitimacy of the monarchy and, along with other factors, contributed to the French revolution that began in 1789.

The combination of a heavily centralized state, the growth of a public sphere, and the events of the French revolution together set the framework within which French identity would be defined and imposed on the population over the next century. During the 19th century, successive French regimes would struggle over the creation of an ideological and symbolic framework that continues to define French identity today. The 19th and early 20th centuries were marked, in France, by tensions between the Catholic Church and the French state. The execution of the king during the revolution of 1789 and the eventual secularization of the state under the French republic were viewed as illegitimate by the Catholic Church. However, by the early 20th century, secularism became a key part of French identity. The development of public education, especially under the French Third Republic (1870–1940), provided an additional key symbol and a tool for establishing French identity. The national education system created a free, secular, and obligatory school system for all French people and, in the process, provided a common set of ideas about what it meant to be French. Education served as an important tool for creating a national identity separate from the church. Military service also served in the 19th and 20th centuries as a key tool for persuading men that they were, in fact, French, by bringing them together with other men from all over the country and by promising upward mobility through service. Finally, the 19th and 20th centuries were marked by the development of the French overseas empire. Education and propaganda surrounding the empire provided French people with a context through which they could develop ideas about what it meant to be French, while drawing contrasts with peoples from around the world who were not French.

One of the central conflicts in French society—a conflict that has endured since the end of the 19th century—concerns whether French identity is produced through the institutions of the republic or if it is rooted in territory and history. A strong centralized French state existed long before the majority of people in France shared a language or other customs and before many thought of themselves as French. Scholars have suggested that French identity became more widespread beginning at the end of the 19th century, although many also believe that considerable diversity of identities and cultural practices continued well into the 20th century, making a unified sense of Frenchness a relatively recent phenomenon. The creation of a national education system at the end of the 19th century has long been cited as one of the primary factors contributing to the unification of France around Republican values. These values include equality, social solidarity, and freedom, along with a broader list of human rights included in the Declaration of the Rights of Man and of the Citizen, a version of which has been part of every French constitution since 1789. The schools also contributed to the spread of the French language and literacy and promoted social mobility. Secularization is also usually invoked as a central Republican value. Public schools are not only promoted as secular spaces, they have long been thought of as one of the main institutions competing with the Catholic Church for the allegiance of the population.

Education in French values is, thus, one manner of making French people. Schools contribute to this by spreading literacy, but also by teaching a view of French history that, from the early monarchy through to the French revolution and the later republics, inevitably results in today's secular republic. Through most of the 20th century, children learned about French history and territory through a book, *Le Tour de La France Par Deux Enfants* (*The Tour of France by Two Children*), that told of the voyage around France of two orphaned refugees from German-occupied Alsace-Lorraine seeking their uncle. Through their story, children learned about to think of the country as a unified whole. Used in public schools until the 1950s, this book marked generations of French people and remains popular today. The French state also uses monuments, cultural institutions, and public rituals to continue to promote the idea of a unified French society. Celebrations around July 14 (Bastille Day) are extensive all over France each year, and the state sponsors many other festivals celebrating aspects of French history and culture throughout the year. Museums and other monuments are heavily subsidized and frequently produce exhibitions that promote French history and culture. Indeed, since the 18th century, the French state has made the promotion and preservation of French language and culture (in both the artistic and national sense) a central part of policy. This mission is pursued today by a large and well-funded Ministry of Culture.

## Alsatians

Alsace, the easternmost province of France, is home to the Alsatians, the French nation's largest and wealthiest ethnic group. For centuries, Alsace had been called the "crossroads of Europe"; today its capital, Strasbourg, is called the "capital of Europe" with reference to the presence of many important European Union bodies and other pan-European institutions. The Protestant/Catholic division, shifts in national identities, and a steadfast provincial allegiance have all shaped Alsatians' sense of self. Alsatians are French nationals but not ethnically French, and while they are Germanic in language and share some cultural history, they are not ethnically German. In Alsace, two distinct systems of identity operate: the French, which ascribes identity on the basis of culture/language use, and the Alsatian (i.e., Germanic), which emphasizes blood, or descent. Politically, Alsatians vote liberal and socialist locally but conservative in national referenda. The "Alsatian paradox" may best be understood as the combination of an internally heterogeneous society whose members nevertheless unify in reaction to external interests and threats.

*Atwood D. Gaines*

Horn blowers at Kientzheim Wine festival, Alsace, France. (Corel)

Although the population is overwhelmingly urban, people in France frequently evoke rural roots. For some, ties to the land—and to history—are central to defining French identity. The historic, linguistic, and cultural diversity of France is considered to be part of the cultural wealth of the country that only people with French roots can understand. However, the French government has developed narratives and policies that bring this perspective into the national identity narrative, by claiming that the diversity of France's regions contributes to the strength of the unified whole. Symbols of French identity, such as cuisine, are often identified by their regional ties, whether for specific dishes or through the wide variety of cheeses, wines, and other foods produced in France. The concept of *terroir*, which refers to the idea that the land, climate, production methods, and even the local culture can be tasted through certain foods, has become central to this idea of French identity in recent years. Similarly, regional languages, traditional forms of clothing, sports, and other customs have been brought into museums that celebrate the popular culture of France and have been incorporated into the national educational curriculum. Even sports events—most notably the Tour de France bicycle race—are used to promote the idea that France's regional diversity contributes to the unified national whole.

If the French state largely succeeded, by the middle of the 20th century, in creating a unified sense of French identity, that identity has, since World War II, faced a number of significant challenges. The French experience in World War II—the collapse of the French military at the beginning of the war and the subsequent collaboration with the German occupation—raised questions about the commitment of French leaders to the values promoted by the republic. Debates about the meaning of this history for contemporary French people are ongoing in the early 21st century.

The demand for self-determination by countries colonized by France and the subsequent decolonization process began, in the 1950s, to undermine the idea that French identity was universally desirable and that it could be adopted by people anywhere in the world. The violent war waged by the French in Algeria (1954–1962) and the exile of thousands of colonists to metropolitan France after the war left a deep and bitter legacy that is still debated, in particular because it highlighted France's failure to live up to its commitment to human rights.

The postwar era was also marked by three decades of rapid economic growth and an expanding population. France assumed a prominent place in world affairs and, as a part of the developing European Union, became part of one of the world's largest economies. Although the growth of the EU contributed to unprecedented wealth in France, it also challenged French people (and other Europeans) to rethink the very idea of national identities. As more and more aspects of economic and social policy are handed off to the European Union—including symbols of national identity, such as currency, with the development of the euro—the framework of the nation-state seems less central to identity formation.

The postwar era was also marked by the migration to France of millions of workers,

## Algerians in France

Approximately 3 million residents in France, or 5 percent of the total population, have family ties to Algeria, a French settler colony from 1830 to 1962. While French law bans the collection of ethnic or racial data, scholars estimate 1.5 million French Muslims are of Algerian origin, roughly evenly divided between Arab and Kabyle (Berber) ethnicities. Another 1.5 million trace their ancestry to *harkis* (Muslims who gained French citizenship by fighting against Algerian nationalists), Algerian Jews, and *pied noirs* (European settlers) who were repatriated to France after Algerian independence. Algerian Muslim men began arriving in France at the end of the 19th century as labor recruits. Algerian soldiers and factory/construction workers later aided the French war efforts and postwar reconstructions, and many eventually settled with their families in the housing projects of Paris, Lyon, and Marseille. Immigrants were active in anticolonial nationalism and suffered harsh police repression. The wounds of the Algerian war remain open today, and Algerians in France, although generally French citizens, still suffer from racism and anti-immigrant discrimination alongside other French Muslims.

*Paul A. Silverstein*

many from former French colonies. Although France has long been a country of immigration (there were also large labor migrations to France, mostly from southern and eastern Europe, in the 1920s), postwar migrants have been the object of ongoing racism and have been seen by many intellectuals and policy makers as more difficult to assimilate than previous waves of migration. Religion is often cited as one of the central issues that renders the assimilation of postwar immigrants difficult. In France, public debates focusing on young women's head scarves in schools—perceived as a symbol of Islamic piety—have been the subject of especially fierce debate. Confronted with racism and discrimination, the children of immigrants have themselves turned to ethnic activism and sometimes to confrontation with

authorities. Although they are usually French citizens, they feel as if the republic has failed to make good on the promise of equality and solidarity in exchange for adopting French values.

France today is still notable for its strong centralized state, its robust political institutions, and its vigorous public sphere. The education system is still focused on making young people into French people through the promotion of French civic values. Many state policies, from education to culture, are designed to assert the ideals of the republic and persuade people of the value of being French. However, the growth of supranational institutions like the European Union, the circulation of globalized media and other products, and the confrontations and debates over how the descendants of immigrants will fit into French society all

## French Antilleans

Between 400,000 and 500,000 people with roots in the French overseas departments of Martinique and Guadeloupe live in metropolitan France. They may be referred to as Antillais, Martinicans, Guadeloupans, noirs, or blacks, among other terms. Antilleans who were born or lived for an extended period in the Caribbean often speak Creole, but French is their dominant language. Most Antilleans in France are Catholic and they are more likely to participate actively in religious life than other French. Although Martinique and Guadeloupe have distinct if related cultures in the Caribbean, within France the experience of racism and discrimination has pushed people from both islands to develop a common identity. Since the 1980s, activists in metropolitan France have sought to organize Antilleans as an ethnic group with a distinct cultural life and particular interests, including the promotion of Creole language and Caribbean music and arts. They hope that recognition of Antillean culture and history within French society will promote equality and reduce racism.

*David Beriss*

contribute to the perception that French identity is, today, increasingly fragile.

*David Beriss*

### Further Reading

Beriss, David. *Black Skins, French Voices: Caribbean Ethnicity and Activism in Urban France*. Boulder, CO: Westview, 2004.

Birnbaum, Pierre. *The Idea of France*. M. B. DeBevoise, trans. New York: Hill and Wang, 2001.

Braudel, Fernand. *The Identity of France*. Vol. 2: *People and Production*. Siân Reynolds, trans. London: Collins 1980.

Brubaker, Rogers. *Citizenship and Nationhood in France and Germany*. Cambridge: Harvard University Press, 1992.

Haine, W. Scott. *The History of France*. Westport, CT: Greenwood, 2000.

Noiriel, Gérard. *The French Melting Pot: Immigration, Citizenship, and National Identity*. Geoffroy de Laforcade, trans. Minneapolis: University of Minnesota Press, 1996.

Weber, Eugen. *Peasants into Frenchmen*. Stanford: Stanford University Press, 1976.

## French-speaking Swiss

The French-speaking Swiss account for roughly 1.5 million people, about 20 percent of the Swiss national population of 7,630,605 (2008). Most live in Romandy—the French-speaking part of Switzerland. Four of Switzerland's 26 cantons (Geneva, Vaud, Neuchatel, and the Jura) are effectively monolingual in French, and three others (Bern, Fribourg, and Valais) are also French-speaking but bilingual with German. These French-speaking cantons (*La Suisse romande*) have a common language and culture, and Roman Catholicism is widely practiced. The French-speaking Swiss could perhaps best be described as an ethnolinguistic group living within a contemporary state structure that is organized as a federal republic. Although Switzerland has four official languages—German (the primary language of 64%), French (20%), Italian (7%), and Romansch (less than 1%)—most Swiss do not fluently speak more than two languages and one of these is now often English.

The historical origins of the French-speaking Swiss can be traced back to the region having been conquered by the Roman Empire in 58 BCE. Switzerland was part of the Roman Empire for nearly five centuries, and the Romans established Latin as the local vernacular language. After the fall of the Empire, various Germanic tribes, culminating with the Franks, controlled Switzerland as it eventually became part of the Holy Roman Empire in 1032. The German-speaking groups dominated the central parts of Switzerland, while what later became the French-speaking population was based in the western zones. In 1291 three German-speaking cantons joined together as a mutual defense and free trade league to form the first Swiss Confederation. This confederation expanded as other city-states and alpine communities became members, and between the 14th and early 19th centuries, French- and Italian-speaking cantons also joined for a range of political and economic reasons. Switzerland was for a brief time part of the Napoleonic Empire, and its present borders and neutrality were guaranteed after the Congress of Vienna in 1815. The Constitution of 1848 codified Switzerland's decentralized state structure and the use of the referendum as a political decision process.

In terms of historical political economy, Switzerland lacked access to the sea, abundant arable land, most natural resources, and a colonial empire, so until the 19th century it was one of the poorer countries in Europe. Tourism in the mid-19th century started to fuel economic prosperity. During the early 20th century, manufacturing of high-value goods (electrical machinery, food products, watches, textiles) contributed to economic growth. After World War II, a combination of tourism, banking, insurance, financial services, industries like chemicals and pharmaceuticals, and a concentration of international organizations' bureaucracies has helped to make Switzerland one of the world's richest countries. Switzerland's state structure developed as a federal model where the individual cantons have a great deal of autonomy within the confederation. This political economy of wealth-generating capitalism and political decentralization has helped guarantee political and social stability within a multiethnic and multilingual nation-state.

Throughout Switzerland's history, religious differences (Protestants versus Catholics) have caused more conflict than linguistic differences. The French-speaking Swiss are predominantly Roman Catholic, while the German-speaking population is fairly evenly divided between Protestant and Catholic religious affiliation. While overt ethnic conflict among the different linguistic groups is limited, there is some degree of ethnic stereotyping between the two largest groups. German-speaking Swiss tend to view themselves as industrious and efficient while French-speaking Swiss often perceive Germans as aggressive, arrogant, and overly serious. The German-speaking Swiss, on the other hand, generally view the French-speaking Swiss in a more positive light by attributing qualities such as "relaxed" and "friendly" to the Francophone population. Traditionally, knowledge of German was important for successful careers in business or national-level civil service, but this is perhaps less true today. Language rights are guaranteed by the Swiss constitution for all four groups.

Canton Jura represents one interesting but complex case study of ethnoregionalist competition and conflict in Switzerland. Jura is primarily French-speaking and Catholic. At the Congress of Vienna in 1815, it became administratively part of the canton of Bern, which is mostly German-speaking and Protestant. However, the northern districts of the Jura are Catholic and have a strong linguistic and cultural connection with France, while the southern districts are Protestant and have a stronger political and religious affiliation with the canton of Bern. Both the northern and southern districts resisted linguistic assimilation into the German-speaking majority. Following World War II, a political autonomy movement emerged that called for the creation of a separate, French-speaking, unified Jura canton. After a long struggle—which included some sporadic violence—several elections were held that finally established the Jura as a separate canton within the Swiss nation-state in 1979. The southern part of the Jura region, however, chose not to join the newly created canton and remained part of Bern. Political discussions continue up to the present about reuniting the southern Bernese Jura districts with the canton of the Jura. This example shows that ethnic and linguistic intergroup relationships in Switzerland are significantly affected by differences based on religious affiliation.

Although Romandy is not an official regional division in the Swiss political system, it does symbolically represent and unify the French-speaking population of the country. Several television channels provide French-language programming to the Romande community. The French vernacular dialect in Switzerland was originally Franco-Provençal, but this variant is no longer widely spoken. Contemporary Swiss French is very similar to standard spoken French, apart from accent and some specific words and expressions.

Ethnic identity among the French-speaking Swiss is complicated by its connection to "Swissness" or Swiss national identity. Swiss society is conceptualized as being founded on an intention to stay together without having a common language or religion ("unity, but not uniformity"). Swiss society has a myth-history narrative about its own origins, a shared political philosophy based on external neutrality, cantonal autonomy, national referendums, and extensive militarization for national defense, as well as the typical symbols of nation-states, including anthems, a flag, passports, currency, and sports teams. French-speaking Swiss have their own territory, language, culture, and customs, and they have a far deeper cultural, social, and ideological connection to France and the broader global Francophone community than Swiss Germans have to Germany or other German-speaking communities. In contemporary Switzerland, French-speaking Swiss are far less likely to learn German in school than in the past, German-speaking Swiss have largely stopped learning French, and the most common second language in the country is now English, reflecting the primacy of that language for global media and commerce. The political, economic, demographic, and linguistic future of the French-speaking Swiss population can best be understood in connection with the larger national and global processes of social change, which are always difficult to predict.

*David Maynard*

## Further Reading

Bouvier, Nicholas, Gordon Craig, and Lionel Grossman. *Geneva, Zurich, Basel: History, Culture and National Identity.* Princeton, NJ: Princeton University Press, 1994.

Butler, Michael, et al. *The Making of Modern Switzerland.* New York: St. Martin's Press, 2000.

Jenkins, John. *Jura Separatism in Switzerland.* Oxford: Oxford University Press, 1986.

Zimmer, Oliver. *A Contested Nation: History, Memory and Nationalism in Switzerland, 1761–1891.* New York: Cambridge University Press, 2003.

# Frisians

Frisians (*Frisons* in French, *Friesen* in German, *Friezen* in Dutch) are a recognized language community in the Netherlands. Their homeland, Frisia (*Friesland* in Dutch, *Fryslân* in Frisian), situated in the northwest of the Low Countries, is surrounded to the west, north, and east by the waters of the Wadden Sea (Waddenzee) and the Ijsselmeer. It is bordered to the east by the province of Groningen and to the southeast by Drenthe and Overijssel. The Wadden islands of Vlieland, Terschelling, Ameland, and Schiermonnikoog are also part of the modern province of Frisia. In 2009, Frisia counted 646,318 inhabitants, making it one of the least densely populated provinces in the country. Frisia's population is distributed over 20 rural communities and 11 cities, of which only its capital Leeuwarden (Ljouwert in Frisian) comes close to 100,000 residents. In 2004 approximately 440,000 inhabitants or 60 percent were native speakers, a reduction by one-third since 1976. Frisians are not striving for some sort of political autonomy. Rather, Frisia derives its identity from being the only Dutch province with its own language. Frisian was officially recognized in a 1989 agreement, and since then provincial administrative institutions have used it as their primary language; since 1997 all place names have been written in Frisian. Currently 80 percent of the province's schools use both Frisian and Dutch as the language of instruction, making the area effectively bilingual. More than half of the population have no religious affiliation, while 30 percent describe themselves as Protestant, 6 percent Catholic, and 2 percent Muslim. Until World War II the agrarian sector represented about half of all economic activities. Despite the dramatic postwar demise of farming, the region still derives its identity as well as a significant amount of economic activity from the land. There are also small numbers of Frisian speakers in extreme northwest Germany, where Frisian is a recognized minority language.

Though the Roman historian Tacitus distinguished between Frisia Maiores and Minores at the northern limes of the Roman Empire, the historic inhabitants cannot be considered ancestors of the modern Frisians. Deteriorating climatic conditions and a rise of the sea level caused depopulation of the coastal areas in the fourth through sixth centuries. In the late fifth and sixth centuries this vacuum was largely filled by the Jutes and Anglo-Saxons, who settled in the coastal region of the Low Countries and Lower Saxony in Germany on their way to England. Developing a strong sense of independence, this amalgam was united under the legendary king Redbad, who founded a Frisian seaborne empire in the seventh century. Unable to withstand Frankish expansion, the Frisians were eventually incorporated into the empire of Charlemagne around 800. After the disintegration of the Carolingian empire, the Frisian lands stretched from the river Zwin in Northern Flanders to the Weser in Germany. Frankish rule also witnessed the gradual Christianization of this larger Frisia. About 400 years later Frisia was dotted with rich convents organizing the cultivation of large agricultural areas.

Danish and Dutch expansion in the 12th century reduced larger Frisia to the northern coastal strip of the Low Countries and Lower Saxony. In this area the idea of the so-called Frisian liberty, which was to be identity-defining for the centuries to come, flourished. The idea that the medieval Frisia was to remain free of any overlord was derived from a privilege supposedly issued by Charlemagne, stating that the Frisians were not to recognize any overlord but the German emperor. The absence of a sovereign overlord made Frisia a feuding society where petty nobles continuously struggled for regional political power. The appointment of a representative of the Habsburg Empire as a ruler in Frisia in 1498, accepted as a means to halt the unbridled warfare that was paralyzing Frisian society, meant the de facto end of its liberty.

The idea of Frisian liberty gained new momentum during the Dutch revolt against Spain, which led to the formation of the Republic of the United Provinces in 1581. Within this federal constellation, Frisia enjoyed considerable administrative autonomy, which found an expression in the 200-year rule of a dynasty of Frisian stadholders (*stadhouder* in Dutch). Illustrative of Friesland's autonomous status was that its stadholder remained a servant of the Frisian Estates (normally, the stadholder served as the king's representative, but there was no king in the Republic). The estates were composed of representatives from the rural and urban communities who appointed the stadholder and provided him with detailed instructions. The Frisian Estates remained powerful until the French occupation of 1795. Friesland definitely lost its federal status after the foundation of the Dutch kingdom in 1815. Since then regional rule stands under the aegis of the national parliament and is coordinated by the Provincial Estates, consisting of elected regional representatives. The estates are headed by a deputy of the king (or queen), first called a governor and since 1850 a commissar, who is nowadays appointed by the Dutch parliament. The adoption of democratic parliamentarism in the 19th century might have prevented the rise of militant Frisian political parties, but the increasing awareness of Frisian language and culture resulted in the founding of the Frisian movement. From the beginning, the movement, which focuses on the preservation of Frisian language and culture, has counted supporters among all mainstream political parties and religious currents. A Frisian National Party has existed since 1966, but it only operates as a regional opposition party without any influence on the national level.

Like German, English, and the Scandinavian Languages, Frisian has its roots in the Ingaevonic, or North Sea German, languages. A forerunner of modern Frisian was introduced by the Jutes and Anglo-Saxons. Old Frisian, as we know it from medieval legal texts, shows many Old English and Old Saxon features. It lost ground to the Frankish language since Merovingian times in the west of the Low Countries. By around 1500 Saxon dialects had taken over in the former Frisian-speaking regions of Groningen and Lower Saxony, reducing the Frisian-speaking area to what is nowadays approximately the province of Frisia, the linguistic island of Saterland in Lower Saxony, and the extreme northwestern coastal region at the German-Danish border. With the introduction of centralized governmental structures around 1500 in Frisia, Old Dutch, which has Frankish roots, was declared the official administrative language. Being reduced to a minority language only spoken in rural areas, the fate of Frisian seemed to be sealed with the rise of the modern national state in the 19th century. A strong counter-movement, inspired by 19th-century Romanticism, sparked its revival as a spoken and written language. The end of the century saw the birth of a standardized Frisian language, which was modernized in 1879, 1945, and 1980. Besides the standard language, four dialects are spoken in the rural regions. Inhabitants of the major urban centers practice a mixture of Dutch and a distinct urban dialect of Frisian.

Frisia's history is closely linked to the rise of Protestantism during the 16th and 17th centuries. In 1580, during the Dutch revolt against the Spanish Habsburg monarchy, the lower German Reformed church was officially declared the only public church in Frisia, meaning that only members of this church were allowed to fulfill public functions. Catholicism and Anabaptism were denounced but nonetheless tolerated as their supporters constituted a majority of the Frisian population for more than a century. Catholics and Anabaptists remained important religious communities until well into the 18th century. After 1834, may Frisians denounced the public church for its loose interpretations of religious dogma and turned toward a stricter Protestant reformism or to the Catholic Church. As elsewhere in the Low Countries, the Protestant and Catholic Church had to cope with strong secularizing tendencies since 1960. As a result, traditional religious communities now only represent a (large) minority in Frisia. The immigration of Turkish and Arabic speakers has seen a rise of Islam, but its influence remains very limited.

Despite the contributions of the 17th-century poet Gysbrecht Japix, Frisian literature only gained maturity under the influence of 19th-century Romanticism. The then-rising Frisian movement owed much of its success to the work of the Halbertsma brothers and their decisive contributions to the reemergence of the Frisian language and literature. In the decades around World War I many considered the Frisian cultural heritage (which had strong agrarian roots) inferior to the Dutch language and literature. This changed after World War II, but acceptance of Frisian culture went along with a shift from being autonomous to being integrated into national and international developments. Music, art, and literature now follow the national and even global trends and are only seldom specifically Frisian. Frisia has its own Scientific Academy, founded in 1938, focusing on Frisian language, history, and social sciences. As a region living under constant threat of sea level rise through the ages, it derives much identity from the landscape. As a land of lakes, terps, and dikes, its landscape was determined by this ongoing struggle. Popular sports like sailing and skating reflect the close link with local lakes and canals. Famous is the 200-kilometer long-distance skating race connecting Frisia's 11 cities, an event that evolved from a heroic event for diehards to a national media spectacle as winter conditions allow it. Its maritime traditions are reflected in the annual *skûtjesrace*, in which 11 traditional freight sailing ships compete. Smaller sports like *Fierljeppen* (canal jumping with a vault) and *kaasten* (a ball game) are typical Frisian sports without leagues outside the province. Frisians never developed their own dance or music, but still adhere to a lively Frisian pop and theater scene.

Despite the arrival of immigrants from Turkey, North Africa, and the Netherlands Antillians in the 1960s through the 1980s, Friesland has actually lost population as the native-born have departed and birthrates have declined. This trend is nowadays only partly compensated for by higher life expectancy figures. Bad economic prospects have not only caused many Frisians, especially the young, to settle outside the province, but also have had a negative impact on the arrival of foreigners. In 1993 only 1.4 percent of the Frisian population was of foreign origin (counting 150 nationalities), while the Dutch average had reached 5 percent.

*Hanno Brand*

## Further Reading

Frieswijk, J., et al., eds. *Geschiedenis van Friesland 1750–1995* (*History of Frisia, 1750–1995*). Amsterdam: Meppel, 1998.

Heidinga, H. A. *Frisia in the First Millenium: An Outline*. Utrecht: Matrijs, 1997.

Hemminga, P., ed. *De Aktueele steat fan Fryslân* (*The Contemporary State of Affairs in Frisia*). Ljouwert: Fryske Akademy, 2001.

Mahmood, Cynthia Keppley. *Frisian and Free: Study of an Ethnic Minority of the Netherlands*. Prospect Heights, IL: Waveland Press, 1989.

Munske, H. M. (ed.). *Handbook of Frisian studies*. Tübingen: De Gruyter, 2001.

van der Schaaf, Sjoerd. *Skiednis fan de Fryske biwegung* (*History of the Frisian Movement*). Ljouwert: De Tille, 1977, republished 2010.

# Friulians

Most Friulians live in Friuli-Venezia Giulia, a region situated in northeastern Italy that was given autonomous status by the 1947 Italian Constitution. The Friulian language, known to speakers as *Furlan* or *Marilenghe*, is of Latin origin and belongs to the Rhaetian subgroup of Romance languages. It is sometimes called Eastern Ladin, since it shares the same roots as Ladin, another Rhaeto-Romance language spoken mainly in the Dolomite area. The Friulian language is predominantly spoken in the provinces of Udine, Pordenone, and Gorizia, but Friulian speakers can be found also in the province of Trieste. According to the Euromosaic study initiated by the European Union, 526,000 out of 1,219,000 inhabitants of Friuli Venezia Giulia use Friulian on a daily basis; unofficial figures estimate 700,000 Friulian speakers throughout the region, making Friulians the majority group in their own region. Nowadays Friulian is spoken more in rural areas than in the cities. Another 170,000 Friulian speakers live elsewhere in Italy, making Friulian the second largest domestic minority language (after Sardinian) in Italy. People of Friulian origin can be found all around the world; most descend from people who emigrated between World War I and World War II. The largest communities of Friulian migrants can be found in North America, with Toronto considered the fourth largest Friulian city in the world (after Udine, Pordenone, and Gorizia). Other large communities have settled in Argentina, Australia, France, and Germany. In big cities Friulian migrants have founded clubs called *Fogolar Furlan* ("Friulian hearthstead") or *Famee Furlane* ("Friulian Family") in order to promote Friulian culture, history, and language. Smaller communities can be found in many other countries. After 1880 Friulians moved to Romania (then part of the Austro-Hungarian Empire), where they worked mainly as craftsmen or in the quarries near the town of Greci. The primary religion of Friulians is Catholicism. In 1998 the Italian Episcopal Conference approved the Friulian translation of the Bible and the Catholic Church recognized the Friulian language as an official liturgical language in 2001.

The origins of Friulians may be traced to the Carni, a population of Celtic origin who settled in the northeast Italic peninsula in 400 BCE. In the second century BCE the area was conquered by the Romans, who founded the city of Aquileia in 181 BCE and later (50 BCE) the Forum Julii (market of Julius), the present-day city of Cividale del Friuli. The contracted name of Forum Julii (Friuli) gave the name to the whole surrounding area. Around 7 BCE the region belonged to the *Regio X Venetia et Histria*, one of the 11 regions into which Caesar divided Italian territory. Allegedly, during the Roman hegemony the Latin language

Family gathers outside home in Italy's northern region of Fruili. (AP/Wide World Photos)

used by the conquerors incorporated elements of the local language. Indeed, some sources claim that Fortunatianus, Bishop of Aquileia from 342 till about 357, wrote commentaries on the Gospels in *sermo rusticus* (the peasant language, which was a combination of Aquileian Latin and the native tongue) because the native people did not understand standard Latin.

After the fall of the Western Roman Empire the Friulians underwent a period of transition under Odoacer, Theodoric, and Justinian until the Lombard invasion in 568, when Cividale del Friuli (previously Forum Julii) became the capital city of their first duchy on the Italian peninsula. During their two-centuries-long domination, the Lombards strongly influenced Friulian artistic and cultural heritage as, for example, in the use of zoomorphic motifs in ornamental compositions or the architecture style of Ara of Rachtis, the Baptistere of Callisto, and the Tempietto Longobardo in Cividale del Friuli. In 776 the Friulian area passed to Charlemagne.

Starting from about CE 1000, Friulian culture flourished during the period of German Patriarchs. On April 3, 1077, Friuli was granted autonomy and sovereignty by the Holy Roman Emperor and German King Henry IV, who conferred the ducal title over Friuli to the Patriarch of Aquileia Sigeart von Beilstein (1068–1077) and his successors. The Patriarch Marquard von Randeck (1365–1381), who had studied canon law in Bologna, gave a deep impetus to the institutional life of the duchy, collecting all previous laws in the *Constitutiones Patriae Foriiulii* (Constitution of Friuli Homeland) that remained in force until 1797.

The Friulian duchy, named Patrie dal Friùl, enjoyed its political independence until June 6, 1420, when the Republic of Venice took it. The Friulian parliament, established in the 12th century, lasted until 1805, but its powers were very limited in its last four centuries. Ultimately, the Patriarchate of Aquileia was suppressed by Pope Benedict XIV in 1751 and replaced by the two archbishoprics of Udine and Gorizia, in order to end the conflicts between the Republic of Venice and the Austrian Empire, which were fighting each other in the Friuli region. The Republic of Venice was defeated by Napoleon Bonaparte in 1797 and, together with other territories, Friuli was delivered to the Austrian Habsburgs according to the Treaty of Campoformio. In 1866 the main part of Friuli came under control of the newborn Italy (1861), but the eastern part (area of Gorizia) joined Italy only at the end of World War I (1918).

The renaissance in the Friuli region under the German Patriarchs also influenced the Friulian language. Most scholars agree that its development dates back to about CE 1000 at the same time as the dialects of the Vernacular Latin (called Vulgar Latin), even if the first written evidence of Friulian is found in administrative documents only from the 13th century. During the 1300s literary works in Friulian (e.g., *Frammenti Letterari*) started to emerge, and commercial, administrative, and legal documents considerably increased. From 1300 onwards, translations from Friulian into Latin were recorded among the exercises assigned at the Schola notariorum (college of notaries) in Cividale del Friuli. On a notary document of 1380 can also be found the ballad *Piruç myo doç inculurit* (probably meaning "My sweet, colored pear"), written in the ancient language spoken at the time in Cividale del Friuli and whose author is assumed to be notary Antonio Porenzoni. There is some evidence that Dante Alighieri's *De Vulgari Eloquentia* (De vulg. eloq. I, 11, 6) makes reference to the language spoken by the people of Aquileia and Istria. Under the German Patriarchate the coexistence, on one side, of Latin and German as official languages and, on the other side, of Friulian as an unofficial language marked Friuli as a multilingual area. Important authors in Friulian include Ermes di Colloredo (1622–1692), Pietro Zorutti (1792–1867), and Pier Paolo Pasolini (1922–1975). Among contemporary Friulian writers mainly writing in Italian is Carlo Sgorlon (b. 1930).

The Friulian minority does not live in a state of isolation, and its members are active in almost all spheres of the society. They take part in the broader Italian culture and society even as they maintain Friulian culture. The protection of cultural traditions is promoted through a wide range of cultural activities and festivals celebrated during the year, as, for example, the *Fieste de Patrie dal Friul* on April 3 for the commemoration of the foundation of the Friulian duchy in 1077, or the Pignarûl, a bonfire ceremony, presumptively of Celtic origin, taking place on January 6. There are also radio and television stations in the Friulian language, such as Radio Onde Furlane and Telefriuli.

Although Friulians have successfully preserved their own culture from foreign dominators since the 15th century, especially in daily, informal relations in the rural areas, they were never officially acknowledged as a people or ethnic minority by the Italian government. It was only on March 22, 1996, that the regional law (number 15) of Friuli Venezia Giulia was passed to protect and promote the Friulian language and culture "as an essential part of the ethnic and historical identity of the regional community" (section 1). This law also established the Regional Observatory for the Friulian language and culture (Italian acronym OLF), later replaced by the Regional Agency for the Friulian language (Italian acronym ARLeF) in 2004. In 2007 this regulation was complemented by another regional law (number 29 in 2007), which has done much to promote the use of the Friulian language through, for example, providing certificates of competency in the Friulian language, erecting bilingual street signs in Friulian and Italian, and permitting use of Friulian in various government offices and proceedings. The Italian parliament passed a 1999 law (number 482) protecting the language and culture of the "historical linguistic minorities," among them people "speaking Friulian," which marked the state's recognition of Friulian as a language effectively used in everyday life. This law also granted financial support for projects promoting the use of Friulian language in, for example, the appointment of Friulian-speaking front-desk officers at the public university.

*Barbara Giovanna Bello*

## Further Reading

Coluzzi, Paolo. *Minority Language Planning and Micronationalism in Italy.* Bern: Peter Lang Publishing, 2007.

Ernst, Gerhard, Martin-Dietrich Gleßgen, Christian Schmitt. and Wolfgang Schweickard. *Romanische Sprachgeschichte 2 / Histoire des Langues Romanes 2 (History of Romance Languages 2)*. New York: De Gruyter, 2006.

Francescato, Giuseppe. *Dialettologia friulana (Friulan Dialectology)*. Udine: Società Filologica Friulana, 1966.

Williamson, Robert Clifford. *Minority Languages and Bilingualism: Case Studies in Maintenance and Shift*. New York: Ablex, 1991.

# G

## Gagauz

The Gagauz (*Gagauz*, pl. *Gagauzlar*) adhere to the Greek Orthodox faith and speak a Turkic language closely related to modern Turkish. Most Gagauz live in their own autonomous region of Gagauz Yeri in southern Moldova (147,500 according to the 2004 census); they inhabit 27 villages there and are clustered in and around the cities of Comrat, Ceadîr-Lunga, and Vulcaneşti, making up 83 percent of the region's population. Other Gagauz are found in southern Ukraine (32,000), where they settled in the 1860s in the vicinities of Odessa and Zaporizhia; in Russia (12,000), especially in the region of Rostov, but also in the region of Tyumen, district of Khabarovsk, Moscow, and St. Petersburg; as well as small contingents in Kazakstan (700) and probably still in Uzbekistan (240). There are also a few Gagauz still residing in Belarus (200), Latvia, Estonia (30), and Georgia. Others live in Dobrogea in southern Romania (2,500 to 3,000) and northern Bulgaria (perhaps 1,400 to 5,000), especially near and in Varna, Kavarna, and Balchik. Only a few hundred have retained their mother tongue in Bulgaria. Outmigration of Gagauz to Turkey, before 1989 for political reasons, nowadays for economic motives, has decreased the number of Gagauz in the Balkans. A small immigrant population of Gagauz, estimated at 2,000, lives in the United States. Some émigrés settled in Canada and Brazil, but no information is available on them. There are also small minorities that call themselves Gagauz living in scattered villages near the town of Nea Zichni in Greek Macedonia (3,500) and in the Edirne region in the European parts of Turkey (15,000). A group of émigrés from the Turkish side lives in the suburbs of the Greek city Nea Oresteida, making up a large portion of the inhabitants in the city. Their relationship with other Gagauz in Moldova and Bulgaria is not clear. In the early 20th century other groups of Turkic-speaking Orthodox Christians—not categorized as Gagauz—lived in Central Anatolia (so-called Karamanlis) and in Mariupol in southeastern Ukraine. Most of these have moved to Greece and are now assimilated in the majority population.

There are several theories, more or less colored by national aspirations, about the origin of the Gagauz. Bulgarian sources argue, for example, that they are Turkified Bulgarians, while Greek sources view them as Turkified Greeks. Another theory claims that the Gagauz have an Anatolian origin. According to this so-called Seljuk hypothesis, the Gagauz are descendants of Seljuk Turks who settled in the eastern Balkans and converted to Christianity in the 13th century. Native Gagauz historians in Moldova usually support this theory. Other scholars advocate the so-called steppe hypothesis, postulating that the Gagauz descend from Bolgars and Cumans,

Local women walk on a muddy road in Chirsova village, south of Chisinau, in the Moldovan autonomous region of Gagauzia March 23, 2007. The Gagauz, a Christian community, settled in this part of Europe after they fled Ottoman rule in what is now Bulgaria. They proclaimed their autonomy in August 1990, but moves to establish a separate administration were suppressed by Moldova until it finally granted the Gagauz self-rule in December 1994. (AFP/Getty Images)

pre-Islamic Turkic tribes pursuing a nomadic existence in medieval times in the Black Sea region and the Balkans. Recent genetic studies provide some support for the Seljuk origins of the Gagauz. Mixed marriages are common with fellow Orthodox Christians among Moldovans, Bulgarians, Russians, and Ukrainians.

Historical records show that many Gagauz began to leave their areas in the Ottoman Balkans for Russia during the wars in the second half of the 1700s. These Christian refugees settled down north of the Danube Delta, near the cities of Bender and Ismaïl. When Bessarabia became Russian in 1812, the Russian state for geopolitical reasons encouraged Gagauz to settle in the border regions in the northeast of present-day Romania. The Gagauz continued to migrate from the Balkans until the majority of them had left the old country. Most Gagauz subsisted on cattle raising and other forms of animal husbandry.

During the so-called Stolypin agrarian reforms in the early 20th century many Gagauz settled in Kazakstan, and in the 1930s, another group moved to Uzbekistan. In 1940, Moldavia became integrated into the Soviet Union and was recognized as a republic within the union, remaining so until its independence as the Republic of Moldova in 1991. The Gagauz received status as a nationality in the Soviet Union. In the early 1960s the language was used in schools, but was soon suspended. During the new open policy in the mid-1980s, it was possible to use the language in schools again.

The cultural awakening was headed by the Gagauz People's Movement. In the late 1980s, glasnost brought more freedom also in Moldova, and in this context, the Gagauz became more radicalized. Already before the collapse of the Soviet Union, Gagauzia was trying to achieve a form of sovereignty. In autumn 1990 it tried to separate from Moldova and establish a 16th Soviet republic. The Gagauz separatist movement was headed by the road engineer Stepan Topal. This movement did not succeed and the area still belongs to Moldova. A referendum in 1991 resulted in 95 percent of votes for independence, but it was declared illegal by the Moldovan government.

On January 24, 1994, the parliament of the Republic of Moldova passed the law, On the Special Legal Status Gagauz Yeri, establishing the autonomous region of Gagauzia. This new form of self-determination for the Gagauz was based on the two principles of ethnicity and territory and won great approval in Europe. It is governed by its own legislature and has its own constitution. Viniculture, cattle breeding, and agriculture make up the foundation of the area's economy. Autonomy and increasing self-awareness have sped up the cultural revitalization of the Gagauz people in Moldova, and also elsewhere. Turkey has in many ways supported this process. Widespread political instability and corruption are major problems for the autonomous region. The Gagauz in Moldova remain mainly rural, although increasing numbers are found in the cities.

Gagauz are Orthodox Christians and members of the autocephalous Orthodox churches in their countries of residence. Translations of parts of the New Testament into Gagauz have become available through foreign Bible societies in Latin, Greek, and Cyrillic script.

The Gagauz speak a Turkic language that belongs, together with Turkish, Azeri, and Khorasan Turkic, to the southwestern or Oghuz branch of Turkic. It is closely related to the Turkish dialects spoken in the southern Balkans, but it also contains elements of northwestern Turkic. Modern Gagauz, which contains a lot Russian and Moldovan loan words, is divided between two main dialects: central and southern Gagauz. Most Gagauz in Moldova and elsewhere in the former Soviet Union are bi- or trilingual. Until recently the language was confined mostly to the family sphere, but it is now used increasingly in schools, government, and the media. Increasing contact with Turkey has also encouraged the interest in the mother tongue. Nowadays it is the official language of Gagauz Yeri, along with Russian and Moldovan. (In Ukraine, Gagauz is recognized officially as a minority language, but in other countries where Gagauz live it receives no protection or support.) From 1957 Gagauz was written with the Cyrillic script (previously they used the Greek and Latin alphabet, although very few publications were available). Since 1996 Gagauz has been written with a 32-letter Latin-based alphabet. It is taught in schools, teachers' colleges, and high schools as well as in Comrat State University. The contemporary culture of the Gagauz is represented by theaters and musical and folklore groups as well as newspapers, books, and modern media. There is a Gagauz ethnographic museum in the village of Bešelma.

*Ingvar Svanberg*

**Further Reading**

Güngör, Harun, and Mustafa Argunsah. *The Gagauz: A Handbook.* London: Curzon Press, 2000.

Menz, Astrid. *Endangered Turkic Languages: The Case of Gagauz.* In *Language Death and Language Maintenance*, eds. M. Janse and S. Tol. Amsterdam: John Benjamins, 2003, 143–155.

Svanberg, Ingvar. "Gagavouzika and Juručki." *Central Asiatic Journal* 32, nos. 1–2 (Wiesbaden 1997): 109–116.

# Galicians

Galicia (sometimes spelled "Galiza" by Galician nationalists) is one of Spain's 18 legally recognized "autonomous communities." (It should not be confused with the similarly titled region that lies between present-day Poland and Germany.) The region's administrative center is the city of Santiago de Compostela (approximately 90,000 inhabitants); its biggest cities are the ports of Vigo (280,000 inhabitants) and A Coruña (240,000). The region is home to some 2.75 million inhabitants. The region's population is aging, and in recent years the number of deaths in the region has on occasion exceeded the number of births. As a result of trans-Atlantic migration in the 19th and 20th centuries, more than 1 million Galicians live abroad, with significant Galician communities in Argentina (particularly Buenos Aires) and in Cuba. Some still follow the old pattern of returning to Galicia for their retirement. Two languages are officially recognized in the region: Castellano (or Spanish) and Galego, a Romance language that shares many common features with Castellano and Portuguese. Estimates of language use in the region vary, and have recently been the subject of some political debate. It is probably accurate to state that most Galicians have extensive ability to speak both Castellano and Galego, and often show an unusual ability to code-switch languages, even in mid-conversation. Galego is used frequently as a teaching language in schools and universities, but there with many exceptions. The majority religion is Catholicism; there are no significant religious minorities. Contemporary Galician identity is defined by a number of overlapping features: a common experience of underdevelopment, identification with Galego (which is not necessarily the same as a proficiency in the use of the language), and shared political and administrative experience as an autonomous community since 1980. Alongside these factors, a looser sense that Galicia can be defined as a Celtic region should also be considered, although—unlike Brittany, Wales, Scotland, the Isle of Man, and Ireland—there is no convincing evidence that a Celtic language was ever the dominant language in this region.

Like other areas of Spain, Galicia experienced multiple incursions by invading and migrating groups during the classical and medieval periods. The archaeological evidence of the castros, prehistoric hill-forts built two thousand years before the Christian era, suggests some significant connections with Celtic cultures elsewhere in Europe. Later Roman incursions were superficial, limited to the formation of an exploitative proto-aristocracy in the region. The Suebes, a tribe from present-day northwest Germany, dominated the region in the 5th century; they converted to Christianity in 429 and were defeated by Visigoths in 456. Moors conquered the region after 714, but only appear to have ruled it for a few decades. The region then came under the control of the neighboring Asturian monarchy, the only part of Iberia that was never conquered by the Moors. In the 9th century, a legend established the site of the tomb of Saint James in Galicia. A new church was constructed there in 899, and the site acquired the name of Santiago de Compostela, derived from either *campus stellae*, field of stars, or *compostum*, burial ground. From the 10th century to the 14th century, this was the preeminent Christian shrine in Europe; it became a symbol of the Reconquest of Spain by new Catholic princes and brought pilgrims and tourists to the city. Thus the first substantial formation of shared identity in the region was constructed around Catholic themes.

Galicia fared less well in the new Christian Spain created in 1492. While its population continued to expand, it was isolated from the centers of Spanish power. The Spanish ships that crossed the Atlantic from the 16th to the 18th centuries left from the southern port of Cadiz, not from Galicia. Relative to other Spanish regions, Galicia became a financially poor and poorly educated agricultural region, dominated by a backward-looking aristocracy and an intolerant church.

In 1764, a liberalizing program, initiated by Charles III, permitted ships to sail from A Coruña to Havana, a measure that was later extended to other Galician ports. The west-facing port cities grew substantially in the succeeding decades. By the 19th century there was a clear contrast between the mass of Galicia's population, living in small, scattered hamlets in inland, mountainous areas and the more cosmopolitan ports. Electoral corruption, a conservative church, and a bewilderingly complex form of land ownership that isolated tenant-farmers on ever-smaller plots of land prevented any substantial reform movement growing in the countryside. Life in scattered hamlets shaped the development of artisanal trades: in place of specialization, the norm was the milmaña, the thousand-handed, multiskilled farmer-artisan. Many Galicians saw migration as their salvation, and an estimated 2 million Galicians may have crossed to Argentina and Cuba between 1836 and 1960. The majority of the migrants were male: some Galician hamlets and villages were therefore run by women, establishing a rural ideal of strong women who could run their households and communities without male direction.

Some dissident and protest movements grew in the 20th century. Republican and later socialist and even anarchist movements were formed in the western cities. Galician nationalism had more varied roots: some democratic and republican strands developed in the cities, but there was an important current of early 20th-century Galician nationalism that developed in the smaller, easterly, towns, which was conservative and antidemocratic in character. The husband and wife team Manuel Murguía (1833–1923) and Rosalía de Castro (1837–1885), respectively a rather deterministic historian and a lyrical poet, were prominent in publicizing and promoting the cause of Galician culture. Murguía's thought resembles developments among other conservative liberal thinkers in Europe: an increasing fascination with biological themes as the defining features of human communities. Castro is different: her poems and lyrics present an eloquent depiction of some of the social problems afflicting Galician society. She wrote with a rare passion about the "migration widows," left by their husbands in the villages. These dissident political currents grew significantly during the Spanish Second Republic (1931–1939), but none of them were strong enough to prevent the rapid conquest of Galicia by rebel generals and ultra-right groups in July 1936.

The Francoist dictatorship (1939–1975) ended the cultural innovations of the Second Republic. (Franco [1892–1975] was born in the Galician port of El Ferrol, but never showed any great sympathy or interest for his homeland.) Castellano (Castilian) was declared to be the sole legal public language. While there were significant moves to crush the use of Basque and Catalan, both associated with the Republican cause, Galego—the language of a conservative region—was less of a target. During the 1940s and 1950s it could be said that the communities of Galician exiles, particularly in Argentina, were more politically representative of Galicia than the repressed and silent towns, villages, and hamlets of the region. The Galician nationalist writer and artist Alfonso Castelao (1886–1950) finished writing his *Sempre en Galicia* (*Forever in Galicia*) in Mexico and Argentina. While retaining the passionate love for Galego and Galician culture expressed by earlier nationalists, Castelao also spoke of the need for a democratic ethos. Galician opposition to the dictatorship grew bolder in the 1960s and early 1970s. There was a revival of cultural nationalism, a series of angry, quasi-insurrectionary strikes, and the formation of two rival strands of ultra-leftist Galician nationalism: one based on an increasingly leftist social-democratic movement, the second inspired by Maoist themes.

Following the establishment of the Autonomous Community and a regional parliament—the Xunta—in 1980, Galicia has largely been run by conservative political groups, which have accepted some aspects of Galician cultural nationalism. One particularly gifted conservative political leader is Manuel Fraga (1922–), who began his political career as a Francoist minister. He was prominent in the creation of the Partido Popular (PP), which developed as Spain's main right-wing party in the 1980s. In Galicia, Fraga led the PP into a policy of working with the Xunta and promoting Galician culture. The PP enjoyed an absolute majority in the Xunta from 1989 to 2005. Substantial challenges to its position have been slow to emerge.

In fact, it was not until 2002 that Galicia's political structures began to change. In November 2002 the Prestige oil tanker sank 149 miles (240 kilometers) off the Galician coast. Despite warnings from experts, no preparations were made for the subsequent oil slick, which represented a significant threat for Galicia's fishing and tourist industries. An angry protest movement—*Nunca Máis* (Never Again)—was formed, and on December 1, 2002, more than 200,000 people marched in protest in Santiago, the largest demonstration in Galician history. The movement represented an exhilarating mixture of ecologists, Galician nationalists, and leftists. In June 2005, a coalition of the PSOE (Spanish Socialist Workers Party) and the BNG (Galician National Bloc) won the regional elections, the first nonconservative government in the region's history. Their victory proved to be short-lived: as the international economic downturn began to affect the region, voters turned back to conservative cultures. In March 2009, the PP was returned to power in the Xunta.

*Sharif Gemie*

**Further Reading**

Gemie, Sharif. *Galicia: A Concise History*. Cardiff: University of Wales Press, 2006.

de Núñez Seixas, Xosé, ed. *La Galicia Austral (Southern Galicia)*. Buenos Aires: Biblios, 2001.

Roseman, Sharon. "'Strong Women' and 'Pretty Girls': Self-Provisioning, Gender, and Class Identity in Rural Galicia (Spain)." *American Anthropologist* 104, no.1 (2002): 23–37.

Villares, Ramón. *Historia de Galicia (History of Galicia)*. 2nd ed. Vigo: Galaxia, 2004.

# Georgians

The Georgians, who call themselves Kartvelians, predominantly live in Georgia, which they call Sakartvelo. The name Georgia is linked to the Arabic (Gurji) and Persian (Gurjistan). Georgia lies to the south of the Russian Federation along the Caucasus Mountains, which form at least part of its northern border. Turkey and Armenia border Georgia to the south, Azerbaijan to the east. Western Georgia has a Black Sea coastline. There are an estimated 4 million Georgians worldwide. The 2002 Georgian census reported 3.6 million Georgians; the 1989 Soviet census reported 3.8 million in the Georgian Socialist Republic. Russia houses the largest Georgian diaspora at 200,000; Georgians also make up the third largest national population of migrants in Russia. Georgian minorities also live in Azerbaijan, Ukraine, Kazakhstan, Turkey, and Iran. The primary language of the Georgians is Georgian (Kartvelian), of the South Caucasian language family. The Georgian cultural identity has several dimensions, both linguistic and regional. The Svans, Laz, and Mingrelians generally self-identify as Georgian but speak different and not mutually intelligible Kartvelian languages. The Svans and Mingrelians live in Georgia (in the Svaneti and Samegrelo regions, respectively), and the Laz reside in northeastern Turkey. Other Georgian regional populations, for example Gurians or Pshavians, maintain unique cultural, historical, and dialectical characteristics, although virtually all speak Georgian natively. Most Georgians identify Orthodox Christianity as their religious affiliation, although there are some Sunni Muslim and Catholic Georgians.

Historians report a proto-Georgian civilization in the Transcaucasus during the Bronze Age (2000 BCE to 1200 BCE) and

Woman sweeps a street in Tbilisi, Georgia. (Corel)

have found evidence of early settlements as far back as 5000 BCE. The Georgian chronicles link the first Georgian tribes to Targamos, grandson of Japeth, son of Noah. Although historians speculate that some of the genealogies found in Georgian histories may be attempts to conform to biblical accounts, they do note that two proto-Georgian tribes, the Tibal and Mushki, existed during the 12th century BCE and are likely to be the Thubal and Mosoch tribes mentioned in the Bible's book of Ezekiel.

Western and eastern Georgia, divided by rivers and mountain formations, followed divergent historical paths. Western Georgia (currently Abkhazia and Imereti) was known as Egrisi and included the kingdom of Colchis, noted in the ancient Greek texts of Strabo and Herodotus. Eastern Georgia in ancient times continued the kingdoms of Iberia and Kartli (current day Mtskheta, Kvemo Kartli, Shida Kartli, and Kakheti). The shifting circumstances of the Georgian kingdoms depended on the rise and fall of surrounding empires. Before the Common Era, Georgia was variously held by the Hittites, Babylonians, Assyrians, Romans, and Persians, among others. In the sixth century BCE, Parnavazi, the first Georgian king, united several eastern tribes to form Kartli-Iberia and established a protofeudalist society. Western Georgians faced greater challenges from the Greek, Roman, and Byzantine armies that sought to control the Black Sea coastline and the trading routes linking Europe to Asia. The Romans reestablished their authority over both western and eastern Georgia by 64 BCE.

For centuries, great empires criss-crossed Georgia and made its kings their vassals. The Romans and Persians competed for control of Transcaucasia, both cultures leaving an impact on the Georgian nation. Roman influence gave way to the Byzantine empire, which likewise vied with the Persians for control and the loyalty of Georgian kings. In the 6th century, Arab forces joined the competition, as did the Khazars (8th century) and the Seljuk Turks (11th century). These opposing imperial interests kept the kingdoms of western and eastern Georgia from unification until the 12th century, when they were joined under the leadership of King David the Builder (Davit Aghmashenebeli), who increased Georgian state territory and diminished the influence of Islam. David's great-granddaughter Tamara (Tamar Mepe) expanded Georgia's power, wealth, and prestige by establishing clients in neighboring states and demanding tributes. The arrival of the Mongol Horde in the 13th century, after her death, put an end to Georgia's greatest epoch. Afterward, the Georgian state dissolved into disparate kingdoms, which were once again dominated by rival states. The Georgian kings began strengthening their ties to the Russian tsars in the late 18th century, which helped diminish the Ottoman and Persian influences. Georgia became a protectorate of the Russian Empire in the early 19th century.

The 1917 revolutions in Russia propelled Georgia into independent statehood in 1918 but the Red Army captured the state in 1921. Joseph Stalin, a Georgian native, played a role in Georgia's Soviet accession as well as helped shape its position in the Soviet Union. The collapse of the USSR paved the way for Georgian independent statehood in 1991. Georgia's first president, Zviad Gamsakhurdia, was elected in October 1990 but was overthrown in a coup in December 1991. Gamsakhurdia and his sympathizers fought a war with the Georgian Military Council that had deposed him and taken power until suffering a final defeat in late fall 1993. Eduard Shevardnadze, First Secretary of the Georgian Communist Party from 1972–1985 and the Foreign Minister of the Soviet Union from 1985–1991, agreed to serve as the chairman of the Georgian Military Council (later the Georgian State Council); he subsequently was elected to the Georgian presidency, a post he held until 2003. The Georgian government fought wars against two secessionist regions, South Ossetia and Abkhazia, the former 1990–1992, the latter 1992–1993. Both ended in ceasefires but without political resolution. Sporadic but minimal violence occurred at times in the 1990s.

Mass protests broke out in November 2003 after fraudulent parliamentary elections results awarded the plurality of seats to a political party associated with Shevardnadze. Decrying government weakness and corruption, Mikheil Saakashvili, formerly minister of justice and head of an opposition party, led a popular and peaceful mobilization, demanding—and receiving—Shevardnadze's resignation. The Rose Revolution, as the movement was named, swept Saakashvili into power as president in January 2004.

Since the collapse of the Soviet empire, Georgian religiosity has surged. According to the 2002 Georgian census, 84 percent of Georgia's population identifies as

Orthodox. Georgian tradition holds that the first messages of Christianity were brought to the area by Simon the Zealot and Saint Andrew. Georgia took Christianity as its state religion under King Mirian in CE 330, in response to the proselytization of Saint Nino of Cappadocia. The symbolism of Georgian Orthodoxy includes the Georgian cross, whose horizontal bar angles down, reflecting the drooping vines of the first cross created by Saint Nino from a grape arbor. The Georgian Orthodox Church, which is autocephalous, is linked to the Greek Orthodox Church.

Other belief systems shared by Georgians include Sunni Islam, practiced by the Ingolitsi in Azerbaijan and Georgian Muslims located in Achara. Acharans, as this latter group was once termed, last had a separate entry in the 1929 Soviet census. Subsequent Soviet censuses, and the 2002 Georgian census, did not include the Acharan category; the 2002 Russian census does report a small number of Acharans. Protestantism is on the rise, although with some controversy given its increasing importance after 1991 and the strong and growing attachment of the Georgian ethnic identity to Orthodoxy.

Roughly 40 percent of Georgians today live in urban areas, with the Georgian capital of Tbilisi containing about a quarter of the Georgian population. In the mountainous regions, such as in Svaneti or Shida Kartli, village communities are predominantly pastoral. The eastern Georgian region of Kakheti is recognized for its wine production. Western Georgia once produced the bulk of Soviet tea, although that cultivation has waned in the post-Soviet period. Georgia has many natural springs and exports mineral water worldwide.

Georgian music and cuisine is renowned. Georgians are known for polyphony, a type of singing with multiple voices. The Georgian polyphony tradition attracts particular attention because of the complexity of its harmonies, the diversity of its forms, and its regional variety. In literature, Georgians celebrate Shota Rustaveli's *Knight in a Panther's Skin*, a medieval epic poem of love, valor, and friendship, written for Tamar Mepe. The Georgian language is notable for its unique verb forms and its consonantal clusters.

Georgia's relationships with its neighbors have been alternatively hostile and friendly, complicated by Georgia's long history of vassalage and the Soviet legacy. Since its independence, Georgia has maintained an uneasy relationship with the Russian Federation. This relationship has been exacerbated by the aspirations of statehood (or annexation by Russia) held by Georgian regions South Ossetia and Abkhazia and Russia's support for their self-determination. In August 2008, the Georgian army entered Tskhinvali, the South Ossetian capital, claiming soon after to have liberated the city from its secessionist government. The Russian army invaded Georgia and established a perimeter around both South Ossetia and Abkhazia, recognizing their independent statehood. Georgia maintains good relationships with its Transcaucasian neighbors, Armenia and Azerbaijan, and has a robust trading relationship with Turkey.

*Julie George*

## Further Reading

Allen, W. E. D. *A History of the Georgian People*. London: Kegan Paul, Trench, Trubner, 1932.

Jones, Stephen. *Socialism in Georgian Colors*. Cambridge, MA: Harvard University Press, 2005.

Lang, David Marshall. *A Modern History of Soviet Georgia*. New York: Grove, 1962.

Suny, Ronald Grigor. *The Making of the Georgian Nation*. Bloomington: Indiana University Press, 1988.

# German-speaking Swiss

German-speaking residents of Switzerland made up 63.7 percent of the Swiss population, or 4,640,359 out of a total of 7,288,010 (2000). German speakers dominate three of the country's most important cities: Zurich, its economic center; Bern, its capital; and Basel. Swiss German (*Deutschschweizer*) is spoken by about 90 percent of the population in the cantons of Zurich, Luzern, Uri, Schwyz, Obwalden, Nidwalden, Glarus, Zug, Solothurn, Basel-Stadt, Basel-Landschaft, Schaffhausen, Appenzell Ausserrhoden, Appenzell Innerrhoden, St. Gallen, Aargau, and Thurgau. German speakers are found in smaller numbers in the cantons of Bern (84%), Fribourg (29.2%), Valais (28.4%), and Graubünden (68.3%). In the French-speaking cantons, the German-speaking population stands at about 4–5 percent, and in Italian-speaking Ticino Swiss German speakers make up 8.3 percent. Most German-speaking Swiss are either Catholic or Protestant, though there are also small Jewish and Muslim minorities, and a growing number is without denomination. Like the French-, Italian-, and Romansh-language populations in Switzerland, German speakers do not regard themselves as an ethnic group. Instead, they give far more weight to their dialects and the resultant regional identities than to being German speakers. They define themselves by place, such as "of Basel, Zurich, or Bern," or relate to even smaller entities like a certain valley.

The foundations of German-speaking Switzerland were laid from the 5th century onward by immigrating Alemanic tribes from the north. From the end of the 11th to the end of the 15th centuries the dialects took roots and various regional linguistic characteristics formed. But the Swiss Germans could never quite deny the influence of written High German, and they absorbed it in the 16th–18th centuries. In the course of the 19th century, in accordance with the nationalism of the time, a new linguistic consciousness emerged that revalued the dialects and cherished them as a national treasure. It should be noted that everyday speech today spans a regionally wide variety of German, or rather Alemanic, dialects without written form. Overall, these dialects are called "Swiss German." In writing, standard High German is used.

German speakers often use the German term *Willensnation* to describe the Swiss nation. This refers to the founding of modern Switzerland in 1848 as a nation "willed" by a people sharing core political principles (federalism, republicanism) and reacting to long-term historical developments. In this, Switzerland deviates from the 19th-century pattern of nationalism in which the nation is defined as people unified by common descent, language, and history.

This particular form of identity, regionally grounded and at the same time nationally differentiated, has prevented the German-speaking Swiss from developing an ethnic consciousness of any relevance beyond generalities. Ethnic homogeneity is rather attributed from outside, that is from the other language groups, which tend to feel dominated by the German speakers. Indeed, while Swiss Germans tend to perceive the members of the other language groups in a positive way, their own dialect use and demeanor are stereotyped rather negatively as provincial, humorless, and narrow-minded.

Switzerland has no political parties that are run or programmed along language groups or interests. The Swiss federal system is built on balance and compromise to such a degree that language disputes are kept from gaining a lasting foothold. Moreover, Swiss language use is strictly regionalized: in some regions German is spoken; in others French, Italian, or Romansh predominates. No language group is accorded minority rights in the form of any support when members live on another language group's territory. For these reasons the concept of ethnicity is never used in politics or in discussions of language group or national identity.

Originally, the whole country was Catholic. Starting with the Reformation and reaching into the 20th century, continuous religious disputes caused conflicts and controversies between Catholics and Protestants, and even broke up cantons. It is one of the defining characteristics of Switzerland that neither linguistic nor religious or any other dividing lines are overlapping. In consequence the changing of coalitions for short- or long-term political and social goals has been a tried and tested course of action.

Switzerland has a number of historical foundation myths and legends, like the Rütli oath and the story of Wilhelm Tell, which played a crucial role in the emergence of a national identity in the 19th and 20th centuries without being bound up with one or another of the national languages. However, it is almost impossible to talk of "the" Swiss German culture. Here as everywhere else, local and cantonal characteristics—which are often marketed as folklore for tourism purposes—turn out to be of far greater importance than elements of a general Swiss German culture. Probably the strongest common denominator is an image of authentic Swissness deriving from a romanticized version of alpine pastoralism. Although this traditional ideal is not limited to Swiss German culture, it is nevertheless most prominent here. On the other hand, the basics of everyday life in the German-speaking part of Switzerland are essentially the same as in most European societies.

Though Swiss Germans are aware of their close cultural ties with neighboring German-speaking Germany and Austria, their self-awareness is to a high degree defined by marking themselves off as a nation. This has historical reasons: the Swiss detached themselves in a century-long process from the Holy Roman Empire and in consequence developed a sense of identity that puts more emphasis on their being Swiss than on the common language.

Today, less than 4 percent of the Swiss work in agriculture. The largest part of the country's gross domestic product is generated in the secondary and tertiary sectors. The secondary sector is dominated by the mechanical, chemical, and pharmaceutical industries. The country is also known as a manufacturer of precision instruments and appliances, as well as for its food industry. Increasingly important are the medical and biotechnical industries. The tertiary sector employs the majority of workers in all regions (72%). Trade, health, and education, as well as banking and insurance, are dominant. For about 150 years tourism has provided essential income in almost all regions of Switzerland.

These days, traditional Swiss language policy is considerably challenged by the growing global dominance of English. Migration, for instance, is transforming the linguistic status quo (21.5% of the population are foreigners). On the one hand, because of diglossia (the simultaneous existence of spoken dialect and written standard language), migrants find it hard to integrate linguistically. On the other hand, given the growing number of immigrants, native German-speaking Swiss feel anxious about preserving their regional identities and a possible diminishing of dialects and cultural traditions. At the same time the number of binational marriages continues to grow.

The Swiss tendency toward neutrality in political relations is counterbalanced by enormous economic interconnectedness. There is occasional talk of being afraid to lose Swiss values amid ongoing Europeanization and globalization. These fears do not concern Swiss German identity particularly, but rather overall Swiss values—which suggests that questions of ethnic identity will remain marginal to future Swiss German discussions of identity.

*Walter Leimgruber*

## Further Reading

Dame, Frederick William. *History of Switzerland.* 3 vols. Lewiston, NY: Edwin Mellen Press, 2003.

Dürmüller, Urs. *Changing Patterns of Multilingualism. From Quadrilingual to Multilingual Switzerland.* Zürich: Pro Helvetia, 1997.

Fahrni, Dieter. *An Outline History of Switzerland. From the Origins to the Present Day.* Zürich: Pro Helvetia, 2003.

Risi, Marius. *Daily Life and Festive Culture in Switzerland. A Brief Anthropology of Cultural Change.* Zurich: Pro Helvetia, 2004.

Zimmer, Oliver. *A Contested Nation: History, Memory and Nationalism in Switzerland 1761–1891.* Cambridge: Cambridge University Press, 2003.

## Germans

The Germans live in Central Europe, mostly in Germany (82.2 million inhabitants, of whom 75 million speak German), and in many countries around the world, both as German expatriates and as citizens of other countries who identify culturally as German and speak the language. Estimates of the total number of Germans in the world range from 100 million to 150 million, depending on how German is defined, but it is probably more appropriate to accept the lower figure. There are many German-speaking people who do not define themselves ethnically as Germans, mainly in Austria (about 8 million), Switzerland (4.9 million), and South Tyrol in Italy (345,000). The largest populations outside of these countries are found in the United States (5 million), Brazil (3 million), the former Soviet Union (2 million), Argentina (500,000), Canada (450,000), Spain (170,000), Australia (110,000), the United Kingdom (100,000), and South Africa (75,000). Most European countries have a significant German population, as do Namibia, Chile, Paraguay, and Israel. In Germany today 31 percent of the population are Catholics, 30 percent are Protestants, and 33 percent adhere to no religious faith, evidence of increasing secularization in recent decades. German identity developed through a long historical process that led, in the late 19th and early 20th centuries, to the definition of the German nation as both a community of descent (*Volksgemeinschaft*)

and shared culture and experience. Today, the German language is the primary though not exclusive criterion of German identity.

If we consider ethnic and national groups as fluid and impermanent today, this holds equally true for the early history of the Germans. It is conventionally believed that Tacitus described the Germanic tribes that were later to become the German nation and *Volksgemeinschaft* in his *Germania* (written around CE 100). In fact, no ethnically or culturally unified society would exist for some time. Instead a mixture of peoples and ethnicities developed through division, combination, absorption, and new developments. After the disintegration of Charlemagne's empire, the Frankenreich, upon his death in 814, the East Frankish German Kingdom arose, dominated by the Duchies of Bavaria, Saxony, Swabia, Franken, and Lorraine, and

Bavarian couple in Munich, Germany. (Corel)

by rivalries among the aristocratic families of the Ottonen, Salians, and Staufer. The kings of the East Frankish Kingdom and later the emperors of the Holy Roman Empire all came from these dynasties. The Holy Roman Empire was not a territory under centralistic rule. At the center of the empire's constitution stood the right of the nobility to elect the king and thereby retain independence and influence, with the balance of power continuously swinging between the king and the principalities. In a series of power-political maneuvers, Otto the Great strengthened the position of the bishops and imperial abbots through land grants and the transfer of sovereign powers. The church became an important factor in politics, resulting in controversies between the pope, kings, and emperors. As a result of this increasingly important role of the church and the reform movement initiated in Cluny, a new religious fervor led to five crusades between 1096 and 1229—wars fought against "the infidels" and for the "liberation" of the Holy Land of Palestine.

This formative phase of European nation-building was also the time of important social and economical revolutions. The German territories were subjected to manorial rule, and the free peasants disappeared. Agriculture adopted the system of three-field crop rotation along with increased market orientation. During the 12th century there was substantial population growth, and cities thrived. The period saw an increase in commercial activities, the founding of trading companies, and specialization and diversification within the arts and crafts. Equally important was German settlement in the East, starting in the 12th century, initially in the wake of military expeditions, whereas the great migrations of the 13th century into new "German" territories (Mecklenburg, East Brandenburg, Pomerania, Silesia, Northern Moravia) were mostly peaceful.

The continued thriving of the cities throughout the late Middle Ages was accompanied by an internationalization of commerce and the rise of a self-confident patriciate. New forms of mobility arose, spearheaded by great explorations. Johannes Gutenberg revolutionized printing (around 1450), and a new understanding of faith and reason emerged, influencing philosophical debates and underwriting an increasingly influential science. In the German territories, the Reformation, commonly associated with Martin Luther, but also with Ulrich Zwingli and Johannes Calvin, marked the beginning of a new era.

In the years between the start of Reformation in the early 16th century and the Peace of Westphalia in 1648, Germany underwent fundamental changes. Initially, Reformation set off a long process of schism accompanied by witch hunts that reached their peak in Germany between 1550 and 1650. The resulting schism of Christianity into Catholicism and Protestantism became a lasting characteristic of Germany. While around 1500 the Holy Roman Empire was on the verge of becoming a vast empire, it now broke down into numerous smaller and middle-sized centers of power, which in the south and southwest found their artistic expression in splendid residences of princes and bishops, inspired by the aesthetic ideas developed in the Renaissance and Baroque periods. The Thirty Years'

War then brought unimaginable suffering, and in Germany alone the population fell from 17 to 10 million.

The Peace of Westphalia gave the seemingly disintegrating Holy Roman Empire a form that assured the continued territorial sovereignty of the German principalities while at the same time allowing for unity and coexistence. Prussia rose to power and became the counterpart of the Habsburg Empire among the German-speaking countries. The enlightenment and its consequences brought more change. The old authorities, church and state, came under criticism, and scientific, political, and social progress superseded older concepts. In Germany, these changes were not the result of popular uprisings but rather of measures taken by elites.

The French Revolution initiated a period, which in Germany has often been called "the long 19th century," whose effects resounded until World War I. In the course of the Napoleonic Wars, Germany fell apart (1806) and the German Confederation was founded, with Prussia and Austria as the two dominating counterparts. Austria was excluded from the German Confederation in 1866, and in 1871, after a victorious war against France, the German Empire was proclaimed with Wilhelm I as its emperor.

The 19th century also brought modernization. The bourgeoisie was the driving power behind the social and economic changes, the key characteristics of which included industrialization (which started relatively late in Germany), capitalism, class society, secularization, and rationalization. There also emerged a fervent nationalism and militarism that was in great part responsible for the catastrophes of the 20th century.

World War I was expected to bring stability, but defeat only aggravated the tensions within German society. Though the Weimar Republic was a time of modernization of the political structures, it also gave rise to increasing antidemocratic tendencies. This period was characterized by a combination of effective modernizations (especially in the media and popular culture) along with a strong antimodern movement that called for a return to the good old times and ways. The continuity of authoritarianism and anti-Semitism along with the economic crisis of the early 1930s promoted the collective march into the catastrophe of Nazism, which was fueled by racism and blind nationalism. Nazism and the Holocaust, along with all the atrocities of the totalitarian regime and horrors of World War II, certainly constitute the darkest chapter in German history. After a period of denial, from the 1960s Germans have grappled publicly with war guilt. This can be seen in the establishment of places of remembrance (*Erinnerungsorte*) and museums in concentration camps, the Memorial to the Murdered Jews of Europe in Berlin, and the Munich Documentation Center for the History of National Socialism.

The end of World War II saw Germany not only disrobed of its delusions of grandeur, but also divided into two states, marking the frontier of a world divided into East and West. West Germany would gradually become a new society, one characterized by enormous economic growth and political openness. The fall of the Berlin Wall on November 9, 1989, marked the start of the process of reunification of the two Germanys, the Federal Republic of Germany and the German Democratic Republic, with the official ratification of the treaty of reunification signed on October 3, 1990. This long-awaited reunification placed heavy burdens on Germans, who were nonetheless able to cope with the economic costs of the project. A more enduring difficulty was posed by the cultural differences between East and West. The remarkable differences in the voting preferences between the eastern and western parts of Germany are among the effects of this divide today.

The greatest challenge for the German society in recent years is globalization and the attendant neoliberal shift in economic policies, which have eroded the social fabric and labor market arrangements established in the postwar period. Environmental challenges, particularly, are also an important political issue. Finally, decades of immigration, which at first was promoted as a means to stabilize the economy, have led to fundamental changes in the German society. Since the 1960s, "guest workers"—especially from southern Europe—have been coming to Germany and were initially expected to return to their home countries after some years. But many of them settled, established families, and introduced new lifestyles, traditions, religious expression, and food styles into German society. The integration of most immigrants proceeded apace, but some differences—especially concerning religion—were highlighted as problems, mainly by right-wing politicians. In the meantime politicians have accepted the reality of Germany being a country with mass immigration. Recently, the citizenship law was modified to make naturalization less restrictive for those long-term residents without German ancestry.

## Turks in Central and Western Europe

Turkish migration to Central and Western Europe began in the 1960s with the signing of bilateral agreements with Germany (and other European states), creating what were called the guest–worker programs in German-speaking countries. The formal policies of labor recruitment in Europe ended in the mid-1970s (in Germany in 1973). Through family reunification programs and political asylum laws, the influx of foreigners, including Turks, continued throughout the 1980s and 1990s, although there were occasional drops fueled by restrictive legislation and promotion of return migration. According to the Turkish Ministry of Labor, today about 3 million Turkish citizens live and work abroad in Europe, with nearly 2 million in Germany alone. Despite continuing debates on their integration to European societies, which emanate from high unemployment, high rates of school dropouts, and notions about the incompatibility of Turkish/Islamic culture with European norms and values, Turks in Europe have over the years formed well-established communities and created strong transnational ties between Europe and Turkey, as well as within Europe.

*Levent Soysal*

The Catholic and Protestant churches, which each count roughly 30 percent of the population as their members, are the dominant churches in Germany. While these two churches witness a continuous loss of members, the percentage of people of Muslim faith has continuously increased and has reached 4.3 percent. People professing no faith are larger in number than any one religion. However, seasonal holidays and festivities of religious origins, above all the Christmas holidays and Easter, remain important for the great majority of Germans. Also important to German cultural life are festivities such as Carnival (*Karneval, Fasching, Fastnacht*), especially in the Catholic regions of the south and southwest of the country. Carnival lasts from Epiphany (*Dreikönigstag*) until the beginning of Lent on Ash Wednesday, with the days prior to Ash Wednesday as the culmination of Carnival. It is a complex phenomenon, which might be described by the terms tradition, amusement, power, prestige, politics, or rebellion. It is the festivity of a temporary counter-world, of irrational and ecstatic moments located beyond conventional social reality and norms. Recurring elements are copious amounts of food and drink, masquerade, music, dance, and parades. Elements of Carnival can be found in other, more regionally specific festivities, of which the Oktoberfest in Munich has gained international renown. The Oktoberfest has evolved from a typical regional popular festivity to a globally known event that bases its attraction on the streamlined presentation of stereotypes of local specifics of a popular festivity.

By European standards, Germany is a large country with much regional variation, making identification of a single German culture difficult. One important aspect of daily life for Germans is sports, in which German teams or athletes are internationally successful, foremost among them the national soccer team. Despite variation, Germans also share eating and drinking habits. Germany registers one of the highest levels of alcohol consumption, with a per capita consumption of nearly 150 liters of alcoholic beverages per year. The greater part, nearly 50 percent of that consumption, is made up of Germany's favorite beverage—beer—while wine and spirits each make up about 20 percent. Germany also tops of the list of countries with the highest number of overweight people in the European Union. Stew is a typical nationwide dish and one with a very long tradition in Germany. In the last decades, barbecuing has become very popular, mostly during summertime. Bread, especially the typical German dark bread, has gained almost mythical status among German expatriates as being the one foodstuff they miss most in their new surroundings. Migration and globalization have had an impact on the eating habits in Germany, with pizza, pasta, kebab, and various fast foods figuring on the list of favorite foods of the Germans.

In terms of high culture and science, two periods of particular importance stand out for Germans. The first is the classic period, connected to such names as J.S. Bach, Ludwig van Beethoven, Wolfgang Amadeus Mozart, and Joseph Haydn in the field of music and Johann Wolfgang Goethe, Friedrich Schiller, and Gottfried Herder in literature. The second one is the Romantic period, and the distinctive personalities are Caspar David Friedrich in the field of painting; Karl Friedrich Schinkel in architecture; Friedrich Hölderlin, Heinrich Heine, E. T. A. Hoffmann, Novalis, and the brothers Grimm in literature; and Johannes Brahms, Franz Schubert, Richard Strauss, and Richard Wagner in music.

There are several other well-known and characteristic aspects of German popular culture. One of them is the symbol of the forest. In a political-nationalistic sense, the forest was regarded as an expression of German culture, a reassuring symbol of enduring Germanness that was touted in times of rapid change, such as the late 19th century. The forest also harbors a strong mythological dimension, which is expressed in Romantic literature and in fairy tales but also in the worldview of ordinary people. As a symbol, the forest has retained its aesthetic meaning, but it has lost its political and mythological meaning. Words like *Gemütlichkeit* and *Heimat* are almost impossible to translate (and are therefore often used in the original German form in other languages) because they are so deeply embedded in a specifically German set of references. *Gemütlichkeit* is usually associated with the middle class and evokes candlelight, soft plush pillows, and naïve paintings of countryside and animals; whatever the social setting, *Gemütlichkeit* always connotes safety and security, and evokes the qualities conveyed by the English term "coziness. " The term *Heimat* is a similar case. On the one hand it means a homeland or hometown, which offers belonging, recognition, and identity, and for which people develop a sense of place. On the other hand it refers to a scenery of wishfulness and longing related to a landscape of desire that "no one has ever been to" (in the words of Ernst Bloch), which strangely enough is used naturally in German discussions about origin, belonging, and identity.

*Johannes Moser*

## Further Reading

Bausinger, Hermann. *Typisch deutsch. Wie deutsch sind die Deutschen? (Typical German. How German Are the Germans?)*. München: Beck, 2000.

Borneman, John. *Belonging in the Two Berlins: Kin, State, Nation*. Cambridge: Cambridge University Press, 1992.

Dirlmeier, Ulf, et al. *Kleine deutsche Geschichte (Small German History)*. Stuttgart: Philipp Reclam, 2006.

Flippo, Hyde. *The German Way: Aspects of Behavior, Attitudes, and Customs in the German-Speaking World*. Lincolnwood, IL: Passport Books, 1998.

François, Etienne, and Hagen Schulze, eds. *Deutsche Erinnerungsorte (German Places of Remembrance)*. München: Beck, 2001.

# Greeks

*Ellines* (Hellenes) is the name by which the majority of the citizens of the nation-state of Greece choose to call themselves. As of 2008, a little over 11 million Greeks inhabited the country's homeland territory, situated at the tip of the Balkan Peninsula. Neo-Hellenes is often used to distinguish these peoples from the ancient Greeks, who serve as their glorious ancestors. Included in the category of the Hellenes, however, are Greek citizens who have migrated to Europe, America, and Australia in search of employment throughout the past century (*apodimos Ellinismos*). Since many chose to stay abroad, hyphenated peoples, such as Greek-Americans, or Greek-Australians, came to be included in the national community under the name *homogeneis Elliness* (of the same genus). In the same umbrella category also belong those who claim Greek descent from ancient or historical times, such as the Pontics from the Black Sea area of the Former Soviet Union or Orthodox Albanians. These people moved to Greece during the past two decades and they are known as the *palinostoundes Ellines* (returning Greeks). Migrants (*metanastes*) from former socialist countries and from all over the developing world also entered Greece in the past two decades in search of employment. Their incorporation into mainstream Greek society is still in the making and problems arise from the cultural and religious diversity they bring into a country that has learned to consider itself homogeneous.

Although Paleolithic cave dwelling has been established as the earliest habitation in the area, Greece's national history usually begins with the arrival of the Hellenes by the second millennium BCE. The most venerated ancestors are those of 5th-century classical antiquity because of their unique innovations in science, politics, arts, and culture. Many foreign peoples invaded the peninsula, such as the Slavs, Franks, and Venetians, not to mention the Ottoman Turks, who stayed for more than

A fisherman rows his boat in a port on the Greek island of Mykonos. One of the most popular of the Greek islands among international tourists, with many bars and a vibrant nightlife, Mykonos is also home to 9,320 inhabitants. (Travel Pictures Gallery)

four centuries (roughly, the 15th–19th centuries). But the putative ancestors are the ancient Greeks who survived foreign occupation. In the Hellenic national imagination, the enemy came from the east, and, while the Persians were the enemies of the ancients, the Turks are still the quintessential enemies and structural opposites of modern Greeks. The battle of Marathon (490 BCE) and the naval battle in Salamis (480 BCE) are historical moments held dear to Hellenes. The fall of Constantinople to the Turks (May 29, 1453) is considered a sacred historical event, and March 25 marks the 1821 onset of the revolution against the Turks and is celebrated both as a national and religious holiday (Annunciation Day). The Asia Minor disaster (*Mikrasiatiki Katastrofi*) of 1922 is another important event that narrates the violence inflicted upon the Hellenes by the Turks. Although the mainlanders originally looked down upon the refugees (*prosfiges*) from Asia Minor, to this day, Hellenes, when asked, distinguish their Asia Minor ancestry in their personal descent narratives. October 28 is the second national holiday celebrated every year and marks the beginning of World War II when the Greeks rebuffed the Italian invasion through southern Albania. The November 17, 1973, demonstration and student massacre at the polytechnic school in Athens by the military dictatorship (1967–1974) is now commemorated as a national holiday.

Key individuals in the history of the Hellenes range from Pericles (495–429 BCE) to Andreas Papandreou (1919–1996): they are usually men in politics and culture, like the ancient Greek statesmen who supposedly invented democracy, mathematicians and philosophers who laid the foundations for modern science, authors of tragedies and comedies, and famous sculptors. Key figures also include Byzantine emperors, like Konstantinos Paleologos (1404–1453), who acted as bastions of Hellenism and Orthodoxy. The heroes of the 1821 war of independence are also revered, and the faces of fighters such as Theodoros Kolokotronis (1770–1843), Georgios Karaiskakis (1780–1827), and even the celebrated woman Bouboulina (1771–1825) adorn the walls of elementary school classrooms.

Many Hellenes imagine their country as sitting at the crossroads of the East and the West, and claim that their ancient forefathers created the cradle of Western civilization. The primary language of the modern Greeks is standardized vernacular (*dimotiki*) Greek and the group's religion is Greek Orthodoxy. The Greeks hold that in order to be Greek, a person must observe Greek Orthodoxy and possess Greek blood and descent as well as a share in the nation's historical continuity. The 1821 struggle for independence united disparate linguistic groups (Greeks, Vlachs, Arvanites, etc.) who shared the Orthodox faith against the Ottomans. The first nation of the Hellenes was born from this cultural mixture and it continued for a century to amalgamate more Orthodox peoples in its national body as the Greek state incorporated new lands such as Thessaly (1881), Epirus (1913), Macedonia (1913), and Thrace (1920). When in the 1920s a population exchange with Turkey brought to the mainland about a million and a half Orthodox Christian refugees from Asia Minor, it was religion again and not language that bonded the peoples together. Ninety-five percent of the country's present population is baptized Orthodox. While the church is slowly losing its sacred character, millions of Hellenes protested in the streets of major cities and towns in 2000 when the European Union introduced new identity cards that would not indicate the religion of the cardholder. Catholics, Protestants, Muslims, Jews, and Armenians comprise the minority religions in the country. With the recent influx of migrants, however, a plethora of religions are now practiced.

In the long run, Orthodoxy alone was not sufficient for national membership. It was also necessary to make co-patriots those from other cultural and linguistic heritages, such as Macedonian Slavs of northern Greece, Vlachs of Epirus, and Arvanites of central Greece, through the adoption of Greek language and civilization. While the revolutionary spirit of the first half of the 19th century begun to subside, the second half of the century witnessed the construction and consolidation of the nation-state both in territorial and ideological terms. European *philhellenes*, while searching for the roots of their own civilization, helped the Greeks construct their own continuity narrative through romantic notions of descent from the ancients. The Byzantine Empire with its Orthodox religion and Greek language served as the missing link between the ancients and the moderns. National history began to be written and historian Konstantinos Paparrigopoulos (1815–1891) was the prominent figure in Athenian intellectual and government circles, who wrote the multivolume *History of the Greek Nation* and established the national continuity narrative, a continuity still taught to children in contemporary schools.

The first president of Greece was Corfu-born Count Ioannis Kapodistrias (1876–1831), who was assassinated in 1831 since his policies undermined traditional Greek elites. The country's parliamentary democracy suffered from internal strife and a problematic relationship with the kings that the Europeans assigned to the new country. The first King Otto arrived in 1833 from Bavaria and ruled the country until he was deported in 1862. Eventually the Danish Glucksburg dynasty established itself in the country (1864–1974).

At the same time, intellectual and political circles were divided into two camps: the modernizers against the traditionalists. Modernizer Kharilaos Trikoupis (1832–1896) oversaw the construction of the Greek state and its bureaucracy during seven terms as prime minister. Having spent his formative years in London, he turned to Greek diaspora circles for the investment capital required to build major public works and railroads.

Another key issue for the young kingdom was the unredeemed brethren still living in Ottoman territories. The Megali Idea (Great Idea) slowly took shape in the capital's political and intellectual circles, and people started imagining a "greater Greece" that could potentially include Constantinople. Liberating those Greeks and incorporating them into the national body provided a topic for debates and activism. Associations for the propagation of Greek letters and culture in these areas were formed in Athens, and teachers and educators were dispatched. Armed men like Pavlos Melas (1870–1904) journeyed to Ottoman Macedonia to combat what he considered Bulgarian propaganda, and the Macedonian Struggle (1904–1908) divided the population between those loyal to the Orthodox patriarchate and the Greek cause and those Slav Macedonian speakers who joined the Bulgarian/Macedonian liberation movement. Following the Balkan Wars of 1912–1913, the New Lands (Macedonia and Thrace) were incorporated, therefore, but the majority of the inhabitants represented diverse linguistic, cultural, and religious groups: Slavs in Macedonia, Vlachs in Epirus, Turkish-speaking Muslims in Thrace, Slav-speaking Muslims in the mountainous border with Bulgaria (Pomaks), as well as a sizeable Sephardic Jewish population living in Salonica and the nomadic Roma. The emphasis in this process was education, and many of these peoples became participants in the Greek national culture. The Jewish population of Salonica, however, suffered near extinction when the majority perished in German concentration camps during World War II.

Cretan-born Eleftherios Venizelos (1864–1936) was the architect of Greece's territorial expansion. In the aftermath of the Asia Minor defeat, he participated in the negotiations that led to the Lausanne Treaty and the exchange of populations between Greece and Turkey. He also began land distribution programs that transformed Greek peasants into smallholders. Most of the countryside still remained poor, however, and the rural poor started migrating to the cities and beyond. Although the country's efforts at industrialization did not prove successful, an urban working class took shape and socialist and

communist ideologies found fertile ground among these peoples. Most of the country's politics since then have been characterized by this sharp left/right distinction, the most dramatic moment of which was the Greek Civil War of 1946–1949.

Greece came out of the violent 1940s poor and totally dependent on foreign aid for reconstruction. Entering the North Atlantic Treaty Organization (NATO) in 1952 gave Hellenes a sense of security, although internal political strife was not over and the years 1950–1974 saw fierce debates centering on the role of the monarchy in democratic times. At the same time, a movement took place for the marginalization of the *katharevousa* language used in schools and bureaucracy, that is, the purified form of Greek language consisting of a mixture of ancient and modern words, constructed by the enlightenment scholar Adamantios Korais (1748–1833). Simultaneously, the teaching of ancient Greek in schools has been debated.

Membership to the European Union has been the most important political and economic development in the last quarter of the past century. Konstantinos Karamanlis (1907–1998), although controversial in his early career, remains a respected statesman who paved the way for Greece to enter the European community. He was also the first prime minister in the history of Greece to come from the New Lands, a small village outside the town of Serres in Greek Macedonia being his place of birth. He eventually became the founder of a family clan of politicians (*tzaki*), and his young nephew, bearing the same name, became a two-term prime minister of Greece 2004–2009. His government is now held responsible for corruption and for bringing Greece to the bankrupt stage it reached in 2010. The Papandreou family is another example of three generations of active political leaders, with present-day Prime Minister George Papandreou bearing the name of his famous grandfather, who led the democratization movement in 1960s Greece. Throughout the two centuries during which the Greek nation-state came into being, clientelism can best describe the way the Hellenes have related to their government. In the absence of a large-scale industrial economic base, the country's economy always depended on agricultural and mercantilist activities. Government jobs were the most desirable, since they offered excellent benefits and retirement options. These jobs were coveted, however, and each time a political party won parliamentary elections, a number of new hires became included in the state's employee rosters. It is this paternalism and clientelism that membership in the European Union aspires to eliminate.

Urbanization and out-migration characterized the life of the Hellenes in the 20th century. In the aftermath of World War II, the devastated countryside begun to export labor to the big cities of Athens and Thessaloniki, as well as to Germany, the United States, Canada, and Australia. While the *rebetika* song genre has its roots in the urban working-class refugee culture of the interwar period, the *ksenitia* (migration) songs of the 1960s are still sung by the Hellenes, with Stelios Kazantzidis (1931–2001) being remembered as the most prominent singer. Manos Chatzidakis (1925–1994) became Greece's internationally acclaimed songwriter, who adapted elements from classical music and from the potentially subversive *rebetika* songs. He, along with Mikis Theodorakis (1925– ), led the songwriting scene in the post–World War II years. The latter became internationally famous through his political activism against the 1967–1974 military junta and wrote the music for the quintessential *Zorba the Greek* movie, directed by Mihalis Kakogiannis (1922– ).

A form of Greek neorealist cinema also developed in the 1950s and 1960s, portraying themes of poverty, urbanization, and socioeconomic class distinctions. Cinemascope pictures that introduced a new form of culture and morality eventually replaced this older black-and-white genre in the early 1970s.

Greeks are proud of Giorgios Seferis (1900–1971) and Odysseas Elytis (1911–1996), who received the Nobel Prize in poetry in 1963 and 1979 respectively. Both of these men, along with Konstantinos Kavafy (1863–1933) and Yiannis Ritsos (1909–1990), are considered to be the major Greek poets of the 20th century. In fiction, the Cretan Nikos Kazantzakis (1883–1957) is the best-known writer. These men of letters, while creating magnificent works of poetry and fiction, also offered a cultural binding link for the Neo-Hellenes.

The Greeks are now a culturally homogeneous group, but they still feel threatened and act defensively when countries/peoples make territorial and descent claims. When the Macedonian Slavs or the Muslims of Thrace, for example, claim a separate, non-Greek identity, then a feeling of danger triggers nationalistic rhetoric. Greek efforts to monopolize the past have been fueled by the discovery of the Vergina ancient

Macedonian tombs in Greek territory in 1979. The Greeks have been adamant in blocking the usage of the name Macedonia by the neighboring republic of Macedonia that gained independence in 1991 following the dissolution of Yugoslavia. The Macedonia issue is one of the greatest controversies in the history of the Greek nation that touches upon the important question of descent. When Greeks demonstrated in the millions throughout the 1990s that Macedonia is Greek and has been so for thousands of years, they were making a statement about their descent from the ancients and their right to exist today.

Another contemporary challenge involves the *palinostoundes* Ellines who are making Greece their homeland. Albanians were the first ones to find their way to Greece through mountain paths. Those who could prove their Greek descent (*homogeneis*) were able to acquire work permits and Greek citizenship. Other Albanians came as economic migrants and faced discrimination in the job market. Greek law now requires that all foreign laborers residing in the country have work permits and benefits. Peoples from the former Soviet Union, with or without Greek descent, have also settled. In addition, hundreds of peoples from Asia enter the country every year illegally: these people do not regard Greece as their destination, but as a means to enter Europe. Greece is thus now charged with guarding the borders of Europe and controlling migration, a task that it does not always do successfully. Georgians, Albanians, Romanians, Russians, Ukrainians, and others paint now the new ethnic and cultural face of Greece. The multiethnic composition of society is a great challenge the Greeks are now asked to face, in addition to the country's bankrupt state economy.

*Anastasia Karakasidou*

## Further Reading

Clogg, Richard. *A Concise History of Greece.* Cambridge: Cambridge University Press, 1992.

Faubion, James D. *Modern Greek Lessons: A Primer in Historical Constructivism.* Princeton, NJ: Princeton University Press, 1993.

Herzfeld, Michael. *Anthropology through the Looking Glass: Critical Ethnography in the Margins of Europe.* Cambridge: Cambridge University Press, 1989.

Karakasidou, Anastasia. *Fields of Wheat, Hills of Blood: Passages to Nationhood in Greek Macedonia, 1870–1980.* Chicago: Chicago University Press, 1997.

Mackridge, Peter. *Language and National Identity in Greece, 1766–1976.* Oxford: Oxford University Press, 2009.

Marchand, Suzanne L. *Down from Olympus: Archaeology and Philhellenism in Germany, 1750–1970.* Princeton, NJ: Princeton University Press, 1996.

Mazower, Mark. *Salonica, City of Ghosts: Christians, Muslims and Jews 1430–1950.* London: HarperCollins Publishers, 2004.

# H

## Hungarians

Hungarians refer to themselves as Magyars (*magyarok* in Hungarian), a designation used as an ethnic label from the original Finno-Ugric root meaning a person from a specific clan. Hungarians are the dominant population in Hungary, a landlocked country of 10 million in central Europe. Hungary's capital, Budapest, straddles the Danube River (Duna in Hungarian), a name that gave rise to the city's designation as Queen of the Danube. As of 2008, the nation's capital counted about 1.7 million residents. Large numbers of Hungarians live in neighboring Romania (about 1.7 million) and Slovakia (700,000) and many fewer in Serbia, Croatia, and Slovenia. The western diaspora numbers about the same, although their proper ethnonational identity is a matter of dispute. The North American diaspora has been purported to be 1.5–2 million, a population that includes descendants of late 19th-century economic migrants as well as those of the 1956 revolution. The predominant religion of the country is Roman Catholicism, with about one-third of the population adhering to the Protestant faith (known as Reformed). Lesser denominations are Greek Orthodox, Evangelical, Baptist, and Jewish. Although a small percentage of believers attend religious services regularly (roughly 15% of the population), affiliation with a church is much higher. Hungarian is a Finno-Ugric language. While the terms Hungarian and Magyar are interchangeable, it has been argued that "Magyar" should be applied only to those who identify themselves ethnically as such, "Hungarian" being considered more apt for all citizens of Hungary regardless of ethnonational identities. In the Middle Ages, Western European university students were registered variously as Hungaricus, Pannonicus, or Transsylvanicus, terms identifying them as ethnically Magyar, from Hungary or Transylvania proper. Neighboring populations variously refer to Hungarians by their self-designation, Magyar (*Madzar*, *Maghiari*, etc.), or versions of the pre-Conquest Onugor such as Venger or Ungur, as evidenced in German (*Ungarisch*), French (*Hongrois*), and English (Hungarian). Greece and Turkey, with which the kingdom of Hungary had considerable but not always amicable relations throughout the centuries, use *Madzari* and *Ugri* as designations for the country's population.

For more than 200 years, linguistic, anthropological, and ethnographic debates have raged concerning the non–Indo-European origin of Hungarians and their language. Two scholarly orientations in particular stand out—the Finno-Ugric and the Turkic proponents. Adherents of the former argue that the basic grammar and core vocabulary of the Magyar language is

Traditional Hungarian dancers. (Corel)

Finno-Ugric of the Uralic language family. The Turkic origins thesis, stressing the more Asiatic background of Hungarians, acquired greater currency when it was used in the latter part of the 19th and the first half of the 20th centuries. Both schools are well established, with research institutions and university language departments as well as cultural contacts with present day "relatives" ranging from Finns, Khanty (Ostyak), and Mansy (Vogul) for the Finno-Ugric school, and Mongols, Uyghurs, Kazakhs, and others for the Asiatic-Turkic idea. More extreme views are also known: Sanskrit, Sumerian, and Etruscan theories of origin have been proposed for the Magyars. Opponents of the Finno-Ugric theory claim that the period of conquest is a figment of the imagination and hold a view that allows for the possibility of prehistoric migrations of Hungarians who have always lived where they reside today.

According to established yet contested theory, the confederation known as the Onogurs ("Ten Arrows" or "Ten Tribes") arrived in the Danubian or Carpathian Basin as part of the last large wave of steppe migrants during the 9th century. Parts of this terrain, known to the Romans as Pannonia and Dacia, were designated as Barbaricum, since it was habited by pagan tribes such as the Goths, Sarmatians, Huns, Alans, Slavs, and Avars. Settlement of the Hungarian tribes, known as the Conquest, took place from the 8th to the beginning of the 10th centuries when a princely state conquered almost the entire Carpathian Basin, a feat that came to a halt when the last raiding troops were defeated by the united German armies in 955 at the battlefield of Lechfeld (near Augsburg in Austria).

The half million Magyars of the Conquest period (recent figures suggest a figure of 1 million, which may be exaggerated) practiced animal husbandry and agriculture. With their first saint king, István (Stephen, 997–1031), the Árpád house established its rule over a vast kingdom that was predominantly Roman Catholic. In 1301, after the death of the last king of the ruling dynasty, various European aristocratic families sat upon the Hungarian throne. From the 11th to 13th centuries, several waves of nomadic groups settled within the parameters of the kingdom, among them the Pechenegs, the Cumans, the Jazygians (sometimes spelled Jassic), the Kalizes, and the Vlachs. German-speaking groups arrived in different waves settling in various parts of the kingdom. By the 15th century, these groups assimilated to the Hungarian (Magyar) majority culture, leaving only broken fragments of their colorful former language, beliefs, and material culture.

Following the fateful battle of Mohács in 1526, one-third of Hungary was under the rule of Ottoman Sultans, an occupation that lasted until 1690. The second third of the Kingdom of Hungary was increasingly taken over by the Habsburgs, and the remaining part became the semi-independent Transylvanian principality. There was considerable, mostly north-south, migration after that time; from the Balkan peninsula, refugee groups found safe haven in Hungary; from the north, economic migrants settled primarily in central and southern Hungary. The Roma/Gypsy appeared in the 14th century, while other groups—notably the Vlach Gypsies—arrived during the 18th and 19th centuries. Similarly, a large group of Germans (known collectively as Schwabians) also arrived between the middle and late 18th century together with a number of Slovaks. Some settled along the Danube, while others scattered on princely estates where they acquired jobs and housing.

From the late 17th century, Hungarians found themselves under the Habsburg yoke. A rising tide of nationalism resulted in a rebellion in 1848–1849, but the ensuing war of independence was crushed by the joined forces of Austria and Russia. A brief terror ensued as thousands fled Hungary or joined the disillusioned classes, further fueling the rising tide of nationalism and anti-Habsburg sentiments. The stalemate came to a halt with the Compromise of 1867, when Hungary and Austria became a Dual Monarchy.

Interethnic relations were dealt a blow during the first decades of the 20th century. The Paris peace treaty following World War I was neither a peaceful settlement nor a treaty based on the wishes of all populations involved. With the collapse of the Dual Monarchy of Hungary and Austria, Hungary lost almost two-thirds of its lands with the northern, eastern, and southern regions acceded to successor states, leaving millions of ethnic Hungarians outside the mother country. This resulted in the Trianon Trauma (referring to the Palace of Versailles where the treaty was concluded): large numbers of ethnic Hungarians resettled to Hungary, encouraging the idea of separatism and nationalism both at home and in the neighboring states. After World War II, ethnic Germans were forcibly uprooted in an exchange program between Hungary, the German Democratic Republic, and Czechoslovakia. Hungarians from the Slovak part of the latter were given only a short time to pack and leave to settle in the empty houses of the expelled Germans.

The case of the largest group, the Hungarians in Romania, offers a special case study in ethnography and national historiography. There are several ethnoregional groups—particularly the Szeklers (*Székely*) and the Csango people—whose cultural traits have been highly valued and thus contested by Hungarian and Romanian elites alike. Regardless of their origin, however, all Hungarians were considered traitors by the new Romanian state after World War II, forcing many to flee to Hungary. This exodus did not cease during the period known as state socialism, when internationalism was to be the main ideological glue of the neighboring ("fraternal") states. According to 1992 statistics, 1.6 million people claimed Hungarian nationality in Romania; by 2002, their numbers decreased to 1.4 million. Sentiment about those living in diasporas still loom large in the minds of Hungarians in Hungary, a notion that fundamentally determines cultural and political ideology concerning nationhood. Both inside and outside Romania, Hungarian elites are quite united in their wish to encourage the establishment of regional autonomous statutes of Transylvanian Hungarians, a political goal that causes nervous reverberations across the Romanian political machinery whenever it is voiced.

Hungary today can be considered a mainly homogeneous country. There are 13 officially recognized minority groups living in the country (that is, those with at least 100 years of proven residence in Hungary as specified by law). One of these, the Roma, is considered an ethnic category, while the remainders are designated as national minorities. According to a 2001 census, approximately 3 percent of Hungarian citizens claimed some non-Magyar ethnic belonging, a figure that is estimated to be as high as 9–10 percent. The most numerous are the Roma/Gypsies (about one-half to one million) followed by Slovaks, Germans, and Romanians. Recently, Chinese migrants in Hungary applied for official ethnonational recognition but were rejected. All the national groups have their own political representation in local governments, elected every four years by a constituency who claim ethnic belonging to that group. The changing nature of ethnicity is notable: in 1998 there were 15 Rusyn (Carpatho-Rusyn) ethnonational local governments, whereas by 2006 this number had doubled to 31. On a daily basis, these minority identities have varying degrees of manifestation.

Citizens of a formerly predominantly agrarian country, Hungarians cherish folk traditions of their ancestors (known collectively as peasant agriculturalist and pastoralist). This has been facilitated by the political-cultural movement referred to as populism. An elite-based revitalization of literary and folk traditions from the 1930s, and more recently in the 1970s, it is based on symbols, values, and folklore of village life, a hallmark of which is the special attention paid to communities away from urban centers such as those situated in present-day Slovakia, Romania, and targeted regions within Hungary where remnants of former lifestyles were found and described by ethnographers (Hortobágy, Sárrét, Kiskunság, Nagykunság, Ormánság, Kisalföld, Palócföld, Jászság, etc.).

Three diaspora areas where Hungarians live outside of Hungary (Subcarpathian Ukraine, Serbia, and the Burgenland region of Austria) are much less valued by ethnographers as their traditions have been eradicated either by forceful or voluntary assimilation. While agricultural ways of life duplicate that of other Europeans, certain features can be considered unique to Hungarians. Cross-fertilized by Slavic, Germanic, Roma, and Romanian culture, Hungarian peasant culture is a mixture of both borrowed and internally developed complexes with considerable regional flavor, illustrated by music displaying pentatonic melodies existing alongside nonharmonic and nonpolyphonic singing. Undoubtedly, such a heritage has been essential in contributing to the development of folk music research since the early 20th century, a tradition that gave the world ethnomusicologists Béla Vikár, Béla Bartók, Zoltán Kodály, and László Lajtha. Most Westerners associate Hungary with Gypsy music since the time of Franz Liszt, which is in fact 19th-century popular music. Roma/Gypsy music resembles tribal music anchored to slow harmonic singing and ballads, together with improvised dancing with little or no contact between men and women during performance.

In contrast, in Hungarian peasant dancing, the stress on virtuoso male solo and small-group dancing is important, such as in archaic female circle dances (*karikázó*), which were required during Lent when instrumental music was forbidden by the church. However, since the mid-20th century, with the waning of agriculture and animal husbandry and the loss of household economy, these forms of music and dance are now relegated to repertoires of folklore ensembles, a pattern that can also be observed with regard to folk customs, dress, and more traditional utensils and furniture. Food ways, especially holiday dishes, are often associated with ethnic pride; to a gourmet it will be obvious that the chicken paprikás, smoked sausages, stuffed cabbage (*töltött káposzta*), jellied pig's feet (*kocsonya*), spicy fishermen's soup (*halászlé*), strudel (*rétes*), and pancake (*palacsinta*) are ethnic characteristics found in flavoring more than in the ingredients. Today, restaurants throughout the country offer traditional as well as international dishes. While pizzerias are common in present-day Hungary, local csárda restaurants, that is, traditional inns where one can hear Gypsy music and taste local food with local wines, still abound and have undergone revitalization since 1990. The internationally recognized wine labels such as Tokaj and Bull's Blood of Eger are increasingly replaced by grapes such as the Kékfrankos, Juhfark, Hárslevelű, Kadarka, Ezerjó, and others.

Urban and intellectual circles have contributed largely to modern cosmopolitan cultural life since the second half of the 19th century, in which the nation's capital, Budapest, has played a crucial role. Most research institutions, theaters, journals, cinemas, and publishing houses are located there, giving perhaps disproportionate emphasis to the capital in comparison to lesser-known cities and towns across the country, where one can also find ample evidence of local traditions and color. Hungarians are proud to claim 13 Nobel Prize-winners, all of whom were born under the Austro-Hungarian Dual Monarchy, among them the nuclear physicists John von Neumann, Edward Teller, Eugene Wiegner, and Leo Szilard. They boast many notable scholars such as historians István Deák and John Lukács, semiotician Thomas Sebeok, psychoanalysts Sándor Ferenczi, Géza Róheim, and George Devereux. The names of philosophers (Karl and Michael Polanyi, Georg Lukács); photographers Robert Capa, Brassai (Gyula Halász), Andre Kertész, Laszlo Moholy-Nagy, Victor Vasarely, and film directors István Szabó, Miklós Jancso, or Márta Mészáros are also world-renowned. Receiving the Nobel Prize for Literature in 2002, the writer Imre Kertész has enlarged the list of famous Hungarians, like the inventor Ernő Rubik who designed the Rubik's cube in 1975. Hungary's soccer sensation, Ferenc Puskás (1927–2006), was beloved by fans all over the world.

After World War II, Hungary was a Moscow-ruled state socialist country, with a single-party system, collectivized agriculture, and nationalized industry. Following the crushed 1956 revolution, during the late 1970s a vibrant, often antistate popular culture and rock music culture helped undermine Communist rule. This led to the revolutionary political events of 1989, a transformation that achieved a new national consciousness and identity together with new symbols associated with a rejuvenated sense of historical memory. Today, apart from the dominant Roman Catholic holidays, there are three major national holidays that are considered genuine in that they represent the Hungarian nation and are not tainted by communism: March 15, celebrating the 1848–1849 revolution and war, August 20 (Saint Stephen's Day) commemorating the foundation of the Hungarian state, and October 23, remembering the outbreak of the 1956 revolution. A member of the European Union since 2004, Hungary remains divided into 19 counties, although there is a strong pressure by the European Union to abandon this county system in favor of a more inclusive regional administrative one. Political and economic transformation aside, there is a considerable population decline: the total number of Hungarians may be about 14 million; in Hungary, in 1999 there were 10,092,000 Hungarians, while a decade later, that number decreased to 10,031,000!

*László Kürti*

**Further Reading**

Frigyesi, Judit. *Béle Bartók and the Turn-of-the-Century Budapest.* Berkeley: University of California Press, 1998.

Kürti, László. *The Remote Borderland: Transylvania in the Hungarian Imagination.* Albany: State University of New York Press, 2001.

Portuges, Catherine. *Screen Memories: The Hungarian Cinema of Márta Mészáros.* Bloomington: Indiana University Press, 1993.

Sugar, Peter F., Péter Hanák, and Tibor Frank, eds. *A History of Hungary.* Bloomington: Indiana University Press, 1990.

Szemere, Anna. *Up from the Underground: The Culture of Rock Music in Postsocialist Hungary.* Philadelphia: Pennsylvania State University Press, 2001.

# Icelanders

Icelanders are the dominant population in Iceland, which is an island of 39,769 square miles (103,000 square kilometers) in the North Atlantic Ocean with a population of nearly 320,000 (2009). The main population of people of Icelandic origin living outside of Iceland reside in the United States and Canada. Contemporary migration flow from Iceland is mostly to other Nordic countries. Icelanders have until recently been a relatively homogenous group, but currently about 10 percent of the population are born outside of Iceland. Icelandic is a North Germanic language descended from Old Norse. The majority of the inhabitants belong to the National Church of Iceland, an Evangelical Lutheran Church.

Icelanders originate from people who migrated to Iceland from Norway, Scotland, and Ireland in the 9th century. The period from the settlement and until the country's entrance into the Norwegian monarchy in the latter part of the 13th century is referred to as the Commonwealth Period. Along with Norway, Iceland came under Danish rule in the 16th century. In 1785, Iceland was granted limited home rule by Denmark, in 1874 it was granted a constitution, and in 1918 it became a sovereign state within Denmark. Full independence was claimed on June 17, 1944, at which time the Icelandic Republic was founded. This occurred while Denmark was occupied by Germany. Iceland was occupied by the British in 1940 and handed over to the United States in 1941. Subsequently a NATO base was established that was located there until 2007. The relations with Denmark and later the presence of the U.S. military have both contributed to the definition of Icelandic nationality.

The establishment of an independent republic was not merely the establishment of a new state according to the nationalistic ideologies then current in Europe, but a self-conscious revival of the independence of the Commonwealth Period. The leader of the nationalist movement, Jón Sigurðsson (1811–1879), researched and published the Sagas of the Commonwealth Period and referred often to the autonomy of that era as he formulated the call for modern Icelandic independence. His birthday—June 17—is celebrated as the national day of Iceland. In spite of the dominant discourse of long and hard struggle against Danish rule, it was not until the 1830s that autonomy claims began to be made in Iceland. The Icelandic language was from the beginning by far the most important aspect of defining Icelandic nationality as distinct from other Nordic nationalities, tightly interconnected with the other main aspect—nature. Language was seen as connecting Icelanders to their history and their land. Because written Icelandic has changed little, modern Icelanders can read the medieval sagas and thereby cultivate a strong sense of connection to their ancestors and homeland. Thus the biological connection, language, and history are all interconnected in Icelandic nationality. For this reason people of Icelandic origin in North America are referred to as West Icelanders even though they rarely speak Icelandic.

As part of the national construction, the standardization of Icelandic was followed by strict language policies purifying the language first of Danish words and later in the 20th century of English influences. The government has reacted to perceived threats to the language by implementing a protectionist language policy aiming to preserve and enhance the language. Great emphasis is put on making new Icelandic words for emergent technologies, such as computer (*tölva*) and telephone (*sími*). The emphasis on preserving Icelandic is also reflected in personal name regulations. From 1951 to 1996, having an Icelandic name was a prerequisite to gaining Icelandic citizenship; today foreign residents no longer have to adopt Icelandic names. However, if one of the parents of a child born in Iceland is or has been a foreign citizen, the parents are allowed to name their child with one foreign name, but they are also required to give the child one Icelandic name or one that can be adjusted to Icelandic grammar. November 16, the birthday of the 19th-century poet Jónas Hallgrímsson, is celebrated as Icelandic language day. The major Icelandic National Broadcasting Service also plays an important role in fostering the Icelandic language, history, and national cultural heritage. In the 1960s the Icelandic authorities, for example, successfully demanded a restriction

on American broadcasting from the NATO base for fear that the English language and American culture might dilute Icelandic ways.

Although the majority of Icelanders identify as religious and 80 percent belong to the National Church of Iceland, an Evangelical Lutheran Church, religion does not play a large role in people's daily lives. The Lutheran Church replaced the Catholic Church in the 16th century as part of the Danish Monarchy. Iceland is today a fairly secular society; there is, for example, a general indifference toward formal marriage, and out-of-wedlock births are not stigmatized. The Hidden People and trolls who populated the beliefs of former rural areas are retained today as folklore. Roads are occasionally constructed in such a way as to prevent damaging rocks where Hidden People are believed to live. A small but growing constituency belongs to the Old Norse religion Ásatrú, a legally recognized revival of the pre-Christian Nordic religion of the early settlers. With growing numbers of immigrants, other religious faiths, mostly Christian, are becoming more common.

Until the 19th century most Icelanders lived as smallhold farmers, with many also taking part in the seasonal fishery. In the end of the 19th century, servants and landless paupers envisioned a better life in the growing fisheries and moved to the coastal villages. Almost one-third of the population moved to North America and some of them formed New Iceland in Manitoba, Canada. The national identity constructed in the late 19th century portrayed the farms as the cradle of Icelandic culture and language. The life in the countryside was contrasted to the supposedly cultureless and cruel lives of the landless day laborers, and the Danish merchants in coastal areas were portrayed as having a bad influence on the language and people.

The 20th century was characterized by growing urbanization and increased wealth, and with this a changing conception of what it means to be an Icelander. Although language continues to be a key symbol in linking the nation together, there are also other symbols presented to tourists such as the Icelandic horse, the wool sweater, and some foodstuff such as rotten shark and blood sausages that are associated in people's minds with the rural past. Following World War II, the development of a modern welfare state emphasized building up of infrastructure and services. An important part of this goal toward the building of a modern society was to modernize the fish industry, which has been the strong base of the economy.

Nature has long figured in the national sense of self. When out on rough seas, fishermen were deemed national heroes providing national wealth and were celebrated in popular songs, but daily life in the villages held little status. Although the purity of nature has been emphasized, the natural perception has for the most part been that of a farmer or hunter and the right to hunt and fish as part of the right of an independent nation. Until recently, environmentalists were seen as a threat to this view. This ideology of common national resource has persisted even though the access to the fish has been privatized with a transferable quota system for more than 20 years.

With the urbanization and forming of a nation-state came the establishment of national theater, a symphony orchestra, and other forms of the arts. Artistic life has been lively in urban and rural areas and in almost every little village there is a music school, commonly with foreign teachers. Musicians who have recently become internationally known include Björk and Sigur Rós. However, literature and poetry have played a larger role in the defining of the group. The heroes of the national movement were poets and writers who wrote about Icelandic nature. Halldór Laxness, a Nobel Prize winner in literature in 1945, was the most influential writer of the 20th century in Iceland in giving meaning to what it was to be an Icelander.

In spite of the privatization of many sectors and growing differences between rich and poor, Icelanders have a strong image of themselves as living in a democratic society characterized by equal access to education and health. From the strong role of women in the settlement of the island to the 1980 election of Vigdís Finnbogadóttir, the first woman president, gender equality is viewed as part of the Icelandic tradition. As Iceland becomes increasingly integrated into a global economy along with restructuring of the industries, tourism, and growing number of immigrants, the ethnic identity of Icelanders is taking on new forms even as it takes up old symbols.

*Unnur Dís Skaptadóttir*

**Further Reading**

Brydon, A. "The Predicament of Nature: Keiko the Whale and The Cultural Politics of Whaling in Iceland." *Anthropological Quarterly* 79 (2006): 225–260.

Hálfdánarson, G. "Severing the Ties—Iceland's Journey from a Union with Denmark to a

Nation-State." *Scandinavian Journal of History* 31 (2006): 237–254.

Hastrup, K. *A Place Apart: An Anthropological Study of the Icelandic World.* Oxford: Clarendon Press, 1998.

Pálsson, G. *The Textual Life of Savants: Ethnography, Iceland, and the Linguistic Turn.* Chur: Harwood Academic, 1995.

Pálsson, G., and E. Paul Durrenberger, eds. *Images of Contemporary Iceland: Everyday Lives and Global Contexts.* Iowa City: University of Iowa Press, 1996.

Skaptadóttir, U.D. "Response to Global Transformations: Gender and Ethnicity in Resource-based Localities in Iceland." *Polar Record* 40 (2004): 1–7.

# Ingush

The Ingush are an indigenous people of the Northern Caucasus numbering less than half a million. Their ethnonym is derived from the first Ingush *a'ul* (village) encountered by the Russians: Angusht. Their own self-designation—*Ghalghay* (*ghal* meaning "fortress" and *ghay* or "inhabitants")—was originally the name of one of the clans into which they are historically divided: Ghalghay, Dgharkhol, Metskhal, Kori, and Kist (Veppi). However, the Kists, especially those living across the main Caucasus range in Georgia, are usually considered a separate ethnic group. The Ingush are Sunni Muslims of the Shafi'i School and speak Ingush, which belongs to the Nakh branch of the Northeast Caucasian language family. The Ingush traditionally inhabited the area between the middle course of the Terek River and the main Caucasus range. Most of them live nowadays in the Ingush Autonomous Republic of the Russian Federation, established in 1992. More than 60,000 Ingush lived in North Ossetia before the Ingush-Osset war (1992) and several thousand in Grozny before the Chechen war (1994–1996). Many thousands live in Central Asia, mainly Kazakhstan, in various parts of the Russian Federation, and in the Middle East, mainly in Turkey.

As far as can be established, the ancestors of the present-day Ingush have been living in their present habitat since around the eighth millennium BCE. Before their encounter with the Russians, the Ingush, together with the Chechens and some smaller groups, were part of a traditional larger ethnic grouping known to its members as Waynakh ("our people"). This sense of common identity has not disappeared despite modern nation-formation. In late 1991, when the Chechens were moving toward, but before they had actually declared, independence, many suggested a united Waynakh independent republic. However, modern nationalism seemed to be stronger and the two peoples parted. The Chechens declared a republic independent of Russia while the Ingush established an autonomous republic within the Russian Federation.

The differentiation between the Ingush and Chechens, which ended in the crystallization of two separate peoples, started before the Russian conquest. By that time—the end of the 18th to the beginning of the 19th century—the Chechens were almost completely Islamicized, while the process had barely started among the Ingush. The Islamicization of the Ingush proceeded mainly in the 19th up to the turn of the 20th century. A major part

Group of Ingush boys wait for a bus to Nazran, in Chermen village at Ossetia on the Ingush border in 2004. (AP/Wide World Photos)

in this process was played by the Qadiri Sufi brotherhood, especially its Battal Hajji *wird* (branch), which resisted the Soviet authorities in the 1930s and 1940s and continues to be of major importance nowadays. Today Islam is a central component of Ingush ethnic identity and cultural tradition. Many, if not most, Ingush are affiliated with Sufi brotherhoods.

It was, however, during the decades of Russian conquest that the gap between the Ingush and Chechens widened, as the formative experience of each group was completely different. The Chechens opposed Imperial Russia with arms since at least the 1780s and played an important part in the 30-year-long Islamic resistance to the Russian conquest (1829–1859) and the

Imamate (Islamic state) it established. The Ingush did not take part in this resistance.

This gap acquired a geographical dimension when, following the final conquest of the eastern Caucasus in 1859, the Orstkhoy (also known as Karabulak)—a transition tribe between the Ingush and the Chechens—migrated en masse to the Ottoman Empire. Further developments, including divide-and-rule policies by both the Russian Imperial and Soviet authorities, resulted in the formation of two separate peoples.

On the other hand, the Ingush and Chechens also share a strongly negative experience under Russian and Soviet rule. During the struggle to conquer the Caucasus the Russian military forcibly transferred the

Waynakhs to the lowlands, only to push them back after the period known as "pacification." Furthermore, both during and especially after the struggle, the most fertile Waynakh lands were distributed among the Cossacks. The spiraling shortage of land and resources coupled with a population explosion drove many Ingush (and Chechens) to brigandage and made the turn of the 20th-century Caucasus into the most lawless province of the Russian Empire.

In the civil war that followed the Russian revolution (1917) most Ingush joined forces with the Bolsheviks. In 1924 the Ingush Autonomous *oblast* (district) was established, and united in 1936 with the Chechen Autonomous *oblast* to form the Chechen-Ingush Autonomous Soviet Socialist Republic. Ingush became a literary language and was provided with a Latin alphabet in the 1920s, and then, in 1938, with a Cyrillic one.

In 1944 the entire Ingush (and Chechen) population was deported to Kazakhstan and Kyrgyzstan, losing in the process between a quarter and a half of its numbers. The Chechen-Ingush ASSR was abolished. In 1957 they were, in Soviet terms, rehabilitated and returned to their ethnic territory, but continued to suffer official and unofficial discrimination. Furthermore, the Ingush were left with an open wound that continued to fester—the problem of the Prigorodnyi district, east of Vladikavkaz.

Following the deportation the Prigorodnyi district was annexed to the North Osset ASSR, and Ossets were settled in it. When the Chechen-Ingush ASSR was reestablished in 1958, the Prigirodnyi district was not restored to it and remained in the North Osset ASSR. Thus, the returning Ingush were not given official permits to return to the district and settled there illegally. The ongoing frustration exploded later in the Soviet period in the form of massive Ingush demonstrations in 1973 demanding the return of the district.

With the dissolution of the USSR the conflict between the Ingush and the Ossets escalated quickly into an all-out war, and in late 1992 the Russian military intervened, evicting the Ingush population from North Ossetia. These, together with Ingush and many thousands of Chechen refugees fleeing the war in Chechnya, created an unbearable refugee problem for the new republic.

Traditionally, the Ingush lived up in the mountains, their economy being based on terrace agriculture and animal breeding. In the old *a'uls* located on the steep slopes and in gorges, medieval dwelling stone towers can still be found. In the 16th and 17th centuries many Ingush migrated to the plains, where they lived in three-story stone houses and engaged in agriculture. The Waynakh were subdivided into tribes and clans. Tribes lived in compact territories and spoke distinct dialects. According to this classification the Ingush were a Waynakh tribe.

Waynakh society was traditionally not divided into classes; instead, each male was considered equal to his peers. Clans too, even if different in size, were equal in status and rejected external authority. Only in response to extreme outside threats would the various clans unite and accept a common temporary and exclusively military leader.

Clans continue to be important even in modern urban life and have a major influence on a person's social life and public behavior. Although nowadays clans are scattered and intermingled, families belonging to the same clan tend to reside compactly in streets or neighborhoods of their own. Strict clan exogamy is universally observed and any Ingush person can trace his/her clan roots to a specific village in the mountains and point at his/her ancestral family tower.

Waynakh morality and codes of behavior are extremely strict. An Ingush man is expected to behave courteously and deferentially to women, to demonstrate respect to his elders in general, and to show obedience to older relatives (especially his father and elder brothers). Although society is patriarchal and women are not considered men's equals, women traditionally enjoyed many more social rights and privileges than in other Islamic societies. Under present-day conditions they have prospects for financial independence, professional careers, and educational achievements too.

The persistence of traditional values and codes of behavior does not mean that the Ingush lack intellectual and cultural dimensions to their way of life or lag behind modernity. Their indigenous artistic and intellectual culture includes a great variety of traditions, legends, epics, tales, proverbs, sayings, songs, music, and dance, a great many of which have been recorded. In addition many Ingush, the highly educated in particular, are very well versed either in the Western or the Islamic (traditional and/or modern) cultures or in both.

*Moshe Gammer*

**Further Reading**

Baddeley, John F., and John Erederic. *The Rugged Flanks of the Caucasus*. London: Oxford University Press and Humphrey Milford, 1940.

Birch, Julian. "Ossetia: A Caucasian Bosnia in Microcosm." *Central Asian Survey* 14, no. 1 (1995): 43–74.

Critchlow, James. *"Punished Peoples" of the Soviet Union: The Continuing Legacy of Stalin's Deportations*. Helsinki Watch Report. New York: Human Rights Watch, 1991.

Goldenberg, Suzanne. *Pride of Small Nations: The Caucasus and Post-Soviet Disorder*. London: Zed, 1994.

Human Rights Watch. *The Ingush-Ossetian Conflict in the Prigorodnyi Region*. New York: Human Rights Watch, 1996.

Matveeva, Anna. "North Ossetia/Ingushetia: A History of the Expulsion and Resettlement of People." In *Searching for Peace in Europe and Eurasia: An Overview of Conflict Prevention and Peace Building Activities*, eds. Paul van Tongeren, Hans van de Veen, and Juliette Verhoeven. Boulder, CO: Lynne Rienner, 2002.

Nichols, Johanna. "The Ingush (with Notes on the Chechen): Background Information." Berkeley: University of California, 1997. Also available at http://ingush.berkeley. edu:7012/ingush_people.html.

# Irish

The Irish are the principal nation/ethnic group on the island of Ireland, which is the homeland of the majority of the approximately 6.2 million inhabitants of the island of Ireland (and where, particularly in Northern Ireland, hundreds of thousands of people identify themselves as British rather than Irish). As an ethnic group, the Irish are also those tens of millions of Irish people and their descendants who are part of the global Irish Diaspora.

These Irish, most of whom descend from those people who emigrated from Ireland during the famine years in the 19th century, form often sizable ethnic minorities in many countries globally, most notably in the United States, Australia, New Zealand, and Argentina. The island of Ireland contains two political entities: the Republic of Ireland (*Poblacht na hÉireann* in Irish, often called *Éire,* or Ireland) occupies five-sixths of the island of Ireland, and, in the northeast of the island, Northern Ireland (a constituent part of the United Kingdom or UK), occupies the remaining sixth of the island. The term Irish denotes the republic's people, language, and culture, and is the primary political and cultural identification for more than 40 percent of the 1.78 million residents (2008) of Northern Ireland. Ethnic and national identification are difficult to ascertain with any certainty in Northern Ireland, where the majority population identify themselves as British within Ireland, but in the UK and elsewhere they often refer to themselves or are often referred to as Irish. The divide between the Irish and the British in Ireland is the product of hundreds of years of colonial relations between the Irish and their more powerful neighbors, but in Northern Ireland the differences in ethnicity between the Irish and the British have been exacerbated since Ireland was divided in 1921, and particularly since the return of violent ethnic conflict in 1969 (which is in most ways ended today via the peace process that has existed since the mid-1990s). Long known as a rural society, over the last generation the majority of the Irish in Ireland have lived in the urban areas of Dublin (capital of the Republic), Belfast (capital of Northern Ireland), Cork, and Galway. The principal languages spoken in Ireland are English and Irish (Gaelic). The majority of Irish in Ireland are Christians; the three largest religions there are Roman Catholic (representing greater than 90% of the populace), the Church of Ireland [Anglican], and Presbyterian.

The Irish culture and language have their origin in the arrival, from the 6th to the 2nd century BCE, of Celtic peoples from the European mainland. Irish Gaelic society developed on the island relatively independently for hundreds of years, but the Irish were far from isolated during this time. Christianity arrived in the course of the 5th century CE, as did the monastic system. Irish monks helped to safeguard the European Christian heritage during the Middle Ages; in the service of humanity and their God they also moved throughout Europe and established monasteries. Norsemen raided Ireland's monasteries and settlements starting in the early 9th century, but later settled along the coasts and waterways of Ireland. In the 12th century the Anglo-Norman migrations to Ireland began, which culminated in the Elizabethan conquest of Ireland. In the 17th century many Irish were forced to vacate their land, a consequence of the English policy of importing immigrants from England and Scotland. Over the course of that century many wars for control of the British Isles were fought in Ireland, some of which, such as the Cromwellian wars and the Glorious Revolution, had significance for wider developments in Europe. Conflicts during the 20th century and the more recent ethnic and nationalist conflicts in Northern Ireland have their roots

Irish farm woman. (Corel)

in the colonial, imperial, and revolutionary clashes of the 17th and 18th centuries, and in the nation-building that occurred in the 19th and early 20th centuries.

Irish ethnic heritage has been heavily influenced by the historical, political, and economic relations between the Irish and their neighbors in Britain and the continent of Europe. The relations with their English neighbors in particular put the Irish into subservient colonial and imperial roles. While the traditional Irish Gaelic social system assimilated many Danes and other Norsemen, as well as the Norman invaders from England after 1169, for four centuries the Anglo-Normans sought to control the island and to institute feudalism and establish parliamentary law and administration. Despite these efforts, by the close of the 15th century English lords controlled only the so-called Pale (the area around Dublin). The Tudors

therefore set out to increase English control, and they did so in part by taking away the lands and power of the Catholic Church in Ireland, actions which helped to forge the long association between Irish Catholicism and Irish nationalism. The Tudor and Stuart conquests and transfer of Irish land to British colonists (1534–1610), the settlement of victorious British troops sponsored by Cromwell (1654), the Williamite war (1689–1691), and the Penal Laws (1695) helped to make Ireland first a colony and later a constituent unit of the United Kingdom of Great Britain and Ireland. This constitutional relationship was broken in 1921, when Ireland, after a War of Independence and a Civil War, was divided into Northern Ireland and the Irish Free State (later the Republic of Ireland).

Generations of political separation and division between the Republic of Ireland

## Northern Ireland Protestants

Ulster Protestants are an ethnic or ethnonational group, established by the "plantation" of English and Scottish settlers in the northern part of Ireland during the first part of the 17th century to suppress the rebellious native Irish inhabitants. This colonization established an ethnonational division between the Catholic Irish population and the Protestant British settler population concentrated in the north. When Ireland became independent in 1920, the country was partitioned because the Ulster Protestants were British in identity and loyalty and preferred to remain a part of the United Kingdom. The 2001 census showed that 895,000 Protestants made up 53 percent of the population of Northern Ireland, and a 1989 identity survey indicated that 68 percent of Protestants identified as British, 16 percent as Northern Irish, 10 percent as Ulster, and 3 percent as Irish. Most grow up in ethnically segregated areas, identify with British culture, history, and identity, attend Protestant churches and state schools separately from Catholics, are loyal to the British crown, want to remain part of the UK, and vote for Unionist political parties.

*Jeffrey Sluka*

and Northern Ireland have resulted in different forms of ethnic, public, and civil culture, which may be seen in dialect, religion, government, politics, sports, and music. For example, the majority population in Northern Ireland count themselves as British nationals; they support the political causes of Unionism and Loyalism and reject calls for unification with the Republic of Ireland. The largest minority population in Northern Ireland, in contrast, self-identify as Irish, and many seek reunification with the republic. In the republic itself, the great majority of Irish people describe themselves as ethnic Irish while far smaller numbers of Irish nationals, known as "Anglo-Irish," stress their British origins. Irish "Travelers" (or "Tinkers"), a minority population found across the island, have long been known as itinerant entertainers, traders, and artisans. At the end of the 20th century, Ireland became for the first time a land of net immigration. Today in both the republic and in Northern Ireland there are growing populations of ethnic minorities who immigrated from elsewhere in Europe, Asia, Africa, and the Americas; many of these people identify themselves as Irish based on various factors of assimilation, intermarriage, affinity, permanent residence, and citizenship.

Irish culture has many origins. By the end of the 18th century there had been centuries of various mixing of Gaelic, Norse, Norman, and English language and customs. Irish ethnicity and nationalism have also been shaped by conquest, colonialism, and rebellion. The cultural nationalism at the heart of the long history of Irish struggles for political and economic autonomy also has many sources that are internal and external to Ireland; paramount

## Northern Ireland Catholics

In Northern Ireland, Catholics are an ethnic or ethnonational group descended from the original Gaelic inhabitants of Ulster. The 2001 census showed that 737,000 Catholics constitute 44 percent of the population of the province, and a 1989 identity survey indicated that among Catholics, 60 percent identified as Irish, 25 percent as Northern Irish, 8 percent as British, and 2 percent as Ulster. They are Catholic in religion and Irish in national identity; they opposed partition in 1920, did not consent to being excluded from the rest of Ireland, and were forced to remain part of the UK. In Northern Ireland, they are an oppressed ethnonational minority subject to political, economic, and cultural discrimination, which led to the 1969–1994 war. Group endogamy is very strong, and in response to extreme ethnic residential and social segregation, most Catholics grow up in segregated districts, identify with Irish culture, history, and identity, attend Catholic churches and schools separately from Protestants, want to become part of a united Ireland, and vote for Republican (nationalist) political parties.

*Jeffrey Sluka*

among these were French and American republicanism, the Catholic emancipation movement of the early 19th century, and the Gaelic Revival of the late 19th century, which was the Anglo-Irish revitalization of Irish language, sport, literature, drama, and poetry.

The various forms of Irish culture have also had a great impact beyond Ireland, most notably among the Irish Diaspora, many of whom had fled the Great Famine (1846–1849), when the staple of the Irish peasantry was destroyed by a potato blight. The diaspora is a significant factor in the creation and persistence of Irish ethnicity and culture around the globe. In addition to the descendants of 19th century emigrants, this population is made up of descendants of both earlier and later Irish emigrants as well as recent arrivals from Ireland itself. Irish communities embrace various aspects of Irish culture, including religion, language, food, drink, dance, music, dress, and secular and religious rituals, such as the St. Patrick's Day parades held around the globe on March 17 wherever Irish ethnic communities are found. While in the past Irish migrants often endured ethnic, racial, and religious prejudice, today Irish people are often known for the strength of their continuing ethnicity as well as their assimilation to majority cultures across the globe. The hyphenated identity of the "Irish-American" is perhaps the best example of how the diaspora has extended and changed Irish ethnicity and heritage. Many in the Irish Diaspora have kept their ties to the homeland and have worked toward a resolution to the ethnic conflict in Northern Ireland. Within the Republic of Ireland itself, ethnic relations may be described as relatively peaceful, but many

## Irish Tinkers/Travelers

Irish "travelers" are a nomadic people of Ireland. In 2006, there were 22,400 travelers in Ireland, about 7,000 in the United States and 15,000–30,000 in Great Britain. In Irish, travelers are called *Lucht Siúil*—"the walking people"—but they refer to themselves as "Pavees." They are also referred to as "tinkers," from the Irish *tincéir* (tinsmith) and are distinguished by their own language (Shelta) and customs. Most live in caravans and travel around the country in pursuit of work. Their origins are unclear, but they may descend from people made homeless by Oliver Cromwell's military campaign in Ireland in 1649–1650 and the "Great Famine" in the 1840s, or, legend has it, from a tinsmith whose line was cursed to travel the Earth for having helped build the cross on which Christ was crucified. They are a socially stigmatized minority suffering from discrimination and racism. Despite passage of the Caravan Sites Act in the United Kingdom (1968), the Irish government still does not recognize them as a distinct "ethnic group."

*Jeffrey Sluka*

A young Irish "tinker," or traveler woman sits with friends on the steps of her caravan. (Dorthea Sheats/National Geographic Society/Corbis)

Irish Travellers and recent immigrants to Ireland from Asia, Africa, and Eastern Europe have suffered from Irish bigotry. In Northern Ireland, ethnic conflict, which is tied to different forms of nationalism, ethnicity, and religion, was high after the return of ethnic violence in 1969 (known as "the Troubles"), but since 1994 paramilitary groups have generally accepted a cease-fire agreement.

Irish culture shares much with its near and far neighbors, but there is also much that is distinctive to Irish ethnicity, in the homeland and globally. The Republic of Ireland has no official state religion, but the Catholic Church has enjoyed a special relationship with political and civil institutions since state independence. Irish Catholicism has also figured prominently in Irish ethnic communities across the globe, but in many situations today in Ireland and elsewhere the differences between Catholic and Protestant are not as pronounced as they were in times past. Worldwide Irish culture is also famous for its achievements in the arts, poetry, literature, and politics. The Anglo-Irish literary renaissance drew inspiration from a long tradition of writing in Irish. Modern Irish writers such as W. B. Yeats, James Joyce, George Bernard Shaw, Seán O'Casey, Samuel Beckett, Frank O'Connor, Seán O Faoláin, Flann O'Brien, and Seamus Heaney are considered to be among the greatest writers in the English language. Among the world-renowned Irish artists of the last century are Jack B. Yeats and Paul Henry. The expressive arts are particularly valued in all forms of Irish culture. Music notables such as U2 and Van Morrison in rock, Daniel O'Donnell in country, James Galway in classical, and The Chieftains in Irish traditional music have had a global impact on the arts. In the last decade there has been an international phenomenon built around the traditional Irish music and dance revival in Riverdance. Many worldwide have appreciated the achievements in cinema of the Hollywood Irish, such as actor James Cagney and director John Ford, and cinema in Ireland has given the world the work of respected directors such as Neil Jordan and Jim Sheridan, and famous actors such as Maureen O'Hara, Liam Neeson, Brendan Gleeson, and Colin Farrell. In civic and public culture the art of informal politics around the globe is often associated with the . machine-style politics that became important in modern Ireland, and was exported to such places and peoples as Tammany Hall in New York, the Daleys of Chicago, and the Kennedys of Massachusetts.

*Thomas M. Wilson*

## Further Reading

Central Statistics Office Ireland (CSO). *Population: Principal Statistics*, 2009. http://www.cso.ie/default.htm.

Foster, Robert Fitzroy. *Modern Ireland, 1600–1972*. New York: Penguin, 1988.

McCall, Cathal, and Thomas M. Wilson, eds. *Hibernicisation and Europeanisation: Ireland and Europe*. New York: Rodopi, 2010.

Northern Ireland Statistics and Research Agency (NISRA). *Population Statistics*, 2009. Also available at http://www.nisra.gov.uk/index.html.

Wilson, Thomas M., and Hastings Donnan. *The Anthropology of Ireland*. Oxford: Berg Publishers, 2006.

# Italians

Italians (*Italiani*) are citizens of the Republic of Italy. The population of Italy was 60,045,068 at the end of 2008, of which 6.5 percent were foreigners. The population has been increasing steadily since the turn of the millennium despite the decline in birthrate, thanks largely to immigration from other countries of the European

Union (EU), Eastern Europe, northern and western Africa, and southern and eastern Asia. In December 2007, 3,649,377 Italians lived outside the country, mostly in other EU countries, the Americas, and Australia. Most of these belong to families that left the country in search of employment in the aftermath of World War II. Populations of ethnic Italians, namely, people who are not necessarily Italian citizens but speak Italian, Italian dialects, and/or identify themselves as Italians are also found in the regions straddling the Italian border, most notably in southeastern France, Corsica, the Canton Ticino of Switzerland, western Slovenia, and the Istrian peninsula of Croatia. The primary language spoken in Italy is Italian (*lingua italiana*), a Romance language based on a Tuscan dialect, adopted by the state after national unification in 1870. Although the Tuscan dialect represents the national standard, several mutually unintelligible regional and local dialects are spoken throughout the country. Some of these, for example, Sardinian in Sardinia, Friulian in Friuli, and Ladin in Trentino-South Tyrol, are considered languages in their own right. The primary religion of Italians is Roman Catholicism. Although nearly 90 percent of Italians identified themselves as Roman Catholics in 2006, only one-third of these described themselves as active members, and the influence of the clergy on social and religious questions is not as great as before World War II. Other Christians found in Italy include Eastern and Greek Orthodox Christians, Pentecostals, and Evangelicals. The Muslim population makes up the largest non-Christian community (1.6%), but only very few of these are Italians. It should be

noted, then, that the Italians, though often described as a homogeneous people, are divided into several culturally, socially, and politically diverse groups throughout the peninsula. Even though the unification of Italy dates back to 1870, there was no historical precedent for the state established then, and identification with an imaginary "Italian nation" still remains problematic.

Although Italians are associated with the nation-state created in 1870, understanding how the term "Italy" (Italia) came into being entails examining Italian identity as an historical process. That the country is home to both the Roman Empire and Catholic Church has been crucial to this identity. The idea that the peninsula represents a homogeneous geographical unit is largely the result of the Roman cultural legacy. Ironically, it was the people inhabiting the southern part of the peninsula that, in the first century CE, first used the term "Italia" to designate a political unit opposed to Rome.

Road building and the process of urbanization of the peninsula undertaken by the Roman empire played a significant role in unifying the territory, yet they also had the effect of furthering strong regional identities. The period following the collapse of the Roman Empire saw the devastating effects of the invasions of the Goths and Vandals. What emerged around the year 1000, then, was a new territory controlled by foreign powers and inhabited by people speaking different (but related) dialects. Most of these dialects developed from Latin that was the only written language in use.

When, in the 13th century, society freed itself from the necessities of a subsistence economy, the towns resumed their function as centers of exchange and market places. This process culminated in the ascendancy of port cities such as Genoa, Pisa, and Venice, and of "communes" (*comuni*) such as Florence, Milan, and Siena (to name a few), whose wealth was based on their control over the surrounding countryside. While these contributed to the emergence of a "national consciousness," their rise also shaped a many-centered universe rife with deep rivalries. The other crucial factor that contributed to the making of a national consciousness in the same period was the process of linguistic (i.e., literary) unification, whose onset is associated with the creation of a circle of poets in Palermo at the court of German emperor Frederick II. At a time when the peninsula was rife with bitter conflicts, Florentine poet Dante Alighieri (1265–1321), still considered by many the father and prophet of a yet unborn Italy, stressed the need of a "national" language purified of elements of dialect and endowed with a fine grammatical and syntactical structure. His emphasis upon a national awareness was later echoed by poet Francesco Petrarca (1304–1374), who described Italy as a country bounded by the sea and the Alps, and the Italians as the legitimate heirs of the Roman tradition.

The connection between the Roman legacy and Italian identity was central to the development of the intellectual movement known as humanism (then called the renaissance) that came to the fore particularly in Tuscany between the 15th and 16th centuries. It consisted of a reexamination of the classical cultural heritage, and affected later developments of Italian and European culture. Italy's central role in European cultural and economic life came to an end during the 16th century following the Ottoman expansion in the eastern Mediterranean, the consolidation of Spanish rule in the peninsula, and the Reformation. The Council of Trent that was the response to the religious schism (1545–1563) did not result in reconciliation with the Reformation, but certainly affirmed the central role of Catholicism in the life of Italians.

The period from the late 16th to the late 18th century saw the consolidation of the power of foreign dynasties on the one hand, and of the church on the other. The 19th century witnessed profound changes in the peninsula as a result of the rise of nationalism in Europe, the growth of the state of Piedmont, and the onset of industrialization. In this context, Giuseppe Mazzini (1805–1872) wrote that a nation has a unity of religion, language, and custom, and influenced the Risorgimento movement that led to the three wars of independence (1848, 1859, and 1866), and then to the capture of Rome and national unification in 1870.

Most Italians are Roman Catholics, and the traditional task of the Catholic Church is to guide and instruct the faithful about their place in the world. Its doctrine retains much of the heritage of the counter-Reformation, most notably an emphasis upon ecclesiastical hierarchy, the submission of women, and the virtues of obedience and acceptance of one's status in life. Private property, the family, and work represented the three pillars of its social doctrine, and affected the political and cultural orientations of most Italians during fascism and the cold war. However, the church is perceived differently in different parts of the country: while in the South the church is still associated with vertical bonds of authority, in the North it succeeded in staying in tune with the transformations of Italian society by developing networks of cultural, recreational, and educational activities alongside the religious ones. Saints play an important role in Catholic doctrine: they may be invoked for help by all believers, and some of them are associated with particular kinds of problems or illnesses. In the Apulian town of Galatina the benevolent intervention of St. Paul was sought to heal those in the state of physical and psychological disorder caused, it was believed, by a spider bite. Saints are also associated with a wide range of identities, which include that of patrons of villages, towns, or occupational groups. The village patron saint, whose statue is carried around the village on patron saint day, provided until recently a way in which local, collective identity was articulated, and is often associated with a miracle. In Naples, for example, the faithful gather three times a year to witness the alleged liquefaction of St. Januarius' blood.

Italy represents a multicentered cultural universe, and every Italian city is characterized by its own flavor: while Genoa, Milan, and Turin are renowned industrial cities, Bologna, Florence, Rome, and Venice are known as cities of amenities. Each city has a major piazza (square), the meeting point for social encounters and the spatial context for commercial activities. It lies at the heart of the historical center, and is surrounded by the main historical buildings such as the town hall, the church, the theater, and the cafés where local residents congregate to have a cup of espresso, read the daily newspapers, play cards, and discuss politics or sport (soccer is by far the most popular). A characteristic of Italian city and town residents is pride in the qualities of one's locality known as *campanilismo* or local chauvinism, which stresses the differences between one's own place and others, but also connotes a narrowness of outlook.

With the aftermath of World War II, the major industrial cities witnessed an influx of immigrants from the South, seeking employment in manufacturing and processing activities. Yet while the postwar economic boom turned the industrialized part of the country into an economic giant, it also widened the gap between the wealthy North and the poorer South, and most northerners and southerners still regard one another as belonging to different cultures. The Italian government has attempted partially to narrow this economic gap by helping to build industrial plants in the South. However, these have not solved any social problems in the area, and the main beneficiaries of state subsidies are often criminal organizations (e.g., mafia in Sicily or camorra in Campania) that rely upon connections with people in high places. Furthermore, in most of the South it is still assumed that one cannot obtain anything without the recommendation (*raccomandazione*) of someone in a position of power, often in exchange for a bribe or a personal favor.

The years that followed unification saw attempts to address internal problems: 78 percent of Italians were illiterate, and the conditions of life were often below subsistence level, especially in the South.

The agricultural crisis of the late 19th century hit Italy very hard, and resulted in massive waves of emigration to richer European countries and the Americas. However, the beginning of the 20th century was characterized by economic growth, most notably by the development of automobile industry, and by a general awakening of the political consciousness of the new working classes. Yet this economic boom was short-lived, and the crisis that affected the steel and automobile industries in 1907 had repercussions in the textile and cotton industries too.

The worsening economic situation and the crisis of the Austro-Hungarian Empire led to the outbreak of World War I. Italy declared war against the empire in 1915. Yet, for Italy, World War I was largely a war of attrition that resulted in the consolidation of an authoritarian state and the death of 600,000 Italians. It was only with the collapse of the Austro-Hungarian Empire in 1918 that Italy could conquer Trentino and the city of Trieste, and later annex German-speaking South Tyrol and the Istrian peninsula with its strong Slavonic minority.

Although Italy emerged victorious from the conflict, it did not succeed in solving its economic problems, and in the war's aftermath the Italian government also had to cope with the rise of socialism. In this context, fascism came to the fore by provoking a climate of civil war in cities where socialists were strong, and subsequently rose to power in 1922. Fascism quickly transformed itself into a regime under the leadership of Benito Mussolini (1883–1945), also known as Il Duce. Central to his rhetoric was the idea that Italy was the natural heir of the Roman Empire. This idea was used to justify the Italian colonization of Libya and East Africa. With the outbreak of World War II, an alliance was signed between Italy and Hitler's Germany. Yet the intervention of the United States in 1941 and Italy's military defeats in Africa and Greece gave fascist Italy severe blows, and the war ended in complete disaster.

American financial help through the Marshall Plan proved decisive in regenerating the Italian economy and in making the Christian Democratic Party (DC) the governing political force instead of the Italian Communist Party (PCI). In joining NATO in 1949, Italy made its choice in foreign policy, and from 1954 economic recovery was very rapid. Until the early 1990s Italy's political landscape was largely shaped by the Cold War, and was characterized by the tension between left and right (or center-right), namely, between Communists and Christian Democrats. Both parties shared an emphasis on solidarity and a denunciation of consumerism. However, the political culture advocated by the DC was the culture of submission to institutional authority (especially the Catholic Church), accompanied by the virtues of mediation, which often turned into advocacy of patron-client relationships. By contrast, central to the political culture of the PCI was the contestation of established authority, the organization of strikes, and collective solutions to collective problems.

In the early 1990s, Italy witnessed dramatic political and economic changes as

## Tyroleans

Just over 1 million German-speaking Tyroleans live in the Austrian region of Tyrol (Tirol) and in the South Tyrol province (Südtirol or Alto Adige) across the Italian border. While the identity of the group is defined primarily by a common language and dialect, until 1918 the Austro-Hungarian region of Tyrol included the above-mentioned territories as well as the Italian-speaking Trentino province. Tyrolean identity was shaped in fundamental ways by the insurrection against Napoleon, led by Andreas Hofer (1809) in his unsuccessful attempt to establish an autonomous peasant republic in the Alps. After World War I Austria surrendered South Tyrol to Italy. Under Fascism, South Tyrol was colonized by Italian industrial workers, and the German speakers remained rural. After World War II the Italian government granted cultural autonomy, but kept economic and social development under its control. Nevertheless, Tyrolean identity

Tyrolean rifleman with red beard at a meeting in the Passeiertal valley, South Tyrol, Italy. (Imagno/Getty Images)

remains fluid, particularly in light of attempts to revive the pre-1918 Tyrolean region in the form of a transnational economic area following Austria's accession to the European Union in 1995.

*Jaro Stacul*

a consequence of the economic recession and the end of the cold war. Among these, the demise of the DC as a consequence of corruption scandals, the division of the PCI into two parties (now three), the decline of the welfare state, and mass immigration are the most significant. Such changes paved the way for the rise of new political forces, of which the Lega Nord/ Northern League and Forza Italia/Let's Go Italy were the most successful. The former contrasts the idea of national identity, promises stern measures to curb immigration, and seeks to transform Italy into a federal state. The latter, founded by media magnate Silvio Berlusconi in 1994, protects the interests of entrepreneurs, and has on its agenda an Italian version of Thatcherism and a residual welfare state. The political changes of the early 1990s also led to the reorganization of the Italian Left, and particularly to the creation of a center-left coalition that includes former communists, the left strand of former Christian Democrats, former socialists, and other minor like-minded movements. Because of the heterogeneity of its membership, the coalition is caught between the legacy of the former Communist Party and the advocacy of economic reforms in order to cope with the challenges posed by neo-liberal globalization.

In the 1980s, Italy ceased to be a country of emigrants, and began to attract waves of immigration primarily from non-European and east European countries. Before such waves, most Italians were quite unprepared for the idea of a multicultural country. The term attached to these immigrants is *extra-comunitari*, which has strong overtones of exclusion and describes people who do not belong to the national community. At the turn of the millennium, many of the new immigrants succeeded in finding jobs and in becoming permanent residents, but the extent to which a civic national community can develop with immigration still remains to be seen.

*Jaro Stacul*

## Further Reading

Barański, Zygmunt, and Rebecca West, eds. *The Cambridge Companion to Modern Italian Culture.* Cambridge: Cambridge University Press, 2001.

De Martino, Ernesto. *The Land of Remorse: A Study of Southern Italian Tarantism.* London: Free Association Books, 2005.

Galli della Loggia, Ernesto. *L'identità italiana (Italian Identity).* Bologna: Il Mulino, 1998.

Ginsborg, Paul. *Italy and Its Discontents: Family, Civil Society, State 1980–2001.* London: Allen Lane/Penguin, 2001.

Procacci, Giuliano. *History of the Italian People.* Harmondsworth: Penguin, 1970.

Silverman, Sydel. *Three Bells of Civilization: The Life of an Italian Hill Town.* New York: Columbia University Press, 1975.

Stacul, Jaro. *The Bounded Field: Localism and Local Identity in an Italian Alpine Valley.* Oxford: Berghahn, 2003.

# Italian-speaking Swiss

The Italian-speaking Swiss make up make up 6.5 percent (470,900) of the national population. Most live in the canton of Ticino (population 306,846 in 2000) and four valleys in the canton of Grigioni (Mesolcina, Calanca, Bregaglia, and Poschiavo) with fewer than 15,000 inhabitants. Italian is the primary language of more than 80 percent of Italian Switzerland's residents. Until a few decades ago most inhabitants spoke the Lombard dialect of Italian in daily life, though the figure has dropped to 30 percent today. Elsewhere in Switzerland reside another 200,000 Italian speakers, who are also fluent in the language of those respective areas. Virtually all Italian-speaking Swiss are Catholic. The Italian-speaking Swiss do not regard themselves as an ethnic group; as is the case with the country's other linguistic groups, they identify with geographical origins and language use.

The earliest evidence of human habitation in the area dates to 5000 BCE. In the Bronze and Iron Ages, pastoralists and hunter-gatherer populations derived a livelihood from Alpine resources. The presence of navigable lakes long facilitated transalpine movements, bringing peoples from north and south into contact. From the sixth century BCE there is evidence of the Lepontii, a Celtic tribe. Archaeological evidence indicates that gradual colonization linked to commercial activity resulted in the Romanization of the area by the end of first century CE.

The introduction of Christianity is documented from the 5th century, spreading out from Milan to the south. A number of impressive monuments testify to a flourishing Romanesque style from CE 1000. The region's role connecting northern and southern Europe was firmly established in the Middle Ages, particularly with the opening to commercial traffic of St. Gotthard's pass in the 13th century. Local residents successfully defended their autonomy and customs from outside nobles seeking to control the region. In the 14th century the area of present-day Ticino was incorporated into the state of Milan, which introduced the use of Italian in government administration and educated discourse. From the 15th century the Swiss Confederates, aided by French incursions into Milanese territory, took an interest in the area, and between 1480 and 1521 Ticino came under Swiss control and remained so until 1798. For their part, the Italian-speaking valleys of neighboring Grigioni chose to join the Republic of Three Leagues (*Leghe retiche*) from the 15th century as a defense against incursions by powerful neighbors such as Venice.

The Swiss respected local autonomy as well as the Italian language of the inhabitants in Ticino. The area became a beachhead in the Counter-Reformation drive against Protestantism. The population, primarily engaged in farming and animal husbandry, also derived a livelihood from transalpine transportation. Historically, Italian Switzerland was characterized by much skilled and typically seasonal migration across Europe; journeying abroad for work were especially those engaged in artistic endeavors (architects, master builders, plasterers, sculptors), but also traders, artisans, itinerant vendors, and so on. The artist tradition, influenced by trends in Italy, reached an apex in the Baroque era with the architect Francesco Borromini and the painter Giovanni Serodine. Internationally recognized artists in the 20th century include Alberto Giacometti and architect Mario Botta. Other notable figures include the philosopher Francesco Soave, educator, politician, and pioneer of statistics Stefano Franscini, and linguist Carlo Salvioni. In 1995, an Italian-language university, complete with a school of architecture, was established. Italian-language public communications (three radio stations and two television channels) play an important role in Italian Swiss culture and identity. In culture, daily habits, and attire the Italian-speaking Swiss are influenced by Italians, whereas in political culture they espouse Swiss federalist values.

With the Swiss revolution (1798) and the arrival of Napoleon Bonaparte, the Italian-speaking areas south of St. Gotthard were reunited to form the canton of Ticino (1803), an autonomous republic of the confederation with its own constitution, government, parliament, and judiciary. The Italian-speaking valleys in Grigioni instead became part of a canton of the same name, seceding from the Republic of the Three Leagues in the same year. Italian was made a national language in 1848, but in keeping with the federal tradition of local autonomy it was officially recognized only in Ticino and Grigioni. Italian Switzerland thus became a recognized component in the Swiss federal system, albeit one with scant demographic or economic weight. The region suffered population loss in the 19th century, with the advent of transatlantic migration and the cessation of traditional temporary migration to Italy. The opening of the railway over St. Gotthard's pass (1882), which linked Italian- and German-speaking Switzerland and placed Ticino squarely in the middle of a modern European commercial corridor, revived hopes for economic development; but the actual economic benefits were meager. However, the discovery of tourism in southern Switzerland and the immigration of several thousand Swiss Germans generated alarms over the Germanization of Ticino. In the 20th century the defense of Italian became an important political theme, and figured in secessionist schemes of Italian aspirations that viewed the area as part of Italy. In the face of the fascist menace in the 1930s there emerged a more favorable climate toward linguistic and cultural minorities, from which, in the name of federal solidarity, Italian Switzerland has certainly benefited.

Since World War II the economy of Italian Switzerland has been transformed from a rural to a service one in which commerce, tourism, and finance figure importantly. Federal employment (postal service, railways, telecommunications), once very important, is in steep decline. Globalization,

the opening of frontiers, and the affirmation of a "competitive federalism" have all renewed a sense of economic and cultural marginalization among the Italian-speaking Swiss, giving impetus to a regionalist political movement (Lega dei Ticinesi) of xenophobic character. The long period of economic growth following World War II gave rise to the mass immigration of Italian workers, and as a result the percentage of Italian speakers in country rose from 5.9 percent in 1950 to 11.9 percent in 1970, only to fall to 6.5 percent in 2000. Among Swiss nationals, however, the numbers have remained stable, with 4 percent in 1950 and 4.3 percent in 2000.

*Marco Marcacci*

**Further Reading**

Bianconi, Sandro. *Lingue di frontiera. Una storia linguistica della Svizzera italiana dal Medioevo al 2000* (*Frontier Languages: A Linguistic History of Swiss-Italian from the Middle Ages to 2000*). Bellinzona: Edizioni Casagrande, 2001.

Ceschi, Raffaello. *Geschichte des Kantons Tessin* (*History of Canton Ticino*). Frauenfeld: Huber, 2003.

Church, Clive H. *The Politics and Government of Switzerland*. New York: Palgrave Macmillan, 2004.

*Guida d'arte della Svizzera italiana* (*Guide to Swiss-Italian Art*). Bellinzona: Edizioni Casagrande, 2007.

Todisco, Vincenzo. *Una finestra sul Grigioni italiano* (*A Window onto Italian Grisons*). Coira: Amt für Volksschule und Sport Lehrmittel Graubünden, 2006.

# K

## Kabards

The Kabards, also known as Kabardins, Kabardians, or Kabardinians, are a subethnic group of the Circassians, who represent the Adyga branch of the Adygo-Abkhaz linguistic group. The vast majority of the Kabards reside in the Republic of Kabardino-Balkaria in the western north Caucasus in the Russian Federation. The capital of the republic is Nalchik. The Adygo-Abkhaz arrived in the Caucasus approximately five thousand years ago. There are just under 400,000 Kabards in Kabardino-Balkaria, and while there are émigré communities in Turkey, Syria, and other countries, most have assimilated into the general Circassian diaspora. The majority of Kabards adhere to Sunni Islam. The Kabards speak Kabardian, a dialect of Circassian (also known as Adyghe or Adyga). Besides Abkhaz and Abaza, the Circassian language has no modern relatives. It should be noted that the Kabards were originally one of numerous Circassian tribes, but because of historical developments they were able to establish a more organized society than the other tribes and developed their own identity. However, all Kabards consider themselves Circassians. Besides other Circassian tribes, their neighbors are: to the south and west the Balkars and Karachays, who speak a Turkic language; to the east the Ossetians, who speak a language related to Farsi; and to the north, Slavic peoples, primarily Russians and Cossacks. In addition, many Slavic peoples live in Kabardino-Balkaria. The Kabards have at times had conflicts with the other indigenous peoples, primarily over the limited arable land of the region, but throughout the vast majority of their history they have enjoyed friendly relations with their neighbors. Relations between Kabards and Slavs are likewise tense at times, but generally good.

Archeological and linguistic evidence has led to the theory that the Adygo-Abkhaz peoples were representatives of the Hatt culture that inhabited central Anatolia prior to the Hittite conquest of the third millennium BCE. Under Hittite pressure they migrated to the eastern shores of the Black Sea. The Kabards emerged as a distinct tribe after the campaigns of the Mongols and Timur depopulated the central Caucasus and the Circassians migrated into those areas. The name "Kabard" may be a reference to the Kabarta River near the Crimea, from which according to legend the chieftain Inal led the Kabards to the central Caucasus in the 1400s. This choice of settlement, between the Kuma River in the west and the Terek River in the east, turned out to be highly beneficial to the development of Kabard society, as its central location shielded them from the majority of raids into the region coming from both east and west, and by 1500 the Kabards possessed the most economically advanced society in the North Caucasus.

Although the Kabards converted to Sunni Islam in the 16th–19th centuries, they have adhered more faithfully to Adyge Khabze, the traditional Circassian code of ethics, which contains precepts similar to other north Caucasus peoples: respect for elders, inviolability of the guest, and friendship treated as a near-sacred institution. The entire Kabard nation was theoretically ruled by a prince known as the *pshi-tkhamade*, while individual villages or clusters of villages were ruled by minor princes. However, the pshi-tkhamade usually held only tenuous control of Kabarda and was frequently challenged by competing families. There were several categories of slaves, although the actual number of slaves was low. The vast majority of the population were free peasants, who nevertheless were bound to the aristocracy by multiple obligations: portions of their crops, the best animals from the herds, and so on. Although it was less oppressive than Russian serfdom, the peasants nevertheless had very few rights and found themselves increasingly bound to the land as Kabarda evolved into a feudal state.

The Kabards' primary livelihood for centuries was sheep herding. They also had herds of cattle. There was some agriculture, but because of the mountainous terrain and poor soil it was insufficient to support their population. The Kabards relied upon trade with their neighbors to acquire such staple items as bread and salt. The Kabards were also master horse breeders.

The only mechanism for dealing with political issues was the *khase*, an ad hoc meeting of representatives from throughout Kabarda. In theory anyone could speak at a khase, but the aristocrats generally monopolized the meetings. The khase suffered from two flaws: all decisions had to be approved unanimously, and there was no enforcement mechanism to assure that the decisions were carried out.

In 1557 Kabard Prince Temriuk signed an alliance with Russian Tsar Ivan IV. The treaty was modified in 1588, linking Russia and Kabarda as allies even more closely. By this time, however, dynastic conflicts had split Kabarda into Greater Kabarda in the west and Lesser Kabarda in the east. As Russian and Ottoman competition for the north Caucasus escalated, Kabarda fragmented further as individual princes made deals with whichever power offered them the most protection at the time.

The most significant event in Kabard history is the Russo-Circassian War. Relations between the two nations deteriorated throughout the 18th century as Russia became more aggressive in its attempt to control Kabarda. Russia began military operations in Circassia in 1804, and many Kabard princes took the Circassian side. Kabarda was ravaged throughout the first half of the 19th century, particularly in the early 1820s by the campaigns of Russian General Alexei Yermolov. When the war concluded in 1864, the vast majority of Circassians were deported to the Ottoman Empire, but Kabards were allowed to remain, leaving them far and away the largest Circassian tribe in the Caucasus.

In 1925 the Soviet Union created the Kabardino-Balkar Autonomous Oblast. The Kabards and Balkars continued their centuries-long tradition of friendly relations with one another until 1944, when the entire Balkar nation was deported to Central Asia. The Balkars were only allowed to return in the late 1950s. Subsequently, the Kabards and Balkars have had tense relations, initially over mutual suspicions concerning the deportations and more recently over land usage. Since the fall of the Soviet Union various organizations have worked at creating a united Circassian homeland in which Kabarda would be included. The Circassian group Adyge Khase was at the forefront of this movement, but recently the Conference of Circassian Youth has taken a more aggressive stance in favor of the creation of a Circassian republic. This has very recently caused serious concerns, particularly among the non-Kabard residents of Kabardino-Balkaria.

On October 15, 2005, a group of perhaps 200 militants led an unsuccessful attack on Nalchik. Numerous theories concerning the motivation for the attack have been forwarded, but the assault appears to have been an anomaly rather than part of an organized rebellion.

*Walter Richmond*

**Further Reading**

Gammer, Moshe, ed. *Ethno-Nationalism, Islam and the State in the Caucasus: Post-Soviet Disorder.* New York: Routledge, 2008.

Jaimoukha, Amjad. *The Circassians: A Handbook.* New York: Palgrave MacMillan, 2001.

Richmond, Walter. *The Northwest Caucasus: Past, Present, Future.* New York: Routledge, 2008.

# Kalmyks

The Kalmyks, Kalmuks, or Khal'mg Tangch, are concentrated in the Republic of Kalmykia in the Russian Federation. This territory is located on the northwest shore of the Caspian Sea southwest of the Volga River. They arrived in this region from western Mongolia or Jungaria (modern day Xinjiang) in the early 17th century. The 2002 Russian Federation census counted almost 174,000 Kalmyks, of which nearly 156,000 lived in the Republic of Kalmykia. They made up a slight majority of the population of this territory. Most of the rest of the republic's population consists of Russians. Around 1,500 people who are descendants of Kalmyks that fled Soviet repression live in New Jersey and Pennsylvania. A small diaspora also lives in France. The ancestral language of the Kalmyk people is closely related to Mongolian, but the primary language used by most of them today is Russian. They have retained a distinct Kalmyk ethnicity based in part upon their traditional adherence to Tibetan Buddhism. Despite living among a much larger Russian population for several centuries and suffering from assimilatory pressures, the Kalmyks remain a distinct ethnic group easily identifiable by physical appearance and religious background from their neighbors.

The early Kalmyk Khanate was a confederation of four nomadic western Mongol (Oirat) tribes that had been excluded from the empire established by Genghis Khan and its successor states. The Kalmyks began moving to the Caspian Sea region from Jungaria in the early 1600s and established a permanent presence in the region of the Volga River by the 1640s. This migration was driven both by conflict with eastern Mongols in Jungaria and the attraction of empty pastureland in the region. The

Kalmyk pilgrims pray after walking miles through a wind-swept field to reach Khurul Monastery, about four miles northeast of the Kalmyk capital Elista, in 2004. (AP/Wide World Photos)

power of the Kalmyk Khanate reached its peak under the rule of Ayuka Khan (1669–1724). After Ayuka's death the Russian Empire increasingly came to dominate politically the Kalmyk Khanate. In particular the loss of pastureland to Russian colonization put severe economic pressure on the Kalmyks. To escape these conditions Viceroy Ubashi led more than 150,000 Kalmyks, out of around 200,000, back to Jungaria. This trek started on January 18, 1771. Most of them died along the way. On October 19, 1771, Catherine the Great abolished the Kalmyk Khanate and integrated the Kalmyks still living in the Volga River region into the Russian Empire. Their descendants are the Kalmyks of today.

After the Bolshevik Revolution, the new Soviet government created a national territory for the Kalmyks in the region of their traditional homeland. On November 4, 1920, the authorities in Moscow created the Kalmyk Autonomous Oblast. They upgraded this territory to the Kalmyk Autonomous Soviet Socialist Republic (ASSR) on October 20, 1935.

The Kalmyks are Tibetan Buddhists of the Yellow Hat order whose traditional religious beliefs and practices closely resemble those of the Tibetans and Mongolians. During the 1930s the Stalin regime closed all the Kalmyk monasteries and temples and persecuted Buddhist religious figures. The Kalmyks maintained many Buddhists practices in private despite the elimination of public worship. Today the vast majority of Kalmyks identify themselves as Buddhists and most of them observe some religious rites. Since 1990 there has been a revival of the public observance of Buddhism in the Republic of Kalmykia and many temples have been reopened.

Historically the Kalmyks were almost entirely nomadic livestock herders. Indeed up until the 1930s the majority of the population remained nomadic. From 1929 to 1937, the Soviet government forcibly settled 95 percent of Kalmyk households on collective farms. Collectivization permanently transformed the rural economy of the Kalmyks from nomadic stock breeding to settled agriculture and animal husbandry.

Soviet repression of Buddhism and the violent collectivization of agriculture created significant resentment among segments of the Kalmyk population. During World War II, the invading German army was able to exploit this resentment to recruit a small number of Kalmyks to fight for them against the Soviet authorities. In order to guard their overstretched supply lines from partisan attacks, the German military formed several Kalmyk units including the Kalmyk Cavalry Corp (KCC) during 1942–1943. Perhaps as many as 5,000 Kalmyks and members of other nationalities participated in the KCC during World War II. The KCC and several thousand other Kalmyks retreated westward to Germany with the German army during 1943–1944.

In contrast, more than 20,000 Kalmyks served in the Red Army during World War II. Despite this loyal service, the Stalin regime accused the entire Kalmyk nation of treason on the basis of the actions of the KCC and other collaborators. As punishment for this alleged crime the Soviet government deported virtually the entire Kalmyk population to Siberia.

This deportation took place December 28–29, 1943. The NKVD (People's Commissariat of Internal Affairs) deported more than 90,000 Kalmyks, including more than 40,000 children, from the Kalmyk ASSR to dispersed settlements in Siberia. Later the Soviet government rounded up the Kalmyks living in other regions of the Soviet Union, including those in the Red Army, and also sent them to Siberia. The total number of Kalmyks subjected to forced resettlement in Siberia exceeded 100,000 people.

The Soviet government forced the Kalmyks to abandon almost all of their property during the deportations, including the livestock upon which their physical survival depended. The Soviet government then failed to provide the Kalmyk deportees in Siberia with adequate food, housing, clothing, and medical care. As a result of the extremely poor living conditions suffered by the Kalmyks in Siberia, close to a fifth of the population perished during the first five years of exile.

The deportations were a demographic disaster for the Kalmyk people. In 1939 there were 134,000 Kalmyks in the Soviet Union. By October 1, 1948, fewer than 80,000 Kalmyks remained alive in the country. Only in 1970 did their population exceed its 1939 levels with 137,200 people.

After February 1957 the Soviet government allowed the Kalmyks to return to their traditional homeland. By the end of 1959, almost 72,700 out of 106,100 Kalmyks in the Soviet Union again lived in the Kalmyk ASSR. This assemblage began the slow process of overcoming the collective damage done to the Kalmyk nation by the deportations. One aspect of this damage has been the massive decline in the use of the Kalmyk language in favor of Russian by Kalmyks. During their 13 years of exile in Siberia the Kalmyks had no access at all to Kalmyk language education and lived dispersed among a largely Russian-speaking population. The lack of native language skills is especially pronounced among young people. A survey in 2004 found that more than 70 percent of Kalmyks between 17 and 26 could not speak Kalmyk, although a majority of them could understand it. Attempts by the government of the Republic of Kalmykia to revive the language have had limited success.

*Jonathan Otto Pohl*

### Further Reading

Khodarkovsky, Michael. *Where Two Worlds Met: The Russian State and the Kalmyk Nomads, 1600–1771*. Ithaca, NY: Cornell University Press, 1992.

Nekrich, Aleksandr M. *The Punished Peoples: The Deportation and Fate of Soviet Minorities at the End of the Second World War*. Trans. George Saunders. New York: Norton, 1978.

Nuksunova, A.N. "The Cultural Identity of Today's Kalmyk Young People." *Russian Social Science Review* 50, no. 5 (September-October 2009): 63–70.

Pohl, J. Otto. *Ethnic Cleansing in the USSR, 1937–1949*. Westport, CT: Greenwood, 1999.

# Karachay

Most Karachays, Muslim Turkic-speakers known to themselves as *qaračaylï*, live in the foothills of Mount Elbrus and neighboring river valleys in the Karachaevo-Cherkessia Republic of Russia. They number altogether around 300,000, and some 222,000 live in their titular republic. Scattered groups are still to be found in Central Asia, as well as in other areas of the former Soviet Union, for instance in Ukraine and Moscow. As is true of many of the mountain peoples of the region, they have a long and varied history of struggle and suppression, but have survived as an independent ethnic unit until the present. According to a common folk etymology Karachay means "black river," but its real meaning remains unclear. When the Caucasus was conquered by Russian forces in the 19th century, many Karachays fled to Anatolia, where there still are villages with Karachay populations, for instance in the Konya and Eskeşehir region. Some Karachays have during the last decades left their poor Anatolian villages for better opportunities as migrants in Germany. There is also a Karachay community in New Jersey in the United States. Some Karachay refugees have recently resettled from the North Caucasus to Scandinavian countries.

As is the case with the closely related Balkars, the Karachay people have a complex history in the North Caucasus region. Turkic-speaking groups settled in the area during the Mongol rule of the 13th and 14th centuries. According to local historians their ethnicity emerged during the late medieval time. However, their ethnonym for a distinct group is mentioned in Russian sources first in the mid-17th century. The Karachays long lived as seminomadic cattle breeders moving their sheep to mountain regions in the summer and the valleys in the winter.

The Karachay have experienced much violence. Russia enlarged its control in the region during the 19th century. In 1864 the Russian conquest of the Karachay territory was completed, although the conflicts continued. Many Karachay left their homeland for Turkey in the 1880s, and again in 1905. In 1922, following the Russian revolution, their territory was turned into the Karachay-Cherkess autonomous territory with Cherkessk as capital; in April 1926 it was split into separate Karachay and Cherkess territories. Ethnic conflicts between Nogais and Karachays continued within the territory in the 1920s. The region was collectivized during the 1930s, and the Karachay elite were to a large extent murdered during the Stalinist terror of the late 1930s. In 1939 there were 75,700 Karachay living in the Karachay Autonomous Region, founded in 1936.

In the fall of 1942 the Nazi troops occupied the area, but a few months later the Red Army reclaimed it. As was the fate of several of the minor ethnic groups of the area, the Karachay were accused by Stalin of collaboration with the Nazi occupiers; using weak minorities as scapegoats for the Soviet war failures was just another way for the Stalinists to conceal their own mistakes. The Karachay were actually the first people to be deported. In early November 1943 all the Karachays who were not on the front were sent to Kazakstan and Uzbekistan. The Karachay autonomous region was abolished, and its southern part was given to Georgia while the larger northern part was united with Stavropol. Many Karachays died in transit, while still others perished from disease and starvation in the initial period of exile. Karachay soldiers in the Red Army were sent from the front directly into exile. After Stalin's death, the Soviet government began to improve the situation for the deported minorities. Nikita Khrushchev's speech denouncing Stalin at the Party Congress in February 1956 made it possible for the Karachays to be rehabilitated and return back home to their valleys in Caucasus. Many homes had been taken over by Russians and others; some therefore chose to settle in urban areas. In January 1957 the Karachay-Cherkess territory was reestablished within its former borders. According to the census of 1959 there were 68,000 Karachays living within the territory.

The exile and the treatment after their return strengthened Karachay identity. While many Karachays work within industry, cattle breeding remains important. Wool production is an important economic activity among women. The relationship with their ethnic neighbors has been strained, and violence has occurred. In 1988 nationalists formed the Karachay national movement Jamagat in order to achieve autonomy for the Karachay people, although without success. Still, Karachay have dominated the Karachaevo-Cherkessia republic's leadership for decades. Interethnic relations between the dominant Karachay population and the more subordinate Circassian population have worsened in recent years.

The Karachays are Sunni Muslims of the Hanafi juridical school. More radical Islamic movements have recently spread across the North Caucasus, and have attracted some younger people. Some have even been accused of taking part in terrorist activities. However, the majority seem to be rather indifferent to their religion, not only as a result of the Communist atheist campaigns in the past, but also by tradition. Popular religion is widely observed, though, and includes many pre-Islamic traits.

Karachay language, which is almost identical with the Balkar written language, belongs to the western subgroup of the Kipchak or the northwestern branch of Turkic languages. A reformed Arabic alphabet was used for Karachay from 1916 to 1926 and was replaced by a Latin script in 1927. Since the late 1930s a Cyrillic script has been used, although an attempt to reintroduce a Latin-based alphabet has been discussed since the early 1990s. Today, most Karachays are bilingual in their native Turkic and in Russian. Since the breakdown of the Soviet rule we can observe a revival of Karachay language and culture, and also a more active diaspora having contacts with their former homeland. The Karachays living in villages in Turkey have to a large extent preserved their language.

*Ingvar Svanberg*

### Further Reading

Comins-Richmond, Walter. "The Karachay Struggle after the Deportation." *Journal of Muslim Minority Affairs* 22 (2002): 63–79.

Grannes, Alf. "The Soviet Deportation in 1943 of the Karachays: A Turkic Muslim People of North Caucasus." *Journal of Muslim Minority Affairs* 12 (1991): 55–68.

# Karelians

Numbering about 220,000, Karelians reside primarily in Russia but also in Finland. The Karelian language, often considered a dialect of Finnish, is currently spoken very infrequently as a mother tongue, having been replaced by either Finnish or Russian, lost respectively to similarity to Finnish and to Russification, though attempts to revive use of Karelian are ongoing. Karelians in Russia tend to practice the Orthodox faith while those in Finland tend to observe Lutheranism. Several significant subgroupings of Karelians exist, primarily based on geographic distinctions; these distinctions tend to accentuate rather than complicate other ethnic definers, such as customary, material, or verbal traditions. Among these groups are the Tver Karelians, Archangel Karelians, Viena Karelians, and Olonets Karelians living in Russian Federation (RF) territory, and the North and South Karelians living in Finland. Karelians are a Balto-Finnic people, related to other groups in the region, such as the Finns to the west and Ingrians to the south toward Estonia, but also more distantly the Sami, Seto, and Livs. Traditional Karelian homelands lie along a very old and frequently contested border between Western and Eastern Europe, one that now stands as the longest between the Russian Federation and a European Union member (Finland).

These homelands stretch from the area of the White Sea in the north, south around Lake Ladoga to Ingria, bordering Finland's Savo region to the west, and Archangel to the east; several migrations pushed Karelians even further south to the Tver region of Russia. In the northern reaches of the territory, evidence of continuous Karelian settlement dates back to the eighth century CE. This traditional territory, with the exception of portions

Member of the Karelian folk-music ensemble plays a balalaika near Petrozavodsk, Russia. (Dave G. Houser/Corbis)

lying inside Finland, serves as the basis for the Republic of Karelia in the Russian Federation. The populations falling on either side of the border between Russia/Novgorod and Finland/Sweden have been separated ideologically if not physically since 1323, when the Treaty of Nöteborg proscribed the border between Sweden and Novgorod lying down the middle of Karelian cultural territory. Since that period, the area inhabited by Karelians in Russia has been transformed from a province of the empire, to the "Karelian Workers' Commune" in 1920, to the Karelian Autonomous Soviet Socialist Republic (ASSR) in 1923, to the Finnish-Karelian Soviet Socialist Republic in 1940 at the culmination of the Winter War and accession of large portions of Finnish-controlled Karelia to the Soviet Union, back to the Karelian ASSR in 1956, and most

recently to the Republic of Karelia in 1991. Throughout this recent history, though titular to the territory, Karelians have themselves been profoundly in the minority since the middle of the 1920s, dropping rapidly to 37.6 percent in 1926 and subsequently falling to a number that consistently hovers around 10 percent of the approximately 800,000 inhabitants of the Republic of Karelia.

Historically, Karelian life was closely tied to traditional agricultural practices that influenced familial and interfamilial relationships through reliance on highly localized power structures and resource use. Karelians typically practiced swidden agriculture. The farmstead was the basic social unit and the primary source of life's necessities for all Karelians. Under these conditions, men and women each had their own tasks: men were responsible for labor in the fields and forests, and women were responsible for caring for livestock and the home. Tied to these methods was the traditional practice of patrilocal, and often arranged, marriage.

Karelians developed a vibrant tradition of oral poetry and song, consisting of epic verse, lyrical poetry, charms, and magic rituals. These traditions were kept by talented singers and storytellers as well as powerful folk sorcerers, or *tietäjät*. Much of the Karelian worldview, with its shamanic influences, is preserved in the songs collected before World War II, after which the tradition seems to have dissipated and all but disappeared. Especially among those Karelians exposed to the Orthodox Church, the most emblematic and distinct tradition still practiced recently is one of lamentation: ritual keening for the dead in funerary rites and for the departure of a young family member in the circumstances of marriage. Other long-lasting traditions of note include typical musical styles and instruments such as the stringed, harp-like kantele.

The epic song tradition has produced the best-known global expression of Karelianism: Kalevala, published in 1835/1849 by collector Elias Lönnrot as *The Finnish National Epic*. Lönnrot edited epic verse he collected from Karelian singers into a cohesive epic poem, which he hoped would help unite Finns during the early period of Finnish National Romanticism. Since that publication, Karelianism has been a powerful item of Finnish cultural identity and was critical in creating the foundation for the modern Finnish nation. Karelianism also inspired the work of Finnish artists, especially composer Jean

Sibelius, and painter Akseli Gallén-Kallela. Karelians were seen as authentically Finnish, despite obvious Russian influence. Karelianism is less characteristic of contemporary Finns, and instead, it has been picked up by ethnic Karelians and their descendants. Many organizations in Finland and Russia have appeared; these organizations strive to revive dying folk traditions through language teaching, cultural events, and performances. The most prominent of these are Karjalanliitto, or The Karelia League, and Juminkeko, both of which organize language classes, events, performances, and cultural education for Karelians and interested non-Karelians alike.

After the Winter War and Continuation War (1939–1940, 1941–1944), 403,000 Karelians were evacuated and resettled into Finland. The resettled Karelians in Finland have had little trouble adapting to modern Finnish society, largely supported by the cultural similarities and closeness that have allowed for all but effortless crossover—however, for this very reason, Karelian identity has largely dissolved into the larger context of Finland. Many traditions practiced in the old homelands have disappeared in contemporary culture. Today, Karelians live and work all over Finland. Most Karelians practice Orthodox faith, especially those from the eastern territories where there is strong Russian influence, though Karelians living in western Karelia are frequently members of the Finnish Lutheran Church.

The multiple Karelian localities as well as subsequent migrations, remigrations, border reformations, and shifting national loyalties mean there is not one but many

Karelias. These same factors have also led to a large-scale dissolution of active folk culture in Karelian communities in both Russia and Finland, and most Karelian activities—including use of the Karelian language—now exist primarily as revival traditions.

*Evan Patrick Wright*

## Further Reading

Jyrkilä, Faina. *The Adaptation of the Resettled Karelian Farmers*. Publications of the Department of Sociology, University of Jyväskylä, nro. 24/1980. Jyväskylä: University of Jyväskylä, 1980.

Nevalainen, Pekka, and Hannes Sihvo Karjala. *Historia, kansa, kulttuuri* (*History, People, Culture*). Helsinki: Suomalaisen Kirjallisuuden Seura, 1998, 705.

Oinas, Felix. *The Karelians*. New Haven, CT: Human Relations Area Files, 1995.

Pentikäinen, Juha. *Oral Repertoire and World View: An Anthropological Study of Marina Takalo's Life History*. FF Communications, no. 219. Helsinki: Suomalainen Tiedeakatemia, 1978.

Stark-Arola, Laura. *Peasants, Pilgrims, and Sacred Promises: Ritual and the Supernatural in Orthodox Karelian Folk Religion*. Helsinki: Finnish Literature Society, 2002.

# Komi

The Komi (*Коми*) inhabit the tundra and taiga forests on the flanks of the Ural Mountains at the eastern edge of Europe. They speak a continuum of languages, subdivided into the Komi-Zyrian and the Komi-Permyak languages; together with the closely related Udmurt who inhabit the region between the Kama and Vyatka Rivers, their languages comprise the Permian languages, a subdivision within the much larger Uralic or Finno-Ugric language family. According to the 2002 Russian Federation census, the Komi-Zyrian numbered 293,406 and the Komi-Permyak 125,235. The Komi are concentrated in three regions of the Russian Federation: the Nenets Autonomous Okrug where the Komi number 4,510 people (10.9% of the population), the Komi Republic (256,464 people or 25.2%), and the former Komi-Permyak Autonomous Okrug (80,327 or 59.0%). The latter okrug has since been merged with the Perm Oblast to form the Perm Krai. A third Komi population, the Komi-Yazva, use a language spoken by fewer than two thousand individuals with a total population numbering approximately five thousand people concentrated in a handful of villages of the Perm Krai. Never integrated into the Komi-Zyrian or Komi-Permyak territories, this group had been written out of the Russian census of 1926, over three thousand individuals relabeled Russian even though they continued to speak a dialect of the Komi language. There has been a push for a linguistic and cultural revival in recent decades with the Komi-Yazva reaffirming their Komi identity. All Komi populations practice Russian Orthodox Christianity.

The original homeland of the Komi is the Upper and Middle Kama River of Russia. In the first millennium BCE, ancestral Komi migrated from the Kama River to the Vychegda and Pechora River basins. By the end of the first millennium, the Komi depended on a mixed economy of agriculture, livestock, hunting, fishing, and foraging. The Medieval Warm Period

A Komi reindeer herder waits for reindeer to arrive to pull his sleds in Nizhnyaya Pesha, Arkhangel'sk, Russia. (Gordon Wiltsie/National Geographic Society/Corbis)

(950–1250) facilitated the ethnic Komi expansion and consolidation.

This expansion would soon come to an end, however, as the Slavic Rus (later to become Russians) moved north, building Orthodox monasteries, founding Slavic farming communities, and imposing tribute on the Komi and other Uralic peoples. The Komi were referred to in The Primary Chronicle as the Perm, and one of the central figures in Komi history was Stephen of Perm (Stefan or *Стефан* in Russian, circa 1340–1396), the Orthodox monk who converted the population to Christianity and was consecrated as the first bishop of Perm in 1383. Scholars speculate that his mother was Perm (Komi), but mirroring the saintly accounts of Cyril and Methodius, Stephen is described as inventing an alphabet for the Perm language with divine intervention. By virtue of entering the Christian fold and having their own liturgical language, the Perm were recognized as the equals of the Rus; the creation of a bishopric accorded the Perm political legitimacy over their territory with Ust-Vym as its new capital.

By the 17th century, the Russian Orthodox Church had reversed its treatment of the Komi. The alphabet that Stephen created was banned, books were destroyed, and only a few fragments of the Permian written language remained. The independent Perm bishopric would lose its independence, being amalgamated and subjugated to the Vologda. After being conquered by Moscow in the 1470s, the Komi emerged as a distinct ethnic group, becoming serfs in the growing Russian Empire. With the decline of written Permian, Komi emerged as the oral language of villagers. The Little Ice Age slowed the Slavic migration, but with the lands to the west and south occupied, the Komi would push northward and eastward. Lacking a unified written language and cultural center, the Komi-Zyrian language alone would develop into 10 different dialects. Coming into contact with the indigenous reindeer-herding Nenets, the Izhma Komi would adopt reindeer herding and trek northward and eastward to the White Sea (Arctic Ocean). Other Komi over the centuries pushed into Siberia, establishing scattered settlements over the Urals. The Komi had facilitated the Russian movement into Siberia as Komi hunters served as guides to the Cossack Ermak, hired by the Stroganovs to lead the conquest of Siberia in the 16th century.

The Komi enjoyed a cultural renaissance in the 19th century. Ivan A. Kuratov (1839–1875) studied in the seminary before working as a teacher. He was the first to write poetry in the Komi language; he translated Russian and European classics into Komi, and produced a Komi grammar. A small Komi intelligentsia was then emerging in the center of Ust-Sysolsk (later renamed Syktyvkar), but the population remained predominantly rural and agricultural.

After the ravages of the civil war following the 1917 Russian Revolution, the Komi achieved their highest levels of political autonomy and cultural development since the time of Stephen. Under the Soviets, the Komi, who had been divided among three different jurisdictions in the Russian Empire, were united in a common territory: in the 1926 census, the ethnic Komi were the overwhelming majority in their territory (86.9%). The Komi area became an autonomous territory in 1921; in 1925 Soviet officials created a separate territory for the Komi Permyak; and in 1929 the Soviet Union divided the northern territories, creating the Nenets Autonomous Okrug, ensuring that the Komi would be landlocked. In 1936, the Soviet Union promoted the Komi territory to a republic, a status that the Komi have maintained in the Russian Federation.

The period following the Revolution marked the apogee of Komi education and literature. In 1918, Komi became the language of instruction in the territory that would later become the republic, and Soviet officials encouraged the development of an indigenous literature. The onslaught of the Great Purge at the end of the 1930s curtailed this progress. Komi leaders were persecuted and Russian replaced Komi as the language of instruction. The establishment of prison camps across the north would move millions of ethnic Russians and others to the distant northern territories of the Soviet Union, including the Komi Republic. After the release of surviving prisoners in the 1950s, most would remain, migrating to the closest cities. In less than a generation, the ethnic Komi dropped to 30.1 percent of the population in their titular republic. With recent industrialization, notably the establishment of the oil industry along with mining, pulp, paper, and lumber concerns, the influx of ethnic Russians reduced the percentage of ethnic Komi further (23.3% in 1989).

With the collapse of the Soviet Union, the Komi established new forms of political representation. A Komi Congress was established, Komi organizing took place within the republic at municipal and republican levels, and Komi also established ties nationally and internationally with the larger Finno-Ugric world. In spite of these recent political achievements, the Komi face significant challenges. The cities where ethnic Russians and the Russian language predominate have seen the lion's share of economic development and job creation, while the villages and rural areas of the Komi Republic, precisely those areas where the Komi language fares best, have been marked by great poverty. Such factors encourage the continued assimilation of the ethnic Komi as the Russian language remains the language of social mobility. Also, the increased mortality and declining birthrates that followed the collapse of the Soviet Union have impacted the Komi, whose numbers in the Komi Republic have declined from 291,542 (1989) to 256,464 (2002).

*Michel Bouchard*

## Further Reading

Habeck, Joachim Otto. *Halle Studies in the Anthropology of Eurasia.* Vol. 5: *What It Means to Be a Herdsman: The Practice and Image of Reindeer Husbandry among the Komi of Northern Russia.* Munster: Lit Verlag, 2006.

Konakov, N.D., et al. "Komi Mythology." In *Encyclopaedia of Uralic Mythologies*, eds. Vladimir Napolskikh, Anna-Leanna Siikala, and Mihaly Hoppal. Budapest: Akademiai Kiado; and Helsinki: Finnish Literature Society, 2003.

## Kumyks

Most of the 422,400 Kumyks (2002 Russian census), who call themselves *qumuq* (pl. *qumuqlar*), live in northeastern and eastern Daghestan. This group comprises almost 13 percent (365,800) of the population of the Republic of Daghestan, now part of the Russian Federation. Others are found in adjacent areas in eastern North Caucasus, including North Ossetia (12,700), Chechnya (8,900), Stavropol Krai (5,700), and other parts of southern Russia. Their homeland borders the western coast of the Caspian Sea. Some Kumyks left their native country in 1861 to escape Russian oppression, settling in northern Anatolia in the Ottoman Empire. Others came to Anatolia a few years later. Small, scattered groups of Kumyks, descendants of these refugees, still live in small villages in Turkey, especially near Tokat and in Istanbul.

Migration during the Soviet period left small numbers of Kumyks living in Estonia (10), Ukraine (700), and Kyrghyzstan (150). Kumyks are Turkic speakers and Muslims.

Even though very little is known about the origin of the Kumyks, historical sources suggest that Turkic speakers had settled in the area west of the Caspian Sea already in the early medieval period. During the 15th and 16th centuries, a group of Kumyks formed an independent principality, based at Tarki, and ruled by a Shamkhal. The Kumyk Shamkhalat survived until the 19th century. The Russians had penetrated the area already in the 16th century and forts were built under Peter I, but it was not until 1867 that the Kumyk Shamkhalat was finally incorporated into Russia.

Most of them lived as sedentary peasants and shepherds at the turn of the last century. Attempts to create an autonomous Kumyk territory after the Russian revolution failed, and their settlement area eventually became part of multiethnic Daghestan. In 1926 the Kumyks numbered around 94,500. In the late 1920s the forced collectivization generated many changes in their way of living, including the suppression of religion, the clan system, and their traditional way of living. During the 1930s many Kumyk leaders were persecuted or deported. After World War II many Kumyks left the countryside for jobs in the new industries. Many mountaineers, belonging to other ethnic groups, began to settle in the Kumyk territory, increasing tensions in the area.

Contemporary Daghestan has around 2 million inhabitants with almost half of the population living on the countryside.

The republic is an ethnoterritorial homeland for more than 30 mainly Muslim and North Caucasian groups, among them, besides the Kumyks, which is the third largest group in the area, also Avars, Dargins, and Lezgins. Daghestan is a mountainous region and is rather economically underdeveloped. The plain coastal areas, where the Kumyks live, have a thriving agriculture, but have also been undergoing industrialization.

In 1989, under the leadership of Salav Aliev, Kumyk nationalists founded Tenglik (Equality), an organization working for territorial autonomy for the Kumyk nation. It has been succeeded by other organizations. Protests and interethnic conflicts have been reported several times over the last decades from the Kumyk area of Daghestan.

The Kumyks are Sunni Muslims of the Shafi'i judicial school. Many of the Kumyks are adherents of the Sufi Naqshbandi brotherhood. However, there are also a minority of Shiites among them, living in Derbent and Makhachkala. Post-Soviet Daghestan is a strong Islamic region, with many new mosques, madrasah, and other religious institutions.

The Kumyk language belongs to the western subgroup of Kipchak or northwestern branch of the Turkic languages and is related to Balkar, Karachay, Crimean Tatar, and Karaim Turkic. It is divided into three dialects: the northern Khasav-Yurt (or Aksay), the central Boynak, and the southern Khaydak. The Kumyk language is to some extent also still used as a lingua franca for the indigenous peoples of Northern Daghestan, although Russian has probably replaced its former importance in many areas. Most Kumyks are bilingual in Kumyk and Russian. The Kumyk language was first written with Arabic script in the late 19th century. The writing system was then changed, first to the Latin script in 1927, then to the Cyrillic in 1938. Already in 1917 periodicals were published in Kumyk, and during the first decades after the Russian Revolution the language was used for instruction in schools. There are a few media in the Kumyk language, but recent attempts to reintroduce the Latin script have failed.

*Ingvar Svanberg*

## Further Reading

Chensiner, Robert. *Daghestan: Tradition and Survival.* New York: St. Martin's Press, 1997.

Mihanan, James B. *One Europe, Many Nations.* Westport, CT: Greenwood Press, 2000.

Olson, James S. *An Ethnohistorical Dictionary of the Russian and Soviet Empires.* Westport, CT: Greenwood Press, 1994.

# L

## Laks

Laks (self-designation Lak) are an indigenous people of the Caucasus who live in mountainous central Dagestan. According to the Russian Federation's 2002 census, 139,732 Laks were living in the Republic of Dagestan out of a total of 156,545 living in the Russian Federation as a whole. They are the fifth largest ethnic group in Dagestan and constitute 5.4 percent of the republic's population. Today Laks are highly urbanized compared to the other populations of the North Caucasus; approximately 80 percent live in cities. The Lak language belongs to the Dargino-Lak group of the Northeast-Caucasian language family. Laks are Sunni Muslims of the Shafi'i School.

Most archeological, linguistic, anthropological, and ethnographic evidence indicates that the Laks are ancient inhabitants of their present lands. Classical sources describe the inhabitants of Dagestan as Legi or Leki, a term very close to the Laks' own term for themselves.

After Arab-Muslim conquerors brought Islam to Dagestan in the 7th century during the Rashidun Caliphate, Laks were among the first in Dagestan to begin the process of conversion. According to Arab sources, the process was completed in the 11th or 12th century.

Kumukh, today the administrative center of the Lakskii district, served for centuries as the hub of Lak cultural and political life. The Arabic title *ghazi*, or warrior, was affixed to the place name as an honorific, and the name Ghazikumukh has been used to refer to the Lak people. The rulers of Kumukh in the 14th century took the title "Shamkhal," which implied prestigious descent from the Arabs of Syria (al-Sham). The Shamkhals came to rule much of central and coastal Dagestan. The Mongols in the 13th century and Timur in the 14th invaded the Lak lands.

Laks took part in the 18th-century struggle against Nadir Shah of Iran and then in the 19th-century Great Caucasian Wars against the Russian Empire. After subduing the mountain peoples in those wars, Russia abolished the Shamkhalate in 1865. The Laks came under Soviet rule following the Bolshevik conquest of Dagestan in 1919.

The Laks among the mountain peoples of Dagestan were first to develop a feudal system, with khans, beks, descendants of beks and women of lower social rank, free peasants, serfs, and slaves constituting the main classes. A system of patriarchal clans (*tukhum*) existed. Exogamous marriage was not forbidden, but endogamous marriage was the norm.

As with most Dagestani mountain peoples, among the Laks customary law (*adat*) regulated village life and interclan relations, including vendetta and blood feud, while Islamic law (sharia) governed matters of family, inheritance, and religious ritual.

Fertile land in mountainous central Dagestan was scarce, so agriculture played only a small role in the traditional economy of the Laks. Transhumance and home industries such as leatherworking, pottery, weaving, and metalwork provided economic mainstays.

Works in written Lak exist from the 15th century, and in the 18th and 19th centuries a substantial religious and didactic literature in Lak emerged. Under Soviet rule Lak was recognized as an official language and taught in schools. The end of Soviet rule resulted in the loss of subsidies for Lak textbooks and a decline in the number of qualified teachers. This downturn, combined with urbanization and economic incentives to learn Russian, the lingua franca in Dagestan, has put the long-term future of the Lak language in doubt.

In 1944 some Laks were resettled from the mountains to lowlands belonging to Chechens who had been deported. Those lands were renamed Novolak and transferred from the Chechen-Ingush Autonomous Soviet Socialist Republic to Dagestan. The return of the Chechens following their rehabilitation in 1956 led to an uneasy coexistence between the two peoples. In 1992 the Russian government resolved to reverse the settlement of the Laks. Only slow progress has been made in returning the Laks, however, and the Novolak region remains a site of ethnic tension.

*Michael A. Reynolds*

**Further Reading**

Bulatova, A. G. "Laktsy." In *Narody Dagestana* (*The Peoples of Dagestan*), eds. S. A. Arutiunov, A. I. Osmanov, and G. A. Sergeeva. Moscow: Nauka, 2002, 348–376.

Marshaev, Ramazan, and Istoriia Laktsev. *The History of the Lak*. Makhachkala: Goskomizdat DSSR, 1991.

Wixman, R. "Laḳ." *Encyclopaedia of Islam*, 2nd ed., vol. 5, p. 617, eds. P. Bearman et al. Boston: Brill, 2009.

# Latgalians

Latgalians are a modern ethnic group of Latvians who reside predominantly in the Latgale region in eastern Latvia. They are also known as Latgallians, Lettigals, Latgolans, and Lettigallians (in Latvian: *Latgaļi*, *Latgalieši*; in Latgalian: *Latgali*, *Latgalīši*). Minor diasporas exist in Russia, Siberia, Western Europe, America, and Canada. The Latgalian language is protected under the Latvian Language Law of 1999 as a variant of the Latvian language. Latgalians are primarily Roman Catholic, unlike the rest of Latvia, which is mostly Lutheran. Advocates for a separate Latgalian ethnicity argue that between Latgale (Latgola) and the other provinces of Latvia, differences in faith, language variations, dissimilar economic conditions, and historical disparities have been greater than between those of certain other sovereign nations, and thus the Latgalians have developed into a separate ethnic group. Others suggest that, in response to historical and economic circumstances, the Latgalians have managed to preserve a more authentic form of the Latvian language and culture. The number of individuals who would self-differentiate as Latgalians, separate from Latvians, is unknown. Estimates span from 200,000 to 500,000. The Latvian government does not consider Latgalians a distinct ethnic group in census data.

The Latgalians (Latgali in historic reference) are of Indo-European origin, part of the Baltic peoples together with other Latvians and Lithuanians (as well as the Prussians, Yotvingans, and Galindians, whose languages and cultures are now extinct). Baltic scholars trace their origins to successive waves of migrations that occurred over an extended period (the second half of the 1st and 2nd centuries CE, the 7th and 8th and possibly the 10th and 11th centuries CE). Baltic tribes (*ciltis*), including the Latgali, migrated to what is now the territory of Latvia and encountered the previous Finno-Ugric inhabitants. In the 12th century German Teutonic knights conquered this region, named it Livonia (for the Finno-Ugric Livs), established a feudal land-tenure system, and endeavored to impose the rituals of Christianity on the territory's polytheistic inhabitants. A series of wars in the 16th century divided Livonia between Polish and Swedish rule. This partition marked a separate existence from the rest of Latvia for Latgalians who inhabited the region of Latgale. The Protestant Reformation instituted Lutheranism in Swedish-ruled Latvia. Latgale or the Polish Inflanty Voivodeship remained Catholic. Imperial Russia acquired the entire territory of present-day Latvia in the 18th century. Governed by Polish and polonized German nobility, Latgalians retained few rights, received little education, and lived in near-poverty conditions. In 1864 printing in Latgalian was banned. Russian anti-Polish financial policies and Russification procedures contributed to the delay in the formation of a middle class and a cultural awakening. Latvia enjoyed a brief period of independence following World War I (1918–1940), but was taken over once again, this time by the Soviet Union (1940–1991).

From archeological excavations, church documents, folk songs, legends, and myths, scholars attempt to reconstruct the early lifestyles and beliefs of the Latgalians. Many customs practiced today appear to have their roots in the early traditions and belief systems of the ancient Latgali. Seventeenth-century Jesuits reported that Latgalians held to polytheistic worldviews characteristic of a wood culture. They buried their dead, in accordance to ancient rituals, in sacred groves. Latgalians considered the birch tree particularly holy. They placed offerings of food and drink for gods and goddesses, including god (*Dīvs*), earth goddess and guardian of women (*Mōra*), and the goddess of fate (*Laima*). Latgalians idolized the oak as a symbol of the masculine and the linden as feminine. One of the most characteristic themes in Latgalian folk culture is the feminine. The sun (*Saule*) is feminine and appears in a multitude of folk songs. *Saule*'s warmth is linked with a mother's love. The moon (*Mieness*) is masculine, as is (*Auseklis*) the rising star and (*Pārkiuņs*) thunder.

Many mothers of nature appear in folklore, such as earth mother, forest mother, and water mother. Latgalian folk songs, as opposed to Latvian, also speak of god's mother (*Dīva muote*), possibly influenced from the Catholic Mary mother of Jesus. *Dīva muote* and *Mōra* were worshipped in similar ways, for instance in beseeching *Dīva* muote to provide a dowry for an orphaned girl. The tradition of song is prevalent in Latgalian culture, such as songs of seasonal celebrations, collective work (*tolka*), and social songs. During the early 20th century Latgalians continued to sing historical songs of *tolka* when working in the fields, and even at times on the collective farms during Soviet rule. Folk songs of seasonal celebrations are now most often sung in local civic halls. Summer solstice (*Juoņi*) is celebrated today as a national holiday when men frequently wear wreaths of oak leaves, the ancient symbol of virility. Feudal and imperial territorial seclusion enhanced Latvian regional distinctions of folk dress, especially in women's clothes. Abrene's regional women's costume of all-white linen with red embroidery, still worn today in song festivals and ethnic holidays, is considered by many characteristic of ancient Baltic dress.

With the Latgalian printing ban lifted in 1904, Latgalians experienced a cultural awakening in the early 20th century. Prominent revival figures are Francis Kemps (1876–1952), Francis Trasuns (1864–1926), Ontōns Skrynda (1881–1918), and Nikodems Rancāns (1870–1933). Latvia's brief period of independence allowed multiple branches of culture to flourish. Latgalians published works representing manifold literary genres, printed newspapers, and established professional theaters. Authors Jānis Klīdzējs (1914–2000), Alberts Sprūdžs (1908–1944), and Ontons Rupaiņs (1906–1976) are renowned for their work from this period. The Soviet government banned the Latgalian language during the occupation period; literature developed legally only in exile: in Germany, Sweden, Canada, and America. In Latgale several authors established a remarkable tradition of handwritten literature; notable are Jōņs Cybuļskis (1911–1997) and Stepons Seiļs (1909–1979). The late 1980s brought a second cultural revival. Latvia

reestablished independence in 1991 and Latgalian cultural societies renewed their work, organized newspapers, and founded the publishing House of Latgalian Culture. The Latgalian language is not used in an official capacity today but is largely spoken in the home in rural areas, and has seen a revival on the Internet. Latgalians are known today for their traditional ceramics, folk music, and folklore ensembles.

*Irene Elksnis Geisler*

## Further Reading

Bukšs, Miķelis. *Latgalu Atmūda: Idejas un Ceiņas (The Latgalian Awakening: Ideas and Struggles)*. Munich: Latgalu Izdevniceiba, 1976. (In Latgalian, summary in German.)

Latkovski, Leonard. Latgale Research Center. Hood College. http://latgaleresearch.com (The Latgale Research Center is a Web site dedicated to informing and educating people on the Latgale region of Latvia.)

Zeile, Pēteris. *Latgales Kultūras Vēsture: No Akmens Laikmeta Līdz Mūsdienai (The Cultural History of Latgale: From the Stone Age Until Present Day)*. Rēzekne: Latvijas Kultūras Centra Izdevniecība, 2006, 720–725. (In Latvian, summary in English.)

Zeps, Valdis J. "Homestead or Village: Eighteenth-Century Evidence for the History of Latgalian Settlement." *Journal of Baltic Studies* 5, no. 4 (1974): 329–338.

Zeps, Valdis J. "Latgalian Literature in Exile." *Journal of Baltic Studies* 26, no. 4 (1995): 313–328.

## Latvians

Latvians, formerly called Letts, make up more than 59 percent of the population in the republic of Latvia, a Baltic country with

2,270,700 residents; its capital, Riga, has more than 700,000 residents. About 40,000 Latvians moved to the United States and Canada from the Displaced Persons Camps after World War II. Many Latvians also have immigrated to Australia, the United Kingdom, Ireland, and Brazil. The Latvian population in Siberia is a result of the deportations of the early and late 1940s. Currently the number of Latvians abroad is estimated to be greater than 215,000 persons. Latvians speak Latvian, a Baltic language of the Indo-European family. The dominant religion is Lutheranism, the practice of which is sometimes mixed in with pagan rituals formed in Latvia's peasant past. Other religions practiced by Latvians include Evangelicalism,

Roman Catholicism, and Russian Orthodoxy. There is also a small Jewish population in Latvia, although its members are primarily regarded as a separate ethnicity from Latvians. The definition of Latvian is many-sided: it refers simultaneously to language, ethnic origin, and nationality, as Latvia, the country, was founded out of a need for ethnic self-determination.

Historians have noted that the term "Latvian" did not become common until the late 1850s with the start of the nationalist movement. Prior to that point the only terms used to describe Latvians were *latvis*, *latvieši* (a Latvian, the Latvians). They were also later called "Letts," as can be seen in the translation of the name of Latvia in other

Couples in traditional Latvian dress folk dancing at fishermen's festival, Riga, Latvia, 1955. (Library of Congress)

languages, such as French (*Lettonie*). But, there were other ethnic groups at the time occupying the same space: Zemgallians, Livs, Kursi, and Latgallians (most of whom were later assimilated into what would become the larger Latvian ethnicity). The dominant narrative traces the origins of the Latvian tribes to 9000 BCE, when the early Baltic tribes arrived in what is now known as Latvia. (Already residing in the area were Finno-Ugric peoples, ancestors of today's Finns, Estonians, and Livs.) The migrating ancestors of the Latvians spoke a Baltic tongue, a language very different from Finno-Ugric but closely related to that of their southern neighbors, the Lithuanians.

The 13th through 16th centuries saw the Livonian period of German rule, followed by the Russian invasion of 1558 and Swedish rule in 1629. In 1651 the Duchy of Courland established territory in the African nation of Gambia and expanded their overseas territory into the island of Tobago (1652–1655). At this time, Courland was ruled by the Duke Jacob (his death in 1682). In 1655, Courland was invaded by the Swedish army, which started the Swedish-Polish War that lasted until 1660. Poland soon had more influence over Courland, starting in 1698 until the Great Northern War (1700–1721) that involved Russia and Sweden along with Russia's allies (including Poland). In 1721, Livland was incorporated into Russia; in 1817 and in 1819 the serfs were emancipated in Livonia and Courland. In the 1850s, Latvian peasants began to move into the cities. At the time, the majority of the land was still owned by wealthy Baltic German landowners and German was the primary language of business and social interactions. In 1867, Russian became the primary language in the Latvian territory although the majority of the peasant estates were under control of the Baltic German aristocracy.

Woman selling warm clothes in Riga, Latvia. (Travel Pictures Gallery)

Key individuals in understanding the early development of the Latvian people are the German-Lutheran clergy, who first wrote down the Latvian language as part of the creation of church liturgy in the Latvian language (songs, prayers); indeed (Baltic) German authors produced the majority of Latvian writing during the 1850s and 1860s. Other key figures were part of the Riga National Association, which founded the first Song and Dance Festival in 1868. Key intellectuals in forming the Latvian cultural and national consciousness were writers Ansis Līventāls (1803–1878) and Juris Nēķins (1826–1878). Later on in the 19th and 20th century, writers such as Rainis (1865–1929) and Aspazija (1865–1943) would contribute to the burgeoning literature being produced in Latvian for Latvians.

The political life and recent history of the Latvians is tied into that of the Latvian nation-state, therefore the struggles of the independent Latvian state are seen as one with the struggles of the Latvian people. On November 18, 1918, the Latvian State declared independence from Russia. Independence brought with it a wave of ethnic and cultural initiatives that included the establishment of Latvian as the official language, a policy of "Latvia for Latvians" that was primarily pushed by Kārlis Ulmanis after his coup in 1934, and the recognition of the rights of ethnic minorities. The independent state would last until 1940, when following the signing of the Molotov-Ribbentrop Pact in 1939 (which divided up Eastern Europe between Germany and the Soviet Union) Latvia was invaded by the Soviet Union and Latvians again found themselves under the control of an occupying power. The year of 1940–1941 is known as the "year of horrors" to commemorate the mass deportations of hundreds of thousands of Latvians to Siberia. In 1941, Latvia was invaded by Nazi Germany and remained occupied until 1945. The occupation brought with it the deaths of much of the Jewish minority, as well as many Latvians who resisted German rule. In 1945, Latvia was reoccupied by the Soviet Union, and Latvians as well as their nation would remain a part of the Soviet Union (and thus be Sovietized) until the adoption of the declaration of independence on May 4, 1990, and the complete reinstatement of Latvia's independence on August 21, 1991.

Since 1991 Latvians have seen a rebirth of ethnic and cultural pride, which includes celebrating their past through the works of famous Latvian authors such as Rainis, Aspazija, and Anna Brigadere, as well as artists such as Janis Rozenthāls (1866–1916) and Vihelms Purvītis (1872–1945), musicians such as Andrejs Jurjāns (1856–1922), Jazeps Vītols (1863–1948), and Raimonds Pauls (1936– ), and numerous scientists (the most famous being Dāvids Hiernīms Grindelis [1776–1836]), athletes, performers, and politicians.

While the majority of Latvians adhere to the beliefs of the Lutheran Church, many Latvians will still describe themselves as "pagan" because many of their holidays and rituals are drawn from the peasant past. Midsummers, now known as St. John's Days (*Jāņi*), are celebrated by dancing around a bonfire, cooking traditional food such as *Jaņu siers* (a special cheese), and wearing *vainags* (floral head-pieces). Christmas is also more commonly known as *Ziemassvētki* (winter celebration), a name carried over from pre-Christian times.

Latvians are also well known for their folk song traditions. The *Dainas* (four-line folk songs) are known by all Latvians and number in the thousands. They were famously catalogued by the writer Krišjānis Barons at the beginning of the 18th century. The Dainas are sung during family gatherings, festivals, and holidays. Every five years sees the arrival of the National Song and Dance Festival (the last one was in 2008 and the next will be in 2013). During the festival, hundreds of choirs from across Latvia and from the Latvian diaspora gather in Riga to sing the best-known folk songs. The event began in 1868, spurred in good measure by the efforts of the Riga National Association. The National Song and Dance Festivals are credited with keeping the culture and language of Latvians alive even during times of foreign occupation and colonization. Song Festivals are also performed abroad; the most well known of these is the North American Song and Dance Festivals, which occur every year and rotate among different cities in the United States and Canada.

Latvians are also known for their fabric work with linen. The designs sewn into the linen are derived from traditional Latvian symbols that can identify the origin of the maker (each region has a specific design), and the type of meaning behind the design. These intricate pieces can be found in many forms, from table runners and blankets to skirts, dresses, and shirts.

Historically, Latvians' relationship to their neighbors has been fraught with tension and occupation. The Latvians have been occupied by the Germans, Russians, and Swedes; these occupations have impacted the Latvian sense of self as well as contemporary relationships with those nationalities. Latvians maintain good relations with their Baltic neighbors, the Estonians to the North and the Lithuanians to the South.

*Lauren Monsein Rhodes*

**Further Reading**

Bleiere, D., et al. *History of Latvia: The 20th Century*. Riga: Jumava, 2006.

Ezergailis, Andrew. *The Holocaust in Latvia, 1941–1944: The Missing Center*. Riga: The Historical Institute of Latvia, 1996.

Misiunas, R., and R. Taagepera. *The Baltic States: Years of Dependence 1940–1990*. Berkeley, CA: University of California Press, 1993.

Plakans, A. *The Latvians: A Short History*. Stanford, CA: Hoover Institution Press, 1995.

Plakans, A. "Peasants, Intellectuals, and Nationalism in the Russian Baltic Provinces, 1820–90." *Journal of Modern History* 46 (1974): 445–475.

von Rauch, G. *The Baltic States: The Years of Independence. Estonia, Latvia, Lithuania, 1917–1940*. London: C. Hurst, 1995 [1974].

# Lezgins

Lezgins (self-designation: *Lezgi* [s.] and *Lezgiiar* [pl.]) are an indigenous people of the Caucasus who live compactly in southern Dagestan and northern Azerbaijan. In 2002, the number of Lezgins in the Russian Federation was 411,500, of which 336,698 were living in the Republic of Dagestan, where they comprise the fourth largest ethnic group and 12 percent of the population. Official statistics from

1994 put the number of Lezgins in Azerbaijan at 171,400, but estimates of the real numbers range from 180,000 to 350,000. The Lezgins are Muslims; the great majority are Sunni of the Shafi'i rite, with small numbers of Lezgins living near or inside Azerbaijan being Shiite. Their language (Lezgin) belongs to the Nakh-Dagestani (or Alordian Northeast Caucasian) group of North Caucasian languages. In culture and way of life Lezgins share much with their neighbors. The term "Lezgin" and its variants have been used through the 19th century to refer to the Muslim mountain peoples of Dagestan in general and not just to the Lezgins. It was only at the beginning of the 20th century that the use of the term began to be restricted to the Lezgins proper.

The Lezgin are an indigenous Caucasian people. Their early history is bound up with that of Caucasian Albania (third century BCE to fifth century CE). Some believe that their name derives from "Lek," the name of one of the largest tribes of Caucasian Albania. The fact that Georgians call the Lezgins "Lek" would seem to lend some support to this idea. Following the fall of Caucasian Albania, the Lezgins came under the rule of the Iranian governor in Derbend.

Arab-Muslim armies conquered the area of southern Dagestan around the city of Derbent in the 7th century during the great Arab-Muslim conquests, making southern Dagestan part of the Rashidun Caliphate. This marked the beginning of Lezgin conversion to Islam. That conversion was completed in the 15th century. Later, the Turkish khanates of Azerbaijan exerted significant influence over the Lezgins. Up until the 19th century, most Lezgins lived in free societies made up of patriarchal clans and extended families, although significant numbers lived at different times under the khanates of Kuba, Derbend, and Kazikumuk. Feudal structures came into existence among these, especially those living in the Kuba khanate.

By 1813, all Lezgins came under nominal Russian rule. Many Lezgins in Dagestan, however, participated in the Great Caucasian War and fought against the Russians alongside the Avar Imam Shamil, who for 25 years (1834–1859) defied Russian rule. It was not until after his defeat in 1859 that the Russians consolidated their rule over Dagestan and the Lezgins.

Social administration and village jurisprudence among the Lezgins, as among other Dagestani peoples, was based on *adat* (Arabic for "customary law") and sharia (Islamic law). *Adat* was used to decide criminal and civil issues such as property, crimes associated with robbery, and others. Sharia was used to decide issues related to religious ritual, family and marriage, weddings, wills, and inheritance. Dispute resolution was oral, with village elders listening to testimony from both sides. The village congregation would express its opinion and majority vote would decide the issue, and a special book of complaints would record the dispute. The principle of blood feud fell under the jurisdiction of *adat*. It served as a means of deterrence and regulation, and was triggered by grave crimes such as murder, assault, and rape.

Home industries (weaving, rug making, leatherworking, pottery, smithing, etc.) and transhumant sheep and goat raising constituted the basis of the Lezgins' traditional economy. In the foothill and lowland areas, cereal crops, gardening, and horticulture were important. The Lezgins regularly used winter pastures in Azerbaijan, and there was a long tradition of seasonal (winter) migratory labor among Lezgin men to the Azerbaijani cities of Baku, Kuba, and Shamakhi. This migration combined with political ties to Azerbaijan reinforced the influence of Azerbaijani culture and language upon the Lezgins until the Soviet period, when Soviet nationality policies strengthened Lezgin identity and weakened the trend toward assimilation.

The material culture of the Lezgins is of the general Dagestani type, with some influence from Azerbaijani material culture. Traditional Lezgin villages all contained at least one mosque and a well. An important part of Lezgin social life was the village square, or *kim*, where villagers (mainly males) would gather to debate and decide issues of village life.

The Lezgin language possesses three main dialects: Kürin, Akhti, and Kuba. Kürin provides the basis of the literary form of the language. Azeri Turkish has influenced all three dialects. In the 19th century Lezgin became a written language and used the Arabic script. Arabic and Persian were the preferred languages for literature and scholarship, and relatively little was written in Lezgin before the Soviet period. During the Soviet period Lezgin was officially recognized and taught in schools.

The advent of Soviet rule brought radical changes to virtually every aspect of Lezgin life. Soviet rule formalized Lezgin identity and made it a fact of bureaucratic and legal life. The collectivization of agriculture and the later conversion of collective farms into state farms overturned the traditional economy and ways of life throughout Dagestan. The changes significantly decreased the amount of land under cultivation and the amount of livestock per capita. Recent years have seen a small, but still fragile, return to individual farming.

The collapse of Soviet Communism in 1991 resulted in the loss of subsidies for textbooks, dictionaries, and other material for the teaching of the Lezgin language and also a decline in the number of qualified teachers of Lezgin. This downturn, combined with incentives to learn Russian, which functions as the lingua franca in Dagestan, has put the long-term future of the Lezgin and other Dagestani languages in doubt.

In 1990, a Lezgin national movement known as Sadval (Unity) emerged in Dagestan to advocate for the establishment of a Lezgin state encompassing the Lezgin territories of southern Dagestan and northern Azerbaijan. The breakup of the Soviet Union and the establishment of an international border between the Russian Republic of Dagestan and Azerbaijan, however, physically divided the Lezgins. In 1998 Sadval split between a radical wing committed to the establishment of single Lezgin state and a moderate wing that aspires to the formation of an autonomous Lezgin entity inside Daghestan. Since then, neither of Sadval's wings has demonstrated a substantial following or influence.

Unemployment is an endemic problem facing Lezgins and other peoples of Dagestan. In fact, rates of unemployment among Lezgins may be as high as 60 percent, nearly twice the Dagestan average.

This job shortage is driving migration into cities. Overall, the fall and economic disintegration of the Soviet Union and the exposure of Dagestan to contemporary globalization in the form of cheap imports have left the Lezgins and other Dagestanis in a prolonged state of economic crisis.

*Michael A. Reynolds*

## Further Reading

Gadzhiev, G. A. and M. Sh. Rizakhanova. "Lezginy." In *Narody Dagestana (The Peoples of Dagestan)*, eds. S. A. Arutiunov, A. I. Osmanov, and G. A. Sergeeva. Moscow: Nauka, 2002, 376–398.

Rizakhanova, M. Sh. *Bytovaia kul'tura Lezgin: 20–90-e gody XX v (The Social Culture of the Lezgins: 1920s to 1990s)*. Makhachkala: Dinem, 2008.

Wixman, R. "Lezgh." *Encyclopaedia of Islam.* 2nd ed. Eds. P. Bearman et al. Leiden: Brill, 2009. Brill Online.

# Liechtensteiners

Liechtensteiners are the national group of Liechtenstein, a tiny principality that sits on the eastern bank of the Rhine, across the river from Switzerland and flanked on its east by Austria. Native Liechtensteiners, for the most part Roman Catholic, number approximately 23,000 across 11 villages, roughly two-thirds of Liechtenstein's population. Because there is little ethnic difference between Liechtensteiners and the neighboring Germans, Swiss, and Austrians—all share the same Allemanic roots and the German language—the distinct Liechtensteiner identity relies heavily on the shared experiences of its native-born population. As such, Liechtensteiners guard this identity keenly through relatively strict immigration policies.

Farm girl, Liechtenstein. (Corel)

Liechtensteiners descend from the same Allemanic ethnic group that controlled the wider region from the fifth century. They derive their name from Prince John Adam Andrew of Liechtenstein who, in 1719, purchased and united Vaduz and Schellenberg—two previously separate, feudal lands on which this group lived. Throughout the next two centuries, Liechtensteiners remained poor, though they eventually forged an alliance with Austria and won extensive liberal rights from its monarchy with a new constitution. After Austro-Hungary's collapse, Liechtensteiners established close ties with Switzerland, and in the past half-century have become one of the most prosperous peoples in Europe through the development of industry and banking. Only one royal family has ruled Liechtensteiners, and the prince has often been the personal guarantor of the people's wealth and security, thereby forming an integral part of their identity.

Historically, Liechtensteiners were and are agrarian people who earn their living through farming and raising livestock. As a result, their villages tend to be close-knit, and native-born Liechtensteiners often descend from centuries-old families. Since World War II, however, the royal family has helped turn Liechtensteiners into a predominantly modern, industrial society. Now, few Liechtensteiners farm; most work in services, banking, or industry centered in two main villages, Vaduz and Schaan. Liechtensteiners are overwhelmingly Roman Catholic, a by-product of their historical ties to Austria, and religion plays a central role in early formal education. With consideration for their small size and similar ethnic background, Liechtensteiners maintain good relations with their neighbors, though there exists an underlying tension surrounding the large numbers of immigrants, mostly from neighboring Germany, Austria, and Switzerland, who live alongside them—approximately one-third of the country's population and nearly two-thirds of its workforce—but do not share their cultural identity.

Attempting to battle fascism, Liechtensteiners formed a consensus government during World War II. This lasted until 1997 when an opposition emerged over the prince's role in political life. After a sometimes bitter and divisive national debate, Liechtensteiners voted in 2003 to grant their prince much greater authority over parliament—the first time this has happened in modern European history. Prince Hans Adam II remains their head of state, though his son, Prince Alois, has handled day-to-day duties since 2004.

*Michael Hass*

## Further Reading

Beattie, David. *Liechtenstein: A Modern History*. London: I. B. Taurus, 2004.

Hass, Michael. "Geopolitics and Nations: Why Liechtensteiners Exist." August 2004. Social Science Research Network. http://ssrn.com.

Raton, Pierre. *Liechtenstein: History and Institutions of the Principality*. Vaduz: Liechtenstein-Verlag, 1970.

Seger, Otto. "A Survey of Liechtenstein History." Vaduz: Press and Information Office of the Government of the Principality of Liechtenstein, 1984.

# Lithuanians

Lithuanians are a Baltic group of approximately 3.4 million people residing in Lithuania, a nation-state in northeastern Europe. Over a million Lithuanians live in the Americas, the United Kingdom, Ireland, Australia, Poland, Latvia, Russia, and elsewhere. Although ethnically homogeneous (83% of the population identify themselves as Lithuanian), Lithuania is also home to Russians, Poles, Jews, Roma, Karaites, and other ethnic minorities. Catholicism dominates, but Orthodoxy, Protestantism, Judaism, and several transnational Christian religions—such as Evangelical Pentecostalism, Mormonism, and Jehovah's Witnesses—are also practiced. The primary language is Lithuanian, one of the two existing Baltic tongues (along with Latvian).

Stretching between the rivers of Vistula (*Wisła*) and Daugava, the prehistoric (2nd to 9th centuries CE) Baltic lands were populated by several tribal groups known as Selonians (*sėliai*), Curonians (*kuršiai*), Samogitians (*žemaičiai*), Prussians (*prūsai*), among others. At the time, Lithuanians (*lietuviai*) inhabited the basin of the Nemunas and Neris rivers. The first written record of this territory appears in a Germanic chronicle produced in Quedlinburg in 1009. The medieval manuscript refers to St. Bruno, a Saxon monk, who was murdered by unwelcoming pagan believers in a land called *Litua* (Lithuania in Latin), while attempting to convert them to Christianity.

Lithuanian woman sells onions. (Travel Pictures Gallery)

Sociopolitically organized in prestate chiefdoms, in the 11th and 12th centuries the Balts relied on grain farming and pastoralism as well as hunting, gathering, and fishing as principal means of subsistence. Called "Vikings of the land," some of these peoples, notably Curonians and Lithuanians, were also known for their marauding raids into neighboring Livonia (contemporary Latvia and Estonia) and into the Slavic territories of Russia and Poland.

In the early 1200s, the pope issued an edict to convert Baltic heathens to Christianity. Resistance to evangelizing Teutonic knights sent by the pontiff united the Balts in a loose confederation, which was further consolidated by their ambitions to expand into Slavic territories. The early 13th century saw the beginning of Lithuanian statehood associated notably with the reign of Mindaugas (1240–1263), the first king to convert to Christianity.

Veneration of land, water, fire, celestial bodies, and plants, among other natural elements and phenomena, was central to the belief system of pre-Christian Lithuanians. Pagan deities were commonly propitiated with sacrificial offerings of domestic animals. Lasting well into the 14th century, burial practices entailed the burning of the dead and disposing of the remains in funerary mounds believed to be gateways to the afterlife. Lithuanians did not officially embrace the Christian faith until 1387— among the last Europeans to do so.

Elements of prehistoric paganism have survived to the present day. In contemporary Lithuania, for example, some Christian crosses are embellished with representations of the moon, sun, and stars, or adorned with images of the oak tree or grass snake, considered to be sacred entities. Referents to paganism can also be detected in traditional handicrafts and textiles, fairy tales and folk songs, as well as in toponyms, personal names, and swear words. Following the demise of atheist socialism in 1990 (see below), there has been a resurgence of interest in pre-Christian faiths.

In the 14th and 15th centuries, Lithuania emerged as a distinct geopolitical entity on the European continent. This historically significant period is remembered for the rule of dukes Gediminas (1316–1341) and Vytautas (1392–1430), the political alliance with Poland, the territorial expansion of the Grand Duchy of Lithuania from the Baltic to the Black Sea, the Duchy's defeat of the Mongol (Tartar) Golden Horde (1362), and the battle of Žalgiris (1410), or Grünwald, where Lithuanian and Polish allies crushed the Teutonic Order, ending its Christianizing missions.

In the 16th century, the strengthening Duchy of Moscovy sought to regain its Slavic principalities in the Polish-Lithuanian Commonwealth. To reinforce their unity against Muscovy's growing threats, the two allied states signed the Treaty of Lublin (1569), which asserted Poland's supremacy and consigned Lithuania to the status of a periphery. This treaty also marked the beginning of "Polonization," a process that erased many cultural differences between Polish and Lithuanian elites, many of whom embraced Polish culture and language as markers of superior civilization. Despite the consolidation of the upper classes, the Commonwealth remained politically and economically weak and ceased to exist in 1795, following the partition of its expansive territory between Russia, Prussia, and Austria. Stripped of its geopolitical status, Lithuania became known as the northwest territory of tsarist Russia.

As resistance to Russian colonialism intensified in the 19th century, tsarist authorities introduced a series of Russification policies intended to assimilate Lithuanians into the multiethnic empire. One such policy stipulated that Roman characters in all Lithuanian publications be replaced with the Cyrillic script. Seen as an attempt to convert Catholic Lithuanians to Orthodoxy and to devalue Lithuanian culture, the alphabet policy was fiercely resisted by the Catholic clergy and the middle class emerging from the peasantry. Russia's heavy-handed strategies of assimilation, paradoxically, led to the strengthening of Lithuanian national consciousness and to increasingly vocal demands for more autonomy within the empire. In 1904, the ban on the Roman alphabet was lifted. Among the key figures of the nationalist movement at the time were historian Simonas Daukantas (1793–1864), bishop Motiejus Valančius (1801–1875), poet Vincas Kudirka (1858–1899), and scholar Jonas Basanavičius (1851–1927).

The easing of Russia's authoritarian grip in the early 20th century brought about more freedom of expression and assembly, and resulted in a proliferation of popular periodicals promoting ideas of national self-determination. The political upheaval created by World War I (1914–1918), the demise of the Russian empire, and the socialist Revolution in 1917 provided Lithuanian nationalists with a historical opportunity to claim political sovereignty.

On February 16, 1918, the northwest territory proclaimed itself an independent nation-state.

During the interwar years (1918–1940), the Republic of Lithuania was largely an agrarian economy with more than half of its population employed in agriculture. Ideas of catching up with Western Europe dominated much of the public discourse at the time. Lithuania's aspirations to move away from the Russian-tsarist past and to align itself with the West, which was seen to be more advanced, were manifest in domains ranging from politics to popular culture, from industrial development to modernist avant-garde trends in literature and art. However, instead of becoming an inclusive liberal democracy, for 15 years the republic was under the authoritarian leadership of President Antanas Smetona, whose political goal was to create a unified, "organic" nation. Interwar Lithuania is often associated with the president's personality cult, sociopolitical conservativism of the Catholic Church, and the rise of agrarian populism and militant nationalism.

As a consequence of the Molotov-Ribbentrop pact signed by the USSR and Nazi Germany, in 1940 Lithuania was annexed to the Soviet Union and lost its sovereignty once again. After the defeat of Hitler's army in 1945, communist Moscow launched a massive Sovietization campaign promising to create a more progressive and just society. Lithuania's political establishment and economy as well as its cultural, social, and educational institutions were demolished and rebuilt according to Marxist-Leninist principles. The so-called Nationalities policy was introduced to eradicate what Moscow called backward forms of nationalism and to make Lithuanians part of the new collectivity of the Soviet people. The state propaganda of socialist patriotism was accompanied with relentless Russification, which entailed resettlement of Russian industrial workers, bureaucrats, and military personnel to Lithuanian cities, the use of the Russian language in many public institutions, promotion of Russian history and culture, and so forth. Labeled a bastion of bourgeois backwardness, the Catholic Church was separated from the atheist Soviet state. Many members of the clergy and the burgeoning middle class, as well as more prosperous farmers, were deported to Siberian labor camps or executed—an estimated 140,000 persons in 1941–1952. Some 60,000 fled to the West. Lithuania remained under Moscow's authoritarian rule for almost five decades.

In the more liberal environment of Mikhail Gorbachev's reforms in the late 1980s, ideas of a sovereign nation powered a well-organized independence movement (Sąjūdis) led by a group of intellectuals, local Communist Party functionaries, and Catholic clergymen. On March 11, 1990, Lithuania was the first Soviet socialist republic to break away from the USSR and to declare independence.

After regaining its freedom, this Baltic nation embraced Western-style liberal democracy and free market in an attempt to redefine itself as a Western, modern country. In the early 2000s, Lithuania's economy grew on average 8 percent annually; in 2004, it became a member of the European Union (EU) and NATO. However, over the past two decades or so, the transformation from Marxist-Leninist socialism to market capitalism has been far from smooth. Deepening socioeconomic differentiation, poverty, lawlessness, shrinking of the population by emigration (approximately 400,000 people since 1990), and low birthrate, disillusionment with the EU, and the reemergence of extreme forms of nationalism are some of the unintended consequences brought about by Lithuania's pursuit of the West after socialism.

*Gediminas Lankauskas*

**Further Reading**

Kiaupa, Zigmas. *The History of Lithuania*. Vilnius: Baltos Lankos, 2002.

Lieven, Anatol. *The Baltic Revolution: Estonia, Latvia, Lithuania and the Path to Independence*. New Haven: Yale University Press, 1994.

Smith, D., et al. *The Baltic States: Estonia, Latvia and Lithuania*. New York: Routledge, 2002.

Sužiedėlis, Saulius. *Historical Dictionary of Lithuania*. Lanham, MD: Scarecrow Press, 1997.

Vardys, S., and J. Sedaitis. *Lithuania, the Rebel Nation*. Boulder, CO: Westview Press, 1997.

# Luxembourgers

The question of what makes a Luxembourger has been of growing importance over recent decades. The Grand Duchy of Luxembourg—the homeland of most Luxembourgers—possesses one of Europe's largest immigrant populations, with 43 percent of its residents in 2009 not owning a Luxembourgian passport. Most of these immigrants are of Portuguese and to a lesser extent Italian and French origin. The multinational character of the country—and its capital especially—is reinforced by the presence of European Union institutions and a cross-border workforce of 150,000 constituting more than 40 percent of its labor market. Most of the latter commute from France and Belgium, but earn their living in Luxembourg's service-based economy, which is built around its flourishing financial center. People who would regard themselves ethnically as Luxembourgers (about 280,000 people possess Luxembourgian nationality and reside within the country) show very few cultural markers to distinguish them from their political neighbors. The Luxembourgish language is very similar to dialects spoken in parts of Western Germany, the country's dominant religion is the same Catholicism found beyond its borders, and likewise it shares most of its political history with neighboring regions, Belgium especially. One could of course argue that the particular mixture of such elements creates Luxembourg's ethnic specificity, but this view neglects actual identifications by Luxembourgers and their constructed character.

Luxembourg's ethnic identity is a child of Luxembourgian national identity, which itself should be considered a relative recent phenomenon. Although mid-20th-century historiography presupposed the existence of a late-medieval and early-modern sense of local particularism, no source material from the period reflects observable feelings of communality or solidarity across social classes based on sharing the same territory. For most of its past, the region that today constitutes the Grand Duchy was part of larger political entities, such as the extended lands of the late-medieval Limburg dynasty within the Holy Roman Empire, or the Habsburg Low Countries during most of modern times. The independent Grand Duchy of Luxembourg, initially only de jure, was created in 1815 as a compromise between Prussia and the United Kingdom of the Netherlands. A national consciousness started to develop in the middle decades of the 19th century as a result of the growing demands by the bourgeoisie for a share in power and the continuing threats posed to the small country's independence by its mightier political neighbors. The threat of political annexation was still real in the first half of the 20th century and considerably reinforced national consciousness. It was most strongly felt after World War I, in the late 1930s, and during the German occupation of World War II.

A significant component of the emerging group identity in the second half of the 19th century was the identification with a common past. By glorifying the medieval counts of Luxembourg, the national master-narrative of history created continuity between the medieval principality and the modern state. It provided Luxembourgers with age-old origins and a historic homeland. It also helped to define Luxembourgers against their principal two "Others": the Belgians, with whom the principality shared much of modern history, and the Prussians, who controlled Luxembourg's fortress until 1867. Around the same time, romantic descriptions of the country and its landscapes appeared alongside attempts to present the country with its own culture. Some of the local religious traditions, such as the pilgrimage to the statue of Our Lady of Luxembourg, gained renewed interest and were increasingly attributed with nationalist overtones.

The first attempts to advance the idea of Luxembourg's inhabitants as a distinct ethnic group stem from around the time of World War I. In 1911, Nicolas Ries presented the Luxembourgers as a distinct race with its own culture and psychology. Unlike their neighbors, Ries argued, the people of Luxembourg represented an ethnic mix of Celtic and Germanic elements, a fusion of the best of French and German aspects, and thus a distinct and "superior eclectic culture." One of the aims was to distance the Luxembourgers from the Germans, who started to take over the role as the principal Other. While these ideas initially emerged in the milieu of the political left, they were quickly adopted by the political right. Furthermore, they had some influence on the legal definition of Luxembourgian nationality and were voiced in parliamentary debates. From 1940 naturalization law changed from the *ius soli* (citizenship based on birth in a country, in Latin literally "right of soil") to the *ius sanguini* (citizenship based on ancestry, in Latin literally "right of blood"). However, the definition of the nation did not entirely shift to an ethnocultural line, since at this point language was not included in the legal definition.

Nonetheless, one perceives a growing emphasis on the Luxembourgish language in media and politics throughout the 20th century, to the degree that it represents nowadays the strongest element of identification for most Luxembourgers. While the local tongue had been largely considered a mere German dialect at the start of the 20th century, it was made a national language by law in 1984 (alongside French and German). Luxembourgish now serves as the main factor to define who is a Luxembourger. Its knowledge is a prerequisite for certain jobs in government and education, making them quasi-inaccessible to non-Luxembourgers. At the same time politicians increasingly insist on language as the prime way to integrate immigrants.

The formation process of a unique Luxembourgian identity, and in consequence ethnic group awareness, has evolved over time—a process still ongoing. Many developments that other nations in Western Europe underwent in the 19th century have begun only relatively recently in Luxembourg. Examples of these developments are the continuing creation of national cultural institutions (e.g., the university in 2003), the establishment of a canon of national literature, and a recent public debate on the content of the national flag (2006–2007).

*Pit Péporté*

## Further Reading

Kmec, Sonja, et al. *Inventing Luxembourg: Representations of the Past, Space, and Language from the Nineteenth to the Twenty-First Century*. Boston: Brill, 2010.

Kmec, Sonja, et al., eds. *Lieux de mémoire au Luxembourg* (*Lieux de mémoire in Luxembourg*). Luxembourg: Editions St. Paul, 2007.

Ries, Nicolas. *Essai de psychologie du peuple luxembourgeois* (*Essay on the Psychology of the Luxembourgian People*). Diekirch: J. Schroell, 1911.

Scuto, Denis. "Qu'est-ce un luxembourgeois?" (*What is a Luxembourger?*). *Hémecht* 58, no. 1 (2006): 73–96.

# M

## Macedonians

Most of the world's approximately 1,750,000 Macedonians live in the Republic of Macedonia in the south-central Balkans. There are also small Macedonian minorities in Bulgaria (5,000), Albania (10,000), Serbia and Kosovo (26,000), and Greece (10,000–30,000), as well as Macedonian diaspora communities in Europe, Canada (38,000), the United States (50,000), and Australia (84,000). Most Macedonians are Christians and belong to the Macedonian Orthodox Church. They speak the Macedonian language, a member of the South Slavic family of languages that includes Slovenian, Bosnian/Croatian/Serbian, and Bulgarian. Macedonian identity and history are extremely controversial subjects; even the name "Macedonian" is contested. Macedonians themselves and scholars throughout the world use the name as a matter of common sense. Bulgaria, however, maintains that Macedonians are really Bulgarians, and Greece insists that only Greeks have the right to use the name Macedonia, inaccurately claiming that "Macedonia was, is, and always will be Greek" because Alexander the Great and the Ancient Macedonians were Greeks.

According to Macedonian nationalist historiography, Macedonians have existed as a distinct nation for thousands of years and are the direct descendants of the ancient Macedonians, whose empire constituted the first Macedonian state. According to Greek nationalist historiography, however, the ancient Macedonians were Greeks, and the modern Macedonian nation is simply an artificial creation of Josip Broz Tito, Yugoslavia's postwar Communist leader, who "baptized" a mosaic of nationalities and with no justification gave them the name "Macedonians." Disinterested scholars know that the linguistic and cultural origins of the modern Macedonians can be traced back to the Slavic tribes who settled in the central and southern Balkans in the sixth century CE. Saints Cyril and Methodius, missionary brothers from Thessaloniki, introduced Christianity to the Slavs and developed the Glagolitic alphabet, in which Old Church Slavonic, the first Slavic literary language, was written, and which was eventually replaced by the Cyrillic alphabet, which is still used for those Slavic languages whose speakers are largely Orthodox Christians.

During the Middle Ages, Macedonia was ruled by a series of empires: the Macedonian kingdom of Samuil, "Tsar of the Bulgars"; the Byzantine Empire under Basil II, known as "Basil the Bulgar Slayer"; and the "Serbian Empire" of Stefan Dušan. From the 14th century to early 20th century, when it was part of the Ottoman Empire, Macedonia's population consisted of such extraordinary ethnic, linguistic, and religious diversity (Bulgarians, Serbs, Albanians, Turks, Greeks,

Macedonians dressed in traditional costume ride horses bearing the former Macedonian flag (1992–1995), during a celebration of the Day of the Republic, August 2, 2001, near Krusevo. (AP/Wide World Photos)

Aroumanians, Jews, Roma, and others) that it inspired the French expression *Macédoine*, a salad of mixed fruit. During this period, the inhabitants of Macedonia were organized into religious communities, known as millets.

The Slavic-speaking Orthodox Christians of the area were under the control of the Greek Orthodox Patriarch in Istanbul. Under the millet system everyday life in rural agricultural communities was characterized by significant corruption and exploitation, despite periodic efforts by Ottoman authorities to improve the efficiency of its provincial administration. During this time, an urban middle class slowly began to grow with the development of small industry and the improvement of communication and transportation networks.

With the decline of the Ottoman Empire and the rise of nationalism in the Balkans, first the Serbs (1815), then the Greeks (1830), and finally the Bulgarians (1878) acquired their own independent states. By the turn of the century what had come to be termed "the Macedonian Struggle" had reached full intensity, as priests, teachers, and irregular bands of guerilla fighters from each country waged a fierce campaign to gain control of Macedonia and instill their idea of the proper sense of national identity in the Christian inhabitants of the area. A distinct Macedonian national identity crystallized at this time. In 1903 Krste Misirkov explicitly called for the "recognition of the Slavs in Macedonia as a separate nationality." The same year Gotse Delchev and other leaders of the Internal Macedonian Revolutionary Movement (VMRO) organized the Ilinden Uprising, which Macedonians consider one of the central events in their long struggle to create an independent Macedonian state. The Ottoman army, however, quickly suppressed this revolt. At the end of the Balkan Wars (1912–1913), the geographical region of Macedonia was divided up among Serbia, Bulgaria, and Greece. From this point on, the fates of the inhabitants of the "three Macedonias," Yugoslav (Vardar) Macedonia, Bulgarian (Pirin) Macedonia, and Greek (Aegean) Macedonia, diverged dramatically.

The portion of Macedonia that came under Serbian control was officially designated South Serbia, and the Slavic-speaking Christians living there were considered South Serbs. During this period, life in rural Macedonia was characterized by a low standard of living and a high birthrate. Agricultural productivity was poor, there was not enough industry to absorb the rural population surplus, and neither domestic nor international markets existed to support significant industrial growth. In addition, the Balkan Wars and World War I had destroyed much of the area's infrastructure, and the newly drawn international borders had disrupted traditional trade routes. Finally, the Serbian government did little to support economic growth in the region.

During World War II, the Yugoslav Communist Party under Tito came to power and declared the formation of a federal

## The Macedonian Question

In the late 19th and early 20th centuries, when Macedonia was still part of the Ottoman Empire, the Macedonian Question was an international conflict between Serbia, Bulgaria, and Greece over which state would control the territory of Macedonia and impose its own national identity on the ethnically diverse population. Since most of the inhabitants of Macedonia were illiterate villagers with no clearly defined sense of national identity, their assimilation into the Serb, Bulgarian, or Greek nations was accomplished by competing campaigns of religious and educational propaganda that often turned violent. H. N. Brailsford, a British journalist traveling through Macedonia in the early 20th century, describes a village that had been "Greek" four years earlier, but had recently become "Bulgarian, "because the Bulgarians had sent the village a teacher and a priest, while the Greeks had only sent a teacher." In this way, he writes, "the legend that Alexander the Great was a Greek goes out by one road and the rival myth that Alexander was a Bulgarian comes in by the other."

*Loring M. Danforth*

Yugoslavia. In August 1944, the Socialist (later People's) Republic of Macedonia was established as one of the six constituent republics of Yugoslavia. The creation of a Macedonian state, even within the framework of a federal Yugoslavia, made possible the recognition of a Macedonian nation. The process of nation-building continued with the standardization of a Macedonian literary language in 1944 and the declaration of an autocephalous Macedonian Orthodox Church in 1967, despite the opposition of the Serbian Orthodox Church.

Under Tito's rule, Macedonians experienced significant improvement in their standard of living in response to increased industrialization and the forced collectivization of agriculture. At the end of World War II, more than half of the Macedonian economy consisted of agriculture and animal husbandry based on small family farms. Postwar land redistribution programs established village agricultural cooperatives and large state-owned industrial enterprises, especially in the areas of textiles, leather, metalworking, and food processing. Improvements in the electricity grid and in road and rail networks, as well as the establishment of shopping centers and tourist resorts, also contributed significantly to Macedonia's economic growth.

The tragic outbreak of nationalist violence and ethnic cleansing of the Yugoslav wars of succession drew worldwide attention during the 1990s. Less well known is the fact that on September 8, 1991, the citizens of Macedonia voted peacefully to establish the Republic of Macedonia as a sovereign and independent state. Successive governments have focused on fighting corruption and organized crime networks engaged in smuggling, racketeering, drug dealing, and human trafficking. They have also faced the difficult task of managing the transition from state ownership to a free market economy.

The Macedonian government has struggled to maintain peaceful relationships between the Christian, Macedonian majority and the Muslim, Albanian minority, which makes up approximately one-quarter of the population. Balancing the legitimate demands of Albanians for the rights of full citizenship with the desire of Macedonian nationalists to preserve the republic as a Macedonian state has proven difficult. Establishing the loyalty of ethnic Albanians to the new Macedonian state is necessary in order to counter the threat of Albanian separatism.

The original preamble of the 1991 constitution described the Republic of Macedonia as "a national state of the Macedonian people in which full equality as citizens and permanent coexistence with the Macedonian people is provided for Albanians, Turks, Vlachs, Romanies, and other nationalities." In 2001 the preamble was revised; it now refers more pluralistically to "the citizens of the Republic of Macedonia, the Macedonian people, as well as citizens living within its borders who are part of the Albanian people, the Turkish people, the Vlach people, the Serbian people, the Romany people, the Bosniac people." The republic is a parliamentary democracy in which the president enjoys significant power. Kiro Gligorov, the first president, was a well-respected senior politician who had served for many years in the federal Yugoslav government. He skillfully guided the republic through its difficult first years, but was seriously wounded in an assassination attempt in 1995. The moderate Democratic Union of Socialists of Macedonia (SDSM), which consisted of former communists and social democrats, held office until 1999, when power shifted to the right and the more nationalist Internal Macedonian Revolutionary Organization—Democratic Party of Macedonian National Unity (VMRO-DPMNE) came to power. The Albanian minority has always voted as a bloc for ethnic Albanian parties, and all governments have been coalitions that included an Albanian party.

During the 1999 war in Kosovo, more than 350,000 Kosovar Albanians sought refuge in Macedonia. As a result of this crisis, living standards in Macedonia fell drastically, exports dropped, and unemployment rose to 33 percent. Political stability in the country was seriously threatened again in 2001, when armed insurgency broke out between an Albanian military group and Macedonian security forces. This conflict ended with the Ohrid Framework Agreement, signed in August 2001, in which the Macedonian government promised to increase local autonomy in areas with large Albanian populations, make Albanian an official language, and increase Albanian representation in the government, the police, and the army. Since then the Macedonian economy has recovered slowly, as gross domestic product (GDP) has grown slowly and inflation has remained under control.

By far the greatest challenge to the republic internationally is the campaign being waged by Greece to prevent Macedonia from being recognized under its constitutional name and from participating in international organizations. Shortly after achieving independence, the Republic of Macedonia sought to gain recognition from the European Community. Although an EC arbitration commission ruled that Macedonia met all of the qualifications for recognition and that the use of the name Macedonia did not imply territorial claims against Greece (as the Greek government had argued), Greece succeeded in blocking the republic's recognition by the EC. In 1993 Macedonia gained admission to the United Nations, but only under the derogatory provisional designation, "the Former Yugoslav Republic of Macedonia."

In a blatant attempt to pressure the republic to drop its claims to the name Macedonia, Greece imposed a devastating economic blockade against it in early 1994. Under increasing international pressure to resolve their differences, Greece and Macedonia signed an Interim Accord in September 1995, according to which Greece agreed to end the embargo and Macedonia agreed to renounce any claims to territory in Greek Macedonia and remove from its flag the 16-ray Sun or Star of Vergina (a symbol of the ancient Macedonian royal family that Greece has claimed as a Greek national symbol). Both countries agreed to submit the name issue to UN-sponsored mediation. In 2004 the United States finally recognized the Republic of Macedonia under its constitutional name. Then in 2009 Greece prevented Macedonia from becoming a member of NATO (in violation of the Interim Accord), again voicing its opposition to the republic's use of the name Macedonia, a term Greece continues to try to monopolize. Bilateral negotiations over the name issue continue under the auspices of the United Nations. From an international legal perspective, however, the issue is perfectly clear. As Louis Henkin and colleagues conclude in *International Law: Cases and Materials*, "There appears to be no basis in international law or practice for Greece's position."

Albania recognizes the existence of its small Macedonian minority and provides some elementary school education in the Macedonian language. The Bulgarian government, however, refuses to recognize its Macedonian minority and has attempted to suppress any expression of a Macedonian national identity among its citizens. Greece also denies the existence of its Macedonian minority. It has consistently subjected Macedonians in northern Greece to a campaign of forced assimilation and harassment. In 1989 a group of Macedonians attempted to establish a nonprofit organization called the House of Macedonian Culture, but was prevented from doing so by the Greek Supreme Court. Nine years later the European Court of Human Rights ruled unanimously against Greece, stating that "mention of the consciousness of belonging to a minority and the preservation and development of a minority's culture" does not constitute a threat to a democratic society.

A variety of Macedonian transnational organizations, such as the United Macedonian Diaspora, the World Macedonian Congress, and Macedonian Human Rights Committees in Australia and Canada, are active in the global cultural war against Greece in which they seek to gain international recognition for the Republic of Macedonia under its constitutional name and to secure full human rights for Macedonian minorities in Greece and other Balkan countries.

A brief survey of important figures in recent Macedonian history must begin with writers and intellectuals who contributed to the Macedonian national renaissance in the second half of the 19th and early 20th centuries, such as Gorgija Pulevski, Kostantin, and Dimitar Miladinov, and Krste Misirkov. Leaders of the 1903 Ilinden Uprising include Dame Gruev, Jane Sandanski, and Goce Delčev. Major literary figures of the 20th century include the poets Kočo Racin, Kole Nedelkovski, and Blaže Koneski, who also made a major contribution to the standardization of the Macedonian literary language in the 1940s. Two of the most important Macedonian politicians of the 20th century are Krste Crvenkovski, one of the leading figures in the liberal revolution of the 1960s, and Kiro Gligorov, the first president of the newly independent Republic of Macedonia.

Macedonians have recently attempted to incorporate Nobel Prize winner Mother Theresa into their canon of national heroes on the grounds that she was born in what is now Skopje in the Republic of Macedonia. Albanians, however, reject this claim since Mother Theresa was born Gonxha Agnes Bojaxhiu to Albanian parents. Mother Theresa herself has said, "By blood I am Albanian. By citizenship I am Indian. By faith I am a Catholic nun. As to my calling, I belong to the world." This last expression of a more cosmopolitan identity stands as a positive alternative to the traditional assertions of narrow ethnic and national identities that have been the source of so much conflict and violence in the Balkans.

*Loring M. Danforth*

## Further Reading

Brown, Keith. *The Past in Question*. Princeton, NJ: Princeton University Press, 2003.

Danforth, Loring M. *The Macedonian Conflict*. Princeton, NJ: Princeton University Press, 1995.

Human Rights Watch/Helsinki. *Denying Ethnic Identity: The Macedonians of Greece*. Helsinki: Human Rights Watch, http://www.hrw.org/, 1994.

Rossos, Andrew. *Macedonia and the Macedonians: A History*. Palo Alto, CA: Hoover Institution Press, 2008.

Roudometof, Victor, ed. *The Macedonian Question*. Boulder, CO: East European Monographs, 2000.

# Maltese

About 400,000 Maltese inhabit three Mediterranean islands; substantial Maltese populations are to be found as well in Australia (110,000), Canada (25,000), the United Kingdom (30,000) and the United States (70,000). Malta lies at the geographical center of the Mediterranean Sea, and like many islands its history is dominated by successive flows of migration, and in Malta's case, colonizing powers. This history of mixing has left its mark on the Maltese, whose repertoire of patronyms reveal Italian, Spanish, Arabic, and British influence; whose language has a Semitic/Arabic structure with substantial Romance loan vocabulary; and who mostly worship a Roman Catholic God they call "Alla." This mixture of cultural influences has led to a popular Maltese saying: "We are all mongrels (*pastardi*), but all pure Maltese." Ethnicity is not a category that sits comfortably with the analysis of Maltese culture and society, mainly because its history has been dominated by deep political conflict, much of which revolves around the question of ethnic, or national, identity.

The islands—an archipelago of five, of which three islands are inhabited—have some of the oldest archaeological monuments in the Mediterranean, demonstrating human habitation from as early as 5000 BCE, and an impressive phase of temple building from around 3300 to 2450 BCE. There is evidence of Phoenician influence from the 7th century BCE, and Roman settlement from around the turn of the millennium and into the Byzantine era. A period of Arab rule was ended by the Normans who controlled Sicily and much of southern Italy in the 11th and 12th centuries. After several hundred years of rule by various European lords, including the Genovese and Aragonese, the islands were given to the Order of the Knights of St. John in 1530. The Knights were replaced in 1798 by a two-year Napoleonic French hegemony, which gave way to British colonial rule. Independence was achieved in 1964 and the Republic of Malta was established in 1974. Malta joined the European Union in 2004.

Maltese party politics developed a distinctively polarizing character during colonial rule, when the Maltese were granted progressively more powerful government under the British. Fault lines established in the 19th century were carried forward into the 20th and 21st centuries, pitting the Christian democratic Partit Nazzjonalist (PN—Nationalist Party) against the socialist Malta Labor Party (MLP—now called the Partit Laburista) in what has effectively become a two-party state. The opposition is, and was, political, but also rooted in a deeper argument about the nature of Malteseness—Maltese ethnicity. The PN have historically been strongly allied to the church, were anti-British, and have promoted an account of Maltese ethnicity as rooted in *Italianitá* (Italian-ness) and *Latinitá* (Latin-ness). The MLP and its antecedents have been predominantly anticlerical, were at times pro-British, and have downplayed the Italian influence to emphasize the Semitic/Arabic roots of Maltese language and culture. They have placed the Maltese in a pan-Mediterranean frame that recognizes kinship with not only the north but also the south shores of the sea.

The conflict between Italianate and Mediterraneanist accounts of Maltese ethnicity first came to a head during the Language Question of the 1920s and 1930s, which pitted the PN against the Constitutional Party (CP)—a predecessor to the MLP. The Question in question had its roots in social class, as did the party political division. The pro-Italian PN was led by the established bourgeoisie—lawyers, priests, and merchants who had strong links with Italy. The pro-British CP was led by Anglo-Maltese administrators, and their followers were proletarian: dockyard workers, who by the turn of the 20th century had begun to galvanize politically with the help of the British trade union movement. The former used Italian in the courts and Latin in the church and aspired to the more general dissemination of this medium. The latter used English in the workplace and Maltese among themselves—it was the language of the Maltese worker. Proposals for educational reform

put language in the political frame, and while the PN argued that Italian was and should be the language of Malta, the CP suggested a bilingual solution, developing English and Maltese pari passu. The PN argument was linked to Italian irredentism promoted within Mussolini's regime and supported by the revisionist archaeology of Luigi Ugolini, which saw Malta as the point of origin for Latin civilization. The CP drew on linguistic similarities between contemporary Maltese and the Phoenician language reconstructed from an inscription found in Malta in 1697. This suggested Semitic rather than Latin roots, and to some—through the theory of the Celts' Phoenician origins—affinity with the Celtic fringe. It also placed Maltese cultural origins in what was subsequently the Holy Land, which is suggestive for a profoundly Roman Catholic population.

The Language Question was answered by the British, who suspended the constitution when the church intervened on the side of the PN. The subsequent outbreak of war, and the bombing of Malta by Italian aircraft, removed the legitimacy of the PN's calls for italianitá, though it maintained an understanding of Maltese cultural roots as fundamentally Latin until the lead-up to independence. By this time the CP's pari passu solution had gained ascendancy and was institutionalized when Maltese and English became the two official languages of independent Malta in 1964. The political polarity between CP and PN continued into postwar and independent Malta, as CP was replaced by MLP. Conflicting accounts of Malta's past, present, and future were pitted against each other, and structures of party leadership, administration, and support generated mutually exclusive networks of association, so much so that Maltese philosopher Peter Serracino-Inglott has argued that at the point of independence, Malta consisted of two nations, not one.

The unifying factor in Maltese ethnicity is Roman Catholicism, with 98 percent of the population baptized into the church. However, religion, like language, has been heavily politicized, with the church issuing interdicts against voting for the CP during the Language Question, and against voting for the MLP in favor of integration with Britain—a proposal brought forward by the MLP government in 1956. Both were viewed by the church as grave—if not mortal—sins, but thousands were prepared to commit them in rebelliously anticlerical, though not necessarily anti-Catholic, activism. Pro- and anticlericalism were also expressed in Catholic popular culture, through competing and antagonistic feast celebrations dedicated to particular patron saints, which continue to have political and economic significance. Catholicism is privileged, as the state religion, in the Maltese constitution, and informs key policy issues—most notably, bans on same-sex marriage, divorce, and abortion. These three issues came to the fore in the lead-up to Malta's accession to the European Union (EU), which many worried would force Malta into legalizing them. In the event, when Malta entered the EU in 2004, it acquired safeguards to maintain these principles of Catholic morality and tradition and protect the Maltese language.

In the decades preceding EU accession, intellectual effort was invested in discussing and codifying Maltese cultural identity, and a number of publications—some directly sponsored by the then-governing PN—emerged with identitá as their subject. What emerged from this was a debate concerning not so much what Maltese identity is, but whether *identity* was a useful or relevant concept for understanding contemporary Maltese life. As this debate petered out in the realpolitik of Maltese-EU relations, it has been partially superseded by a newer wave of ethnicity-speak. Since EU accession, increasing numbers of asylum seekers and irregular migrants have arrived in Malta, mostly from sub-Saharan Africa. This has provoked in some circles a renewed interest in defining and protecting Maltese ethnicity. A handful of neonationalist groups have emerged, some returning to a racial notion of Latinitá, to mark the difference between themselves and the migrant "other."

*Jon P. Mitchell*

## Further Reading

Boissevain, J. *Saints and Fireworks: Religion and Politics in Rural Malta.* 2nd ed. Malta: Progress Press, 1993. First edition published in London by Athlone Press.

Cassar, C. *Society, Culture, and Identity in Early Modern Malta.* Malta: Mireva Publications, 2000.

Mitchell, J.P. *Ambivalent Europeans: Ritual, Memory, and the Public Sphere in Malta.* London: Routledge, 2002.

Mitchell, J.P. "Looking Forward to the Past: National Identity and History in Malta." *Identities: Global Studies in Culture and Power* 10 (2003): 377–398.

Sant Cassia, P. "History, Anthropology, and Folklore in Malta." *Journal of Mediterranean Studies* 3 (1993): 291–315.

# Manx

The term *Manx* relates to people with a familial tie to the Isle of Man, an island in the Irish Sea (British Isles) lying almost equidistant from its neighbors. Of the growing population of 82,000 (2006), less than 50 percent are island born. The latter are British citizens (the Isle of Man is a British Crown Dependency), but the island is not part of the United Kingdom (UK). The primary language is English, although Manx Gaelic is spoken by a growing minority, and Manx Gaelic-medium schooling is available. The official religion is Church of England, but Nonconformism is also spiritually and culturally significant. A diasporic community exists (particularly in the United States and Australia), and links are actively maintained.

The island's Celtic prehistory is evidenced by visible archaeology in the landscape. By the 11th century the Isle of Man was under the rule of Norse kings, as part of the Kingdom of Mann and the Isles. In 1266 it was ceded to Scotland, and then in 1289 it came under English control. Granted by the crown to English nobles who became "Lords of Mann," it remained independent until revested in the British Crown in 1765. Despite these changes, the island's parliament, the Tynwald Court, survived. Said to be the world's longest continuous parliament, today Tynwald is both a symbol of the Island's Norse heritage and of the fact that it is, again, largely self-governing and independent.

Celtic roots are evident in the Manx Gaelic language, and in typical Manx surnames such as Kewley and Quayle, the K or Q sound being what remains of the Gaelic mac (son of). Norse/Celtic duality continues to color the island's political and cultural life, but the last few decades have also seen a rapid influx of workers for the international finance sector on which the economy now largely depends. As its position geographically, politically, and fiscally vis-à-vis its neighbors dictates, the Isle of Man has always absorbed settlers (known colloquially as "comeovers") who have, in time, become Manx, but this latest and most dramatic influx of foreign workers has resulted instead in ethnic tension.

That tension was expressed through direct protest in the early 1970s and late 1980s. However, it also prompted a grassroots revival of cultural expression that has prevailed: examples include Yn Cruinnaght, the island's annual inter-Celtic festival, and a reinvigoration of the fair that accompanies the annual open-air sitting of Tynwald (July 5). The Manx Heritage Foundation (established 1982) supports the growing interest in the island's Gaelic language, and its music, dance, and poetic traditions. Manx National Heritage, a government department, has guardianship of the nation's natural and tangible heritage, and archives. Manx cultural engagement, open to all residents, now enables different forms of identity and identification—ethnic and cultural—on which both island-born and settled "comeovers" can call, as appropriate.

*Susan Lewis*

## Further Reading

See Manx entries in J. T. Koch, *Celtic Culture: A Historical Encyclopedia*. Santa Barbara, CA: ABC-Clio, 2006.

# Maris

The Maris, also known as the Cheremises, live in their own republic, Mari El (8,996 square miles or 23,300 square kilometers), part of the Russian federation and situated on the shores of the middle reaches of the River Volga. The area of Mari settlement is not confined to the boundaries of the republic, but continues beyond these, east as far as the Urals, with sporadic linguistic enclaves found in the republics of Bashkortostan and Tatarstan, as well as in the Kirov and Yekaterinburg areas. About half of the Maris dwell outside of the titular republic. According to the last census of the Soviet Union (1989) there were 671,000 Maris, of which 81 percent (about 540,000) spoke their mother tongue. As claimed by the first census of Russia (2002), the number of Maris

had decreased 6 percent. The Mari language belongs to the Volgaic branch of the Finno-Ugric languages. Since the 1920s the Maris have developed two literary languages. The dominant Eastern Literary Language, based on the Central and Eastern dialects, is spoken by 92 percent of Maris. The other literary language, based on the Western or what is often called the Hill dialect, is spoken by about 35,000 people. The traditional religion of the Maris is animistic. Despite the official atheism of the Soviet period, traditional religion endured and has been preserved up to the present day, particularly in the eastern diaspora areas. After the demise of the Soviet Union it was considered by many to be a cornerstone of Mari identity. The Western Maris were converted to the Orthodox faith as early as the 14th century.

Peasants play cards in the village of Nur-Shari, 560 miles east of Moscow, August 18, 2002 in Mari-El, an autonomous republic of the Russian Federation. (Oleg Nikishin/Getty Images)

The ancestors of the Maris dwelled in roughly same areas as do the Maris today. A distinct Maris ethnicity began to emerge about 3,000 years ago. As early as CE 1000 the Mari tribes had shaped themselves into the form we now know. After the 9th century the Maris were in contact with the Turkic-speaking Volga Bulgars, who established a trading nation situated at the Volga Bend. In the 13th century the area fell into the hands of the Tatars, who established a powerful nation (the Golden Horde and later the Khanate of Kazan). The Maris lived in subjection to the Tatars until 1552, when the Russians conquered the Khanate of Kazan and took possession of its lands. They rebelled three times against the Russians at the end of the 16th century, but were eventually beaten. During these so-called Cheremis Wars half of the Mari population perished. From the beginning of the 17th century the Maris began to flee eastward away from Russian power and compulsory conversions, creating the Mari diaspora.

The traditional religion of the Maris is animistic: everything that lives has a soul and the supreme divinity is the god of heaven, with many assistants. The Maris have no religious architecture. They commune with their deities at communal events organized in sacred, fenced-off groves, where the priests of the Mari ethnic religion perform animal or food sacrifices while reciting prayers for the prosperity and livelihood of the people.

The Maris have long been farmers and cattle owners. Hunting and fishing have also survived as important means of livelihood. Beekeeping is a very common secondary occupation. In the 18th and 19th centuries the Maris were also important manufacturers of bast products. The Maris have dwelt in the provinces right up to the present day. There are only a few towns in Mari El (capital Yoshkar-Ola), and the majority of inhabitants of these are Russians or other nationalities.

The Maris have been in constant contact first with the Volga Bulgars and their Chuvash descendants and later with the Tatars, both of whom remain their neighbors. The effect of these Turkic peoples on the Maris is clearly seen in language (structure, vocabulary) and culture (music, folk songs).

Song and dance play an essential role in Mari tradition. The songs are short and lyrical in nature. Song and dance are accompanied on the accordion, with drums and pipes. Among the Western Maris the gusli is a common instrument. Mari music is pentatonic. Mari prayers are very long and recited in a special sacral form that differs from the normal language. The first literary relics are from the 18th century. The national writer of the Maris is Sergey Chavayn (1888–1937), poet and prosaist. The most eminent poet is the lyricist Valentin Kolumb (1935–1974).

In the 1920s the literary (or written) languages were created with the support of the Soviets; Mari theater, literature, and the press all emerged, as did education in the Mari language. The Maris were granted their own autonomous territory. This was changed to the Mari Autonomous Socialist Soviet Republic in 1936, and in the 1990s to Mari El. The late 1930s, during the administration of Joseph Stalin, saw the beginning of the purging of all the minority peoples in the Soviet Union. In 1937 the entire Mari intelligentsia, charged with nationalism and conspiracy against the state, was eliminated. The purges dealt a significant blow to Mari identity. From the 1950s through the 1980s, education in the mother tongue declined. Nowadays the Mari languages are only taught in the rural schools in the first grade, and then only as a subject; Russian, not Mari, continues to be the language of instruction. In 1989, 19 percent of Maris were unable to speak the Mari language, a percentage that continues to grow because large numbers of Maris youth do not speak the language.

The fall of the Soviet Union raised the spirits of many in the Mari territory, giving impetus to an embryonic democracy. The economic collapse in Russia in the mid-1990s, however, threw Mari El into a difficult economic situation, cutting short the national revival. In the 21st century the new pro-Russian administration in Mari El reduced the rights of the Maris. National institutions are once again threatened, and Mari activists came under assault. Reforms implemented during the period of Vladimir Putin have weakened the rights of linguistic and national minorities in legislation and education, for example, with deleterious effects on Mari identity.

*Sirkka Saarinen*

**Further Reading**

Konuykhov, Alexey K., ed. *Finno-Ugric Ethnicities in Russia: Yesterday, Today, and Tomorrow*. Trans. Pavel Krotov. Syktyvkar: Society Finland–Russia and Komi vojtyr, 2009.

Lallukka, Seppo. *The East Finnic Minorities in the Soviet Union. An Appraisal of the Erosive Trends*. Helsinki: The Finnish Academy of Science and Letters. B:252. 1990.

Lallukka, Seppo. *From Fugitive Peasants to Diaspora. The Eastern Mari in Tsarist and Federal Russia*. Helsinki: The Finnish Academy of Science and Letters, 2003. Humaniora 328.

# Mingrelians

The Mingrelians (also referred to in English as Megrelians and occasionally Megrels or Mingrels, and called *margali* in Mingrelian and *megreli* in Georgian) are concentrated in the western littoral province of Mingrelia (also referred to by its Georgian name Samegrelo and in historical sources as Odishi) of the Republic of Georgia and the province of Gali, the southernmost district of the disputed territory of Abkhazia, formerly the Autonomous Republic of Abkhazia within Soviet Georgia. Mingrelians also live dispersed throughout Georgia. No reliable figures for the numbers of Mingrelians exist, but they are thought to number between 400,000 and 500,000. The principal distinguishing marker of Mingrelian identity is the Mingrelian language, a vernacular language belonging to the Kartvelian language family. Mingrelian is closely related to, but not mutually intelligible with, Georgian. Mingrelian identity is also denoted by characteristic surname endings in -ia, -ava, and -aia, although bearers of these surnames are by no means all competent in the Mingrelian language. In terms of religious identity Mingrelians are indistinguishable from other Georgians in adhering to the Georgian Orthodox faith.

Theories differ as to how and when differentiation took place within the Kartvelian language family; the mainstream view is that the Zan language branched off in about the eighth century BCE, and later differentiated into Mingrelian and Laz, which is now spoken by the Laz ethnic group living along the Turkish Black Sea Coast and by a very small number of people in southwest Georgia. Mingrelian and Laz have in the past been described as dialects of the Zan language, but it is no longer customary to do so today.

Contemporary Mingrelia covers part of the territory of the ancient Black Sea littoral kingdom of Colchis-Egrisi, which united with the eastern Georgian kingdom of Iberia in the 3rd century BCE. Mingrelia formed part of the centralized Bagratid kingdom from 1008 to 1442. Following the fragmentation of the kingdom on account of Mongol invasions, Mingrelia survived as a relatively autonomous principality. From the 11th until the late 17th century Mingrelia was ruled by the Dadiani dynasty, with the result that this family name became synonymous with the title of ruler in the principality. In 1691 rule over Mingrelia passed to the Chikovani family, related to the Dadiani, who then adopted their name. Mingrelia was incorporated into the Russian Empire in 1857 with loose promises of autonomy, but was later incorporated into the Kutaisi *guberniya* (province) with no special status.

Throughout the early modern period Georgian remained the language of worship and elite discourse in Mingrelia. Today virtually all Mingrelians use Georgian as their literary language; there are negligible numbers of monolingual Mingrelians in rural areas of Mingrelia and Gali who do not speak Georgian. Some Mingrelians living in Abkhazia in the late Soviet period used Russian as their literary language, possessing only a poor or passive knowledge of Georgian; this reflected the more Russophone environment in Abkhazia.

There have been sporadic attempts by outsiders to create a written language for Mingrelian; these efforts have been seen as controversial in Georgia, where they have been interpreted as efforts to divide Mingrelians from their Georgian national identity. In the late 19th century the Russian Empire attempted to establish a Mingrelian-language liturgy, although the project was abandoned. In the early 1930s the Soviet regime published a number of Mingrelian-language newspapers, using the Georgian script, apparently aimed at disseminating communist ideology to rural populations in Mingrelia unable to read Georgian. Soviet ethnographers also classified Mingrelians as a separate census category, along with a number of other subgroups later classified as Georgians distinguished by vernacular language or religion (for example, Svans, Laz, Ajarians). These were consolidated, however, in the mid-1930s into a single Georgian identity category, after which these subgroup identities were stigmatized as "backward." The notion of a separate Mingrelian identity was nonetheless still plausible enough to form the basis for a purge of Georgian Communist Party officials of Mingrelian origin during 1951–1952. Framed as the purge of a Mingrelian nationalist ring, this development was more likely a reflection of regional clan rivalries within the Communist Party.

Figures identifiable as Mingrelian from their surnames featured prominently in the Georgian national revival of the late

1980s, notably including independent Georgia's first president, Zviad Gamsakhurdia. Gamsakhurdia was removed in a coup in early 1992, after which Mingrelia continued to be identified with his supporters, known as "Zviadists." A Zviadist uprising took place in Mingrelia in autumn 1993, coinciding with Georgia's military defeat in Abkhazia. The revolt was brutally suppressed by *mkhedrioni* paramilitary bands, one of the forces behind Gamsakhurdia's removal from power in Tbilisi in December 1991.

Debates over the nexus between Mingrelian and Georgian identities are overshadowed by Georgia's experience of territorial fragmentation following conflicts in Abkhazia and South Ossetia in the 1990s and again in 2008. It should also be noted that the majority of the approximately 250,000 people displaced from Abkhazia as a result of the Georgian-Abkhaz conflict of 1992–1993 were Mingrelian. A contested and in any case seasonally fluctuating number ranging from 45,000 to 70,000 have been able to return to Gali. During the 1990s the de facto authorities in Abkhazia intermittently sponsored experimentation with a Mingrelian press in the form of a Russian-Abkhaz-Mingrelian newspaper, directed at the Mingrelian population in the Gali district. Mingrelians in Gali today receive their primary and secondary education in Georgian in more remote areas, but in Russian in Gali town and its surroundings, with Georgian being taught as a subject only.

In Mingrelia itself there was a small-scale revival of interest during the 1990s–2000s in the Mingrelian language in the form of folkloric and lexicographical works. This never developed, however, into significant demands among Mingrelians for the institutionalization of Mingrelian. Rather, a Mingrelian identity is expressed through local variations in the realms of folklore and cuisine. It also finds expression in the continued use of the Mingrelian language in a relationship to Georgian that broadly corresponds to diglossia—the use by a speech community of different language varieties for different domains (often understood as high-prestige and low-prestige). However, the prestige of a given language variety for its speakers cannot be read mechanically from its use in one or another domain; Mingrelian is one interesting example of a language variety spoken in low-prestige domains that nonetheless has considerable symbolic prestige for its speakers.

*Laurence Broers*

## Further Reading

Borozdin, K. A. 1885. *Zakavkazskiya Vospominaniya. Mingreliya i Svanetiya c 1854 po 1861 god (Transcaucasian Memoirs. Mingrelia and Svaneti from 1854 to 1861).* St. Petersburg.

Broers, Laurence. "Two Sons of One Mother: Georgian, Mingrelian and the Challenge of Nested Primordialisms." Chapter 7 in "Containing the Nation, Building the State: Coping with Nationalism, Minorities and Conflict in Post-Soviet Georgia." PhD diss., School of Oriental and African Studies, University of London, 2004.

Feurstein, W. "Mingrelisch, Lazisch, Swanisch: Alte sprachen und Kulturen der Kolchis vor dem baldigen Untergang," In *Caucasian Perspectives*, ed. G. Hewitt. Unterschleissheim/Munchen: Lincom Europa, 1992, 285–328.

Mak'alatia, S. *Samegrelos et'nograpia* [*The Ethnography of Mingrelia*]. Tbilisi, 1941.

## Moldovans

The Republic of Moldova, a landlocked state with Romania to the west and Ukraine to the north, east, and south, is home to approximately 2.6 million self-identified Moldovans who make up 76 percent of the country's population of 3.4 million. The country includes the Gaugaz Autonomous Region in the south and the disputed Transnistrian region in the east. Most Moldovans profess the Christian Orthodox faith. Moldovans speak what most linguists categorize as a dialect of Romanian. It should be noted that the ethnic category of Moldovan is contested and that the question of ethnicity involves a political debate both inside and outside of the country. Some claim that Moldovans are ethnically, culturally, and linguistically very similar to neighboring Romanians, while others, including the current Moldovan government, contend that Moldovans are a distinct ethnic, cultural, and linguistic group. Language is also a political issue, and those who refer to the language as Romanian may reflect the former claim, while those who refer to it as Moldovan may reflect the latter. Some Romanians refer to Moldovans as Bessarabians to distinguish them from Romanian citizens who live in the Moldovan region of Eastern Romania.

Moldovans are descendants of the ancient Dacian people, who were colonized by the Roman Emperor Trajan in the 1st century CE. The Romans brought the Latin language to the country, which provided the basis for the development of the Romanian language. Legend has it that a Romanian prince, Dragoş, founded Moldova

A girl flashes the victory sign in front of Moldova's flag in the capital, Chisinau, during a 2002 protest against the government's intention to impose Russian as one of the country's official languages. (AP/Wide World Photos)

in the early 14th century during a hunting expedition where his favorite dog, Molda, was gored by an ox. According to the legend, Dragoș named the region Moldova. Today the ox is incorporated in the state emblem and flag. In 1359, Moldova became a principality independent from medieval Romania (Țara Românească) under the rule of Bogdan. Medieval Moldova (sometimes referred to as Moldavia) was twice the size of the present-day state, with its borders extending from the Dniester River in the east to the Carpathian Mountains in the west. Stephen the Great (Ștefan cel Mare) is the most notable medieval ruler and famously defeated the Ottomans in 1475. Today, Stephen the Great is celebrated as the patron of Moldova, and his image is featured on church icons, public statues, the state currency, and folk art. Moldova remained a medieval Romanian principality from 1359 until 1538, when it became a vassal state of the Ottoman Empire.

With its moderate climate and fertile soil, Moldova is a rich agricultural country. Half of the population lives in rural areas. Moldovans are traditionally farmers, and agricultural symbols and themes are prevalent in folk traditions and holidays, such as Hram. Throughout the calendar year, each village, town, and city celebrates Hram, which marks the day of each municipality's settlement. The outdoor festivities may include circle dancing (*hora*), performances by folkloric dance troops, presentations of folkloric tableaus, and craft and agricultural displays. Folk costumes combine elements of traditional Romanian dress, such as elaborately embroidered cotton blouses for women, with regional modifications, such as boots instead of traditional moccasins as worn in Romania.

Moldova has a rich tradition of folk music and dance. Folk musicians play a range of instruments from traditional pan flutes to modern accordions. The centuries-old folk ballad "Miorița" continues to be performed today and is reflected in modern life: verses from the "Miorița" are inscribed on national banknotes, and the popular rock band Zdob și Zdub titled a song after it. Moldova has a national folk dance ensemble, Joc, and a national folk chorus ensemble, Doina, as well as many other regional folk groups throughout the country. Moldovans are well known for their brightly colored flat-weave carpets that incorporate floral motifs against a black background and their earthenware pottery that is made throughout the country. Moldovans are best known for their wine and hospitality, which are a great source of individual and national pride. The state-owned vineyard Cricova, with its miles of limestone cellars, is considered a national treasure. Families throughout the countryside make their own house version (*vin de casa*). Offering a guest a glass of house-made wine (often from an earthenware pitcher) is the utmost sign of Moldovan hospitality. Moldovans in urban areas also adhere to the same high standards of hospitality, although their wine may come from a relative's home in the countryside. Celebrated cultural figures include scholar Dimitrie Cantemir, poet Mihai Eminescu, humorist Ion Creanga, and writer Gheorghe Asachi. These cultural icons, like many of Moldova's folk traditions, are also celebrated in Romania.

Approximately 98 percent of Moldovans are Christian Orthodox and follow the Eastern or Russian Orthodox calendar, unlike their Romanian neighbors. Since the independence from the USSR in 1991, religious elements, such as prayers or icons, are increasingly prevalent in public life, including schools. Most Moldovan families have a religious icon in a corner of their home and adhere to organized religious practices and activities, such as house blessings, baptisms, and Christmas and Easter celebrations. Christmas is celebrated with traditional carols (*colinde*) and religious services. In recent years, Santa Claus (*Moş Craciun*) and Christmas trees have become popular. Easter is an especially symbolic and important holiday. Special bread (*pasca*), shaped like a ring to celebrate the renewal of life, and eggs, dyed red to symbolize the blood of Christ, are prepared for the Easter Vigil and blessed by local priests before consumption on Easter Sunday. A week after Orthodox Easter Sunday or Monday, Moldovans celebrate their dead ancestors at the cemetery with wine, traditional dishes, and blessings from the local priest. This day is called Easter of the Dead (*Paştele Blajinilor* or *Paştele Morţilor*). Secular holidays, such as New Year's Day (January 1), Women's Day (March 8), and Victory Day (May 9), are widely celebrated.

From the Ottoman Empire, the Russian Empire annexed the eastern part of Moldova (the land between the Prut and Dniester Rivers) in 1812 and established the territory that most closely corresponds with the present-day state. Russian authorities renamed the region "Bessarabia" to distinguish this tsarist entity from the western part of Moldova that today is part of Romania. Russian authorities reshaped the demographics of the region by settling tens of thousands of Russians and Ukrainians into Bessarabia, as well as by encouraging Bulgarians, Germans, Poles, and other Eastern Europeans, including Jews, to move to the region. The country continues to be a multiethnic state today. At the time of the Bolshevik Revolution and the end of tsarist Russia, the Bessarabian parliament voted to establish the Moldovan Democratic Republic in December of 1917. This independence was brief, and, in March of 1918, the government voted to unify with the Romanian kingdom. In June of 1940, the German-Russian non-aggression pact of Ribbentrop-Molotov in 1939 allowed the Soviet Union to seize Bessarabia. It became an official Soviet state in 1944. The Soviets incorporated the southern and northern areas of Bessarabia into Ukraine and consolidated the central part of the territory with the present-day Transistria. The Soviet state corresponds with the present-day borders.

The Republic of Moldova became independent in 1991 after the collapse of the Soviet Union. Today it is a parliamentary republic. Since independence, Moldova has struggled with economic development and is one of the poorest countries in Europe. This poverty had created massive emigration, with an estimated 1 million of the total population (all ethnicities) working legally and illegally abroad outside of Moldova. Remittances from abroad account for more than a third the country's gross domestic product. Human trafficking and government corruption are also considerable challenges facing the Moldovan state and nation.

*Elizabeth Anderson Worden*

**Further Reading**

Brezianu, Andrei, and Vlad Spanu. *Historical Dictionary of Moldova*. 2nd ed. Lanham, MD: Scarecrow Press, 2007.

Ciscel, Matthew H. *The Language of the Moldovans: Romania, Russia, and Identity in an Ex-Soviet Republic*. Lanham, MD: Lexington Books, 2007.

Dima, Nicholas. *Moldova and the Transdnestr Republic*. East European Monograph Series. New York: Columbia University, 2001.

Dyer, Donald L., ed. *Studies in Moldovan: The History, Culture, Language and Contemporary Politics*. Eastern European Monograph Series. New York: Columbia University, 1996.

Heintz, Monica, ed. *Weak State, Uncertain Citizenship: Moldova*. Berlin: Peter Lang, 2008.

King, Charles. *The Moldovans: Romania, Russia, and the Politics of Culture*. Stanford: Hoover Institution Press, 2000.

# Montenegrins

Montenegrins (*Crnogorci*) are a South Slav people who inhabit the Republic of Montenegro but also have a substantial diasporic presence in Serbia, Italy, the United States, and Argentina. The highly ambiguous and historically changing character of the Montenegrin identity, whereby some Montenegrins see themselves as Serbs too, makes it difficult to establish a precise number of the population, but it is estimated that there are more than 400,000 Montenegrins in the world. Most Montenegrins speak the ijekavian variant of the Shtokavian dialect of the Serbo-Croatian language, which in the 2007 Constitution of the Republic of Montenegro is defined as Montenegrin—the official language of the state. Traditionally Montenegrins have been Eastern Orthodox Christians with most nominally belonging to the Serbian Orthodox Church and the rest adhering to the Montenegrin Orthodox Church, Roman Catholicism, or Sunni Islam, except for self-declared atheists. It should be noted that the questions of religious affiliation, language, and ethnic attachment are all deeply contested as a large number of people in Montenegro have historically oscillated in their self-designation; identification has ranged from being exclusively Serb, to expressing simultaneous Montenegrin and Serb identities, toward developing an exclusively Montenegrin identity. Furthermore the very existence of the separate Montenegrin ethnicity has been contested and denied not only by the many political and cultural organizations in Montenegro's largest neighbor, Serbia, but also by a significant number of Montenegro's own inhabitants.

There is a little reliable information on the origins of Montenegrins. It is apparent that following the early large-scale migrations of the Slavs from the fifth century onward, the Slavic populations become a majority in the territory of the present-day Montenegro by the sixth century. The name Montenegro (*Crna Gora*) is first mentioned in a papal epistle of 1053. The medieval period was characterized by intensive power struggles between the aristocratic households with the prominent presence of the Serbian nobility. This period also saw the establishment of the first

Independence supporters wave Montenegrin flags amid celebrations in Montenegro's administrative capital, Podgorica, on May 21, 2006 after Montenegro voted for independence from Serbia in a historic referendum that split the former Yugoslav republics. More than 55 percent of the tiny Balkan state's voters chose to separate from Serbia—slightly more than the minimum required for the European Union's approval. On June 13, the United States officially recognized Montenegro as an independent and sovereign state. (AFP/Getty Images)

forms of medieval statehood; the principalities of Dioclea and Zeta proved the most durable of these and are now recognized as the predecessors of the modern Montenegrin state. From 1276 to 1309 Zeta was an autonomous principality within the medieval Serbian state governed by Queen Jelena, widow of the Serbian king Uroš I. In 1496 Zeta fell under Ottoman rule but the Montenegrin tribes retained control of the hills. Although the Ottomans ruled the territories of Montenegro for nearly four centuries they were unable to gain control in the mountainous villages where the majority of Montenegrin population lived. For most of this period Montenegrin society was organized in a segmentary fashion, with the patrilocal extended families forming distinct clans (*bratstvo*) belonging to a larger tribal unit (*pleme*). Despite adhering to common traditional tribal codes and sharing a common Christian Orthodox religion, the tribes were notoriously autonomous and disunited. This distinct social order had a loosely organized theocratic structure with the metropolitan of the Orthodox Church (*vladika*) acting as a both religious and secular authority. It was only during the rule of the House of Petrović in the 18th and early 19th centuries that tribal loyalties started to weaken at the expense of the broader pan-Montenegrin territorial identity. The three Orthodox Metropolitans of the House of Petrović—Petar I, Petar II, and Danilo—were decisive in modernizing Montenegrin society and in uniting divided tribes. While Petar I and Petar II were instrumental in devising unified legal and fiscal systems, more centralized state structure with a proper police force, and the first educational institutions, Danilo was successful in separating religious from secular authority and in instituting the first unified and standardized military force. Furthermore, Danilo proclaimed Montenegro an independent principality and was crowned the prince of Montenegro in 1852. Full independence from the Ottoman Empire was formally acknowledged at the Congress of Berlin in 1878 when Montenegro became internationally recognized as a sovereign nation-state.

The history of protracted warfare coupled with the durable existence of the traditional tribal organization over several centuries generated a set of cultural codes and values that are unique to the Montenegrin population. Among these cultural codes two ethical ideals stand out: *Čojstvo* (roughly translated as humanity and manliness) and *Junaštvo* (heroism). These normative principles are derived from the warrior ethos that developed over the centuries of Ottoman rule and sporadic conflicts with Venetians and Hapsburgs, and were reinforced in the wars of the early 20th century: the Balkan wars, World War I, and World War II. Whereas traditionally these cultural codes stipulated rules for the virtuous behavior of soldiers, they gradually infused the civilian sphere too and became the moral parameters for the entire Montenegrin society. These traditional normative codes emphasized the need to act with integrity and rectitude, to treat adversaries with dignity, to show humility and respect for others, to behave fairly to other human beings, and most of all to be willing to sacrifice oneself for other members of community. While in previous times this implied fighting to death—as

being captured brought shame not only on the respective warrior but on the entire extended family—in recent periods *čojstvo* and *junaštvo* have found reflection in the conspicuously stoic attitude to everyday life shared by many Montenegrins. As various anthropological and sociological studies have demonstrated over the years, despite a nominal commitment to Eastern Orthodox Christianity, most Montenegrins are not particularly religious. This is evident from the fairly low rates of church attendances and little or no observance of religious practices. Instead the ethical ideals of *čojstvo* and *junaštvo* that underpin the popularly accepted stoic worldview still have far greater resonance among the contemporary Montenegrin population.

These moral principles were articulated and reinforced through highly developed Montenegrin traditions of folk epic poetry. Historically this epic poetry was centered on depicting the heroic events and personalities from the various battles, wars, and popular rebellions against Ottoman, Venetian, Austro-Hungarian, and Italian imperial rule. Usually a storyteller would sing or recite the epic poems in decasyllabic verse while simultaneously playing the gusle, a one-stringed instrument. Building on this folk tradition, Montenegro's greatest poet, writer, and ruler, the above-mentioned Metropolitan Petar II Petrović Njegoš, created the highly acclaimed epic book, *The Mountain Wreath* (1846), which still serves as a cornerstone of the Montenegrin literary tradition. The book's focus on the oppressive character of the Ottoman rule proved inspirational not only to the various resistance movements among south Slavs but its contents have appealed to the variety of national movements throughout 19th- and early 20th-century Europe.

The importance of the Montenegrin warrior ethos was also visible in 20th-century warfare, where despite the nation's numerically small size, Montenegrins have been highly represented. The Montenegrin military proved extremely resilient in the 1912–1913 Balkan wars and World War I, as a result of which Montenegro doubled the size of its territory. In World War II Montenegrins were enthusiastic participants in the Yugoslav partisan resistance forces and proved themselves again stubborn soldiers, able to expel Italian occupiers without external help. Consequently one-third of all officers in the communist Yugoslav People's Army were of Montenegrin origin and a large number of generals and high-ranking party officials were Montenegrins.

The collapse of communist Yugoslavia in the early 1990s and in particular the breakup of the joint federal state of Serbia and Montenegro in 2006 had a decisive impact on the transformation of Montenegrin identities. Although the communist period proved crucial for establishing all major Montenegrin cultural and political institutions, the communist state also preserved the ethnonational ambiguities with no clear distinction between the Montenegrin and Serb identities. Even though census results over four decades of communist rule all indicated that the overwhelming majority of the population declared themselves as Montenegrins, this information in itself was no reliable indicator of the strength of Montenegrin identity, as many individuals understood Montenegrin-ness to be a segment of the broader Serbian identity. This identity concept became apparent in the 1990s when the political turmoil brought about by the wars of Yugoslav succession put an end to these ethnonational ambiguities. The adverse geopolitical environment polarized and radicalized the population of Montenegro by fostering the eventual split into two mutually opposing ethnicities: Serbs and Montenegrins. This dramatic social transformation was registered in the latest census data (2003), which shows a clear split between those who self-identify as Montenegrins (43%) and those who see themselves as Serbs in Montenegro (32%). Although this split is present throughout the entire country it also has a strong geographical basis, with much of the south expressing strong Montenegrin consciousness and the north being more pro-Serbian. Following the tight result of the referendum on independence (55.5% in favor) held in May 2006, Montenegro became an independent and sovereign state. However, independence did not bring an end to the ethnopolitical divide within the Montenegrin population. Instead the government's decision to institute Montenegrin as the official language of the new state and to support the highly contested Montenegrin Orthodox Church has further polarized the population of Montenegro.

*Siniša Malešević*

## Further Reading

Andrijašević, Z., and S. Rastoder. *The History of Montenegro from Ancient Times to 2003.* Podgorica: Montenegro Diaspora Centre, 2006.

Bieber, F., ed. *Montenegro in Transition: Problems of Identity and Statehood.* Baden-Baden: Nomos, 2003.

Boehm, C. *Montenegrin Social Organization and Values.* New York: AMS Press, 1983.

Malešević, S., and G. Uzelac. "A Nation-State without the Nation: The Trajectories of Nation-Formation in Montenegro." *Nations and Nationalism* 13, no. 4 (2007): 695–716.

Morrison, K. *Montenegro: A Modern History.* London: I. B. Taurus, 2008.

Roberts, E. *Realm of the Black Mountain: A History of Montenegro.* Ithaca, NY: Cornell University Press, 2007.

# Mordvins

Mordvins are divided into two groups, Erzyas and Mokshas. Mordvins reside in their own republic within the Russian Federation (9,755 square miles or 25,266 square kilometers), in the territory between the Volga tributaries, the Oka and Sura. Only 27 percent of the Mordvins dwell in the titular republic; the majority live in scattered enclaves over a very extensive area to the north and south of the republic as well eastward to the Ural Mountains. According to the last Soviet census (1989) there were 1,154,000 Mordvins; the first Russian census (2002) estimated the number of Mordvins to have decreased by 21 percent, to 845,000. Of those who speak Mordvin, about two-thirds speak Erzya and one-third Moksha, which to some extent are mutually understandable. Literary languages for both groups were developed in the 1920s. The Mordvin languages belong to the Volgaic branch of the Finno-Ugric language family. The Russians began converting the Mordvins to the Orthodox faith as early as the 15th century. Although the conversion work was completed by the 18th century, even in the early 20th century the traditional polytheistic religion survived in places alongside Christianity.

The ancestors of the Mordvins inhabited the same area as do their descendants today. A distinct Mordvin identity began to form about 3,000 years ago. A common Mordvin language can be dated from about CE 300; by the end of the millennium it had diverged into Erzya and Moksha. In the 8th century the Mordvins came into contact with the Turkic Volga Bulgars, whose mercantile state was situated in the Middle Volga, and to which the surrounding nations paid tribute. In the 11th and 12th centuries the Russians penetrated Mordvin territory, but their advance was halted by the arrival of the Tatars. The Tatars established a powerful state on the Volga (the Golden Horde and later the Khanate of Kazan), to whom the Mokshas in particular were subjected, while the Erzyas remained in territory controlled by the Russians. The Russians overthrew the Khanate of Kazan in 1552. The flight of the Mordvins to the east and south from their core area commenced at the end of the 16th century. The Mordvins participated in many rebellions against Russian rule, and after the resulting defeats, migration continued up to the 18th century. Even in the 19th century Mordvins migrated in large numbers to Siberia and Kazakhstan. In the 1920s 11 percent of Mordvins dwelt in Siberia.

Traditional Mordvin religion was polytheist, the most important deities of which were the god-creator and his relatives. The gods lived in the Upper World, and they were petitioned to ensure the success of one's own life and livelihood. The essentials for human life were all determined by the so-called mothers: female spirits (e.g., earth spirit, field spirit, water spirit). In the Lower World lived the departed.

The main occupations of the Mordvins during the last one thousand years have been agriculture and cattle husbandry. Hunting and fishing have provided a secondary means of livelihood. In forest areas beekeeping has also played a vital part. The Mordvins are mainly country folk. In the capital, Saransk, as in the other towns, the majority of inhabitants are Russians.

The Mordvins were in close contact first with the Volga Bulgars, then with the Tatars, from whom the Mokshas in particular have assimilated certain cultural features. The Russian influence began partly as early as the 12th century but gained momentum toward the end of the 16th. The Russian influence is evident in the language (structure, loan words) and in culture (building style).

The Mordvins have long mythic and heroic songs, as well as ballads and lyrical songs. These songs observe a strict syllabic meter with parallelisms and extensive use of formulas. Songs are performed either in unison or as part-singing. There is also a tradition of long fairy tales. In Mordvin tradition the lamentation (wedding, funeral, and recruitment laments) had a central place until the second half of the 20th century. Some epics have been composed on the basis of themes from Mordvin epic poetry. Of these the most significant is *Mastorava* ("Mother Earth"), published in 1994.

A few books were published in Erzya and Moksha in the 19th century, but for the most part the Erzya and Moksha literary languages began to develop in and

after the 1920s with the support of the Soviets. The most renowned Mordvin artist is Stepan Erzya (1876–1953). His powerful, often massive sculptures depicted mythic and biblical figures just as often as they did emotional space.

In the 1920s, development of the Erzya and Moksha literary languages commenced, and Mordvin language cultural institutions were established. In 1928 the Autonomous District of Mordvins was established, and in 1934 it was made into an Autonomous Socialist Republic that in 1994 became the Republic of Mordovia. However, only 32 percent of the inhabitants are ethnic Mordvins. In the latter part of the 1930s, during Joseph Stalin's administration, the terrors began and the entire Mordvin intelligentsia was either imprisoned or put to death on the basis of fabricated charges. The national identity began to deteriorate as a result of the purges. Imposed school reform in the 1950s caused instruction in the mother tongue to diminish, so that nowadays Mordvin is taught for a few hours in the week only in the first grade. In 1989, the proportion of Mordvins who did not know their own language stood at 33 percent; most of these belong to the younger age groups, a feature that will accelerate the language change process in the coming decades. The scattered nature of Mordvin settlement has made the people very susceptible to assimilation.

The disintegration of the Soviet Union and the democratization of Russia triggered a fragile national revival even in the Mordvin territories, but it was caught in the bud quickly with the emergence of economic difficulties. During the presidency of Vladimir Putin (2000–2008), centralized power in Russia was reinforced and the rights of minority nations in legislative matters and education, for example, have suffered.

*Sirkka Saarinen*

## Further Reading

Konuykhov, Alexey K., ed. *Finno-Ugric Ethnicities in Russia: Yesterday, Today, and Tomorrow*. Trans. Pavel Krotov. Syktyvkar: Society Finland–Russia and Komi vojtyr, 2009.

Lallukka, Seppo. *The East Finnic Minorities in the Soviet Union. An Appraisal of the Erosive Trends*. Helsinki: The Finnish Academy of Science and Letters, 1990. B:252.

Nanofszky, György, ed. *The Finno-Ugric World*. Budapest: Teleki László Foundation, 2004.

# N

## Nogai

The Nogai people (self-designation *Noğay*) live in scattered groups over a large area in northern Caucasus and Dagestan of the Russian Federation. According to the 2002 census, the number of Nogai in Russia was 90,700. About 20,000 live in the Stavropol district north of the Caucasus, 16,000 in the Karachaevo-Cherkessia Republic, 3,500 in Chechnya, a small number in Ingushetia, and 38,000 on the Nogai Steppe in northern Dagestan. A few still live in the Crimean Peninsula of Ukraine. Nogai minorities are also to be found in a few villages (estimated at a few thousand) in Dobrogea in southern Romania as well as in several villages near the shores of Tuz Gölü in the Konya area of Turkey (estimated at 90,000). A few Anatolian Nogais have migrated for work to northwestern Europe, for instance to Germany, the Netherlands, and Sweden. Small groups of Nogais are still also to be found in Wadi El Sir in Jordan. The Nogai are Turkic-speaking Muslims.

The origin of the Nogais is related to the Golden Horde in the 13th and 14th centuries. Their ethnonym (noğay means "dog" in Mongolian) seems to have emerged among them under the leadership of Amir Nogay. In the first half of the 17th century a number of Nogai tribes were nomadic on the steppes between the Danube and the Caspian. With the invasion of the Mongolian Kalmyks many Nogais were forced to leave their steppes and they settled on the foothills of the North Caucasus. By the Kuban River they encountered the Adyghs. In the 17th century some of the Nogay leaders entered into an alliance with the tsarist government and fought at times together with the Russians against the Kabards, the Kalmyks, and peoples of Dagestan. Since the early 19th century the majority of the Nogais have settled in North Caucasia. After the Russian conquest of the Caucasus in 1859–1864 many left for the Ottoman Empire and are therefore still to be found in the Balkan Peninsula, Anatolia, and Jordan. Contemporary Nogais in Russia and Turkey live on cattle breeding and agriculture.

Nogais organized themselves after the fall of the Soviet Union, and a nationalist movement, Birlik ("Unity") exists. It represents the Nogais in Dagestan, and in the early 1990s it called for a separate Nogai state. Some clashes between Nogais and other ethnic groups have been reported. The war in Chechnya forced many Nogais to settle in neighboring republics. However, Nogai groups are scattered over a wide area, and attempts to unite them have so far not been successful. However, in 2007 the Nogais in the Karachaevo-Cherkessia Republic formed their own administrative region.

The Nogais converted to Islam during the 14th century. Nowadays most of them profess Sunni Islam of the Hanafi juridical school, and since the early 1990s there has been a revival of institutions and connections with the broader Muslim world. Some young Nogai have been influenced by more radical movements, especially in Chechnya.

The Nogai language belongs to the southern subgroup of the Kipchak or northwestern branch of the Turkic languages, and is related to Kazak and Karakalpak. It is usually divided into three dialects: Kara Nogai spoken in Dagestan, Central Nogai in the Stavropol area, and Ak Nogai by the Kuban River. The importance of the language has been restricted to village level, while the scattered groups of Nogai have used various neighboring languages, especially Russian, in contacts with the outsiders. These contacts have also left a deep impact on the language and culture of the Nogai.

The first written Nogai language was based on the Arabic alphabet. In 1928 the Latin alphabet was introduced, but was replaced by a Cyrillic script in 1938. Few Nogai language newspapers and other media exist, and very little literature exists. Attempts to reintroduce the Latin script in the early 1990s failed. Nogai is considered an endangered language.

*Ingvar Svanberg*

## Further Reading

Akiner, Shirin. *Islamic Peoples of the Soviet Union: An Historical and Statistical Handbook*. London: KPI, 1986.

Krag, Helen, and Lars Funch. *The North Caucasus: Minorities at Crossroads*. London: Minority Rights Group, 1994.

# Norwegians

Norwegians are the dominant ethnic group of the constitutional monarchy of Norway, numbering about 4 million of a total population of 4.5 million (2009), the rest comprising the indigenous group Saami (ca. 40,000), recent immigrants and their descendants (ca. 450,000), as well as tiny minorities of Roma, Travellers, Kven (Finnish-speakers), and Jews. These minorities are often citizens and thus Norwegian in a political sense, if not in an ethnic sense. There are, moreover, several million people of Norwegian descent in North America, but they are not usually considered Norwegians. Lutheranism is the state religion in Norway, though few regularly attend church. Along with the other Scandinavian peoples, Norwegians speak a North Germanic language, largely mutually intelligible with Swedish and Danish and also related to German, English, Dutch, and Afrikaans. Norwegian exists in two official varieties, *riksmål* ("state language") or *bokmål* ("book language") and *nynorsk* ("new Norwegian").

Norwegians are descendants of Germanic speakers who settled in northwestern Europe before 100 BCE. The ethnonym (*nordmann, norsk*) can be traced back to the Viking age (8th to 10th centuries), but local and regional identities would then necessarily have been stronger than the common ethnic identity.

Although Norway was an independent kingdom in the Middle Ages, it became increasingly dominated by Denmark from the late 14th century and was an integral part of the Danish kingdom from 1537 to 1814, and the written language remained

Danish until the late 19th century. The language reformer Ivar Aasen (1813–1896) single-handedly designed a new written language based on rural dialects (particularly from western Norway), and drawing on considerable popular and parliamentary support in an age of strong national romanticism, *nynorsk* (then *landsmaal*, "rural language") became an official language, along with *riksmål* (Dano-Norwegian) in 1885. *Nynorsk* remains a minority variety, chiefly used in Western Norway outside the main urban centers, but it has a strong position in literature and some of the media. *Riksmål*/*bokmål* has also been reformed several times, bringing it closer to spoken language and somewhat more distant from Danish.

The language issue reflects the diverse history of Norwegians. The major towns and cities have been oriented toward the continent, while rural culture has arguably retained more of its Norse origins. Many contemporary political controversies are founded in rural-urban conflicts over interests.

This tension also has a bearing on the question of national identity. In the shaping of a distinct, modern Norwegian identity in the 19th century, the close cultural and historical affinities with Danes and Swedes presented a problem, since Norwegian identity had to appear as unique. As a result, nation-builders of the period, as influenced by German Romanticism in cultural matters as they were by the ideals of the Enlightenment in politics, developed an image of Norwegianness based on rural culture, especially from the mountain valleys of southern Norway. Customs and traditions from these areas came to be

seen as archetypal of Norway—foods such as *rømmegrøt* (sour cream porridge) and *spekeskinke* (cured ham), folk music based on the Hardanger fiddle and dances such as the halling but also local adaptations of imported dances such as the Rheinländer (known as reinlender in Norway) and the polka, became symbols of Norwegianness along with other aspects of peasant life, although they were scarcely representative at the time and became much less so as the 20th century progressed. However, peasant culture had the virtue of being distinctly Norwegian, as opposed to Swedish and Danish, defining the new nation (but much older ethnic group) in no uncertain terms.

Two sets of historical events have been crucial in the development of Norwegian identity and the self-understanding of Norwegians. Although the Viking era is well known, and forms the focus of a number of popular plays (*spel*) performed annually in many communities, it has had a weak impact on national identity, as that period is correctly seen as too distant in time to be relevant for the present era. However, when, in the aftermath of the Napoleonic wars, Denmark lost Norway, local elites saw the possibilities of full independence and signed a constitution on May 17, 1814. Although Norway months later entered into a union with Sweden that would last until 1905, the Swedish-Norwegian union was a loose one, and Norwegians largely ran their own country with little interference from the Swedish king. From the mid-19th century, May 17—Constitution Day—has been celebrated as Norway's national day, with almost universal participation in public rituals involving children's parades, speeches by notable men and women, and memorial services, making it the single most important public ritual in the country. The signing of the constitution in 1814 still reverberates in Norwegian society.

The second formative event was the war and subsequent occupation by the German Nazi regime (1940–1945). Norway had acceded to full independence only a generation before the German invasion of March 9, 1940, and its status as an independent country seemed fragile in the years of the occupation. From 1945 up to the present, innumerable books, films, and documentaries have detailed the Norwegian resistance against the Nazis. In spite of the publication of the acclaimed biographies of Vidkun Quisling, the Norwegian Nazi leader and chief minister during the occupation, there has been much less interest in the very widespread Norwegian collaboration with the Nazis and the participation of Norwegian soldiers in Hitler's army. Anti-Semitism was also strong in Norway before and during the war.

The occupation and subsequent defeat of Nazism also had cultural consequences. Before 1945, Norwegian artists and intellectuals were strongly oriented towards Germany, a country with which one felt linguistically and culturally close, often spending substantial periods in German cities. After 1945, the focus shifted toward the United States and the United Kingdom. As a result, the second language of contemporary Norwegians is English, German is no longer widely understood, and few German books are translated into Norwegian.

Before the 11th century, the majority of Norwegians worshipped and sacrificed to Norse gods such as Odin, Thor, and Frøya. The Christian faith gained a substantial foothold in the group around CE 1000, and Christianity became the dominant religion after the Battle of Stiklestad in 1030. As a result of the Reformation, which reached the country in 1537, the Catholic faith was replaced by Lutheranism, which is still the state religion. However, influenced by secularization and increased pluralism, few Norwegians go regularly to church outside of weddings, funerals, and other major rituals, and there is general consensus that the church has lost much of its power since the last decades of the 20th century. On the other hand, it can be argued that many of the cultural values associated with Protestantism remain strong among Norwegians. Frugality and a positive evaluation of simplicity (as opposed to the opulence of the Catholic church) are often mentioned in this respect.

Until the end of the 19th century, Norwegians were generally rural, and as mentioned, the national identity still associates the essence of Norwegianness with the rural life. Hindered by the harsh climate and rugged topography, feudalism was never predominant—the surplus generated by Norwegian agriculture was not sufficient to support a feudal class except in the most favorable regions. Along the coast, however, shipbuilding and merchant shipping developed as important industries, and the export of fish and other maritime products (such as whale oil) were for centuries very important, indicated in the fact that the western port of Bergen was for a long time the only substantial city in the country. Timber has also traditionally been an important export commodity. However, poverty was rife, and an estimated one-third of the population emigrated, mostly to North America, in the 19th and early 20th centuries.

Norwegian high culture arguably reached its zenith in the latter half of the 19th century, a period that witnessed an unprecedented blossoming of the arts, when, notably, the composer Edvard Grieg, the playwright Henrik Ibsen, and the writer Bjørnstjerne Bjørnson (Nobel laureate 1903) reached a wide international audience. Major artists active in the early 20th century include Knut Hamsun (whose reputation was tainted by his unrepentant Nazism) and Sigrid Undset (both Nobel laureates), as well as the painter Edvard Munch.

Winter sports such as cross-country skiing and alpine skiing are enormously popular in Norway, both at the competitive and the leisure level. Norwegians are also renowned ice skaters. The love of nature is seen as a national characteristic, and well over half the population has easy access to a cabin in the mountains or countryside.

Today, Norwegians live in one of the safest and richest countries in the world, thanks to early to mid-20th century industrialization, the wealth of natural resources and, since the 1980s, North Sea oil. Their present and future challenge as a group with a distinctive identity tied to the Norwegian nation-state concerns their relationship to the outside world. Having voted no to membership in the European Union twice (1972 and 1994), Norwegians are concerned with maintaining their identity while being at the same time totally dependent on a globalized economy and knowledge industry. The growing number of immigrants and their descendants poses a similar challenge concerning the boundaries and contents of future Norwegianness; whether it should be based on origins, language, way of life, or simply citizenship. This debate is bound to continue for many years still.

*Thomas Hylland Eriksen*

## Further Reading

Brochmann, Grete. *History of Immigration: The Case of Norway 900–2000.* Oslo: Universitetsforlaget, 2008.

Danielsen, Rolf, et al. *Basic Features of Norwegian History. From the Viking Age to the Present.* Oslo: Universitetsforlaget, 1995.

Kiel, Anne Cohen, ed. *Continuity and Change: Aspects of Modern Norway.* Oslo: Universitetsforlaget, 1991.

Gullestad, Marianne. *The Art of Social Relations: Essays on Culture, Social Action, and Everyday Life in Modern Norway.* Oslo: Universitetsforlaget, 1992.

Osterud, Oyvind, ed. *Norway in Transition.* London: Routledge, 2006.

## Ossetians

Ossetians or Alans refer to themselves as *Allon* in their literary language and as *Iron* and *Dygoron* in their two dialects. In the Middle Ages Ossetians were known as *Alans* (in the West), *Asi* (in the East), and *Jasi* (in Eastern Europe). The name *Ossetians* appeared in Russian in the 18th century, deriving from Georgian *Oseti* (from the "country of Osi" or Alania). The territory of Alania-Ossetia (the homeland of Ossetians) in located in the Central Caucasus on both slopes of the main Caucasus. Major Ossetian cities include Vladikavkaz-Dzaudjikau, Tskhinval, Beslan, Mozdok, Ardon, Digora, and Kvaisa. The Ossetian diaspora is found mainly in Georgia, Turkey, and the Russian Federation (Moscow, Kabardyno-Balkaria, Stavropol krai). The total number of Ossetians globally exceeds 650,000, of whom 510,000 live in Ossetia (450,000 in North Ossetia and 60,000 in South Ossetia). The Ossetian language belongs to the eastern subgroup of the Iranian branch of the Indo-European language family and stands out in an area populated by speakers of Turkic and Caucasian languages. Literary Ossetian has two variants: the eastern (based on Iron dialect) and western (based on Digora dialect); the Iron dialect is spoken by the majority. Most Ossetians follow Eastern Orthodoxy and about 15 percent profess Islam.

Ancestors of Ossetians, the Scythians, inhabited the foothills of the Caucasus range and in the eighth–fourth centuries BCE occupied the mountainous part of the Central Caucasus. In the third–second centuries BCE, Caucasian Scythia was invaded by kindred tribes of Sarmatians. In the 1st century CE, a strong Scythian-Sarmatian alliance became known by a common name (Alans). In the fourth–fifth centuries, Alans established a number of kingdoms on the territories of Gallia and Northern Africa. Caucasus Alania is known as one of the richest and most influential medieval states in Eastern Europe. The South Caucasus part of the Great Silk Road passed through Alan territories, and Alanian kings Sarosy, Itaz, Dorgolel, and Khudan took part in the most significant international events of their day. In the 13th century, Alania was invaded by Tatar-Mongols. The struggle for independence continued until 14th century, when the last Alanian king, Bagatar, died. Late in the 14th century, the plain of Alania was laid waste by the invasions of Tamerlan, and surviving Alans established themselves in mountain valleys of the Central Caucasus. In the 15th–18th centuries, Alania was a confederation of 11 counties with its own citizenship, representative democracy, and parliament. A citizen owned an inherited allotment of land, managed an independent household, and enjoyed the right to vote. The community regulated the community relationships without allowing feudal lords to infringe upon the rights of the lower classes.

In 1749–1752, the Confederation Embassy headed by Zurab Magkati agreed in St. Petersburg to the integration of Alania-Ossetia with Russia. The integration act was documented in 1774, after the Russian-Turkish War; the Kuchuk-Kainarjiy Treaty lifted the barriers to Russia's sovereignty in the Caucasus. In the first half of the 19th century, a massive return of Ossetians to the lowlands took place.

St. Andrew the Apostle introduced Christianity to Alania, and from the early 10th century Eastern Orthodoxy was the state religion. A Muslim minority has existed since the 13th century. Ossetian religious culture is characterized by strong monotheism, strict ritual rules, and absence of clerical structure.

Rituals are led by the head of the family or community. Three cheese pies are required for rituals because they symbolize the harmony of the universe, consisting of the upper, middle, and lower worlds. Since the 10th century, state policy has called for combining images of saints and harmonization of calendar rituals, and unification of original hieratic patterns of Alan monotheism and Orthodox Christianity was followed. Today, the complementary parallelism is fundamental to religious beliefs.

The traditional forms of household economy varied by region, with cattle breeding and terrace farming in the hills and plough farming and farmhouse cattle breeding on the plain. The development of a market economy, construction, and mineral resource industries, as well as food production started in the mid-19th century, the same period that saw land tenure reforms and the abolition of feudalism. The second half of the 19th century and the beginning of the 20th century was a period of intensive modernization, a time when national cultural institutions were created. Today Ossetians work in all sectors and exhibit high levels of education.

Traditional Ossetian culture celebrates the warrior. Embodied in the epic folklore, classic literature, arts, and theater, the Solitary Knight, who values dignity more highly than life, serves as the archetype of the national character. The openness typical of the national culture is reflected in the credo of the prominent poet Kosta Khetagkati: "My world is a temple, my shrine is my love, my Motherland is the Universe." These features complement the multiethnic composition of the population in Ossetia and the absence of cultural and interconfessional tensions with neighbors. Significant Ossetians include Grigory Tokati (the constructor of the U.S. Apollo spacecraft and shuttle in the 1960s), conductor Valery Gergiev, and football (soccer) coach Valery Gazzaev.

During the Russian Empire, Ossetia was divided between Terskaya oblast and Tiflis and Kutaisi provinces. After the Bolshevik Revolution in 1917, territorial and administrative unity was restored by popular demand. After the civil war, the Bolsheviks forcefully divided Ossetia once again. The South Ossetian Autonomous Oblast became a part of the Georgian Soviet Republic (as did some parts of the Kazbegi district) and the North Ossetian Autonomous Republic formed part of the Russian Soviet Republic.

With the dissolution of the Soviet Union, Georgia refused to grant greater South Ossetian autonomy, ultimately leading to a war in which many soldiers and civilians were killed. In 1990–1992, 100,000 Ossetians from Georgia and 20,000 from South Ossetia found refuge in North Ossetia. In order to protect lives and property of people, the Autonomous Oblast utilized proclaimed itself an independent Republic of South Ossetia. In 2008, the Russian Federation and Nicaragua opened the process of international recognition of the republic.

In 1992, armed groups from the neighboring entity Ingushetia entered into North Ossetia with the goal of seizing the eastern part of Prigorodny *rayon* with a mixed (Ingush and Ossetian) population. The Ossetian-Ingush political conflict is now close to settlement, and the majority of displaced persons have returned to their former residences. The denationalization policy in the USSR led to limiting the use of the Ossetian language to that of everyday life. After the dissolution of the USSR, the Ossetian language has gained the status of an official language and is now in use in the educational system and record keeping.

*Ruslan Bzarov*

**Further Reading**

Alemany, A. *Sources on the Alans. A Critical Compilation.* Leiden-Boston-Koln: Brill Academic Publishers, 2000.

Bachrach, B. S. *A History of the Alans in the West.* Minneapolis: University of Minnesota Press, 1973.

Littleton, C. Scott, and Linda A. Malkor. *From Scythia to Camelot.* New York: Garland Publishing, 2000.

Bliev, M., and Bzarov, R. *A History of Ossetia.* Vladikavkaz: Ir, 2000. (In Russian: Блиев М.М., Бзаров Р.С. История Осетии. Владикавказ: Ир,, 2000.)

# P

## Poles

Poles are a Slavic group whose traditional homeland is in Central Europe, in the country of Poland. An estimated 37 million ethnic Poles live in Poland, comprising nearly 97 percent of the country's population. Approximately 1.2 million Poles live in long-standing communities in Ukraine, Lithuania, and Belarus. In addition, there are large immigrant communities of Poles in the United States and Germany. Since Poland became a member of the European Union in 2004, there has been a sharp rise in temporary migration; an estimated 2 million Poles live in other member countries, roughly half of whom are in Great Britain and Ireland. Poles' primary language is Polish, and their primary religion is Roman Catholic.

Historically, Poland has engaged in frequent wars to expand, protect, and regain territory, but lacked the centralized structures to maintain control, especially in

An Easter procession in Radomysl, Poland. The great majority of the Polish population is Roman Catholic. (EPA Photo/Stanislaw Ciok)

the face of expansionist neighbors. Slavic tribes moved into the region of contemporary Poland in the second half of the 5th century. The origin of the Polish state is most commonly associated with the conversion to Catholicism of Mieszko I in 966 during a period of territorial expansion of the Polanie, "the People of the Field." Mieszko's son Bolesław became the first crowned king, and extended control over Silesia, Pomerania, and Małopolska (the Kraków region), and briefly controlled parts of what are now the Czech Republic, Slovakia, and Ukraine. In the beginning of the 11th century, the Polish seat of power moved from Gniezno to Krakow. Centralization under the Piast dynasty was challenged by the lack of a uniform standard of succession, a relatively large and powerful nobility (roughly 8–10% of the population), and incursions by Mongols and Teutonic Knights. Following a long period of fragmentation, in the 14th century, Władysław I and his son, Kazimierz III, reclaimed much of the land that had been lost, and expanded Piast control eastward into Rus regions (parts of contemporary Belarus and Ukraine).

At the end of the 14th century, the Polish-Lithuanian Union was established upon the marriage of the Lithuanian Jagiełło and Polish Jadwiga. Jadwiga held the title King of Poland because she was a monarch in her own right, not via marriage to a king. Thus began the Jagiellonian dynasty, whose reign included the defeat of the Teutonic Knights at Grunwald in 1410. The period 1466–1576 is commonly called Poland's golden age. The united Polish and Lithuanian lands reached nearly to the Black Sea. Extended trade and cultural contacts provided resources for a flourishing of arts and architecture, particularly in Kraków and Gdańsk. Also, a unique political system developed, in which the power of the hereditary monarch was limited by a parliament (*sejm*) of nobility and clergymen, and laws protected the rights of the nobility.

Upon the death of Zygmunt August, the last Jagiellonian king, in 1572, the king became an elected position, selected by parliament. Increasingly important because of its central location between Kraków and Vilnius, Warsaw became Poland's capitol in 1596. Despite military successes against the Swedes and Russians in the early 17th century, and the defeat of the Turks at Vienna in 1683 under the leadership of King Jan Sobieski, internal political rivalries and ongoing challenges from outside prevented Poland from solidifying control over its vast territory. Members of parliament resisted efforts to strengthen the power of the king, and exercised the liberum veto, whereby a single member could defeat any legislation. Thus fragmented from within, neighboring powers Russia, Prussia, and Austria steadily encroached upon Polish territory. On May 3, 1791, inspired by political reforms in the United States and France, the Polish parliament ratified a new constitution that laid the groundwork for extending democratic liberties. By 1795, the weakened Polish state was powerless to resist further partitions, and Poland disappeared as an autonomous country.

Poles are overwhelmingly Roman Catholic (95% of the citizens of Poland), and religion has historically served as a central marker of distinction with neighboring groups (especially Orthodox Rus/Ukrainians and Russians and Protestant Germans). Furthermore, religious practice has played an important part in maintaining Polish communities outside of Poland and in the absence of an autonomous Polish state. Central to Polish Catholicism is the Black Madonna of Częstochowa; annually, as many as 4 million Poles make the pilgrimage to this holy icon of the Virgin Mary. Reproductions of the icon hang in churches and homes throughout Poland and, like the original, are said to have the power to grant miracles. The Black Madonna is also closely linked to the Polish nation; named "the Queen of Poland," it is believed to have protected Poland from various foreign invasions, and continues to play an important symbolic role in contemporary politics. Important rites associated with religious holidays include church mass, prayers, and blessings, as well as social and sometimes even humorous practices. For November 1, All Saints Day, families clean graves and decorate them with flowers and candle lanterns; crowds visit the cemeteries, which at night are aglow with candlelight. On the Monday after Easter, called Śmingus Dingus, it is customary to throw water over people. Wigilia, Christmas Eve, traditionally brings together extended family, and is celebrated with a 12-course meal that includes fish but no other meat. Instead of birthdays, most Poles celebrate their saint's day, the day associated with a saint who shares their name. Important rites of passage include infant baptism, first communion at age nine, and a church wedding.

The first Polish university was established in Krakow in 1364; the Polish language started to be used in church sermons in the 13th century and in literature in the early 16th century. The term *naród*, nation, referred to the collectivity of nobility in the 15th century, and was associated with the rights and responsibilities of citizenship, a code of honor and courage, and values of hospitality and liberty. In the 19th century, *naród* took on a more modern significance as Romantic nationalists, many of whom lived in exile, used the arts and literature to inspire nationalist sentiment, political and military mobilization, and the reestablishment of an autonomous Polish state.

Well into the 20th century, Polish society was mostly agrarian and even today farmers make up more than 20 percent of workers. Historically, most land was held by the nobility, while the vast majority of the population worked as peasants or serfs on noble estates. For centuries, towns remained small and relatively weak, hindered from growth by restrictions on guilds, land ownership for townspeople, and peasant migration. When Western Europe moved toward industrialization, Poland continued to rely on agriculture, and supplied raw materials and agricultural products in exchange for inexpensive manufactured goods. The nobility was a diversified group, ranging from extremely powerful magnates who controlled massive estates to those of modest means who nevertheless were nominal equals within the political body, the *sejm*. As the magnates' power grew in the 16th and 17th centuries, they extracted so much from the peasants that many farmers lost their land, personal rights, and legal freedoms. This loss of autonomy, which persisted into the 19th century, is sometimes called the "second serfdom." Much of the peasant population lacked a well-developed sense of ethnicity; rather, they identified with their particular place of residence and their religion.

In modern times, social, cultural, and political preferences tend to distinguish occupational groups, especially farmers, workers, and intelligentsia. In recent years, a class of entrepreneurs and businessmen has also emerged. These groups also tend to have different levels of education, and to be further divided by urban and rural residence. Polish women tend to be better educated and more religious than men. Birthrates, which have tended to be above the European average, dropped sharply after 1990 to become one of the lowest in Europe in the early 2000s.

Until World War II, Poles lived in mixed ethnic communities with Germans, Ukrainians, Belarusians, Lithuanians, and Jews. Known for its religious tolerance, in the 16th century Poland became a haven for Jews escaping persecution elsewhere in Europe. Jews settled primarily in towns and cities and played an important role in the trades, and later in industry. Nearly all of the 3 million Polish Jews were exterminated during World War II. After the war, Poland reemerged more ethnically homogeneous than it had ever been, shaped by the Holocaust, border shifts, and population movements. Small populations remain of (in order of size) Silesians, Germans, Belarusians, Ukrainians, Roma, and Łemko. Other distinctive regional groups include Górale in the southern mountains and Kashubians in the northeast.

The culture and history of the Polish people are strongly linked not only to the existence of a Polish state, but also to its absence. In the late 18th and throughout the19th centuries, when other countries in Europe were solidifying their centralized states and legitimating that power via constructions of the nation, Poland remained divided among Russia, Prussia, and Austria. Poland regained its political autonomy at the end of World War I, but securing that independence was a challenge. During the war, a half million Poles lost their lives and numerous others became refugees. Border disputes needed to be settled with Germany, Czechoslovakia, and Bolshevik Russia. When fighting ceased in 1921, the country's western border ran from the Free City of Gdańsk to Poznań to Katowice and Kraków, while the eastern border extended beyond Vilnius and Lviv (Polish Lwów). Ethnic minorities comprised roughly 30 percent of the country's population. Ethnic Poles in Silesia and elsewhere fell outside of the new Polish State.

Politically, the period between the world wars was characterized by deep divisions among Roman Dmowski's National Democrats, General Józef Piłsudski's Polish Socialist Party, and other parties representing various regional and political interests. In 1926, Piłsudski gained dominance following a military coup, and remained in power until his death in 1935. Piłsudski worked to integrate the Polish economy, administration, armed forces, and infrastructure, though the country was hit hard by the depression of the 1930s and faced ongoing pressure from neighbors Germany and Russia. In 1939, Nazi forces attacked Poland, leading France and England to declare war on Germany and beginning World War II. Opposition to the Nazis continued in Poland as well, and included two major uprisings. During the war, the Nazis forced Jews into ghettos and concentration camps, where most perished. In 1943, some Jews fought back in the Warsaw Ghetto Uprising. Throughout the occupation, an active Polish underground maintained universities, the arts, and military forces (Armia Krajowa, the Polish Home Army), and sought to liberate the capital city in the Warsaw Uprising of 1944. Twenty percent of Poland's population died in the war, and much of the country, especially Warsaw, was devastated by sustained Nazi bombing.

After the defeat of the Germans, Poland's new borders shifted westward; they encompass Silesia and part of Pomerania, but exclude Lviv and Vilnius. With the consent of the other Allies, the USSR declared the states along its western border, including Poland, part of its sphere of influence and used its power to establish state socialist governments in them. Immediately after the war, Poles focused on rebuilding and developing infrastructure and industry. Though their political freedom was curtailed, the economy grew amidst mass migration to cities. By the mid-1970s, economic growth halted, encumbered by the inefficiencies of the centralized economy and the need to repay foreign debt. Although there had been organized protests in 1956 and 1968, the biggest opposition emerged in the Solidarity Movement of 1980 under the leadership of Lech Wałęsa. In 1981, President Jaruzelski declared martial law and outlawed the increasingly political protest movement. State socialism crumbled when in 1989 the government agreed to hold free parliamentary elections, and the Communist Party lost all but one contested seat. With no response from the USSR, similar events occurred throughout the Soviet Bloc. Great symbolic significance in the struggle for Polish autonomy has also been attributed to the election of a Pole to become Pope John Paul II in 1978. Since 1989, Poland has instituted liberal market and democratic reforms, and strengthened its ties with Western Europe by entering NATO in 1999 and the European Union in 2004. At present, the position of the Polish state is more secure than it has perhaps ever been, strengthened by strong international alliances, a growing economy, and higher educational achievement. It also faces challenges, most particularly increased social and economic inequality that disproportionately affects retirees, the less educated, and rural residents.

*Marysia Galbraith*

## Further Reading

Davies, Norman. *Heart of Europe: A Short History of Poland*. Oxford: Oxford University Press, 1984.

Dunn, Elizabeth. *Privatizing Poland: Baby Food, Big Business, and the Remaking of Labor*. Ithaca, NY: Cornell University Press, 2004.

Pogonowski, Iwo C. *Poland: A Historical Atlas*. Rev. ed. New York: Dorset Press, 1988.

Sanford, George. *Poland: The Conquest of History*. Amsterdam: Harwood Academic Publishers, 1999.

Stauter-Halsted, Keely. *The Nation in the Village: The Genesis of Peasant National Identity in Austrian Poland 1848–1914*. Ithaca, NY: Cornell University Press, 2001.

Wedel, Janine. *The Private Poland*. New York: Facts on File, 1986.

Zubrzycki, Genevieve. *The Crosses of Auschwitz: Nationalism and Religion in Post-Communist Poland*. Chicago: University of Chicago Press, 2006.

## Pomaks

Pomaks (Bulgarian, *Pomatsi*; also known as *Achrjanis*, in Greece; in Bulgarian state usage, *Bulgari-miosliolmani* or "Bulgarian Muslims") reside on the Balkan Peninsula. Concentrated in the Rhodope Mountains of southwestern Bulgaria and Greek northern Thrace, a significant population lives in Turkey with smaller communities in Romania, Macedonia, and Albania. The Bulgarian census does not provide a category for Pomak identity, and estimates for their population range between 130,000 and 250,000 based on correlating separate categories for mother tongue and religious confession. In Turkey as many as a quarter of a million inhabitants are of Pomak descent, including historic communities, émigrés from Bulgaria, and a much larger number who assimilated into Turkish identity. The population in Greece is roughly 30,000. The Torbeshi of Macedonia, also a Slavic-speaking Muslim community, are sometimes included within the larger Pomak community, but scholarly disagreements on their ethnic relation to Pomaks parallel those on Macedonian-Bulgarian relations. Pomaks speak a dialect of Bulgarian, although many (particularly in Greece and Turkey) also speak Turkish. Bulgarian, Greek, and Turkish scholars propose different origin stories for Pomaks, often to highlight claims of ethnic kinship.

The presence of Slavic-speaking villages of Muslim belief in the Rhodope Mountains can be traced to mass conversions to Islam in the 15th through the 17th centuries CE during Ottoman rule. Although some Bulgarian historians characterize this as forced conversion, historical accounts are unclear and Ottoman rule created material incentives to conversion since Christians were subject to additional taxes and social restrictions. The location of the Pomak homeland suggests possible Ottoman state motives for conversion, given its geographic proximity to the approaches to Istanbul and to the north of Salonica, a major Ottoman commercial and military center. Politically motivated scholarship has advanced different national claims. For example, some Greek theories suggest that Pomaks were either originally Greek or Hellenized Thracians, subsequently Slavicized and later converted to Islam. Turkish scholars have argued that Pomaks are the descendants of Arabs, Cumans, Pechenegs, and/or Konyar Turks who settled in the region in the 11th through the 13th centuries, before the Ottoman conquests. Most Bulgarian scholars emphasize linguistic elements, pointing to the preservation of archaic Bulgarian elements in Pomak dialect to categorize them as a historically Bulgarian ethnic population that converted to Islam but, confined by their mountainous geographic isolation, were not fully assimilated into a Turkish identity. Such scholarly positions have recently been expanded to include studies of genetic markers and blood types, but results remain contested.

Pomaks are Sunni Muslims, generally of the Hanafi school, although some individuals and communities have converted to the Bulgarian Orthodox Church. Major Islamic holidays and customs are generally followed, although some regional Christian traditions can be observed such as the celebration of the feast days of Orthodox saints. Similarly, in some Pomak communities Islamic strictures against alcohol and the eating of pork have not been historically followed. As with other Muslims in Bulgaria, the 1920s saw state efforts to encourage traditionalism (including retaining sharia among the Muslim community) as a form of resistance to the lure of Kemal Ataturk's reformist efforts in neighboring Turkey. Subsequent modernization efforts targeted specifically Muslim customs that could be perceived as Turkish influence, particularly personal names, the use of the Turkish language, and clothing. Despite such efforts, the *shamiia* (woman's headscarf) remains in common use, although traditional handwoven clothing— particularly the *shalwar*, or Turkish-style loose trousers for women—are increasingly displaced in daily wear by industrially produced clothing. The male fez and turban are similarly often displaced in daily wear by the influx of contemporary Bulgarian fashion. Pomak villages are, agriculturally, similar to other alpine groups in Bulgaria and the Balkans and mix pastoral occupations, self-sufficient farming, and the growing of tobacco.

As with other Muslim inhabitants of southeastern Europe, the end of Ottoman

rule and emergence of independent states overturned political and social hierarchies, usually to their detriment. Pomak militias served with other Ottoman forces to suppress the April 1876 Bulgarian uprising; following the Russo-Turkish War of 1877–1878, Pomaks in the Rhodope mountains rebelled against both the new Bulgarian state and the sultan, creating a brief autonomous state before acceding to Ottoman control in 1885. The Balkan Wars of 1912–1913 saw the Rhodope Mountains being divided between Bulgaria and Greece. Most Pomak communities were integrated into Bulgaria, accompanied by a campaign to forcibly convert Muslims to Christianity and to impose Bulgarian ethnicity, a policy reversed in 1913. Intensive state assimilation campaigns supposedly to redeem the Bulgarian ethnic identity of Pomaks were undertaken in the 1930s, 1950s, and 1970s–1980s, each time giving way to moderation. Such campaigns were partially led by Pomak groups such as Rodina ("Homeland") seeking modernization and Bulgarianization, retaining a Muslim confessional identity while fully embracing both Bulgarian national identity as well as modern customs. The Greek state similarly restricted Pomak-inhabited regions along the Greek-Bulgarian border, briefly attempting in the 1970s to Christianize and Hellenize the region. Such campaigns were exacerbated by security concerns during the cold war that led to the forcible removal of some communities from border regions, and restrictions on travel to and from the region.

In the socialist period (1944–1989) in Bulgaria, widespread emigration to Turkey from Bulgaria meant a slight population decline. Socialist economic development in the Rhodope Mountains reduced incentives for internal migration to the cities, however. State projects to bring electricity and transportation links to Pomak towns and villages were followed with small factories for textiles and timber, mining, and the expansion of commercial agriculture, principally of tobacco. Such development has continued subsequent to the transition to democracy and market capitalism after 1989. Although assertions of a Bulgarian national identity for Pomaks remains a point of political rhetoric, restrictions on Muslim confession and folk customs have largely been eased (although some travel restrictions remain in Greece regarding Pomak-inhabited areas).

*James Frusetta*

**Further Reading**

Brunnbauer, Ulf. "Diverging (Hi-)stories: The Contested Identity of the Bulgarian Pomaks." *Ethnologia Balkanica* 3, no. 1 (1999): 35–50.

Eminov, Ali. *Turkish and Other Muslim Minorities in Bulgaria*. New York: Routledge, 1997.

Neuberger, Mary. *The Orient Within: Muslim Minorities and the Negotiation of Nationhood in Modern Bulgaria*. Ithaca: Cornell University Press, 2004.

Turan, Ömer. "Pomaks, Their Past and Present." *Journal of Muslim Minority Affairs* 19, no. 1 (1999): 69–83.

# Portuguese

Portuguese also refer to themselves as Lusitanians (the Roman name for the local residents encountered in that area during the Roman conquest). The Portuguese make up the dominant population in the state of Portugal, which has a population of 10.7 million. The largest city in Portugal is the capital (Lisbon); if the suburbs are included, about one-third (3.3 million) live and work in this metropolitan area. Porto, the second largest city, and its environs make up 30 percent of the population (3 million). While Coimbra is not next in size, culturally it is the third most important city. Between 1960 and 1973 more than 1.5 million Portuguese emigrated, leaving the nation with a negative population growth rate. As a result, after Lisbon the second largest "Portuguese" city became Paris rather than Porto. Many left for Northern Europe to labor in the dirty jobs (for example, construction, janitorial services, farm laborers) that the locals did not want. They also migrated to most other West European countries such as Spain, France, the Benelux nations, and Switzerland for similar employment. Other major destinations, beyond the Portuguese colonies, were Venezuela, South Africa, Canada, and Australia. Portugal is almost exclusively a Roman Catholic country where almost everyone speaks Portuguese. The culture is Iberian with Spanish Galicia being especially similar to Portugal in language and culture. Portugal has had a strong national identity, and has been a homogeneous nation regarding language, religion, culture, and ethnicity for about a millennium. Military conscription for the colonial wars in the 1960s, national television broadcasts, the expansion of health care and social security, schooling, and postal and banking networks spread throughout the nation to make it an even more tightly knit society.

Fisherman repairing nets, Nazare, Portugal. (Corel)

Portugal is one of the oldest, geographically most stable nations in Europe. Its 800-year history as a nation-state has led to a high degree of cultural unity. It has one of the world's most stable frontiers, and has seen hardly any change to its continental boundaries since it became an Iberian nation in the 13th century.

Until the Roman invasions around 200 BCE, the Lusitanians continued to dominate the western part of the peninsula. With the fall of the Roman Empire in the fifth century CE, the Swabians, a Germanic tribe, created a kingdom in Western Iberia. In 1128 Portugal emerged as an independent nation under the rule of Afonso Henrique (Portugal's first king). By 1249 Afonso III captured the Algarve region from the Moors, which established the present boundaries of Portugal, with the exception of languishing skirmishes with Castille (Spain) that stabilized in 1295. Four centuries of Moorish rule left its mark on Portuguese customs and culture. Agricultural advances, such as irrigated orchards, were introduced. Southern Portugal still showcases the architecturally distinctive white housing and place names beginning with "al" (for example, Algarve). The carpet weaving craft from Arraiolos to Portalegre is another vestige of this influence, as is the use of tile throughout the nation.

By the 15th century, much earlier than other major European powers, Portugal was already enjoying a strong sense of national unity. It was relatively free of civil strife and was governed by a strong, institutionalized, monarchical government. Since Portugal had firm territorial boundaries, its militaristic aristocracy turned its attention to the sea. The focus became one of exploration, maritime trade, and colonization.

Whereas the Netherlands' and England's industrialization was primarily financed by the middle or entrepreneurial classes, in Portugal significant capital was never accumulated by these ranks. It remained in the hands of the elite, who used the wealth to build expensive churches and to purchase luxuries. They preferred to import these goods rather than invest in their domestic production. The end result was the "old country's" transformation into a giant sieve through which its wealth passed to help northern Europe finance its industrial revolution, leaving Portugal on the sidelines well into the 20th century.

By the 16th century, Portugal began to see a fall of profits from the colonies. The combination of a series of weak kings and the decrease in revenues led to serious foreign debt problems. The 60-year Spanish rule that followed the end of the Aviz dynasty did not help matters. Even during the Marquis of Pombal's restoration period (he governed the nation for King José from 1750 to 1777) little attention was devoted to Portuguese development. Through his authoritarian, highly centralized government, Pombal introduced the enlightenment (rationalism) to Portugal, but even these conditions did not produce the middle class that Portugal needed to one day take its place alongside the industrial nations.

Until the 19th century, Portugal remained free of the antimonarchical civil unrest and coups occurring in many other nations. From the 1820s on, however (ever since the crown's flight to Brazil during the Napoleonic invasions and its reluctance to return to Portugal after Napoleon's defeat), the upper-middle-class and military elements assumed a broader role in Portuguese politics. Increasingly, liberal ideas such as democracy, equality, and popular sovereignty began to influence these nascent political groups until they created a constitution in 1822 that limited royal power.

In 1910 a revolution created the first republic in Portugal and the third in Europe following the French and Swiss. Governments under the republic were short-lived, averaging one every four months (45 governments, 7 parliamentary elections, and 8 presidential elections were held during this period). Political violence, involvement in World War I, budget deficits, bread shortages, capital flight, a backward agricultural sector, and currency devaluation added to the instability and to increasing unhappiness. By 1926 a general unhappiness began to infiltrate all sectors of society, and the majority of Portuguese acquiesced to the need for a right-wing, nonrepublican solution.

A military coup in 1926 successfully ended Portugal's experiment in liberal democracy. By 1930 the military and the dictator, António Salazar, succeeded in returning political stability to the nation. The values of God, family, and the nation were given the highest priority. Change was controlled, partly through the use of a secret police used for political surveillance. Corporatism became the Portuguese solution to alien radical transformations such as socialism, liberalism, or communism. In 1968, Salazar suffered an incapacitating stroke and was succeeded by the scholar Marcello Caetano.

In 1974, a military coup was carried out by mid-level officers. Given the widespread dissatisfaction with the Salazar/

Caetano dictatorship, popular support soon transformed the coup into a revolution. A brief summary of the resulting major changes would include: (1) the breakup of the colonial empire, (2) the government's increased involvement in the economy, (3) the emergence of political parties, (4) an increase in labor rights and Portuguese Communist Party domination of unions, (5) a reorganization of local governments, and (6) a limited agrarian reform. The Armed Forces Movement's major goals were democratization, decolonization, and development. From 1974 to 1976 there was a prolonged national debate on what new form of government and social organization the country should adopt. After six provisional governments, three elections, and two failed coups, the Portuguese settled on a west European style of democracy, and Portugal inaugurated its new democratic regime on July 23, 1976. Portugal joined the European Union (EU) in 1986.

Portugal is primarily a Roman Catholic country, partly as a result of the forced conversions of non-Catholics (Moors were defeated and the Inquisition persecuted the Jews, Moors, and Protestants). The Pyrenees also insulated the Iberian Peninsula from the Protestant Reformation that swept Europe north of the mountain range. During the Salazar/Caetano dictatorship, Catholicism was designated the official state religion and was integrated into school curriculums. Today Jehovah's Witnesses, Mormons, and other religious groups are beginning to make inroads, but Catholicism still dominates.

Despite national unity and identity, the Portuguese today, especially the younger generation, are quickly being assimilated into globalized world culture, responding mainly to the influence of foreign, especially American, cinema and music. While they are hardworking, they are economically peripheral in Western Europe. Portuguese often have a fatalistic perspective on life, accepting the cards they have been dealt in life rather than trying to change their destiny. Fittingly, this attitude is reflected in Portugal's national music called *Fado*, with its plaintive and melancholic songs of lost love and life's hardships. This fatalistic perspective contradicts the adventurousness of the 15th- and 16th-century explorers and 20th-century emigrants. Their inherent melancholy does not alter their ability to enjoy themselves while facing their difficulties, and many take comfort in simply being surrounded by family and friends. Almost every weekend the Portuguese make merry at dances or festivals. They love music; and unless they are mourning a death in the family, they actively participate in playing, singing, or dancing. They are a people proud of their culture and accomplishments, yet also see themselves as developmentally inferior to peoples in North America or Northern Europe. They readily embrace new technologies, continue to make important and cutting-edge contributions to architecture, create innovative social programs, and show a strong commitment to cultural enhancement.

Despite Portugal's small size, regional diversity exists, including a dualism between rural and urban society in all cities and even towns. While the rural areas have modernized somewhat in the last 30 years as electrification and improved roadways have spread throughout the nation, there is still a significant cultural difference between traditional, rural life and more modern, urban culture. The continental regions can be divided into the Noreoeste Cismontano, Alto Portugal, Nordeste Transmontano, Beira Douro, Beira Alta, Beira Litoral, Beira Serra, Beira Baixa, Estremadura, Sado e Ribatejo, Alentejo, Algarve, and the two autonomous Atlantic Ocean archipelagos Açores (Azores [nine inhabited islands]) and Madeira (two inhabited islands). Each island speaks Portuguese with its own distinctive accent, and there is a good-natured rivalry between islanders and the mainlanders, with each group using the other as the punch line of demeaning humor.

One of the most dramatic changes in the last few decades is that the nation has become a destination for immigrants. By the mid-1990s legal foreign residents accounted for close to 2 percent of the population. Since then the inflow of East Europeans has increased this figure to nearly 4 percent. As of 2005 Brazilians made up the largest group of immigrants, with Ukrainians second, and Cape Verdeans third.

In 2004 the economy remained at the bottom of the 15 western European Union members, surpassed even by the new member Slovenia and averaging only 75 percent of the EU's standard of living. Overall, the economy has experienced tertiarization, coastalization, and urbanization. Nevertheless, seeing Portugal today, with its improved economy, large middle class, progressive commitment to technological development, and the value placed on its cultural heritage, it is hard to believe that only 35 years ago, the Portuguese were living under a repressive, insular dictatorship.

In 1950 Portugal had the youngest population in Europe. As throughout the continent, however, the Portuguese are having fewer children (in 2001 family size was 2.8 people per household) so that since the late 1990s those older than 65 have surpassed those under 15. Nevertheless, family is central in Portuguese society, so it should not be remarkable that many Portuguese celebrations follow the family-centered life cycle. After the United Kingdom, Portugal has the highest rate of marriage in Europe. Most children live with their parents until they wed (between the ages of 20 and 30). Under pressure of modernization and urbanization the extended family is being replaced by the nuclear family.

Historically, gender roles in Portugal have followed traditional lines and division of labor, with males being the breadwinners, and women taking charge of the household and raising children. Today, in order to maintain a middle-class standard of living it is necessary for both parents to work. Economic pressures have forced women into the workforce, where they are now found at all levels of the professions. Despite entering the labor force, most women are still in charge of laundry and ironing, housecleaning, cooking, and caring for the ill. Men generally make small repairs around the house. Yet the majority of women do not think it unfair that they spend 19 hours per week on domestic chores while the men only spend three.

Gay, lesbian, bisexual, and transgender individuals have had a difficult time considering Portugal's conservative, moral standards influenced by centuries of Catholicism and nonexistent social debate. It is only in the last decade that homosexuals have begun coming out of the closet to openly declare their sexual orientation.

Contemporary Portugal is an outward-looking, modern, democratic, and European state with a legacy of a relatively recent traditional, colonial, and often inward-looking past that continues to shape and influence its development in the 21st century. The modernity is evident in the new highways, apartment buildings, hypermarkets, and mobile phones (there are more active cell phones than people in Portugal). What was until the 1970s a traditional society increasingly conforms to a model of an advanced European state in economic structure, democratic political traditions, social organization, welfare services, and the aspirations and expectations of its citizens. Socioeconomic indicators show a rapid convergence with European norms in diet and demographic characteristics. Because Portugal took half the time (two to three decades) to make these changes compared to most other Western European nations, current social and economic conditions are more fragile and vulnerable. For example, there are still significant gaps with the rest of Europe in terms of the diversity and strength of the economy, levels of education and training, and the quality and efficiency of its public services. Old-country traditions persist in that the dominant political elites have survived and traditional lifestyles endure in the countryside. With modernization comes a new set of tensions and paradoxes; a dichotomy is created between traditional and modern forms of production, consumption, and social reproduction. These new demands and maturity have confronted the Portuguese with many of the problems of advanced Western nations such as falling electoral turnout, immigration, drug abuse, and increased crime.

The nation has changed drastically since the 1974 revolution in ways that have affected its customs and culture. Alterations to its colonial empire, increased involvement in international relations, and patterns of emigration and immigration have caused Portugal to have a broader global vision. Additionally, social change, democratic consolidation, European integration and the accompanying economic development, and national identity, as well as the character of contemporary literature and art, have had enormous impact on diversifying perspectives in Portugal. Thus, the Lusitanian uniqueness of the past may not endure into the future.

*Carlos Cunha*

## Further Reading

Gallagher, Tom. *Portugal: A Twentieth-Century Interpretation*. Manchester: Manchester University Press, 1983.

Keefe, Eugene, et al. *Area Handbook for Portugal*. Washington: U.S. Government Printing Office, 1977.

Marques, A. H. de Oliveira. *History of Portugal*. New York: Columbia University Press, 1972.

Payne, Stanley G. *Spain and Portugal*. Madison: University of Wisconsin Press, 1973.

Pinto, António Costa, ed. *Contemporary Portugal: Politics, Society, and Culture*. Boulder, CO: Social Science Monographs, 2003.

# R

## Roma

The Roma, sometimes known as Gypsies, comprise the largest minority group in Europe, numbering approximately 10 million. In response to a long and ongoing history of discrimination, those who identify in other social contexts as Roma may be reluctant to do so for census takers; therefore, exact population figures are difficult to ascertain. Romani groups live primarily in Central and Eastern Europe but are also found around the world. Most scholars consider the Roma to be a diaspora that migrated west from India beginning in the 11th century, entering Eastern Europe between the 12th and 14th centuries. Virtually all Roma speak the language of the country in which they reside, but according to linguist Yaron Matras, at least 3.5 million also speak a form of Romani, an Indo-Aryan language sharing roots with Sanskrit. Today almost as many Romani dialects exist as there are distinct Roma groups. The Roma are often viewed as a homogeneous population, but they are in fact an internally diverse amalgamation of ethnic communities bound together as a political project. Those identified as Roma self-differentiate into many distinct subgroups. These include, but are not limited to, Sinti (Germany), Gitano (Spain), Beash (Hungary and Romania), Romungro (Hungary), Romanichal (United Kingdom), Kalderash (Romania and Ukraine),

and Domari (Middle East). The Travellers of the British Isles are also sometimes considered in this group. English Romanichal Travellers speak a dialect of Romani. Other subgroups like the Scottish and Irish Travellers do not share an Indian origin or speak Romani. However, in all Travellers' itinerant way of life, academics, political officials, and some activists see similar cultural features. The religious identity of Roma varies widely, from nonbelievers to Roman Catholic, Orthodox, and Pentecostal Christians to Muslims.

The historical trajectory of the Roma is widely debated in academic literature. Based on linguistic evidence, most scholars assert that the Roma are an Indian diaspora that migrated from the northwestern part of the Indian subcontinent to the Middle East and Europe in the Middle Ages. Anthropologist Judith Okely was the first to point out that evidence for the Indian migration hypothesis was based on incomplete documents, accounts from the 19th composed by non-Roma, and linguistic evidence that falsely equates language with ethnicity. Contemporary connections to an Indian homeland are negligible because Roma have lived in Europe for more than 500 years.

Evidence of the Roma presence in Europe was first documented in writings as early as the 13th century, and they were firmly established in most Central and Eastern European countries by the 14th

Roma children in a school hallway in Hungary. As a result of ethnic segregation, Roma children are often expected to use separate classrooms and lavatories, eat separately in the dining hall, and play separately in the schoolyard. (AP/Wide World Photos)

and 15th centuries. At this time, the origins of the Roma were not known and the members of this minority group were largely viewed with suspicion and distrust. According to Ian Hancock, the Roma were originally misidentified as Egyptian migrants and the term "Gypsy" emerged from this mistaken identity. Today, the Roma are also known as Gypsy or a similar cognate in all regions where they live (*cigány* in Hungarian, *ţsigan* in Romanian, *zigeuner* in German). Gypsy and related terms are now considered pejorative, but in some contexts, the terms are used with no ill will intended.

The Roma have faced persecution, suspicion, and discrimination wherever they have attempted to settle in Europe. Perhaps the most appalling example is the enslavement of the Roma in Wallachia and Moldova (now Romania) from their arrival in the region until the late 19th century. Even in regions where slavery was not prominent, the Roma found it impossible to gain any social standing in established guilds or gain access to land. They developed trades and livelihoods that depended upon exchange with members of the larger society even as it set Roma apart, a division that exists to this day.

The Roma are often considered to be nomadic, but today there are only a few traveling groups, primarily concentrated in France and the British Isles. The large majority live in established neighborhoods and villages and, for the most part, have resided in these areas for several generations. In some cases, Roma lived nomadic lives because political efforts to regulate them prevented them from establishing and maintaining residences. Exclusion from land ownership compelled Roma to make their living by engaging in such trades as shoeing horses, working metals, repairing and selling used goods, and making music. They traveled to settlements, selling their goods and services. When these economic niches closed, they generally tended to settle in one place. In the 18th and 19th centuries, reform-minded monarchs attempted to permanently settle itinerant Romani groups. For example, the Austrian Habsburg Empress Maria Theresa effected several measures in the 18th century that forced Roma to abandon their nomadic ways. These regulations also made Roma subject to taxation and attempted to force them to adopt lifestyles similar to those of "good" Austrians or Hungarians. Most contemporary Roma are now settled, but like members of other groups, they may migrate during times of war and hardship. During the Balkan civil wars of the 1990s, settled Roma were displaced from their homes and they sought asylum in Western Europe, but this latest wave of migration should not be attributed to nomadism. When Roma from Eastern Europe today migrate to Spain, Italy, and other western European countries for seasonal work in agriculture, construction, and the service economy, they are typically following the migration patterns of their non-Roma compatriots.

Because the Roma are such a diverse group, it is impossible to depict a single, unified belief system or way of life that could be characterized as "Roma culture." Roma across different countries use a number of cultural symbols when they refer to their common heritage, such as the horse or the wheel, which appears in the Romani flag designed by international Roma activists.

The Romani language provides a source of shared identity for Roma in many parts of the world. Although the language has a wide array of dialects, many common words are shared, and speakers of different Romani dialects can usually carry on simple conversations with one another despite the variations. Some languages spoken by Romani—such as Beash—derive from different roots but nonetheless convey ethnic pride. Roma activists in many countries have led language revitalization efforts and worked for recognition of Romani as a foreign language certified in higher education systems.

A strong tradition of arts and craftsmanship is a source of ethnic pride among many Roma. Traditional Roma skills with horses and metalwork sometimes find contemporary expression in hobbies such as racing horse-drawn carriages and rebuilding classic cars. For centuries, Roma have earned recognition from other Europeans through their skills in music and performance, and their influence can be heard in much of the folk music traditions of Eastern Europe. Django Reinhardt, a French Rom, developed the popular musical style known as "Gypsy jazz." Today, Roma musicians draw an international audience, whether performing new interpretations of traditional wedding music and folk ballads (Taraf de Haidouks, Kalyi Jag) or world-beat influenced pop music (Esma Redzepova). More recently, Roma artists have moved into other fields in the creative arts. Twenty thousand people visited the first Roma Pavilion in 1997 at the Venice Biennale, presenting the work of 15 Roma visual artists.

In everyday life, poverty and social exclusion are the primary ways in which the Roma are differentiated as a group separate from other Europeans. Members of majority groups commonly misattribute to Gypsy culture a range of negative characteristics—such as poor hygiene, illiteracy, dependence upon state aid, criminality, and begging—that are in fact rooted in poverty and oppression. Such descriptions have led to harmful practices such as the establishment of Gypsy crimes divisions in police departments, forced sterilizations of Roma women, denial of health care services, and limiting access to schooling for the youth.

In the past century, Roma groups throughout Europe faced persecution and genocide, changing socioeconomic conditions, and major shifts in political systems. Like the European Jews, Roma were targeted for extermination on the basis of ethnicity during the Nazi genocide. The Romani term *o Porrajmos* ("The Devouring") refers to the Roma Holocaust, but Roma from Eastern Europe strongly object to this term, which has sexual connotations in some dialects. More than 220,000 Roma—over one-quarter of all European Roma—were killed between 1933 and 1945. Nazi eugenics researchers deemed the Roma to be mentally unfit and genetically sick. From the mid-1930s, German racial hygiene laws forbade Roma from intermarriage with those identified as Aryans, and persecution intensified in 1938 with Nazi decrees to deport Roma and Sinti from German lands. Roma in Germany and other Axis countries were sent to forced labor and concentration camps and were executed in large numbers. The practice of forcibly sterilizing Roma women also began during this time, a human rights abuse that persists in some countries today, according to the Center for Reproductive Rights. Concentration camp survivors were reluctant to discuss their experiences, and scholars of the Nazi atrocities against the Roma only began to publish their research in the 1990s. Unfortunately, the Nazi genocide of the Roma has received relatively little attention, and repatriations and recognition for Roma survivors have been slow in coming.

In Central and Eastern Europe, the Roma way of life changed dramatically during the state socialist era. Initially, Communist Party officials in many countries considered the Roma to be a group outside the class system and excluded them from land redistribution, citizenship papers, and formal employment in state firms. By the late 1950s, however, officials attempted to integrate the Roma as workers. Many were introduced into the industrial work force for the first time and there was a corresponding move from rural, isolated areas to the city. While some policies of the state socialist period resulted in far greater inclusion of the Roma in education and formal employment, other policies prohibited them from organizing as an ethnic group to preserve Romani language and culture. When state socialism ended, Roma lost their jobs, and poverty and discrimination are critical problems.

Many Roma live in isolated settlements and have a much lower standard of living than their majority counterparts. A recent Hungarian public health survey published by Zsigmond Kósa, for example, examined environmental indicators including access to indoor plumbing and distance from waste dumps and found that Roma neighborhoods have significantly less infrastructure and more environmental hazards than non-Roma ones. Although tens of thousands of Bulgarian Roma have lived in Sofia's Fakulteta district since the late 1940s, the neighborhood has no access to sewerage and little access to electricity. In several places in eastern Slovakia, Roma were evicted from the town centers and forced to resettle in abandoned industrial areas and outlying woodlands, where they are exposed to toxic waste dumps and are vulnerable to flooding. Roma families displaced by the war in Kosovo were moved to refugee camps in Mitrovica built on a former lead mine, exposing hundreds of people to toxic heavy metals.

Throughout Europe, the Roma fall disproportionately in the lower socioeconomic status. Like any other social group, the Roma comprise members of different socioeconomic classes. The elite are educated intellectuals, business people, nongovernmental leaders, and politicians who may not be recognizable to the broader society as Roma. The middle class is made up of those Roma who have been able to maintain employment and, in Central and Eastern Europe, stayed in the system after the 1989 regime change that left most unemployed. For example, Kalderash metalworkers in Russia and the former Soviet Union translated their welding and metallurgy skills into a secure middle-class livelihood. The remainder of Roma are severely marginalized, undereducated, and unemployed. This marginalization is maintained because Roma youth have largely been excluded from the education system by being segregated into low-quality schools and classrooms or schools for the mentally disabled. They are routinely tracked into vocational schooling and prohibited from attending high-quality high schools. As such, there is a notable lack of Roma in higher education.

The Roma minority will play a significant role in the future of Europe because of its relative growth in birth rates. Like non-Roma women in Europe, contemporary Roma women generally are having fewer children than did their mothers and grandmothers. Nevertheless, Roma population growth remains positive at a moment when the birthrate of ethnic majority groups in most European countries is below replacement. On the one hand, this has led to demographic panics about an ever-larger Roma population. On the other hand, this reality leads humanitarian workers to stress the need for increased investment in the education and well-being of Roma youth.

Wherever they reside, those identified as Roma are subject to distrust, suspicion, and persecution from majority society. The 2009 European Union Minorities and Discrimination Survey commissioned by the European Union Agency for Fundamental Rights found that in a 12-month period, approximately 50 percent of Roma experienced some form of discrimination, one in four experienced a personal assault, and one in five were the victim of racially motivated harassment. At the same time, a very small percentage reported these attacks because they did not have confidence that reporting the crimes would change the situation. A 2008 European Commission "Eurobarometer" survey on discrimination found that intolerance of and violence toward Roma is on the rise. Roma communities in Italy, Hungary, and the Czech Republic have all been the recent victims of pogroms and violent attacks.

Much of the extreme prejudice against the Roma stems from their lack of a national homeland, a fact that perplexes members of majority populations who imagine the nation-state as an ethnically homogenous unit. In recent decades, however, new forms of Roma political mobilization appeared at the local, national, and international levels. Roma groups in some countries recognize a traditional leader (sometimes called a king or *vajda*), but there is no universal Roma leader. Local-level political organization may include traditional leaders, state-recognized minority representatives, Roma candidates for municipal offices, or civil organizations. Roma political leaders have sought national-level office as candidates for mainstream and Roma ethnic political parties in Hungary, Slovakia, Macedonia, and other countries.

Roma began organizing at the international level with the First World Romani Congress in 1971, and in subsequent years, Roma activists have formed international committees such as the European Roma and Travellers Forum of the Council of Europe. Since the population of the Roma in the European Union increased dramatically with the 2004 and 2007 expansions, there has been a proliferation of European-level programs, including the Decade for Roma Inclusion launched in 2005, the European Roma Information Office, and the European Roma Rights Center. Roma gained new political representation with the first two Roma Members for the European Parliament (MEPs), Livia Jaróka and Viktória Mohácsi of Hungary. Roma-led nongovernmental and grassroots organizations are growing in number, and there are greater resources at the international level for Roma organizations.

*Krista Harper and Andria Timmer*

## Further Reading

Cahn, Claude. *Roma Rights: Race, Justice, and Strategies for Equality.* New York: International Debate Education Association, 2002.

Crowe, David M. *A History of the Gypsies of Eastern Europe and Russia.* New York: St. Martin's Griffin, 1996.

Hancock, Ian. *We Are the Romani People.* Hertfordshire: University of Hertfordshire Press, 2003.

Ládanyi, János, and Iván Szelényi. *Patterns of Exclusion: Constructing Gypsy Ethnicity and the Making of an Underclass in Transitional Societies of Europe.* Boulder, CO: East European Monographs, 2006.

Okely, Judith. *The Traveller-Gypsy.* Cambridge: Cambridge University Press, 1983.

Ringold, Dena, Mitchell A. Orenstein, and Erika Wilkens. *Roma in an Expanding Europe: Breaking the Cycle of Poverty.* Washington, DC: The World Bank, 2005.

Stewart, Michael. *The Time of the Gypsies.* Boulder, CO: Westview Press, 1997.

Vermeersch, Peter. *The Romani Movement: Minority Politics and Ethnic Mobilization in Contemporary Central Europe.* New York: Berghahn Books, 2007.

## Romanians

Romanians are the dominant population of Romania. As of the 2002 census, Romanians represent 90 percent of a population of 22 million, the largest ethnic minorities being Hungarians (approximately 7%) and Roma. Significant Romanian diasporas exist in Italy, Spain, Germany, France, Israel, Canada, and the United States. Romanian is a Romance language, together with Spanish, Portuguese, French, and Italian, and is spoken by approximately 26 million people, of which 20 million live in Romania. Romanian is also the official language in the Republic of Moldova (known there as Moldovan) and Vojvodina (Serbia). Whereas the language differentiates Romania from its neighbors, the dominant Orthodox Christianity (87% of the population) provides connections with nearby countries such as Bulgaria, Ukraine, Russia, and Greece.

The origins of Romanians are intensely debated by historians. A point of view widely accepted by Romanian historians emphasizes the mixture of Romans and Dacians after the Second Dacian War (CE 105–106), when the Roman Empire conquered and administered Dacia until CE 271, when Aurelian ordered the withdrawal of Roman troops from this territory. The latter does not coincide with a total withdrawal of Roman colonizers as many had already formed families in Dacia. This theory finds support in the current structure of the Romanian language with a large Latin component, the geographical positioning

Festival in Secuiesc, Romania. (Corel)

of Romania that coincides with a vast territory of Dacia, and much archaeological evidence discovered in the last century. Following this track, the key figures for the early Romanian history are two Dacian leaders—Burebista, who unified the tribes around 60 BCE, and Decebalus, who resisted the Romans in their first war (CE 101–102)—and Trajan, the Roman emperor who conquered Dacia and started the colonization process.

A different perspective claims that Romanians formed south of the Danube and migrated to the current Romanian territory after the Hungarian and Slavic invasions in the mid-13th century. Proponents of this view point to the short-term colonization of Dacia by Romans (only 165 years), the long-lasting presence of Romans in the regions to south of the Danube, language commonalities between Albanian and Romanian languages, and the existence of populations sharing traits with Romanians (for example, Aromanians in the southern Balkans and Megleno-Romanians in Greece, Turkey, and Macedonia). However, this theory finds support neither in the medieval chronicles, which do not mention a migration from the Balkans, nor in the Hungarian chronicles that mention existing populations on the Romanian territory when they arrived. Moreover, the very few common words between Romanian and Albanian may indicate legacies from the Dacian language.

Until the mid-19th century Romanians lived in three principalities formed between the 12th and 14th centuries: the Romanian Country (Walachia), Moldova, and Transylvania (founded as Voievodat, became principality in 1541). The founding rulers—Basarab I in Walachia, Bogdan-Voda in Moldova—are key figures for early Romanian history. In Moldova, Stefan cel Mare (Steven the Great) is an emblematic ruler known for his military successes, churches, and monasteries. In Transylvania, Iancu de Hunedoara is known for his battles against Ottomans, the latter becoming suzerains of Transylvania in less than a century (1541) after Iancu's death. In Walachia, Mircea cel Batran (Mircea the Old), Vlad Tepes (Vlad the Impaler who inspired Stoker's Dracula character), and Mihai Viteazul (Michael the Brave) were the main leaders of the struggle against the Ottomans in the 14th through 16th centuries. The latter plays a prominent role in Romanian history as the first ruler to conquer and unify the three principalities for a few months in 1600. Transylvania becomes part of the Austrian Empire in the 17th century, whereas Walachia and Moldova are controlled from the 18th by rulers appointed by the Ottomans.

The period saw several upheavals. In 1784, a rebellion uniting Romanians, Hungarians, and Germans against feudal constraints in Transylvania was crushed. The 1821 Walachian uprising, though crushed, spelled the end of Ottoman appointed rulers. Revolution struck in 1848 in all three regions, against the Ottomans in Walachia, the Russians in Moldova, and the Habsburgs in Transylvania; the revolution failed in all three areas, though there was a short-lived independent government (1848–1849) in Walachia. In 1859, the so-called Small Unification brought Walachia and Moldova together, as nationalist leaders took advantage of the Paris Peace Treaty (1856) to elect the same leader,

Alexandru Ioan Cuza. The name of Romania was adopted for the newly founded country, and the country was officially recognized by all, including the Ottoman Empire in 1862. Starting in 1866, Romania was ruled by Carol I of Hohennzolern-Sigmaringen for 48 years (the longest period in Romanian history) and gained its independence after a war against the Ottomans (1877–1878), becoming a kingdom in 1881.

Romania's involvement in World War I on the winning side brings the unification of all the principalities of Walachia, Moldova, and Transylvania in 1918. After the death of King Carol I, King Ferdinand led the country until his death in 1927. This was followed by the regency of his nephew Mihai I (Michael I), preferred over Carol II, the son of Ferdinand. Carol II became king in 1930 and installed a dictatorship in 1938, banning political parties. In 1940, after a coup d'etat, the pro-German general Ion Antonescu (prime minister at that time) took control, installing King Michael I on the throne, and Romania joined World War II on Germany's side. This action resulted in territorial losses to the Union of Soviet Socialist Republics (Basarabia and Northern Bucovina—parts of Romanian Moldova). Romania changed sides on August 23, 1944, when Antonescu was dismissed by King Michael I and arrested. Michael was forced to abdicate in 1947, the year a republic was established; Communists, who held control from 1945, then achieved the power they would hold for almost half a century.

The medieval principalities were the settings for the early development of Romanian culture and traditions. In Transylvania, the developments followed a different track than in Moldova and Walachia, as the former was under Hungarian and Austrian influence intensely and from an early stage. The Christian faith of Romanians is linked with the process of Christianization initiated by about CE 250 by the Romans in Dacia (Dacians were initially polytheist). The archaeological evidence dating back into the 6th century appears to favor such a hypothesis. As none of the migrants entering Romanian territory were Christian, the continuity appears to make sense. As Romanians are the only Latin people to adopt Orthodoxy, their choice can be linked with the earlier organization and Christianization of Bulgarians and Russians, neighbors who could influence the religious development in Moldova and Walachia. There is clear evidence that Romanian spirituality was heavily influenced by the Orthodox world. During the 14th through 17th centuries, religious writings dominated the field of literature, and rulers of Moldova and Walachia built monasteries and churches that have lasted until today. The historical chronicle (*Letopisețul Țării Moldovei*) of Grigore Ureche was the most important document of the period; this work was continued in the beginning of the next century by Miron Costin and Ion Neculce. The cultural life in Walachia was complemented by Constantin Brancoveanu, known for the architectural style used for the buildings in his time. In the 18th century, Moldovan culture was synonymous with Dimitrie Cantemir, a Voivode of Moldova whose work encompassed a wide range of fields, including philosophy, history, linguistics, ethnography, and geography. His investigation of Romanian history was complemented by Latin works on Moldova and the rise and decline of the Ottoman Empire, republished in English, French, and German a few decades afterwards.

Romanians have long cultivated a multitude of customs, traditions, ballads, poems, and stories that relate to deep beliefs about relationships between people, love, hate, and fairy tale characters (kings, princesses, witches). Even today, Romanians maintain traditions related to specific periods of the year: Christmas carols, for example, or the custom of giving trinkets to ladies on March 1 in celebration of spring. "Miorita" is one of the famous ballads depicting pastoralism (inherited from Dacians) and portrays in a philosophical manner the life of a shepherd, full of symbols about life and death. Situated for centuries at the confluence of empires, the Romanians long traded with others. The main objects for exchange were animal products (including skins) and foodstuffs. In Transylvania, with its ethnic mixture of Romanians, Hungarians, and Germans, the latter organized fortress-cities that served as commercial centers. The principalities were hierarchically organized with a ruler and council of wealthy people (*boieri*) in charge of the political body, the Great Assembly. Each principality had its own territorial divisions, with specific names, where local rulers were installed. The oppression of the peasantry, which involved serfdom and even slavery, lasted until the 18th century in all three principalities under different names: *rumânie* in Walachia, *vecinie* in Moldova, and *iobăgie/şerbie* in Transylvania.

As borders changed dramatically in medieval times, the relationships with neighbors included peace and conflict. Moldova fought numerous wars with Ottomans and Poles, but enjoyed peaceful relations with Russia under Dimitrie Cantemir and Czar Peter I. Walachia fought the Ottomans, but intensified relations with Bulgarians, sharing a common state in the 11th century and fighting for their liberation in 1877–1878. Transylvania fought wars with Moldova and Walachia in different periods, but became part of the same country as soon as the situation allowed. Transylvania also witnessed the peaceful cohabitation of Romanians, Hungarians, and Germans until 1784, when representatives of all three populations participated in a short-lived upheaval against feudal constraints. Through the centuries Romania had separate territorial conflicts with Hungary and Russia, with gains and losses on both sides.

Romania has produced a number of important cultural figures, from the 19th century. This includes writers and poets like Vasile Alecsandri, Ion Creanga, Ioan Slavici, Ion Luca Caragiale, George Cosbuc, Mihai Eminescu (considered the national poet), Liviu Rebreanu, Mihail Sadoveanu Tudor Arghezi, George Bacovia, Tristan Tzara, Lucian Blaga, Mircea Eliade, Eugene Ionesco, and Marin Preda. Nicolae Grigorescu and Stefan Luchian are the founding fathers of modern Romanian painting. Ciprian Porumbescu and George Enescu are key names for Romanian music. Constantin Brancusi became an internationally known sculptor thanks to the appeal within his work to the primordial sources of popular culture, whereas Emil Cioran, Constantin Noica, and Petre Tutea were known for their philosophical writings all over the world.

Romanian Communism was characterized by nationalism and the personality cult of Ceausescu, whose absolute rule resembled that of Mao in China and Kim Il-Sung in North Korea. Communist rule brought heavy industry, relocations of people from rural to urban areas in order to decrease disparities, the leveling of interethnic relations, limited individual and collective rights, the monopoly of the state over production, and a one-party state. Romania was the only former Eastern bloc country that violently replaced the old rulers (thousands died in the streets) by condemning to death Ceausescu (1989). With no negotiated transition and no strong opposition in the beginning, the winners of the first free elections (1990) were former communists. Violence was used in the first years of the transition whenever Ion Iliescu, the elected president, faced opposition on the streets or by the prime minister. The first democratic government was formed only after 1996, too late to meet the NATO accession requirements. Romania joined NATO in 2002 and the European Union in 2007, missing the first chance for accession in 2004 because of slow or nonexistent reforms in crucial sectors such as justice, environment, and competition. The slow democratization process was finalized around 2000, with most of the institutions in place and democratic benchmarks on the right track. The fall of communism allowed ethnic minorities to seek representation and collective rights. Hungarians organized and their party has succeeded in every election starting in 1992, being twice in the coalition government (1996 and 2004) and once having a separate agreement with the governing coalition (2000). The right to education at all levels in the Hungarian language represents a major gain for this ethnic group; they aim to obtain the right to autonomy in the counties in which they represent the majority. Romania provides the chance for 18 other ethnic minorities to elect one representative each in the Chamber of Deputies through a special quota for representation. Although Romania is the seventh most populous member state in the EU and the ninth largest territory, the country faces serious demographic challenges imposed by migration and low birth rates. In the post-EU accession period approximately 3 million Romanians fled the country for better-paid jobs abroad; recently Romanian immigrants have come into conflict with locals in Italy.

*Sergiu Gherghina*

## Further Reading

Barbu, Daniel. *Firea romanilor* (*The Features of Romanians*). Bucharest: Nemira, 2000.

Calinescu, George. *Istoria literaturii romane de la origini pana in prezent* (*The History of Romanian Literature from Its Origins until Present*). Bucharest: Minerva, 1985.

Deletant, Dennis, et al. *Istoria Romaniei* (*The History of Romania*). Bucharest: Editura Enciclopedica, 1998.

Gallagher, Tom. *The Theft of a Nation: Romania since Communism*. London: C. Hurst, 2005.

Giurescu, Constantin C. *Istoria Romanilor* (*The History of Romanians*). Bucharest: All, 2008.

Stowe, Debbie. *Romania—Culture Smart! A Quick Guide to Customs and Etiquette*. New York: Random House, 2008.

Treptow, Kurt. *Tradition and Modernity in Romanian Culture and Civilization*. Iasi: Center for Romanian Studies, 2002.

Verdery, Katherine. *National Ideology under Socialism: Identity and Cultural Politics in Ceausescu's Romania*. Berkeley and Los Angeles: University of California Press, 1991.

# Romansh

The Romansh are speakers of the Romansh language (also: Rumantsch, Roman(s)ch, Rh(a)eto-Romance) in Switzerland. They are the smallest of Switzerland's four linguistic groups, making up about 0.5 percent (35,095) of the nation's population. Most reside in Grisons (Graubünden), a trilingual canton in the southeast where they constitute 14.5 percent of the population (68.3% speak German as a first language and 10.2% Italian). The Romansh can be divided in five subgroups based on written forms: the three Rhine idioms Sursilvan, Sutsilvan, and Surmiran and the two Engadine or Ladin idioms, Puter and Vallader. Today all Romansh are at least bilingual (Romansh, German). About two-thirds of them are Roman Catholic (especially Sursilvans) with the remainder Protestants (especially Engadines). The Romansh do not view themselves as an ethnic group; like other Swiss populations, the Romansh identify themselves primarily on the basis of geopolitical origins and dialect.

The Romansh are descendants of Raetic and Celtic people who were Romanized in the wake of conquest by Drusus and Tiberius in 15 BCE. Romansh, a neo-Latin language, developed out of the Vulgar Latin language spoken during Roman rule. Under the Romans the Province of Raetia (Raetia prima, with the capital at Chur, and Raetia secunda, with the capital at Augsburg) reached from Regensburg to Trient and from Konstanz to Kufstein. The invasion of Germanic peoples (Alemanni and Bavarii) began in the third century. Raetia secunda was Germanized during the 5th century. After the fall of the Western Roman Empire and the rise of the Osthrogoths (493–536/7), Raetia prima became part of the Frankish Empire and was called Raetia Curiensis (Churrätien). With political and ecclesiastic reorganizations, there emerged a German-speaking dominant class. Later, the immigration of German-speaking Walser people from the late 13th century reduced the Romansh territory. In the Free State of the Three Leagues (Freistaat Gemeiner Drei Bünde), established in 1524, German definitely replaced Latin as the official written language of government, while Romansh remained the language of the populace.

The continuous diminution of the Romansh territory and people slowed in the 16th century with the development of a literary tradition, primarily built on religious texts inspired by the Reformation and Counter-Reformation. However, given its religious, political, and topographical divergences the Romansh language was already written in different idioms. The decline of Romansh continued in the 19th century with industrialization, tourism, and mobility. The political incorporation of Grisons in the Swiss Confederation in 1803 reinforced the influence of the German language. In the second half of the 19th century a "Romansh Renaissance" emerged, as some intellectuals began to campaign for the preservation of the threatened Romansh language and culture, founding regional language-maintenance organizations. In 1919 they established the Romansh umbrella organization Lia Rumantscha. The claim for recognition as the fourth national language of Switzerland became urgent when Italian Irredentists argued that Romansh was an Italian dialect, meaning that Romansh- and Italian-speaking Grisons as well as the residents of Italian-speaking Ticino should be considered as part of Italy. In 1938 nearly 92 percent of the Swiss (male) voters approved Romansh as national language, along with German, French, and Italian.

Living in the rural and alpine regions of Grisons, most Romansh gained a livelihood as peasants and craftsmen until the 19th century; emigration and activity associated with commercial traffic through passes in the Alps were also important sources of income. With the beginning of alpine tourism, the service sector expanded, becoming today's most important economic sector. Nowadays tourism professionals promote Grisons as the "holiday-corner of Switzerland" and Romansh as a "unique selling proposition."

The tradition of political and legal communal autonomy fostered strong, local cultural identities in Grisons, a tendency compounded by religious, linguistic, and topographic barriers to interaction. The resulting variations in ecclesiastical and popular traditions were documented by Casper Decurtins in *Rätoromanische Chrestomathie* (1896–1919), the most important collection of Romansh cultural history and folklore. And since 1939, an excellent source of Romansh language and culture has been the *Dicziunari Rumantsch Grischun*, one of the four national dictionaries of Switzerland, which document the spoken and written language and the (material) culture of the four Swiss language regions.

Today also the remotest alpine valleys and Romansh villages are connected with the world, and cultural life has changed. But in some regions some ancient customs are still (or again) cultivated. Some still banish winter by throwing wooden fire-discs (*trer schibettas*) or cowbells (*Chalandamarz*) and Catholic villages cultivate processions and (culinary) celebrations of their local patron saint (*Perdonanza*). As in other rural regions, Romansh villages have a strongly organized social life, particularly youth associations and choral, music, drama, and sports societies.

As the population of Grisons shares the culture of residents of other alpine regions, the only exclusive Romansh cultural trait is the Romansh language. A considerable quantity of literature has been written since the "Romansh Renaissance." The traditional local and peasant literature served primarily as an instrument in the struggle for language maintenance and as the local literature for school and population. Recent decades have seen the emergence of more literary forms of the language, though such efforts contend with small numbers of readers and their preference of their regional written Romansh as well as the availability of a vast German-language literature.

Half of the population of Grisons spoke Romansh until the middle of the 19th century. Nevertheless Romansh was considered as a crude peasant language and an obstacle to economic and cultural development. German was and remains the language of professional and social advancement. Today the stereotype of the backward Romansh has diminished. Official recognition of multilingualism valorizes Romansh, but German remains the dominant language.

In the 1970s and 1980s, political efforts were made to provide a sound basis for the maintenance of this endangered language. National and cantonal subventions for the Romansh umbrella organization (Lia Rumantscha) were augmented substantially. Since 1996 Romansh is not only a national language but also a semi-official language of Switzerland. Grisons has enforced the legal status of Romansh with a language law (2008), and a national language law will be enacted in 2010. The Romansh have a full-time radio channel in their mother tongue and can see about 90 minutes a week of Romansh broadcasting on public television. A small Romansh daily newspaper is published, and recently a publishing house for Romansh literature has been started.

An important challenge for the Romansh today is the new supraregional written variety initiated by the Lia Rumantscha; Rumantsch Grischun was created in 1982 on the basis of the three major written Romansh varieties in order to facilitate the use of Romansh in the public domain. Rumantsch Grischun now serves as the official language of national and cantonal administration, and it will replace the regional varieties in Romansh primary schools. Many Romansh object to it as an artificial language without history,

tradition, or soul. Given the expansion of foreign language instruction in Swiss primary schools, above all of English, the introduction of this new language instead of the familiar regional varieties creates further concerns in Romansh schools.

Demographic trends suggest that the decline of the Romansh population has not abated. Many young Romansh emigrate for education and work opportunities. Recently efforts have been made to support the language among children in the Romansh diaspora, but the success of these efforts seems unlikely.

*Renata Coray*

## Further Reading

Billigmeier, Robert H. *A Crisis in Swiss Pluralism*. The Hague: Mouton, 1979.

Coray, Renata. *Von der Mumma Romontscha zum Retortenbaby Rumantsch Grischun. Rätoromanische Sprachmythen* (*From Romansh Mother to Test Tube Baby Rumansh Grischum: Romansh Language Myths*). Chur: Bündner Monatsblatt Verlag Desertina, 2008.

Gross, Manfred, ed. *Romansh Facts and Figures*. 2nd revised edition. Chur: Lia Rumantscha, 2004.

Grünert, Matthias, et al. *Das Funktionieren der Dreisprachigkeit im Kanton Graubünden* (*Functioning of Trilingualism in the Canton of Grisons*). Tübingen/Basel: Romanica Helvetica 127, 2008.

# Russians

Russians (*русские* or *russkie* in Russian) are the dominant ethnic population in the Russian Federation, the world's largest state. According to the 2002 census, ethnic Russians represent 79.8 percent

(115,889,107) of the country's population. Outside of Russia, the largest concentrations of ethnic Russians are found in the surrounding republics that were part of the Soviet Union until its dissolution in 1991; in terms of absolute numbers, the largest concentrations of Russians are found in Ukraine (over 8 million) and Kazakhstan (nearly 4 million). However, at the time of the dissolution of the Soviet Union, ethnic Russians and Russian-speakers had become near majorities in many neighboring regions or countries. Additionally, the worldwide Russian diaspora numbers in the millions, with the largest numbers found in the United States and Canada. The Russian Orthodox Church remains the largest religious congregation in Russia, though many are not observant or celebrate other faiths. Russian, an Eastern Slavic tongue, is the official language of the Russian Federation.

The ancient Slavs colonized vast tracts of Europe, leaving little trace of the languages spoken there prior to their arrival. Linguists have suggested that the word "Slav" originated from the word *slovo* or "speech." Slavs would come to predominate across much of Europe before pushing farther northwards and eastwards into what is now Russia. The genesis of the Russian ethnic identity can be traced back to Kievan Rus. This political entity is historically contested as it is seen as the ancestral root of not only the Russian nation, but also the Ukrainian, Belarusian, and often disputed Rusyn identities. The creation of a political entity at the end of the first millennium permitted the promotion and consolidation of a common identity,

A Russian woman places a candle during a Christmas service in the Christ the Savior Cathedral in Moscow on January 7, 2002. (AP/Wide World Photos)

one that rose above the tribal identities and was more constrained than the overarching Slavic identity. In this period the Slavic Rus pushed deep into what is now central and northern Russia, displacing or assimilating the indigenous Finno-Ugrian peoples and establishing a "Russian land" (Русьская земля referring to the lands of Rus, not the modern Russia). This political consolidation was buttressed by the arrival of Christianity, which provided not only a written literature but also access to a new religious ideology encouraging ethnic consolidation.

One of the oldest undisputed Eastern Slavic written sources, *The Primary Chronicle*, recounts the establishment of a dynasty of princes that would rule in Rus and the successor principalities until the end of the 16th century. Here we read that Varangians (Norse Vikings) under the leadership of Rurik were invited to rule over Novgorod in 862 and their descendants would come to rule over Kiev and a series of cities stretching from Novgorod to Kiev. Ninth-century annals from Western Europe recount the arrival of emissaries from "Rhos" who are Swedes; and 10th-century treaties drawn up between the "Rus" and Byzantium were signed by warriors with Scandinavian names who were from the "land of the Rus." By the end of the 9th century, a large territory was politically united under the rule of a noble line that quickly assimilated as Slavic speakers. Slavic farmers would follow the warriors and merchants, and Slavic Rus came to predominate linguistically and ethnically over an ever-larger territory.

Kievan Rus extended its power and territory by subduing neighboring tribes, exacting tribute and soldiers to help the conquerors lead expeditions farther afield. At the core of Kievan Rus was the territory surrounding Kiev, inner Rus. The main settlement in the northern territories of Rus was Novgorod ("New City") and Pskov. Archaeological evidence suggests that fortified settlements were established in scattered locations through the northern forests. Slavs and Scandinavians vied for control of the region, seeking to monopolize the collection of tribute and trade from the peoples inhabiting the forest. Kiev extended its control over these northern Slavic cities and tribes in the 10th century.

Under the rule of Vladimir or Volodymyr, who reigned from 980–1015, Rus reached its apogee, but tribal identities remained. Seemingly to foster a common identity, Vladimir attempted to establish a cult that would transcend tribal identities and customs. Vladimir later reconsidered these policies. Legend has Vladimir sending out emissaries to collect information on the various faiths (Christianity Eastern and Western, Judaism and Islam), and according to tradition he chose to accept Orthodoxy as the faith of Kievan Rus through his baptism in 988.

The rise of a centralized, Orthodox state promoted a common culture. In accepting Orthodoxy, Kievan Rus gained literacy. The alphabet that developed in the southern Slavic territories was transferred to Rus. Initially conducted in Slavonic, the liturgy used in the churches of Russia gradually converged with the local dialect to become Old Russian. Christianity promoted a common ethnic identity: the *Sermon on Law and Grace* penned by Ilarion, the first metropolitan from Rus appointed in 1051, describes how the spread of Christianity promoted common symbols among the Rus. The religious zeal of converts also led to the settlement of new territories. Russian monks pushed far northward, establishing monasteries in distant lands, as far as the borders of the Arctic Ocean (White Sea). The start of the second millennium was marked by a period of global warming, facilitating the spread of farmers northward, and the forest would have provided greater protection against the marauding warriors of the steppe to the south of Kiev and central Rus. Religious and ecological forces promoted a growing Slavic population in northern territories, a population with a Rus identity, speaking a language that they called "Rusian" (руський or руский), and sharing a common faith.

The Mongol invasions of Rus and sacking of Kiev in 1240 ended the preeminence of Kiev. The western territories of Rus would fall under the domination of western states: the Lithuanians, the Poles, and finally the Austro-Hungarian Empire. This division of the Eastern Slavs led to linguistic divergence, splitting the Rus into distinct languages and national identities. Though dialectical differences existed between the central Rus territories and the north where the language was influenced by the languages of the neighboring Finno-Ugrian tribes, the splitting of western Rus from the east would lead to the emergence of distinct Ukrainian and Belorussian languages as well as religious schisms.

The shaping of the Russian ethnos is closely tied to the conquests of the princes of Moscow. A minor settlement before the Mongol invasions, Moscow gained its first Rurik prince when Daniil, son of Alexander Nevsky, settled in Moscow. As the seat of the metropolitan and later patriarch and as a growing principality, Moscow would eventually lay claim to all the territories of Rus. In the 15th century, Moscow began conquering neighboring principalities, notably Novgorod, and Muscovy soon ruled over much of the former lands of northern and eastern Rus. With the marriage of the prince of Moscow to Sophia, last princess of Constantinople, Moscow princes claimed the title of Caesar (czar or tsar), claiming Moscow would be the third and final Rome. Subsequent conquests increased the territory of the Russian Empire over the Urals all the way to the Pacific Ocean and down to the Caucasus Mountains and the Black Sea. Peasants would follow, spreading Russians across Siberia and far to the south. The Russian Empire integrated much of the western lands of Rus in the 18th century.

Despite vigorous Russification policies, older ethnic and cultural diversity remained and new hybrid identities emerged across the Empire. Dozens of communities that are classified as Russian could be defined as separate ethnic groups. These include Russian Cossacks (казаки or *kazaki*); the Pomory (Поморы), descendants of settlers from Novgorod who established themselves in the Russian far north prior to Moscow's conquest of Novgorod; and the Jakutjane (Якутяне), who are descended from ethnic Russians and the indigenous Sakha of the Russian far east. Though such groups tend to be small and dispersed, they do highlight the heterogeneity that nonetheless exists under the Russian heading.

The rise of Peter the Great and the Romanov dynasty consolidated tsarist power and led to the emergence of modern Russian culture. Peter spearheaded the modernization of the empire, a policy pursued by later leaders. Under Peter, a Russian Navy was established and the nobility was forced to adopt Western European dress and manners, notably in shaving off their beards, in the 18th century. Peter oversaw construction of his new capital, St. Petersburg, a city built using modern Western European design and aesthetics. In the 19th century, Russian authors developed a modern literary language and tradition, starting with Pushkin and reaching a crescendo with such authors as Lev Tolstoy and Fyodor Dostoyevsky. Likewise, composers and directors wrote and staged Russian-language operas and Russian ballet performances as well as world-renowned symphonies. These works became the basis of a standardized language and cultural tradition that would be taught in schools in the 20th century. Nonetheless, while a modern Russian identity was emerging, a rich cultural tradition of popular music, folklore, and folkways continued in the villages and countryside, where more than 90 percent of the population lived. Local communities participated in a shared culture, with regional variations, which included folk tales, dances, and popular religious beliefs that were a syncretism of ancient pagan traditions and popular Orthodox Christianity. At the same time localities were linked to Russian identity because significant moments of the history of Rus were preserved in *byliny* (былины), Russian epic poems.

After the Bolshevik Revolution of 1917, the newly created Soviet Union promoted Russian language and culture through policy and the movement of ethnic Russians into new territories across the Soviet Union. The resulting Russian diaspora remains to the present: approximately 25 millions Russians inhabit Ukraine, Kazakhstan, Belarus, and the other neighboring independent states that were formerly republics in the Soviet Union. During Soviet times, the Russian language gained its greatest reach. Promoted as an international language, the language of national friendship and brotherhood, Russian was spoken by half of the population as a mother tongue according to the 1989 census and was taught as a second language across the Soviet Union and in many of the Communist satellite states of the Eastern bloc. Though attempts to promote the Russian language as a compulsory second language in Soviet schools met with limited success, at the height of Soviet power at least an additional 100 million people spoke some Russian as a second language in the Soviet Union, Europe, and elsewhere.

The Soviet Union transformed the countryside, resulting in a largely urban Russian population. Both in Russia and in the diaspora, ethnic Russians are concentrated in cities. In the Russian Federation, close to 77 percent of all ethnic Russians live in urban areas as opposed to 73 percent of the population of the Russian Federation. Likewise, in the former states of the Soviet Union ethnic Russians are concentrated in industrial and urban centers. The ethnic landscape of the Russian Federation is being transformed as some ethnicities have higher birthrates and consequently younger and growing populations, while others are declining both in

## Soviet Policy on Nationality and Ethnicity

In the 1920s, the Bolsheviks set out on a radical path of nation-building and political reorganization within a federal system. Large non-Russian populations were recognized as nations and became republics, while smaller groups were deemed ethnicities and granted language and cultural rights within territorial and political entities that included autonomous ethnic provinces (oblasts) and regions. In this euphoric period of nation-building, alphabets were invented for languages, literatures encouraged, and schools and other institutions established in ethnic autonomous regions to promote indigenous cultures. Though the Soviet Union's 1924 constitution embraced the Wilsonian ideal of national self-determination, the Communist Party nonetheless was never divided along ethnic lines, and power remained firmly centralized in Moscow. The progressive policies of the 1920s were followed by repression, including the forced relocation of millions, in the 1930s. Later, the push toward industrialization, along with the Communist Party's battle against the perceived dangers of petty-bourgeois nationalism, only exacerbated these demographic shifts as new policies favored ethnic Russians and Russian language and culture.

*Michel Bouchard*

terms of their absolute numbers and relative importance. Concurrently, internal migration within the Russian Federation is favoring large urban centers and central Russia to the detriment of the Russian Far East and other economically peripheral regions of Russia.

Also notable is growing immigration to Russia, with the majority (96% in 2008) of migrants coming from former Soviet republics. While some of the migrants are ethnic Russians, they include many who are neither Russian nor Slavic. This influx of groups, along with growing numbers of ultraconservatives and neo-Nazis in the Russian Federation, has led to ethnic conflict, with visible minorities being targeted for attack. While the Russian Federation must deal with the

rise of very conservative and aggressive forms of Russian nationalism, ethnic Russians in turn must negotiate with political forces in other states as they press for their rights. Quite often these center on whether the Russian language should be an official state language (debated in Ukraine) or whether there should be Russian-language schools (debated in the Baltic states of Estonia and Latvia).

With the fall of the Soviet Union in 1991, a veritable 20th-century empire, Russians saw themselves as losing global prestige. Successor states such as Estonia and Latvia soon dropped the Russian language as a compulsory subject in schools and required ethnic Russian and Russian-speaking minorities to learn their respective national languages. The 1990s in Russia were marked by economic and social dislocation. The economic turmoil of this period—hyperinflation, rising unemployment, the inability of business and the state to pay salaries and pensions and a reliance on barter and individuals producing what they could to survive—resulted in high death rates and low birthrates among ethnic Russians. Though the symptoms were starting to appear in the latter years of the Soviet Union, social ills such as rising alcoholism and drug abuse contributed to the higher mortality of Russians across post-Soviet states. Other Soviet legacies included ecological degradation and the lack of viability of entire industrial sectors and cities. That and rising criminality and corruption called into question the long-term prospects of the Russian Federation and the very future of Russians themselves. However, Russia's abundant natural resources together with rising commodity prices fueled a growing economy in the first decade of the second millennium. Russians felt a growing national pride and described the country as having "risen from its knees" on the world stage.

Following the collapse of the Soviet Union, old identities had to be either jettisoned or reworked. Soviet identity was quickly set aside, even by fervent Communists, as a new Russian state and ethnic identity emerged. Central to this identity was the growing preeminence of Russian Orthodoxy. Though the Russian Federation is multiethnic and the Russian Orthodox Church is but one of a number of religious faiths given official recognition, the Russian Orthodox Church has been growing in importance, with old churches being restored and new churches being built. Likewise, large numbers of Russians have been baptized and politicians have been visibly demonstrating their Orthodox faith. Nonetheless, there has also been a growth in conversion to Protestantism in Russia as missionaries seek converts in the wake of the Soviet collapse.

This has led to conflict as the church has sought the support of the state in curbing the influx of foreign missionaries and new churches within the federation. Similar struggles were under way elsewhere as people worked to reconcile the Soviet past. Typical of this process was the selection of a new national anthem. In the 1990s, under President Boris Yeltsin, a new hymn was selected with no lyrics. Then, under Putin, the Soviet anthem's melody was chosen as the new national hymn and the lyrics of the old Soviet hymn reworked. A new Russian national identity is therefore emerging that integrates Soviet history into Russia's self-proclaimed thousand-year history.

Along with the willingness to incorporate old Soviet symbols into the new Russian Federation, there has been a growing centralization of a vertical power whereby under the banner of sovereign-democracy the state administration has been actively managing democracy and the media. Opposition parties have been marginalized and the major media, notably television, has come under state control as Russia's national television stations are either under state ownership or owned by state-controlled corporations. The short-lived war against Georgia in 2008 also highlighted the Russian Federation's willingness to use military force to achieve political ends.

*Michel Bouchard*

## Further Reading

Barford, P. M. *The Early Slavs: Culture and Society in Early Medieval Eastern Europe*. London: British Museum Press, 2001.

Dolukhanov, Pavel M. *The Early Slavs: Eastern Europe from the Initial Settlement to the Kievan Rus*. New York: Longman, 1996.

Hosking, Geoffrey. *Russia: People and Empire, 1552–1917*. Cambridge: Harvard University Press, 1997.

# S

## Saami

The Saami (sometimes spelled Sámi or Sami, in earlier literature known as Lapps or Finns, terms also used by their Scandinavian neighbors in a rather derogatory manner) are an indigenous people and an ethnic minority living in the northern parts of Norway, Sweden, and Finland and on the Kola Peninsula of Russia. The Saami refer to their traditional homeland as *Sápmi*. This settlement area covers the coastal and inland parts of northern Norway, the inland parts of northern Sweden, the northernmost part of Finland, and most of the Kola Peninsula. Only in a few municipalities within this area do they form a majority, however. During the postwar era a relatively large number have emigrated to the south, mainly to the capital areas of the Nordic countries. Forms of public registration vary, so their number can only be estimated, but most sources operate with 40,000–50,000 Saami in Norway, 15,000–20,000 in Sweden, 7,000–8,000 in Finland, and close to 2,000 in Russia, for a total population of 65,000–80,000. Acculturation processes and assimilation policies over a long period caused many Saami to identify themselves as mixed or as belonging to the majority, but some have in recent years taken part in an ethnopolitical revitalization process and come to embrace a Saami identity. The Saami language belongs to the Finno-Ugric family and is completely different from Norwegian, Swedish, and Russian but is related to Finnish. The total number of Saami speakers has not been registered, but may be estimated at 40,000–50,000. As many as 90 percent of them speak North Saami, which means that a number of the smaller dialects are in danger of extinction. State borders cut across the language boundaries and separate language communities. Those Saami who profess a faith typically adhere to Lutheranism.

The origin of the Saami is lost in the mist of history. Their ancestors may have been present in the Fenno-Scandic area since the Stone Age some 6,000–8,000 years ago and are believed to have immigrated from the east, but as a people with a distinct language the Saami seem to have originated during the last millennium BCE, when they came in contact with other peoples to the south and the east with contrasting cultural repertoires (language), social organization (chiefdoms) and ecological adaptations (agriculture). The oldest written firsthand source (CE 890) tells about a peripatetic hunting people with a few domesticated reindeer used for transport and as decoy animals in hunting. By the end of the Middle Ages, when they had been subject to heavy taxation by the state powers of the time (Denmark, Sweden, and Russia), their extensive hunting activities changed to a livelihood based on nomadic reindeer herding, and, on the Norwegian coast and fiord

Saami woman feeding a reindeer in Finland. (PhotoDisc, Inc.)

areas, to fishing and farming like their Norwegian neighbors. During the 18th century they lost the ownership of their farm land and became tenants. In the 19th century, governments in Sweden and Norway declared the reindeer pasture areas ownerless property (*terra nullius*) and consequently state owned, but without negotiating any treaty agreement. In addition, the closing of state borders prohibited access to some of their traditional pasture areas.

The pre-Christian Saami religion worshipped a number of male and female deities believed to control forces in nature and protect humans. The shaman (*noai'de*) had a central role in sustaining the spiritual relationship to nature, ancestors, and gods, in predicting future events, and so forth. Christian missionaries in the 17th and 18th centuries managed to convert the Saami to Christianity, and their

ancient religion was suppressed and went into hiding or oblivion. A religious movement called Laestadianism spread to most parts of Sápmi during the second half of the 19th century with a gospel of renunciation of things of the world, and particularly renouncing the use of alcohol, encouraging repentance of sins, and enacting the followers' obligation of mutual forgiveness. The revivalist movement appealed not only to Saami, but also to Kvens (people of Finnish ancestry) and even to parts of the majority peasantry.

The Saami are commonly associated with reindeer pastoralism, but fewer than 10 percent are actually herders. In Norway reindeer nomadism is characterized by the seasonal movements from the inland to the coast in spring and back again in the autumn, and in Sweden between the winter pastures in the lowlands in the east and the summer pastures in the mountains. In both countries reindeer breeding is a Saami privilege, but in Finland and on the Kola it is also practiced by neighboring peoples. Sedentary Saami traditionally practice a mixed economy of fishing and farming and in later years a whole range of other occupations as well.

A governmental policy of assimilation was initiated around the middle of the 19th century as a conscious effort to eradicate Saami culture and language. This policy was particularly efficient in Norway, where the political and cultural élite of the time was aiming to create an independent nation-state (Norway was in a union with Sweden from 1814 to 1905). The dominant instrument of the assimilation policy was the school system, which prohibited the use of the Saami language and excluded knowledge of Saami culture and history from its curriculum. According to the social Darwinism prevalent at the time, reindeer nomadism was considered a culture in decline and doomed to disappear.

Over the last 50 years an ethnopolitical movement has swept over Sápmi and engendered cultural revitalization and a stronger self-consciousness. The conflict over the damming of the Alta River in Norway (1979–1981) attracted international attention and marks the start of a new era when the Saamis' status as an indigenous people has been achieved, as manifested in a growing space for self-government. Saami parliaments have been established in the three Nordic countries, with a predominant role as advisers to the governments on Saami issues. Land rights have also to some extent been recognized, but this development has caused some protest from the majority, claiming equal rights for all citizens and no ethnic privileges.

*Trond Thuen*

## Further Reading

Gaski, Harald, ed. *Sami Culture in a New Era. The Norwegian Sami Experience.* Seattle: University of Washington Press, 1997.

Lehtola, Veli-Pekka. *The Sámi People. Traditions in Transition.* Fairbanks: University of Alaska Press, 2004.

Paine, Robert. *Herds of the Tundra. A Portrait of Saami Reindeer Pastoralism.* Washington: Smithsonian Institution Press, 1994.

Paine, Robert. *Camps of the Tundra. Politics through Reindeer among Saami Pastoralists.* Oslo: Institute for Comparative Research in Human Culture, 2009.

Svensson, Tom G. *The Sámi and Their Land.* Oslo: Novus forlag/The Institute for Comparative Research in Human Culture, 1997.

Thuen, Trond. *Quest for Equity. Norway and the Saami Challenge.* St. John's: ISER Books, 1995.

## Sardinians

Sardinians constitute the majority of inhabitants of Sardinia, the second-largest island of the Mediterranean Sea, with a surface area of 9,301 square miles (24,090 square kilometers). The resident population is 1,665,617 (2008); the main urban centers are Cagliari, the regional capital, with 158,041 inhabitants, and Sassari, with 129,086. Population density is historically lower here than in the rest of Italy, with 68 inhabitants per square kilometer versus 189. It is difficult to establish the size of the Sardinian diaspora in the world. According to regional government estimates, as many as 600,000 Sardinians may have emigrated from the end of the 19th century to the present (2009). The majority of these, approximately 350,000, moved to the Italian peninsula, but there are also large communities of Sardinians in France, Germany, Switzerland, and Belgium. In the rest of the world the biggest community is found in Argentina, with smaller ones in North America and Australia. As elsewhere in Italy, the main religion in Sardinia is Roman Catholicism. It is not easy to define the characteristics of Sardinians as an ethnic group, but certainly the common linguistic tradition (both Sardinian and Italian are spoken) and insularity are two crucial elements.

According to genetic evidence and population models, Sardinia's original population came from the Italian mainland and Greece, which in turn moved from the Middle East and Greece. The earliest settlements date from 6,000 to 2,800 BCE, in the Neolithic. The Nuragic civilization prospered between the Neolithic age and Bronze Age, 1800–238 BCE. Nuraghi are megalithic edifices in the shape of truncated conical towers, made with large stones and a false-cupola vault. Around these structures, often very large and consisting of various sections, were originally built villages, with dwellings in the form of stone huts. This civilization left a deep mark on the territory: there are currently approximately 7,000 nuraghi still visible, in various states of preservation. The nuraghe of Barumini, discovered by the Sardinian archaeologist Giovanni Lilliu, was added to the UNESCO World Heritage Site list in 1997.

Sardinia was subsequently colonized by several civilizations, including the Phoenicians and Carthaginians (800–238 BCE),

Rome (238–467 BCE), and the Vandals. Christianity came to the island in the 6th century with the Byzantines, who ruled until CE 1000. In response to repeated attacks from North Africa, the head of the Byzantine administration (the so-called "judge") delegated power to four lieutenants. By the 9th century, the leaders in Cagliari, Arborea, Logudoro, and Gallura had become kings (*judikes* in Sardinian). In these sovereign states, the king did not transfer power to heirs and the populace influenced government through popular assemblies. This phase ended with the Pisan dominion, and subsequently, Aragonese and Spanish rule (1326–1718). In 1847 Sardinia was admitted to the peninsula and became part of the Italian state. The Italian Kingdom was proclaimed in 1861.

It is difficult to conceive of Sardinian culture as a homogenous whole, despite the region's insularity and its unique history. It is, however, possible to highlight some distinctive themes in its popular culture. In the field of music, for example, this is the case with the *launeddas*, a woodwind instrument consisting of three pipes, played in accompaniment to religious processions and dances. The *canto a tenore* is a type of polyphonic folk singing with four male voices; it was made part of the UNESCO World Heritage Site list in 2005. Sardinian popular religiosity and its rituality are characterized by several original elements interwoven with pre-Christian as well as more recent Spanish borrowings. The annual religious cycle of celebrations is still observed throughout the island and includes Carnival, Holy Week, patron saint feasts in rural shrines, and sea processions in fishing communities' feasts.

Sardinia's population is bilingual: the national language, Italian, which is the language of institutional education and public administration, coexists with the Sardinian language (Sardo) in all its varieties. Thanks to the extensive work of the linguist Max Leopold Wagner, Sardo is considered a Romance language like Italian, French, Spanish, and Portuguese. The Sardinian language originated in the third century BCE following the Roman conquest, and some of its variants still show original Latin elements. The variants are specifically associated with location: the Logudorese variant is spoken in the north, the Barbaricino in the center, and the Campidanese in the south. Within main language groups are numerous subgroups. The language itself carries layers of pre-Latin linguistic elements and layers of subsequent introductions laid by Roman rule and Italian influence. In addition to Sardo, other languages are spoken: Catalan is spoken in Alghero, and on the island of San Pietro, inhabited since 1738 by fishing communities that migrated from Liguria in Northern Italy, a dialect of Ligurian, called Tabarchino, is spoken; its name originates from Tabarka in Tunisia. In northern Sardinia two more sublanguages are found, whose roots are within the Corsican-Sardinian linguistic group: Sassarese in the town of Sassari and Gallurese in the Gallura area. Sardinian was recognized by a 1999 national law as one of Italy's minority languages. According to a 2006 decision by the regional assembly, regional, provincial, and local governments may issue their decisions in Sardinian as well as Italian, though the Italian text stands as the official document.

The second half of the 20th century saw radical transformations with the foundation of the Regione Autonoma della Sardegna (Autonomous Region of Sardinia; Sardinia was granted a special autonomous regional government within Italy) in 1948, the eradication of malaria with the support of the Rockfeller Foundation (1946–1950), and the industrial development implemented by the large-scale, government-financed development (Piano di Rinascita [literally, Rebirth or Renaissance Plan]), particularly in the 1960s and 1970s. Malaria's defeat created the basis for the development of tourism on the coasts. Emigration resulted in the depopulation of the interior, producing a shift in the average population age. Furthermore, there was a general tendency to move from the interior areas toward the coast and the main cities, which offer ports, airports, public and commercial administration, higher education, and factories. Like the rest of the country, Sardinia is nowadays a destination for Eastern European, Asian, and African immigrants. The larger immigrant communities are originally from Romania, Ukraine, China, the Philippines, Morocco, and Senegal.

Sardinians have always participated in and significantly contributed to Italian national life. Sardinians are, in fact, some of the most important national political leaders: Francesco Cocco Ortu (1842–1929), liberal, minister of the Italian Kingdom; Antonio Gramsci (1891–1937), political philosopher and founder of the Communist Party; Emilio Lussu (1890–1975), writer and politician, minister in the first Republican governments. Lussu cofounded the Sardinian Action Party (Partito Sardo d'Azione), prominent in the antifascist movement Justice and Liberty (Giustizia e Libertà) and in the Action Party (Partito d'Azione). More significant contributors include Antonio Segni (1891–1972), of the Christian Democratic Party, fourth president of the Italian Republic; Enrico Berlinguer (1922–1984), national secretary of the Communist Party; and finally Francesco Cossiga (1928), of the Christian Democratic Party, eighth president of the Italian Republic.

Like other semiperipheral areas of Europe, since the beginning of the modern age Sardinia has been characterized by specialized agricultural production (extensive grain growth) and seasonally mobile sheep farming. Agricultural and pastoral society in Sardinia typically has been based on the nuclear family, with bilateral kinship reckoning and neolocal postmarital residence. The domestic unit corresponds to the household farm as a productive and reproductive center, mostly a subsistence orientation. This type of economy also involves exchange; wheat and farming produce always provided material for market transactions. Cheese, in particular, according to Fernand Braudel, has been exported in northern Europe since the 16th century. As several historians (Maurice Le Lannou, Giulio Angioni, Giannetta Murru, Pier Giorgio Solinas) have shown, agriculture and animal farming are not mutually exclusive activities but are rather complementary. This can be seen in specific microregional cases, such as in the mountainous areas of central Sardinia, where transhumance farming was once common. It can be argued that nowadays all transhumance farming activities have ceased and shepherds are mostly sedentary. State-financed, large-scale farms, using technology, specialized machinery, and sophisticated irrigation, have replaced small, family-run farms. This phenomenon increased in the early 1960s with the migration of shepherds to Tuscany and Lazio and the creation of state-financed farms. Agriculture and farming are still fundamental in the overall economy of Sardinia. Today as in the past, wheat, vegetables, fruit, olive oil, wine, cheese, bread, and sweets circulate in the market.

Artisanal production has always played a crucial role in the Sardinian economy. The French geographer Maurice Le Lannou singled out specific products and related production areas in the first half of the 20th century. Nowadays there are original developments in various fields, including ceramics, tapestry, weavings, collectors' knives, copper kitchen utensils, gold and coral jewelry, wooden and natural fiber objects, and cork and granite. Sardinia has also been a mining region, well known for centuries for its mining deposits of silver, lead, copper, and coal; its mines were exploited until very recently. At present the mining structures are part of a geomining park. Overall, what was once essentially a rural area is currently a modern country with the same population distribution patterns as those found in the rest of Italy and other industrial countries. Eight percent of Sardinian residents work in the primary sector, 24 percent in the industrial sector, and 68 percent in the service industry.

*Franco Lai*

**Further Reading**

Assmuth, Laura. *Women's Work, Women's Worth. Changing Lifecourses in Highland*

*Sardinia*. Helsinki: Finnish Anthropological Society, 1997.

Cavalli-Sforza, Luigi Luca, Paolo Menozzi, and Alberto Piazza. *The History and Geography of Human Genes*. Princeton, NJ: Princeton University Press, 1994.

Counihan, Carole. "Bread as World. Food Habits and Social Relations in Modernizing Sardinia." In *The Anthropology of Food and Body*, ed. Carole Counihan, 25–42. New York: Routledge, 1999.

Lortat-Jacob, Bernard. *Sardinian Chronicles*. Chicago: The University of Chicago Press, 1995.

Magliocco, Sabina. *The Two Madonnas: The Politics of Festival in a Sardinian Community*. Long Grove, IL: Waveland Press, 2005.

people"). "Scottish" is an adjective, not a collective noun (thus, "the Scottish flag"), unlike the term "English" which doubles as both collective noun and adjective for things English (as in "the English" and "the English flag"). "Scotch," as both collective noun and adjective, in use mainly in the 19th century, has largely fallen into disuse. People in Scotland speak English (or more precisely, Scottish Standard English) but with vocabulary, grammar, and syntax with origins in the variant of northern English known as Scots. Scots are not an ethnic group nor do they consider themselves a national minority living within the British state. Rather, they are a collectivity

## Scots

The Scots are native to Scotland, a country currently making up part of the United Kingdom. Some 5 million reside in Scotland; Glasgow, Edinburgh, Aberdeen, and Dundee are the largest urban areas in the country. About 10–15 million people elsewhere in the world claim Scottish ancestry, mainly in English-speaking countries such as the United States, Canada, Australia, and New Zealand. Scotland is nowadays a mainly secular society, with around half of the population claiming some religious affiliation, mainly to the (Protestant) Church of Scotland, but only one in four Scots attend church regularly. "Scots" is the collective noun for people who consider themselves Scottish (correct usage is "the Scots," not "the Scottish"). Scots also refers to the language used in Scotland, and is sometimes used as an adjective ("the Scots

Scottish bagpipper at Pitlochry Highland Games. (Corel)

defined by territory, above all by place of birth, residence, and ancestry. Being Scottish derives from having a sense of place, as "coming from" Scotland as a national territory, rather than a sense of tribe.

According to historians, Scotland has five founding peoples: (1) Picts (Roman invaders referred to them as Picti—painted people), who spoke a form of P-Celtic (similar to Welsh) and who settled in northeastern Scotland; (2) Scots, who came from Ireland, bringing their language—Q-Celtic or Gaelic—to western and northern Scotland, and who gave their name to the country—Scot-land; (3) Norse, from what is now Norway, who settled the Northern (Shetland and Orkney) and Western Isles; (4) Britons, speakers of P-Celtic (Brythonic), who settled in south and west Scotland; and (5) Angles, who migrated into Scotland from northern and eastern England, making their capital in Edinburgh, and who spoke early Norse/English, which transformed into Scots. The diversity of founding peoples is celebrated in modern times as making Scotland a "mongrel nation," without a narrow ethnic definition or identity, and helping to generate an inclusive sense of Scottish identity.

Scotland (Scotia) was established in CE 843 as a separate Gaelic-speaking kingdom north of the river Forth by Kenneth MacAlpin, who united the Scots in the west and the Picts in the east. By 1034, Scotland extended south of the Forth to the river Tweed, more or less the present border with England. Invasion by the English state in the late 13th century saw resistance in the Wars of Independence, first by William Wallace and then by Robert Bruce, culminating in the victory of the Scots at the battle of Bannockburn in 1314, and the Declaration of Arbroath in 1320, which affirmed Scottish independence from the English crown and maintained its status as a separate state.

Prior to 1560, Scotland was a Catholic kingdom, reflecting the religion of the then-monarch, Mary, Queen of Scots. Thereafter, it was formally Protestant, with a strong Calvinistic ethos and Presbyterian rulership. The national church became the Church of Scotland, which later saw schisms in the mid-19th century over the appointment of clergy. Migration from Ireland in the second half of the century saw a revival of Catholicism, particularly in west-central Scotland. By the 21st century, Scotland had to all intents and purposes become a secular society, with only one in four active worshippers, although around half of Scots claimed to be nominally religious.

The Union of Crowns in 1603 saw the Scottish king James VI succeed to the English crown and thereafter move his court to London, thereby diminishing Scottish cultural autonomy. In 1707, the Union of Parliaments amalgamated the legislatures of Scotland and England, further eroding Scottish political autonomy and ending the separation of Scottish (and English) states, creating Great Britain, thereafter (1801) the United Kingdom of Great Britain and Ireland.

Scotland, like England, became an industrialized and urbanized country in the early 19th century, with its population concentrated in the "Central Belt" from Glasgow in the west (the "second city of the Empire") to Edinburgh, the former capital city, in the east. Other cities include

Aberdeen, Dundee, Inverness, and Perth. The Gàidhealtachd in the northwest suffered population, economic, and cultural erosion, especially after the failed Jacobite wars of the 18th century. All parts of Scotland, but especially the Gàidhealtachd, saw massive emigration in the 19th and 20th centuries, mainly to parts of the British Empire. Gaels in particular migrated to eastern Canada where Gaelic continues to be a significant language and cultural signifier.

As a language with roots in Old Norse and Old English, Scots is closely related to English, and evolved as the language of state in Scotland from the 15th to the 18th centuries. The unions of Crowns (1603) and Parliaments (1707) helped to demote the status of Scots to that of a dialect. The 20th century saw a revival of Scots as a literary language (known as Lallans or Doric) linked to a more general revival in Scottish (as opposed to British) identity. Ulster Scots is spoken in Northern Ireland, among the descendants of 17th-century Scots settlers. A more distinctive language, spoken by around 2 percent of people in Scotland, is Gaelic, mainly in the north and west of Scotland in the area known as the Gàidhealtachd. Scots Gaelic derives from Q-Celtic (Goidelic) and is closely related to Irish, reflecting historic migration patterns from Ireland to Scotland across the North Channel between the two countries. Once spoken across much of northern and western Scotland, Gaelic has receded to the northwest and Hebridean islands.

There is no clear-cut relationship between politics and Scottish national identity, which is by and large cultural. Scottish culture has deep roots: its exemplars are the intellects of the Scottish Enlightenment (Adam Smith, David Hume, Adam Ferguson), the novels of Walter Scott, and the poetry of Robert Burns. The cultural revivals in literature, art, and music, first in the 1920s, and later in the 1960s, led to a stronger connection between national identity and political change. Scottish culture thrives on diversity and hybridity: its literary traditions range from standard English (e.g., Muriel Spark), to "Scots" (known as Doric/Lallans, e.g., Hugh MacDiarmid and Lewis Grassic Gibbon), and Gaelic (e.g., Sorley MacLean). It draws on regional traditions: in art and architecture it includes Charles Rennie Mackintosh (Art Nouveau), the Glasgow Boys (Impressionism), and postwar diversity (e.g., Anne Redpath, Joan Eardley, John Bellany). The revival of folk music draws upon regional traditions and Irish influences. Artistic and cultural life is underpinned by institutions like the Edinburgh International Festival (1948), and the National Theatre of Scotland (2004).

After the 1707 Union, Scotland retained its institutional autonomy: in religion, a separate legal system ("Scots law"), education, and the use of "Scottish" currency banknotes within the sterling area. These were important carriers of a strong sense of Scottish identity, even though Scotland was formally governed by the British government at Westminster in London. The inherent tensions between Scottish institutional and cultural autonomy, and the lack of formal self-government, helped to create a national, devolved parliament with primary lawmaking powers in Edinburgh in 1999.

Scots are Scottish first, and British second; in this respect, their nationality differs from their citizenship. Only one in 20 people living in Scotland give priority to being British, although most would include this as a minor descriptor. Nevertheless, national identity is not a political matter, defining attitudes to whether or not Scotland should remain within the British Union. Being Scottish is a cultural rather than a political issue. Scottish self-government post-1999 was an outcome, not a cause, of a growing sense of being Scottish.

Since 2007, Scotland has had a Nationalist (minority) government, elected by the proportional representation election system. Formal independence is supported by around one-third of people in Scotland. Nevertheless, around two-thirds of Scots want a more powerful parliament than the one created by the 1999 settlement, indicating that self-government is unfinished constitutional business.

In terms of national identification, relations with Scotland's largest neighbor, England, help to define the national "other." The ratio of England to Scotland in terms of land mass is 3:2; the population ratio is 10:1. About 800,000 Scots (people born in Scotland) live in England; and 400,000 English-born people live in Scotland. The interplay of national identities (Scottish and English) with British state (citizenship) is complex, with Scots far more likely to emphasize the national over state identities, compared with the English. Nevertheless, it seems that people in England are expressing their English identity and becoming better able to distinguish it from being British.

In terms of national identity, Scotland shares similarities with other "understated" nations such as Catalunya/Catalonia and Euskal Herria/Basque Country in Spain, Flanders in Belgium, Quebec in Canada, as well as Wales in the United Kingdom. Nevertheless, Scots are comparatively unusual in that linguistic distinctiveness, an important carrier in these other countries, is a weak marker of national identity. Despite, or possibly because of, this lack of close association between language and national identity, Scottish nationalism is widespread, for the criteria for being Scottish are diffuse and do not require incomers to be proficient, for example, in the national language. Scottishness is carried by a range of institutional markers, suggesting that Scots have a civic rather than an ethnic sense of national identity; this gives it greater potential for national inclusion. Around 2 percent of people living in Scotland are nonwhite—mainly of Asian Pakistani origin. They have greater propensity to self-describe as Scottish (as in "Scottish Muslims/Pakistanis") than similar ethnic groups in England who tend to use a British rather than an English descriptor. The Scots, in short, are less of an ethnic group than a national one, whose strong sense of identity derives from residence and/or birthplace within the territorial-jurisdictional boundaries of Scotland.

*David McCrone*

## Further Reading

Bechhofer, F., and D. McCrone, eds. *National Identity, Nationalism, and Constitutional Change*. New York: Palgrave, 2009.

Devine, T. *The Scottish Nation: 1700–2000*. New York: Penguin, 1999.

Houston, R. A. B. *Scotland: A Short Introduction*. New York: Oxford University Press, 2008.

McCrone, D. *Understanding Scotland: The Sociology of a Nation*. New York: Routledge, 2001.

# Sephardic Jews

Sephardic Jews (Sephardim) are generally held to be Jews of non-Ashkenazi origin, mostly from the Mediterranean region and including North African, Middle Eastern, and Central Asian Jewries. However, the term Sephardim, derived from Sepharad, a toponym first used to designate the Iberian Peninsula in the Aramaic translation of the Hebrew Bible, specifically refers to Jews who trace their ancestry to medieval Spain and Portugal. (North African Jews are often classified separately as Maghrebim or together with Middle Eastern and Central Asian Jewries as Mizrahim.) Dispersed following expulsions in the 15th and 16th centuries, Jews and some Jewish converts to Christianity (conversos) fleeing the Inquisition formed two main groups outside the Iberian Peninsula: Eastern Sephardim in cities of the Ottoman Empire and a smaller contingent of Western Sephardim, mostly former conversos, in western European cities. Italy served as a crossroads between the two. Western Sephardim utilized normative Portuguese and Spanish because they maintained contact with Iberia, whereas Eastern Sephardim developed a distinct language, called Ladino (Judeo-Spanish), based on medieval Castilian and other Iberian dialects with admixtures of Hebrew, Turkish, Italian, and French, and written in Hebrew characters. From the 18th century, the paths of the two groups further diverged: those in Western Europe came to be overwhelmed demographically by an influx of Ashkenazim, whereas the dissolution of the Ottoman Empire and emergence of successor nation-states splintered Eastern Sephardim. The Holocaust decimated Sephardic communities throughout Europe.

Jews inhabited the Iberian Peninsula during the Roman era, Visigoth period, and Arab conquest (711). The formation of a Jewish courtier class, equipped with commercial, administrative, and diplomatic skills, represented a legendary golden age (10th–12th centuries). Prominent Jews included statesmen Hasdai ibn-Shaprut and Samuel ha-Nagid, and poets and philosophers Moses ibn-Ezra, Solomon ibn-Gabirol, Judah ha-Levi, and Moses Maimonides. The Almohad invasion (1148) resulted in forced conversions; Jews fled northward to Christian kingdoms pursuing the Reconquista and helped administer territories conquered by Christian kings. Jewish scholars also developed the kabbalah (Jewish mysticism) and compiled its central text, the Zohar (13th century).

Anti-Jewish animus accompanied the Reconquista. The preaching of Dominican friars, compounded by economic crisis, provided the context for the massacre and forced conversion of Jews in Seville (1391). While many converted Jews (conversos or "New Christians") became devout Catho-

Isidor Aysner, a Jew of mixed Sephardic and Ashkenazi heritage, poses by former Sephardic synagogue for the thriving Jewish community in pre-WWII Bulgaria. (Time Life Pictures/Getty Images)

lics, others persisted in practicing Judaism secretly. Pejoratively labeled Marranos ("swine"), conversos became the target of "purity of blood" statutes and attacks, first in Toledo (1449). The Spanish Inquisition (1478) sought to combat the heresy of "judaizing" among conversos. Ferdinand and Isabella expelled the Jews (1492) to prevent them from encouraging conversos to judaize.

Approximately 100,000–150,000 Jews fled Spain in 1492. Some settled in North Africa. Many went to Portugal; they were forcibly baptized en masse (1497) and suffered a massacre in Lisbon (1506). Since Portugal did not establish its Inquisition until 1536, crypto-Judaism, the secretive practice of Jewish rituals, became common. Converso religiosity frequently combined beliefs and practices from Judaism and Christianity. Some conversos and their descendants, some fleeing the Inquisition, became involved in trans-Mediterranean and trans-Atlantic trade. They constituted the Western Sephardic dispersion, referred to themselves as Hebrews of the Portuguese nation, and traded wine, wood, and sugar from the New World and diamonds and spices from Asia. Mercantile policies and the toleration on the part of the Calvinist Dutch Republic made Amsterdam the center of the Western Sephardim; 3,000 resided there (1675), where they readopted the normative practice of rabbinic Judaism. Its Ets Ahaim Yeshiva trained rabbis, who also served satellite communities in London, Hamburg, Bordeaux, Bayonne, Curaçao, and New Amsterdam. A dowry society (Dotar) linked enclaves of Sephardim in Western Europe and Italy and aided young women in their marriage preparations.

Iberian Catholic, Dutch Calvinist, and Sephardic Jewish intellectual currents that converged in Amsterdam impacted the literary production of Western Sephardim. Menasseh Ben-Israel operated an important printing press and sought to convince Cromwell to readmit Jews to England. Daniel Levi de Barrios wrote numerous plays in Spanish. Baruch Spinoza, excommunicated for his heterodox beliefs (1656), composed major philosophical works. Some Western Sephardic families served as patrons to the Dutch masters and subjects of paintings by Rembrandt.

The Eastern Sephardim in the Ottoman Empire formed the demographic core of Sephardic Jewry after 1492. They arrived from Iberia in the immediate wake of the expulsion, and during the 16th and 17th centuries, either as conversos from Portugal or after sojourning in Italy or North Africa. Permitted under Islam to worship and maintain communal autonomy in exchange for taxes, Jews settled in newly conquered Ottoman cities, such as Istanbul and Salonica, where they formed congregations named after the regions in Iberia or Italy from which they came and organized their living quarters around shared courtyards, or *kortijos*. Other centers of settlement included: Izmir, Edirne, Bitola (Monastir), Sarajevo, Belgrade, Zagreb, Skopje, Sofia, Bucharest, Rhodes, Safed, Jerusalem, Cairo, and Aleppo. Bringing important skills and technologies they served as translators, merchants, tax farmers, and doctors; established the first printing press in the Ottoman empire (1493); and developed the textile industry,

producing uniforms for the janissaries, the sultan's military.

Sephardic Jews assimilated smaller, long-established populations of Romaniotes, Greek-speaking Jews resident in the Mediterranean basin since antiquity. Some communities of Romaniotes, such as in Ioannina, Greece, retained distinct traditions until the 20th century.

Renowned Sephardic rabbinic centers, led by Joseph Taitazak, Samuel de Medina, and Moses Almosnino, flourished in Salonica, Istanbul, Edirne, and Safed. Joseph Caro wrote the Shulhan Arukh, adopted by Sephardim and Ashkenazim as the standard rabbinic legal code. Ladino translations of the Bible appeared in Istanbul (1547) and Ferrara (1553). Caro, Moses Cordovero, Isaac Luria, and Salomon Alkabes also developed kabbalah. Alkabes composed a Sabbath hymn, Lecha Dodi, still chanted today in synagogues of all denominations.

Until the 20th century, Eastern Sephardim conducted a portion of their liturgies in Ladino, in addition to Hebrew, based on melodies adopted from Ottoman high court music. Eastern Sephardim also developed an extensive repertoire of *romansas*, or secular ballads, sung in Ladino especially by women. Sephardi women also adhered to a distinctive sartorial code, characterized especially by several styles of headdress, such as the *tokado* in Izmir and Rhodes or the *kofya* in Salonica, believed to have origins in medieval Iberia.

The eschatological implications of the expulsion, combined with the dissemination of kabbalah, sparked the messianic movement of Sabbetai Sevi of Izmir (1665) that drew wide support. Sevi converted to

Islam and undermined his support base. Some followers converted to Islam and formed a distinct group (*dönme*). The failure of the Sabbetean movement coincided with Ottoman military defeats and economic downturn, which adversely impacted Eastern Sephardim, who took a secondary role in commerce behind Greeks and Armenians.

In the 18th century, the trajectories of Western and Eastern Sephardim further diverged. Western Sephardim replaced Spanish and Portuguese with the national language wherever they resided. Those in southwestern France became the first Jews in Europe to receive full civil rights (1790). A massive influx of Ashkenazim from Eastern Europe during the 19th century overwhelmed Western Sephardim, who became a small minority of the total Jewish population.

In the Ottoman Empire, measures to incorporate Jews into the Ottoman polity did not yet emerge. Eastern Sephardim developed print culture in Ladino. Most famously, Jacob Huli's *Meam Loez* (1730) made rabbinic knowledge accessible to the masses. Ethical literature (*musar*) proliferated. Contributing to the Jewish Enlightenment, David Attias advocated that Ottoman Jews study secular subjects and foreign languages.

The reorganization of the Ottoman administration, the introduction of modern schooling, and the advent of Ladino newspapers transformed Eastern Sephardic life in the 19th century. Reform decrees (1839, 1856, 1869) sought to centralize Ottoman authority, grant equal rights to non-Muslims, and develop Ottoman citizenship, although without state-sponsored education. Filling this void, the Paris-based Alliance Israélite Universelle established Jewish schools throughout the Ottoman Empire that sought to regenerate the impoverished classes, taught religious and secular subjects (in French), and trained artisans and craftsmen. New cultural forms of expression emerged in the vernacular, such as belles lettres, the theater, and Ladino newspapers, like *El Tiempo* (Istanbul) and *La Epoka* (Salonica), which supported modern education and served as forums for competing political ideologies, including Zionism, diaspora nationalism, assimilationism, and socialism after the Young Turk Revolution (1908).

The dissolution of the Ottoman Empire ruptured the center of the Eastern Sephardim. Around 1900, there were 177,500 Jews living in the Ottoman Empire: the largest concentrations were found in the cities of Salonica (75,000), Istanbul (60,000), Izmir (25,500), and Edirne (17,000). The Ottoman loss of Sarajevo (1878), Sofia (1908), and Salonica (1912) reduced Ottoman Jewish communities to the boundaries of present-day Turkey. Many Jews emigrated to France, the Americas, and Palestine. The majority, who remained in Turkey, Greece, Bulgaria, and Yugoslavia, were subjected to nationalizing linguistic and economic policies. Anti-Jewish sentiment also increased: pogroms erupted in Salonica (1931) and Edirne (1934).

The Holocaust destroyed the Eastern Sephardim. Jews in Serbia, under German control, were executed in labor camps or murdered in gas vans (1941–1942). The Ustaša of Croatia collaborated with the Nazis; 6,500 of 9,000 Sephardim in Sarajevo perished (1941–1943). Jews in Greece suffered one of the highest mortality rates of any Jewish community in Europe (87%). Forty-eight thousand Jews from Salonica were deported to Auschwitz and Bergen-Belsen (1943). Bulgaria, allied with Germany, deported "foreign" Jews from occupied Thrace and Macedonia to Treblinka (1943); few survived. Neutral Turkey compelled non-Muslims (including Jews and *dönme*) to pay a capital tax (1942–1944). Of Eastern Sephardim who immigrated to France, 10,000 were deported under the Vichy regime. The Holocaust also decimated Western Sephardim: 4,300 in the Netherlands were deported to Nazi camps; 800 survived.

With the creation of the State of Israel, 35,089 Jews from Bulgaria, 30,657 from Turkey, 6,596 from Yugoslavia, and 1,540 from Greece immigrated (1948–1949). Few remain today in the Eastern Sephardic heartland, with the exception of 25,000 in Turkey. Few speak Ladino (about 100,000 worldwide). The last Ladino newspaper published in Hebrew characters folded in 1948, and postwar generations have been educated in the languages of the countries in which they reside. Communities in Istanbul and Salonica maintain synagogues, schools, museums, and choirs. Emigration, intermarriage, and anti-Semitism continue to challenge group identity. Western Sephardim have had even greater difficulty in preserving their identity. Their synagogues, museums, or cemeteries can be visited in London, Amsterdam, Hamburg, Curaçao, and New York. Institutions for the study of Sephardim operate in Israel, Spain, France, and the United States.

*Devin E. Naar*

## Further Reading

Benbassa, Esther, and Aron Rodrigue. *Sephardi Jewry: A History of the Judeo-Spanish Community, 14th–20th Centuries*. Berkeley: University of California, 2000.

Gerber, Jane. *The Jews of Spain: A History of the Sephardic Experience*. New York: Free Press, 1992.

Harris, Tracy. *Death of a Language: The History of Judeo-Spanish*. London: Associated University Presses, 1994.

Kaplan, Yosef. *An Alternative Path to Modernity: The Sephardi Diaspora in Western Europe*. Leiden: Brill, 2000.

## Serbs

Serbs live mainly in the western part of the Central Balkan Peninsula. The majority of Serbs inhabit the state of Serbia (with its capital at Belgrade). According to the 2002 census, Serbia has 7,498,001 inhabitants, of which 6,212,838 (82.9%) self-identify as Serbs. These figures exclude the province of Kosovo, where perhaps 150,000 (7.5% of a population of 2 million) are Serbs; Kosovo has been under United Nations protection since 1999, and in 2008 the Albanian majority unilaterally declared Kosovo's independence, a move disputed by Serbia. Serbs also reside elsewhere in countries formerly making up the Federal Republic of Yugoslavia, namely Slovenia, Croatia, Bosnia and Herzegovina, Montenegro, and Macedonia; in Bosnia and Herzegovina, Serbs represent the majority of the population in Republika Srpska, one of its two contemporary parts (1,267,000 or about 88%). Serbs also reside in Romania, Hungary, and Albania; in Western Europe (especially Germany and Austria); and overseas (the United

States, Canada, Australia). The total official estimated number of Serbs living outside of Serbia is 3.5 million. Serbs speak Serbian, which belongs to the South Slavic branch of Indo-European Slavic languages. Serbian has two alphabets—Cyrillic and Latin; the official alphabet in contemporary Serbia is Cyrillic, but the Latin alphabet is also widely used. The primary religion of Serbs is Serbian Orthodox.

Serbs belong to the South Slavic peoples. The name *Serbs* is one of the old Slavic tribal names, traces of which can be found in toponymy of the ancient Slavic homeland (today's Germany, Russia, and Poland). The ancestors of Serbs settled in the Balkans in the 6th and 7th centuries CE. With gradual tribal unification and under the influence of neighboring powers, a Medieval Serbian state emerged. Christianity and literacy arrived in the late 9th century, spread by Byzantine missionaries Cyril and Methodius and their disciples. Decisive moments in the development of the Serbian state include the establishment of the House of Nemanjić (the royal house of Serbia from 1168 to 1371), the archbishopric in 1219, as well as the church cult of the same royal house, starting with its founder, Stefan Nemanja (St. Simeon) and his son Rastko (St. Sava). This new state was known as the "Serbian land" and also as Raška (Rascia) and was centered in southern Serbia. The medieval state reached the peak during the rule of Tsar Dušan (1331–1355), when its borders encompassed present-day Serbia south of the Danube and the Sava rivers, Montenegro, Albania, Macedonia, and most of Greece.

Dušan's heirs proved incapable of resisting the advancing Ottomans. The Battle of Kosovo (1389) is often viewed as the

Traditionally dressed Serbian folk singers. (Corel)

decisive event in the collapse of the Serbian state; the fall of Smederevo in 1459 marked its actual end. The Turks would remain until the 19th century in central Serbia and until the beginning of the 20th century in southern Serbia. Only what is today known as Vojvodina was within the Ottoman Empire for a shorter period of time, from 1521 to 1688, when it became part of the Habsburg Monarchy. With the gradual dismemberment of the state, the elites, joined by large numbers of lower classes, moved mostly to the Habsburg Monarchy or to inaccessible mountainous regions. During the 18th century, there emerged a Serbian middle class consisting of merchants and artisans living in urban centers in the Habsburg Monarchy (Vienna, Budapest, Timisoara, Novi Sad, Trieste) with modern cultural and political views on, for example, nationalism. South of the Sava and the Danube rivers, Ottoman influences were strongest in cities. During the Ottoman rule a part of the local population converted to Islam. While non-Muslims did enjoy considerable autonomy, converts were eligible for social advancement. For example, Sokollu Mehmed Pasha, Grand Vizier of the Ottoman Empire (1565–1579), was of Serbian descent.

The territory of modern Serbia was thus a meeting point of cultures. Serbian tradition represented a complex mixture of Slavic, Balkan, Byzantine, Ottoman, Mediterranean, Central European, and other influences. The elites that created the national culture during the 19th and 20th centuries attempted to reduce cultural pluralism and eclecticism, emphasizing above all Slavic relationships, as well as belonging to Byzantine legacy. The national identity of Serbs has above all else been founded on the language and religion, as well as on glorification of heroism and martyrdom in struggle against foreign rule.

The modern history of the Serbs starts with the First (1804) and Second (1815) Serbian Uprisings, which led to gradual liberation from Turkish rule. Serbia gained full independence from the Ottoman Empire in 1878, and in 1882 it was proclaimed a kingdom. Two dynasties originating from the uprising leaders, the Houses of Karađorđević and Obrenović, took turns at the throne. Dominating the political and social scene, particularly in the second half of the 19th century, was the goal, through "wars for national liberation and unification," to expand Serbian borders to encompass all Serbs living under Ottoman and Austro-Hungarian rule. World War I and the collapse of Austria-Hungary led to the unification of South Slavic lands in a single new state, the Kingdom of Serbs, Croats, and Slovenes (renamed Kingdom of Yugoslavia in 1929). Serbs perceived themselves as a pillar of the new state; Serbian elites however, underestimated its complexity and fragility, and the intranational political relations soon became extremely tense. In 1929, King Aleksandar Karađorđević declared a dictatorship, which only made matters worse and led to the king's assassination in 1934 in Marseilles, France, by Croatian and Macedonian nationalists. In World War II, Yugoslavia was divided among different occupation forces. With the king and political elite in London, the antifascist movement, led by the Communist Party and Josip Broz Tito, continued to gain supporters in Yugoslavia and recognition abroad. Tito's forces prevailed against the Serbian nationalist royalist Chetnik movement, whose collaboration with Axis powers is still disputed, but which undoubtedly committed many war crimes, and the Nazi puppet Ustaše regime in Croatia. This regime, among other misdeeds, committed mass murders of Serbian and other "objectionable" populations in its territory.

Severe conflicts during the last two centuries occurred between the Serbs and several neighboring peoples in the period of developing nationalism, but intensive cultural cooperation occurred as well, particularly among Southern Slavs, which enabled the creation of a common state in 1918. The first Yugoslavia (1918–1941) attempted to solve national diversity by creating unitary Yugoslavian citizenship, while the second Yugoslavia, socialist and federal (1945–1991), tried to accomplish the same goal with a specific form of multiculturalism. In the period of socialism, openness toward the world and elements of market economy, as opposed to the Soviet bloc, from which Yugoslavia managed to secede in 1948, led to greater Western influence in everyday life. A consumer society has been developing in Serbia since the end of the 1960s. During the period of Yugoslavia's dissolution in the 1990s, Serbia became an independent state, which opened the process of reconstruction of its national identity. That process unfolded during the largest crisis in modern Serbian history, characterized by attempts to fill in ideological and identity emptiness by the revival or reinvention of national culture and tradition. In addition, today globalization and influence of media on culture and everyday life are evident.

Ever since the times of their arrival in the Balkans, Serbs have devoted themselves to agriculture. In the early 20th century, 84 percent of Serbs were still farmers. However, urban population began to grow and political and economic elites were formed during the 19th and 20th centuries. These elites held opposing views regarding modernization. Some were in favor of Europeanization and some supported the anti-Europeanizing movements. Part of the elite perceived the village, peasantry, and *zadruga* (a characteristic type of traditional large family) as the national ideal. A belated industrialization, however, changed Serbian society. The capital, Belgrade, increased its population 15-fold from the mid-19th to the mid-20th century and became a local hub of urban culture. Urbanization spread to smaller towns as well, though the integration of rural migrants was not without problems and a rural-urban contrast remains even today.

A key event in the cultural development of Serbs was the linguistic reform of the first half of the 19th century, in which the Cyrillic alphabet was adjusted to the phonetic principles and everyday speech that formed the basis of written Serbian. A key figure in contemporary cultural and literary developments was Vuk Stefanović Karadžić (1787–1864). With his disciples, Karadžić collected a large body of material on traditional life and oral traditions. What would come to be considered Serbian national culture is rooted in Karadžić's work, especially his collections of epic ballads. Indeed, the singing of decasyllabic heroic poems with the *gusle* (a single-stringed instrument) according to traditional pattern is still alive in some parts of Serbia. While most forms of traditional culture have disappeared over the past century, dancing traditions were maintained through the folkloristic work of cultural artistic associations supported by the socialist state. Traditional music exerts a certain influence on today's popular music and is also affirmed as a form of national music.

Serbs traditionally observed the Orthodox religion and have an autocephalous church headed by a patriarch. However, the residues of pre-Christian religions, especially the cults of nature and the dead, remain recognizable under the Christian layers even today. A trend toward secularization dates to modernization, a process emphasized during the socialist era, when religion was largely suppressed. Recent changes in Serbia and the Balkans have given new impetus to religion, which is again thought central to national identity. Some of the rituals and customs, particularly *slava* (a feast celebration of family patron saint) and the manner of celebration of Christmas, are popularly accepted as symbols of ethnic distinctiveness in relation to other peoples.

The symbolic borders between Serbs and others have been linguistic and religious in character. Since the end of the 19th century, when the language was shared with the others, religion played the distinguishing role—thus Serbs were different from Catholic Croats and Muslims/Bosniaks. The relation toward Montenegrins was more complex, owing to shared religion, language, and traditions; the establishment of separate states allowed room for the emergence, albeit contested,

## Ethnic policy in the former Yugoslavia

The principle of ethnic/national equality (brotherhood and unity) was an ideological cornerstone of socialist Yugoslavia (1945–1991). The Federation consisted of six republics—Slovenia, Croatia, Bosnia and Herzegovina (BH), Serbia, Montenegro, and Macedonia—which were considered constitutive nations of SFRY. Serbia also had two autonomous provinces (Vojvodina, and Kosovo and Metohija) on the basis of significant multiethnicity. The state also recognized numerous national minorities, with Albanians and Hungarians being the largest. The Yugoslav model was not a melting pot, but rather a form of managed pluralism. The constitution guaranteed equal rights to all nations and national minorities. In the case of the latter the rights primarily covered the right to their own languages, culture, and education. The one-party state balanced and manipulated the multiethnic reality. Federal party and state officials were selected by applying the "national key" principle calling for equal representation and cyclical rotation of members of all nations and large minorities. The state and party intervened in case of ethnic conflicts or tensions.

*Mladena Prelić*

of separate national identities. At the beginning of 20th century, Serbian elites also saw Macedonia as Serbian in character, but this conflict was overcome by the creation of Yugoslavia, within which Macedonians were a recognized nation.

After World War II, Yugoslavia became a socialist federal republic with a single-party system. It consisted of six federal units, with Serbia being one of them. Josip Broz Tito was the head of the state, army, and party until his death in 1980. Tito's death was followed by a crisis of federal government regarding its legitimacy and ideology. In Serbia a hybrid regime emerged, combining a conservative monoparty system and populist nationalism. The breakup of Yugoslavia into its federal units (1991–1995) was accompanied by a series of devastating wars. Subjected to Slobodan Milošević's autocratic leadership and his regime's role in the 1990s events, Serbia was for several years placed under United Nations sanctions. As a consequence of Serbia's armed attempts to prevent secession of the province of Kosovo, in 1999 a three-month-long NATO bombing campaign ensued. Among the consequences of the events of the 1990s was the arrival of large numbers of Serbian refugees from the other, war-torn parts of the former Yugoslavia. Opposition to the regime had very limited influence until 2000, when it finally gained an absolute electoral majority. After the dissolution of Yugoslavia, Serbia remained in federation with Montenegro, under the name of the Federal Republic of Yugoslavia, known after 2003 as Serbia and Montenegro. When Montenegro seceded and declared its independence in 2006, the country became the Republic of Serbia. The weakness of the democratic state in Serbia was demonstrated when its prime minister, Zoran Đinđić, who led modernization processes, was assassinated in 2003. Populism in political life as well as an underdeveloped civil society still represents serious obstacles for the advancement of democracy in Serbia. The Serbian economy suffered devastating decay during the 1990s, and the transition from socialism to market orientation brought about new challenges. Yet another problem facing Serbia today is depopulation caused by low birthrates and emigration, particularly of young and educated people.

*Mladena Prelić*

## Further Reading

Calic, Marie-Janine. *Sozialgeschichte Serbiens 1815–1941: Der aufhaltsame Fortschritt während der Industrialisierung* (*Social History of Serbia 1815–1941: Slow Progress in Industrialization*). München: Südosteuropäische Arbeiten 92, R. Ouldenbourg Verlag, 1994.

Ćirković, Sima. *The Serbs*. Malden: Blackwell Publishing, 2004.

Ćorović, Vladimir. *Istorija Srba* (*The History of Serbs*). 3 vols. Beograd: BIGZ, 1989.

Pavlowitch, Stevan K. *Serbia: The History behind the Name*. London: C. Hurst, 2002.

Petrovich, Michael Boro. *A History of Modern Serbia 1804–1918*. 2 vols. New York: Harcourt Brace Jovanovich, 1976.

Sundhaussen, Holm. *Geschichte Serbiens: 19.-21. Jahrhundert* (*History of Serbia: From 19th to 21st Centuries*). Wien: Bohlau Verlag Ges.m.b.H und Co.KG, 2007.

# Silesians

The term Silesian refers to four distinct ethnic groups that are closely associated with the territory of Silesia, which is defined as the area from the Oder River (from its sources in the Tatra Mountains) to, roughly, its conjunction with the Lusatian Neisse. Since 1945, when the borders of Poland were significantly revised, almost all of Silesia has been within Poland. (There is some discussion about whether the land immediately west of the Lusatian Neisse, which lies within Germany, should be considered a part of Silesia or of Lusatia.) Moving from west to east, Lower Silesia, extending from the Lusatian Neisse to approximately the Glatzer Neisse, was inhabited until 1945 by monolingual speakers of German, the descendants of medieval settlers from western German territories. Most of this population was Lutheran, though some were Roman Catholic. They were displaced to the two Germanies following the end of World War II; their descendants maintain ethnic organizations devoted to culture and politics there. At the same time, Poles displaced from territories absorbed into the Soviet Union settled in Lower Silesia. Some members of the postwar generations now claim Silesian as their regional identity, while others identify simply as Polish. East of the Glatzer Neisse, Silesia can be divided into two further regions, Opole Silesia, centered on the city of Opole, and Upper Silesia, centered on the city of Katowice (German sources usually conflate the two, while Polish sources distinguish them). Silesians in both regions are multilingual, with distinct dialects of Polish, German, and standard Polish in use. These Silesians share the Roman Catholic faith of their Czech and Polish neighbors. Extensive emigration to the industrial heartland of western Germany has resulted in a substantial diaspora of Opole Silesians and Upper Silesians there. Because ethnic identification is a vexed issue for all four groups, it is not possible to estimate the number of members of any one of them; however, their combined population does not exceed several million.

The multilingual population of contemporary Opole and Upper Silesia traces its origins to West Slavic-speaking peoples who inhabited Silesia prior to the first consolidation of Poland as a kingdom, under the Piast dynasty in the 10th century. Silesia came into a western political orbit when Casimir the Great reunified Poland and ceded Silesia to the Bohemian sovereign, John of Luxembourg (1339). Silesia thus became Czech, which in turn became Austrian (in 1526); from 1740 to 1742, Prussia wrested Silesia from Austria in the War of the Austrian Succession. This was one of the first political moves by which Prussia consolidated territories into what became modern Germany. Prior to the 10th century, Lower Silesia was also populated by West Slavic speakers; however, the Piast monarchs as well as their Czech, Austrian, and Prussian successors all encouraged immigration from western German territories, and German-speaking communities slowly replaced Slavic ones from the west eastward. The replacement of Slavic speakers slowed in the mid-18th century, and did not extend into the eastern reaches of Silesia (Opole and Upper Silesia). However, the eastern, Slavic population came under heavy German influence with the development of industry, rail transportation, primary education, and military service.

The German-speaking Silesians of Lower Silesia slowly developed their own, distinct dialect of German. The West Slavic Silesian dialects are considered transitional Polish-Czech dialects at base, sharing enough defining characteristics with Polish that they are usually classified as Polish dialects. However, by the early 20th century they exhibited heavy German influence in vocabulary and grammar; Silesian-German bilingualism had also become almost universal by then. Since 1945, many of these German words have been replaced by standard Polish words, and standard Polish has been added to the linguistic repertoire.

The boundary between multilingual, Slavic Silesians and monolingual, German Silesians largely corresponded to a Roman Catholic/Lutheran divide, and this had implications for folk practices and dress. When the monolingual German-speaking population was displaced and replaced by monolingual, and Roman Catholic, Polish speakers, the significant differences became those concerning folk Catholic practices, cultural attitudes toward household and agricultural management, and language. In the east, the boundary between Opole Silesians and Upper Silesians formed, and continues to focus, on differing economic bases: Upper Silesians are industrial workers and city dwellers, while Opole Silesians rely on a mixed economy of industrial work, agriculture for subsistence and a local market, and service sector work. Since the mid-18th century, both groups have engaged in labor migration and emigration to western Germany, and continue to do so. There are also linguistic differences between Upper Silesian dialects and Opole Silesian dialects that are significant enough to inhibit communication, though the similarities are obvious enough that speakers of both sets of dialects easily recognize the other as Silesian. Additionally, the fact that Upper Silesia was awarded to Poland after World War I, while Opole Silesia remained in Germany, has meant that Upper Silesians tend to see Silesian identity within the context of Polish identity, and to focus their political energies on attaining greater regional autonomy within Poland; Opole Silesians, on the other hand, tend to see their identity as an inherently mixed one, and to focus their energies not only on Silesian distinctiveness, but also on maintaining their cultural, linguistic, and political ties to Germany. In the immediate postcommunist period, this emphasis on continuing ties to Germany led to considerable interethnic tension in Opole Province between indigenous and postwar immigrant populations; however, close cooperation between the German consulate and the provincial government with regard to public education and reassurance avoided the escalation of this tension beyond harsh words and graffiti. In Opole Silesia and Upper Silesia, the boundary between Silesians and Poles is also reinforced by the greater mobility within the European Union afforded to Silesians by virtue of dual Polish-German citizenship. This high rate of dual citizenship among Silesians places them in a different relationship to the immigration and labor migration laws of Germany, the Netherlands, and the United Kingdom, to cite three preferred destinations.

*Elizabeth Vann*

## Further Reading

Davies, Norman. *God's Playground: A History of Poland.* New York: Columbia University Press, 1982.

Mach, Zdzisław. "Case Study: Migration to a Deserted Land." In *Symbols, Conflict and Identity.* Albany: State University of New York Press, 1993, 184–210.

Rose, William. *The Drama of Upper Silesia.* Brattleboro, Vermont: Stephen Daye Press, 1935.

Tooley, T. Hunt. *National Identity and Weimar Germany: Upper Silesia and the Eastern Border, 1918–1922.* Lincoln: University of Nebraska Press, 1997.

Urban, Thomas. *Deutsche in Polen: Geschichte und Gegenwart einer Minderheit (Germans in Poland: History and Present of a Minority).* Munich: C. H. Beck, 1994.

## Slovaks

Slovaks [*Slováci*] are a Slavic people concentrated primarily in Central Europe, and the Slovak Republic houses nearly 5 million Slovaks, with Slovak minorities residing in neighboring Czech Republic and Hungary, as well as the United States and Serbia. Under centuries of Magyar and Austrian domination, most Slovaks profess the Catholic faith. The Slovak language is a West Slavic language very similar to Czech. To Westerners, Slovaks are associated with the country of Czechoslovakia,

a state that existed in one form or another from 1918 to 1993. The histories of the Czechs and the Slovaks are, however, quite different, and their union in the form of Czechoslovakia served political expediency more than historical consanguinity.

From around 500 BCE, Celtic tribes known to the Romans as Boii occupied the area of today's Slovakia. The first Slavs settled the region in the fifth and sixth centuries, having migrated from the northeast (today's Belarus and Ukraine). By the first decades of the sixth century, they had reached the banks of the Danube River. The first independent Slavic state arose in the south of today's Moravia as a counterbalance to the nomadic Avars invading from the east, and the Slavs freed themselves

Woman harvests grapes near Bratislava, the capital of Slovakia. (EPA Photo/CTK/Jana Misauerova)

from Avar domination in 623, led by the Franconian merchant Samo. The western part of present-day Slovakia became the center of Samo's empire in the seventh century. Around 830, Moimír I united the Slavic tribes north of the Danube, and present-day Moravia became the center of the Great Moravian Empire, which lasted until 906 and included Bohemia, Moravia, and parts of today's Slovakia, Poland, Germany, and Hungary.

In western and southern Europe, the political and religious center of gravity had shifted from the western to the eastern part of the Mediterranean. Rome had been laid low by constant invasion, and Constantinople (known today as Istanbul) had become the seat of Christianity throughout the world. In 863, the Great Moravian leader Rastislav (846–869) sought to weaken Frankish religious influence from the west and decided his denizens required the earthly and otherworldly benefits of Christianity. In response to his request, Byzantine emperor Michael III dispatched two missionaries, the brothers Cyril and Methodius, to Moravia. Before their departure, Cyril, a linguist, philosopher, and diplomat, devised a written alphabet for the Slavic language called Glagolitic. The alphabet was based on the Slavic dialect spoken in their hometown on the Balkan Peninsula and was composed of a mixture of Greek and other eastern letters. Cyril's followers created the simpler Cyrillic alphabet from Glagolitic, which is still used in Russia, Bulgaria, Serbia, Ukraine, and Belarus. It was from Moravia that Christianity spread throughout the Slavic lands. The Great Moravian Empire, however,

was destroyed by Hungarians and Germans around 907, and Bohemia to the west became the principle Slavic state in the area. Hungarians conquered the Slovaks, who were cut off from the Czechs for a thousand years until the collapse of the Austro-Hungarian Empire in 1918. Hungarian influence can be seen especially in Slovak music and cuisine.

At the end of the Ottoman-Habsburg wars in 1699 most of the Kingdom of Hungary came under Austrian control; this included the area of the present-day Republic of Hungary; Slovakia; Transylvania, in what is now Romania; most of Croatia; parts of Serbia; and Carpathian Ruthenia.

The 19th century saw the rise of various nationalistic movements throughout the realm of the Habsburg monarchy, which were brought about in part by a 1786 decree issued by Holy Roman Emperor Josef II compelling government officials to explain legislation in the vernacular of the various peoples of the monarchy. The leader of the Slovak National Revival was Ľudovít Štúr (1815–1856), who codified the contemporary Slovak literary language. He explained the grammar of his new language standard in *Nauka reči Slovenskej* (*The Study of the Slovak Language*, 1846).

During the Slovak National Revival, the Czechs and Slovaks were still under the Austrian Monarchy and began agitating for more autonomy. When World War I erupted in 1914, Czechs and Slovaks were in no way eager to fight for their Austrian overseers. When called up for service, they defected in droves and even formed a coordinated fighting force in Russia comprising several thousand volunteers, which became known as the Czechoslovak Legion. When the empire collapsed at the end of the war, the Czechoslovak Republic was proclaimed in Prague on October 28, 1918, and on November 14, the National Assembly elected Tomáš Garrigue Masaryk as the Republic's first president.

Between the world wars, Czechoslovakia was an island of democracy in Central Europe surrounded by authoritarian and fascist regimes. It was the 10th most industrialized country in the world, comprising over 14 million people, with a nationality breakdown of (according to the 1930 census): 5.5 million Czechs, 3.5 million Slovaks, 3.2 million Germans, 700,000 Hungarians, 549,000 Ukrainians, 80,000 Poles, 186,000 Jews (both Czech and German), and 50,000 "other." Between the wars, Czechoslovak society was complex, with large landholders, middling farmers, tenants, landless laborers, and a host of specialists in the countryside such as herders, smiths, teachers, clerics, and local officials. The urban scene was equally diverse, with hundreds of thousands of small-scale manufacturers, shopkeepers, tradesmen, craftsmen, and an articulate intelligentsia. Moreover, the country lacked the extremes in wealth and poverty that marked so much of Central and Eastern Europe during this period.

With the arrival of the Great Depression, however, industrial reform lagged from lack of money and resources, and ethnic conflicts were exacerbated. The Slovaks and Ukrainians felt they had not been granted the degree of autonomy they had been promised, and by the middle of the 1930s, a large number of Czechoslovakia's German speakers—who were massed mainly along the German and Austrian borders in the so-called Sudetenland—were claiming discrimination by the Czechs and agitating for secession from Czechoslovakia to link up with Greater Germany.

German chancellor Adolf Hitler officially declared his support for a self-determined Sudetenland on September 12, 1938. When Hitler pressed, Britain and France, anxious to avoid war, urged Eduard Beneš, the president of Czechoslovakia, to relent and surrender the Czechoslovak border regions. On September 29, 1938, the dictators of Germany and Italy and the prime ministers of Britain and France gathered together in Munich to sign the so-called Munich Agreement, according to which Czechoslovakia was to surrender to Germany its borderlands. The British prime minister, Neville Chamberlain, defended the decision to give part of Czech territory to Hitler in an infamous radio address: "How horrible, fantastic, incredible it is that we should be digging trenches and trying on gas-masks here because of a quarrel in a faraway country between people of whom we know nothing." Czechoslovakia lost one-third of its territory along its western and northern borders, which included its best military fortifications, natural defenses, and vast economic resources. At the incitement of Hitler, Poland and Hungary took advantage of the situation to seize long-disputed border territories. Altogether, Czechoslovakia lost 4.8 million people, one-fourth of whom were Czechs and Slovaks.

The Slovaks, too, took advantage of the Czechs' weakness, and ancient and recent grievances against the Czechs came bubbling to the surface. They declared an autonomous government in March of 1939, elected Jozef Tiso as their president, and allied themselves with Germany. On March 13, Hitler summoned Tiso to Berlin, and the following day the Slovak Diet convened and unanimously declared Slovak independence. Tiso immediately banned all opposition political parties and instituted Nazi-inspired censorship as well as the deportation of Jews to be exterminated. During the war more than 73,000 Slovak Jews were dispatched to and murdered in concentration camps. When it was clear that the Nazis were in retreat, the Slovak anti-Nazi resistance group staged an uprising in the summer of 1944, and Soviet and Romanian troops finally liberated Slovakia in April 1945.

After the war, the Czechoslovak Republic was revived, and according to the Beneš decrees enacted during and after the war, around 3 million Germans and Hungarians were forcibly removed from Czechoslovak territory, which forever changed the makeup of the region. After the communist coup in February of 1948, Czechoslovakia began taking orders from Moscow and became a Soviet satellite until the Velvet Revolution of 1989. The brief relaxation of hard-line rule known as the Prague Spring was crushed by Warsaw Pact troops in August of 1968.

In 1989 the communist governments in Central and Eastern Europe collapsed like a house of cards. Following the reforms of Mikhail Gorbachev in the Soviet Union in the mid-1980s—*glasnost* and *perestroika*—Poland and Hungary took advantage of the reformist mood of the region and began a series of protests of their respective governments. Finally the Czechoslovak government negotiated the terms of their resignation in December 1989, and Václav Havel was elected president of the new republic. The overcoming of Czechoslovak communism became known as the Velvet Revolution—both for the peaceful way in which it was conducted and Havel's favorite rock band, the Velvet Underground.

In the immediate years after 1989, Slovakia suffered disproportionately during the transition to a market economy, and the June 1992 elections brought to power the left-leaning nationalist Movement for a Democratic Slovakia (Hnutie za demokratické Slovensko—HDZS), led by the fiery and controversial autocrat Vladimír Mečiar, a Soviet-trained lawyer and firm believer in Slovak independence. In July, the Slovak parliament voted to secede from the republic, and despite numerous efforts, leaders could not agree on a compromise. On January 1, 1993, Czechoslovakia once again ceased to exist, becoming the Czech and Slovak Republics. The divorce, compared to other national separations in the region, was relatively smooth. Václav Havel was elected president of the Czech Republic, and Mečiar became prime minister of Slovakia. Slovakia joined the North Atlantic Treaty Organization on March 29, 2004, and the European Union on May 1, 2004. It adopted the euro on January 1, 2009. Today Slovakia's economy is considered a "tiger economy," known as the Tatra Tiger. In 2007 it had the highest sustained GDP growth in the European Union.

*Craig Cravens*

**Further Reading**

Busik, Josef, et al. *The Slovak Republic. Country Report.* Vienna: Bank Austria AG, 1993.

Kirschbaum, Stanislav J. *A History of Slovakia: The Struggle for Survival.* New York: St. Martin's Griffin, 1995.

Wolchik, Sharon. "Czechoslovakia." In *The Columbia History of Eastern Europe in the Twentieth Century*, ed. Josef Held. New York: Columbia University Press, 1992, 119–163.

# Slovenians

Slovenians (*Slovenci*, pl.) are a Slavic people who make up the dominant population of Slovenia, with a population of 2,010,377 (2006). Historically, Slovenians were called *Kranjci* (German, *Crainer*), from the name of the Austro-Hungarian imperial province Crain (Latin, *Carniola*) that was for centuries the central imperial province with a Slovenian populace. The linguistic and political borders of Slovenian territory shifted considerably throughout the early and medieval times and were resolved to the present-day territory of the Republic of Slovenia only after World War I and World War II. Important centers of Slovenian culture developed during the late 19th century in Ljubljana, the present capital and largest city, Maribor, Celje, and outside the present state of Slovenia, in Vienna, Klagenfurt, and Trieste. There

still live Slovenian speakers in neighboring countries that are politically organized and enjoy minority protection.

Throughout the 19th century for mostly economic reasons, and during the 20th century for predominantly political reasons, Slovenians migrated first to the United States, Argentina, and Australia, and then to France and Germany, where there exist organized diaspora communities. The Republic of Slovenia legally recognizes these "Slovenians without Slovenian citizenship" and grants their members a specific position within the Slovenian legal order. Slovenians are traditionally Roman Catholic (57.8% according to the 2002 census), although 42 other religious groups are registered in Slovenia. Slovenians speak Slovenian, a South Slav language that has numerous diverse spoken dialects and three different historic written standards of which two are in use in Slovenia and northern Italy, respectively. The earliest document of Slovenian language dates back to CE 1000 (the Freising/Brežinje codex).

Archeological evidence indicates continuous human habitation in what is today Slovenian territory since the Neolithic, notably the settlements on stilts in the Ljubljana marshes from the Hallstatt period. Romans came into contact with the Celtic Noric tribe by the second century BCE. By CE 10, Noricum and neighboring Pannonia were incorporated into the Roman Empire, which already included Istria (part of the Italian region of Venetia et Histria), and the early inhabitants of the Slovenian territory were subsequently Latinized and later Christianized.

In the late sixth century, unidentified Slavic tribes settled in and engaged in military conflicts and cultural interaction with neighboring Lombards and Bavarians. In the mid-seventh century a Slavic feudal kingdom, Carantania, was founded that included the northernmost parts of what is now Slovenian territory and southern Austria. Carantanian feudal rulers were supposedly elected in a special ritual that remains part of the Slovenian political tradition and has recently caused political conflict with the neighboring Austria over the symbolic ownership of the ritual. Independent Carantania lasted only until the early ninth century, when it was incorporated into the Frankish feudal lands and Germanic nobility replaced the emerging Slavic nobility. After the fall of Carantania, Slovenians were distinguished primarily by language and status as a low social class subordinated to foreign elites.

In the early Middle Ages, eight monasteries were founded, as were several medieval commercial towns (coastal towns that had existed without interruption since the antiquity developed a specific Mediterranean culture). Slovenians were serfs to feudal lords of several kingdoms, such noble dynasties as the dukes of Carinthia, the patriarchs of Aquileia, the Andech, the Traungau, the Babenberg, the Spanheim, and in particular the Habsburg that conquered most of the Slovenian lands by the early 15th century. Their only serious competitors in the late Middle Ages were the Counts of Cilli, whose ascent ended with the absence of descendants in the mid-15th century. Intensification of Ottoman attacks in the late 15th century precipitated peasant rebellions, while

the Reformation in the mid-16th century produced the first books in the Slovenian language under the influence of the Protestant preacher Primož Trubar. The counter-Reformation that followed reinforced the grip of the Roman Catholic Church on the Slovenian peasant population, a grip further strengthened by Habsburg absolutism. However, in the course of the 18th century, enlightened Habsburg absolutist rulers such as Marie Therese modernized education, transportation, and economy in Slovenian lands. Finally, Joseph II partially abolished feudalism in 1782 and opened the way for the emergence of a Slovenian-oriented small nobility and bourgeoisie, partially influenced by enlightenment ideas; notable members included the baron Sigismund Zois, Anton Tomaž Linhart, and Janez Vajkard Valvasor. Despite these gains, a relatively small number of German-, Italian-, and Hungarian-speaking nobility and bourgeoisie continued to dominate towns in Slovenian majority territories.

In reaction to the liberal ideas of the French Revolution, briefly introduced in the period of French rule, when Slovenian lands were made part of Napoleon's Illyrian provinces (1809–1813), Slovenian nationalism emerged. Nationalism found a voice in burgeoning literary production in the Slovenian language. By 1848 modern written Slovenian had been modeled on the dominant German culture of the Austrian (Habsburg) empire. Slovenian intellectuals were divided into liberals, the so-called "Prešeren circle" after the Goethe-inspired poet France Prešeren (1800–1849), and conservatives, dominated by the Catholic bishop Anton Martin Slomšek and the linguist Jernej Kopitar, an ideological split that was found in many other Central European ethnic communities. The first half of the 19th century gave rise to local pan-Slavic linguistic ideas, notably in the works of Stanko Vraz (1810–1851), but they were rejected by Prešeren, the linguist and literary historian Matija Čop (1797–1835), and other liberals.

Nineteenth-century Romanticism inspired Slovenian intellectual elites, like their peers across Central Europe, to engage in the German-style invention of folk culture. Language was consistently seen, as it is to this day, as the most endangered and the most important sign of Slovenian culture and nationhood (as the two were conceptually equated). Aspects of peasant culture were elevated to the status of national symbols, as was the case of the supposedly unique Slovenian hayrack (*kozolec*). In the early 20th century figures such as Franc Saleški Finžgar (1871–1962) produced literary works celebrating the ancient history of Slovenians while writers such as Prežihov Voranc (1893–1950) offered poetic interpretations of the hardships of peasant life. A distinctively Slovenian high culture emerged only during the early 20th century; key figures include Jožef Plečnik (1872–1957) in architecture, Rihard Jakopič (1869–1943) in Impressionist painting, and Ivan Cankar (1876–1918) in the Modernist literary movement. The Socialist Realism of the post-World War II period likewise produced lasting artistic accomplishments such as the so-called Partisan literature and poetry, architectural Functionalism, and sculpture on the theme of resistance and revolution. During the 1970s and 1980s, Slovenian artists and intellectuals gained national and international acclaim, including the philosopher Slavoj Žižek (1949–), the pop/punk group Laibach (notably its holistic artistic project entitled *Neue Slowenische Kunst*), and writers Svetlana Makarovič (1939–), Drago Jančar (1948–), and comic strip author Tomaž Lavrič (1964–).

On October 1918, following the demise of the Austro-Hungarian Empire, Slovenia became part of the State of Slovenians, Croats, and Serbs with Zagreb as capital; in December 1918 this entity merged with the Kingdom of Serbia to become the Kingdom of Serbs, Croats, and Slovenians. In 1929, the state was renamed the Kingdom of Yugoslavia (that is, the Kingdom of Southern Slavs). The kingdom dissolved during World War II; in its place, the Communist Democratic Federative Yugoslavia was proclaimed on November 25, 1945, renamed Federative People' Republic of Yugoslavia a year later, and finally the Socialist Federative Republic of Yugoslavia (SFRY) in 1963. During the 1980s, civil movements in Slovenia increasingly opposed the post-Tito regime in Yugoslavia, the rise of Serbian ethnic nationalism in Kosovo, and Yugoslav legislation and military organization. In May 1988, the Slovenian branch of Yugoslav secret police and the Yugoslav Army arrested four leading Slovenian opposition journalists and political workers under the charge of antirevolutionary activity and military espionage. The Trial of the Four (Janez Janša, David Borštnar, David Tasič, Franci Zavrl) instigated a mass civil resistance movement (Board for the Protection of Human Rights) against communism and the Yugoslav state.

On May 8, 1989, new political parties published the so-called May Declaration, demanding the formation of a sovereign, democratic, and pluralist Slovenian state, echoing the historic May Declaration of 1917 of Slovenian, Croat, and Serbian representatives in the Viennese parliament that demanded the formation of the state of Southern Slavs in view of the imminent demise of the Austro-Hungarian Empire. On the basis of a plebiscite for independence (December 26, 1990) that had gained support from 88.5 percent of registered voters, Slovenia proclaimed independence on July 25, 1991. Croatia declared independence the next day, and the SFRY, decaying under Serbian militarism led by Slobodan Milošević, quickly dissolved. In the so-called Ten-Days War that followed the proclamation of independence, the Yugoslav army sought to reverse the actions of the Slovenian parliament and government. Slovenia agreed to a cease-fire and a temporary suspension of further activities related to independence with the Brioni declaration of July 7, 1991, mediated by a diplomatic "troika" of EU Member States' foreign ministers. Led by a pragmatic coalition of anticommunist parties (DEMOS), Slovenia adopted its new constitution as a democratic country and a social welfare state with a capitalist economy on December 23, 1991. During 1992, Slovenia was officially recognized by most countries. It became a member of the UN in 2002, NATO in 2004, and the European Union in 2004. It adopted the Euro in 2007 and Slovenia presided over the Council of European Union in 2008.

The DEMOS coalition dissolved in 1992 when the first democratic elections were held under the new constitution. In the first decade of independence (1992–2002), the broad-coalition governments were marked by the personality of leftist liberal democratic Prime Minister Janez Drnovšek (1950–2008) and Milan Kučan (1941–), two-term President of the Republic (1992–1997, 1997–2002) and former Communist leader of Slovenia. In the 2004 elections, the opposition leader, independence fighter, and DEMOS' Minister of Defense during the Ten-Days War, Janez Janša (1958–), and his Slovenian Social Democrat party assembled the first rightist coalition to last for its entire elected term. The steadfast rivalry between Kučan as a symbol of preindependence political "continuity" and Janša as the leader of the Pro-Catholic, nationalist right stabilized into a 50-50 national division between liberals and traditionalists, the left and the right, reflecting an ideological split that reaches back at least to the revolutionary 1840s.

Today self-identified Slovenians make up over 83 percent of the country's population. Minority populations consist of Italians and Hungarians at the border areas who enjoy special constitutional and legal protection as a consequence of peace treaties following World War I and World War II; the Roma, which are also legally protected as a minority since 2006; migrants and descendants of migrants from all ex-Yugoslav federal republics; and migrants, predominantly noncitizens from nonneighboring countries. Slovenia shares, with other ex-Socialist countries, a plethora of political and social dysfunctions, among them scavenger privatization, a chaotic economy, severely downgraded systems of social and health care, outdated industrial infrastructure, a complete collapse of the judiciary, an aging society with negative natality and no organized migration policy, the all-pervasive equating of the traditional, single social class, ethnic community with the modern civil state, and the systematic inability of the media to professionally assert their prodemocratic function. Ethnic exclusivism, xenophobia, nepotism, and the absence of professionalism and meritocracy at all levels, the burgeoning of bureaucracy, and passionate disputes about the past all figure importantly in national debates. The elections of 2008 brought to power a leftist coalition led by the successors of the old Communist Party; however, no fresh ideas and leaders seem to be in sight.

*Irena Šumi and Cirila Toplak*

**Further Reading**

Blitz, Brad K., ed. *War and Change in the Balkans: Nationalism, Conflict, and Cooperation.* Cambridge, UK: Cambridge University Press, 2006.

Čop, Jaka, and Tone Cevc. *Slovenski kozolec (Slovene Hay-Rack).* Žirovnica: Agens, 1993.

Cox, John. *Slovenia: Evolving Loyalties.* New York: Routledge, 2005.

Grdina, Igor. *Preroki, doktrinarji, epigoni: idejni boji na Slovenskem v prvi polovici 20. stoletja (Prophets, Doctrinaries, Epigones: Ideational Struggles in Slovenia in the First Half of the 20th Century).* Ljubljana: Inštitut za civilizacijo in kulturo—ICK, 2005.

Luthar, Oto, ed. *The Land Between: A History of Slovenia.* Frankurt/Main: Peter Lang, 2008.

Monroe, Alexei. *Interrogation Machine: Laibach and NSK.* Massachusetts: MIT Press, 2005.

Rotar, Drago B. *Odbiranje iz preteklosti: okviri, mreže, orientirji, časi kulturnega življenja v dolgem 19. stoletju (Picking from the Past: Frames, Networks, Orientation Marks, Times of Cultural Life During the Long 19th Century).* Koper: Annales, 2007.

Vezjak, Boris. *Sproščena ideologija Slovencev: o političnih implikacijah filozofema sproščenost (The Relaxed Ideology of the Slovenes: On the Political Implications of the Philosopheme Relaxedness).* Ljubljana: Mirovni inštitut/Peace Institute, 2007.

## Sorbs

Sorbs or Wends are a Slavic people living predominantly in the countryside, in the federal states of Brandenburg and Saxony (region of Lusatia) in the Federal Republic of Germany. Sorbs are known as *Serbja* (Sorbian), *Sorben* or *Wenden* (German), and Sorbs or Wends (English). The Federal Ministry of the Interior estimates there are about 20,000 Sorbs in Brandenburg and 40,000 in Saxony. They speak Upper Sorbian (in Saxony) and Lower Sorbian (in Brandenburg). Both languages belong to the Western Slavonic group of languages. All Sorbs are proficient in the German language. Approximately three-quarters of Sorbs are Protestant and one-quarter Roman Catholic.

The Slav tribes lived from the 6th century in what is today the eastern part of Germany and were subject to German authority from the 10th century. They mixed with migrating German settlers and were assimilated. The Sorbs were only able to maintain their Slav language, culture, and identity in Lusatia, which lay on the periphery and was colonized later.

Sorbian language and culture blossomed in the wake of the Reformation. The translation of the Bible (completed in 1728) led to the training of Sorbian-speaking priests and later teachers as well as the development of Sorbian-language religious texts and later secular literature. Sorbian newspapers and journals started to appear in the middle of the 19th century. A national political and cultural movement against assimilatory pressures from the German state (Germanization) was formed in the 19th century. The Sorbian minority did not receive any state support until 1945. Only basic Sorbian language instruction was given in schools. The Sorbian political and cultural umbrella organization Domowina (founded in 1912), other organizations, and the Sorbian media were all banned by the Nazis in 1937, and active Sorbs were persecuted.

The communist regime in the German Democratic Republic recognized the Sorbs as a national minority (1948 Law on the Protection of the Rights of the Sorbian People). Sorbian state schools, cultural organizations, and media were founded. However, Communist Party members held positions of authority in Domowina and other Sorb organizations, effectively stifling an independent Sorb voice, and Sorbs who refused to accept the terms of the one-party state were discriminated in school, at work, and in cultural affairs.

After the reunification of Germany, protection and support for the Sorbs were legally guaranteed by the state (in the form of an article in the constitutions and Sorbian laws in both federal states). The political interests of the Sorbs continue to be represented by Domowina, an umbrella organization representing 15 cultural and other organizations and counting some 8,000 members.

Important centers of Sorbian culture are the towns of Bautzen/Budyšin (Saxony) and Cottbus/Chośebuz (Brandenburg), which have grammar schools, academic institutions, museums, and a publishing house. Additionally, Bautzen hosts a bilingual theater and the Sorbian National Ensemble. There are 30 primary schools, 10 middle schools and 2 grammar schools with Sorbian as the language of instruction or Sorbian language classes. The total number of pupils is about 4,000. Research on the language, history, and culture of the Sorbs is conducted by the Sorbian Institute in Bautzen, and Sorbian studies are taught at the University of Leipzig. Modern Sorbian culture includes literature, theatre, music, and folklore adaptations. Handrij Zejler (1804–1872) and Jakub Bart-Ćišinski (1856–1909) are considered to be the national poets; significant artists in the 20th century are the writers Jurij Brězan (1916–2006) and Kito Lorenc (1938–) and the composers Jan Rawp (1928–2007) and Juro Mětšk (1954–). Sorbian customs and traditions are still cultivated in rural areas. Some older women wear Sorbian costumes every day, while younger women and girls wear them on festive occasions. Sorbs are for the most part employed in industry, services, and the public sector, with around 10 percent making a living in agriculture. For the last 120 years there has been open cast lignite mining in the Sorbian area, in particular in Brandenburg; given the dense settlement pattern in this part of Germany, the opening of mines has led to the resettlement of some 15,000 people from 80 villages and towns.

Several hundred of Sorbs emigrated to the United States in the 19th century. They maintained their language in the Texan villages of Serbin and Giddings up to the beginning of the 20th century. The Wendish Heritage Museum in Serbin keeps alive the memory of the Sorbian migrants.

*Ludwig Elle*

**Further Reading**

Barker, Peter. *Slavs in Germany: The Sorbian Minority and the German State since 1945.* Studies in German Thought and History 20. Lewiston: Edwin Mellen Press, 2000.

Kasper, Martin, ed. *Language and Culture of the Lusatian Sorbs throughout Their History.* Berlin: Akademie-Verlag, 1987.

Stone, Gerald. *The Smallest Slavonic Nation: The Sorbs of Lusatia.* London: Athlone Press, 1972.

## Spaniards

Spaniards are the citizens of Spain. There are also important diasporic communities of Spaniards and their descendants in the Americas, France, Germany, and Switzerland. Spain has a population of 46 million people. Spanish, or Castilian, is spoken throughout the whole country, although Catalan, Galician, and Basque are also spoken in some regions. Catholicism has traditionally been the religion of the group, but nowadays just a minority is observant. It should be noted that Spaniards self-differentiate themselves into distinct subgroups, including Castilians, Andalusians, Catalans, Galicians, Basques, Valencians, Aragonese, Canary Islanders, and Navarrese. Historically, Roma have constituted the

main ethnic minority in Spain. At present, there are over half a million Spanish Roma living in the country.

The Iberian Peninsula has been inhabited for at least 35,000 years. The first ethnic group known to inhabit the region were the Iberians, an Iron Age culture that settled in the east and south of the peninsula at the beginning of the third millennium. In the ninth century BCE, Celtic peoples colonized the north of the Iberian Peninsula. Their interaction with the Iberians led to the formation of the Celtiberian culture in the central plateau of the peninsula. The Celtíberos had contact with Greeks and Phoenicians, who established trading settlements along the eastern and southern coasts. The latter also named the Iberian Peninsula "Hispania," literally "land of rabbits." Following a period of Carthaginian domination in the third century BCE, the Romans gradually took control of the whole peninsula. The provinces of Hispania were fully integrated into the imperial system, and Roman culture and Latin language expanded. The decline of Roman power led to a series of invasions of the peninsula by Swabians, Vandals, Alans, and Visigoths in the fifth century CE. Of all the Germanic invaders, the Visigoths emerged dominant. By the seventh century CE, they had been Romanized, converted to Christianity, and established the Kingdom of Toledo, which loosely controlled the entire peninsula.

The realm of Toledo came to an abrupt end following the Muslim invasion of the Peninsula (711–718). Soon after, the Umayyad dynasty (736–1031) created an emirate, with its capital in Cordova. The Umayyad developed cities, such as

Seville and Toledo, which became famous throughout Europe for their advanced learning and modern industries. They also granted a certain level of religious toleration to their subjects, and large numbers of Jews and Christians lived together with Muslims. Yet the peaceful coexistence of diverse religious groups was eventually challenged by Christian rebels. A number of small Christian kingdoms emerged in the northern mountains and slowly drove the Muslims southwards. By late 13th century, the whole Iberian Peninsula was in Christian hands, with the exception of the Kingdom of Granada. War also led to a process of territorial amalgamation and Castile, Aragon, and Portugal emerged as the biggest kingdoms of the Iberian Peninsula. In 1469, the marriage of Isabella and Ferdinand II led to the union of the realms of Castile and Aragon and the creation of the Spanish monarchy. The incorporation of the Kingdom of Granada into Castile (1492) and the annexation of Navarre (1511–1514) completed the unification of peninsular Spain.

Christian control of the Iberian Peninsula meant the forceful expulsion of Jews (1492) and Muslims (1609). Many Jews and Muslims nominally converted to Christianity but continued to practice their original religion. Christian expansion also led to the dissemination of the Castilian language. A Romance language, Castilian developed and expanded in the late Middle Ages by incorporating numerous terms from Arab, Basque, Aragonese, Catalan, Astur-Leonés, and Galaico-Portuguese. Following the dynastic union of Castile and Aragon, the Castilian language began to be known also as Spanish. Castilian grew in the Americas,

Africa, and the Philippines, as it became the language of choice of the Spanish imperial administration. The Spanish empire of the Habsburgs (16th and 17th centuries) and the Bourbons (18th and early 19th century) also imposed the Catholic faith in the newly conquered lands. In Europe, the Habsburg monarchs tended to side with the Vatican in the 16th- and 17th-century wars of religion, which gradually led to identifying Spaniards with Catholicism. The 16th and the 17th centuries also witnessed the Spanish Golden Age in the arts. The writings of Miguel de Cervantes, Francisco Quevedo, and Pedro Calderón de la Barca as well as the paintings of Diego Velázquez and Bartolomé Murillo are good examples of Spanish art of the period.

As in all European countries, it was the end of the old order that led to the creation of the modern nation in Spain. Throughout the 19th century two models of Spanish nationalism emerged: liberal and traditionalist. In the main, the liberal canon emphasized civic features and understood Spain as a community of destiny defined by a common body of law, that is, a constitution, which applied to all citizens. Traditionalists defined Spaniards in ethnic terms and considered Catholicism as the defining feature of the Spanish people. Underneath these conflicting ideas of the nature of Spaniards lay two antagonistic political projects. While liberals gradually advocated a democratic Spain, traditionalists defended authoritarianism as the best manner of governing the country. Both views were to clash in a number of military conflicts of which the Spanish Civil War (1936–1939) was the most violent. The victory of General Francisco Franco and the subsequent dictatorship signaled the triumph of the ethnic canon based on Catholicism and the Castilian language as the hallmarks of Spanishness.

Yet the establishment of a new democratic system in the late 1970s reinstalled a more civic and multicultural conception of Spaniards. The current Constitution of 1978 declares Castilian the official language of the country but grants Catalan, Basque, and Galician co-official status in the regions where the latter are spoken. The constitution also states that no religion shall have a state character and guarantees freedom of ideology and worship to individuals and communities. Today, the main political parties describe Spaniards as a multicultural civic community loyal to the 1978 Constitution. Regardless of linguistic, geographical, and religious background, one's Spanish identity is now seen as following directly from one's Spanish citizenship. Nevertheless, it is worth noting that some of the old ethnic associations between Spaniards, Catholicism, and the Castilian language are still operating. For example, the immigration policies of José María Aznar's government displayed a certain ethnic concern. In 2002, the conservative government authorized the entrance of 1 million immigrants in response to Spain's economic need of cheap labor, but this authorization was restricted to Latin Americans—rather than the geographically more sensible choice of North Africans—on account of the religious and linguistic affinity of the former and perceived assimilation problems pertaining to the latter.

Some school textbooks still give an ethnic vision of Spaniards and portray Christianity and the wars against the Muslims as the core of the nation's historical formation. In Spanish popular culture, the figure of the Moroccan continues to signify the barbarian "other." The endurance of the concept of the Moor as the alien that defines what Spanishness is not, and therefore links the nation to Christianity, may come as a surprise in a society that has dramatically secularized its habits in the last 30 years. Yet the power of this idea arises from its role as the foundational myth of the nation rather than from the number of Spaniards who still practice their Catholic faith. The idea that Spain was built by Christians against Muslims persists in popular consciousness, regardless of the fact that nowadays less than 18 percent of Spaniards are practicing Christians.

Democracy and a rapid economic growth have radically transformed Spain in the last 30 years. The trend by which over a million Spaniards migrated to Western European countries in the last years of the Franco dictatorship has been dramatically reversed. Excluding illegal immigration, there are over 5,500,000 foreigners living in Spain, which means that 12 percent of the country's population was born abroad. These figures place Spain at the top of the European Union immigration rates. But what really makes Spain unique is the pace with which its substantial immigrant community had come into being. It rose 10-fold between 1996 and 2009.

The last three decades have also witnessed an important cultural transformation. Spain has become a fully urbanized, modern country that plays a central role in the European Union. Pedro Almodóvar, Antonio Banderas, and Penélope

Cruz represent a new generation of artists and have replaced 20th-century Federico García Lorca, Pablo Picasso, and Salvador Dalí as iconic figures of Spain. Some of the traditional activities such as bullfighting are losing ground, whereas other, more globalized forms of entertainment have become extremely popular among young Spaniards.

The constitutional system created in the late 1970s established a highly decentralized Spain. The country is divided into 17 regions, or "autonomous communities," with their own governments, parliaments, public officers, and media. The regional governments have powers over many areas, including education, policing, health care and, in some autonomous communities, tax collection. This semifederal state structure has led to the emergence of regional political elites that have shown a keen interest in promoting the identities of their own autonomous communities. The fostering of regional identities from above has effectively contributed to the fact that nowadays most Spaniards identify with both their autonomous community and Spain. Strengthening regional identities has proven compatible to upholding a common Spanish identity.

The same pattern can be observed in autonomous communities with robust regional nationalist movements, such as Catalonia and the Basque country. Decentralization has bolstered regional feelings in Spain, just as devolution reinforced the identities of Quebecers and Scots in Canada and the United Kingdom, respectively. However, the increasing level of identification with the Basque country and Catalonia has not weakened the level of affinity with Spain of Catalans and Basques. If anything, self-government in these autonomous communities has encouraged the emergence of dual identities. Nowadays, the vast majority of Catalans (80%) and most Basques (61%) declare a feeling of identification with both their autonomous community and Spain. These multiple identities are possible because national and regional identities in these cases are generally considered to be compatible rather than antagonistic, even though some sections of public opinion in Catalonia and, especially, the Basque Country do identify exclusively with one or the other.

Spaniards also feel deeply European. Surveys regularly show that Spanish identification with Europe is one of the highest in the European Union. One of the reasons for the strength of this rapport with Europe is that for most of the 20th century, and in particular under the unpopular Franco dictatorship, it signified modernity and democracy for Spaniards who aspired to both. In the current democratic system, Europeanism is not seen as a threat to national uniformity but rather as a complement to Spanish and regional identities.

In a postmodern world where identities are multiple and fragmented, Spanishness has been radically transformed. In the last three decades, economic globalization, European integration, and massive immigration have simply changed what it means to be a Spaniard. Nowadays, Spaniards are defined in terms of citizenship, civic values, multiculturalism, and loyalty to the 1978 Constitution. Yet the old ethnic perceptions, rooted in a mythological common origin, Catholicism, and the Castilian language, still exert a significant influence on the way Spaniards perceive themselves and are seen abroad.

*Alejandro Quiroga*

## Further Reading

Balfour, Sebastian, and Alejandro Quiroga. *The Reinvention of Spain. Nation and Identity since Democracy*. Oxford: Oxford University Press, 2007.

Díez Medrano, Juan, and Paula Gutiérrez. "Nested Identities: National and European Identity in Spain." *Ethnic and Racial Studies* 24, no. 5 (2001): 773–778.

Hooper, John. *The New Spaniards*. London: Penguin, 2006.

Kamen, Henry. *Imagining Spain. Historical Myth and National Identity*. New Haven: Yale University Press, 2008.

Mar-Molinero, Clare, and Angel Smith, eds. *Nationalism and the Nation in the Iberian Peninsula*. Oxford: Berg, 1996.

Muro, Diego, and Alejandro Quiroga. "Spanish Nationalism. Ethnic or Civic?" *Ethnicities* 5, no. 4 (2005): 567–569.

Tremlett, Giles. *Ghosts of Spain: Travels through a Country's Hidden Past*. London: Faber and Faber, 2006.

# Svans

Svans (*mushuan* in Svan; *svani* in Georgian) are concentrated in the northwestern mountainous province of Svaneti (sometimes referred to as Svanetia, and in classical sources as Suania) of the Republic of Georgia. Svaneti has traditionally been divided into upper (Zemo Svaneti) and lower (Kvemo Svaneti) parts, reflecting the region's geography; Svans also live dispersed throughout Georgia. Until August 2008 Svans also populated the Kodori gorge in the seceded territory of Abkhazia, formerly the Autonomous Republic of Abkhazia within Soviet Georgia. There are no reliable figures for numbers of Svans, but they are thought to number not more than 30,000. The principal distinguishing marker of Svan identity is the Svan language, a vernacular language belonging to the Kartvelian language family and itself differentiated into a large number of localized Upper Svan and Lower Svan dialects. Svan is thought to have branched off from the Kartvelian languages' common ancestor in the 18th century BCE, and is not mutually intelligible with any other language in the family. Svan identity is also denoted by characteristic surname endings in -niani and -ani, although bearers of these surnames are by no means all competent in the Svan language. In terms of religious identity Svans are indistinguishable from other Georgians in adhering to the Georgian Orthodox faith; however, pre-Christian traditions are prominent in Svan folklore. Svans use Georgian as their literary language.

Isolated by its extremely remote and hazardous geography, Svaneti has historically retained a strong local identity, rooted in a strong martial tradition, and resisted easy incorporation into neighboring polities. For the same reasons the region also served as a refuge for exiles from political struggles elsewhere in Georgia. Svaneti was loosely incorporated into the centralized Bagratid kingdom from 1008–1442. Following the fragmentation of the kingdom on account of Mongol invasions, Svaneti survived as a principality, with different areas under the control of different dynasties, notably the Dadeshkeliani in Upper Svaneti. Internal instability led the Dadeshkeliani to seek protectorate status from the Russian Empire in 1833. Svaneti was eventually incorporated directly into the Russian Empire in 1858, and later, after a brief spell as part of independent Georgia 1918–1921, the Soviet Union.

Early Soviet ethnographers classified Svans as a separate census category, along with a number of other subgroups later classified as Georgians distinguished by vernacular language or religion (for example, Mingrelians, Laz, Ajarians). These were consolidated, however, in the mid-1930s into a single Georgian identity category, after which these subgroup identities were stigmatized as backward. Interest in Svan identity was restricted after this time to linguistics and ethnography. Depopulation in Svaneti became a concern during the late Soviet period, a process accelerated by the economically difficult conditions of the post-Soviet period. As a result of the Georgian-Russian-South Ossetian conflict in August 2008, just under 2,000 Svans were forcibly displaced from the Kodori gorge in Abkhazia, when Georgian control over the gorge, reestablished in 2006, was again lost. They remain displaced as of this writing.

In light of the dispersal of Svans correlating with the depopulation of Svaneti, there is growing concern among linguists regarding the future of the Svan language amid evidence of reduced competence in the language among young Svans. Unfortunately discussion of this theme in Geor-

gia remains politicized by the country's recent history of secessionist conflict.

*Laurence Broers*

## Further Reading

Topuria, V., and M. Kaldani. *Svanuri leksikoni (Svan Dictionary)*. Tbilisi: Kartuli Ena, 2000.

Tuite, Kevin. "Svan." *Languages of the World/ Materials*, vol. 139. Munich: LINCOM Europa, 1997.

# Swedes

Swedes make up the majority of the more than 9 million people inhabiting Sweden, a constitutional monarchy located on the Scandinavian Peninsula. The largest cities are Stockholm (just under 2 million) and Gothenburg (just under 500,000). The country has experienced considerable immigration in recent decades, and almost 20 percent of the populace is of foreign origins. The largest diasporic community of Swedes is found in the United States, particularly in the upper Midwest. Most Swedes are members of the Lutheran Church, though the number of adherents has dropped recently. Swedish is the principal language of the country; in addition, Finnish, Meänkieli, Yiddish, Romani, and Saami are recognized as official minority languages.

Swedes originate from hunter-gatherer groups who settled in the Scandinavian Peninsula 12,000–13,000 years ago. Modern population genetic studies indicate that 85 percent of present-day ethnic Swedes originate from those first hunter-gatherers.

St. Lucia's Day is observed in communities throughout Sweden with the selection of young women to portray St. Lucia for the day. In Swedish families, the eldest daughter dresses in a white gown and wears a crown of lighted candles and lingonberry leaves. (AFP/Getty Images)

Starting about four thousand years ago, agriculture and metalworking (first bronze, then iron) spread across the peninsula. During the Viking Age (793–1050), locally based chiefdoms spreading into neighboring Norway, where they cooperated and competed for power at home and for lucrative trade and plunder abroad. Swedish Vikings in particular grew rich from the trade in slaves and furs in the Baltic Sea and into western Russia. By the end of the Viking period, the principal centers of population and power were the central area (Svealand) and southern area (Götaland). (*Sverige*, the country's name in Swedish,

is thought to originate from Svea Rike, the presumed medieval kingdom or state in central Sweden.) The country was unified under a single king (Sverker) early in the 12th century. Stockholm was founded in 1252 by Birger Jarl and became Sweden's political center in the 17th century.

The most powerful and influential king in Sweden was Gustav Vasa (1496–1560). He was of common origin, but became sovereign as the leader of a rebellion against the so-called Kalmar Union, a union linking the kingdoms of Denmark, Norway, and Sweden, created in 1397 and lasting till 1523. The union incorporated areas like Finland, Iceland, the Faeroe Islands, Greenland, the Orkney Islands, and the Shetland Islands. Denmark and Norway remained united until 1536. Gustav Vasa put an end to elected kings and introduced instead hereditary monarchy in Sweden, an institution that remains today, albeit without real power. From 1610 Sweden developed into a great north European power, including the Baltic States and considerable parts of North Germany.

The Nordic countries (Sweden, Denmark, Norway, Finland, and Iceland) are politically interwoven, earlier through wars, later by friendship and cooperation. Norway and Denmark especially figure prominently in Swedish history and culture, and these countries' languages are mutually understood. All of them have developed from Old Norse, as has Icelandic. During the 16th and 17th centuries several violent wars were fought between Sweden and Denmark. When the final one came to an end in the 1720s, five Danish districts had been incorporated into Sweden. In 1814 Sweden and Norway were united in a political union, which was peacefully dissolved in 1905. After the period of Nordic wars ended, peaceful relations have remained between the five Scandinavian countries and today there is a strong sense of community and cultural affinity. The countries' common history and (except for Finland) a shared linguistic heritage and shared religious history within the Lutheran Church contribute to this.

Throughout history Swedes have also been influenced by northern Europeans. During the 16th and 17th centuries, for instance, German traders and craftsmen settled in Sweden. The numbers were relatively small, but they came to have an important impact on Swedish society. Their language influenced the Swedish language, which now has many German-based words, and prosperous merchant families from England and Holland brought significant business knowledge to Sweden. The 1800s saw French influence, especially at the royal court and among the nobility. Those immigrants groups were the internationalists of their time and their field of action was Europe, not just Sweden.

The first Christian missionary (St. Ansgar) arrived in Sweden in the 9th century, and by the 12th century most of the country had dropped the Viking gods for Christianity. Sweden got its first archbishopric (Uppsala) in 1164 and remained Catholic till 1525, when King Gustav Vasa broke the bond with Rome by himself appointing a clergyman friend—Laurentius Petri, who incidentally would soon marry—as archbishop and not letting the pope consecrate him. The New Testament was published in Swedish in 1526 and the full Bible in 1541; in 1544 Lutheranism became the official religion. In the course of the 18th and 19th centuries the Swedish church was influenced by Pietism, which stressed personal religious experience. In keeping with the increasingly ecumenical stance of the church and country, from 1952 Swedes were able to withdraw from the church. Then, in 2000, the Swedish Parliament decided to sever the Lutheran church from the state, in keeping with the view that the state should not prescribe a particular ideological/religious orientation to its citizens. Sweden is now one of the most secular societies in the world.

Swedish is a North Germanic language, closely related to Norwegian and other Nordic languages. Modern Swedish is based on the dialects spoken in central Sweden in the early 16th century. The translation of the New Testament is generally acknowledged as the beginning of modern Swedish. The establishment of the Swedish Academy (1786), an institution devoted to the preservation and celebration of Swedish (as well as literature generally), marked the state's commitment to the language. A standardized form (*rikssvenska*) of Swedish was promoted from the late 19th century, but regionally distinct dialects continue to be spoken. Swedish is an official language of Finland, along with Finnish.

Sweden was urbanized late and its lifestyle still reflects the peasant heritage to a certain extent, for instance, in a preference for small groups of friends who share similar views and values. Another Swedish characteristic is the love of the countryside and a need for solitude. According to World Values Surveys (1999–2002), leisure stands out as more important to Swedes than most other nationalities, and almost half of the households have a second home, either in a rural area, in the mountains, or at the sea, something which is unique to Sweden. Youth pursue a more urban lifestyle than earlier generations, and eating out has now become the most popular leisure activity in Sweden. This is most certainly a consequence of cheap foreign travel, in combination with the abundance of ethnic restaurants run by immigrants. In the same survey Sweden stands out as one of the most individualistic societies; about half of Swedish households consist of only one person, the highest percentage in Europe.

Until the end of the 19th century, Sweden was a comparatively poor country, and it remained so overwhelmingly into the 20th. After World War II Sweden rapidly became a global industrial power. This transition was made possible by Sweden's neutrality in World War II, which had left the productive capacity unscathed and Sweden ready to supply much-needed materials and products to war-torn Europe. Sweden also became internationally renowned for its social democratic system with a high standard of living, social security system, radical public planning, high taxation, and balanced distribution of income.

Internationally known Swedes include: Carl von Linné or Linnaeus (botanist, 1707–1778), Alfred Nobel (inventor of dynamite and founder of the Nobel Price, 1833–1896), August Strindberg (writer and dramatist, 1849–1912), Greta Garbo (film actress, 1905–1990), Dag Hammarskjöld (Secretary General of the United Nations, 1905–1961), Astrid Lindgren (children's writer, 1907–2002), Raoul Wallenberg (leader of rescue action for the Jews in Hungary during World War II, from 1912 probably until 1947), Ingmar Bergman (film director, 1918–2007), Birgit Nilsson (opera singer, 1918–2005), Ingemar Johansson (world champion heavyweight boxer, 1933–2009) and Björn Borg (tennis player, 1956– ).

During World War II Sweden adopted a policy of neutrality applicable to armed conflicts, combined with a policy of nonalignment. This policy might reflect a national mentality characterized by conflict avoidance, an inclination to listen rather than speak, and a willingness to strive for agreement and consensus and to compromise.

These tendencies are expressed in Sweden's particularly active peacekeeping operations and have become a hallmark of the country's international commitments. This was especially evident in Dag Hammarskjöld's work as Secretary General of the United Nations (1953–1961), tragically cut short in a plane crash in Zambia.

Sweden remained long as one of the most ethnically homogeneous countries in Europe. However, in the last decades this changed and at the beginning of the 20th century approximately 20 percent of the total population of 9 million are foreigners (i.e., born abroad, or both parents born abroad).

In the late 1940s immigration to Sweden began with the recruitment of foreign labor from southern European countries like Italy, Yugoslavia, and Greece, supplemented by war refugees from Eastern Europe. From the mid-1970s, however, only asylum seekers are allowed to immigrate and from the 1980s mainly those originating in the Middle East and South America. Sweden's generous welfare system has made it the preferred choice among asylum seekers in recent years. At the same time it must be said that another reason for the liberal refugee policy was (and still is) Sweden's fast-growing aging population. A smaller number of working people will have to support the growing number of elderly. Relative to its population Sweden has given far more residence permits to asylum seekers than any other country in Europe; Sweden has also granted asylum to more individuals from Iraq than the United States and Canada together. This development stands in historic contrast to the period 1850–1930

when about 1,200,000 Swedes emigrated for America, driven by famine and religious persecution and attracted by "the land of the future."

At the beginning of the new millennium Sweden has become a multicultural society: in 2005, balancing Sweden's low birthrate, foreigners accounted for 94 percent of the population growth. This transformation has not been without problems, and immigration has become a multifarious problem area, in most cases with no simple solutions. Rising unemployment has increased resistance among Swedish employers to hiring non-Europeans, especially those with language problems and insufficient professional skills. Prejudice and discrimination have surfaced (especially Islamophobia), and ethnic segregation has developed on housing estates. Vandalism has increased and previously almost unknown offenses, such as organized crime, trafficking, and drug smuggling, have entered into Swedish society.

*Åke Daun*

## Further Reading

Daun, Åke. *Swedish Mentality*. University Park: Pennsylvania State University Press, 2005.

Kent, Neil. *A Concise History of Sweden*. New York: Cambridge University Press, 2008.

Lindqvist, Herman. *A History of Sweden. From the Ice Age to Our Age*. Stockholm: Norstedts, 2006.

Setterdahl, Lilly. *Minnesota Swedes*. East Moline, IL: American Friends of the Swedish Emigrant Institute of Sweden, 1996.

Weibull, Jörgen. *Swedish History in Outline*. Stockholm: Almqvist & Wiksell International, 1997.

# T

## Tabasarans

Tabasarans are an indigenous people of the Caucasus who live compactly in southeast Dagestan. Their neighbors include the Aguls, Lezgins, Kaitag Dargins, and Azerbaijanis. In 2002 the number of Tabasarans in the Russian Federation was 131,785 and of these 110,152 lived in the Republic of Dagestan. The Tabasaran language belongs to the Lezgic subgroup of the Nakh-Dagestani group of North Caucasian languages. Tabasarans are Sunni Muslims of the Shafi School.

Tabasarans began converting to Islam when the first Arab-Muslim conquerors arrived in southern Dagestan in the 7th century, and the process of conversion was completed sometime in the 11th and 12th centuries. Aspects of pre-Islamic belief, such as the names of deities and the celebration of spring known as Ebeltsan, remain to this day.

Much evidence suggests that the Tabasaran homeland was part of Caucasian Albania. Armenian and Arabic sources attest that after the fall of Caucasian Albania, Tabasaran (Tavasporan, Tabarsaran)

School and youth teams march in a parade October 4, 2003 celebrating the 5,000th birthday of the ancient city of Derbent, on the Caspian Sea in Dagestan, Russia. (Scott Peterson/ Getty Images)

existed as an independent region. Living as they do near the great pass at Derbent on the Caspian shore, Tabasarans have experienced a great many invasions, and fought the Huns, Sassanid Persians, Khazars, and Arabs, later the Mongols and Timur, and then the Safavid Persians. Tabasarans came under Russian rule in 1813.

Traditionally Tabasarans have been farmers and herders. The climate of Tabasaran territory is mild and warm, and contains a great variety of flora and fauna as well as abundant water. Tabasarans accordingly engage in various forms of agriculture, including grain farming, orchards, and viticulture. Domestic industries include carpet weaving, woolen clothing, woodworking, leatherworking, and beekeeping.

The village *jamaat* (Arabic for "congregation") formed the basic unit of Tabasaran social life. Guided by *adat* (customary law) and sharia (Islamic law), the *jamaat* decided important questions by consensus of adult males. A council of elected elders handled questions of administration. *Adat* regulated civil and criminal matters, including blood feuds, while sharia regulated matters of marriage, inheritance, and religious ritual.

Tabasaran material culture belongs to the general Dagestani type. Under Soviet rule, the Tabasaran language became an official language of Dagestan and remains one today. It has one of the world's languages' most complex case systems, and its nouns have 48 cases.

Soviet rule, characterized by collectivization of agriculture, repression of religion, and bureaucratization of ethnic identity, had a tremendous impact on the Tabasaran people, as it did on other Dagestanis. Much of that legacy was negative, but during the Soviet period the population did increase fourfold and did see an overall rise in living standards. Many Tabasarans moved down from the mountains to lowlands in the Soviet period. Today, toughly 40 percent of Tabasarans live in cities. According to the 2002 Russian Census, 97 percent of Tabasarans speak their native tongue and 87 percent know Russian (other estimates are 95.9% and 62.5%, respectively). Smaller numbers speak Azeri and Lezgi.

*Michael A. Reynolds*

**Further Reading**

Alimova, B. M., and R. I. Seferbekov. "Tabasarantsy." In *Narody Dagestana* (*The Peoples of Dagestan*), eds. S. A. Arutiunov, A. I. Osmanov, and G. A. Sergeeva. Moscow: Nauka, 2002.

Bosworth, C. E. "Ṭabarsarān." In *Encyclopaedia of Islam*, ed. P. Bearman et al. 2nd ed., vol. 10. Leiden: Brill, 2009, 22.

Ikhilov, M. M. "Tabasarany." In *Narody Dagestana: sbronik statei* (*The Peoples of Dagestan: A Collection of Articles*), eds. M. O. Kosven and Kh.-M. O. Khashaev. Moscow: Izdatel'stvo Akademii nauk SSSR, 1955, 179–191.

# Tatars

The term Tatar is an umbrella category for several Turkic-speaking, more or less related ethnic groups in Russia and Siberia. The ethnonym Tatar existed already in the 16th century, defining not only Turkic speakers but other Muslims as well within the Russian Empire. In the first Soviet census of 1926, various Turkic speakers in the Volga region and western Siberia were identified and recognized as separate ethnic groups. Later, however, they were again categorized as one group, called in general Tatars. As a consequence, they were regarded as a linguistic and cultural unit, and the same standard Tatar written language, based on the Kazan Tatar dialect, has been used for all these scattered groups. They do not necessarily share the same historical roots.

Since the fall of the Soviet Union, various Tatar groups have again emerged as separate ethnic units, looking for recognition. During the Russian census of 2002, Tatars were divided into Volga, Astrakhan, Keräshen, and Siberian Tatars. Most of the Volga Tatars are the so-called Kazan Tatars, who make up the majority in Tatarstan, one of the constituent republics of the Russian Federation. Many Tatars live also in the Republic of Bashkortostan.

Closely related to the Kazan Tatars are Mishär Tatars, still mentioned in the census of 1937, living south of Volga in the Nizhniy Novgorod, Tambov, Penza, and Ryazan districts of Russia, as well as in the Chuvash, Mordova, and the Mari-El Republics. The Qasim Tatars live in and around the city of Kasimov, Russia. Another related group is the Tiptärs in Ural. Siberian Tatars include the Barabins in the Baraba steppe, as well as the Bukharlyks (descendants of Sart merchants from Bukhara who established trading colonies in Siberia, but integrated with Tatars since the beginning of the 19th century) and other scattered groups in Tyumen, Tura, Tobol, and Tara. Out of half a million Tatars in Siberia, the indigenous Siberian Tatars make up almost 200,000; others are mostly Volga Tatars.

About 70,000 Astrakhan Tatars live in Astrakhan, along the Caspian Sea in southern Russia. Crimean Tatars constitute a separate ethnic group, speaking their own language, previously resident on the Crimean peninsula and now living in Central Asia, Turkey, Bulgaria, and Romania. Many Crimean Tatars left the peninsula to escape the Crimean war in the 1850s and settled in the Ottoman Empire, especially the Balkans. The remaining Tatars were forced to leave their homeland in 1944, but as many as 250,000 have recently returned to the Crimea, which since 1991 belongs to Ukraine.

Diaspora populations of especially Kazan and Mishär Tatars are found in and outside Russia, especially in Finland, Estonia, Latvia, Sweden, western China (Xinjiang), Japan, Australia, and the United States, but also in Central Asian republics, particularly Uzbekistan, Kazakhstan, Tajikistan, Kyrgyzstan, and Turkmenistan. In most countries Tatars have created small, close-knit, and active communities that since 1991 have taken up relations with Tatarstan. Poland, Belarus, and Lithuania are home to a few thousand Tatars nowadays speaking mainly Slavic languages, although they originate from Turkic speakers that settled in the area in the 18th century or even earlier.

Most Tatars are Muslims, but according to the 2002 census, 27,000 Keräshen Tatars in the Tatarstan, Udmurtia, Bashkortostan, and Chelyabinsk regions belong to the Russian Orthodox Church. There are probably many more Keräshen, maybe 300,000, but recognition of this group as a separate ethnic unit has encountered resistance among Tatar politicians.

Although Tatars are again divided into many smaller groups they altogether number close to 7 million in Russia, and another million live in other countries. Two million live in the Republic of Tatarstan, making up close to 53 percent of the population, followed by 40 percent Russians. Tatarstan has developed into the cultural center and symbolic homeland to Tatars of various backgrounds all over the world and keeps active contact with most communities abroad.

The Tatars have a complex history. Some Tatar forefathers were the descendants of Turkic-speaking groups who lived in the Volga area and the steppes several centuries before the Mongols. These are for instance the Bolgars, Kypchaks, and Pechenegs, who were defeated and subjugated by the Mongols in the 13th century, which further contributed to the ethnic mix. Others are Turkified autochthonous groups, often of Finno-Ugric background.

After the disintegration of the Mongol Golden Horde, several Tatar khanates were established by Mongol and Turkic rulers. Contemporary Tatar groups identify themselves as descendants of these diverse khanates, Kazan, Astrakhan, Siberia, and Crimea being the most important. Tatars from different regions do not necessarily feel close or even related, even though the general concept of being Tatar gives them some common ground.

The Kazan khanate was destroyed by the Muscovites in 1552, and the Kazan and Volga Tatars subjected to Russian rule were resettled and forbidden for several decades to enter the city of Kazan. A few years later the other Tatar khanates fell as well. After the Russian conquest, when villages were destroyed, land stolen, and Islamic sites damaged, many Tatars migrated eastwards toward Siberia. Later Tatars played an important role as army units in the conquest of Siberia and several Russian wars.

Russian empress Catherine II created the Orenburg Spiritual Assembly in 1788, making Islam one of the official faiths in Russia. At this time, many Tatars were merchants and traded all over the empire, creating colonies in several towns. Volga Tatars were and are the most integrated of all Tatars in Russian society.

Volga Tatars, with their cultural center in Kazan, went through a modernization process in the late 19th and early 20th century. The Islamic Jadidist movement and the students and academics of Kazan University and Simbirsk Teachers' College played an essential role in this reform process, which extended into Central Asia, to Turkic peoples in China, and into Siberia with the help of Tatar teachers and publications. Volga Tatars created a short-lived independent state in 1918, but already in 1920 an autonomous Tatar Soviet republic was established. As other people within the Soviet Union, the Tatars were allowed to engage in a kind of nation-building, however without nationalism. Islam was suppressed or at least very little tolerated, and kept a low profile. In 1991, the Tatar national homeland was transformed into the Republic of Tatarstan, which is located in the east of European Russia, within the Russian Federation. Tatarstan, with the city of Kazan as its capital, borders the republics of Bashkortostan, Chuvashia, Mari-El, and Udmurtia, all with substantial Tatar minorities.

The Tatars are mainly Sunni Muslims of the Hanafi School of jurisprudence. Islam is part of the national identity, but many Tatars are rather secularized. A more universalist vision of Islam has come with the younger generation of religious leaders who have trained abroad, and there is some religious revival; several mosques have been restored or built since 1991. However, religion plays hardly any political role in contemporary Tatarstan or among Tatars abroad. There are, as already mentioned, a group of Orthodox Christian Tatars in Russia.

The Tatar languages belong to the northern subgroup of Kypchak, which is the northwestern branch of the Turkic languages, and they are related to Bashkir. The western dialects are spoken by Mishärs and some related groups in Russia, the central dialects by Kazan Tatars, and the eastern dialects by Siberian Tatars. Astrakhan Tatar, which includes three various dialects and belongs to the southern subgroup, sometimes also defined as a separate language, is related to Nogai and Kazak.

Tatars used a modified Arabic script until the beginning of the 20th century; the written language was mostly Kazan Tatar with local variations. This written language had a great impact on other Turkic groups in Russia, central Asia, and western China in the 19th and 20th centuries. The Keräshen Tatars developed in the 18th century a distinct literary language for religious purposes, using the Cyrillic script.

In 1927, a Latin alphabet was introduced for Tatar, only to be replaced by Cyrillic in 1939 by order of Soviet authorities. Although Tatar written language had a rather limited social importance during the Soviet era, it was also used among Turkic groups in Siberia and elsewhere.

Since the early 1990s, Tatar culture and language are experiencing a revival through literature, music, and other forms of cultural expression and exchange between Tatar groups in different regions and countries.

*Ingvar Svanberg*

## Further Reading

Akiner, Shirin. *Islamic Peoples of the Soviet Union*. London: KPI, 1986.

Bennigsen Broxup, Marie. "Volga Tatars." In *The Nationalities Question in the Post-Soviet States*, ed. Graham Smith. London: Longman, 1996, 210–222.

Khakimov, R. S. "The Tatars." *Anthropology & Archeology of Eurasia* 43 (2005): 45–61.

Rorlich, Azade-Ayşe. *The Volga Tatars: A Profile in National Resilience*. Stanford, CA: Hoover Institute Press, 1986.

Tomilov, Nikolai A. "Ethnic Processes within the Turkic Population of West Siberian Plane." *Cahiers du Monde Russe* 41 (2000): 221–232.

# Turks

The population of Turks in the European part of contemporary Turkey, an area of 9,175 square miles (23,764 square kilometers) (3% of the total area of the country), is close to 10 million, about one-eighth of the total population of the Republic. The area in question includes the three major cities located in Thrace (Edirne, Kırklareli, and Tekirdağ) and the European parts of Istanbul and Çanakkale, located on the shores of the Bosphorous and Dardanelles, respectively.

This population is comprised mostly of ethnic Turks who moved into the area as the Turks began their incursions into Europe from Anatolia in the early days of the Ottoman Empire, and even before; a small but visible minority of Roma people, and a very small number of Jews, who settled in the city of Edirne during their expulsion from Spain in the 15th century; as well as Jews, Greeks, Armenians, and other minorities of Istanbul. The population also includes Turks who migrated from the Balkans back to Turkey at various epochs of the tumultuous history of the area. Turks speak Turkish, a Turkic language, and most practice Islam.

Limiting the presence of Turks in Europe to an arbitrary geographical definition is problematic. Istanbul's total population officially stands at 12 million, about 8 million of whom live in the so-called European side. Leaving Istanbul in or out radically alters the composition of the area and there is almost no sound categorical division to be made between the European and Anatolian sides of Istanbul. Moreover, the presence of Turks in Europe dates back to times prior to the conquest of Istanbul by the Ottomans. In 1352 Ottoman Turks got hold of Gallipoli and in 1402 they made Edirne (Adrianople) their capital and ruled the empire from Europe, so to speak, for half a century. The second major wave of Turkish settlement in Europe happened with the labor recruitment programs set in motion in the 1960s between the core states of Europe (Germany, France, Belgium, the Netherlands) and Turkey. Though the official programs ended in the mid-1970s, the movement of populations between Europe and Turkey has continued without losing momentum and attained a complex transnational character. There is also

Farmer in Ephesus, Turkey. (Corel)

a Turkish Cypriot presence in the United Kingdom (more than 100,000 according to estimates).

Considering that the Greek part of Cyprus is a European Union (EU) member and Turkey is an EU candidate country, accounting for Turks in Europe is both a diachronically and synchronically complicated matter. Overall, in the larger geography of Europe, the total population of Turks, excluding the Republic of Turkey, approximately amounts to 9 million, significantly varying from country to country—from 53 in Malta, to 100,000 in Russia, to 3 million in Germany. These notwithstanding, it is possible to narrate a Turkish presence in European Turkey, if one expands the story to the Balkans.

Historically, up until the late 19th century, European lands that were ruled by the Ottoman Empire were called European Turkey, *La Turquie d'Europe*, by European travelers, historians, and politicians. Roughly speaking, this area now constitutes the successor states of the empire (Greece, Bulgaria, the former Yugoslavia, Romania), and includes Moldavia and parts of Hungary. The term "Balkans" is a rather new invention. Even when the Ottoman Empire was breaking up the term Balkans was not very much in currency. With the onset of the 20th century and the Balkan wars, European Turkey had become the Balkans, designating not only a political but also a cultural entity.

During their rule—more or less 600 years, a long stretch by any measure—the Ottomans established a substantial Turkish/Muslim presence in the region, not only demographically but also architecturally and culturally. They did not, however, realize this at the expense of extant Christian populations of the area. Under the *millet* (nation) system that was operationalized by the Ottomans as a ruling strategy, local Christian populations enjoyed living by their own customs and religious edicts, and were on the whole ruled by their own elites and aristocracies. Coercion was not absent but conversion was not the rule.

The Balkans have remained predominantly Christian, about 80 percent in the 17th century, while urban populations were mostly Muslim. Among the new settlements built up by the Ottomans, Sarajevo, Banja Luka, Mostar, and Tirana stand out to this day. Other important centers in the Balkans were Edirne, Thessalonica, Belgrade, and Skopje. Mostar and Sarajevo lived through the most brutal days of the wars that led to the breakup of former Yugoslavia. Istanbul has always been the city of paramount importance in European Turkey, serving as capital not only to the Ottomans but also to the Eastern Roman Empire before them. By the 17th century, Istanbul was the largest city in the whole of Europe, with a population of more than a quarter million, while at the time Paris had a population of some 220,000, Rome 100,000, and other capitals such as Berlin and Vienna trailed behind with less than 100,000.

Cities all in all were vibrant centers of trade, politics, and culture. The revolutionary national movements of the 19th century, including the Young Turks movement, brewed in the cities of the Balkans. The activists of various nationalities saw the Ottoman Empire as an obstacle to modernization and strove for the liberation of their own nations, which led the way to the foundation of numerous nation-states in the Balkans. In 1908, a division of the Ottoman army moved from the Balkans to Istanbul to restore the parliament and reinforced the role of Young Turks of the *İttihat ve Terakki* (Union and Progress) party in ruling the empire. The reign of the three Pashas of the ruling party, Enver, Cemal, and Talat, lasted until the end of World War I, when the failed Ottoman Empire surrendered to the Triple Entente. After a war of independence against the invading armies of the French, Italians, Greeks, and British, the Republic of Turkey was founded in 1923, and the Treaty of Lausanne established the current borders of the new nation-state, leaving only a portion of European Turkey within the borders of the republic.

In the very early days of the republic, Greece and Turkey agreed to exchange populations. More than 1 million *Rum* (Greek Orthodox) citizens of the Empire left for Greece, while Turkey received close to 400,000 Muslims from Greece, with the exception of Greeks in Istanbul and Muslims in Eastern Thrace. This was not the first instance of population exchange in European Turkey. In fact, exchanges and purges were not uncommon in the region. As early as the beginning of the 19th century, Muslim populations were purged from or left the Balkans for the safer regions of the empire, leaving Crete, Thrace, and Bulgaria and settling in Anatolia. With the foundation of these nation-states, every other new state exercised population exchange, forced or voluntary, as a way to strengthen their national stock. Another instrument employed to achieve ethnic unity was the forced changing of names; minorities in Greece were made to adopt surnames ending with "os" or "is," in Bulgaria ending with "off," and in Serbia with "itch." Consequently the Balkans, not entirely but to a greater extent, became ethnically coherent.

The question of minorities, however, is far from being resolved and seriously conditions the relations between the states of the region despite their membership in the EU and the North Atlantic Treaty Organization (NATO), and growing economic cooperation. In September 1955, following right-wing riots in Istanbul aimed at minorities, noncitizen Greeks living in the city were forced to leave the country. In the waning days of the communist regime in Bulgaria, after yet another act of forced name conversion, close to 300,000 Muslim Turks left Bulgaria for Turkey in a span of a few months. Some 130,000 later returned to Bulgaria. Greece to this day refuses to call members of ethnically Turkish populations Turks, formally categorizing them as Muslims.

Not all movements between Turkey and the nation-states that emerged in former European Turkey have been unwelcoming. Though not in great numbers, the former Greek residents of Istanbul visited their city; Muslims in Thrace, Bulgaria, and former Yugoslavia made trips to Turkey, engaging in informal trade; and the Roma people crisscrossed the region, all despite the burdensome disincentives and stringent passport and border controls imposed by nation-states. Today Turkish/Muslim populations residing in the former European Turkey approximately amounts to 1.3 million, with roughly 50,000 in Bosnia-Herzegovina, 50,000 in Kosovo, 55,000 in Romania, 150,000 in Greece, 200,000 in the Republic of Macedonia, 750,000 in Bulgaria, and the rest living in various Balkan countries. This estimate does not include those citizens of Turkey who work and reside in the Balkans as businesspersons, workers, and students, as well as husbands and wives.

The long history of Turkish/Muslim presence in what was called European Turkey up until the 19th century leaves little room for cultural differentiation among the various ethnic populations in the Balkans, aside perhaps from what is strictly mandated by religious rules and customs. Even there, heterodox practices are not uncommon, such as conversion of Christian saints into Muslim saints, and giving alms to them in order to make the unmarried marry, the infertile get pregnant, and the disabled walk. The food and dietary customs, with the exceptional prohibition on pork, show strong similarities. What is known as shepherd salad in Turkey, a concoction of tomatoes, cucumbers, and onions, is called Greek salad in Greece and Bulgarian salad in Bulgaria, with the addition of shaved white cheese. The culture wars over the ownership of *Karagöz* and *Karagiosiz,* a traditional shadow play, and over food—*baklava*, *dolma* (stuffed grape leaves), and *musakka* (an eggplant dish)—between Greece and Turkey serve only as reminders of the commonality of tastes and culture, rather than difference. *Köfte*, *ćevapčići*, and *souvlaki*, a grilled meat dish made from minced meat and revered all over the region, is only a case of variation on a theme. Tekirdağ in Turkey is famous for its *köfte*; in Ljubljana, the most famous *ćevapčići* place is called *Harambaša* (an

Ottoman military term for sergeant); and in Athens, the most famous *souvlaki* place is called *Bayraktaris*, a family name with origins in Anatolian Turkey. The traditions of folk dance and song display a mélange of rhythm, costume, and choreography. Wedding ceremonies borrow traditions from each other (mixed marriages were not uncommon) and the spoken language of everyday is recognizably enriched by foreign words acquired from the languages of the region.

Cultural commonality is not limited to the domain of the vernacular. Intellectual national traditions, if they are to be called as such, emerged and developed in the heyday of the national movements, after enjoying a centuries-long elite patronage under the Ottoman rule. The national movements, while struggling for the right of their own nations for statehood, implicitly agreed upon the need for European-style modernization in the areas of economy, education, the arts, and culture. The models they employed and enacted were tested and tried before in the West, following a line of progress from the days of the renaissance and the enlightenment to the French Revolution and Wilsonian principles.

Later, and particularly after World War II, the relations between intellectual elites have always been strong, though limited to the oppositional circles of the right or left in their respective countries. The community associations of migrants from Greece and Bulgaria have never lost their contacts with their homeland, first under the rubric of a generic anticommunism and nationalism, and now under identity politics and claims for cultural rights. Greeks from

Istanbul have always kept their Istanbulite identity and ties with their city. Turkish and Greek intellectuals have struggled to break through the barriers of national enmity by organizing joint art events and concerts, and today increasingly focus their efforts in divesting school textbooks of language breeding ethnic animosity. In Bulgaria, the Movement for Rights and Freedom, a political party of Bulgarian Turks founded after the fall of the Soviet bloc, is a coalition partner.

As the countries of former European Turkey are getting formally reintegrated to Europe in the postsocialist era, and Turkey's accession negotiations with the EU are progressing, economic and cultural ties between Turkey and Balkan states are becoming more hospitable and neighborly, and minorities are in a better position to claim political and cultural rights.

*Levent Soysal*

## Further Reading

Herzfeld, Michael. *Anthropology through the Looking Glass: Critical Ethnography in the Margins of Europe.* Cambridge: Cambridge University Press, 1989.

İnalcık, Halil, and Donald Quartet, eds. *An Economic and Social History of the Ottoman Empire,* vols. 1–2. Cambridge: Cambridge University Press, 1997.

Kasaba, Reşat, ed. *Cambridge History of Turkey: Turkey in the Modern World,* vol. 4. Cambridge: Cambridge University Press, 2008.

Mazower, Mark. *The Balkans: A Short History.* New York: The Modern Library, 2002.

Todorova, Maria. *Imagining the Balkans.* Oxford: Oxford University Press., 2009.

# U

## Udmurts

The Udmurts, also known as the Votyaks, live in the Republic of Udmurtia within the Russian Federation, between the Rivers Vyatka and Kama, tributaries of the Volga. Two-thirds of the Udmurts live in their titular republic while the remainder dwell to the south, southwest, and southeast in the republics of Tatarstan and Bashkortostan, and in the districts of Perm and Kirov. According to the last (1989) census of the Soviet Union there were 746,000 Udmurts, and 69 percent of these spoke Udmurt. The first Russian census (2002) showed a decrease of 11 percent in their numbers. The Udmurt language belongs to the Permic branch of the Finno-Ugric language family. The traditional religion of the Udmurts is based on ancestor worship and has in some places continued until the present day. Especially in the northern areas, Orthodox Christianity was introduced long before the arrival of the official atheism of the Soviet Union.

The forefathers of the Udmurts lived on the same territory as the Udmurts of today. Together with the Komi the Udmurts formed the Proto-Permian national group, from which the Udmurts separated as late as the 9th century, when the Komi started to move northwards. Even before the separation, the Permians came into contact with the mercantile state of the Volga Bolgars, and the Udmurts would continue to pay tribute to it for many hundreds of years. In the 13th century the area was subjugated by the Tatars, who established a powerful state of their own (the Golden Horde and the Khanate of Kazan). The Russians were already holding the northern parts of the Udmurt territory by the 15th century, but it was not until 1552 that the Udmurts became totally subject to Russian power, when Ivan the Terrible conquered the Khanate of Kazan. In response, many Udmurts fled eastwards and later migrated in many directions.

The traditional Udmurt religion is founded on respect for one's ancestors. As late as the early 20th century each family possessed its own guardian spirit (*vorshud*) for whom a box was kept in the back corner of a hut in the yard. Meals would be prepared in the hut in the summer, and it was here that sacrifices were conducted in the midst of the family. The whole family took their name from this *vorshud* spirit. Ancestors were regarded as having decreed the norms of which they were the protectors and guardian spirits. Larger sacrificial feasts in honor of all of the ancestors of larger family groupings—in, for example, wedding celebrations—were led by priests and performed in groves or fenced woods, where animals and food were given in sacrifice. Also, *Inmar* (the god of the sky) was worshipped there along with the spirits of natural forms like mother earth. Udmurt religious practice was repressed by the Soviets, but after the fall of the Soviet Union Udmurt religion has been revived in many areas.

The Udmurts have always been agriculturalists and cattle breeders. Hunting too has been an important means of livelihood, especially in the northern areas. Beekeeping is a common secondary occupation among the Udmurts and other populations in the Volga area. There are gas and oil deposits in the territory of Udmurtia. Heavy industry is concentrated in the towns (e.g., in the capital Izhevsk), where most inhabitants are ethnic Russians. Udmurt culture survives mainly in the rural areas, and only in the city of Glazov in northern Udmurtia has there been a tradition of Udmurt handicrafts since the 19th century.

The Udmurts were in close contact with the Volga Bolgars and subsequently the Tatars. Tatars still live in many areas alongside Udmurts. The influence of these Turkic peoples is quite evident both in the Udmurt language (e.g., loanwords) and Udmurt culture (e.g., short lyrical songs). Russian culture has influenced the Udmurts since the end of the 16th century, but this influence was most intense during the Soviet period.

Udmurt folksongs are short and lyrical; most are composed of four lines. They may be performed anywhere, at feasts as well as in connection with the passages of life or freely according to one's mood. The earliest texts in the Udmurt language date from the end of the 18th century, while during the 19th century a few dozen publications appeared in different dialects. The literary language was formulated in the 1920s on the basis of several dialects. The most renowned figure in Udmurt literature is the poet Kuzebay Gerd (1898–1937), who also published articles on the subjects of folklore and literature.

For minority nationalities such as the Udmurts, the early Soviet era of the 1920s was a positive time in terms of cultural development. The Autonomous Soviet Socialist Republic of Udmurtia was established in 1934. After the collapse of the Soviet Union this became the Republic of Udmurtia, now part of the Russian Federation. In 1937, during Josef Stalin's administration, most of the Udmurt intelligentsia were killed or sent to camps, a fate that befell members of many other minorities. Udmurt identity suffered a further blow with the educational reform of the Nikita Khrushchev administration, which reduced instruction in Udmurt to a few hours a week in the primary classes. By 1989, 30 percent of Udmurts no longer knew their own mother tongue. Because youth in particular lack proficiency in the language, fluency in Udmurt is declining quickly. The Udmurt language and culture are best preserved in the rural areas.

The fall of the Soviet Union and subsequent attempts at democratization in the 1990s enlivened Udmurt culture; for example, the practice of the Udmurt religion gained strength. However, centralization was again reinforced in Russia during the Vladimir Putin administration, and rights of minority nationalities—with respect to legislation and education, for example— were curtailed. This trend constitutes a threat to all of the minority nationalities in the Russian Federation, including the Udmurts.

*Sirkka Saarinen*

## Further Reading

György Nanofszky, ed. *The Finno-Ugric World*. Budapest: Teleki László Foundation, 2004.

Konuykhov, Alexey K., ed. *Finno-Ugric Ethnicities in Russia: Yesterday, Today, and Tomorrow.* Trans. Pavel Krotov. Syktyvkar: Society Finland–Russia and Komi vojtyr, 2009.

Lallukka, Seppo. *The East Finnic Minorities in the Soviet Union. An Appraisal of the Erosive Trends.* Helsinki: The Finnish Academy of Science and Letters, 1990, B:252.

# Ukrainians

Ukrainians are a Slavic people making up the majority population of Ukraine. The country's major population centers are Kiev (Kyiv), Donetsk, Dnipropetrovsk, Kharkiv (Kharkiv), Odesa, and Lviv. The Ukrainian diaspora includes large concentrations in Russia (where it constitutes the second largest national minority), the United States, Canada, Brazil, and the United Kingdom. Large numbers of migrant workers live in Portugal, Italy, and the United Kingdom. Ukraine's population has declined from 52 million (1989) to 47 million (2001). The 2001 census registered 78 percent Ukrainian, 17 percent Russian, and a remainder that includes more than 100 smaller nationalities. In 2001, 68 percent of Ukrainians listed Ukrainian as their native language, while 30 percent selected Russian. Ukrainian became the state language with a 1989 law that was enshrined in the 1996 and 2006 constitutions. Russian is widely spoken in eastern and southern Ukraine, particularly in urban centers. The two main religions are Orthodoxy and Greek-Catholicism with a majority of the parishes of both churches located in western and central

Ukrainian leftists rally in Kiev in 2003 to mark the anniversary of the Bolshevik revolution and to protest economic hardship. The country is politically divided, with eastern Ukrainians tending to favor Soviet institutions and western Ukrainians supporting market reform. (AP/Wide World Photos)

Ukraine. Ukrainians are defined as one of three eastern Slavic groups but the Ukrainian language is intelligible to both (western Slavic) Poles and Russians. Ukraine's cultural traditions draw on both eastern and western Slavic traditions, as well as pre-Slavic cultural legacies (Trypillians, Scythians). Both main churches—Russian and Ukrainian Orthodox as well as Greek Catholic—follow the Byzantine rite. The Crimea has Tatar, Greek, and eastern Slavic traditions.

Ukrainians are believed to descend from one of the oldest cultures in Europe, the Trypillya culture dating from the fifth to third millennia BCE. The Trypillian culture built the largest settlements in Europe from 4000 to 3000 BCE in the area which today is Ukraine. The Celts and Scythians settled in Ukraine where they left their cultural mark. The Greeks (Byzantines), Romans, Goths, and Huns established colonies in the Crimea, which from the 13th century became a center of Tatar culture.

The first Slavic state—Kievan (Kyivan) Rus—was founded around one of the oldest Slavic cities of Kiev as early as the fifth century CE, nearly 700 years before Moscow. In 1982, Kiev celebrated its 1,500th anniversary. Kievan Rus stretched as far north as the Baltic Sea and south to the Black Sea, to the Carpathians and Volga River in the east, thereby covering much of contemporary European Russia and Belarus. The original base of Kievan Rus lay in what is now central and northeastern Ukraine.

In 988, Kievan Rus converted to Byzantine Christianity, which integrated the state into Europe. Christianity assisted in the development of urban centers. The roots of modern Ukrainian are traced back to the Kievan Rus state of the 11th to 12th centuries. The legacy of Kievan Rus has been fought over by Russian, Soviet, and Ukrainian historiography as to whether it is a proto-Ukrainian state, part of Russian (i.e., eastern Slavic) history or as a kernel of the three future Eastern Slavic peoples (Russians, Ukrainians, Belarusians). Historiography in independent Ukraine defines Kievan Rus as a proto-Ukrainian state whose traditions after it was destroyed by a Mongol invasion in 1240 continued in the Galician-Volhynian principality in what is now western Ukraine.

Following prolonged internal strife between principalities and the eventual destruction of Kievan Rus, the western region maintained its independence in the Galician-Volhynian principality that was later annexed by the emerging Grand Duchy of Lithuania. The later Polish-Lithuanian Commonwealth annexed a large portion of contemporary Ukrainian territory (the original core lands of Kievan Rus) and Belarus between the 14th and 15th centuries. Ottoman Turkey controlled the Crimea, which was dominated by the remnants of the Mongol Golden Horde. To the northeast of Ukraine a new emerging power was Muscovy that emerged from the Novgorod and Vladimir-Suzdal principalities that had overthrown the Tatar occupation.

In the 16th to 18th centuries, Ukraine was dominated by the freebooting Cossacks who had fled into the no-man's-land of southern Ukraine, where they created the Zaporizhian *Sich* (Host) immortalized in the fictitious *Taras Bulba* epic written by the Ukrainian Nikolai (Mykola) Gogol. The Cossacks defended their freedoms from serfdom introduced by landlords and foreign rulers (who tended to be the same). They also saw themselves as defenders of Ukrainian cultural traditions and the Orthodox religion.

In the mid-17th century, under the leadership of Hetman (military-political leader) Bohdan Khmelnytsky, the Cossacks established an independent state. In 1654 Khmelnytsky signed a military alliance, the Treaty of Pereiaslav with Muscovy (the future Russian empire). The Treaty of Pereiaslav has been a source of historical and political dispute ever since. Ukrainian Cossack leaders saw the treaty as a military alliance of Orthodox believers against Catholic Poland-Lithuania and the Muslim Ottoman empire, both pressing on Cossack lands from the west and south. Russian and Soviet historiography depicted the treaty, most notably in the 1954 anniversary, as the eternal striving of Ukrainians for the reunion of Ukraine with Russia. Some Ukrainian Cossack leaders believed that the tsar had reneged on his promises and therefore Ukrainians had a legal right to break what might be called the contract, a view that has become predominant in Ukrainian historiography. Ukrainian Cossacks defeated an invading Muscovite army at Konotop in 1659 but Hetman Ivan Mazepa together with his Swedish allies were defeated at the important 1709 Battle of Poltava. The anniversary of the Battle of Poltava in 2009 was crowned with the unveiling of a monument to Mazepa in Ukraine to loud protests from Russia. Mazepa was defined by imperial Russian, Soviet, and post-Soviet Russian historiography as a traitor who sought to break Ukrainian-Russian unity.

Poltava proved to be an important turning point in Russian history where Muscovy transformed into the Russian empire following the occupation of Ukrainian Cossack lands. This opened the way for Russia to expand south to the Black Sea coast. In the last two decades of the 18th century the Russian empire fully incorporated Ukraine as *gubernia* (provinces) after abolishing its autonomous status as a Hetmanate dominion (where Cossacks had controlled domestic affairs but the Russian state controlled foreign and defense policies). In the 1870s the Russian empire annexed the Crimea and in the next century hundreds of thousands of Tatars emigrated to the Ottoman empire. Serfdom was introduced into Ukrainian Cossack lands and the last vestiges of traditional Cossack liberties were destroyed.

Not all Ukrainian lands fell under tsarist rule; western Ukraine remained within the Austrian empire, which had important governmental and cultural differences from the Russian empire. In addition, within the Russian empire pro-Western influences continued to remain strong: Kiev remained an important Polish city until the Polish uprising of the mid-19th century; and the Greek-Catholic Church, a fusion of Roman Catholic and Byzantine Orthodox traditions established in Brest in 1569, was influential in central Ukraine until it was banned in the 1830s.

Life for the Ukrainian population in the Austrian (later Austro-Hungarian) empire was very different from that in the Russian. The more liberal governing regime permitted Ukrainian-language education, civil society, and political life, and practiced religious tolerance. Austrian rulers supported Ukrainian national rights against the Poles, who were dominant in the ruling classes. These liberal Austrian policies contributed to what could be considered Ukrainian nation-building with the emergence in the late 19th century of Ukrainians as a self-conscious people with their own literature, culture, and political, scholarly, and religious elites.

In the Russian Empire, Ukrainians faced a more repressive regime bent on preventing the emergence of self-conscious Ukrainians in what was seen as Austrian-backed separatism. The Ukrainian language was banned in two decrees in the 1860s and 1870s, the only language to face this fate in the Russian empire. The language ban affected education and all manner of

Ukrainian cultural activities while the tsarist secret police (*Okhrana*) kept a watchful eye on Ukrainian political life. Ukraine's bard, poet, and writer, Taras Shevchenko, was arrested, forcibly conscripted into the army, and sent into Siberian exile. Ukrainians in tsarist Russia also had fewer opportunities to emerge as free landowning peasants, as serfdom was maintained longer and more strictly than in the Austrian empire.

Ukrainian political parties and groups emerged in both Russian and Austrian Ukraine in the late 19th and early 20th centuries, some advocating federalism and Ukrainian autonomy within the existing empire while others sought Ukrainian independence. The disintegration of both empires in 1917–1918 led to a struggle for independence in western and eastern (termed "Greater") Ukraine. As in the 17th century, Ukraine was pressed on many sides by countries seeking to expand into territories where ethnic Ukrainians were in a majority: Poles and Romanians in the west and Bolshevik Russia in the east and south. The Russian White armies refused to accept Ukrainians' right to autonomy (let alone independence) and were defeated by their short-sighted nationalities policies toward the non-Russian peoples of the empire.

The attempt to establish an independent Ukrainian state between 1917 and 1920 failed, weakened by internal opposition from anarchist groups led by Nestor Makhno and from supporters of an indivisible Russian empire. Ukrainian nationalists also faced the obstacle of a weak ethnic Ukrainian presence in cities and towns, disorganized and ill-disciplined armed forces, and external invasions from Poles and Russians. The West Ukrainian Peoples Republic sought to unite with the Kiev-based Ukrainian Peoples Republic in 1918, but it was overrun by Polish forces that had been trained and had fought in France in World War I. Galicia and Volhynia were occupied by Poland, Trans-Carpathia by the Czechoslovak state, which failed to adhere to its promise to provide autonomy, and Bukovina by Romania. Greater (eastern) Ukraine was incorporated into the Union of Soviet Socialist Republics (USSR) in 1921 as a Soviet republic.

The borders of the Soviet Ukrainian republic were expanded 1945–1954 with the addition of territories with ethnic Ukrainian majorities in Poland, Trans-Carpathia and Bukovina, and the Crimea, which had an ethnic Russian majority. The remaining Crimean Tatars were expelled in 1944 on allegations of collaboration with the invading Nazis. The Crimea was elevated to an autonomous republic within the Soviet Ukrainian republic in 1990, a status it had possessed 1921–1944 within the Russian Socialist Federated Soviet Republic, and became an autonomous republic in independent Ukraine.

Soviet Ukraine suffered the worst excesses of totalitarianism, both Soviet and Nazi, in the 1930s and 1940s. Estimates indicate that 12–15 million people in Ukraine died in the course of three major sets of events: the 1933 artificial famine, the Stalinist Great Terror, and the Nazi occupation of 1941–1944. A mass burial ground near Kiev contains more than 100,000 victims of the Stalinist Great Terror. The majority of the estimated 4–7 million who died in the famine were ethnic

Ukrainian peasants while the majority of the estimated 6 million who perished in World War II were Jews. All nationalities died from the onslaught of the Nazi terror machine, whose ideology perceived Ukrainians and Slavs as subhuman. In World War II, most Ukrainians fought in the Soviet Army. Independent Ukraine has led a campaign to denounce the crimes against humanity committed by the Soviet regime with a particular focus on the "genocide-famine." This denunciation of Stalinism and the "genocide-famine" has led to poor relations with Russia, where a campaign to rehabilitate Jozef Stalin as a great wartime leader has purposefully ignored the crimes committed by his regime.

The four decades following World War II witnessed a continuation of the industrialization and urbanization of Soviet Ukraine that had begun in the 1930s. This modernization project brought with it two contradictory developments. Ethnic Ukrainians became dominant in Ukrainian cities for the first time since the Middle Ages, an example being the capital city of Kiev, where the proportion of ethic Ukrainians grew from 22.2 percent in 1897 to 82.2 percent in the 2001 census. The process of Sovietization was accompanied by Russification in educational, cultural, and language policies. Ukrainian liberal dissidents and nationalist activists protested against these Russification policies and human rights abuses, thereby becoming the largest proportional ethnic group incarcerated in the Soviet Gulag (camp prisons).

Ukraine was one of the republics active in the popular protests and opposition movements in the Mikhail Gorbachev era. The Popular Movement for Restructuring (known by its Ukrainian abbreviation Rukh) spearheaded the opposition with a strong base of support in western Ukraine and Kiev. The gradual disintegration of the USSR, loss of control over events by President Gorbachev, semifree parliamentary elections in March 1990 to the republican parliament that gave Rukh and its allies a quarter of seats, and growing divisions in the Communist Party in Ukraine were the backdrop to the August 24, 1991, declaration of independence. The Soviet Ukrainian parliament voted overwhelmingly for independence after a hard-line coup d'état in Moscow failed. The declaration was endorsed by 91 percent of Ukrainians in a referendum held on December 1 that year. On the same day, former Communist Party ideological secretary Leonid Kravchuk was elected president.

Independent Ukraine held its first free parliamentary and presidential elections in 1994, with Leonid Kuchma defeating Kravchuk and becoming president. Political parties only began to dominate the political scene from the 1998 elections. The Communist Party was banned in August 1991 and only relegalized in October 1993 after which it acted as the main opposition throughout the 1990s when Ukraine was in severe recession in its transition to a market economy.

Ukraine was the last former Soviet republic to adopt a new presidential constitution in 1996, replacing the 1978 Soviet Ukrainian constitution that had been amended many times after the USSR disintegrated. The Crimean autonomous republican constitution was adopted two years later. The constitution was amended into a semiparliamentary system in 2006.

President Kuchma was reelected in 1999 after defeating the Communist leader but lost popular support after November 2000 with the onset of popular protests in the "Kuchmagate" crisis, sparked by allegations that he had ordered violence against an opposition journalist—Georgi Gongadze—who was found murdered. The democratic opposition won its first election in 2002 and thereafter support for the Communist Party collapsed. Opposition leader Viktor Yushchenko won the 2004 presidential elections following mass protests known as the Orange Revolution, in which one in five Ukrainians participated, primarily from western-central Ukraine.

*Taras Kuzio*

## Further Reading

Kuzio, Taras. *A Contemporary History of Ukraine.* London: Reaktion Books, 2010.

Kuzio, Taras. *Ukraine. State and Nation Building.* London: Routledge, 1998.

Magocsi, Paul Robert. *A History of Ukraine.* Toronto: University of Toronto Press, 1996.

Marples, David. *Heroes and Villains: Creating National History in Contemporary Ukraine.* New York: Central European University Press, 2007.

Sasse, Gwendolyn. *The Crimea Question: Identity, Transition, and Conflict.* Cambridge, MA: Harvard University Press, 2007.

Subtelny, Oest. *Ukraine. A History.* 3rd ed. Toronto: University of Toronto Press, 2001.

Yekelchyk, Serhiy. *Ukraine. Birth of a Modern Nation.* New York: Oxford University Press, 2007.

# W

## Walloons

The Walloons (in French, *Wallons*) are a community of 4 million people who speak French and live in Belgium, a constitutional and parliamentary monarchy counting 11 million inhabitants. Wallonia, for the most part Catholic, is composed of the southern territories of the country while the northern part, better known as Flanders, is inhabited by the Flemish people. A small German-speaking community has been present in the area bordering Germany since the end of World War II. Although Walloons are in general consistent consumers of French culture by reason of shared language and geographical proximity, their respective mentalities are significantly different. While the French are conscious of belonging to a country with a glorious history, Walloons generally do not feel the same regarding Wallonia or even Belgium. The cultural identity of French-speaking Belgium differs depending on the point of reference—it is one thing in Brussels, which is mostly French-speaking but located in Flanders, and another in Wallonia itself, for example in the cities of Liège, Charleroi, or Namur (the capital). From a historical point of view, it is difficult to define Wallonia; at the crossroads of larger European powers, the territories and boundaries of the area have shifted often. The name Wallonia was used for the first time only in 1844. The area became a political entity known as the Walloon Region with the revision of the Belgian Constitution of 1970–1971. In fact, books dedicated to Wallonia's history date only to the second half of the 20th century, as a reaction to the creation of Belgium's two language communities.

During antiquity, the territories that composed Wallonia belonged to northern Gaul. Caesar had conquered it in 57 BCE after defeating the resident Celtic tribes such as the Belgae. South of the Cologne-Bavay axis, five centuries of the *pax romana* largely influenced the Romanization of this Belgian province and explains the Romance languages (French and dialects such as Walloon, Wallo-Picard, Wallo-Lorrain, and Chapenois) spoken today in Wallonia.

With the fall of the Roman Empire, Gaul was carved up. For the Germanic tribes who took over areas abandoned by the Romans, the Gallo-Romans of northern Gaul were known as the *Walhah* (Walloon). In following centuries these territories would form the cradle of the Carolingian Empire. Intensive evangelization as well as the creation of dioceses (sixth century) and the establishment of many abbeys (from the seventh century) ensured the maintenance of the Latin language and reinforced the Roman heritage in culture and language. Religious centers enjoyed autonomy and were centers of cultural development, for example in silversmithing and the production of

People hold yellow flags with images of red roosters, the emblem of Wallonia, during the feasts of Wallonia, in Namur, Belgium on September 18, 2010. Wallonia is the predominantly French-speaking southern region of Belgium; each of the country's autonomous regions observes its own Feast Day. (AFP/Getty Images)

illuminated manuscripts. Indeed, the first literary text in the *oïl* language (the ancestor of standard French), *Cantilène de Sainte Eulalie* (880), was penned near Tournai.

These northern Roman regions were brought within the fold of the Germanic Empire (925) but their integration was not achieved. Principalities were created (the Earldoms of Hainaut and Namur, the Dukedoms of Brabant and Luxemburg, and the ecclesiastical Principalities of Liège and Stavelot-Malmedy) that developed over the 10th century and later obtained their independence. In the Low Middle Ages, they achieved political autonomy; the most important were the Prince-Bishopric of Liège and the Principality of Stavelot-Malmedy.

During the 15th century, through an alliances-and-heritage game, the Roman principalities became possessions of the House of Burgundy—except for Liège and Stavelot-Malmedy, which were only under their protectorate. Burgundian rule weighed heavily on the population, a trend continued under Charles V. The city of Liège rebelled but was plundered by Charles the Bold in 1468 for this disobedience, as revealed by Philippe de Commines in his *Chronicles* (1447–1511). At the Duke's death (1477), Liège regained its autonomy. Later, the principality was cut in two as the Burgundian Netherlands was inherited by Spain (and later Austria), a situation that lasted until 1794.

Lacking sea access, Wallonia had a rather mediocre position in international trade during the 15th and 16th centuries in comparison to Bruges and Antwerp in

Flanders. Only Tournai, famous for its traditional tapestry, was able to project itself as an agricultural market and a commercial center where traders from the Netherlands and France would meet. Nevertheless, Wallonia maintained profitable commercial relations, mainly regarding coal, steel, iron industry, and drapery, with France, the Prince-Bishopric of Liege, and some German states. During the 18th century, industrial development brought increased commercial contacts throughout Europe.

Until the 19th century the politically scattered Walloon territories were deeply influenced by French culture. Paris set the tone, especially in the Prince-Bishopric. French intellectuals or writers were often exiled there, and the cities of Liège and Bouillon not coincidentally became famous publishing and press centers. During the French Revolution of 1789, the Principality of Liège, sharing the same spirit of liberty, led its own revolution. A bit later, the old Netherlands and the principality would be added to the French Republic and then to Napoleon's Empire.

After Waterloo (1815), "Belgian" territories were included in the Kingdom of the Netherlands under William I of Orange. Soon, Belgians, among whom the entire aristocracy was French-speaking and Catholic, refused the Dutch Prince's domination, protesting and claiming their independence in 1830. A fusion in the French-speaking part took place, and Wallonia became a whole, where Liège, the Hainaut, and Namur were no longer distinguished. In an effort to consolidate support for the new state, local identities were minimized, as Henri Pirenne's *History of Belgium* (1899) makes clear. At the beginning, the country

also needed to emphasize its distinctiveness with regard to France, so Flemish history and mythology, as a clear alternative to French culture, have been overemphasized by the French-speaking aristocracy in order to give a heart to the hypothetical "Belgian soul" praised by Edmond Picard (in "L'Âme belge," 1897).

During the 19th century, Belgium ranked as the second industrial power in the world thanks to the considerable development in the steel industry, metallurgy, and coal extraction around the Sambre-et-Meuse's field. Walloon engineers' know-how was widely admired. In a few decades Eugène Solvay, John Cockerill, Zénobe Gramme, Georges Nagelmakers, and Albert Thys built veritable empires, mainly thanks to the export of materials and techniques and to the establishment of railroad networks in Belgium and France, but also later on in China and the Congo. Edouard Empain was responsible for the construction of the Metro in Paris. This improvement went together with the arrival of progressive working-class movements and the creation of unions, which goes a long way toward explaining why the political orientation in Wallonia remains essentially socialist to this day.

At the end of the century, in reaction to the emerging Flemish nationalist movements that sought increased representation on behalf of the larger Flemish population, the Walloon Movement was led by Jules Destrée. A congress was held in 1905 and again in 1912. The new Walloon Assembly provided Wallonia with an emblem, a red rooster on a yellow background; a feast celebrated the last weekend of September; and an anthem, "The Walloon's Song," composed in Walloon dialect from Liège around 1900.

Prosperity in Wallonia ended with World War I. The German occupation destroyed the infrastructure, sapped economic potential, and decimated livestock in the countryside. Germany was not able to repay Belgium for the wartime damages stipulated by the Treaty of Versailles (1919). The resources of the Congolese colony saved the economy temporarily, but between the two World Wars many crises arose and the politicians adopted a defensive investment policy for Wallonia. Rather than innovating or converting formerly strong industries, monies were directed to shore up the condemned coal, steel, and iron industries. To this day Wallonia remains poorer than prospering Flanders.

During the 20th century, artists from Wallonia (and Brussels) became celebrated in a number of genres. Their originality found expression in architecture (Alphonse Balat, Roger Bastin, Jacques Dupuis, Victor Horta); social films (the brothers Dardenne); and various literary and pictoral genres, many nontraditional, including cartoons (Hergé, Morris, Peyo, Walthéry, Philippe Geluck), detective novels (Georges Simenon), surrealism (Christian Dotremont, Marcel Mariën, Achille Chavée, Paul Nougé, Paul Delvaux, René Magritte), the fantastic (Jean Ray), regionalism (Hubert Krains, Hubert Juin, Conrad Detrez, Jean Louvet), and magical realism (André Delvaux).

After World War II, the Flemish and Walloon language community positions became more extreme. An irreversible federalization process was started in 1962, based on a series of linguistic laws that provoked successive revisions of the Constitution. Since April 23, 1993, Belgium has been a complex federal state made up of Regions and Communities, and Wallonia and Flanders each have their own parliament and government. While the Flemish generally favor greater regional autonomy—a quarter of them even demanded independence in 2010—Walloons are for the most part reluctant to continue dismantling the state, even if a minority argue for being reattached to France.

The status of Brussels, historically Flemish but largely French-speaking, remains problematic. This situation has already provoked many institutional crises and there is no doubt many more will arise in the future, without however the prospects of a satisfying solution. Besides, its population exhibits multiple influences, from the coexistence of Flemish and French-speaking communities, to the numerous migrants and the presence of significant European Union and international institutions. However, owing to its status as the capital of the European Union, the Brussels Region is compelled to put aside the regionalist considerations common elsewhere in the country.

*Marie-Agnès Boxus*

**Further Reading**

Beyen, Marnix, and Philippe Destatte. *Un autre pays* (*Another country*). Bruxelles: Le Cri, 2009.

Cook, Bernard A. *Belgium: A History*. New York: Peter Lang, 2002.

Delforge, Paul. *Encyclopédie du mouvement wallon* (*Encyclopedia of the Walloon Movement*). 3 vols. Charleroi: Institut Destrée, 2000 and 2001.

Demoulin, Bruno, and Jean-Louis Kupper. *Histoire de la Wallonie de la préhistoire au XXIe siècle (History of Wallonia from Prehistory to the 21st Century)*. Toulouse: Privat, 2004.

Vos, Louis. *Nationalism in Belgium*. London: MacMillan Press, 1998.

## Welsh

The Welsh occupy a small country located along the western shore of Britain. The Welsh call themselves *Y Cymry* (fellow Welsh), their country *Cymru* (Wales), and their language *Cymraeg* (Welsh). The major population centers are the metropolitan ports of Cardiff, Swansea, Newport, and their related densely settled valley systems in the south. Significant Welsh settlement abroad is confined to the English-speaking world of North America, South Africa, Australia, and New Zealand, with one Welsh-speaking colony in Patagonia. Increasing numbers of Welsh people today reside in neighboring states in Europe. The population of Wales is about 3 million, of whom 22 percent are Welsh-speaking, and language remains the most distinctive aspect of national identity. The most prominent religious groups are Christian, subdivided into affiliates of the Church in Wales, the Roman Catholic Church, and the myriad nonconformist and dissenting denominations. In most respects the Welsh share demographic, institutional, cultural, and sociopolitical ties with the English, who constitute some 48 million out of a United Kingdom (UK) population of 61.4 million in 2009.

An elderly Welsh woman smiles for the photographer during the Rugby World Cup in 1999. (AFP/Getty Images)

The origins of the Welsh may be traced to a fusion of the indigenous Neolithic together with Celtic and later migrants who arrived from mainland Europe after 500 BCE. Welsh constitutes one of six Celtic languages, the others being Cornish, Irish, Manx, and Scottish Gaelic in the British Isles and Breton in France. The Roman conquest in the first century CE and four subsequent centuries of occupation incorporated Wales into a wider European orbit. The Roman occupation exerted a significant impact on the language, landscape, religion, urban structure, and communication system of Wales. Their Anglo-Saxon successors called the Romanized, partly Christian inhabitants of West Britain

*Weleas* (foreigners). Saxon incursions into Wales and Welsh raids on Lowland England created prolonged tensions along the border; in response, Offa, King of Mercia, oversaw the construction of a massive earthwork military frontier during the last decades of the eighth century that would in effect become the national boundary separating England from Wales.

After CE 1100 the Normans conquered coastal Wales and the Welsh Marches. The Normans sought to incorporate the native Celtic Church into a wider Norman-based Catholic system. They also developed an indigenous Norman-Welsh aristocracy, many of whom were responsible for the Norman invasion and occupation of Ireland. Over the next two centuries, the Welsh princes, most notably Llywelyn, the last indigenous Prince of Wales, failed to resist incorporation into England's expanding Plantagenet kingdom. The Edwardian conquest of Wales, CE 1282–1283, heralded the gradual incorporation of the landed gentry throughout the later Middle Ages and transformed Wales from a rebellious periphery to a fairly tranquil, if not quite domiciled, border region of England. Following the Henrican Acts of Union of England and Wales in 1536 and 1542 a county system of administration was established and English law was instituted in Wales by means of county sheriffs and justices of the peace. Having proscribed Welsh from official life, the Acts of Union required all public officialdom that was transacted in the Welsh principality to be in English and this convention was maintained until the restitution of Welsh under the Welsh Language Acts of 1967 and 1993. Fearful of Catholic home-grown threats and those originating from Ireland, the Tudor State sanctioned the translation of the New Testament (1536) and Book of Common Prayer by William Salesbury in 1567 and the complete Bible into Welsh by Bishop William Morgan in 1588, ostensibly to seal the populace within the Protestant faith through the promotion of Welsh literacy. These reforms produced an elegant standardized form of Welsh, which facilitated the language's survival throughout many centuries of struggle and active state incorporation.

A vibrant culture developed despite the proscription of Welsh in official circles. Between the Tudor and Victorian periods the old bardic literary tradition was displaced by the challenges of the Renaissance, the rise of dissenting nonconformity, and popular print culture, especially the denominational newspapers and ballad broadsheets. A key figure was the naturalist Edward Llwyd, Keeper of the Ashmolean Museum in Oxford (1691–1709), who inaugurated comparative Celtic philology and composed a geological and natural history of Celtic lands. The Cymmrodorion Society founded by London Welshmen in 1751 promoted scientific and scholarly work and was followed by a host of county and local historical, antiquarian, literary, and agricultural improvement societies throughout Wales. It was in the great age of nonconformist dissent from the mid-18th century to the period of Liberal Radicalism at the turn of the 20th century that the lasting values of modern Wales were formed. The Welsh Methodist Revival 1735–1790s was a formative event as it revitalized religion and witnessed the emergence of national figures such as Howell Harris (1714–1773), influential preacher and founder of the Calvinistic Methodist Church in Wales; Griffith Jones (1684–1761), founder of the circulating school movement, by means of which more than 200,000 people learned to read the scriptures during his lifetime; William Williams (1717–1791), the most significant Welsh hymn writer; and Daniel Rowlands (1713–1790), a powerful preacher and religious revivalist.

During the latter part of the 19th century, rapid Anglicization occurred as a result of industrialization and urbanization produced by the massive expansion of iron and coal exploitation together with steel production and engineering. The predominantly monolingual social structure was refashioned into a bilingual society by the redistribution of a growing population consequent to industrial expansion, which gave a fresh impetus to the indigenous language and culture, institutionalizing them within new modernizing industrial domains.

Welsh-medium mass culture was reflected through popular involvement in chapel-based social activities, choral festivals, Eisteddfodau competitions in music, drama, and poetry, a brass band tradition, miners' libraries, national sporting federations, and a vibrant publishing industry. However, imperial economic advances and state intervention following the Education Act of 1870 and the Welsh Intermediate Education Act of 1889 bred a new awareness of English values, culture, and employment prospects and stimulated the process of Anglicization, which encouraged the transmission of Welsh identity through the medium of English. Between roughly 1930 and 1960, the population of industrial Wales abandoned Welsh as a first language while English was perceived as the language of progress, equality, prosperity, commerce, and mass entertainment.

In the Liberal heyday, 1880s–1920s, Wales established a set of national institutions, including the federal University of Wales (1883), the National Library of Wales at Aberystwyth, and the National Museum of Wales at Cardiff, the latter two established in 1907, while the Church in Wales was created following the Act of Disestablishment in 1920. The Liberal Party championed individual liberty and free trade. Its most charismatic leader, David Lloyd George, introduced as chancellor in 1911 social reforms that created the welfare state. He became prime minister (1916–1922), steered the United Kingdom through World War I, and negotiated the Paris Peace Conference of 1919, which redrew the political geography of Europe, giving substance to the early Cymru Fydd ambition of national self-determination. In 1922 the Liberal era was displaced by Labour hegemony, which has dominated Welsh electoral politics ever since. Key figures include the trade unionist James Keir Hardie (1856–1915) and Aneurin Bevan (1897–1960), minister of health in Clement Attlee's postwar cabinet, who introduced the National Health Service and other social and housing reforms that radically transformed the quality of life of working people. Labour continues to dominate local government and the bilingual National Assembly for Wales (NAfW), which it established following the devolution program in 1999, although the power of trade unionism on which the Labour Party was formed has waned considerably.

In 1925, Plaid Genedlaethol Cymru (the Welsh National Party) was formed by intellectuals such as Saunders Lewis, a university lecturer and playwright; the Reverend Lewis Valentine, a Baptist minister; and D. J. Davies, an economist. Their goal was the preservation of Welsh cultural and spiritual values through the maintenance of a predominantly rural, communitarian lifestyle. The party has championed a radical bilingual Wales, with a strong program aimed at strengthening the economic and social basis of its communities. It has grown in electoral strength and capacity to influence political events, such that by 2007 it became the Labour Party's junior partner in a coalition government within the NAfW. The direct-action pressure group Cymdeithas yr Iaith Gymraeg (the Welsh Language Society), formed in 1963, was concerned in campaigning in favor of the production of official bilingual forms and licenses, a separate Welsh-medium television channel, and a greater equality between Welsh and English in judicial affairs. Its current impact has been strengthened by an alliance of 13 language-focused organizations under the umbrella of Mudiad Dathlu'r Gymraeg (Movement to Celebrate Welsh).

Following a century of decline, since 1991 the Welsh-speaking population rose from 510,920 (18.7%) to 582,000 (20.8%) in 2001. This is due to the development of Welsh-medium education and the Education Reform Act (1988), which granted core subject status for Welsh in all schools within the statutory education age range (ages 5–16). The Welsh Language Act of 1993 provided a statutory framework for the equal treatment of English and Welsh, mainly through the 543 Language Schemes coordinated by public bodies with the Welsh Language Board, whose promotional work has also had a profound effect on increasing opportunities to use Welsh through marketing campaigns and the use of Welsh software and information technology.

In 2007 the Labour Party and Plaid formed a coalition within the Wales Assembly Government, whose "One Wales" policy sought to transfer more powers from Westminster to Cardiff, to strengthen Welsh-medium education and language legislation, harness sustainable development and ecological practices, and boost the role Wales plays in the international community. In March 2010 the Welsh Assembly passed a Welsh Language Measure, which heralded a new era in legislative devolution and the development of distinct national policy areas.

Modern Wales has produced many talented individuals, including scientists and philosophers Alfred Russell Wallace, Bertrand Russell, Brian David Josephson, Martin Evans, and Steve Jones; explorers David Thompson and Morton Stanley; literary and creative artists W. H. Davies, Dylan Thomas, R. S. Thomas, Saunders Lewis, Raymond Williams, William Clough-Ellis, and Kyffin Williams; actors and entertainers Richard Burton, Anthony Hopkins, Tom Jones, and Catherine Zeta-Jones; musicians Ivor Novello, Bryn Terfel, and John Cale; sports stars John Charles, Jimmy Wilde, Jim Driscoll, Gareth Edwards, Lyn Davies, Colin Jackson, and Tanni Grey-Thompson; and religious leaders such as Archbishop of Canterbury Rowan Williams.

*Colin H. Williams*

## Further Reading

Davies, John. *The History of Wales.* New rev. ed. New York: Penguin, 2007.

Davies, John, et al., eds. *The Welsh Academy Encyclopaedia of Wales.* Cardiff: University of Wales Press, 2008.

Jenkins, Geraint, and Mari A. Williams, eds. *"Let's Do Our Best For the Ancient Tongue": The Welsh Language in the Twentieth Century.* Cardiff: University of Wales Press, 2000.

Rawlings, Richard. *Delineating Wales: Constitutional, Legal, and Administrative Aspects of National Devolution.* Cardiff: University of Wales Press, 2003.

Stephens, Meic, ed. *The New Companion to the Literature of Wales.* Cardiff: University of Wales Press, 1998.

# Contributor List

Karen Armstrong
*University of Helsinki, Finland*

Barbara Giovanna Bello
*University of Milan, Italy*

David Beriss
*University of New Orleans*

Paul J. Best
*Southern Connecticut State University*

Michel Bouchard
*University of Northern British Columbia, Canada*

Marie-Agnès Boxus
*Haute Ecole Charlemagne, Belgium*

Hanno Brand
*Fryske Akademy, Netherlands*

Laurence Broers
*Conciliation Resources*

Ruslan Bzarov
*North Ossetian State University, Russia*

Jasna Čapo
*Institute of Ethnology and Folklore Research, Croatia*

Jeffrey E. Cole
*Connecticut College*

Peter Collins
*Durham University, United Kingdom*

Renata Coray
*University of Zurich*

Craig Cravens
*University of Texas, Austin*

Carlos Cunha
*Dowling College*

Loring M. Danforth
*Bates College*

Åke Daun
*Stockholm University, Sweden*

Sarah H. Davis
*Emory University*

Jeroen DeWulf
*University of California, Berkeley*

Ludwig Elle
*Sorbian Institute, Germany*

Murat Erdal Ilican
*Oxford University, United Kingdom*

Thomas Hylland Eriksen
*University of Oslo, Norway*

James Frusetta
*Hampden-Sydney College*

Atwood D. Gaines
*Case Western Reserve University*

Firouz Gaini
*University of the Faroe Islands, Denmark*

Marysia Galbraith
*University of Alabama*

Moshe Gammer
*Tel Aviv University, Israel*

Irene Elksnis Geisler
*Western Michigan University*

Sharif Gemie
*University of Glamorgan, United Kingdom*

Julie George
*Queens College, City University of New York*

Sergiu Gherghina
*University of Leiden, Netherlands*

Toomas Gross
*University of Helsinki, Finland*

Valentina Gulin Zrnić
*Institute of Ethnology and Folklore Research, Croatia*

Krista Harper
*University of Massachusetts, Amherst*

Michael Hass
*Independent researcher and writer*

Miroslav Hroch
*Charles University, Czech Republic*

Anastasia Karakasidou
*Wellesley College*

Hasan Ali Karasar
*Bilkent University, Turkey*

Fethi Keles
*Syracuse University*

Hakan Kirimli
*Bilkent University, Turkey*

László Kürti
*University of Miskolc, Hungary*

Taras Kuzio
*University of Toronto, Canada*

Franco Lai
*University of Sassari, Italy*

Gediminas Lankauskas
*University of Regina, Canada*

Walter Leimgruber
*University of Basel, Switzerland*

Susan Lewis
*University of Durham, United Kingdom*

Siniša Malešević
*National University of Ireland at Galway, Ireland*

Jan Mansvelt Beck
*University of Amsterdam, Netherlands*

Marco Marcacci
*Independent researcher and writer*

Sean Martin
*Western Reserve Historical Society*

David Maynard
*State University of New York, Stony Brook*

David McCrone
*University of Edinburgh, United Kingdom*

Gary Wray McDonogh
*Bryn Mawr College*

Jon P. Mitchell
*University of Sussex, United Kingdom*

Christian Moe
*Independent researcher and writer*

Johannes Moser
*Ludwig Maximilian University of Munich, Germany*

Devin E. Naar
*Stanford University*

Vasiliki Neofotistos
*State University of New York, Buffalo*

Stephan E. Nikolov
*Independent scholar*

Donnacha Ó Beacháin
*Dublin City University, Ireland*

Uffe Østergaard
*Copenhagen Business School, Denmark*

Yiannis Papadakis
*University of Cyprus*

Pit Péporté
*University of Luxembourg*

Jonathan Otto Pohl
*American University of Central Asia, Kyrgyzstan*

Mladena Prelić
*Institute of Ethnography, Serbian Academy of Sciences and Arts, Serbia*

Alejandro Quiroga
*University of Newcastle, United Kingdom*

Michael A. Reynolds
*Princeton University*

Lauren Monsein Rhodes
*University of Washington*

Walter Richmond
*Occidental College*

Sirkka Saarinen
*University of Turku, Finland*

Pietro Saitta
*University of Messina, Italy*

Paul A. Silverstein
*Reed College*

Unnur Dís Skaptadóttir
*University of Iceland*

Jeffrey Sluka
*Massey University, New Zealand*

Levent Soysal
*Kadir Has University, Turkey*

Jaro Stacul
*Grant MacEwan University, Canada*

Irena Šumi
*Maribor University, Slovenia*

Ingvar Svanberg
*Uppsala University, Sweden*

Julie Thorpe
*University of Western Sydney*

Trond Thuen
*University of Tromsø, Norway*

Andria Timmer
*University of Iowa*

Hege Toje
*University of Bergen, Norway*

Cirila Toplak
*University of Ljubljana, Slovenia*

Elizabeth Vann
*Brockton High School*

Brian Glyn Williams
*University of Massachusetts, Dartmouth*

Colin H. Williams
*Cardiff University, United Kingdom*

Thomas M. Wilson
*State University of New York, Binghamton*

Elizabeth Anderson Worden
*American University*

Evan Patrick Wright
*University of Washington*

# Geographical Index

# Index